Réunion Mauritius Seychelles

R.M.S. ang. 1

Note to readers

Each island is described according to itineraries. The ■ symbolise possible stops. In order to facilitate the preparation of your trip, hotel and restaurant prices are given by category (double occupancy basis) and in US dollars. Only the prices of some services or purchases are indicated in local currency.
Due to the variations in the cost of living and opening times and the speed with which hotels and particularly restaurants have a tendency to open and close, the practical information and prices within this guide are likely to have changed since the date of publication.

Michelin Travel Publications
Published in 2000

NEOS

New – In the NEOS guides emphasis is placed on the discovery and enjoyment of a new destination through meeting the people, tasting the food and absorbing the exotic atmosphere. In addition to recommendations on which sights to see, we give details on the most suitable places to stay and eat, on what to look out for in traditional markets and where to go in search of the hidden character of the region, its crafts and its dancing rhythms. For those keen to explore places on foot, we provide guidelines and useful addresses in order to help organise walks to suit all tastes.

Expert – The NEOS guides are written by people who have travelled in the country and researched the sites before recommending them by the allocation of stars. Accommodation and restaurants are similarly recommended by a on the grounds of quality and value for money. Cartographers have drawn easy-to-use maps with clearly marked itineraries, as well as detailed plans of towns, archeological sites and large museums.

Open to all cultures, the NEOS guides provide an insight into the daily lives of the local people. In a world that is becoming ever more accessible, it is vital that religious practices, regional etiquette, traditional customs and languages be understood and respected by all travellers. Equipped with this knowledge, visitors can seek to share and enjoy with confidence the best of the local cuisine, musical harmonies and the skills involved in the production of arts and crafts.

Sensitive to the atmosphere and heritage of a foreign land, the NEOS guides encourage travellers to see, hear, smell and feel a country, through words and images. Take inspiration from the enthusiasm of our experienced travel writers and make this a journey full of discovery and enchantment.

C. Vaisse/HOA QUI

Réunion

Mauritius

The Seychelles

The following colour plates are common to Réunion, Mauritius and Seychelles. They illustrate the chapters on flora, fauna and traditional architecture in each island. In the texts covering these subjects, animals, plants and architectural terms illustrated by a drawing are in bold typeface.

A FEW SHELLS

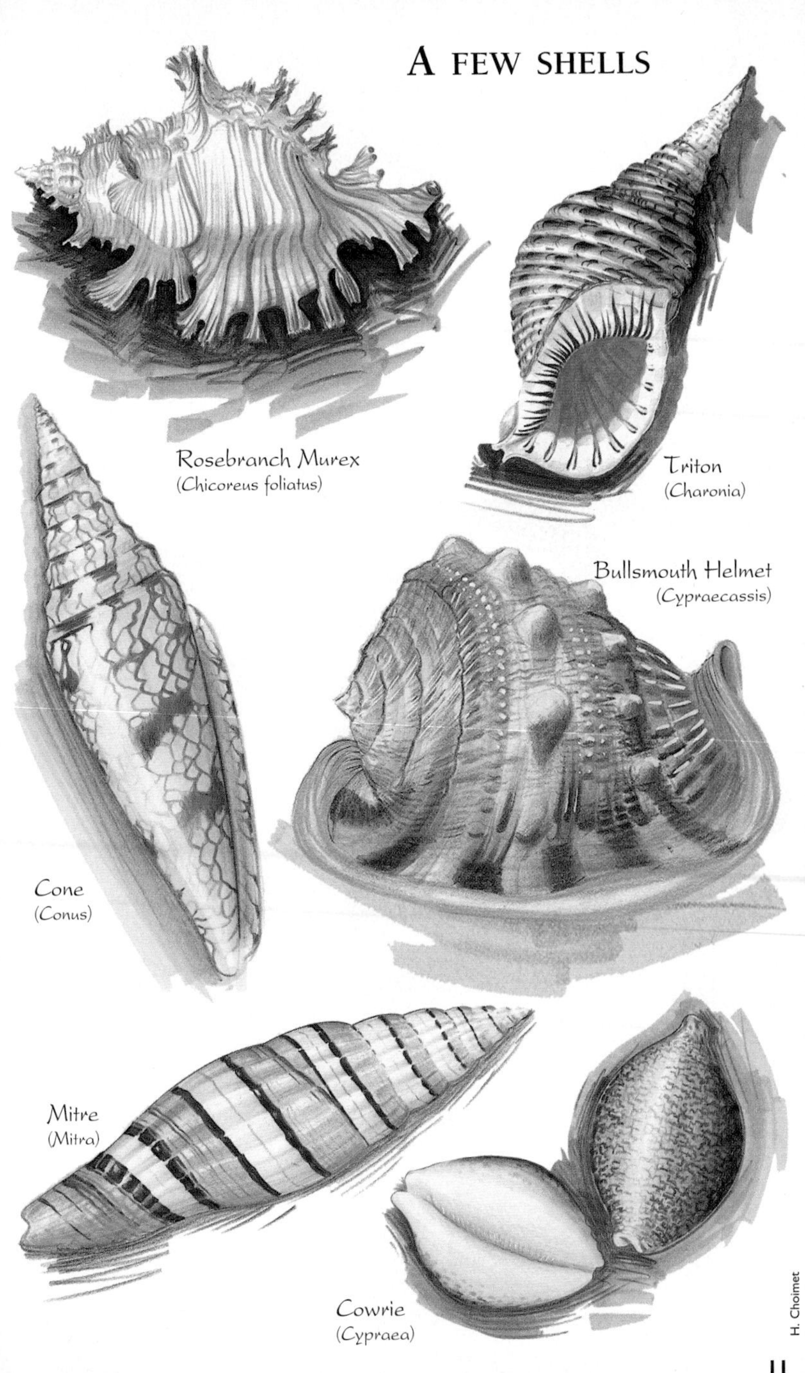
Rosebranch Murex
(Chicoreus foliatus)
Triton
(Charonia)
Bullsmouth Helmet
(Cypraecassis)
Cone
(Conus)
Mitre
(Mitra)
Cowrie
(Cypraea)
H. Choimet

Common fish

Tomato Grouper
rouge z'ananas
(Cephalopholis sonnerati)
Longfin Bannerfish
(Heniochus acuminatus)
Clown
Triggerfish
(Balistides
conspicillum)
Teardrop Butterflyfish
(Chaethodon unimaculatus)
Parrotfish
(scarus)
Emperor Angelfish
(Pomacanthus imperator)
H. Choimet

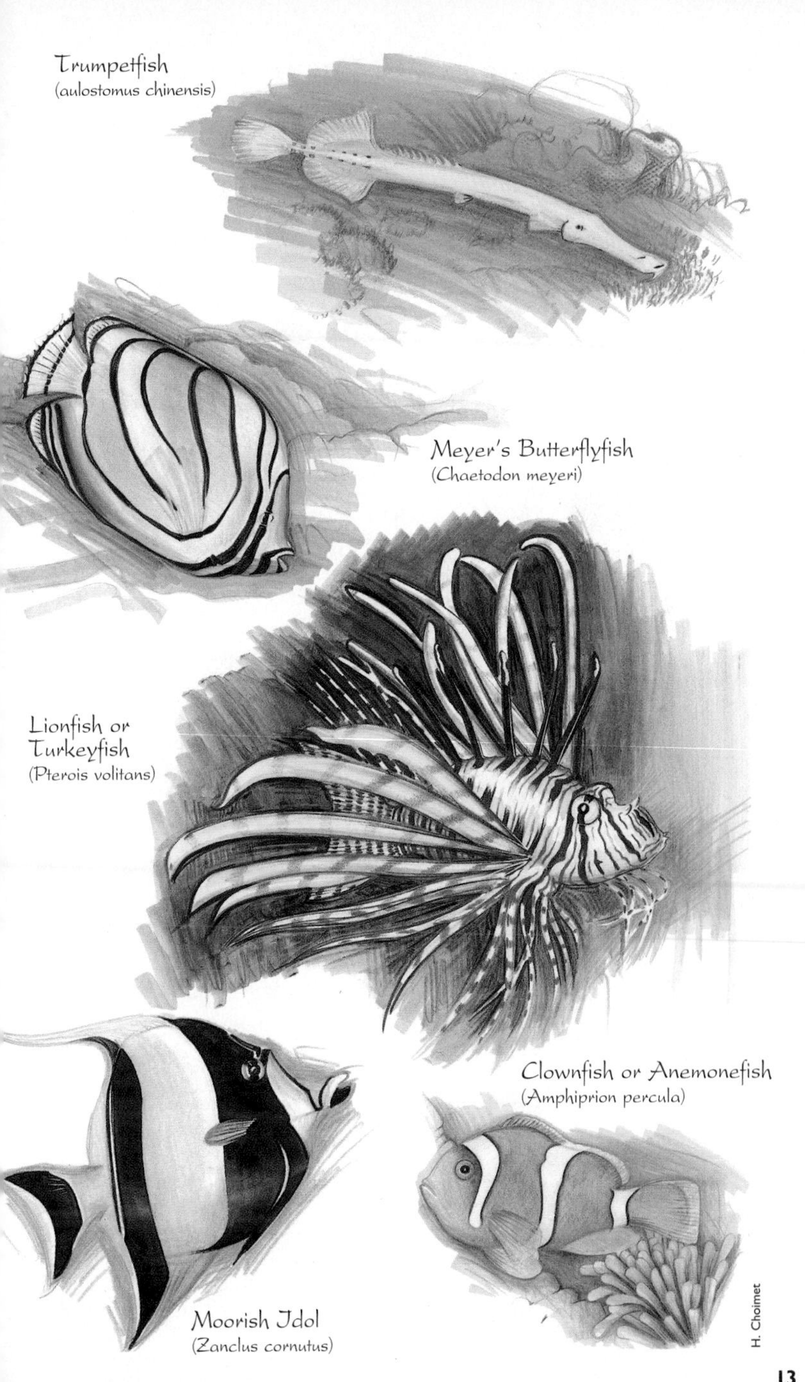
Trumpetfish
(aulostomus chinensis)
Meyer's Butterflyfish
(Chaetodon meyeri)
Lionfish or
Turkeyfish
(Pterois volitans)
Clownfish or Anemonefish
(Amphiprion percula)
Moorish Idol
(Zanclus cornutus)
H. Choimet

Distinctive birds

Red-tailed
Tropic Bird
Paille-en-queue
(Phaeton rubricanda)
Common or Brown Noddi
Anous stolidus pileatus
Sooty Tern
Goelette
(Sterna fuscata
nubilosa)
Crab Plover
Cavalier
Doromas ardeola
Cattle Egret
Madam Paton
(Bubulcus ibis)
H. Choimet

VARIOUS PLANTS

Bird of Paradise or
Crown Bird Flower
(Strelitzia reginae)
Torch Ginger
(Amomum magnificum)
Red Hibiscus
(Hibiscus rosa-sinensis)
Allamanda
alamanda jaune
(Allamanda cathartica)
Bouganvillea
villea
(Bougainvillea
glabra)
Anthurium
White Frangipani
Tree
frangipane blanc
(Plumeria obtusa)
H. Choimet

Creole houses

Bright colours, diamond-shaped decorations, serrated lambrequins and charming gardens planted with flowering shrubs characterise the typical little corrugated-iron shack.

Carefully contrived timber houses, weather-boarded against the elements and topped with rust-red sloping roofs to ensure the inhabitants are kept dry

Courant: The house exterior and roof are covered with wooden slats nailed to a wooden framework. Windows and doorways are fitted with shutters and a small parapet to prevent rainwater draining through.

Detached townhouses are usually set back from the street and separated off by a decorative gate (le baro) fitted to masonry pillars. On the corner, there may be a look-out (le guetali) so that street-life can be watched unobtrusively.

H. Choimet

Elegant planter homesteads

The four towers have been added after the gabled roof. A row of turned wooden balusters grace the balconies on the first floor. All openings are carefully aligned so as to encourage a through-draught of fresh air. The house is raised on a platform so as to ensure against flooding and prevent damp when the ground is waterlogged.

Elegant neo-classical columns grace this verandah. Most houses are white-washed with lime made from coral. A permanganate coating applied to the shutters to prevent infestation by termites, lends a blue tint to the paint-work.

Cane blinds on the verandah provide both shade from the sun and privacy from prying eyes. The pond gracing the front garden is also a symbol of wealth. Decorative parapets and finials ornament the dormer windows and the roof.

Réunion

Area: 2 512sqkm
Population: 705 072
Capital: St Denis
Currency: French franc (FF)

Setting the scene

E Valentin/HOA QUI

Bébour-
Bélouve Forest

VOLCANIC BEGINNINGS

Réunion is not the dreamy tropical paradise promoted by glossy advertisements for there are no turquoise lagoons, white sand beaches or swaying coconut palms in this land: only a few wild beaches to while away the time between long walks in the hills. Unlike other islands, this one conceals her beauty in the Uplands of the hinterland. There, the scenery is diverse and dramatic: the dense vegetation is both exotic and fragrant, the relief is wild and craggy, and in the middle of it all stands a mysterious volcano, one of the most active but least dangerous in the world.

A Mascarene island

Réunion lies in the midst of the Indian Ocean at latitude 21° south and longitude 55° east, 660km from the east coast of Madagascar. Together with Mauritius (220km to the northeast) and Rodrigues (727km away), it forms part of the **Mascarene** archipelago.

The juxtaposition of two volcanic outcrops have fashioned the elliptical shape of the island, 50km by 70km, which claims to have a 220km fairly regular coastline and an irregular relief over 2 512sqkm.

A young volcanic island

Over five million years ago, a small volcano began taking shape on the ocean floor at a depth of some 4 000m – presumably as a result of tectonic movement and the release of molten magma from a pressure point. During the initial phase of activity, a great lava flow was expelled to form a huge platform 200km across. The ensuing volcanic activity was so intense that the submerged outcrop grew rapidly: two million years later it emerged above the ocean surface.

Today, this land mass reaching 3 069m above sea level is termed a "shield volcano". Given its true dimensions (7 000m including the section below the sea), it is considered one of the largest volcanoes in the world. The first hot-spot, or primary volcano, which caused the island to be formed is known as **Piton des Neiges**, and this has been dormant for approximately 20 000 years. During that time, landslides and natural erosion have combined to produce three amphitheatres. Meanwhile the second peak, **Piton de la Fournaise**, has been regularly erupting for 350 000 years.

Wild and broken coastline

Réunion's coast is ringed with pebble beaches – as a result of debris brought down from the ravines – white sandy beaches, produced by the banks of accumulated broken coral, and black sand banks emanating from eroded volcanic rock. Precipitous and therefore wild basalt cliffs, pounded by the sea, encircle much of the island. As the rock plunges steeply downwards, there is almost no continental shelf to provide for sheltered lagoons. The few stretches on the western side of the island were formed fairly recently and rarely exceed much more than a metre deep. Beyond the line of foaming breakers that marks the edge of the volcanic platform, the land mass falls away completely. With no barrier to protect the steep coastline and no shallows to abate the mighty onslaught of the elements, there are very few sheltered spots other than the two bays accommodating the harbours at St-Paul and La Possession.

The west coast is covered with great swathes of savannah dotted with aloes. As drought settles upon the undulating countryside, the tall grasses shimmering in the breeze, pale and turn golden. Two major risks now threaten the landscape: either some maniac or criminal will set fire to it, reducing it to a black and barren desert, or some developer will manage to snatch away another plot on which to build, extending the encroachment of urbanisation on any available space. Indeed, most of the population lives on the narrow coastal plains, where the towns and hamlets are concentrated.

The Uplands

Long, fairly gentle slopes stretch down towards the sea. The main flanks are given over to extensive sugarcane plantations that in places extend all the way out to the coast. And so, with each season, the scenery changes: in January, the ploughed earth becomes covered with tender green shoots that grow to form a thick, lush mantle in the weeks and months that follow. Once the plants reach a height of 3m, they burst into flower, producing great sheaves of plumes that appear orange-yellow at dawn, silvery white in full sunlight and mauve at dusk. At harvest time, the vegetation is cropped and the island is quite bare. The simple houses that for so long were hidden amongst the fields are suddenly exposed to all and sundry, while the larger planter's houses, graced with avenues of coconut palms, are revealed in all their splendour. For a time, the brown earth is laid bare until, at last, the cycle of the seasons begins again. Contrast is imparted to the countryside by a number of large **ravines** that shelter attractive valleys or deep gorges full of vivid bright green crops or flourishing vegetation at variance with the light green sugarcane. The south-eastern highlands, exposed to the unpredictable volcano, are characterised by a more rugged scenery. Superimposed layers of subtle black and brown volcanic rock and lava are a testimony to the island's formation. Exposed patches of basalt have in time been tempered by nature, weathered little by little with touches of green and grey. The slopes of **Grand Brûlé,** meanwhile, are covered with patches of dense forest luxuriating in the hot and humid conditions and impenetrable jungles of exotic species stimulated by high levels of rainfall.

At the centre of the island, two high plateaux – **Plaine des Palmistes** and **Plaine des Cafres** (1 300-1 700m) – separate the two volcanic peaks. These elevated areas are allocated to arable and stock farming, but being as they are at 1 300-1 700m above sea level, they are far more reminiscent of an alpine landscape than of a tropical island. In winter, when a thick mist settles upon the island interior and temperatures drop, ribbons of smoke rise from the chimneys of the houses.

Among the mountain peaks

Beyond the plains, a road leads up to the volcano. Shapeless blocks of basalt strew the ground endowing a bleakness to the "lunar" landscape. The vegetation along the way becomes stunted and more disparate before disappearing altogether from the **Plaine des Sables**, where the only colour is imparted by the glinting metallic-grey and reddish rocks and sand. A sparse patch of green and white vegetation relieves the black austerity and then, round a corner, **Piton de la Fournaise** stands proudly erect, towering above its lava plateau stretching out towards the sea.

The tallest peak is **Piton des Neiges**, a pointed mass serrated with rampart-like cliffs visible from all around the island. A large extent of the hinterland is taken up by the outcrop and three vast, gaping **circus-like arenas** that surround it. These are largely the result of landslides and erosion caused by interacting wind and rain over the millennia, which also fashioned this astonishingly rugged landscape. The small flat areas cut off by deep gorges harbour a few closely built houses, while the larger plateaux accommodate whole villages. Water cascades several hundred metres to the ground below over sheer rockfaces and sharp outcrops. In places, the mountainsides are completely covered with dense

G. Coulon/ALTITUDE

Piton de la Fournaise erupting, March 1986

forest, elsewhere this has been cleared and replaced by plantations of crops suitable to the environment. This relief continues to be shaped by erosion which is more powerful than ever. Great clefts in the rocks mark the entrances to the amphitheatres, which are drained by sleepy rivers, and the rounded basalt pebbles reveal just how fast these water courses can rage when swollen.

Tropical climate

The climate in Réunion alternates between two seasons that complement those of the northern hemisphere. The **southern winter**, the drier and cooler season, is fanned by the very strong southeast trade winds. The hot and wet **southern summer**, from November to April, is subjected to frequent tropical depressions sweeping usually from the northeast and bringing torrential rain. They also herald the annual cyclone season. Perhaps the most memorable in recent years was cyclone Hyacinth, which ravaged the island in 1980 with winds that gusted at 300km/hr; 1.17m of rain fell in 12hr at Grand Îlet and more than 6m in 11 days at Commerson!

Despite the distinct seasons, the weather varies considerably with altitude and orientation so that there are more than two hundred different **micro-climates** on the island: temperatures on the coast can be 30°C when it is only 5°C at the top of the volcano, and it can be raining hard on the plateaux while the coast a few miles away basks in bright sunshine.

The island's relief and prevailing winds combine to split the country into two distinctive regions: the eastern flank, exposed to strong winds and rain, is regarded as the **windward side** while the more sheltered western part is the **leeward side**. In the more humid areas, cloud tends to collect around the mountain peaks over 800m and thick mists blanket out the lower reaches of the ravines and amphitheatres.

Flora past and present

When the island emerged from the ocean three million years ago, it was devoid of any animal or plant life. In time, a great variety of nuts and seeds were conveyed to the barren shores from distant lands with the help of birds, winds, cyclones and sea currents, where they took root and grew in profusion. As the different species vied for nutrients and space in which to grow, some plants adapted to their new environment while others evolved. Once a balance was established, these plant variants became endemic to Réunion.

Scented woods and leaves, flowers of every colour and shape, together with the sheer luxuriance of the forests combined to dazzle the first people who landed there into thinking it was the lost Garden of Eden.

Alas, three centuries of human colonisation have severely and irrevocably damaged this haven of plant life. Radical clearing, intensive agriculture, rapid urban growth and the introduction of exotic species have in turn decimated much of the native forest and many of the unique plants that once thrived so happily. Today, there are approximately 700 indigenous plants and 160 endemics that are recognised officially and protected in nature reserves.

A few definitions

The indigenous species describe those plants that were growing on the island before the arrival of man.

The endemic species comprise the indigenous plants that have slowly mutated and adapted themselves in order to respond effectively to the ambient conditions on the island, so as to become a variant of a species that is peculiar and specific to that land.

The exotics include all those species introduced by man from another country.

A broad range of vegetation proliferates in concentric zones between the coast and sea level and the high Uplands at 2 200m. Additional variants are provided by the different conditions on the eastern windward and western leeward flanks.

The local people are particularly discerning when it comes to the subject of plants, and that they are delighted at the opportunity of sharing this love and knowledge with interested parties.

The species in bold are illustrated on p 16-17.

Tropical forest on a large scale

Nearly two-fifths of the island is covered by forest, probably less than half of what there was before the advent of man. Besides the extraction of timber, the natural vegetation has been ravaged relentlessly by clearing for agriculture, by grazing and by fire. However, the national forestry commission (ONF) is now attempting to reverse the destruction. Vested with the responsibility for protecting, regenerating and maintaining the forest areas, it is also developing various tourist facilities by heightening awareness of and respect for this valuable and unique natural resource.

Specialists have isolated five distinct types of forest in Réunion.

Endemic tamarinds predominate in the forested upland regions and the Plaine des Tamarins at Mafate. Their tortured shapes provide carpenters and cabinet-makers with a finely grained wood suitable for furniture. The trees grow in symbiosis with *calumets des Hauts*, a kind of bamboo that is specific to the island. The Highland Acacias – imported from abroad – are linked to the cultivation of geraniums and provide locals with a source of fuel, notably for distilling alcohol. The Upland forests have some fifty different kinds of tree with coloured wood, including the *mapou* (Pisonia with reddish bark), the *tan rouge* and the *tan maigre*.

Below 300m, a different set of trees with exotic woods grow, such as the small and large *nattes* (Sideroxylon), styrax, camphor, *takamaka* (Alexandrian laurel), *bois puant*, *bois savon*, *bois noir*, feathery-leafed *Fanjans* or **tree-ferns**, elegant *bois de fer* and the pink-flowering tree hibiscus *(mahot)* along with many others. Perhaps the most wonderful specimens are to be found in and around Bébour-Bélouve, Plaine des Palmistes, Mare Longue and St-Philippe.

Common *cryptomerias*, a resilient and fast-growing conifer destined for industrial uses, are grown more and more, particularly in the amphitheatres. Their wood is turned into cheap furniture, building materials and forestry/agricultural fencing posts.

Elsewhere on the island, a kind of scrub-land predominates, made up of heather, gorse, broom and ferns.

Coastal regions

The great banyan tree is a member of the ficus *(Moraceae)* family that takes on rather a strange appearance as it produces long aerial roots that hang down from the branches to take root in the ground below. As a result, they provide a shady spot for people to meet under (as at St-Denis or on the seafront at Terre Sainte) or for a quiet siesta. The ficus is regarded as sacred both by Hindus and Buddhists (as it is said, Buddha received Enlightenment under such a tree), and so the roots provide a private corner for a Tamil shrine or for prayer (as at St-Paul) away from prying eyes.

On the whole, there are fewer coconut trees and traveller's palms on Réunion than on other tropical islands. This is also the case for the *palmiste* palm *(Deckenia nobilis)*, which once grew in profusion around Plaine des Palmistes, but which has been over-exploited for its delicate and highly prized palm-heart, served in special dishes like "Millionaire's Salad".

Great numbers of casuarinas are to be seen everywhere, having been introduced originally as a means of combating soil erosion. They especially proliferate among the dunes of Étang Salé and in the unstable soil in the amphitheatres, particularly at Salazie.

Pandanus or **vacoa** seem to thrive on the eastern and southeastern coasts and have become associated with St-Philippe where they are used to make mats and baskets.

Flowering species

Many ornamental plants and imported exotics blossom all the year round and so are given pride of place by their owners in the garden: do not be surprised, therefore, to find dahlias, ranunculas, geraniums, gladioli, begonias, tea-roses and such like growing side by side.

Additional colour is provided along the roads and streets across the island by flowering shrubs: yellow **allamanda**, pink **hibiscus**, rich magenta, red, pink, white and yellow **bougainvillaea**, exquisite orchid flowers projecting from an unlikely mossy cranny, delicate white arum lilies and **poinsettias** with vivid

E Valentin/HOA QUI

Pandanus and vanilla

red leaves all grow together without offending the eye. Trees also burst into bloom and shower the pavements with petals: the **flame trees** *(flamboyants)* – often associated with Kenya – produce bright red flowers throughout the southern summer, large-leafed jacarandas turn a glorious mauve in contrast with more familiar varieties like acacias, silky oak and broom. The wonderful sweet-scented yellow and white flowers of the **frangipani** are also considered special by Tamils and so are often planted beside temples – a practice that might have been copied by Catholics to shade some of their cemeteries.

Among the multitude of orchids, one has been especially prized and has earned an international reputation, the Bourbon vanilla orchid, which was introduced to Réunion in the early 19C. This climbing plant's favourite host is the **Pandanus**. Other distinctive features include its long oval leaves that alternate up the stem, from which a long, green fleshy fruit might hang. It seems to be best suited to the climate on the east of the island *(see insert on vanilla, p 147)*.

Exotic fruits

Whatever the season, the Réunion marketstalls display a range of exquisitely juicy and tasty fruit to savour and enjoy. Despite this broad selection, additional varieties grown in private gardens are swapped and exchanged between friends and neighbours and so remain beyond the reach of restaurateurs, hotel-caterers and market stall-holders.

The southern summer, around December, is best for lychees and mangoes; later come the longans – a small round fruit with smooth beige skin and juicy sweet translucent flesh. In winter, you can pick the tart-tasting red and yellow guavas that grow in the Uplands. Various different types of banana grow on the eastern side of the island, not to mention another assortment of fruit and vegetables that alternate with the seasons: Victoria pineapples, star fruit or *caramboles*, avocados, breadfruit, papayas and pink pepper from the false pepper tree, sour-sop *(corossols)*, *cœurs de bœuf* (a custard apple-like fruit), jack-fruit, mangosteens and rambutans.

Fragrant oils and spices

During the 18C Réunion earned itself a reputation for producing exotic spices for export although this trade has largely dwindled. Only pepper is still grown commercially, while cloves, cinnamon, nutmeg, cardamom and turmeric (locally known as *saffran*) are only really to be seen growing in botanical gardens.

The dwindling demand for rare essential oils continues to be satisfied by a few small-scale growers cultivating geraniums in the western Uplands, *vetiver* (lemon-grass) in and around Tampon and St-Joseph, and, to a lesser extent, ylang-ylang.

Tiresome weeds

Several exotics introduced by man have become so well acclimatised to their environment that they are choking out various indigenous species. Probably the most virulent pest is the brown vine, which spreads itself in a tangle of shoots. Even the guava which produces succulent (and rather sharp) fruit and the delicately-flavoured rose apple are considered to be harmful, invasive and destructive.

A NEGLECTED FAUNA

Three hundred years ago, Réunion could have been proud of its particularly rich and colourful fauna: blue wood pigeons, black and white flamingos, multi-coloured parrots and giant tortoises all contributed to its image as a paradise island. Alas, only a fraction of the species recorded by the island's first visitors can be seen today, either because they managed to conceal themselves in inaccessible corners, or because their flesh was uneatable. Among the most famous creatures to have died out are the land tortoise and the endemic Réunion ibis known as *solitaire. Species in bold are illustrated on p 11-15.*

Birds

Réunion's diverse climate and rich plant life support a tremendous variety of birds, which, for the most part, are concentrated in the forest areas. Those that once inhabited the lowland plains, water courses and the coast have largely or completely disappeared as growing numbers of people and houses encroach upon their unprotected habitats.

The *papangue* (harrier), a graceful bird of prey, can still be seen haunting the interior reaches between 500m and 1 500m above sea level. There are the simply named *oiseau blanc* – a small and round, grey and brown bird with a white mark on its back – and the *oiseau lunettes vert,* which is similar but green and with two white rings around the eyes. The **cardinal** (or red fody) earns its name from the male's red plumage. The *tec-tec* (stone chat) – a small endemic bird with brown and white colouring – pops up everywhere on the island. ..The almost tame Mascarene paradise flycatcher – referred to by locals as *l'oiseau-la-vierge* – is another sociable bird that enjoys following people out walking. The brazen **condé** (or *bulbul*) has a shaggy black crest, while his cousin *martin* **(mynah bird)** is brown with yellow beak and legs. Towards the end of the day, flocks of bright yellow *belliers* (canaries) congregate in the banyan trees and chatter loudly. The male *tuit-tuit* or *merle blanc* (cuckoo shrike) is grey with a white tip on the tail: it is one of the rarest birds in the world and lives exclusively on the Plaine des Chicots. The last survivors (numbering some 160) all reside on Réunion.

By comparison, there are fewer species of sea bird to be seen. *Barau's petrel*, an endemic sea bird, spends his days fishing at sea but then returns to roost among the uplands above 2 000m. In the wilder coastal regions, you may spot the common (or brown) **noddi** *(maqua)*, the **sooty tern** *(sterne fulgineuse)* or the endearing **paille-en-queue** (white tailed tropic bird) with its long tapering white tail and graceful flight down and over ravines and cliffs. You may also get the chance to see the small swift-like bird known locally as a *salangane* which makes an edible nest from seaweed, as well as various species of shearwater and quail.

Land animals

The *tangue* (tenrec) is a small hedgehog-like mammal with a long nose and long hair that predominantly resides in the ravines and forests; occasionally, they are to be seen walking with young through private gardens. In the hinterland, goats scamper around open craggy areas, nimbly moving across the loose scree.

All the reptiles you are likely to meet in Réunion are harmless. The most common is the gecko; he ably scales walls and ceilings in search of mosquitoes and other small flying insects which he is able to gobble up with a flick of the tongue. Each successful catch is celebrated by a series of short sharp cries – a sound that soon becomes reassuringly familiar. His distant cousin, *the endormi*, a wonderful slow-moving green chameleon with red, blue and yellow patches, is a far rarer sight, although he occasionally ventures out into people's gardens. The *Manapy green lizard*, meanwhile, is usually to be found lounging among the trunks of *pandanus*, especially in and around St-Joseph.

Réunion is a veritable haven for insects and can claim to have a number of endemic species. Do not be put off by the size of the cockroaches and the large spiders *(babouks)* which are completely harmless. There are mosquitoes all year around, particularly on the coast and when the weather is humid. Although none are actually dangerous, it is worth keeping an eye out for the large yellow wasps and small scorpions – occasionally spotted on the west coast – and the large millipedes *(cent-pieds)* with brown markings that can deliver a very painful sting and precipitate heart palpitations *(in which case alert the emergency services immediately)*. The many multicoloured butterflies flitting among the garden flowers are far more endearing.

Marine Life

Remember that it is forbidden to collect pieces of coral and/or shells from the sea or in any quantities from the beach.

Réunion is a relatively young island surrounded by warm waters (22-28°C) that was formed by a series of volcanic explosions. As the rock plunges almost vertically down to the ocean floor, there is little to no continental shelf for colonies of coral to grow, save 15sqkm of reef on the western side.

In the shallower waters, the sea floor is scattered with large black or beige sausage-shaped holothuria commonly known as "sea cucumbers" or "sea caterpillars". Other hazards include sea urchins, patches of seaweed and pieces of broken coral *so it is worth wearing plastic shoes* when out exploring the shallow waters. Further out, where the water is deeper and around rocky outcrops, you will find sea-fans with yellow, red and black excrescences gracefully swaying in the current, sponges, sea anemones, crustaceans, many molluscs, cephalopoda (octopus, squid and cuttlefish) and shells. The distinctive types of shells include the common **cones**, **cowries**, *terebridae* (elongated spindle shells), *lambis* (spider conchs) and giant clams, as well as the rarer *cassis* (**helmet shells**), *Oliva*, **mitres** and **tritons** that have long been pillaged by unscrupulous collectors.

The shallow inter-tidal areas attract a prolific number of startlingly beautiful tropical fish, such as the appropriately-named **damsel**, **butterfly** and **trumpet**, as well as the less refined **grouper** *(gros rouge z'ananas)*, blue surgeon fish, **moorish idols**, **standards leopard**, **clown** and **parrot** fish.

Beyond the reefs, in the deep blue sea, lurk the larger species. Some use camouflage to help them stalk food or for defending themselves from predators: be wary, therefore, of the stone fish that cunningly blends into its surroundings and the **rascasse** or scorpion fish that possesses a series of poisonous dorsal spines, which can deliver a vicious sting that is capable of triggering heartpalpitations. Beware of banks of catfish, which often move in shoals, that also have poisonous spines. *Should you feel a sting and detect a red area, leave the water and alert the emergency services.*

Out in the ocean seas roam the big fish that fishermen and gourmets delight in catching: barracuda, marlin, bonito, tuna, sea bream, swordfish and *emperor* fish. You may also catch sight of dancing rays, curious and playful dolphins as well as the odd shy turtle breaking the surface to catch its breath before disappearing again. Be aware that blue and white sharks are also to be found around the island, so be careful if you venture out to swim, windsurf and dive beyond the sheltered and shallow waters. *(In short: it is recommended that visitors to the island stay near supervised beaches and only swim during the day.)*

Three centuries of history

14C	The Arabs discovered **Dina Moghrabin**.
1512	The Portuguese christened Mauritius, Rodrigues and Réunion the **Mascarene** archipelago.
1638	The French set foot on **Mascarin**.
1642	Governor **Pronis** took possession of Mascarin.
1646	12 mutineers were exiled to the island.
1649	The island was renamed **Île Bourbon**.
1664	The Compagnie des Indes became the **French East India Company**.
1723	The **Code Noir** institutionalised slavery.
1735	**Mahé de La Bourdonnais** was appointed Governor of Bourbon.
1738	**St-Denis** established as the capital of the island.
1764	Collapse of the French East India Company; the responsibility for government reverted to the French Crown.
1793	The island was renamed "**La Réunion**" in the aftermath of the revolution and presided over by the Colonial Assembly.
1806	For a brief period the island assumed the name **Bonaparte**.
1810	Possession passed to the English after Napoleon's defeat by the *"habits rouges"*.
1815	Under the **Treaty of Paris, Bourbon** was ceded back to the French.
1848	Abolition of slavery. The island assumed its definitive name, **La Réunion**.
1946	Réunion was made a **Département Français d'Outre Mer** (DOM).
1982	The French "département" was raised to the status of **région**.
1986	Camille Sudre founded "**Télé Free DOM**" to counter the monopoly of French mainland TV.
1991	Rioting in **Chaudron**.
1998	Commemoration of the 150th anniversary of the abolition of slavery.

Discovery and colonisation

The story of Réunion only really begins to take shape in the second half of the 17C. Before that time, the island was visited by a variety of explorer-cum-navigators who each gave it a different name: in the 14C it was referred to by the Arabs as **Dina Moghrabin**; in the 16C it was known to the Portuguese navigator, Diego Lopes de Sequera, as **Santa Appolonia**. A little later, Pedro Mascarenhas bestowed his own name upon the islands of Rodrigues, Mauritius and Réunion, calling them the **Mascarenes**. For the period between 1520 and 1620, the name Réunion changed each time the English and Dutch made a landing there.

In 1638 the French established themselves on Madagascar; four years later they settled on the island of **Mascarin**. By 1642, the **French East India Company** (Compagnie de l'Orient) ordered Governor Prontis, who was in charge of trade and commerce in Madagascar, to take official possession of Mascarin. Rather than imprison 12 mutineers, he banished them to Réunion to live on their wits. Three years later they returned home in the best of spirits and blooming health, full of colourful accounts of this marvellous island paradise. The island was henceforth named **Île Bourbon** after the reigning French dynasty. In 1664, when the Compagnie de l'Orient had been reformed by Colbert as the **Compagnie**

des Indes orientales, the authorities decided to establish a permanent presence there that might prove advantageous during Madagascar's colonisation. In 1665, **Etienne Régnault**, the newly appointed governor of the territory, landed on the island accompanied by 20 volunteers – seduced by the prospects painted by the French authorities of a promised land.

East India Company outpost

The population on the island grew very slowly. In 1675, after the French were expelled from Madagascar, there were only a hundred settlers resident there including a number of Malagasy and Indian people. Each was allocated a generous land concession, bounded by ravines, that stretched "from the breaking waves to the mountain tops" and was instructed by the **French East India Company** to concentrate on rearing stock or cultivating crops that were suitable for provisioning passing ships. Despite this edict, only one ship put into port between 1690 and 1694.

The resident population, left very much to their own devices, struggled to be self-sufficient. Their survival was determined by their meagre produce being illicitly supplemented by English and Dutch contraband and by plundering the local game and edible fruits of the forest. In so doing, however, they decimated certain species of flora and fauna and drove others to extinction.

The East India Company resumed its control over the colony in 1715, shortly after the French conquered Mauritius.

As the vogue for drinking coffee swept through Europe's high society, the plant was introduced to Bourbon and grown on a speculative basis. The lower regions and the coastal areas were gradually denuded of their tropical jungle to make way for coffee plantations. Soon Bourbon monopolised the trade in coffee. As the growers became more affluent, the population of the island expanded from 270 in 1680 to 35 500 in 1780. What hitherto had been unofficial slavery was institutionalised under the tyrannical French law known as the **Code Noir** in 1723. More or less at the same time, various ruthless pirates, who had sowed fear in the hearts of all who sailed across the Indian Ocean, decided to repent and retire on the island.

Prosperity and poverty

Throughout his reign as governor (1735-46), **Mahé de La Bourdonnais** actively took part in the development of the Île Bourbon and Île de France (Mauritius). While all efforts on the Île de France were channelled into increasing her commercial standing, Bourbon – considered the "poor relation" – was relegated to providing perishable foodstuffs and basic staples.

As competition from the West Indies gradually undermined Bourbon's coffee monopoly, planters began to diversify into other crops like rice, wheat and other such produce for the home markets while maintaining production of coffee and cotton for export.

Meanwhile, as inroads were being made by rival nations into conquering the spice-rich lands of the East, the French sent parties out into the jungle to collect samples of the most promising plants that could be introduced to their own colonies. With unflinching determination, **Pierre Poivre** fought off opposition to secure for himself what was required for growing cinnamon, pepper, ginger, and – more importantly – cloves and nutmeg. Having been successful in establishing these potentially lucrative exotics, the island began to enjoy the prospect of prosperity. Not all the residents shared in this wealth, however, for the planters with rights over the land accounted for a mere 20 % of the total population. Out of a total of 46 000 inhabitants, some 35 000 were slaves and that number was on the increase.

Furthermore, a conservative figure of a thousand has been estimated for people of mixed race occupying an unspecified place in society. With each successive generation, the white planters' land-holdings were parcelled out amongst their heirs; as plots became smaller, the concessions became less profitable and the fortunes of the "**p'tits Blancs**" degenerated to nothing short of extreme poverty. The loss of France's territories in India and the East incited **Louis XV** to reassert his naval superiority in the Indian Ocean, most especially in the face of the British threat. While war raged in Europe, the fortunes of the French East India Company degenerated. The king acquired the Mascarene archipelago as his own in 1764, and subjugated the islands to a selected "royal" administration.

Short-lived British conquest

The effects of the French Revolution reverberated on the colony several months after the events in Paris. In 1793, the authorities renamed the territory **Réunion**, in reference to the 'union' between the National Guard and the Marseilles battalion on 10 August 1792; it was also decreed that slavery should be abolished but the residents categorically refused to comply.

As Napoleon began to build up his empire in Europe, uncertainty ravaged the offshore territories. The island, which by 1806 had assumed the name **Bonaparte**, was suffering from a teetering economy and the devastating outcome of two cyclones when the British chose to impose a crippling blockade around it.

Franco-British rivalry for the Indies and colonisation of strategic islands in the Indian Ocean was at its height. In 1809, the British went ashore at St-Paul and spent three weeks there. Following four days of fighting in July 1810, they took control of St-Denis which had become the capital in 1738.

The island reverted to being called **Île Bourbon** while Île de France – conquered by the British – was renamed Mauritius. The defeat of Napoleon at Waterloo in 1815 put an end to the Napoleonic Wars. The Congress of Vienna sealed the peace in Europe while the **Treaty of Paris** reviewed territories abroad: Bourbon was ceded to the French; **Mauritius**, Rodrigues and the Seychelles came under British jurisdiction.

The island's economy, ravaged by war and a series of natural disasters, needed to be rebuilt. Although Réunion was now free to compete commercially with Mauritius, she suffered on the short term from losing such an important market for her agricultural produce. Growers switched to planting sugarcane safe in the knowledge that France's demand for the commodity would increase as she recovered from 25 devastating years of war.

Colonial era

In 1817, **Charles Desbassyns** installed a steam-powered sugar-refining plant on his Chaudron estate. Plantations across the island of coffee, cloves and other perishable foodstuffs were uprooted and replaced with fields of sugarcane. The island that once depended on exporting her fruit and vegetables was now obliged to import grain, rice and even fruit. By 1830, many of the land-holdings were merged to form great estates and the refineries were nationalised. By 1860 more than half of the agricultural land was given over to growing sugarcane.

In January 1848, the Second Republic had outlawed slavery. On 20 December of the same year, slavery was permanently abolished in Réunion. Commissioner **Sarda Garriga** was given the responsibility of assuaging the apprehensions of the larger land-owners and calmly overseeing the issue of contracts binding all the freed slaves to work for their former masters as before.

C Pavard/HOA QUI

Sugar refinery at Kerveguen, 1884 (Album de Roussin)

In the same year, the island returned to calling itself **Réunion**. The labour crisis provoked by the liberation of the slaves was now resolved by allowing boatloads of "**recruited labourers**" from Madagascar, East Africa, but more especially from northeastern and southern India, China and the Comoros to volunteer to come and work on the island. Although the working conditions resembled those of slavery in all but name, the migrants settled there and went on to provide the island with its multi-ethnic population.

Meanwhile, the plight of the "**p'tits Blancs**" worsened. Like the emancipated slave workers, they were reluctant to seek work on the big estates, so by 1850, more than half of the population was living in poverty. The only solution was to move deeper into the uncharted hinterland in the hope of finding new areas where they could grow fresh staples. The development of the hitherto untouched Uplands and amphitheatres had been encouraged since 1830 but now their conquest began in earnest, although life there remained precarious.

Little changed otherwise on the island until **Hubert Delisle** was appointed Governor – the first Creole to be so honoured. Between 1852-58 he set about building a new infrastructure for the island. Roads and bridges were put in place so as to open up access to the Uplands and to improve communications across the territory.

The established local bourgeoisie, a refined but frivolous social set, instigated the construction of elegant villas in which to peacefully pass the languid days. **St-Denis** assumed the attributes of a provincial capital, complete with its line of administrative premises, religious buildings and its gracious avenues in which all and sundry might take a Sunday afternoon stroll and parade their finery.

Colony in crisis

Several crises put an end to this period of optimism and expansion. Shortly after the **Suez Canal** was opened, Réunion's isolation was exacerbated when it found itself outside the route plied by the merchant vessels. The brand new facilities provided by the harbour at Pointe des Galets were found to be incapable of handling large shipments of freight. More or less at the same time, the price of sugar plummeted on the international markets, unable to sustain the competition from Cuban suppliers. Many of the plantations were declared bankrupt.

The population was decimated as epidemics of cholera, smallpox and the plague swept through the community up to the 1920s; the poor resettled in the suburban outskirts of town.

Réunion was run down, malaria was rife and the people struggled against rising infant mortality, illiteracy and alcoholism. Despite this, immigrants continued to arrive from afar, right up to the closing years of the 19C when droves of **Chinese** and **Indian Moslems** elected to move there.

Fragile solutions – Once France had gained control over **Madagascar** in 1895, she was quick to lose interest in the smaller struggling territory. Many of the most enterprising entrepreneurs left Réunion in order to escape from the collapsed economy and social chaos.

To safeguard against further socio-economic problems affecting the Uplands, the cultivation of geraniums was initiated to supply essential oil to the perfumery industry. Other plants – like sisal (used in making rope) and vetiver (lemongrass) – were also grown although their success was to be short-lived.

1882 also saw the inauguration of the island's first railway line between St-Benoît and St-Pierre. Although its primary function was to facilitate the transport of sugar, it allowed people to move more freely around the island.

Repercussions of two world wars – Of the 10 000 volunteers who left Réunion to fight for France in the **First World War**, more than 1 000 lost their lives. Between the wars, the economic crisis affecting almost every aspect of farming continued. A fatal strain of Spanish 'flu swept through the population, already weakened by malaria, killing several thousand people. Meanwhile, the first steps towards modernisation materialised: a shipment of motor cars was unloaded, the television was launched and aircraft began landing on the island on a regular basis.

In 1940, the fate of the entire territory was put in the balance when Governor Aubert declared his support for the **Vichy** regime. The British immediately blockaded Réunion with reinforcements based in Mauritius, cutting it off from the outside world until 1942, when the **Free French Forces** landed there and saved the island from famine.

A French département

On 19 March 1946, it was decided that the easiest way of pulling the colony into the modern era was to make it a **département français d'Outre-mer,** in other words, an overseas county or state of mainland France. This having been done, the island's fortunes did not change overnight.

The first efforts were directed at reducing the infant mortality rate by improving medical facilities and eradicating the endemic malaria. The next phase involved setting up a system for assessing and distributing benefits, launching a series of considerable building projects and instigating better housing for the people. It was not until the Gaullist Deputy, **Michel Debré,** was appointed in the 1960s that these plans were brought to fruition. As Réunion began transforming itself, the population figures exploded. The social and economic climate was profoundly changed. However, given the island's size and remoteness, the French government thought it inappropriate to subsidise the local economy too much.

A few years later, as agriculture remained in a state of crisis and unemployment figures boomed, central government was obliged to intervene by sending ever larger amounts of capital.

Search for the voice of Réunion

In 1981, the first independent radio station, **Free-DOM,** began broadcasting. Other voices started to compete with the state-controlled station RFO (Radio France d'Outremer) for audiences. In the same year, the first celebrations were held to commemorate the abolition of slavery and *mayola* – a traditional kind of music based on songs sung by slaves that was hitherto banned – was revived *(see Music & Dance p 55)*.

1981 also saw the launch of **TV Freedom.** This pirate channel transmitted unconventional programmes in Creole that reflected the true interests of the Réunion people, in stark contrast with the official public network which continued to show programmes in French.

In 1991, the pirate station was banned by the authorities for candidly deepening the malaise from the protracted economic depression. Such a radical move provoked rioting and pillage in the **Chaudron** district that lasted several days. The rapid deployment of force was quick to contain the insurrection and restore order but this only masked the island's profound social unease.

On the brink of a new millennium

Réunion is not only a French département – one of the smallest at that – but also a region made up of 24 districts – making it one of the largest in France. It is represented on a national level in the French parliament by three senators and five députés. For a long time now, the political scene has been dominated by large land-owners and eminent people from the liberal professions. During the 1980s, a major effort was made to decentralise the class-system. As a result, a new kind of politician was allowed to emerge, this time from a more modest background and detached from the intrigues and corruption hitherto associated with politics. Life in the public domain is almost always eventful, and Réunion has had her share of financial scandals. The island has also been influenced by rather surprising coalitions between the **Réunion Communist Party** and the right-wing parties. Despite their ideological differences, they are continuously sustaining each other when it comes to fighting for an extra seat or backing a particular motion. In 1992, the people of Réunion rejected the traditional parties and elected Camille Sudre, head of TV-Freedom, as president of the regional council. The revelation that some irregularity rendered the election invalid eventually lead to the appointment of his wife, **Margie Sudre,** instead.

The issues of independence or autonomy no longer make headline news, but as the 20C draws to a close, there are many other matters that need to be resolved – namely to minimise the present economic and social inequalities, tackle the population explosion, to maintain good relations with Paris and successfully realign itself for better integration into the European Community.

A subsidised economy

Colonial inheritance

The local economy continues to be highly dependent on producing **sugarcane** for the French market, for which it receives large subsidies from France and the EC. While comprising three-quarters of the territory's exports, it represents only a third of the agricultural output. Facilities for refining the sugar have recently been streamlined and are now concentrated around two factories, one at Gol in the St-Louis district and one at Bois Rouge in St-André. During the harvest season – from July to December – you will see the great big trucks known locally as *cachalots* (ie whales) transporting the cane from the fields to the refineries.

Towards self-sufficiency

Food fads and healthier eating practices, together with the increased spending power of consumers, have boosted the demand for **fresh-farm produce** – especially fruit and vegetables. The reduced cost of air-freighting perishables abroad and the lack of any exchange rate have also boosted the profit margins of French importers-cum-distributors of pineapples and lychees in particular, thus increasing the market potential for commodities grown in Réunion. As long as revenues from exportable "exotic" produce outpace those from fruit and vegetables for local consumption, the island will continue to struggle for self-sufficiency, especially when prices soar to spectacular heights after a cyclone. Similar improvements are to be found in **stock farming,** although the demand for meat and milk still outweigh supply. Both inshore and offshore **fishing** are regarded as being secondary in importance.

Limited industry

For a long time, sugar-refining was the only industry on the island. Now it represents only a quarter of the region's economy with a larger share coming from growing **perishable foodstuffs**. The third player is the **construction** industry, which is charged with undertaking large-scale building works and supplying the infrastructure of all public amenities (power, water, sewage etc). In order to satisfy the insatiable demand for housing and lessen the social and economic burden of unemployment, the state is relaxing its stance on property speculation and development by providing homeowners with certain financial advantages.

Looking to the future, the prospects of greater industrialisation are bleak. Not only will the territory continue to be hampered by the constraints dictated by a small home market, but it will forever be faced with exorbitant costs of importing rawmaterials.

Service industries

Some 75 % of Réunion's GNP is generated by the service industries, with **commerce** playing a leading role. Since the 1980s, when the concept of the package holiday was expanded to include charter flights, **tourism** has come to be the island's most dynamic sector. During 1998, the island welcomed over 390 000 visitors, thereby generating nearly US$6 500 million.

Unemployment and consumerism

The younger generation is facing bleak prospects, with unemployment levels at 42.8 % – the highest in France.

At the same time, household revenues are at a record high, artificially inflated by handouts from the State (family and sickness benefits), with three out of five of the population dependent on social security payments.

Over the past two decades, household expenditure has been transformed, with priority being given to an ever increasing number of domestic appliances and **consumer products**. The total number of cars has tripled in the last 10 years with more new cars than babies being registered per year! Due to this consumer age, 90 % of homes now have television.

Given the true economic situation of the region, this boom has only been possible because of **credit** and **social security** funding.

This former colony, which always had a precarious economy, is still looking to find a model on which to pin its aspirations for self-sufficiency and political autonomy

Meeting the people

Y. Arthus-Bertrand/ALTITUDE

St-Paul market,
aerial view

A CORNER OF FRANCE IN THE INDIAN OCEAN

A growing population

The last census (1990) to be undertaken in Réunion recorded a relatively young adult population of 705 072: predictions, meanwhile, estimate this figure will rapidly increase to 1 000 000 by the year 2010. For since the island was made a French *département*, improved healthcare during the 1950s and the eradication of malaria have radically reduced infant mortality. The resulting repercussions of the population explosion are being felt now – with at least half the nation under the age of 25.

A cast of many

The people of Réunion are all extremely diverse, being born of varied ancestries from ten countries and three continents, be they European colonists, African slaves or Asian workers. Whether of white, black, yellow or mixed stock, and irrespective of their creed celebrated in church, mosque, temple or pagoda, the inhabitants of Réunion live peacefully with one another and respect each other's cultural identity. Despite ethnic and religious differences, they all speak Creole, attend French schools and consider themselves first and foremost "Réunionnais". Today, at the close of the 20C, the rigid system that at one time segregated communities according to strict social and economic categories has largely been displaced by a strong Creole identity and a positive attitude towards multi-ethnicity.

Creoles

The largest group is the Creole community, which to all intents and purposes is descended from early European sailors and settlers of (predominantly) French, Dutch, English, Spanish, Italian and Polish origins. In fact, the word "Creole" was initially devised to denote those people born on the island; today, the term is colloquially used to refer to the island inhabitants who are not of Kaffir, Comorian, Chinese, Indian or mainland French stock and who collectively represent some 40 % of the population.

Among this social group there are the **"p'tits Blancs des Hauts",** made up of impoverished working-class whites who, having been forced to abandon the large plantations when slavery was formally abolished (1848), migrated to the island interior where they lived from subsistence farming. A number of groups continue to eke out a miserable existence up in the remote corners of the Upland regions, and, being so isolated, these are often affected by the debilitating consequences of interbreeding.

The **"gros Blancs"** – descended from similar European forebears – comprise the local aristocracy, born into privileged families of planters and islanders of consequence. These are the large land-owners, who have managed to safeguard their tenures on agriculture, commerce and business. By controlling the output of cane and the price of sugar, they rose to power in politics and government, although, since the social structure of the island has evolved, this group has become less autocratic.

J. Du Boisberranger/HEMISPHERES

Fête de la Salette, St-Leu

Over the years, there has been an increase in mixed-marriages and a proliferation of **"People of Colour"**, born out of a mingling of two cultures. As a result, a happy profusion of different physical features and skincolour combine to make a remarkably diverse population. On the whole, the majority of these people are Catholics and are to be found working in agriculture and / or administrative jobs.

Finally, there are the **"Z'oreils"** or "*métros*" – the French from the mainland metropolis. The Creole name meaning "ears" is thought to derive from the Frenchmen's inability to understand the local pigeon language and their need to strain their ears to listen to what was being said. This community is of vital importance to the social structure of the island, as it is from this group that many well-educated middle-management workers are drawn both for the private and public sectors. Some may have come to Réunion on temporary assignments, others have chosen to settle there on a permanent basis.

Creoles abroad – It should be remarked, however, that someone who is born into a family that has been established in Réunion for several generations considers himself a "Creole" when abroad. For the islanders' identity – irrespective of whether they are Kaffirs or Indians at home – is best represented as "Creole". Furthermore, the politicians of Réunion will refer collectively to their electorate as being Creole.

Kaffirs

The Kaffirs (from the Arab *cafir* "infidel") are descended from the East African slaves who were brought to the island in the 17C and 18C from Mozambique,

Widespread flight into the hills

In 1750, shortly after the abolition of slavery, there were five slaves to every free man. From the start, it was inevitable that many of the slaves engaged in forced labour on the large estates would attempt to run away into the hinterland. In the mid-18C, these numbers escalated, sometimes with dire and violent consequences. Many were unaccustomed to fending for themselves, and so had little option other than to band together and sally forth at night in search of food. In order to safeguard the petrified town folk, Mahé de La Bourdonnais set up a special militia, charged with mercilessly killing the runaways and being rewarded accordingly. One such bounty-hunter, the colonist François Mussard, became notorious for implacably tracking down runaway slaves around Mafate and Cilaos between 1743 and 1771.

Tanzania, Somalia and Madagascar. During colonial times, those who managed to escape to the remote Upland regions were usually referred to as *"marrons"* – meaning "brown" for short. Many disappeared without trace, having been tracked down and killed by white bounty-hunters looking to cash in on the rewards paid for each body turned in.

Among those who survived the witch hunt, many ended up living with the *p'tits Blancs des Hauts*. Their offspring, in turn, became assimilated into the Creole population. The true black "kaffirs", therefore, are more likely to be direct descendants of the slaves who were freed in 1848. The majority continue to work in the cane fields and sugar refineries, and practise a distinctive form of Catholicism, tinged by animist rituals inherited from their ancestors.

Indians

The "Indians" denote those people whose forebears chose to migrate to Réunion in their tens of thousands between 1848 (abolition of slavery) and 1882 (at which time it was no longer possible to hire them) in search of work on the plantations that had been abandoned by the runaway slaves, where they were subjected to the same abject conditions endured by their predecessors.

The first distinctive group is made up by the **Malabars** (or Malbars), who came from the southwest Indian Malabar coast and from the Tamil states in the south and southwest of the country. They form a close-knit community (comprising some 25 % of the population), and maintain their traditional rituals handed down from generation to generation. It is highly possible that one or other Tamil festival might be celebrated sometime during your stay: look out for signs of special ceremonies taking place at one of the many brightly-coloured temples dotted around the island. A large proportion of Malabars continue to live in the vicinity of a former sugar refinery, notably somewhere along the east coast.

The **"Z'arabes"** are Indian Moslems who, for the most part, are involved in the rag trade (off-the-peg clothing) and hardware shops. The majority moved to Réunion between 1870 and 1914, in the hope of seeking their fortune in a French colony and escaping the economic hardships at home in Gujarat, a region bordering Pakistan on the northeast coast of India. The reason they became known as "*Z'arabes*" was that on arrival, the Creoles mistakenly identified these Moslems as Arabs.

They form a small and closed – but nonetheless significant – minority (less than 5 % of the population), partly as a result of the considerable influence they can bring to bear on economic and political issues. They tend to congregate in the major centres like St-Denis, St-Pierre and St-Benoît, where they control a number of valuable assets in terms of land and business.

Chinese

The Chinese or *Sinois* community, which amounts to less than 5 % of the island's population, originates from Malaya, although a subsequent wave of immigrants came from southeast China (mainly Canton province). The first boatloads arrived during 1860-70 and found work as farm labourers; successive groups coming between 1910-20 became retailers. Still today, the streets are lined with *boutiks* offering a multitude of goods outside the range of an average grocery, stationer's, bar and hardware store combined. The Chinese are discreet and hard-working, and show great solidarity among themselves.

Other minorities

Additional colour is added to this cosmopolitan island by small groups of indigenous people, among others, from Indo-China, Yemen, Malaysia, Java and Australasia. At the close of the 20C, the largest proportion of recent arrivals comes from **Madagascar**, **Comoros** and **Mayotte**: islands wracked by hardship and poverty. Alas, Réunion has troubles of its own – including growing unemployment and unsustainable socio-economic problems – so these foreigners are rarely given the asylum they seek, and more often than not are left to do the menial jobs that residents refuse to undertake.

Religions in Réunion

In the same way that harmony resides among the different ethnic communities of Réunion, so there is a healthy religious tolerance.

Creole Christianity

All 24 districts of Réunion bear the names of Catholic saints given to them by the early colonists. Its evangelisation began in earnest in the 17C when a band of Lazarist preachers were sent there by Louis XIV; a series of monks of various denominations and orders followed behind them intent on building parishes and baptising all incoming immigrants, including slaves, and then, later in the 19C, attempting to convert the Indian "recruited workers" and the freed Black slaves.

Although 90 % of Christians are Catholics, there is an active Protestant faction on the island.

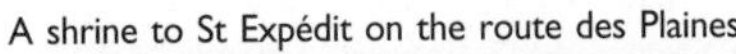

A shrine to St Expédit on the route des Plaines

M Lemerle/ MICHELIN

On the whole, the inhabitants of Réunion are a pious people, although their religion tends to be relatively liberal, incorporating such principles as the Ten Commandments into an eclectic blend of beliefs. A certain number of **pagan cults** pertain to missionary fathers or local divinities, to whom miracles or other powers have been attributed.

Every day, pilgrims gather before the **Black Virgin** at St-Marie, **Notre-Dame de la Salette** in St-Leu or beside the **Vierge au Parasol** at Ste-Rose.

Signs of religious devotion are in evidence everywhere: in addition to churches, there are little shrines know as **"ti bon dié"** dotted along the main roads and paths. Elsewhere, you might notice effigies of a soldier with a red cloak, bearing a cross in his hand representing **St Expédit**, the most venerated local saint (despite not being recognised by the Church), decorated with paintings and red cloth, candles and flowers. He has the reputation of swiftly granting the wishes of the faithful and is often invoked in vengeance: once the wish has been granted, the supplicant must leave an offering lest he be punished in his turn.

Other **popular beliefs** expressed in the form of black magic, witchcraft, voodoo and superstition have been traditionally transferred from one generation to another by god-fearing individuals from Africa, Madagascar and India. Such practices continue to be exercised by a small minority, who leave traces of their nocturnal rites in specific cemeteries (such as at St-Pierre), road intersections, by the sea, on trees, and so on. You might see cigarette ends, glasses of rum, coconuts, flowers and spices or offerings such as a dead cockerel, sacrificed according to occult rituals. Despite being condemned by the Catholic Church, sorcerers and healers continue to practise their art for those in the know. Indeed many islanders remain **superstitious** at heart and will do all they can to avoid evil spirits affecting their lives on a daily basis. To this end, it is common to find unlikely objects – a knife, a doll or salt – scattered around a house, warding off evil spirits.

Hinduism from overseas

Hinduism was brought to the shores of Réunion by Indian migrants in search of work in the 19C. Although its practice was formally opposed by the colonial authorities and the Church, the faith was sustained within the closed communities and now ranks as the second most important religion. Baptised shortly after arriving on Réunion, they were nevertheless allowed by their employers to revert to their native religions. Special areas were designated and set aside within factory courtyards for employees to build small shrines. It will come as no surprise, therefore, to find numerous Malabar "chapels" close to the precincts of the old sugar refineries on the east coast, often shaded by a banyan tree – revered as sacred in India.

Through time, the Indian religion has assimilated local beliefs and practices that make Creole Hinduism into something quite unique. Without the Brahmins (Hindu priests who remained in India), the Malabars chose to develop their own popular rituals around the worship of the deity **Kali,** in whose honour animals are sacrificed, **Pandialé**, for whom people walk over hot coals, and the god **Mourouga** (youngest son of Shiva).

Inevitably, there are adherents to the more traditional and orthodox Hinduism, and those who opt for the divergent Creole form found in Réunion.

For more on Hinduism and its divinities, see p 207.

A moderate form of Islam

Islam was introduced to Réunion by a wave of Moslem migrants from Southern India in the 19C. Since then, numbers attending the island's thirteen mosques have been increased by the arrival of believers from Mayotte and the Comoros. United by faith, the Indo-Moslem community rigorously adheres to the precepts of Islam: affirmation of the one and only Allah, regular prayer, the giving of alms, the fast at Ramadan and, if possible, the pilgrimage to Mecca. Every Friday, the faithful gather at the mosque to listen to the Imam and offer up their prayers. Young Moslems enrolled at the ordinary French schools are free to receive a religious education at the Medersa or Koranic school and learn Arabic and /or their parents' mother tongue, Urdu or *Gujurati*. They are encouraged to be flexible and moderate in their interpretation of the teachings of the Koran, and to be very tolerant in their devotion. Some women wear the veil while the majority prefer to don jeans and tee-shirts. Alcohol is freely available everywhere.

Most Moslems in Réunion are **Sunni**; there is also a smaller group of **Shi'ites** who arrived later.

Buddhism and Chinese cults

Many Chinese converted to Catholicism on their arrival in Réunion in the 19C. There is only a small minority of Buddhists and these have incorporated various Taoïst and Confucian elements into their rituals. Whatever their actual religion, this community remain faithful to the cult of ancestors and the service of the dead.

Mixed celebrations

Religious festivals provide islanders of all faiths and denominations with a chance to come together. It comes as no surprise, therefore, to find Malabars attending churches or *Z'arabes* taking part in Tamil celebrations, proof of the island's deep-rooted cultural mix.

Christian festivals

Every Christian holy day is celebrated with great enthusiasm, be it Christmas, Easter, Assumption (15 August) or All Saints' Day. Furthermore, such important feasts are usually marked with processions.

Probably the most universally celebrated of the annual festivities is **Christmas**, when everyone, irrespective of his or her creed, partakes in the ritual of decorating trees and exchanging presents. Father Christmas appears in all the shop windows during December, appealing to children from all communities together.

The period of Lent leading up to **Easter** is still observed by some people, although the main holiday is Easter Monday, when it is traditional for families to spend the day on the beach with a picnic.

For **All Saints'** (1 November), people flock to the cemeteries much as they do in other Catholic countries to remember the dead and decorate the graves of loved ones with flowers. In certain places, Creoles maintain an ancient African ritual of honouring their belief in the afterlife, by sprinkling the ground with water and/or offering up a complete meal to the dead.

Hindu festivals

Notice of the more important Malabar festivals is posted up on walls and sometimes advertised in newspapers and on the radio. Visitors are usually welcome at celebrations, and may even be formally invited to assist at the ceremonial meal and partake of food presented on a banana leaf and eaten with fingers. Do not hesitate in accepting such invitations, although guests should be familiar with, and respectful of, the etiquette observed at such events (rules are listed outside the entrances to Hindu temples – *see p 59*). The largest gatherings tend to be at St-Denis, La Possession and St-André.

Certain festivals attract huge crowds comprising several thousand followers. Whatever the occasion, these colourful celebrations could be the highlight of any visitor's holiday. Even if he/she is unable to appreciate the significance of every ritual, soaking up the pervasive festive atmosphere and devotional excitement, and sharing the joy – sometimes even the suffering – make for a truly memorable experience. Such affairs provide the perfect excuse for participants to dress up in their finest saris and brightest jewellery, to deck monuments with garlands of flowers and strings of lights and to fill the air with the most exotic incense.

To honour the goddess Pandialé, followers undertake such impressive feats as **walking over burning coals** at the time of the summer and winter solstices, sometime towards the end of December/early January and the end of June/early July. To do this, penitents must observe a period of 18 days of purification by fasting, self-control, meditation and prayer before participating in the procession, headed by a sacred float *(tell)* accompanied by the sound of drums. On their heads they wear a pyramid of fruit and yellow flowers – known as a *karlon* – which is offered up to the divinity. One by one, they follow the religious leader in walking three times across a six metre-long ditch filled with red-hot coals, prepared earlier that morning in front of the temple. Just as Pandialé was spared her suffering by her spiritual purity, so these penitents are protected from the searing pain by their abstinence through fasting. Despite this, bowls of milk are on hand to soothe burnt and blistered feet after the event.

The reason people might wish to do this lies in a personal desire or need to atone for sinning, to thank a divinity for granting a particular request, or to affirm a special vow. Believers are never required or obliged to perform such an act.

The ritual of sacrificing an animal – usually a cockerel or a goat – is performed in honour of the goddess **Kali**, to whom red flowers are dedicated. At the end of the ceremony, the sacrificial meat *(massalé coq* or *cabri massalé)* is eaten as part of a feast.

Cavadee, **Divali** and **Holi**: *see how these festivals are celebrated in Mauritius on p 209.*

Chinese festivals

Chinese New Year or the **Spring Festival**: *see p 213.*

Every year, the Chinese celebrate the **Guan Di festival** *(fête du Guan Di)*, which honours a notably brave and upright soldier who has been elevated to the rank of a hero and god in war, literature and commerce.

During the annually-held **Festival of The Dead** *(fête des morts)*, the Chinese remember the departed. On that day, each family goes to the cemetery before proceeding to the temple and praying for their dead ancestors.

C. Vaisse/HOA QUI

Z'arabes at prayer

The **Mid-Autumn Festival** *(fête de la mi-automne)*, which is held in September, commemorates the Chinese victory over the Mongols. For the occasion, special "moon biscuits" *(gâteaux de lune)* are baked and eaten. According to tradition, the date of the insurrection was marked on the cookies until banned at the revolution.

Moslem Festivals

See p 212.

DAILY LIFE

Architectural heritage

The days of the really traditional Creole *"case"* are numbered, and, slowly, the term is becoming a collective term for any of the island's simple dwellings or more substantial houses, built of wood, corrugated iron or concrete breeze blocks. Only the larger and grander homes remain exempt as these are commonly referred to as *"châteaux"*.

With time, all the little ramshackle houses along the roadsides are being replaced by standardised, and therefore commonplace, constructions. The more traditional, substantial and sophisticated family residences cost a fortune to maintain in a habitable state. These elegant buildings that comprise Réunion's architectural heritage have suffered the consequences of neglect over the long term, a lack of investment, devastating cyclones and fires, and, above all, a complete lack of interest.

On the whole, with a little effort, several distinctive styles of house may be discerned. In the wilds of the south, the houses tend to be small; in the Plaine des Palmistes, they are built for summer use; in the smarter residential streets of St-Denis, elegant townhouses grace the likes of the rue de Paris while out in the country, large planter's houses emerge from among the sugarcane fields. But how much longer will these traditional styles prevail?

Turn to the illustrations p 18-19.

Creole "ti'cases"

Most people in Réunion live in their own separate houses. First and foremost, these are designed as far as possible to withstand cyclones. To date, local hardwoods *(bois de fer, bois de rempart)* have been employed in the construction of the framework and roof joists as these are solid yet flexible, resistant to termites and impervious to rot. Four-sided roofs tend to be favoured over normal two-part roofs and gable walls because they prevent rain from lashing at the walls and seeping through the masonry during cyclones.

In recent times, concrete and corrugated iron have come to replace the traditional thatch of palm fronds and plaited vetiver, and displaced the need for weatherboarding and protective wooden shuttering against the elements.

The underlying simplicity of the basic structures is often offset by a profusion of colour and ornament. Red roofs rise up above the luxuriant green gardens; shutters are painted to resemble windows; finely-detailed fretwork **lambrequins** – of carved wood or wrought ironwork – ornament the eaves; **frontages** are marked out with decorative lozenge patterning; walls are insulated with **protective slats** of tamarind wood help to fuse the houses with their garden settings.

The **verandah** also is adapted to suit the local climate. In the Lowlands, it is used like a roofed terrace that opens out onto the garden; in the Uplands, it takes the form of a glazed conservatory where one might entertain friends to tea or coffee, or enjoy some other idle pursuit. In either case, this terrace area is furnished with comfortable chairs made of cane or rattan and groups of flourishing green pot-plants and flowers. It provides a lovely cool and airy space in which to sit away from the heat of the day, and a sheltered spot out of the wind and rain during a storm.

Whatever kind of house they have, the islanders derive great pride and joy from their **kour,** or garden, where they are able to indulge in their love for all kinds of flowering species. In the odd case, the overall impression is one of tangled confusion: this is by design. Elsewhere, you may find ordered beds planted with vegetables or a clutch of hens, ducks and bantams being raised for domestic use. The corner of some gardens may be given over to the kitchen, or *boucan,* that comprises a shabby-looking corrugated-iron shack in which the curry is left to simmer over a wood fire.

A growing number of city-dwellers are choosing to abandon the traditional forms of housing in favour of purpose-built apartment blocks, most especially since the 1960s when the local population boom required several housing estates to be hastily built – hence such deplorable complexes as the Michel Debré estate in Chaudron on the outskirts of St-Denis. Nowadays, the state planning department is actively sponsoring a more measured and carefully-planned building programme that might help to resolve certain social problems and replace the more squalid premises around. It will probably take another twenty or so years before every family has a decent home.

Fragments of a grander era

In the course of your wanderings about the countryside, look out for the straight avenues of coconut palms cutting a swathe through the sugarcane plantations that lead up to the *habitation* – where the landowner lives. These residences comprise a series of buildings housing the kitchen (constructed away from the main house to minimise the risk of fire), the cow-shed, the stable and the *camps* where the servants and estate workers were accommodated.

As with the *ti'cases*, the front of these more sophisticated establishments was graced with the typical **lambrequins** and a **verandah**, only this time made of stone or painted wooden slats. Additional features might also include decorative **columns** and **awnings**.

The most elegant buildings have long gone; other more modest homesteads survive. In the Upland regions, many of the fine larger family houses are in fact secondary residences belonging to wealthy folk who escape to the cool hills during the hot summer season.

Colonial town buildings

Many of the municipal buildings put up in the 18C by the French East India Company remain standing: notably the prefecture in St-Denis and the town hall in St-Pierre. Although designed for use by the army and for warehousing, they currently provide offices for regional and local council administrations. Their modern function is well suited to the rather formal and severe style of building, with its heavy colonnades and lime-washed walls dramatically articulated by black basalt stone dressing.

The old quarters, like the neighbourhoods around the Cathedral in St-Denis and rue des Bons Enfants in St-Pierre, date from the same period and reflect a similar architectural style. As might be expected, the buildings were regimented into rigid blocks along rectilinear streets by the Company

Ground-coral lime and mortar

For centuries, lime has been mixed with stone and used to cement blocks of masonry together or added to water and applied to walls like a wash. In Réunion, there are no limestone cliffs and so lime was made from grinding up the dead coral washed up from the lagoon. The last functioning lime-kiln on the island was at St-Leu which closed in 1995, to the advantage of the ecology of the lagoon.

surveyor. The overall effect is less formal, however, partly because of the reduced scale, partly because of the relief provided by the finely worked wrought-iron balcony balustrades along the Promenade.

On the whole, the planters enjoyed flaunting their wealth: hence the string of beautifully crafted wrought-iron gates – known as **baro** (from the French *barreaux* meaning bars) – lining the main street. The houses beyond the grilles were designed to show that no expense was spared as regards the building materials used and the nature of the applied decorative ornament. Each is furnished with a small **guetali**: a belvedere-cum-pavilion strategically placed at the corner of the house or in the garden, from which residents could keep a watchful eye over the street without being seen.

How the day is divided

Weekdays

For most islanders, the day begins between 5am and 6am. For many this is followed by an hour or two stuck in a traffic jam. School starts at about 7.30am, offices sometime between 7.30am and 8.30am. The majority dine fairly early, at around 7.30pm or 8pm and retire to bed soon after. Do take this into account before making a telephone call after 9pm lest you haul someone out of bed!

Weekends

Sunday picnics are a real institution: do not be surprised to encounter the most delicious smell of cooking *massalé* wafting your way when out walking in the hills at the weekend. First thing in the morning, family expeditions set out for a special site in the woods, by a waterfall or on the beach, say, and set about putting up the trestle tables and chairs. Out come the groundsheets and the umbrella, the cooking pots, ingredients and utensils required in the preparation of the gently-simmered *cari*: everything is there save the kitchen sink. Several generations find themselves collected together around the family table. Then it is time to while away the hours with a siesta, a game of cards, dominoes or bowls, while in the background, radios blare out the catchy rhythms of the latest popular song or *séga* tune.

Saturday-night fever

Discos and *kabars* (open-air dances) attract crowds of people intent on dancing the night away. The atmosphere is maintained by liberal quantities of rum and *dodo* (local beer). The traffic on the roads is even heavier than usual and pile-ups are a regular occurrence. The party spirit carries on during Sunday: minibuses do the rounds of the villages whisking the younger generation off dancing, while the older people may set out for a picnic in the country.

Networking

During the week, people tend to stay at home rather than go out on the town. Rarely do the islanders venture out to a restaurant or to one of the few bars and cafés unless they are residents of St-Denis, St-Gilles or St-Pierre. The most popular places in which to meet up with friends tend to be the boutiks, grocery-cum-hardware store-cum-bar, where hot gossip is exchanged, or in the street, where people might draw up a seat for a chat or a game of cards.

Cars

A bird's-eye view of Réunion in 1999 would have included a car every 100m; since then, the number of vehicles is fast approaching saturation point for this small, hilly island's limited road network. Despite this, the "limousine" continues to be regarded as a reflection on social status, and so it is lovingly washed and polished each weekend in the river or at a waterfall using large quantities of soap, while the hi-fi systems boom out their sounds and drown out the competition.

Gambling

The Réunion population makes up a considerable proportion of those taking part in the two main French national lotteries (La Française des Jeux and the PMU). In 1999, the share for Réunion amounted to nearly US$13 thousand million: twice as much as in mainland France. Prize-winners incite other islanders to chance their own fortunes and so queues form on a daily and weekly basis outside the various lottery outlets and ticket booths.

Television

90% of homes now have television and watching TV is one of the most popular pastimes.

Sport

Réunion is a land of sporting fanatics and many of the young are both keen and talented when it comes to handling a round ball. Running is popular as well, with people jogging all over the place, sprinting along the fast lane of the main road or on the Montagne road and along La Barachois. Groups of eager enthusiasts congregate in the early evening for training sessions, the football pitches engage in feverish action, while the running circuits are pounded by indefatigable joggers.

Food

"Un ti peu la morue grillée"... the subject of cooking comes into a surprising number of local songs. Practically everyone knows how to prepare the traditional *cari*, *rougail* and rum punches that play such an essential part in their day-to-day lives.

However, diet and eating habits are changing fast, partly as a result of major improvements in the refrigeration and distribution of perishable foodstuffs, and partly since bread was introduced and established as a popular staple and more meat is readily available for easy consumption.

Women

Women occupy an important place in Réunion society. Over the past 20 years, they have gradually become increasingly independent, both in social and economic terms. This has been achieved by encouraging women to study for longer periods and to higher standards, by providing better job opportunities (in the service and hotel industries) and though state benefits for single mothers. The heaviest burden on single-parent families – which make up a quarter of the total number of family households – tends to be the custody and education of the children in which the mother plays a vital role. Furthermore, it is the women of the household who tend to assume the responsibility for all the administrative tasks and smooth running of the home.

Dress

Most people now wear western-style clothes although many, especially among the Malabar and *Z'arabe* communities, still dress in traditional attire. This is especially evident in and around the temples and mosques when followers of the faith rally to prayer dressed in brightly-coloured saris or spotless white tunics, transparent veils or knitted skullcaps.

Cyclone alert

Cyclone alerts are tense times. As soon as cyclone warnings are announced *(see p 69* Cyclone alert!) people rush to the supermarkets to buy stocks of food, mineral water, torch-lights, batteries and candles. Hour after hour, the media broadcasts bulletins on the state and whereabouts of the depression. When the orange alert is given, the population is seized with apprehension as it stops to listen out for information from its transistor radios. Now that there are progressively fewer corrugated-iron shacks, the dreaded consequences of a serious cyclone have abated. Indeed, some people arrange to get together during the red alert phase and settle down to playing games indoors – cards and dominoes usually – when it is forbidden to go outdoors. The red alert is maintained during the lull that follows the eye of the storm, as the tail can bring further devastation. At last, when the gales have subsided and the cyclone has moved away, the orange alert is sounded and it is time to take stock of the outcome: fallen trees, damaged roofs, roads washed away... After the suspense, the rhythm of daily life returns to normal.

Shouldering a billhook

P. Baker/SUNSET

Art and folklore

Music and dance

The sound of music permeates the home, the street, the beach, the discos and the *kabars* (dances out in the open air). It provides a rhythm to life on the island, and, day after day, reflects the harmonious intermingling of the different cultures. The two main traditional dances, the *Maloya* and *Séga*, are an extension of this mix, blended and performed by the Creoles using tempi and instruments from Africa, Madagascar and Europe.

Maloya

This dance is a primitive form of the *séga* *(see below)* and recalls the songs sung by the slaves born in Madagascar and Mozambique. The name *maloya* is derived from the Madagascan expression for "I'm fed up". The musical accompaniment is played on African and Madagascan instruments including: the **rouleur**, a goat-hide and wooden drum made from a barrel (originally this would probably have been a hollow tree trunk) astride which the player sits, the **bobre**, a stringed instrument contrived from a split and dried gourd, a string and a length of wood, and the **cayamb**, a flat contraption created out of fine cane shoots filled with seeds, which is shaken like a rattle.

The *maloya* is more than just a dance: the full-blooded and heart-rending songs that relate to the hardships and chores of daily life or to love call for a reaction from the dancer. As the soloist intones his lament, the dancer responds by moving sensuously and lasciviously. The musicians quicken the beat and the pace becomes frenzied; the dancers, entranced by the rhythms, let themselves go. Couples come together and separate, without ever touching, combining harmonious and suggestive movements. For a long time, the strains of the *maloya* allowed the dispossessed to vent their despair, resentment and outrage. In the 1930s, this anger abated and the songs were silenced until the 1960s when the Réunion Communist Party revived their popularity.

For this music expressed discontent: it was, therefore, ideally suited to rallying the Creole people into formulating their identity and claiming their independence. As a result, the authorities banned the *maloya* for a period of fifteen years. Then during the 1970s, singers and groups like **Danyel Waro, Granmoun lélé** and **Ziskakan** managed to introduce it into their performances at free concerts and, eventually, at the first Creole festival.

The revival of *maloya* was officially marked by the Left being elected to power in 1981: since that time, new bands have responded to the example of **Ti Fock** and **Baster** and combined the spirit of the *maloya* with reggae to produce a sound called **maloggae** (Racine, Tatane, Patrick Persée), and jazz (Sabouk, Teddy Baptiste), rock (Rapidos, Joe Sparing), rap and other popular genres.

Séga

Séga was originally introduced to Réunion from Mauritius, and soon became the rage among bourgeois society in the second half of the 19C. Its bittersweet songs speak of love and the trials of daily life. In colonial times, they were danced by slaves. Later, after the First World War, the dances were brought into Creole middle-class drawing rooms. The music's present, contemporary form reflects current tastes, which in time have displaced the traditional instruments in favour of the synthesiser, modern drum kits and electric guitars. Like the *maloya*, the *séga* borrows a number of elements from other types of music: combined with reggae, it becomes **seggae –** jazz, rap, etc.

Foreign influences

As Réunion became more prosperous, a new social class evolved: soon European forms of dancing were introduced and became the rage at the large private house-parties. The music was played by Black musicians and they imparted their own rhythms and energy to it, interpreting the happy-go-lucky tunes in a distinctively Creole way. So, by the end of the 19C, the most fashionable dances included **quadrilles**, **polkas** and **Scottish dancing,** with accompaniments provided by an accordion, violin and banjo. These strains continue to be enjoyed in the Upland regions among the *p'tits Blancs,* where a number of bands manage to keep alive an interest and taste for some of the old-fashioned kinds of music.

Craft

Most of the souvenir shops display cheaply-made wares imported from Madagascar, India, China and Africa. Among the traditional handicraft skills still practised in Réunion, probably the most distinctive is **basket-work,** using textured fibres from the *pandanus*, *vetiver*, *choka* and coconut trees. Although the finished items are usually intended to be functional, the hats, bags, baskets and slippers available on the market stalls can be extremely decorative.

Another notable speciality, associated with Cilaos since the 19C and still practised to this day, is the **jours de Cilaos**: an intricate kind of lace through which one can see "daylight" – hence the name. The same women do the most wonderfully intricate embroidery too, which they make up into tablecloths, handkerchiefs and other household linen.

Another typical form of needlework is the recycling of dress fabric into patchwork. These quilts are locally known as **tapis "mendiants",** probably because the little hexagonal patches could be added wherever the family was stationed at the time. The same remnants are often made into little dolls.

Skilled **cabinet-making** and fine joinery were introduced to the island population by the East India Company. As a result, wood-workers have learnt to exploit the various textures and coloured grains of such rare woods as tamarind, camphor, cinnamon, styrax and sideroxylon, especially for turning out reproductions of colonial furniture or creating decorative carved objects and inlaid boxes.

Literature

Réunion's literature asserts its own peculiar Creole quality. During the 19C, the written word mainly consisted of **poetry** that celebrated the beauty and charm of the island. Among the most distinctive, there is Leconte de Lisle, the founder of the French Parnassian circle that rejected Romanticism, the Pre-Romantic poet, Évariste de Parny, and Eugène Dayot. After the Second World War, a new genre emerged that was more in touch with the people and their grievances, when penned by the likes of Jean Albany and Jean-Henry Azéma.

The **novel**, which was so dominated at the outset by the highly conventional authors Marius and Ary Leblond, evolved during the 1970s when writers began drawing upon the history and cultural diversity of the island for their inspiration. The prime figures to emerge among the new generation include Daniel Vaxelaire and Jean-François Sam-Long who wrote about the *Black slave-hunters* and Madame Desbassyns and Dhavid and Guy Douyère, who produced colourful accounts of their childhood. However, the most well-known is probably Axel Gauvin, who wrote moving novels in which French and Creole are blended, thus helping to assert a specific Réunion identity.

Séga dancing

SOCIAL ETIQUETTE

How to mix with the locals

The people of Réunion may, at first, appear slightly distant, a little cold maybe and sometimes almost disagreeable. However, if you set this first impression aside and make the effort to talk to them by engaging in conversation, asking questions about their homeland, commenting on the island's flora, or chatting about religious festivals, you will find them to be open and friendly.
Relations are made even easier if you choose the right place and time. The following subjects provide a good basis for starting a conversation:

T Perri /HOA QUI

Outside the Ravine du Pont café

- For a more authentic experience of daily life, opt for a bed and breakfast or a guest-house rather than a hotel, and frequent the picturesque and cheap eating-places around the market area or snack-bars rather than formal restaurants.
- Walk out to the more remote Creole houses: with a little luck and tact, you may be invited in to share tea and / or a chat.
- If you are invited for a meal, this will probably be served out on the veranda rather than in the house itself. You will also be taken around the garden, or *kour*, by your host and shown each different plant.
- An easy way to engage in conversation in the market is to enquire how to prepare the fruit and vegetables displayed.
- The majority of people enjoy cooking and love to talk about it. This usually leads into an exchange of tips and recipes, or a recommendation of where to eat something particularly special. Ask about the different kinds of *cari* or the thousand and one ways of preparing a rum punch, for each family has its own private recipe.

• On the bus, locals often engage in discussions with tourists and "métros" from mainland France who are unfamiliar with the island: they are often happy to suggest things and make recommendations on what to avoid.

• If you are a fan of football, do not hesitate in talking about the local teams and any league matches broadcast on television: many local people are passionate about football, which they call "ballon-rond".

• Linger around the temples, mosques or churches after prayer meetings at the end of the day or at weekends, and enjoy the bustle as people stop for an idle chat before heading homewards. Find out about any festivals due to take place and try to attend the festivities – from a discreet and respectful distance.

Forewarned is forearmed

• Remove shoes before entering a mosque or Hindu temple. Check that your shoulders are covered, and avoid – if possible – wearing short shorts and skirts (ie baring your legs) and plunging necklines. Do not enter Hindu temples carrying or wearing any form of leather (belts, bags or pouches), as it is considered impure.

• It is best to ask permission before taking someone's photograph. Women, in particular, might turn their head away when they notice a lens focused upon them. Children, on the other hand, hasten to pose in front of the camera, thus ruining any hope of catching a spontaneous shot.

• Say "in the Metropolis" rather than "in France", because time and again you will be reminded that Réunion is a French *département*.

• When sitting down to a meal, remember that *cari* dishes are served in a particular order: first the rice, then the pulses, followed by the meat, and finally the *rougail* (tomato condiment).

• In Indian restaurants, do not reproach the waiter for being overly familiar if he spreads your napkin on your knees.

• When you set out to visit someone at home, if there is no doorbell, announce yourself confidently at the *baro* (gate) by calling "*na pwin person*?" (is anyone there?)

• When driving, be wary of any plastic bags deposited in the middle of the cross-roads: these are likely to contain offerings, which, according to Malabar practices, are designed to attract evil spirits.

Eating and drinking

Tastes and flavours

Réunion's cultural diversity is reflected in its colourful, spicy and aromatic cuisine. The early French settlers established a taste for gently stewed meat, the Africans introduced their fondness for root vegetables, like *manioc* (cassava) and *patates douces* (sweet potatoes), whereas the Madagascans launched *brèdes* (green leaf vegetable), and vanilla and ginger. In time, the Indians introduced the use of distinctive and subtly blended spices – turmeric, coriander, cumin, *calou pilé* and *massalé* – and the Chinese oyster sauce and *siav* (soy sauce), which they used to flavour their lightly cooked vegetables tossed in a *wok*. What cannot be attributed to any particular influence is the widespread use of hot chilli, which is added liberally to many dishes or served as a condiment.

Either way, food forms a vital and colourful part of Creole life and a fundamental element to the island's culture.

Regional specialities

The two basic staples of Creole cooking are the **cari** and its variant, **rougail** (shorthand for *rougail marmite*). In both cases, chopped onions, garlic and spices (mainly ground turmeric/*saffran pays/massalé* and chilli) are gently fried together; then ginger and tomatoes are added, followed by the cubed meat, fish, *z'ourite* (octopus) or seared prawns. These are then left to simmer gently until cooked. The main dish is usually served with boiled rice, some kind of pulse – like lentils, dried haricot beans or Cape peas – and a spicy hot condiment simply referred to as *rougail* or *rougail pilon* (chopped or crushed raw chillies, garlic and/or onion flavoured with lemon juice, tomato, green mango, peanuts, avocado or aubergine/egg plant). Alternatively, there might be a form of the local pickle know as *achards* (finely sliced raw vegetables, poached in spiced vinegar and preserved in aromatic oil). Local etiquette dictates that the rice should be spooned onto the plate first, followed by the pulses, the meat and finally the "*sauce*".

Other specialities include cured meats – collectively referred to as **charcuterie-pays** – comprising a variety of home-prepared sausages and pork scratchings (deep-fried rind/crackling), often served as a stew or *cari*.

Certain dishes remain peculiar to a particular region: *bichiques* at St-Benoît; vanilla-flavoured goodies on the east coast; grilled tuna, swordfish and marlin on the west coast; *chouchou* from Salazie; lentils from Cilaos; duck with guava in the Plaine des Palmistes, and so on. More exotic specialities – *palm-heart* Millionaire's Salad, geranium mushrooms (only available in the Uplands, and at a specific time of year), swallow's nests or wasp larvae – are considered true delicacies.

A limited number of establishments pride themselves on offering a range of local dishes, featuring surprisingly delicious – even if simple – cooking, using home-grown ingredients that once were eaten solely by the initiated, such as *gratin de songe à L'Embuscade*, *cari baba-figue*, *choca bleu* in Roche Plate.

The islanders have only recently begun to produce their own cheeses, which they sometimes flavour with different spices or lemon *(combava)*. These tend to be eaten when soft and fresh, and accompanied by guava jam. Sweet-addicts may be disappointed to find that there are no sugary treats to satisfy their cravings other than the usual fruit fritters and ice-creams made with lychees, guava, mangoes and passion-fruit. Another staple is the rather heavy and dense-textured cake made with sweet potato, colocasia *(songe)* or *manioc*. These are wholesome and nutritious if a little bland, but are ideal for taking on long hikes as fallbacks when hungry and tired.

Creole munchies

All sorts of delicious snacks are available everywhere and anywhere in town, in the market, from the roadside and parking lot, on the beach or from village stores or *boutiks*.

Samossas are north Indian specialities consisting of small deep-fried triangular pastry-cases filled with seasoned vegetables and / or spiced meat or fish. The **bonbon-piment** is a different kind of fritter made with a special type of spiced flour – do not worry, it is not as fiery as its name implies. **Bouchons** are dim-sum parcels – a Chinese form of ravioli made with rice flour, stuffed with pork and steamed. The **sarcive**, which are also Chinese in origin, are fine slices of smoked and honeyed loin of pork.

Creole thirst-quenchers

Creole meals are regularly preceded by a rum-based **fruit-punch** aperitif, and rounded off with a rum digestif drink or **"rhum arrangé",** which consists of rum in which fruit and spices (star anis, cinnamon, zest of orange, vanilla, lemon grass citronella, *fahem*...) have been macerated for several months.

A popular and less potent alternative is *dodo*, a Bourbon form of lager that can be consumed in large quantities. More recently several new local beers, made by the same company, have also appeared on the market: "Bourbon la Rousse" and "Bourbon la Blanche". The **wine of Cilaos**, which in the early days was fermented using Isabelle grapes and had a reputation for causing people to become deranged, is becoming more palatable since new kinds of vines were introduced.

C Vaisse/HOA QUI

Spoilt for choice

Language

The **Creole spoken in Réunion** is slightly different from the forms spoken in Mauritius, Rodrigues or the Seychelles, although the inhabitants of the various islands have no trouble in understanding each other.

Creole, a form of pigeon-French, was developed in the 18C during colonial times: the need for a common language was not only prompted by the need for masters to be understood by their slaves, but also for slaves of various nationalities to be able to communicate between themselves. As a result, the French language was gradually simplified and corrupted by the illiterate labourers on the plantations. Foreign words imported from African and Madagascan dialects enabled this class of subordinates to express nuance and assert their own "language". Over time, this was further enriched with words assimilated from English, Hindi and Chinese. Within particular communities of immigrants, close families and religious groups, however, the mother tongue continued to be spoken.

For generations, Creole remained a hybrid spoken language that was common to all and used on a daily basis; only recently has it evolved a consistent system of grammar and spelling that has allowed it to be written down. For French speakers, it is easy to follow the gist of a sentence as many words are derived from the French and pronounced phonetically. Others, meanwhile, will appreciate the distinctive cadences of the language and the expressive intonation of words which often are onomatopoeic.

Because Creole was considered to be an insular language of the people, regulations banned it from being taught in schools and broadcast on the media. This was finally changed in the 1970s. After years of almost clandestine use, it is now in favour again and is widely used in literature, music, and, since 1982, in the public domain and media.

Despite this, **French** remains the official language that is taught in school and spoken on public occasions and at formal functions. It is also the language of administration and bureaucracy, justice and business.

Helpful phrases

Pronunciation

"ch" is pronounced "s"	Les Sinois (the Chinese)
"g" and "j" are pronounced "z"	L'arzent (money)
Vowels are preceded by "z", "n" or "l"	Le z'ananas (the pineapple),
mon l'auto (my car)	
The masculine is nearly always used	
even for feminine words	Mon l'auto, son caze (his house)
"même" is used for emphasis	lé bon même (it's really good)

In short – what's what

Achards	Pickled vegetables and chillies preserved in spiced oil, used as a condiment.
Bagasse	Sugarcane waste used as compost or burnt as fuel.

Baro/Barreau	Grille outside a Creole house, its height and width being indicative of the householder's wealth.
Bazar	Market.
Bertelle	Flat knapsack woven from pandanus, worn on the back.
Bichiques	Young fish or fry newly hatched at sea that swim up river to live to maturity. Highly prized delicacy.
Bois	Used to denote a variety of tall plants (literally "wood").
Bonbon	General word for sweetmeats/candies as well as savoury biscuits.
Bonbon piment	Spicy savoury fritter made from ground pulses.
Boucan	In old usage, to denote a fisherman's small shack; today, this might be a small outside wooden cookhouse with a corrugated-iron roof.
Boucané	Smoked belly of pork.
Bouchon	Tasty meatball wrapped in rice-flour paste.
Brèdes	Leafy spinach-like vegetable usually eaten boiled in broth or stir-fried.
Bringelle	Aubergine/eggplant.
Café coulé	Brewed-up home-roasted coffee, sometimes flavoured with vanilla.
Cabri	Goat, often prepared by Tamils in a hot spicy stew.
Cachalot	Articulated truck loaded with sugarcane.
Cafre	The word Kafir in English, used to describe Black people from Africa and, therefore, the descendants of Negro slaves. As in English, the term can be both pejorative or affectionate in its meaning.
Camaron	Large prawn.
Cap	Large rock or headland.
Cari	Staple dish in Creole cooking, adapted from the Indian curry.
Case/Kaz	A general word for a dwelling that might range from a small corrugated-iron shack to a largish family concrete breeze-block house. The very large and elegant villas, however, are called "château".
Chouchou	A rather bland-tasting gourd-like vegetable grown on a vine up a trellis, equivalent to the "choko" of Australia and a "christophine" or "choyote" in Europe.
Combava	Small green fruit resembling a lime. Zest is used in cooking.
Dodo	Colloquial name for the Bourbon beer – after the solitaire or dronte, a bird which, after becoming extinct, came to be considered as mythical.
Écart	Remote village.
Faham	Special kind of orchid sometimes used to flavour herbal tea or rum drinks.
Fanjan	Tree-fern.
Farine	Fine rain or drizzle.
Figue	Banana.
Gaulette	Old French measure equivalent to 15 King's paces (5m), still used to describe cane crop coverage. The word can also allude to a pole or fishing rod.
Giraumon	Red pumpkin.
Grains	Dried pulses (beans, lentils) served with cari.
Gramoune	Old person, grandfather.

Grègue	Rustic white metal coffee-can.
Guetali	Small pavilion standing in the corner of a garden or sticking out of the external walls from which one could survey the street unseen (from guetter = to watch out for).
Habitation	A large country estate inclusive of the house and surrounding land.
Îlet	Remote hill village in the circus region, perched on a plateau or volcanic scree.
Kabar	Musical celebration-cum-party, associated with maloya.
Kour	Garden.
Lambrequins	Ornamental designs cut into the woodwork or ironwork for decoration, very often in the form of a geometric edging applied to the underside of the eaves or verandahs.
Lontan	In the olden days.
Malabar/Malbar	Person from the extreme southwestern Malabar coast of India.
Marmaille	Child.
Marron	Fugitive, wild – and by implication illicit, clandestine when referring to the runaway slaves in the mountains, or to a wild animal or plant.
Massalé	Indian mixture of spices.
Morne	Small rounded hill, standing alone in the middle of a barren plain.
Moukater	To mock, make tittle-tattle, spread gossip.
Pistache	Peanut.
Pois	General term for pulses (beans, broad beans, lentils).
Rack	Ordinary rum.
Rempart	Sheer cliff.
Rhum arrangé	Rum in which fruit and spices have been steeped for several months.
Rougail	Either a slowly simmered stew (rougail marmite) or a fiery condiment (rougail pilon).
Safran pays	Ground turmeric: widely used yellow powder made from the ground root.
Samossa	Small Indian deep-fried pasty, stuffed with spicy meat, fish or vegetables.
Sarcive	Chinese-style grilled spare-ribs, marinated in honey and soy sauce.
Sari	2-piece dress worn by Indian women comprising a long piece of fabric wrapped around the waist and draped over the shoulder.
Siave	Chinese soy sauce.
Tente	Basket woven from pandanus leaves.
Varangue	The open or glazed verandah of a Creole house on one or more sides.
Yab	Pejorative term for the "p'tits Blancs des Hauts".
Zamal	Cannabis.
Z'arabe	Asian Moslem originally from the Indian sub-continent.
Z'embrocal	A dish comprising rice, vegetables and turmeric.
Z'oreil	A pejorative allusion to a French person from mainland France.
Z'ourite	Octopus.

Just for fun...

Amarrer son cou	To protect oneself from a chill.
Argent braguette	Family credit.
Bat'un carré	Go for a turn or a stroll.
Blanc rouillé	A white person with red hair.
Bonbon la fesse	Suppository.
Un bon peu	A great deal.
Bouchonné	Constipated.
Cari la faiblesse	Vegetable curry, with no meat.
Casser un contour	To turn.
Cass papaye sans gaulette	A tall person.
Un chauffe galet	A lazy-bones or lay-about, always sitting down.
Coco	The head.
Colodent	Toffee-coated peanuts, sometimes described as "nougat pays".
Conserves	Spectacles.
Coup de sec	Glass of rum.
Être en bois carré	In good health, great shape.
Faire dentelle	To be affected, pretentious.
Le fait-clair	Daylight.
Une femme manze la corde	A fickle woman (who chews the rope to escape).
Le fénoir	Night time.
Le jour y vieillit	Twilight (literally translated as: the day is getting old).
Ladilafé	Tittle-tattle, lies.
Lé gayar	That's fine, that's good, that's super.
La loi	The police.
Mangosier y bat' quat'cylindres	I'm very hungry (I could eat a horse).
Moin lé pas en ordre	I don't feel well, not myself.
Mon femme lé génée	My wife is pregnant.
Navé napi	There was some, there is none left (in a shop).
Parasol	Sunshade.
La peau du bois	Tree bark.
Pied de riz	A good match, a woman who manages to support the household well.
Pile plate	Flask of white rum.
Poulet-gasoil/ poulet-la-route	Roast chicken sold along the roadside.
Racleur la mousse	Surfer.
Rale-poussé	A provocative push/ shove.
Soulier vernis	Aubergine/eggplant (literally: polished shoe).
Sourire tranche papaye	A big smile, a broad grin.

Helpful phrases

Practical Information

A. Venturi/VISA

Canyoning at Aigrettes waterfall

BEFORE GOING

• Local time

Réunion is 4hr ahead of London in the winter and 3hr in the summer and 9hr ahead of Eastern Standard Time (EST). When it's 9am in Britain, it's either 12noon or 1pm in Réunion, depending on the season, and when it's 9am in New York and Toronto, it's 6pm or 7pm in Réunion, depending on the season.

• How to call Réunion

Dial international + 262 + the number you wish to call.

• When to go

As Réunion is in the southern hemisphere, summer and winter are the opposite of our European or North American climates. Réunion can be visited all year round, but the humid, tropical climate does make the summers rather hot and heavy. The most pleasant time to visit is from **April to December**, with a slight preference for the **April-May** and **September-October** periods.

Although the island does have two distinct seasons, the terrain and trade winds create a multitude of **microclimates** with large differences in temperature between the coasts and the Uplands and in rainfall between the drier west coast and the more humid east coast.

Even though the mornings are bright and sunny, the Réunion sky has a tendency to cloud over from midday onwards, so only the early birds get the most out of Réunion's landscapes.

The sun rises between 5am and 6.30am all year round and sets around 5.30pm in the summer and 6.30pm in the winter.

Southern wintertime

Winter, or the dry season, runs from May to October when the climate is dominated by the cool easterly to southeasterly trade winds. Temperatures remain warm and it rains less, especially on the West Coast.

During July and August, average coastal temperatures are over 20°C, at which period the beaches are deserted by the locals. In the Uplands, temperatures can drop to below 0°C (Plaine des Cafres and the uppermost summits).

Temperatures rise again in October and the vegetation is once again a feast of colour and variety in November.

This dry season is the best time for walking and most other outdoor activities. The low temperatures can, however, come as a surprise, particularly in the July-August period.

Southern summertime

Between **November and April**, Réunion is subject to northeasterly winds bringing with them warm, humid weather. Temperatures can rise to as much as 34°C on the west coast. Temperatures are dependent on the terrain with a daily average of 14°C over 2 000m. Officially, this is the **cyclone season**, but the riskiest period generally runs from January to March, when it's best to avoid the area because the combination of cyclones and heavy rains can make getting about and activities difficult. Furthermore, this is when Réunion schools are on holiday (end of December to early February) and tourist facilities are generally pretty busy.

In November and December, the warm climate is particularly suited to deep-sea diving.

Cyclone alert!

If you decide to visit the island between December and April, you must be aware of the four alert phases in use.

1) Cyclone watch – the zone is subject to a depression which represents a potential threat. There is no immediate danger, but all inhabitants and visitors must keep an ear on the radio or ring *Météo France* for weather updates (☎ 0836 680 808) and cyclone update information (in French). All mountain walks or boat trips are cancelled and supplies (tinned food, drinking water, candles, batteries, radio) should also be checked.

2) Orange alert – the cyclone may represent a danger to the island within the next 24 hours. Business continues as normal but schools and nurseries close. Residents must put away anything that the wind can blow away, keep pets indoors, protect windows and doors and keep the radio on.

3) Red alert – the cyclone represents an imminent danger. A 3hr forewarning is given before a red alert is declared in order to enable residents to reach a safe area. After this three-hour period, no one must leave the protection of their homes (apart from the danger, fines are extremely heavy for offenders). If the eye of the cyclone passes just overhead, a lull is felt throughout the island. Beware, though: the wind will begin to blow again just as violently and very suddenly. Phone calls must be restricted to absolute necessity, because the emergency services need all the lines they can get. Accommodation centres are open throughout the island in case of need.

4) After the cyclone – the danger is not yet over. Tap water must be treated and only bottled water drunk. Facilitate access to emergency services. Do not cross flooded ravines (most accidents are due to drowning). Do not touch any fallen electrical wires.

• Packing list

Take light-weight cotton garments, but also a raincoat of some sort and a few warm jumpers, especially if planning to go during the summer (southern winter). Good walking shoes (with very tough soles for the volcano) are essential for any prospective walkers. Plastic sandals are recommended if you intend to go swimming. A hat and sunglasses are also a must.

• A trip for everyone

Travelling with children

Réunion organises a large number of activities for children: swimming in the lagoon, easy nature walks, tobogganing, horse riding and so on. Few hotels provide specific child-care centres or activities, but many do have reduced rates for children. However, getting around towns with a pushchair is quite an ordeal due to the narrow pavements.

Women travelling alone

Women travelling alone run no particular risks, but they would do better to avoid hitchhiking or walking alone. Alone or accompanied, women will encounter the rather blatant stares of Réunion men, who may occasionally attempt to strike up a conversation.

Elderly people

Elderly people will encounter no specific problems, but it must, however, be remembered that Réunion is a mountainous island and visiting the Uplands and the island's interior is one of the high-spots of any trip. Such visits can be extremely tiring, especially due to the abrupt changes in altitude and temperature. Avoid January and February, which are particularly hot and humid. The least tiring solution is to opt for comfortable bus excursions.

Disabled persons

Réunion is, unfortunately, very poorly equipped to receive disabled tourists. Just getting about in town is practically impossible due to the narrow, very busy pavements.

• Address Book

Tourist Information Offices

Australia – 25 Bligh Street, Sydney, NSW 2000, ☎ (29) 231 5244, Fax (29) 221 8682

Canada – 1981 avenue MacGill College, Office 490, Montreal H3A2W9, ☎ (514) 288 4264, Fax (514) 845 4868

United Kingdom – 178 Piccadilly, London, W1V OAL, ☎ (171) 493 5174, Fax (0171) 493 6594

USA – 444 Madison Avenue (16th floor), New York, NY 10022, ☎ (212) 838 7800 (7029), Fax (212) 838 7855

Web Sites

www.la-reunion-tourisme.com

Embassies and Consulates

Australia – 6 Perth Avenue, Yarralumla, Canberra, ACT 2600, ☎ (26) 216 0100, Fax (26) 216 0127

Canada – 42 Sussex Drive, Ottowa, Ontario, K1M 2C9, ☎ (613) 789 1795, Fax (613) 562 3790

United Kingdom – 58 Knightsbridge, London SW1X 7JT, ☎ (171) 838 2000

USA – Chancery, 4101 Reservoir Road NW, Washington DC 20007, ☎ (202) 944 6000, Fax (202) 944 6166

• Formalities

Identity Papers

Réunion is a French département and the same rules apply to tourists travelling to Réunion as to France. European Union nationals must have a valid identity card or passport. Nationals of other countries must have a valid passport, a visa in some cases (South African citizens) and a return or onward ticket.

Sanitary regulations

Imports of plants, vegetables or fruit of any kind are strictly prohibited and subject to heavy fines, because the island's insular environment encourages the rapid development of plant illnesses and parasites.

Pets

It is possible to take pets from the European Union to Réunion accompanied by the appropriate health certificates. Information from **Réunion Veterinary Services Department**, bvd de la Providence, 97488 St-Denis Cedex, ☎ 48 61 00.

Vaccinations

No vaccinations are necessary, except for those visitors who have spent time in countries where cholera and yellow fever are endemic.

Driving licence

An international driving licence (held for over a year) is required to rent a car, motorbike or 80cc scooter.

• Currency

Cash

The national currency in Réunion is the French Franc. US$1= approximately 6.45 FF.

Money Exchange

You can change money at the airport and in the larger city banks. Some hotels will accept payment in foreign currencies.

Travellers' Cheques

Travellers' cheques are rarely used in Réunion, but they can be exchanged in all the large banks.

Credit Cards

Credit cards can be used for the majority of purchases in Réunion (Visa, Mastercard, Diner's, Eurocard, American Express). Automatic cash distributors, known as *gabier*, whilst common in city centres, are relatively rare in the Uplands.

• Spending money

The cost of living in Réunion is even more expensive than in Europe or the United States. Although eating out is relatively cheap (you can find dishes from US$6), no cheap accommodation is available, with the exception of camping or *gîtes* (lodges) (around US$10). Renting a car is almost essential and will cost from US$25 to 45 per day or US$250 to 330 per week. For more details, see the transport, accommodation and restaurant sections in the following pages.

• Booking in advance

If planning to travel in the July-August or January-February periods, you will need to book accommodation and a car at least two months before you leave. During other periods, it's best to book a few weeks before departure. In the shoulder season (March-April and particularly June), make sure you ask about reduced rates, as hotels are rarely full at these times.

• Repatriation insurance

Remember to take out repatriation insurance. This can be done through your bank: some bank cards include special insurance policies. If you booked through a tour operator, emergency / repatriation insurance is often included in the price of your trip. The following may however prove useful.

Travel Insurance Agency, Suite 2, Percy Mews, 755B High Rd, North Finchley, London NI2 8JY, UK, ☎ 181 446 5414, Fax 181 446 5417, info@travelinsurers.com

Travel Insurance Services, 2930 Camino Diablo, Suite 200, PO Box 299, Walnut Creek, CA94596, USA, ☎ 800 937 1387, Fax 925 932 0442, webinfo@travelinsure.com

• Gifts to offer

Réunion stores are as well stocked as French stores and distributing gifts in the street is not a common practice. If invited for dinner or drinks, you can take whatever you would normally take if invited out at home: a bottle of wine, flowers or, most appreciated but more difficult to keep fresh, chocolates.

GETTING THERE

• By air

Scheduled flights

It is not possible to fly direct to Réunion from Australia, Canada, the UK or the USA. Travellers will have to take a connecting flight in Europe, mainly Paris, or in Singapore if travelling from Australia

Air France operates nine weekly flights, including 7 direct, out of Paris. Information: callers within France ☎ 0802 802 802, callers outside France ☎ 33 0802 802 802, www.airfrance.fr

British Airways, in conjunction with Air Liberté, operates 4 weekly flights out of Paris Orly. Information: callers within the UK ☎ 0345 222 111, callers outside the UK ☎ 44 141 222 2222, www.britishairways.com

Swissair, Sabena and **Austrian Airlines** also operate flights to Réunion, often in conjunction with another smaller airline.

Charter flights

Charter flights do exist but primarily via French tour operators.

Flights to other locations in the Indian Ocean from Réunion

Air Austral, 4 rue de Nice, BP 611, St-Denis Cédex, ☎ 90 90 90.
Flights to Madagascar, Comores, Kenya, Mayotte, Mauritius, Seychelles and Johannesburg.

Air France, 7 av de la Victoire, 97477 St-Denis, ☎ 40 38 38, flights between Réunion, Seychelles, Mauritius, Madagascar

Air Madagascar, 2 rue Mac Auliffe, St-Denis, ☎ 41 23 26, flies to Madagascar several times a week.

Air Mauritius, 13 rue Charles Gounod, St-Denis, ☎ 94 83 83, flies between Réunion and Mauritius for around US$220 return.

Air Seychelles, Air France Offices, 7 av de la Victoire, St-Denis, ☎ 40 38 38, flies once a week to Réunion from Seychelles.

Gillot-Roland Garros International Airport

The airport is situated some 7km from the centre of St-Denis, on the island's north coast. It houses several stores, snack-bars, restaurants, a post office, bank and exchange counter, representatives of the airlines and car rental companies, and an air-freight service for unaccompanied luggage. It is best to check the departure time of flights (particularly in the cyclone season) by telephoning a few hours in advance (☎ 28 16 16).

Duty-free shops

Passengers arriving from abroad do not have access to the duty-free shop, which is only open to passengers leaving the country.

Confirmation

It is essential to confirm your return flight 72hr ahead as overbooking is practically systematic.

Airport tax

Generally included in the cost of the airfare, the airport tax is roughly US$3.

• Package deals

It can be a good idea to book your flight, accommodation and car rental from the same tour operator.

In addition to contacting the tourist offices of each country you wish to visit (see the appropriate pages in each *Making the most of* sections), you might also contact the following, perhaps via e-mail.

Indian Ocean Angling Adventures, PO Box 367, Westville, 3630, South Africa, ☎ 27 31 266 6772 / 4747, Fax 27 31 266 7481, ioaa@iafrica.com As the name suggests, deep-sea fishing, primarily in the Seychelles.

Sun Kids, Sun International Indian Ocean, Le Saint Geran Hotel, Belle-Mare, Mauritius, ☎ 230 415 1825, Fax 230 415 1539, web site: www.sunkids.com Specialises in family holidays, mainly in Mauritius.

Thomas Cook Ltd, 6 Midford Place, London W1A 1EB, UK, ☎ 44 8705 666 222, web site: www.thomascook.com

Thompsons Tours, 1st Floor Dunkeld West Shopping Centre, Cnr Bompas Rd and Jan Smuts Ave, Dunkeld West, Johannesburg, South Africa, ☎ 27 11 770 7700, Fax 27 11 788 2664, web site: www.thompsons.co.za Specialises in Indian Ocean destinations.

Travel Wizard Inc, 5675 Lucas Valley Rd, Nicasio, CA94946, USA, ☎ 1 800 330 8820, Fax 1 415 662 2505, web site: www.tropicalislandvacation.com Specialises in island destinations.

Tropical Places, Freshfield House, Lewes Rd, Forest Row, East Sussex, RH185ES UK, ☎ 44 800 018 2256, Fax 44 1342 822 364, web site: www.tropical.co.uk/

• By boat

The cargo-ship, *Mauritius Pride*, runs a regular service between Réunion and Mauritius (the night crossing lasts around 12hr and costs between US$120 and 200 return, depending on the class). Another ship, "L'Alimora", also operates a regular weekly service with Mauritius (around 6hr, US$130).

SCOAM, 47 rue Évariste-de-Parny, 94720 Le Port, Réunion, ☎ 42 19 45, Fax 43 25 47.

Mauritius Shipping Corporation, Nova Building, 1 route Militaire, Port Louis, Mauritius, ☎ 242 52 55, Fax 242 54 45

Mr Ocean Line Co Ltd, rue Sir William Newton, 2nd floor, Orchid Tower, Port Louis, Mauritius, ☎ 210 7104, Fax 210 6961.

Blue Line Shipping, rue St-Paul, Le Port, Réunion, ☎ 55 23 25.

THE BASICS

• Address book

Most of the tourist information about the island is in French, which is the case of *Run,* an excellent little magazine, distributed free and regularly updated. Otherwise, there is a tourist map in English and French with hiking and excursion ideas around the island.

Tourist Information

Tourist Office

Each town has its own tourist office, with a wide variety of brochures, also mostly in French. The *Maison de Montagne*, in St-Denis and Cilaos, is an essential stop-off for anyone who wants information about lodges (*gîtes*) or activities in Réunion. The tourist offices and interactive information terminals, *Guetali*, can also provide useful information about leisure activities.

Tourist Office – 10 rue Pasteur, St-Denis, ☎ 41 83 00, Fax 21 37 76. Monday-Saturday, 8.30am-6pm, Sundays, 9am-12noon.

Maison de la Montagne – 10, place Sarda Garriga, St-Denis, ☎ 90 78 78, Fax 41 84 29. Monday to Thursday, 9am-5.30pm, Fridays, 9am-4.30pm and Saturdays, 9am-4pm.

Réunion Tourism Committee – 4 place du 20 décembre 1848, St-Denis, ☎ 21 00 41, Fax 21 00 21.

Embassies and Consulates

As Réunion is not an independent state but a French territory, most countries do not in fact have diplomatic representation on the island.

• Opening and closing times

Banks

In the main towns, banks are open Monday to Friday, 7.45am-3.45pm or 8am-4pm and closed on weekends. Elsewhere, opening hours vary, but in general banks are open from 9am-12noon or 12.30pm and 1.30pm-4pm or 4.30pm. A few rare branches are open on Saturdays, notably at St-Gilles-les-Bains.

Post Offices

In the main towns, post offices are open Monday to Friday, 8am-5pm; Saturdays, 8am-11am. Elsewhere they are open Monday to Friday, 8am-11am and 1pm-4pm, Saturdays, 8am-11am.

Shops

Opening times are in general 9am or 9.30am-12noon and 2.30pm-6pm. All shops are closed on Sundays, with the exception of a few grocery stores or "boutiques" that are open on Sunday morning.

Markets

St-Denis – Little market (Petit Marché) for food and the big market (Grand Marché) for crafts: everyday except Sunday. Le Chaudron: Wednesday mornings and Sundays. Les Camélias: Friday mornings.

St-Paul – All day Friday and Saturday mornings (food and crafts).

St-Pierre – Covered market: everyday except Sunday. Craft market on the sea front: Saturday mornings (food and crafts).

Restaurants

As a general rule, restaurants are open from 11.30am-1.30pm and from 7pm-9.30pm.

Offices

Office opening hours are Monday to Friday, 7.30am or 8am-4.30pm or 5.30pm, with a lunch break between 11.30am and 1.30pm.

• Museums and gardens

Hours

Open for the most part from 9am to 5pm. Often closed on Mondays and sometimes at lunchtime. For more details, see the *Exploring Réunion* section of this guide and the local magazines.

Entrance fees

If not free, entrance fees vary from US$1.50 to 5.00.

• Postal service

Postal charges are the roughly the same as in Europe. Stamps can be bought from post offices, tobacco outlets and some stores. Any mail weighing over 20g (ordinary letter or card) sent outside of Réunion is subject to an air tax. It costs around US$11 per kg to send a parcel abroad (not including Africa). The end of the afternoon is the least busy period in most post offices, particularly in small towns where queues can be very long.

• Phone and fax

A network of **France Télécom** public phone boxes, identical to those in France, works with phone cards that can be bought from post offices, tobacco outlets, certain stores and occasionally with credit cards. These boxes are located all over the island. You can also send faxes from post offices or hotels (exorbitant prices). The **GSM** network operates on the island.

International calls

Telephoning abroad can be done from any public phone boxes and rates are lower between 12.30pm and 1.30pm and between 6pm and 8am (remember the time difference though!).

Codes

To make a call to someone else in Réunion, dial the six-digit phone number.
To call abroad from Réunion, first dial 00 + country code + phone number
Codes of other countries – United Kingdom: 44; USA/Canada: 1; Australia: 61.

Directory Enquiries

Local directory enquiries: dial 12
International directory enquiries: dial 00 262 12 + country code.

• Public holidays

1 January	New Year's Day
April	Easter Monday
1 May	Labour Day
8 May	1945 Victory
May	Ascension Day (Thursday)
May	Whit Monday
14 July	National Holiday
15 August	Assumption Day
1 November	All Saints' Day
11 November	1918 Armistice
20 December	Freedom Holiday (abolition of slavery in Réunion)
25 December	Christmas Day

• Other religious holidays

January	Cavadee (Tamil)
February	Chinese New Year
April	Tamil New Year
July	Fire walking (Tamil)
November	Divali (Tamil)

• Regional holidays

January	Green honey festival at Plaine des Cafres (craft and agricultural fair)
February	Wine harvesting at Cilaos
	Pineapple festival at Ste-Clotilde
May	Chouchou (local vegetable) festival at Salazie
July	Goyavier (local fruit) festival at Plaine des Palmistes

August	Vacoa (locally produced rope) festival at St-Philippe
	Saffron festival at St-Joseph
September	Ecological tourism festival at Ste-Rose
	Heritage day "Visit a garden" (organised by the Ministry of Culture)
November	Lentil festival at Cilaos
	Vetiver festival at St-Joseph

• School holidays

Exact dates vary from year to year, but globally the periods remain the same.

All Saints'	31 October to 13 November
Christmas	19 December to 5 February
Easter	21 March to 2 April
Winter	20 May to 2 June
Summer holidays	29 July to end of August-early September

GETTING AROUND

• By car

The best way to get around Réunion is to rent a car, and it's possible to drive round the island in a day.

Car rentals

To rent a car you must be 21 years of age or over, have an international driving licence (held for over a year) and you must leave a deposit or credit card imprint. We recommend renting primarily from agencies which belong to the **French National Car Syndicate (CNPA)** and which can be identified by a special logo. They will provide reliable vehicles with standard rental contracts. Most international rental companies have representatives in Réunion, located at the airport and in the major hotels. The island also comprises a large number of competitive smaller agencies, particularly in the St-Gilles-les-Bains region. Renting a car costs between US$25-45 per day or US$230-300 per week.

Road network

A network of 360km of national multi-lane highways, 750km of secondary roads and 1 500km of tracks cover the island. While correctly maintained for the most part, some of the High Plains roads are regularly damaged by heavy rainfall and lack maintenance. Others are subject to frequent landslides, such as the coastal or Cilaos road. It is preferable to check on the state of the roads, particularly after heavy rains, either by listening to the (French-speaking) radio or by calling an official **Road Transport** answering machine (again in French) ☎ 97 77 77.
A well-maintained coastal road surrounds the island. A large number of roads around towns are built for four-lane traffic. Visitors can't avoid using these large roads to a certain extent, but it's not difficult to get off them and enjoy the opportunity of visiting some of the smaller towns in the Uplands.
During the rainy season, the four-lane coastal road between St-Denis and La Possession is regularly covered by landslides, turning it into a normal two-lane road and creating impressive tailbacks. It can occasionally be closed completely. If you have to get to St-Denis, we suggest taking the small mountain road (*route de la Montagne* – approx. 3hr) or the Uplands road *(route des Plaines)* if you're coming from the south. If the *route du Cap la Houssaye* is closed, take the *rampes de St-Paul* (D6) and the *route du Théâtre* (D10).

Driving

Cars drive on the right side of the road. Speeds are limited to 50km/hr in urban areas and 110km/hr on four-lane roads. Accidents are frequent and drivers should keep a lookout at all times for dangerous overtaking or lane-changing on four-lane roads, slow vehicles such as tractors on express routes, crazy motorcyclists weaving in and out or the numerous stray dogs that haunt the roads at night.

Traffic jams are a daily feature of Réunion life, particularly around the capital, and the situation worsens considerably when the coastal road is closed. Generally speaking, driving in the larger towns is difficult during the traditional peak periods when offices and schools open and close. Avoid the following times if at all possible:

On weekday mornings (7am-9am): western and eastern approaches to St-Denis; west coast, from la Saline to the entrance to the St-Paul four-lane road (northbound). Afternoons (4pm-6pm): la Saline, (southbound); St-Denis East exit.

At weekends, late afternoon: west coast, from Souris Chaude to the St-Paul four-lane highway, northbound (people leaving the beach).

Fuel

The island has a good network of fuel stations, most of which are open from 6.30am to 7pm and generally closed on Sundays. On the main road (RN from La Possession, St-Gilles, St-Denis), some stations are open 24 hours, with payment by banker's card. Fuel prices are more or less equivalent to those of Europe and vary very little throughout the island.

Parking

Parking in towns can prove as difficult as driving in them. Paying car parks in St-Denis and St-Pierre are closely monitored.

In case of accidents

Call either the fire brigade (☎ 18) or the ambulance service (SAMU ☎ 15 or ☎ 20 10 10).

• By taxi

Taxis are not only few and far between, but also expensive. The main taxi ranks are at the airport (the fare between the airport and St-Denis will cost under US$20) and in the town centres.

• By group taxi

Group taxis which are less expensive and more widespread than regular taxis, operate primarily in the Uplands. Times and information can be obtained from town bus stations.

• By bus

A shuttle service operates between St-Denis bus station and the airport (US$4). St-Denis has an urban bus service.

Cars Jaunes runs 13 lines around the island between 4.45am and 7.20pm (only on weekdays), but some rural areas are still poorly served. Allow around US$6 for a St-Denis to St-Pierre trip. The bus stations will be able to supply information about times, routes and prices. In the St-Paul area, a minibus network called **Pastel** (☎ 22 54 65) runs a service in the Uplands and the St-Leu town also operates a relatively recent minibus service, **Ti'Cars Jaunes**, in the Uplands.

• Hitch hiking

This is a widespread form of transport that works pretty well during the day, especially around the coast, and can occasionally compensate for the shortcomings of public transport. The best hiking spots are bus stops, either in towns or on the edge of two-lane roads. Patience is necessary as the competition is fierce. Avoid the evenings or if travelling alone, especially for women.

• Renting a bike

Biking enthusiasts would do well to respect a few basic safety rules: drive in the middle of the road, a little to the left, never on the right to avoid hazardous overtaking; watch out for the early summer rains and for numerous patches of diesel oil that can make roads extremely slippery; keep an eye open for gravel on bends and roundabouts in the Uplands.

Motorbikes – Most of the island's rental companies are located along the west coast and in St-Denis. A 125cc bike costs around US$30 a day and US$45 for a 650cc. You will be asked to show you have held a driving licence for at least 2 years and to leave a deposit of US$800.

Scooters – A 50cc costs just under US$20 a day and US$90 for a week. You must be over 21 and have a full driving licence to rent an 80cc or 125cc.

Bicycles – Using the bicycle lanes, shown by green stripes on the edges of some of the four-lane routes, is inadvisable, and bicycling on the other busy roads is downright dangerous. What's more, the island's terrain doesn't really lend itself to bicycling as a means of transport. You could, however, rent a mountain bike in the Uplands *(see the Sports and pastimes section, p 81)*.

• Organised tours and excursions

Information on organised tours and excursions can be obtained from tourist offices, the *Maison de la Montagne* or specialised agencies:

Bourbon Tourisme, 14 rue Rontaunay, St-Denis, ☎ 94 76 94.
Papangue Tours, 5 rue de Nice, St-Denis, ☎ 21 74 08.
Réussir Voyages, 45 rue Juliette Dodu, St-Denis, ☎ 41 55 66.
Agora Voyages, 192 rue du Général de Gaulle, St-Gilles-les-Bains, ☎ 33 08 08.

BED AND BOARD

• Where to stay

Accommodation is widely available throughout the island, but the majority of the hotels and tourist facilities are located on the west coast, which has the best climate and the only sandy beaches. There is a wide choice, from busy seaside resorts such as the very touristy St-Gilles to the more authentic calm of little towns such as St-Leu, Étang Salé-les-Bains or St-Pierre. The size of the island is such that it's possible to book into one place for the duration of your stay, leaving each day to travel around. However, it would be a pity not to spend a few nights in the amphitheatres and near the volcano, especially to make sure you can enjoy the best time of the day to go walking. Whatever your choice, it is essential to book in advance if planning to visit during the July-August or December-January periods.

• Various categories

Réunion has a vast range of accommodation at prices to suit all budgets. If travelling alone or as a couple, hotels and bed and breakfast-style accommodation are cheapest. If travelling with a group or a family, the rural lodge *(gîte)* option would be cheaper.

Hotels

Most of the coastal towns, the amphitheatres in Cilaos and Salazie and parts of the Uplands have hotels. The most luxurious are around St-Gilles and Boucan Canot, but quality can vary widely from one establishment to another.

A double rooms costs around US$40 a day in an average hotel and up to US$190 in a luxury hotel. Breakfast is rarely included in the price. Prices will also vary depending on the length of stay and the season. Prices should be systematically negotiated during the shoulder season, particularly in the more upmarket establishments.

Rural lodges (gîtes), bed and breakfast and stopover lodges (gîtes d'étapes)

Réunion has over 100 rural lodges *(gîtes)*, 190 bed and breakfast rooms and 20 stopover lodges *(gîtes d'étape)*, all of which are ideal to get to know the island and its inhabitants. Most of the rural lodges are located in the Uplands or halfway up, some are on the coast, to the south and east of the island. Some have gardens. For a group of two to 14, prices per week in a rural lodge can vary from US$150 to US$380.

Bed and breakfast accommodation is practically the same for 1 person or for a couple. Prices vary from around US$25 to US$38 per night, including breakfast. In stopover lodges, the average price is US$11 (between US$7-25) per person per night. Breakfast is not always included.

Relais départemental des Gîtes de France, 10 place Sarda Garriga, 97400 St-Denis, ☎ 90 78 90, Fax 41 84 29.

Family holiday villages

The island comprises four family holiday village resorts (VVF), at St-Gilles-les-Bains, La Saline, St-Leu and Cilaos. If interested, you will need to book far in advance as they are highly popular amongst the locals, who often book from one year to the next. Information, ☎ 24 29 29.

Guest houses

This is an informal and not very commonplace form of accommodation, which exists mainly in St-Denis and St-Pierre.

Youth hostels

The island counts three youth hostels, at Hell-Bourg (Salazie amphitheatre), Bernica in the St-Paul Uplands and at Entre-Deux.

Fédération des Auberges de Jeunesse, ☎ 41 15 34 (US$7 per person, per night plus breakfast).

Camping

Réunion only has four campsites, at St-Gilles-les-Bains (only open during the local school holidays), at Rivière des roches (Bras Panon), at Grand Anse (Petite Île) and at Cilaos. Very popular amongst the Reunionese, music and atmosphere guaranteed!

CTR, ☎ 21 00 41.

If travelling in a group, you can camp rough in the heart of the island.

To rent camping equipment – Possession Tourist Office, 27 rue Waldeck-Rocher, ☎ 22 26 66.

• Eating out

In hotels and guesthouses

All the medium and upmarket hotels have restaurants, most of which are open to non-residents, serving local and French cuisine. Most have gargantuan breakfast buffets (for under US$10) and you can take advantage of them to have a dip in the hotel's pool.

In restaurants

The island's numerous restaurants (mainly in towns) offer a wide range of cooking traditions – Creole, Chinese, Indian or French. A *cari* or a salad will cost a minimum of US$7 and a full meal around US$15. Town restaurants are busiest between 12noon and 1pm, during the midday lunch break, and it's best to book a table in the better known restaurants. Closing days vary, but Sunday is the traditional closing day when you might fancy trying one of the more regional dishes served in *table d'hôte* establishments, which are often open during the weekend.

Tables d'hôtes and auberge farms

This is a traditionally French custom whereby farms or other private houses turn themselves into impromptu restaurants, generally offering set meals of local cuisine. In Réunion, most are located in very pleasant settings in the Uplands and offer a set menu of Réunion home cooking. Unfortunately, the local tradition whereby the host eats with his or her guests is dying out, particularly in the larger establishments. A full meal costs between US$10 and US$15. It's advisable to book a table, sometimes several days ahead, either direct or via **Gîtes de France** (☎ 90 78 90).

In the street

Most of the towns have "bars on wheels", particularly on the seashore, with extremely cheap local specialities to eat there or take away: *samossas, bouchons, sarcives*, sandwiches, *caris*, etc. In streets and on roadsides, travelling salesmen sell roast chicken, called *poulets gasoil* or *poulets-la-route* (diesel chickens or roadside chickens - around US$5), mainly at weekends and more rarely during the week.

Drinks

Tap water can be drunk everywhere in Réunion, but should, however, be avoided after heavy rains or cyclones. Don't miss the chance to taste the local brew, *dodo*, a very light beer, or rum, most often served in punches as an aperitif or after dinner.

H. Choimet

SPORTS AND PASTIMES

• On land

Walking

Réunion is a **walker's paradise** and walking is by far the best way of getting to know the island's fauna, flora, people and landscapes. Over 1 000km of marked paths for all, whether novice or enthusiast, young or old, fit or not so fit. The most well-known wind their way around Piton des Neiges, the volcano and the Mafate amphitheatre. Never start out on a hiking trip if bad weather is forecast. In addition, paths are often damaged after a cyclone, so it's best to check conditions before leaving. Protective sun cream is essential for everyone, particularly on the volcano, even if the sky is cloudy. Leave early in the morning to make the most of the daylight luminosity and distant horizons, because the Uplands have a tendency to become blanketed in mist by midday. Temperatures can also be surprisingly chilly, particularly during July and August. If planning a long walk, hikers should remember that night falls between 6pm and 7pm.

Maison de la Montagne, 10 place Sarda Garriga, 97400 St-Denis, ☎ 90 78 78. For information, advice, the state of paths, accommodation bookings, organised hikes, etc.

Magma Rando, 41ter, ligne Berthaud, St-Gilles-les-Hauts, ☎ 55 72 22. Run by an excellent mountain guide, Geneviève Planchad Brave, who will introduce you not only to the desolate basalt ranges and the volcano, but also to the rest of the island. Her enthusiasm for Réunion and its nature is very compelling.

Mountain biking

The island has over 700km of bicycle paths, signposted by the French Federation of Cycling, and six authorised mountain bike centres. Bicycles can be rented near the paths, with or without guides, for a definitely energetic way of getting to know Réunion. Renting a bike costs from around US$10 per half day and around US$15 a day. *See the Making the most of sections.*

4WD expeditions

A possibility for excursions off the beaten track, if, for instance, you want to go to Dimitile, Rivière des Remparts or the volcano by going up the ravine beds.

Indi 4x4 adventure, ☎ 24 23 87 (around US$100 per person, half-price for children, including lunch).

Réunion Escapade Tout Terrain, ☎ 21 87 20.

Canyoning and climbing

A fairly recent addition to the island's leisure activities, both activities are accessible to enthusiasts of all levels: the three St-Gilles basins serve as a practice area, whereas the Cilaos and Salazie amphitheatres require more technique. Experienced guides are available to take travellers round Réunion's gorges and waterfalls. Around US$40 per half-day and US$70 for a whole day.

Information from **Maison de la Montagne**, at St-Denis or **Pays d'Accueil** *(addresses in the regional Making the most of sections).*

White water sports

The turbulent rivers in the east offer the choice between rafting, up-river kayaking or aquatic hiking. All are subject to the level of the water in the rivers. Around US$40 for a half day and US$70 for a whole day.

Contact **Kalanoro** or **Mahan**, Maison de la Montagne, 10 place Sarda-Garriga, 97400 St-Denis, ☎ 90 78 78, for a team of professional, serious and very welcoming state-diploma guides.

Riding

You don't have to be an experienced rider to go out for a hack on the calm *Méren* horses. The clubs around Plaine des Cafres, the volcano, the west Uplands or Entre-Deux *(see the Making the most of sections)* have a whole range of wonderful treks for an original way of getting to know the island. From US$15 -20 an hour or around US$150 for a whole weekend.

Golf

Réunion has three different golf courses: a flat course in the dry vegetation around Étang Salé, Colorado golf course with a view of the ocean over St-Denis and the more technical and energetic Bassin Bleu course, above the three St-Gilles basins. The green fees are around US$25 per day during the week.

• The sea

The regulation flags positioned on beaches are not for decoration but are highly serious and bathers should respect them at all times, particularly at Boucan Canot and Étang Salé, where the currents and waves can be strong enough to prevent swimmers from returning to the beach. If this happens, let yourself be carried by the current until help arrives. After heavy rainfall or a cyclone, avoid swimming in the lagoon for at least two weeks.

Swimming

It's possible to go swimming in the public swimming baths and in some hotel pools. Swimming in the sea is only possible along the west coast, but even this can be jeopardised by the waves, currents and shallowness of some of the lagoons. All the island's beaches are public.

Scuba diving

Even though the island's marine beds are not spectacular, some sites are still well worth exploring, such as those around the west and southeast coasts. Most diving clubs are located in St-Leu and St-Gilles *(see the corresponding Making the most of sections)*. Around US$25 for an initiation dive.

Surfing and windsurfing

St-Leu and Trois Bassins are internationally renowned in the surfing world, where it is also possible to try *moree*, also available at Boucan Canot and Roches Noires. Windsurfing can be done inside the lagoon and also beyond by experienced surfers. Renting a board costs around US$15 to US$20 per hour. Avoid the bay of St-Paul and the Jamaique area in St-Denis, where sharks have killed more than one rash surfer. Remember that sharks hunt mainly at sunset.

Ligue Réunionnaise de Surf, ☎ 24 33 10.

Deep-sea fishing

The best deep-sea fishing season is between October and May. Outings cost around US$70 per person for a half-day (two to four people). Boats leave from Le Port, St-Gilles or St-Pierre *(see the corresponding Making the most of sections)*.

H. Choimet

Glass-bottom boats

Explore the sea bed without getting wet (US$11 for adults and US$6 for children). For best visibility, choose a sunny, windless day and check the condition of the "glass-bottom" for scratches before embarking.

St-Gilles-les-Bains Port, ☎ 24 47 77.

• Up in the air

Paragliding and hang-gliding

Renowned for its international competitions and champions, Réunion is a fully fledged member of the world's free-flight circuit. Flying is possible almost everyday and in a whole host of breathtaking sites *(for addresses, see the corresponding Making the most of sections). Prices range from US$45 for an initiation flight and US$230 for an initiation course (2 long flights).*

Microlight aircraft

An original and exciting way to take a look at Réunion's landscapes. A wide variety of different circuits are available and prices range from US$25 for an initiation flight (15min) to US$100 for a flight along the coast and over Mafate or US$200 over the Volcano. *For addresses, see the Making the most of the West Coast section, p 119.*

Plane and helicopter

These are two activities that take place early in the morning, before the Uplands are deep in a blanket of mist. An unforgettable flight around the island in a plane costs between US$45 to US$60 per person for a 1hr flight. Information from the Gillot or Pierrefonds Airclubs at St-Pierre. Even more sensational is a helicopter tour of the island (US$215 per person) or of the amphitheatres (US$150). Stops are sometimes possible at Mafate. *For addresses, see the Making the most of the West Coast section, p 119.*

• Nightlife

Concerts

The island's musical life beats to the rhythm of numerous *maloya, séga* and other local groups. Réunion also welcomes a large number of French and foreign artists during the **Festival Africolor**, which is held primarily in October. There are lots of high quality concerts, particularly from June to November. An evening out at the wonderful open-air amphitheatre at St-Gilles is always a must. During the weekends, the **Espace Jeumont** (St-Denis) and the **Bato Fou** at St-Pierre open their stages to local groups.

Cinema

Most towns have cinemas, but the programming is not very exciting and almost exclusively in French. Programmes can be found in the local daily newspapers.

Theatre

A few dynamic troupes, such as **Acte 3** (at St-Benoît) or **Compagnie Vollard**, put on lively shows with themes that often refer to Réunion history. Dialogues are in Creole, but relatively easy to understand, providing you speak a little French! They are always lively and animated, and spectators are often invited on to the stage to take part in the show. It is occasionally possible to eat at the theatre with the actors during the intermission (ask when booking seats).

Casino

The island has three casinos in St-Gilles, St-Denis and St-Pierre.

Bars and nightclubs

The Réunionese love to dance. Most young people go out to nightclubs all Saturday night and often on Sunday afternoons. However, there are very few bars. *See the corresponding Making the most of sections.*

SHOPPING

• What's on offer

Arts and Crafts

Various stores and local, mainly Madagascan, craft markets sell small wooden sculptures, embroidered tablecloths, cloths, wickerwork, etc. *(see p 57)*.

Food

Bourbon vanilla, one of the best in the world, is sold in the markets, in the vanilla cooperative and in the large food stores. Check its origin. Long-lasting, it can be used to perfume sugar, for example. Stock up on Creole spices, *achards* and hot spicy pastes to try a little Creole cuisine on your return home. Exotic fruit-flavoured punch, lychee or *combava* flavoured alcohol or vintage rum are also other favourites. It's also possible to invent your own concoction by macerating fruit, vanilla or mixtures of spices and herbs bought in the market in rum for at least three months. You could also send back a **Colipays** (☎ 28 99 99) basket with an assortment of exotic fruit and other regional specialities, delivered within 48hr (around US$50). Guaranteed fresh.

Clothes

The markets and some stores sell t-shirts with exotic prints, colourful pareos and other lightweight clothes.

Plants

It's possible to take home orchids or shoots of exotic trees. To do so, ask for a special air package or contact **Colipays** *(see above)*.

Others

A poster of Réunion fauna, flora or architecture, or illustrated diaries or calendars with photos of the island are another gift or souvenir idea.

• Where to shop

See the Making the most of sections of the guide for addresses.

Markets

In addition to spices and fresh produce, the markets also have a wide range of arts and crafts. The St-Denis market is undoubtedly the best, but St-Paul and St-Pierre markets are more typical.

Stores

The island has all sorts of different types of craft shops. For a wide range of local produce and souvenirs, books, video cassettes, prints, posters and watercolours, you could also try **Lacaze**, 10 place Sarda Garriga in St-Denis, ☎ 21 55 47.

Supermarkets

Although less picturesque, they are often cheaper and have a wider choice of, for example, rum, punch, jams, spices, vanilla, but also video or music cassettes, books and posters.

• Posting purchases

Purchases can be posted by parcel (10kg maximum and of limited size): ask at a post office. By airmail: ask an airline.

HEALTH AND SAFETY

• Precautions

Réunion has no tropical illnesses or cases of malaria. The only precautions required concern possible allergies to plants or flowers throughout the year. The sun is also another possible source of illness.

However, the main dangers are related to the sea. If stung by a venomous fish (rascasse or stone fish), contact a doctor immediately and keep the part stung in water as hot as you can stand.

• Medical kit

Make sure you bring with you or buy on arrival (more expensive) a good sun block cream, a mosquito repellent and antihistamines if you suffer from pollen allergies.

• Health services

Hospitals

Réunion is equipped with the most modern hospital structure in the Indian Ocean and its facilities are quite comparable to those of France.

CHD Félix Guyon, Bellepierre, St-Denis, ☎ 90 50 50.

Centre hospitalier general de Terre Sainte, St-Pierre, ☎ 35 90 00.

Centre hospitalier Gabriel Martin, rue La Bourdonnais, St-Paul, ☎ 45 30 30.

Pharmacies

Réunion has over 200 chemists, dotted all round the island.

Doctors

Over 1 000 doctors, GPs and specialists, practice in Réunion. Doctors and chemists on call at the weekend are listed in the daily newspapers. In case of an emergency, you can also call **SOS Médecins** in St-Denis, (☎ 97 44 44), in St-Paul (☎ 45 45 02) and in St-Pierre (☎ 35 02 02).

Dentists

There are a large number of dentist's surgeries on the island, who also run an evening and weekend emergency service.

• Emergencies

Dial 18 for the **fire brigade**, 15 or 20 10 10 for an **ambulance** or 17 for the **police**.

FROM A TO Z

• Bartering

With the exception of the big St-Denis market, bartering is not all commonplace and may well result in offence.

• Drinking water

Tap water can be drunk all over the island, but it is advisable to avoid drinking it after heavy rainfall or a cyclone. When out walking, don't drink ravine water, but fill up your water-bottle with bottled mineral water before setting out.

• Electricity

Electricity is standard European 220 volts. Most lodges do now have electricity but this is solar-powered and voltage can be weak.

• Internet

The development of the net is such that a whole range of establishments now have their own web site. The most practical remains www.guetali.fr, which has links to a great many other sites on the island.

• Laundry Service

Some hotels do have a laundry service. There are also a few dry cleaners but very few automatic launderettes (St-Gilles-les-Bains, St-Denis, St-Pierre, St-Leu).

• Local Guides (Guides Pays)

Local guides (generally French-speaking) are available to take you round the island and give you a more colourful and more anecdotal description than that generally provided. Reservations from the Travel Office in St-Denis: ☎ 86 32 88.

• Newspapers

It's not difficult to find the international press in supermarkets, stationers *(papeterie) or at the airport*. The best range of foreign press can be found at **Le Tabac du Rallye** in St-Denis. All the local press is in French, but on Wednesdays, Le Quotidien has a page of news in English.

• Photography

It's possible to find all types of films, but developing is relatively expensive and not always of very good quality.

• Radio and television

All the programmes broadcast are in French but not necessarily of French origin (Belgium, Switzerland, Quebec), and there is a very wide choice of TV and radio programmes, including government-run stations and a whole score of 'free' stations.

• Thefts

The standard precautions applicable anywhere should be observed. Don't leave valuables unattended on the beach, in a car or even in a hotel room.

• Tipping / gratuities

Although not common, tips are appreciated.

• Units of Measurement

Distances in this guide are given in kilometres. As a rule of thumb, one kilometre is five-eighths of a mile: 5 miles is therefore about 8 kilometres, 10 miles is about 16 kilometres and 20 miles is about 32 kilometres.

Consult the table below for other useful metric equivalents:

Degrees Celsius	35°	30°	25°	20°	15°	10°	5°	0°	-5°	-10°
Degrees Fahrenheit	95°	86°	77°	68°	59°	50°	41°	32°	23°	15°

1 centimetre (cm) = 0.4 inch
1 metre (m) = 3.3 feet
1 metre (m) = 1.09 yards
1 litre = 1.06 quart
1 litre = 0.22 gallon
1 kilogram (kg) = 2.2 pounds

• Weather forecasts

All weather forecasts are in French.
Forthcoming 24 hours: ☎ 08 36 68 00 00.
Local current weather conditions: ☎ 08 36 68 02 02.
Cyclone updates: ☎ 08 36 65 01 01.
Sailing conditions: ☎ 08 36 68 08 08.

LOOK AND LEARN

It must be said that practically everything written about Réunion has been written in French. The following cover the Indian Ocean in general, but the majority include section(s) or chapter(s) on Réunion.

• General

BUTLER Reg, ***The Indian Ocean***, 1998

GILHAM Mary E, ***Islands of the Trade Winds; An Indian Ocean Odyssey***, Minerva Publications, 1999.

HUC Claude, ***L'Ile de la Réunion***. English text included.

SIMPSON Colin, ***Blue Africa***, A chapter on Réunion.

• Children's books

PENNY Malcolm, ***The Indian Ocean***, Raintree Publications, 1997. Children's nature guide.

• Fauna and flora

BOCK K, ***Common Reef Fishes of the West Indian Ocean***, 1999

HALL TR, ***Fishes of the Indian Ocean***, Calypso Publications, 1998

LIESKE Ewald, ***Coral Reef Fishes, Caribbean, Indian Ocean and Pacific Ocean***, Princeton University Press, 1999.

QASIM S Z, ***Glimpses of the Indian Ocean***, Sangam Books, 1998.

SINCLAIR Ian, ***Chamberlain's Guide to the Birds of the Indian Ocean Islands***, C. Struik, South Africa, 1998.

• History

CHANDRA, ***Indian Ocean and its Islands (Strategic Scientific and Historical Perspectives)***, 1992.

CHANDRA, SATISH, ***The Indian Ocean Explorations in History, Commerce and Politics***, 1987.

MACPHERSON Ken, ***Indian Ocean; A history of people and the sea***, Oxford UP, India, 1998

SCARR Deryck, ***Slaving and slavery in the Indian Ocean***, 1998.

• Maps

Réunion – Africa, Indian Ocean Series, 1997

Mauritius/Réunion – Africa, Indian Ocean Series, 1989

• People and Culture

GEORGES Eliane, ***The Indian Ocean***, B Taschen Verlag, Germany, 1998. Coffee table book.

• Religion

PARKIN David, ***Islamic Prayer along the Indian Ocean Littoral***, Curzon Press, 1999.

• Sport

HEIKELL Rod, ***Indian Ocean Cruising Guide***, Imray, 1999.

JACKSON Jack, ***Diving in the Indian Ocean***, Rizzoli Publications, 1999.

Exploring Réunion

C. Vaisse/HOA QUI

Panorama
of Mafate

St-Denis ★

Pop 131 480

Main town, administrative centre and capital of Réunion

Not to be missed

The Creole houses in the town centre.

The "Petit Marché".

A stroll along rue du Maréchal Leclerc.

An aperitif on the terrace of the "Roland Garros" café.

And remember

Visit the town centre on foot.

Avoid weekends (frenetically busy Saturdays, empty and abandoned Sundays).

Keep away during the rush hours (7am-8am and 4.30pm-6pm).

Arrange excursions and places to stay at the Maison de la Montagne.

St-Denis has an endearing provincial charm about it, and so provides a good introduction to Réunion. The town centre, which is best explored on foot, is networked with straight streets that recall a more formal colonial age, lined with admirable Creole houses redolent of a former way of life. Then, to catch a feel of Réunion's present, continue your amble through the Barachois district or the Jardin d'État.

Some visitors will be drawn by the museums and monuments, others may be happier to observe the world passing by and find entertainment at street level. Against a background of shaded gardens alternating with elegant Creole building fronts, St-Denis bustles with smiling people with a love for bright colours, delicious smells and the power of communicating in a variety of languages. The overwhelming celebration of diversity is to be seen in everything about you: mosques look out over churches and Tamil temples jostle with pagodas; women dress in a choice of floral prints, Indian saris, Moslem djellabas or Creole mini-skirts. In the narrow side streets, an open doorway may reveal a faded, time-worn poster of Mike Brant and Claude François on the wall, while allowing various cooking smells of simmering curry or rice to permeate the air. Whenever you fail to communicate with language or gesture, you will probably find a broad smile works just as well and dispels the need for words.

At the top of the town, it may be good to stretch the legs by taking a short – or long – walk around the Hauts de St-Denis, pausing here and there to admire the wonderful views.

Former colonial capital

The name St-Denis was imparted to the place largely as a result of misadventure. For it was here that the *St-Denis* took shelter during a bad storm after losing contact with the rest of the East India Company fleet, by anchoring in a bay off the Île Bourbon in the shallows of a river estuary. Thereafter, both the river and the town took the vessel's name.

The story of St-Denis really begins in 1669, when **Étienne Régnault**, a general in the East India Company, left St-Paul in order to settle in the north of the island. The small settlement, comprising a handful of houses along the seafront (close to the present Council headquarters), a warehouse, a chapel and a small harbour of sorts, depended on seafaring and commerce.

In time, the plantations became more lucrative and the village grew. The land was parcelled into concessions in 1723, and on this basis the town evolved over the ensuing ten years. The same arrangement survives, with some modification,

A
B

ST DENIS

0 200 m

HOTELS

- Fleur de Mai .... ①
- Manguiers (Les) .... ②
- Marianne (La) ....③
- Mercure Créolia (Le).... ④
- Mascareignes (Le) .... ⑤
- Select .... ⑥
- Jardins de Bourbon (Les) ⑦
- Juliette Dodu (Le)........ ⑧

N
Indian Ocean
SWIMMING POOL
Place de la Pointe des Jardins
Place Sarda Garriga
LE BARACHOIS
R. de l'Artillerie
Maison de la Montagne
Place du 20 Décembre 1848
Rue Mac Auliffe
R. du Four à chaux
Ruelle Floricourt
R. du Moulin à vent
Rue Nice
Rue Juliette
Rue de Jean
R. Neuve
Boulevard
R. de la Batterie
Place E. Regnault
Joffre
Ruelle Cologon
R. des Sables
Rue Jules
Place du Gl De Gaulle
Bd Gabriel
R. Doret
Rue de l'Amiral Lacaze
R. du Mât du pavillon
Avenue de la Victoire
Place de la Préfecture
Square La Bourdonnais
Préfecture
Rontaunay
La Bourdonnais
Villeneuve
R. des Moulins
Rue du Gouvernement
Place Leconte de Lisle
St-Pierre
Le Port
Ruelle Edouard
R. St-Paul
Cathedral
Rue Alexis de Villeneuve
Dodu
Charles
Auber
R. Victor Mac Auliffe
Rue Châtel
Compagnie
R. Pasteur
Ruelle Rebeca
R. d'Assas
Bd Lancastel
Rue de la Gare routière
St-Benoît
Ste-Clotilde
Rue de la Boulangerie
R. de l'Abattoir
R. du Pont
Old Hospital
Monument aux morts
Rue de la Compagnie
Pasteur
Mosque
Gounod
R. de la Ferrière
Rue de l'Est
Limites
R. du Maréchal Leclerc
Old Town Hall
Quai Ouest
Quai Est
Ruelle Tortue
Maison Barre
Rue du Maréchal Leclerc
Rue Felix Guyon
Chinese Pagoda
Petit marché
Tamil Temple
Rue de l'Océan
Grand marché
Rue de la République
Rue Lucien Gasparin
Rue de Paris
Rue Sainte Anne
Jules Garros
Rue des Jules Olivier
Bd de Montreuil
Rue Ste Marie
R. Joseph Hubert
Frère Denis
BAS DE LA RIVIÈRE
Rue Jean Châtel
Rolland
Marie
Beaumont
Artothèque
Rue Ste
Musée Léon Dierx
Monseigneur
Rue A. Bédier
Rue St Bernard
R. ST-Denis
Digue
R. de la Rampe Ozoux
Bd Lacaussade
Rue du Général de Gaulle
Place de Metz
Main Police Station
Rue Malartic
R. Suffren
R. Liancourt
R. Colbert
Jardin d'État
Source
Muséum d'histoire naturelle
Rue Poivre
Rue Decaen
Ruelle Esparon
Rue Roncereau
Rue Acoly
Rue Monthyon
Rue des Noirs
R. Milius
Rue Fénelon
Impasse Leroy
Ruelle de l'Hôpital
R. Molières
Tourette
Rue Philibert
Chemin des Anglais
La Montagne
Rue Bertin
R. Bertin
R. de Parny
R. de Cremont
Ruelle Boulot
Rue des Manguiers
Rue du Bois de Nèfles
Rue Gibert des Molières
Ruelle Routier
Ruelle des Bassins
R. Camp Ozoux
R. des Topazes
Bagatelle
R. de l'Escouble
Rue St-Philippe
Rue de la Source
Leblond
Rue du Couvent
LA SOURCE
Ravine des Noirs
Rue du Ruisseau des Noirs
Rue N. de la Serve
Mazagran
Cascade du Chaudron
Centre Hospitalier Félix Guyon
BELLEPIERRE
Rue Hubert Delisle
La Roche Écrite
Le Brûlé

to the present day. In 1735, **Mahé de La Bourdonnais**, the governor of "Îles de France et de Bourbon" elected to transfer his seat of government to St-Denis because it would be easier to defend than St-Paul.

St-Denis became the **capital** of Bourbon in 1738. It was then that various important buildings were erected, such as the prison and the Lazariste College (now houses some of the university's departments). In time, new suburbs pushed back the town boundaries. Districts were developed up towards the hills so that the affluent middle-classes might escape the crushing heat of summer, while others transformed the area around the mouth of the St-Denis and Butor rivers.

During the early 19C, including a brief period of occupation by the British (1810-15), the town grew to be extremely prosperous. This, in turn, generated the wherewithal for improving local amenities, such as roads, schools and a harbour. By 1860, the town's population stood at 30 000, including the majority of the island's élite.

Then, suddenly, the tide turned and the town was ravaged by a succession of disasters, plunging it into a period of crisis lasting several decades: sugar prices plummeted, epidemics decimated the population and cyclones obliterated the harbour. The people abandoned their homes in town, the suburban outskirts fell to rack and ruin, while the well-heeled sought refuge in the Uplands.

In 1946, Réunion was formally made into a French *département*, and St-Denis assumed the role of provincial **capital**. The local population proliferated, so the authorities were forced to launch an ambitious building programme to extend the town eastwards. The Michel Debré estate in the Chaudron district was put up during the 1960s, then the Champ Fleury district was developed in the 1980s. Meanwhile, rigorous controls were implemented to protect the historic towncentre.

At the close of the 20C, St-Denis has a population of more than 120 000 and continues to flourish. Do not be surprised, therefore, by the number of active building sites around town, nor indeed by the major traffic congestion in the streets, as a large portion of the island's economic activity is concentrated here.

Town

Allow a whole day.

Le Barachois (A1)

The gateway to St-Denis is the Barachois district which faces out to sea. Originally, this part of town grew up around the old harbour that was destroyed in 1874. Today, the seafront is known as **place Sarda Garrigua** in honour of the Republic's commissioner, who proclaimed the abolition of slavery there on 20 December 1848 and emancipated 62 000 slaves.

The shaded gardens stretching along the seafront recall the days when St-Denis was a well-fortified maritime and military outpost. A series of **cannons**, although a mere reproduction of the great battery installed there in the past, still point out to sea.

The long square stone buildings that have a somewhat austere presence about them comprise some of the contemporary depositories and warehouses used by the French East India Company. In the rue de Nice, level with the swimming pool, stand the former **military barracks** and **artillery depot** that now

Le Barachois

accommodate the Radio-France overseas service and the local administration for Public Works (responsible for amenities and building projects).

The fine vaulted entranceway for 10 place Sarda Garrigua leads into an elegantly arcaded courtyard. There you will find the **Maison de Montagne**, which provides detailed information for hiking and excursions into the hinterland.

Freedom celebrations

On 20 December of every year since 1981, a "Kaffir Festival" has been held here to commemorate the abolition of slavery in Réunion. Right across the island, the public holiday is marked with bands and open-air Creole-style street parties locally known as "kabars". These are among the very rare occasions when a hand-to-hand combat or "moringue" between disguised participants is enacted, much as it was in the days of slavery. In 1998, special festivities were organised to commemorate the 150th anniversary of the abolition of slavery.

The Barachois has become a favourite place for locals to congregate and idle away the day with a game or two of French bowls *(pétanque)*. Perhaps the best time to loiter under the *ficus* trees, or take a stroll round and about is a Sunday afternoon when the area is closed to cars and various bands play.

Cross boulevard Gabriel Macé.

This part of town is well-suited to meeting friends and relaxing at one of the bars, for both truly well-known St-Denis terrace cafés are situated here: the "Rally" and the "Roland Garros". The statue of **Roland Garros** (1888-1918) in front of the café honours the Réunion-born aviator, who was the first to fly across the Mediterranean and who developed a way of firing a pistol through a spinning propeller.

On the corner of the Roland Garros café, turn right along the seafront as if to turn your back on it.

Place de la Préfecture (A1), the parade ground once known as the Place d'Armes, has provided the context for several momentous events in the history of Réunion, most notably when the British handed the island back to the French in 1815, and more recently, when Réunion was declared a French "département" in 1946. The statue in the middle of the square portrays Governor Mahé de La Bourdonnais (1699-1753), the man who did so much to develop the two "sister islands" of Mauritius and Réunion.

The **Hôtel de la Préfecture** (Town Hall) dates from 1730, when it was built by the French East India Company as a kind of showcase-cum-shop; in 1764, however, it was converted for use as the governor's residence. As such, this elegant building – one of the oldest in Réunion – illustrates all that is best about colonial architecture, notably its sober design comprising a central block flanked by symmetrical wings, relieved by carved columns, a wooden roof and shaded verandas.

Continue along avenue de la Victoire which, beyond the war memorial, becomes rue de Paris.

Avenue de la Victoire and rue de Paris★★

Place Leconte de Lisle (A1), off rue Rontaunay, is proudly named after the famous French poet and Academician who was born in St-Paul in 1818. Further down the street on the left sits the neo-Tuscan **Cathedral** (A1), built between 1829-32 in the neo-classical style before being completed between 1861 and 1863 by the addition of a porch. This listed historic monument is currently being renovated.

The old Town Hall

Just next door is the **former city hall** (A2), which dates from the mid 19C. Under renovation since 1995, the city intends to use it for official receptions when it's finished.

The **former hospital** (A2) on the right, built in 1829, now houses the district and local council administrative offices. The bust by the entrance is a portrait of **Victor Mac Auliffe**, a famous doctor born in 1870.

A war memorial marks the point where avenue de la Victoire ends and rue de Paris begins. The **Monument aux Morts** (A2), erected in 1923 in honour of the missing soldiers of the First World War, is affectionately know as **Zanz'an l'air** (*l'ange en l'air* or the angel above the pillar), as it always presides over official ceremonies, demonstrations or other such occasions.

Just beyond it stands the old town hall (1846-60) – **l'ancien Hôtel de Ville** (A2). Plans are in hand for it to be used for council offices.

Many of the **town houses** (A2) lining the rue de Paris are a reminder of the prosperous times enjoyed by Réunion in the early 19C. Just imagine the gossip that was exchanged by society ladies concealed in the *guetalis* – the small, specially designed arbours from which it is possible to see out but not in. Each one has its own character and charm. If you stop before any of the *baros* (gates) you will see just how much loving care has gone into each detail. The roof is covered with wooden slats, the front is decorated with carvings and stitched hangings, the garden is lush and well-tended, and the open veranda is furnished with deep comfortable Creole armchairs that look so enticing. All that is missing is an iced-glass of rum punch!

N° 15 was where the former French Prime Minister, Raymond Barre, was born; today, it houses the island's design and planning department. **N° 25** was once owned by a late French senator called Repiquet. **N° 26** – further along on the right – is a fine restored Créole house. Now home to the **Artothèque**⋆ (A2) (☎ 41 75 50 9am-12noon / 1pm-6pm; closed Monday. No charge), it is an art gallery which organises exhibitions of Indian Ocean artists. It is also known for the rather unusual service of lending out works of art, at moderate rates, to art-lovers.

The house next door, n° 28, was built in 1845 to accommodate the local bishop: today, it houses the **Musée Léon Dierx*** (A2) *(9am-12noon / 1pm-5pm;. closed Mondays. No charge)*. The museum was named after a Parnassian painter and poet, Léon Dierx (1838-1912), who was born in the same place as Raymond Barre (French politician), at n° 15. First set up in 1911 by writers Ary and Marius Leblond, in 1947, the museum was left a bequest by Lucien Vollard, brother of the picture-dealer Ambroise Vollard, who had sold the work of Cézanne and Renoir. The now restored picture collection includes Impressionist and Cubist pieces from the dawn of the modern era to more recent and contemporary works (minor works by Gauguin, Picasso, Émile Bernard, Maurice Denis, Bourdelle and Bugati; engravings by Georges Rouault; pieces by Jean Le Gac, Karkis, Ange Leccia and Gilbert Clain, for example). Colourful examples by several Réunion artists are also represented.

At the far end of rue de Paris you come to the **Jardin d'État** (A3-B3) *(7am-6.30pm. No charge)*. These gardens – a good place for a cool drink and a break from sightseeing – were laid out by the French East India Company in 1770 as a kind of nursery for new species of plants imported from afar. Here, they could be carefully tended and monitored before being planted out for commercial exploitation. The "Jardin du Roy", to give it its official name, also hosted public entertainments and exhibitions.
In amongst the rows of plants are several exotic specimens such as the Talipot palm *(Corypha umbraculifera)* which only flowers every 30-40 years, a unique variant of the rubber plant, the bottle gourd tree and the "sausage tree".
The busts portray **Pierre Poivre**, who introduced cloves and the nutmeg tree to Réunion, and **Joseph Hubert**, who is credited with the import of various fruit trees, notably the lychee.

The former colonial palace at the end of the garden shelters the charming local natural history museum – **Muséum d'Histoire Naturelle*** (B3) (☎ 20 02 19 10am-7pm; closed Sundays. Entry charge). The small permanent displays, although rather old-fashioned, provide some insight into the land and sea animals living on and around the island. Star features include the **solitaire** (dodo), the Bourbon tortoise and the coelacanth (a primitive fish).

Turn right out of the garden into rue Général de Gaulle and take the second left.

In contrast with rue de Paris, **rue Juliette Dodu** (B2) boasts a number of more modest Creole houses or **cases**, notably at n° 140 and n° 142, behind tall bushy gardens.

Rue Maréchal Leclerc runs at right angles to rue Juliette Dodu.

Rue du Maréchal Leclerc

If you walk across town, you will soon realise that it is commercial competition rather than race or creed that divides and distinguishes the various districts of town. Although within the ethnic mix, you may notice that some communities are more disposed towards one form of trade than another. Nowhere is this more evident than in rue Maréchal Leclerc, where Madagascans, Chinese, *Z'arabes*, Creoles, Malabars and *Métros* all rub shoulders together to share in the frenzied competition for business. This is the main "high street", where everyone likes to come to buy and sell their wares and services. Crowds of people mill along the narrow pavements, overflowing occasionally onto the street where tails of traffic are as likely as not to be at a standstill.

A good place to start is the covered market at 2 rue Maréchal Leclerc. The **Grand Marché**★ (A2) *(9am-6pm; closed Sundays)* comprises a large hall surrounded by wrought-iron railings, where stall-holders set up business proffering hand-crafted goods from Madagascar: embroidered tablecloths, carved wooden knick-knacks and basket-ware.
Go back to rue de Paris and cross to the opposite side of the street: at n° 121 a tall minaret situates the **Mosquée** (B2) *(9am-12pm / 2pm-4pm. No charge)*, which rises up above the shopping arcade at street level. The mosque's quiet, white and green, sun-filled courtyard provides respite from the frenzied business of the world outside. Please show respect for the place by being dressed appropriately and removing your shoes.

The atmosphere of the **Petit Marché** (B2) *(Monday to Saturday, 5am-7pm and Sunday morning)* located some way down rue Maréchal Leclerc is also busy and colourful. Depending on the season, you will find stalls laid out with delicately flavoured and juicy lychees, mangoes, pineapples and small bananas. Others will be laden with exotic bunches of cut flowers: red *anthurium*, white arum lilies or tropical garden vegetables such as *chouchou* (a pale green gourd-like vegetable) and *brèdes* (a green leaf vegetable that resembles spinach). Among the plastic packages and labelled bottles spread before the spice-seller, you will find vanilla and nutmegs, star anis and fennel – and before you move on, ask him to let you sniff the powerful scent of ylang-ylang.

On leaving the Petit Marché, find rue Ste-Anne and push open the gates of n° 63.

The Chinese pagoda – **Pagode Chinoise** (B2) *(8am-6pm. No charge)* – is a discreet, if slightly austere building with an air of mystery that removes it from the hustle and bustle of the street.
A short way beyond the pagoda at 261 rue Maréchal Leclerc, sits one of the finest Tamil temples on the island. The **Temple Tamoul**★ (B2) *(6am-7pm. No charge)* is open to visitors not wearing or carrying leather (bags, belt, watch-strap, shoes or other).

Excursions to the Hauts de St-Denis

Anyone who enjoys walking – be they lovers of the countryside or hardened hikers – will be captivated by the beauty and diversity of the scenery in the Hauts de St-Denis.

Route de la Montagne *Allow 1hr by car*

Take the western road (RD41) out of St-Denis, sign-posted "La Montagne", for 33km as far as La Possession.

Whether travelled by day or by night, this road provides ample opportunities to stop and enjoy a number of **extensive views** down over the town.

Chemin des Anglais★

Follow the RD41 (route de la Montagne) and after 15km turn right to the St-Bernard stadium. From here follow the track (9km, 450m broken section, allow 6hr including a halt at la Grande Chaloupe) to La Possession, coming out onto the route de la Montagne. Bus from La Possession to St-Denis.

The attraction of this hike is the promise of wonderful **views**★ across the wooded mountain landscape and the shining sea sparkling in the sunshine. The flat stones scattered along the track are a reminder of days gone by, when the first settlers passed this way after landing at **la Grande Chaloupe**. On the edge of the village stand the proud vestiges of the Réunion railway – affectionately known as the *ti'train* – complete with carriages that are open to the public.

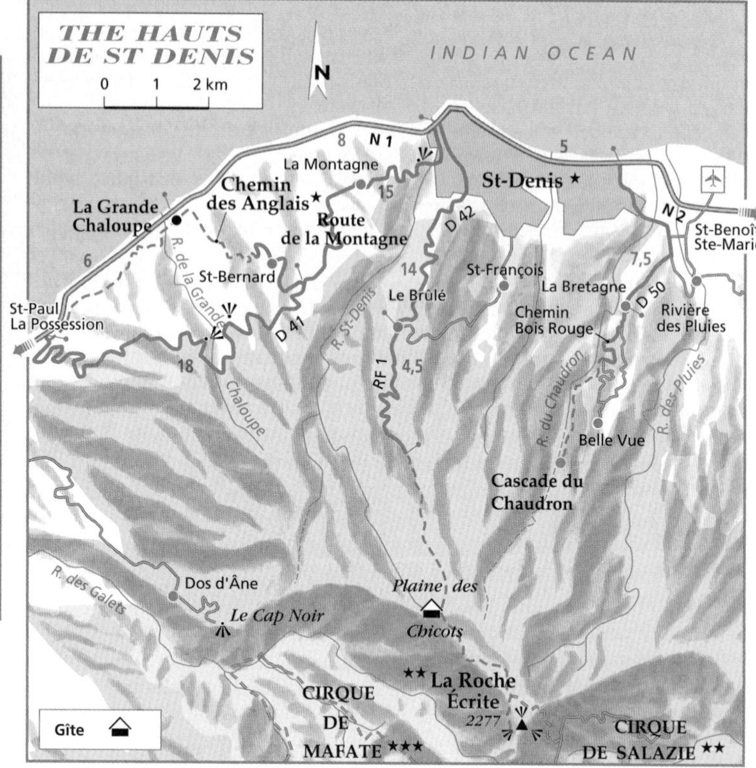

Cascade du Chaudron

Head east out of St-Denis towards La Bretagne and Bois Rouge. Park the car by the pumping station. The path branches off from the chemin du lavoir (90min there and back; easy walking).

You will feel yourself to be both very close to and very far from civilisation all along this walk. Very quickly, the track plunges into the dense vegetation of the tropical forest scattered with *chocas* (aloes) and agaves, although in the near distance, the sound of mopeds is perceptible over and above the noise of a town. The way ahead follows that of a water-conduit, built in 1860 to supply St-Denis, before crossing a footbridge to a ledge running along the sheer side of a ravine, through a tunnel and out to the waterfall. Those liable to suffer from vertigo can take a lower path to the cascade du Chaudron.

Roche Écrite★★

Take the road south (RD42) out of St-Denis and follow it to Le Brûlé. Continue along the RF1 to the car park where the hike begins (19km there and back; entails a 910m climb; allow 7hr). Perhaps the most ideal way to do this is over two days, with an overnight stay at the gîte on Plaine de Chicots (reservations at the Maison de Montagne).

The most rewarding aspect of this excursion on foot through the forest landscape of the Hauts de St-Denis is the splendid view from the top, at 2 277m above sea level. The first section rises steeply through lush woodland, made up of *cryptomeria* trees, tree ferns, *bois de remparts* and *calumus* reeds, to the mountain hostel set among tamarinds and *mahots* (pink flowering trees), where you will enjoy a tasty and well-earned *cari*. The second, more gentle "leg" to the summit is up and over bare rocks. As the vegetation is rather sparse up here, it is imperative that you take precautions against sunburn (hat, sunscreen, long-sleeved shirt). Roche Écrite itself is covered with inscriptions while all around, an extensive **view**** extends over the Cirque de Salazie on the left and the Cirque de Mafate on the right, and on the skyline, the Piton des Neiges and the round-headed volcano beyond.

Making the most of St-Denis

Getting there

From the airport – Allow 15min by taxi (around US$17), by bus (US$4) or by hire-car.

By car – Leave the car in the Barachois district on the western side of town on the seafront or in front of the Town Hall.

By bus – The bus station is situated in Boulevard Joffre (☎ 41 51 10), at the entrance to the town, 5min from the Barachois seafront. Buses go right around the island, stopping in all the towns on the way.

Getting around

On foot – The easiest and best way to explore the town is on foot, thereby saving you from tiresome traffic jams and the problem of find parking spaces.

By car – Be warned: keep in mind that vehicles coming from the right always have right of way in town, that almost every other street is restricted by the one-way system, and that the no-entry sign may be lost among a profusion of other road signs.

Address book

Tourist information – ***Maison de la Montagne***, 53 rue Pasteur, ☎ 90 78 78, Fax 41 84 29. Monday to Thursday, 9.30am-5.30pm; Friday, 9am-4.30pm; Saturday 9am-4pm. Absolutely vital when it comes to advice on hiking or reserving accommodation in the hills, although places can be booked over the telephone.

Office de tourisme, 10 place Sarda Garriga ☎ 41 83 00, Fax 21 37 76.

RUN is a free magazine distributed through various outlets that lists up-dated addresses and information on places to stay, places to eat, shops and activities.

Banks and money – Be sure you have sufficient cash when travelling inland or on excursions, as ATMs are only available in town centres and in coastal resorts.

Banque de la Réunion, 27 rue Jean Châtel ☎ 40 01 23. ATM instructions in Creole only.

BNPI, 67 rue Juliette Dodu, ☎ 40 30 30.

Crédit Agricole, 14 rue Félix Guyon, ☎ 90 91 00 .

Caisse d'Épargne, 55 rue de Paris ☎ 94 80 00.

BRED, 33 rue Mac Auliffe, ☎ 90 15 60.

Post Office – ***Main Post Office***, 62 rue du Maréchal Leclerc, ☎ 40 17 17. Other smaller branches are dotted around the island.

Telephones – There are public phone booths all over town.

Medical emergencies – ***Centre hospitalier départemental Félix Guyon*** (A3), rue des Topazes, Bellepierre ☎ 90 50 50.

Details of which chemists are on night-duty are published in the daily press and in their shop windows.

Airline offices – *Air Austral*, 4 rue de Nice, ☎ 90 90 90.

Air France, 7 av de la Victoire, ☎ 40 38 60.

Air Mauritius, 13 rue Charles Gounod, ☎ 20 25 00.

Car rentals – Most of the car rental agencies are located in the north of the island, where prices are also higher. The following prices are based on unlimited mileage, not including fuel. Deposits are relatively high, between US$770-950, paid by credit card.

Garcia Location, place de la Gare, ☎ 21 20 20, Fax 90 98 25, jmgarcia@guetali.fr A little, local company with some of the most competitive rates around. Three-door car from US$15 a day. Pleasant staff, bookings advisable.

ERL, Ste-Clotilde, ☎ 21 66 81. Local company with offices at St-Gilles where cars can be dropped off. More expensive but reasonable, from US$30 a day for a three-door car.

ADA, 9 bd Doret, ☎ 21 59 01. Well-known car rental agency with rates under the average. All the vehicles are nearly new. From US$35 a day for a three-door car.

WHERE TO STAY

There are some twenty or so different establishments with a variety of facilities in St-Denis, although it is not the nicest place in which to stay. There are no charming family-run or Creole-style hotels. You may wish to spend one or maybe two nights there while visiting the town, but certainly no more. Furthermore, the scheduled departure times of aircraft do mean that you have to spend a night close to the airport. The prices quoted are based on the cost per night of a double room with breakfast.

US$30-45

Le Mascareignes Hôtel, 3 rue Lafférière, ☎ 21 15 28, Fax 21 24 19 – 12rm CC This unsophisticated little hotel is located in a quiet street, parallel to rue du Maréchal Leclerc. Guests will appreciate the warm family atmosphere and friendly welcome. All the rooms are clean and comfortable. If you would rather have a quiet breakfast, ask for a room with a terrace.

Hotel Fleur de Mai, 1 rue du Moulin à Vent ☎ 41 51 81, Fax 94 11 60 – 10rm CC This small, unpretentious and well-kept Creole house is set in pleasant gardens. Situated close to the Barachois district and the bus station, it is convenient for exploring the town. Remember to ask for a room with a window and a balcony.

US$45-70

La Marianne, 5 ruelle Boulot ☎ 21 80 80, Fax 21 85 00 – 24rm TV CC Good value accommodation. Small, modern purpose-built block with simple but clean rooms situated close to the Jardin d'État. The spacious bedrooms are attractively arranged with rattan furniture, although they are not particularly well insulated against noise. If possible, choose a room upstairs: although there is no lift, your luggage will be willingly delivered to your door.

Select Hôtel, 1bis rue des Lataniers, ☎ 41 13 50, Fax 41 67 07 – 54 rm TV CC This modern hotel, located in a road parallel to rue Monthyon, 10min from the Jardin d'État, offers excellent value for money. Although not very typically Creole, it is well situated, the welcome is friendly and the rooms are clean and quiet. Ask for one of the upstairs rooms and enjoy the view over the roofs of St-Denis. The hotel also provides car rentals with a very reasonably priced room+car deal.

Les Manguiers, 9 rue des Manguiers ☎ 21 25 95, Fax 20 22 23 – 20rm TV CC This establishment, situated close to the Jardin d'État, has a number of self-contained studio-apartments that may be ideal for anyone in search of a base for an extensive stay in town. The view from the upper room balconies extends over the town.

Les Jardins de Bourbon, 18 rue du Verger, ☎ 40 72 40, Fax 30 32 28, hotelbourbon@la-reunion.com – 187rm TV CC This large, modern residency is set at the foot of the St-François ramps. Spacious, comfortable rooms able to sleep up to three people. The best ones are those overlooking the city. The hotel offers reduced rates for visits of over a week, which makes it ideal for long stays in St-Denis. An oasis of calm, close to the city centre, excellent value for money.

Over US$70

Le Juliette Dodu, 31 rue Juliette Dodu, ☎ 20 91 20, Fax 20 91 21 – 43rm Situated in the birthplace of the famous resistance fighter after whom it's named, this hotel combines an efficient welcome with charm and quite reasonable prices given the quality of the services offered. Superbly decorated with design furniture, the Juliette Dodu is one of the city centre's most luxurious establishments. If possible, take a suite and admire the original parquet floors.

Le Mercure Créolia, 14 rue du Stade, Montgaillard (B3 indicated off the town plan) ☎ 94 26 26, Fax 94 27 27 – 108rm This large hotel equipped with a variety of excellent facilities enjoys a fine position on the slopes of St-Denis. Panoramic views extend over the surrounding landscape from the large swimming pool. You will find all the staff extremely friendly and helpful, especially when it comes to arranging and co-ordinating the various activities on offer. The professionalism of the staff and the highly competitive car rental rates more than compensate for the hotel's remoteness (15min by car to the town centre).

Domaine des Jamroses, 6 chemin du Colorado, La Montagne, ☎ 23 59 00, Fax 23 93 37, jamroses@runresa.com – 12 rm Set in a two-acre tropical park overlooking St-Denis, this calm, welcoming hotel is full of the charm of olde worlde Creole cottages, with its period furniture and elegant verandas. Spacious rooms, four in the luxury category overlooking the sea. At the top of the park, a 10min walk through the forest takes guests to the nearby Colorado leisure centre (golf, riding, tennis). Half-board possible. Seminar rooms, keep-fit, sauna, jacuzzi, pool table.

WHERE TO EAT

Snack bars

Less than US$7

For a quick bite or an aperitif, head for one of the roadside cafés that serve freshly made samossas and "*bouchons*" – a local speciality.

Chez Kaï, 35 rue de Nice (A1) ☎ 21 90 98. Lunch and dinner; closed Sunday lunchtime. Chinese specialities, excellent fritters (prawns, "*songes*"– a leafy green vegetable, salt-cod) and stuffed flat breads or na'an. The place itself is nothing much to look at, although the food is good and you can always take it to eat outside overlooking the sea.

Chekouri, place Sarda Garriga (A1) (on the Barachois seafront, opposite the RFO HQ, under the huge ficus trees) ☎ 41 72 72. Lunch and dinner. A convenient spot for a quick dish of local curry before resuming your sightseeing although you may find it rather noisy.

Les Calumets – Chez l'oncle Sam, 71 allée des Topazes, ☎ 21 33 89. Lunch and dinner; closed Sundays. The reputation of this little snack bar, just next door to the Felix Guyon Hospital, has grown due to its delicious samoussas (duck with vanilla, deer, shark, etc). It is even rumoured that the very popular cheese samoussa was born here. They also serve very reasonably priced caris. A somewhat indifferent welcome and setting are the only two drawbacks.

La Terrasse, 30 rue Félix Guyon, ☎ 20 07 85. Lunch and dinner; closed Sundays. In the shade of the veranda of this rustic Créole cottage, set in the heart of the city, you can eat either snails in garlic sauce from France or more traditional caris. The best table is in the old guetali, although very noisy, it provides diners with an excellent, yet protected, view of the street.

Le Massalé, 30 rue Alexis de Villeneuve (A1) ☎ 21 75 06. Lunch and dinner until 8pm; closed Friday lunchtime. Wide range of deep-fried Indian savouries and delicious sweet munchies of all flavours (rose, almond, vanilla) and colours to eat there or takeaway. Excellent tea and very friendly staff.

Creole cooking

US$7-25

Le Reflet des Îles, 27 rue de l'Est (B1) ☎ 21 73 82. Lunch and dinner ; closed Saturday lunchtime, Sundays and bank holidays. Here, you will get a warm welcome and excellent Creole food at a reasonable price. Typical dishes include locally made sausages, "ti-jacque" – green jackfruit – salad, tomato and onion-based stews, not to mention a long list of different tasty curries. To round off your meal, they offer a range of rum-based cocktails. Great service.

Le Vieux Portail, 43 rue Victor Mac Auliffe (B1) ☎ 41 09 42. Lunch and dinner; closed Saturday lunchtime and all day Monday. You will see the old "baro" (barred gate) standing before this recently restored Réunion house. The dining area is arranged around a patio below a lovely open-rafted veranda. The delicious smell of cooking spices emanating from the kitchen are enough to make the mouth water before the dishes actually arrive at the table. Forget all your worries and savour the cool atmosphere and delicious food.

Le Fangourin, 11 bd Doret, at the foot of Camélias hill, ☎ 20 27 92. Lunch and dinner; closed Saturday lunchtimes and Sundays. This restaurant, set in an elegant Créole house, serves delicious Créole cuisine at quite reasonable prices. Definitely worth a try.

Chinese cooking

US$7-25

Les délices de l'Orient, 59 rue Juliettte Dodu (A1-A2) ☎ 41 44 20. Lunch and dinner; closed all day Sunday. Good food served although the place is rather kitsch. Slow service.

Le New Escale, 1 rue De Lattre de Tassigny (first floor) (B2 indicated off the town plan in the direction of St-Benoit) ☎ 41 22 20. Lunch and dinner; closed all day Monday. Good food served in a grandiose Chinese restaurant interior.

Le Saigon, 11 rue Gilbert des Molières, ☎ 41 13 67. Lunch and dinner; closed Mondays. Although the décor is nothing special, the Vietnamese cuisine is without a doubt the best in St-Denis. A very warm welcome and magnificent beef sarthé. Ask for a table on the veranda.

Indian cooking

US$7-25

Le Goujrat, boulevard Gabriel Macé (A1), above the Barachois swimming baths ☎ 21 60 61. Lunch and dinner; closed Sundays and Monday evening. A friendly welcome is imparted by a sari-clad attendant. Atmosphere is provided by piped Indian music. Good range of Indian dishes. Request a table with a view of the pool.

French cooking

Less than US$7

L'Igloo, 67 rue Jean Châtel (A1-A2) ☎ 21 34 69 (advance booking recommended especially at lunchtime). Lunch and dinner. A range of excellent salads and light dishes. Wonderful choice of desserts (great "vacherins" with meringue, ice cream, whipped cream and fruit). Notable for its cocktails and ice creams.

Cyclone Café, 24 rue Jean Châtel (A1) ☎ 20 00 23. Lunch and dinner; closed Saturday lunchtime and all day Sunday. Atmospheric Mexican-style establishment full of colour and ingenious ideas. Tasty food although the quantities will only assuage very meagre appetites.

US$7-25

L'Hélios, 88 rue Pasteur (A2) ☎ 20 21 50 (reservations advised). Lunch and dinner; closed all day Sunday and Monday. Delicious tuna-steak tartare and/or open-fire barbecued dishes to be savoured on a shaded terrace. A popular place among wine-drinkers.

US$25-40

Bonnat-Vola, 22bis rue Suffren, on the corner of rue du Ruisseau des Noirs (B3) ☎ 41 65 48. Lunch and dinner; closed Saturday lunchtime and all day Sunday. Original decor comprising thousands of different small knick-knacks and coloured objects sculpted and arranged by Mme Vola. Superb French food including a tempting-sounding langoustine pie followed by a tender filet of venison stuffed with wild cherries and walnuts. Taste the raspberry dessert served with a coulis of red berries.

WHERE TO HAVE A DRINK

Bars, ice cream parlours and tea rooms – *Le Rallye*, 3 avenue de la Victoire (A1) ☎ 21 34 27. Café with tables outside that make it a popular meeting place for a specific circle of habitués. Live music on Sundays played by a local band.

Le Roland Garros, 2 place du 20 décembre 1848 (A1) ☎ 41 44 37. Old-fashioned basalt town-house converted to accommodate an informal and convivial bar, imbued with the relaxed atmosphere of the tropics and the style of a metropolitan brasserie. Try a mango sorbet from the ice cream parlour next to the restaurant, recently opened by the manager of the Roland Garros. Mini prices and delicious flavours.

L'Igloo. This establishment is as busy now as it was when it opened. The variety of flavours and varieties (milk shakes, ice cream cakes, cakes) explain the success of the island's best ice cream parlour. Not to be missed. See also "Where to Eat".

Le Cadre Noir, 11 rue de Paris (A2). This small Creole house with a walled garden conceals both a picture gallery and a lovely tea room.

Cyclone Café. The restaurant turns into a bar in the evenings. The "in" place for all the city's students. See also "Where to Eat".

La Terrasse, See "Where to Eat".

Café Moda, 75 rue Pasteur, ☎ 41 99 41. Closed Sundays. After a meal at the Hélios restaurant, just opposite, go and have a drink on the terrace of the Café Moda. Lively and friendly, particularly on Tuesday evenings, when there's dancing.

Entertainment – *L'Espace Palaxa*, Ste-Clotilde (B2 indicated off the town plan in the direction of Ste-Clotilde) ☎ 21 31 13. Check the press for details of live concerts given by Creole bands (Fridays usually).

Champ Fleuri, avenue André Malraux, Ste-Clotilde (B2 indicated off the town plan in the direction of Ste-Clotilde) ☎ 41 11 41. Large hall with a 900-seat capacity used for a variety of shows (Indian and/or contemporary dancing, live bands, etc).

Théâtre du Grand Marché, rue du Maréchal Leclerc, ☎ 20 33 99. This theatre, which replaces the old Fourcade Theatre, is located behind the big market. It also houses the Indian Ocean Drama Centre, which, in an auditorium painted with Ndebele-style paintings (South African ethnic art), puts on productions about Réunion and its neighbouring islands.

Théâtre Vollard, 23 rue Léopold Rambaud, Ste-Clotilde, ☎ 21 25 26. The island's most famous theatre, which occasionally exports its productions to Paris. All the work put on is based on Réunion's history. Not to be missed.

SHOPPING

Arts and crafts – Several shops selling a variety of hand-crafted goods from Réunion, Madagascar and India are to be found along rue Juliette Dodu, rue Jean Châtel and rue Maréchal Leclerc.

Lacaze, place Sarda Garriga (A1). This shop caters mainly for tourists in search of gifts and mementoes of their stay in Réunion. To this end, a range of locally made goods are on offer alongside books, rum and spices. Prices are very much in keeping with those charged for similar items in the centre of town.

Grand Marché, rue Maréchal Leclerc (A2). This shop essentially imports its wares from Madagascar. Do not hesitate to bargain over prices, especially if you are considering buying several things.

Le Mahal, 50 rue du Maréchal Leclerc, ☎ 41 63 98. Excellent choice of Indian craftsmanship at very reasonable prices. Better than Ali Baba's cave.

Art galleries – *Le Cadre Noir* (see above).

Galérie L'Océane, 51 rue de Paris. This pretty little Creole house doesn't have a permanent exhibition, but travellers lucky enough to be in St-Denis during an exhibition of local artists should seize the opportunity.

Books and newspapers – *Le Rallye* (see above). Open daily and into the early evening for cards, books about the island, newspapers, etc.

Librairie Gérard, 5ter rue de la Compagnie.

L'Entrepôt, 42 rue Juliette Dodu (A1).

THE WEST COAST★★

ST-DENIS TO ST-LOUIS

Approx 80km of coast road
Allow 2 days
Sunshine, high temperatures and low rainfall

Not to be missed
View from Maïdo.
A stroll through St-Paul market on Friday evening.
A swim off Boucan Canot.
The Stella Matutina Museum.

And remember
Avoid weekends, if possible.
Start out on hikes early in the morning, equipped with plenty of drinking water, a waterproof and suitable walking shoes.

The west coast is essentially dedicated to catering for seaside holidays. For this side shelters Réunion's only shallow lagoons, as well as the best white or black sand beaches. It also provides the most favourable conditions for windsurfing and scuba-diving in the lee of the trade winds and the swell. For the same reasons, it was here on the **"leeward" coast** that the early settlers landed and set up their base camps – hence the number of scattered vestiges to be seen in the area. In addition to the draw of the historical remains, there is the scenery, comprising great swathes of golden savannah succeeded by fields of sugarcane and then, on the higher slopes, stretches of dense forest and scraggy patches of gorse.

St-Denis to St-Paul

27km by car or bus. Avoid the morning and evening rush hours on a weekday and the heavy traffic back into St-Denis on a Sunday evening. Under normal conditions, estimate 20min by car.

Coastal Road

The main trunk road west out of St-Denis is reputed to be the most expensive stretch of road in France, as it was largely built (1963), and then widened to four lanes (1976), on land reclaimed from the sea. Used by 40 000 vehicles a day, it is the bane of many an islander's life as congestion regularly causes traffic jams which, in turn, quickly gridlock the system across the region. Nonetheless, the road stands as a remarkable feat of engineering as it picks its way between the sea and a succession of fractured basalt cliffs and volcanic lava flows that are turned into great big gushing waterfalls after heavy rain. The view of the scenery on either side is magnificent, especially at sunset when the steep rocks are bathed in deep shadow and mellow reflected light. Despite the different safety devices installed along the cliffs, including the netting designed to minimise the dangers of rock falls, accidents do occur and traffic is often temporarily halted.

It was at **La Grande Chaloupe**, 8km west of St-Denis, that the British troops landed in 1810; today, the village preserves its old railway station, sections of the tracks and an 1885 **Creusot locomotive**, classed as a historic monument. A little outside of the village is the former Lazaret; although in ruins for many years, it has recently been undergoing renovation and should soon house the Department of Environment. The Grande Chaloupe's interest lies in the beauty

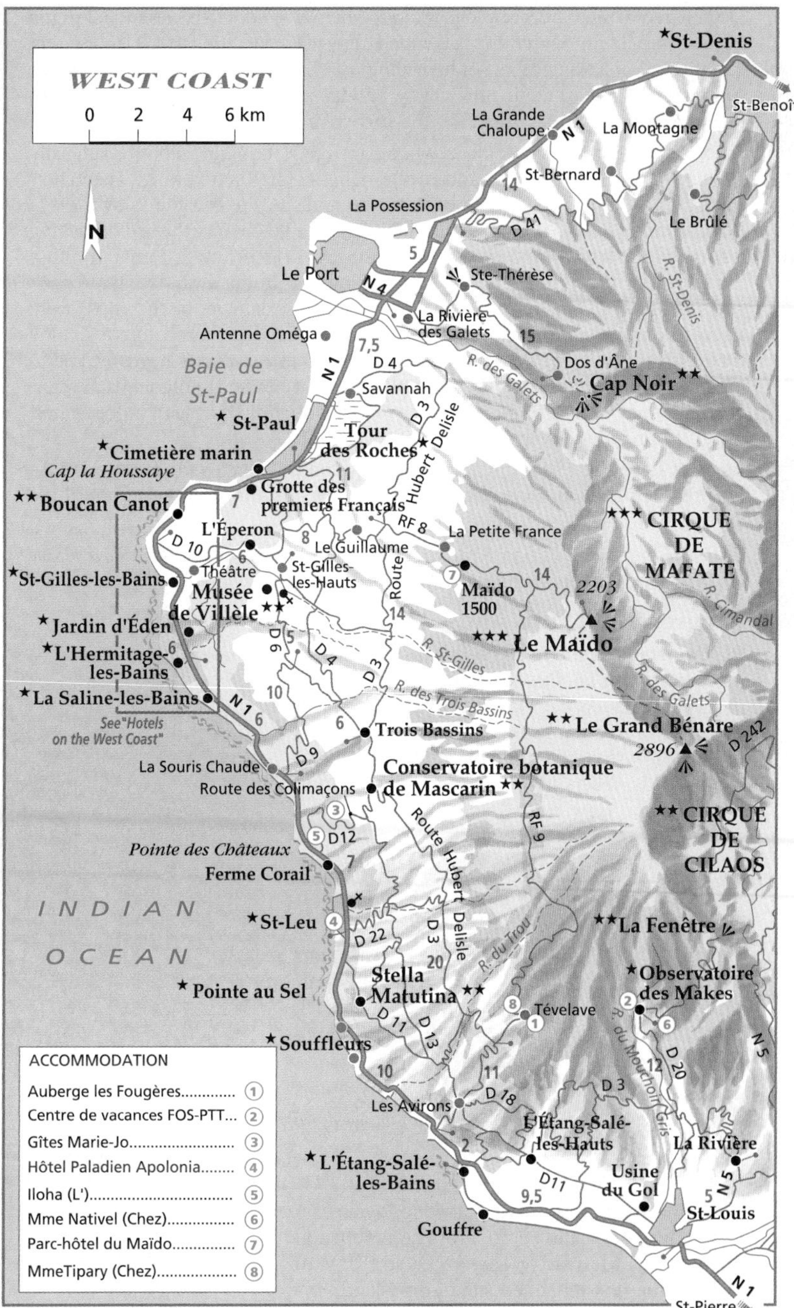

WEST COAST
0 2 4 6 km
N
St-Denis
St-Benoît
La Grande Chaloupe
La Montagne
St-Bernard
Le Brûlé
La Possession
R. St-Denis
Le Port
Ste-Thérèse
La Rivière des Galets
Antenne Oméga
Baie de St-Paul
R. des Galets
Dos d'Âne
Cap Noir
Savannah
St-Paul
Tour des Roches
Hubert Delisle
Cimetière marin
Cap la Houssaye
Grotte des premiers Français
Boucan Canot
CIRQUE DE MAFATE
L'Éperon
La Petite France
Le Guillaume
Théâtre
St-Gilles-les-Hauts
St-Gilles-les-Bains
Musée de Villèle
Maïdo 1500
2203
R. Cimandal
Jardin d'Éden
Le Maïdo
L'Hermitage-les-Bains
R. St-Gilles
R. des Galets
La Saline-les-Bains
R. des Trois Bassins
See "Hotels on the West Coast"
Le Grand Bénare
2896
Trois Bassins
La Souris Chaude
Conservatoire botanique de Mascarin
Route des Colimaçons
CIRQUE DE CILAOS
Pointe des Châteaux
Ferme Corail
Route Hubert Delisle
INDIAN OCEAN
St-Leu
La Fenêtre
R. du Trou
Observatoire des Makes
Stella Matutina
Pointe au Sel
Tévelave
R. du Mouchoir Gris
Souffleurs
Les Avirons
L'Étang-Salé-les-Hauts
La Rivière
L'Étang-Salé-les-Bains
Usine du Gol
St-Louis
Gouffre
St-Pierre
ACCOMMODATION
Auberge les Fougères 1
Centre de vacances FOS-PTT 2
Gîtes Marie-Jo 3
Hôtel Paladien Apolonia 4
Iloha (L') 5
Mme Nativel (Chez) 6
Parc-hôtel du Maïdo 7
MmeTipary (Chez) 8

of the Creole '*cases*', recently repainted in the old style. Every year the Tangue festival is held in September, at which time all generations of islanders get together to eat a *tangue* (sort of hedgehog) *cari* and organise a traditional *kabar*. Alternatively, one can enjoy the village and its surrounding countryside by following the **Chemin des Anglais**★, the first paved road on the island *(see p 98)*.

La Possession marks the place where, in 1649, Captain Lebourg officially claimed possession of the island in the name of the French king. Thereafter, the island assumed the named of **Bourbon** and the site became known as "la Possession du Roy". Up to the end of the 19C, La Possession thrived on having a successful boatyard and being the last staging post before St-Denis. In those days, the island's principal town was a good two hours away by stage-coach and passengers, after experiencing the perils and dangers of the road, were likely to require some restorative refreshment from a local inn before resuming their onward journey. When the railway was built, the town's heyday came to an end, then the coast road was completed and it became a remote backwater. Nowadays, La Possession is essentially a residential district, with a population of 20 000 relying largely on jobs in St-Denis or Le Port.

Le Port developed as a town around its harbour activities during the 1890s. Its precisely laid out avenues and modern architecture, however, hold little appeal for tourists.

Follow the road sign-posted for Rivière des Galets and continue through the village. At the junction, take the D1 marked for Dos d'Âne (15km drive, winding steeply uphill; 20min).

Excursion to Dos d'Âne★

Rivière des Galets developed out of a small settlement down by the river as a place for Creole families to escape to at the height of the summer. As the road twists uphill, you will come to a place known as Halte-Là – so named because it was a favourite place for outlaws to "hold-up" travellers before robbing them – from which a fine **view** extends down over Le Port. Eventually, the road leads up to **Dos d'Âne**, an attractive hamlet at 1 000m above sea level.

Continue towards Cap Noir and leave the car in the car park.

An easy walk (20min) along a level path contouring the hillside takes you to a viewing platform with a splendid **view**★★ of Mafate. The track then continues in a great loop to **Roche Verre Bouteille** (75min there and back).

From Cap Noir you can walk back to St-Denis via Plaine d'Affouches or Plaine des Chicots, or go down into Mafate and come out by Deux Bras.

Drive back to the RN1 and follow directions to St-Paul.

The main road crosses over the wide Rivière des Galets, recently dammed up. From here, stop and enjoy the splendid **view**★ over the bay of St-Paul, the first inhabited site of the island.

St-Paul to St-Gilles-les-Bains

15km by the main coastal road. Allow 10min by car.
Allow at least 2hr to reach Maïdo via Les Hauts.

■ **St-Paul★ –** The bay of St-Paul is one of the few places in which boats can safely moor, and it was here that the *St-Alexis* cast her anchor in 1638. Naturally sheltered from the swell and the wind, the bay seemed to promise the first colonists a good situation for a settlement that, in time, might become the capital of the island. During the 18C, the early settlers ventured out towards the marsh and along the coast, gleaning subsistence from fishing, hunting and small cultivated plots. When fire destroyed part of the town, many residents moved to St-Denis.
For a time thereafter, St-Paul flourished as a result of coffee and cotton; the centre of town became graced with fine planter's houses. Then, towards the close of the 19C, St-Paul's prosperity came to an end. The demand on the international markets for sugarcane declined and prices fell accordingly, local businessmen suffered the loss of successive contracts as new harbour facilities became available at Pointe des Galets, and, finally, malaria swept through the town decimating the population.

The bay of St-Paul, once referred to as the "best bay in which to anchor", has not lost its original vocation, however, for each year, when a cyclone is forecast, all the cruise-boats in the area collect here and wait for the danger to pass.

Come off the RN1 and head for the town centre.

JF Galmiche

Friday afternoon in the market at St-Paul

The **Chaussée Royale**, built by royal decree in 1769, is still lined with a series of fine old planter's houses. On the right, at N° 233, stands the former Franco-Chinese school overlooking the **Grand Cour**, one of three houses once owned by Mrs Desbassyns *(see p 111)* built in the IndoPortuguese style of Pondichéry.

Otherwise, St-Paul's **town centre** preserves very few traditional old houses, although an enduring charm is provided by the Chinese-managed wooden shops and elderly locals cycling through the streets. The main thoroughfare running across the picturesque commercial centre is presided over by the **town hall**, built in 1667 by the French East India Company. Other 17C buildings from the same era (fire station, council offices), behind coconut palms and casuarinas, line the **seafront**. The cannons, which once stood at the ready to protect the town up on the Bernica Cliff, also date from the same period.

This area overlooking the sea also accommodates the island's most charming **market**** *(Friday and Saturday morning)*. Stall-holders proffer freshly collected fruit and vegetables from their gardens, others sell sweet-smelling herbs, packaged spices and mysterious bottles of "sauce", or colourful examples of Madagascan handicraft. This is a perfect opportunity for tasting one of those appetising *samossas* and *bonbons-piments* before taking a seat at the *"Ti'case en Paille"* by the bar or on the terrace facing the sea, to enjoy a bite to eat and to listen to a group of *gramounes* (elderly) musicians that regularly plays there.

Follow signs out of town to St-Gilles and park in front of the grotte des premiers Français

The sailors' cemetery – **Cimetière Marin*** – will appeal most to romantic souls who enjoy absorbing the serenity of a place steeped in history while allowing the imagination to reconstruct the open sea. The concept of time is quickly blurred as the senses succumb to the powerful scent of the frangipani, the glinting sea, the heat of the day and the thought of marauding pirates... Many of the tombstones list the names of the island's first inhabitants – founding families and local dignitaries, like the poet **Leconte de Lisle** (1818-94) or individuals who ended their lives there, like the shipwrecked Breton sailors from the *Ker Anna* (1894), and Olivier Levasseur, commonly known as **La Buse**, who became one of the most notorious pirates of the Indian Ocean and is reputed to have hidden his treasure in the Bernica ravine (*see p 420* La Buse's Treasure). It is not unusual for people to come here at night and surreptitiously leave an ex-voto, a packet of cigarettes or some rum at the foot of the cross beside his tomb.

The same reflective mood should accompany you across the main road where, opposite the cemetery, you will find the legendary cave known as the **grotte des premiers français**. It was here in the hollow of the cliff that the first men to set foot on Réunion are reputed to have taken shelter. It may be worth taking a look, and being tempted into having a refreshing drink of coconut milk juice *(eau coco)* or a piece of chicken grilled on the open coals from one of the trucks parked up there. More often than not, you will find the place crowded with locals enjoying their Sunday picnic or watching a smiling couple of newly-weds posing for photographs.

Go back to the RN1 in the direction of St-Denis and turn off to follow indications for the town centre. Then keep right for Grande Fontaine. Please note that the following excursion (approx 5km) should not be undertaken after heavy rain.

The **Tour des Roches*** consists of a short drive around the marsh of St-Paul, thereby completing another foray into history, to see where the early settlers came to hunt and gather food. The best time to go is in the early morning or at sunset when the scenery is infused with light and colour. It is as if you have been transported to a place in Africa, inhabited by Africans and planted with verdant tropical vegetation. The last of the island's coconut plantations also has bananas, clumps of green-leafed colocasia, bamboo, papyrus and watercress beds. A few Madagascan *moufia* palms, which are rare in these parts, grow proudly up on the cliffs overlooking the marsh. The path comes out beside a series of buildings on the left that once formed part of the **Savannah** sugarcane refinery.

To rejoin the RN1, turn left after the Savannah roundabout. Once you reach St-Paul, look out for and follow directions to Plateau Caillou, Fleurimont and Le Guillaume, where you will find indications (barely visible) bearing right for Maïdo (RF8).

Excursion to Maïdo**

Allow 1hr to reach the summit. Leave early in the morning at around 6am-7am. The road to Maïdo is long and tortuous. As the weather can unexpectedly change for the worse, it is best to make straight for the top and make regular stops to admire the scenery on the way down.

Virgin forest covered the Hauts de St-Paul until the 1920s when it was cleared to make way for geranium plantations. All along the **Maïdo road** you will see the landscape exploited for sugarcane, fruit and vegetables and geraniums before you come to the areas forested with tamarinds and *cryptomerias* – a kind of conifer imported from Japan and widely planted by the ONF (Forestry Commission) after the Second World War.

The word *Maïdo* means "scorched earth" in Madagascan. At an altitude of 2 204m, it is inevitable that the vegetation is rather stunted and windswept. It is here that the **Balcon de Mafate***** opens out over an extensive panorama embracing the island's highest peaks. Straight ahead rise **Gros Morne** (2 991m), **Piton des Neiges** (3 070m) and **Grand Bénare** (2 896m). Here and there in this grandiose landscape, the sunlight is caught and reflected off the tin roof of a shack that stands isolated in amongst the undergrowth or in huddled groups. To the left, a walkway provides an uninterrupted view of the whole Rivière des Galets amphitheatre.

The small footpath branching right leads to Grand Bénare (6hr there and back; fairly arduous).

Be it a blisteringly hot day or a cold windy one, the hike up to **Grand Bénare** is best undertaken in the morning. You reap your reward at the top when you take in the great **view**** over the Mafate and Cilaos amphitheatres.

On your way back along the RF8, there are several places to stop off. The leisure centre **Maïdo 1 500** *(School holidays, 8am-5pm; otherwise Wednesdays, Saturdays, Sundays and public holidays. Separate charge for each activity)* is surrounded by a green and pleasant estate. Those who enjoy the thrill of travelling at high speeds may like to go for a ride on the summer **toboggan**. The secrets involved in the distillation of geranium to extract its essential oil are revealed by the demonstration of a roadside **working still**, one of the few left on the island. Additional facilities are laid on at the hotel-restaurant "Maïdo 1 500" on the edge of the complex (*see p 119*).

G. Guittot/DIAF

Geranium still

A little further down lies the **Petite France** estate (1 200m). The first owner, who acquired the land in 1850, wanted to create a cool, pleasant garden, reminiscent of France, in a glade of trees with different coloured barks. He set about seeding oaks, silver birches and lime trees, together with a wide variety of **geraniums**. Somewhere in amongst the fields of geraniums, you may have the opportunity of seeing how the flowers are distilled to produce an oily extract that is used in medicinal preparations and perfumery.

At Le Guillaume, at the bottom of the Maïdo road, fork left towards St-Gilles-les-Hauts (D7 then D4 or D8). Drive right through the village and turn right towards the Villèle museum.

■ **St-Gilles-les-Hauts –** At one time, all the land around these parts belonged to the **Panon-Desbassyns** family, one of Réunion's major dynasties of plantation-owners. In the latter half of the 18C, three houses were built for the three daughters: the "Grand Cour" in St-Paul, the "Maison Blanche" at Bernica and one at Villèle (1787), which in 1971 became a museum. All three were modelled on the Indo-Portuguese style that was the norm in Pondichéry, a former French colony, where Mr Desbassyns had served in the Royal Army against the British.

The guide to the **musée de Villèle**** (☎ *22 73 34/55 64 10, 9.30am-12noon and 2pm-5pm; closed Tuesday. Entrance fee*), who conducts tours of this great big house, was the former family chauffeur. The house, built of volcanic stone and brick, conforms to a rigorously symmetrical plan and is covered with a flat *armagaste* roof (made of lime mixed with sugar and egg, as found in India). The two-tiered **veranda**, lined with marble and terracotta tiles, opens out onto the large **garden** planted with over 95 different species of trees and plants. Part of the museum is dedicated to portraying conditions on a sugar and coffee plantation in the 18C. A fine collection of **furniture** and household effects is on display to illustrate the kind of home comforts available to a Creole dignitary in the 18C and 19C: a dark wood-panelled drawing room, a bedroom furnished in tamarind wood, furnishings acquired from the French East India Company, Cantonese porcelain, a clock given to Mrs Desbassyns by Napoleon, Gobelins tapestries. A fresco in the large drawing-room illustrates a scene from *Paul et Virginie*, the novel written by Bernardin de Saint-Pierre, who was a close friend of the family, the heroine of which was modelled on one of Mr Desbassyns's cousins.

The main house, which until 1971 remained in the family, would have had several annexes around it, including the *boucan* (kitchen), built apart so as to avoid the risk of fire, a dispensary for treating the slaves and a sugar-refining plant now in ruins.

On the slope across the road, planted with eucalyptus trees, stands the **Chapelle Pointue** *(9am-12noon / 1pm-5pm; closed Tuesdays. No charge)*, a mausoleum with an elegant neo-Gothic roof built for Mrs Desbassyns who is buried there.

Follow directions to St-Paul (CD10), leaving St-Gilles-les-Hauts behind you on the left.

Colonial era personified

Mrs Desbassyns's reputation is legendary when it comes to the history of Réunion, although she remains a controversial figure. She was certainly admired in her own time as someone endowed with great entrepreneurial skill which she exercised in improving the cultivation of sugarcane with irrigation schemes, building factories and lime works, founding schools and a hospital. She was toasted for her generous hospitality at "l'habitation" – one of the biggest homesteads on the island, where she entertained almost everyone passing through as a guest, including the British officers in charge of the ships captured off the coast. The wealthiest woman on the island, who lived through the fall of the Monarchy, the Revolution, Napoleon's Empire and the Restoration, also came to represent the success of Colonialism founded on slavery. At her death in 1846, she left an estate of 500 hectares and a workforce of 300 slaves. The person, who to some was a saintly carer of the poor (St Providence des Pauvres), was attributed by others to be ruthlessly cruel, forcing her slaves to be whipped and branded, or worse, having their limbs amputated. Later, when the volcano showed signs of erupting, it is said that elderly islanders were heard to mutter "burn burn, Mrs Desbassyns"...

Route du Théâtre

This road takes you through an attractive stretch of the countryside including the village of **l'Éperon**, which has a large Malabar community. Occasional cock-fighting sessions attract huddles of animated spectators to the area before one of the many temples. Look out, in particular, for the large and gaudily decorated **Tamil Temple** at the beginning of the track to Tamatave on the left-hand side (1km). A former sugar-refining plant, now converted into a **craft-centre**, displays an array of local handicraft: pottery, painted fabrics, jams and pickles, artwork, etc.

Further down the road, the entrance to the **Ravine St-Gilles*** is lost behind the gaggle of mobile snack-cars and sightseeing coaches. Beyond, footpaths pick their way through leafy tropical vegetation to reach three pools, fed by waterfalls, in which you can take a refreshing dip. If you walk through the channel to the left of the path, you will come to the sapphire-blue pool known as the **Bassin Bleu**. A track branching off to the right will take you steeply downhill to the **Bassin des Aigrettes**. A third track runs between the two and leads to the **Bassin des Cormorans**. It is well worth putting off a visit to these pools until after the weekend, when they are particularly crowded, or heading for the northeastern part of the island where there are other just as lovely and quieter pools to enjoy (*see p 148*).
Before the road reaches the coast, you will notice on your left the St-Gilles **open-air theatre** (théâtre de plein air), where many a memorable evening concert and recital has been held *(details published in the local press)*.

The beaches between Boucan Canot and Trois-Bassins

For 25km, stretches of white and black sand beaches alternate along the west coast. Although the landscape on this side is not typical of the island as a whole, it does provide some of the few spots where it is possible to swim and practise other water sports in complete safety. However, you may be shocked to find that since Réunion was made a *département* of France and developed an infrastructure for tourism, building promoters have transformed the St-Gilles coast into a single holiday-village conurbation.

Y. Arthus-Bertrand/ALTITUDE

Aerial view of the St-Gilles coastline

Do be careful when bathing, as certain sections of beach (notably off Boucan Canot and Roches Noires) have no protective barrier reef to shelter them from undercurrents powerful enough to drag an adult out to sea. Where there are reefs, do not attempt to venture beyond them. Never swim alone. Keep an eye on children playing in the water at all times, even near the shore, in case they are swept away by a strong wave. Every beach displays notices indicating where the danger spots are. Feeding sharks swim into shore in the early morning, at nightfall, after heavy rain and in cloudy water.

The different beaches are marked along the coastal road (RN1) leading out of St-Paul.

■ **Boucan Canot** – The first headland, **Cap de la Marianne**, is so called since the profile of Marianne (the personification of the French Republic wearing her Phrigian cap) in the cliff was painted blue, white and red to celebrate the bicentenary of the French Revolution. The next cape – **Cap la Houssaye** – is a good place to go diving, after which the rocks melt into a fine sand to form the Boucan Canot **beach**** that is considered the most beautiful on Réunion.

As with the Roches Noires beach at St-Gilles, the shallows very quickly give way to deep water – hence their popularity for diving, surfing and body-surfing (known locally as *moree*). Streams of people come from St-Denis to spend the weekend at the seaside, causing long tailbacks of cars and motorbikes along the roads and queues up to the mobile snack bars to buy *bouchons* and *samossas*, a cool beer or a guava juice.

■ **St-Gilles-les-Bains** – The small fishing village on the edge of the Desbassyns estate largely depended upon its landlords for its survival right up to the close of the 19C. Things began to change in 1863 when the road from St-Paul was completed, although further developments in tourist facilities had to wait until Réunion was made a French *département*.

Only a few fragments from the past survive, save the odd traditional house in amongst the invasion of banal seaside-resort buildings put up in modern times, filled with cheap restaurants or clothes and souvenirs shops.

The **plage des Roches Noires*** consists of a long gentle sweep of pale sand beach lapped by the Indian Ocean. Similar facilities are laid on for the same range of water sports as at Boucan Canot. The nearby, recently enlarged and improved **harbour** provides moorings for small boats and fishing smacks while, further out, larger diving-club and deep-sea fishing vessels lie at anchor.

■ **L'Hermitage and Saline-les-Bains** – The original communities to populate this area were based in hamlets up in the hills behind, south of St-Gilles-les-Hauts. Then, when the new road was built in the 19C, the seaside resorts began to take shape.
The beach here is protected by a coral barrier-reef, so the water in the lagoon is calm, warm and shallow. If you have them, it is well-worth donning plastic shoes or jelly sandals (to protect your feet from sharp coral and sea-urchins) at the same time as mask and snorkel, before going out to swim among the myriad of coloured damsel-, clown-, parrot- and butterfly fish. Rest assured that the rather repulsive-looking dark sausage-like creatures known as sea-cucumbers on the sea-bed are no threat whatsoever.
The long white sandy **beaches***, lined with rows of casuarinas, are extremely attractive to visitors and local residents alike, especially at the weekend, so they can become extremely crowded.
To differentiate the various sections of beach, regulars have allocated them the names of the nearest mobile snack bar. Right in front of **Toboggan**, at L'Hermitage, you will find the reefs populated with a profusion of tropical fish. Further south at Saline, **Planche Alizés** is known for its deck-chairs, rowing-boats and pedalos as well as its cosmopolitan habitués.

For those who get impatient with lying on the beach all day, there is the **Jardin d'Eden*** to explore *(opposite Avenue de la Mer, RN1, L'Hermitage, ☎ 33 83 16. 10am-6pm; closed Mondays. Entrance fee. Allow 90min)*. This peaceful and shaded miniature tropical garden provides an excellent introduction to the proliferation of locally found species: spices, succulents, aquatic plants, some edible, others with aphrodisiac, magic and / or malicious properties, including some that are regarded as sacred by the Hindus. Each plant has its Creole name and a specific use, be it culinary, medicinal or merely superstitious.

Exploring the Hauts de l'Ouest*

The western Upland region is split into sections by densely overgrown ravines. Several minor roads provide local farmers and labourers with access to their fields, so the traffic you will encounter will largely consist of tarpaulin-covered pick-ups or pedestrians shouldering their *bertelle* (flat woven-palm basket worn on the back).

Take the N1 out of Saline-les-Bains and continue through the place known as "la Souris Chaude"; at the junction, take the D9 left and follow it to where it joins the D3 at Trois-Bassins.

The **route Hubert Delisle (D3)** is named after the governor who commissioned its construction in 1858. Its completion enabled people to move further into the hinterland and develop agricultural holdings at and above 800m. For visitors to the island, the road is an excuse for a lovely 50km drive between St-Paul and St-Louis, to enjoy the wonderful **panoramas** that open out over the coast. It also provides an insight into the pace and nonchalance of life in the upland villages.

From Trois-Bassins, you can either head northwards to **Guillaume** (above St-Paul) or continue southwards to **Colimaçons** and rejoin the coast road near St-Leu.

The wooded area over and above 1 200m, between **Petite France** (on the Maïdo road) and **Tévelave**, is bisected by a multitude of small **forestry tracks*** (RF). These make for a fine outing by car or motorbike, or provide remote spots for a picnic followed by a walk in the hills.

The coast between St-Leu and St-Louis

20km - 15min by the RN1

As you journey south, you will notice how the landscape becomes progressively more sparsely populated. The parched slopes are interrupted here and there by the exposed escarpments of each deep and densely overgrown ravine. The rugged land mass abruptly falls away in a series of precipitous cliffs that continue along the coast to L'Étang-Salé. Far removed from the modernity of St-Denis and the seaside kitsch of St-Gilles, you will find the people in the south enjoying a peaceable existence and a more traditional rhythm of life.

On the right of the RN1, just before St-Leu when coming from l'Hermitage, level with the RD12.

Ferme Corail to Colimaçons

Ferme Corail (*Pointe des Chateaux ☎ 34 81 10. 9am-6pm. Entrance fee*) is primarily a **tortoise** sanctuary. There, you will find several dozen specimens, graded by age, being monitored and interbred to safeguard the species from extinction. It is surprising, therefore, to discover the farm **shop** promoting the pharmaceutical, cosmetic and nutritional benefits of tortoise derivatives and selling souvenirs and jewellery made of genuine tortoiseshell!

Opposite Ferme Corail, fork left off the RN1 onto the RD12.

The D12 or "route des Colimaçons" leads up to the **Conservatoire Botanique de Mascarin**** (*Colimaçons-les-Hauts ☎ 24 92 27. 9am-5pm; closed Mondays. Entrance fee, guided tours at 10am, 11am, 2.30pm, 3.30pm*). The botanic gardens, dedicated to preserving rare and endangered species, continue the work initiated by Mr de Chateauvieux on his estate. Since 1986, the Conservatoire has been charged with combining scientific research with promoting a greater awareness and respect for the island's flora through education and sophisticated tourist facilities. Three hectares of garden, recently made accessible to the general public, and a number of glass-houses shelter thriving specimens of fruit tree, orchids and carnivorous plants.

Passionate amateur botanist

Sosthènes de Châteauvieux, who was employed as a steward to the Desbassyns family, settled in Colimaçons in 1857 on what had been a reconnaissance station. In time, his estate grew to some 600 hectares. In 1865, he had a special chapel built modelled on the typical church found back home in France. Here the Marquis was able to pursue his other great passion which was to import suitable plants from abroad and acclimatise them in his private nursery. In this way, such trees as the eucalyptus, jacaranda and monkey puzzle came to be introduced to Réunion, and that quinine was grown essentially as an antidote for malaria (as first prescribed by the British physician Thomas Sydenham in 1666).

Go back to the RN1 following directions to St-Pierre, and continue to the centre of St-Leu.

■ **St-Leu*** – A relaxed nonchalance and holiday atmosphere pervades the heart of this small town at all times of year. Fishermen sell their catches of lobster, blue fish and other kinds of parrot-fish fresh from their nets along the side of the road. In the background, surfers ride the famous "*gauche de St-Leu*", a regular succession of waves famous across the world since the inauguration of a major **surfing** competition held annually in June. A small supervised beach with deeper water lies in wait behind the Hotel Apolonia.

On the left of the roundabout at the entrance of the town sits the **Church of Notre-Dame de la Salette***, which was hurriedly built into the cliff in 1859 while a cholera epidemic was sweeping through the island. As if by miracle, the spread of the disease was halted by the town gates: this remarkable event continues to be celebrated on **19 September** each year by a pilgrimage.

As the main road continues into the town centre and becomes the high street, you will find the **town hall** presiding over matters on the right hand side. In actual fact, the building originally served as a warehouse for the French East India Company and recalls a time when the town enjoyed a certain degree of success from its production of Bourbon coffee, for which Louis XV had a particular liking. Indeed, the considerable workforce employed there at that time enabled the town to repel an attack by the British in 1796. Its eventual decline was precipitated by a series of cyclones followed by a major slave revolt in 1811.

A few other attractive buildings down along the **seafront**, now converted into offices, date from the same era. The musical rhythms and the enticing smell of grilled chicken emanating from the mobile snack bars under the casuarinas provide ample reason for a short break here.

Beyond St-Leu

Head out of St-Leu along the RN1 towards St-Pierre, and turn left along the RD11.

An old sugar-refining plant provides a suitable home for the **musée agricole et industriel de Stella Matutina**** *(☎ 34 26 14, 9.30am-5.30pm; closed Mondays and between 2nd to 4th Tuesday of September. Entrance fee. Allow 2hr)* which aims both to instruct and amuse. The large (5 000sqm) complex has been sensitively renovated for use as "the" Réunion museum, outlining the history and economy of the island. Displays relate the importance and changing fortunes of the coffee, sugarcane, spices, vanilla and geranium plantations over the centuries. The ground floor is largely devoted to the island's **history**, with sections set aside for its geology and volcanoes, its weather patterns and cyclones; additional space is reserved for temporary exhibitions which are usually very good. On the first floor, the story of sugar is retold, with particular reference to its extraction from the cane and its refining process using steam-powered boilers. There is also a working model of a three-masted schooner of the type used by the French East India Company and a wonderful **sweet shop** that will appeal to both young and old. The second floor provides information on the flora of the island, together with an **Odorama** for identifying the various herbs and spices. Before you leave, key in a selection of numbers into the **juke-box** and go out into the street with the rhythm of a song ringing in your ears.

Return to the RN1 and continue towards St-Pierre.

Some way along the road, the mesmerising smell of the frangipani trees fill the air: on the left sits St-Leu's colourful **public cemetery***, enclosed with a rectangular wall, overlooking the sea.

Before the road broadens into a dual carriageway, turn right by the bus stop down a badly marked track.

Pointe au Sel* is a headland that has been classified as a protected site of special scientific interest and that is well worth a detour. The naturally austere landscape falls abruptly, exposing rather forbidding cliffs to the merciless sea

(Swimming prohibited because of dangerous currents). The **salt pans** *(7am-12pm/ 1pm-4pm. No charge unless you join a guided tour)*, built in 1942 and recently renovated comprise a series of interconnected terraced pools where the water is allowed to evaporate, thus leaving a deposit of salt crystals to form. The dried salt is collected in the morning and small sachets of it are on sale there.

Continue along the RN1 towards St-Pierre. Stop at the car park, 4km outside St-Leu.

When the sea is rough, you will hear the roaring sound emanating from the **blowholes*** *(souffleurs)*, which is produced when the water surges violently up into the hollowed rocks, pushing the air and spray up through a small aperture. *(Do be careful not to get too close as a powerful wave could catch you unawares)*.

4km or so beyond the blowholes, turn left up to the village called les Avirons. From there, you have two options: either you can head back northwest across the Tévelave forest to join the Hauts-sous-le-Vent forestry road (RF9) that links up with the Maïdo road; or you can continue south along the D11 that forks right towards Étang-Salé-les-Hauts.

■ **L'Étang-Salé** – The first people to settle in the area were drawn to the Uplands rather than the coast, which was developed only after the railway was built in 1882.

The community of **L'Étang-Salé-les-Hauts** earns its livelihood from sugarcane, maize, groundnut and banana plantations. It is here that the famous **Gol cane-chairs** and **capelines** – a local hat made from latanier fibre – are still made.

The D17E picks its way down towards the sea between rows of fabulous *cytisus* and *flamboyants* before cutting through L'Étang-Salé estate **woodland area**, which is predominantly planted with casuarinas, eucalyptus, tamarinds and Siamese cassias and provides locals with ample opportunities for a Sunday afternoon stroll. The lower reaches are taken up by an 18-hole **golf-course** that is renowned throughout the countries of the Indian Ocean.

Since the major four-lane bypass was built, peace has in part returned to the small and attractive seaside resort of **L'Étang-Salé-les-Bains.** Here the long **beach*** has black sand and so it is vital to don shoes before venturing across it during the heat of the day lest you burn the underside of your feet. Be careful to bathe in areas that are supervised because the currents can be deceptively strong in places. The southernmost section of the rocky coastline extending beyond the town, is cut by a deep crevasse. Here, the sea thunders between the basalt cliffs sending foam and spray high into the air.

Plaine du Gol

The population living up on the fertile plain, now covered almost completely with fields of sugarcane, is concentrated in the village of St-Louis, which was founded in around 1720 and is located a good distance from the coastal salt-marshes. Up here, there is a fine **view** across to the foothills of Tévelave, Makes and L'Entre-Deux. To the left of the dual-carriageway lies what is perhaps one of Réunion's most beautiful **avenues of coconut trees***.

If you are in the area just outside St-Louis any time between July and December, you will be struck by the sweet smell coming from the **Gol Sugar Refinery** (*Usine Sucrière du Gol: ☎ 26 10 02. Guided tours booked in advance, open every day*). In the olden days, the island claimed to have a hundred sugar-refineries: since 1995, there are only two left in working order – this one and the Bois-Rouge plant at St-André.

Go back down towards the centre of St-Louis.

St-Louis consists of a single high street bordered with Chinese-owned shops. It enjoys a warm, dry climate and has an old-fashioned and rather provincial

Y. Arthus-Bertrand/ALTITUDE

Low tide

feel to it. Among its handful of buildings, you will note the **church** and a large **Hindu temple** *(remove shoes before entering and check that no leather is being worn).*

Take the RN5 leading out of the centre towards La Rivière.

Beyond St-Louis

The striking feature of **La Rivière** is its flowers. To learn more about the different varieties, take a walk around the **Creole garden** belonging to Mrs Merlot *(203 route de Cilaos ☎ 39 08 87. 8am-6pm. Entrance fee).*

The road through the hamlet continues up to the **Cirque de Cilaos**** *(see p 171).*

Follow the D20 towards les Makes up a 15km winding road above St-Louis.

The D20 shadows the deep **Ravine du Mouchoir Gris**, providing panoramic views over the undulating sugarcane country. The little village of **Makes**, surrounded by trees, provides the local people with "a change of air" to use a Creole expression.

The **Observatoire astronomique de la Réunion*** *(☎ 37 86 83 access by prior arrangement 9am-12noon / 2pm-5pm; Sundays, 9pm-12midnight. Entrance fee. The best season for stargazing is during the southern winter between June and August)* organises evenings when the public are invited to study the stars. Through the lenses of a telescope, space may be seen to be crowded with constellations, other planets and their galaxies. Given Réunion's proximity to the Tropic of Capricorn and its distance from any major landmass, visibility tends to be extremely good.

The **Fenêtre viewing platform**** 10km above Makes (RF14) provides the ideal spot from which to contemplate the landscape around Cilaos.

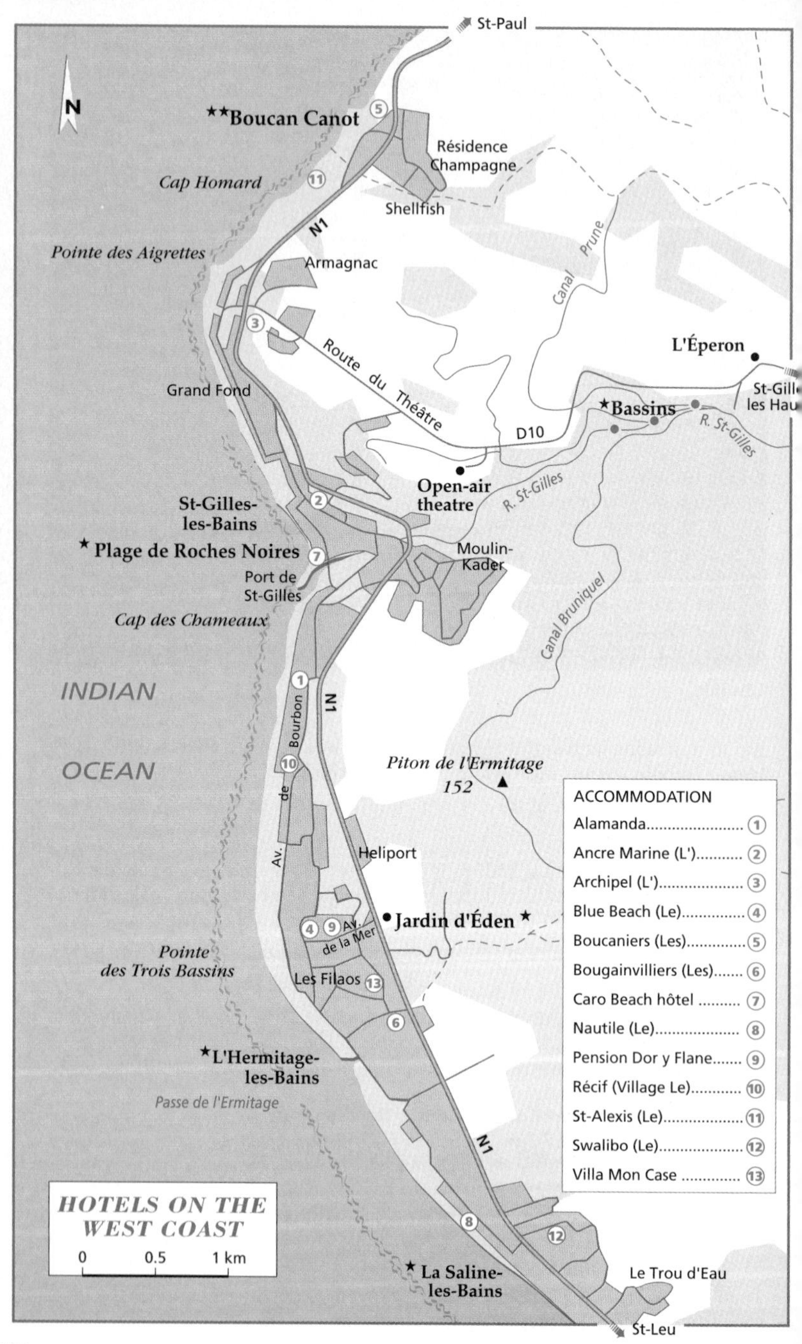
St-Paul
N
★★Boucan Canot
Résidence Champagne
Cap Homard
Shellfish
N1
Pointe des Aigrettes
Armagnac
Canal Prune
Route du Théâtre
L'Éperon
Grand Fond
St-Gilles-les-Hauts
★Bassins
R. St-Gilles
D10
Open-air theatre
R. St-Gilles
St-Gilles-les-Bains
★ Plage de Roches Noires
Moulin-Kader
Port de St-Gilles
Cap des Chameaux
Canal Bruniquel
INDIAN
OCEAN
Av. de Bourbon
N1
Piton de l'Ermitage
152
Heliport
Jardin d'Éden ★
Av. de la Mer
Pointe des Trois Bassins
Les Filaos
★L'Hermitage-les-Bains
Passe de l'Ermitage
N1
HOTELS ON THE WEST COAST
0 0.5 1 km
★ La Saline-les-Bains
Le Trou d'Eau
St-Leu
ACCOMMODATION
Alamanda 1
Ancre Marine (L') 2
Archipel (L') 3
Blue Beach (Le) 4
Boucaniers (Les) 5
Bougainvilliers (Les) 6
Caro Beach hôtel 7
Nautile (Le) 8
Pension Dor y Flane 9
Récif (Village Le) 10
St-Alexis (Le) 11
Swalibo (Le) 12
Villa Mon Case 13

Making the most of the West Coast

GETTING THERE

By bus – Regular services operate out of St-Denis and stop at the main coastal towns. Additional ***Pastel*** and ***Ti'cars jaunes*** minibuses serve the Uplands communities.

By car – The coastline is accessible by main road; secondary roads and forestry roads network the Upland areas.

ADDRESS BOOK

Tourist information – *Office du tourisme de l'Ouest*, Galerie Amandine, St-Gilles-les-Bains ☎ 24 57 47, Fax 24 34 40. Tuesday to Friday, 8.30am-12.30pm/1pm-6pm; Saturday, 9am-5pm; Monday, 9am-12noon/1pm-6pm.

Office du tourisme de l'Étang-Salé, 74 avenue Octave Bénard, L'Étang-Salé-les-Bains ☎ 26 67 32, Fax 26 67 92. Monday to Friday, 8.30am-12noon/2.30pm-6pm; Saturday, 9.30am-12noon/3pm-6pm; closed Sunday.

Banks – Most banks have offices at St-Paul, St-Gilles-les-Bains, St-Louis and St-Leu.

Post offices – Post offices are to be found in the centre of St-Paul, St-Gilles-les-Bains, St-Leu, L'Étang-Salé-les-Bains, St-Louis.

Telephone – Public telephones are scattered throughout this area.

Vehicle rentals – Agents are located in the centre of St-Paul, St-Gilles-les-Bains, St-Leu and around the many hotels at l'Hermitage.

It is advisable to approach one of the smaller local agents whose rates are often much more advantageous than those of the larger, more well-known rental companies. The following offer attractive rates with unlimited mileage and will deliver cars wherever asked.

Gégé Location, 167 ter, rue du Général de Gaulle, St-Gilles, ☎/Fax 24 59 77. Single fixed rate (150FF per day) for minimum of three days.

GIS, 180 av du Général Leclerc, ☎ 24 09 73, Fax 24 55 20. Slightly more expensive than the former (from 210FF/day for a three-door car). GIS has a wide choice of cars and requires less deposit (2000FF) than its competitors. two days rental minimum.

Medical services – Chemists abound in the centres of town and in the tourist resorts. Many of the beaches manned by coastguards will have a first-aid unit. Should you require a doctor, make enquiries at your hotel.

WHERE TO STAY

Unless stated otherwise, the prices quoted are based on the cost per night of a double room with breakfast.

• St-Paul

Around US$75

Parc-hôtel du Maïdo, route du Maïdo, le Guillaume. ☎ 32 52 52, Fax 32.52.00, maidoh@oceanes.fr – 24rm Mini-tennis, volleyball, boules, billiards, toboggans, pony-trekking. One of the attractions of this well appointed bungalow-accommodation in the hills (1 500m) is the variety of facilities on offer from the neighbouring sports centre, including the hire of cross-country bikes. This is a perfect place from which to explore the Maïdo area.

• Boucan Canot

US$45-60

Les Boucaniers, 27 route de la plage de Boucan Canot, ☎ 24 23 89, Fax 24 45 96– 15rm Ideally located opposite Boucan Canot beach, this hotel residence provides a mixture of comfortable clean rooms and small, well equipped bungalows. The highly impressive restaurant totally dominates the beach, but self-catering facilities are also available, because the rooms are equipped with a tiny kitchenette. Each room also has a balcony or terrace. Room no8 is the biggest and most comfortable and costs almost the same as the others.

Over US$150

Le St Alexis, 44 route de Boucan Canot, ☎ 24 42 04, Fax 24 00 13– 42rm Although it may initially appear remote and off-putting, this luxurious building is not devoid of charm. A swimming pool winds its way through the various buildings opposite the lagoon. The luxuriously furnished wood-panelled rooms each have a jacuzzi. Panoramic restaurants overlooking the ocean. Excellent breakfasts.

• **St-Gilles-les-Bains**

Before settling on a particular hotel, it is well worth enquiring after any special promotional deals or premium rates available on offer from the larger establishments, which are rarely fully booked.

US$30-45

Pension Dor Y Flane, 21 avenue de la Mer, l'Hermitage. ☎ 33 82 41, Fax 33 98 52 (advance booking recommended) – 13rm Subject to availability, you can choose to stay in the large main house which has rooms of varying quality, or in flats in a spacious and comfortable residence (with kitchen, television and bathroom facilities). Shared kitchen, terrace and seating areas. The owner, a talkative person with a great personality, usually welcomes her guests with a delicious home-made punch on her veranda.

Les Bougainvilliers, 27 ruelle des Bougainvilliers, l'Hermitage. ☎/Fax 33 82 48 – 9rm Pretty family-run bed-and-breakfast located in a peaceful residential quarter 300m from the beach. Friendly reception, charming and fresh in feel. Self-catering facilities available to those staying more than four consecutive nights.

US$45-75

Villa Mon Case, 7 boulevard des Cocotiers, l'Hermitage. ☎ 33 81 15, Fax 33 93 92 – 3rm Three-nights minimum stay. Book well in advance to save being disappointed. Well-equipped bungalows (sleeping two-six; washing-machine, kitchen) overlooking a small patio-garden with barbecue, set in a green and peaceful backwater, 5min from the beach. Very convivial reception.

Hôtel l'Ancre Marine, centre commercial le Forum, rue General de Gaulle. ☎ 24 31 32, Fax 24 35 85 – 17rm These simply furnished rooms are situated on the top floor of a small modern and clean shopping mall, with a terrace. During the day, the noise of the busy high street can be rather off-putting, although in the evening, you are ideally placed to enjoy the nightlife of St-Gilles.

Hôtel Alamanda, 81 av de Bourbon, ☎ 33 10 10, Fax 24 02 42, alamanda.hotel@wanadoo.fr – 58rm Located opposite St-Gilles Casino, and 2min from the local nightclubs and cinema, this hotel is ideally located for those who want to combine daily outings without missing out on the nightlife. The hotel overlooks a large, quiet park and a generously sized swimming pool. The rooms are simple but functional. Insist on a room overlooking the park or the swimming pool.

US$75-95

Village le Récif, avenue de Bourbon, l'Hermitage. ☎ 24 50 51, Fax 24 38 85 – 76rm Spacious rooms or bungalows arranged around a lovely lawn shaded by coconut trees. Huge swimming pool and bar festooned with Creole decorations. Attentive and efficient staff.

Le Swalibo, 9 rue des Salines, Saline-les-Bains. ☎ 24 10 97, Fax 24 64 29 – 30rm Welcoming establishment tastefully furnished and decorated with bunches of fresh tropical flowers, attentive and discreet staff. Separate jacuzzi provides private moments of complete relaxation.

US$95-110

Le Blue Beach, avenue de la Mer, l'Hermitage. ☎ 24 50 25, Fax 24 36 22 – 56rm All the rooms with private balcony overlook the curvaceous swimming pool and the open restaurant dining area. The rumble of the air-conditioning units and the nightlife can be irksome, so ask for an end room, if possible. Thoughtfully conceived and comfortable. 200m from the beach.

L'Archipel, Grand Fond. ☎ 24 05 34, Fax 24 47 24 – 66rm Free bus service shuttles guests to the beach at Boucan Canot and the centre of St-Gilles. Despite this hotel's rather unattractive site close to the main road, it is well conceived and quite pleasant. The rooms, attractively furnished with rosewood furniture and Chinese decorative details, are arranged in 12 Creole-style bungalows. Both the lounge area and restaurant open onto the large swimming pool.

US$110-140

Caro Beach Hôtel, 46 rue Roland Garros, Roches Noires. ☎ 24 42 49, Fax 24 34 46 – 48rm Modern hotel situated right in the centre of town, slightly removed from the noisy shopping areas. Request a room overlooking the bay and the Roches Noires beach. If travelling in a party, ask for one of the apartments.

Le Nautile, 60 rue Lacaussade, Saline-les-Bains, ☎ 33 88 88, Fax 33 88 89, nautili@runnet.com – 43rm This recently built, quite magnificent hotel is the twin sister of the Juliette Dodu in St-Denis. Here also, the charm and good taste are impeccable: old-fashioned tiling, bright colours, a superb swimming pool with jacuzzi and well-furnished rooms. The hotel's location is quiet, without being isolated, and the welcome flawless. The suites are very luxurious. Music once or twice a week.

• St-Leu

Less than US$30

Gîtes Marie-Jo, 69 chemin du Buisson (route des Colimaçons). ☎ 34 83 11, Fax 34 78 12 – 8rm Small self-contained studios and apartments available for a week at a time. What this accommodation lacks in charm it makes up for in practicality, providing families with a more economical option than a hotel.

US$60-110

L'Iloha, Pointe des Châteaux, ☎ 34 89 89, Fax 34 89 90, iloha@oceanes.fr – 64rm This impressive colonial-style hotel has rooms ranging from the simplest to the most luxurious, depending on your budget. It also has an unmatched view over the Bay of St-Leu. Each bungalow (more expensive) has a pleasant veranda. Every week the hotel organises a wide range of activities and musical evenings.

US$110-125

Paladien Apolonia (Nouvelles Frontières), boulevard Bonnier. ☎ 34 62 62, Fax 34 61 61 – 133rm The sound of piped music permeates every corner of this huge hotel-club. Convivial and social areas around the bar and the long indoor swimming pool. Many free activities on offer to 3-77 year-olds. Supervised public beach, deep clear water 50m from the hotel. Large proportion of guests travelling in groups.

• Les Avirons

US$15-30

Chez Mme Tipary, 14 route du Tévelave, ☎ 38 00 71 – 2rm An authentic Creole case, still full of olde world charm and set in a beautiful garden. Unpretentious rooms and a family atmosphere. Mrs Tipary's energy and warmth delight all who meet her. Meals, on request, evoke a little taste of "Far-off Réunion": in addition to the traditional chicken cari, you may also be able to taste brede, sorrel and herring pie or a Ti Jacques cari. Excellent value for money.

US$45-60

Auberge les Fougères, 53 route des Merles, Le Tévelave. ☎ 38 32 96, Fax 38 30 26 – 16rm Apart from being brand new, this hotel enjoys a wonderfully quiet and cool position right on the edge of the forest high up in the hills. It is also both welcoming and comfortable, although it is best to avoid the ground-floor rooms. Terrace with panoramic views of the coast. Restaurant: see Where to eat, *p 123*.

• St-Louis

Less than US$23

Chez M. et Mme Nativel, Route de la Fenêtre, Les Makes ☎ 37 85 37– 2rm The gîte is located in a new 'Creole'-style house. Each room is clean, well-equipped and comfortable and has its own little veranda leading into the pretty Creole garden. Excellent Creole cooking on request and an impressive collection of Réunion rums. Very friendly.

Centre de vacances FOS-PTT, 13 rue Georges Bizet, Les Makes. ☎ 37 85 92, Fax 37 86 19 – 5rm and two dormitories. Situated opposite the observatory. Studios and dormitories arranged around communal areas such as the refectory, kitchen and playroom. After contemplating the stars, you can lay your head on a pillow and dream of new horizons.

WHERE TO EAT

• St-Paul

US$7-15

La Baie des Pirates, 17 route des Premiers Français, ☎ 45 23 23 CC Lunch and dinner; closed Saturday lunchtime and Sundays. Although it might look like a local buccaneers' den, this roadside restaurant, just before the marine cemetery, serves an excellent fillet of shark or grilled swordfish at very reasonable prices. It must be said that despite somewhat kitsch false spiders' webs and murals depicting marine battles, the place is still very pleasant.

US$15-20

Le Loup, 192 rue Marius et Ary Leblond. ☎ 45 60 13. Lunch and dinner; closed Saturday lunchtimes, all day Sunday and Monday. Excellent swordfish 'tartare', zébu (beef from Madagascar) steak and assortment of grilled fish or meat; unctuous floating islands and crème brûlée followed by a glass of rum on the house to round things off. Nice atmosphere.

Chez Floris, 48bis rue la Croix, Étang-St-Paul (near the town centre). ☎ 22 69 81. Lunch and dinner; closed Sundays. Low-lighting, fishing nets, lifebelts and old propeller-driven engines provide a congenial backdrop to this restaurant which specialises in Creole dishes: typical sausages in tomato and onion sauce, meat and fish freshly cooked over a wood-fire, the best swordfish 'au combava' (marinated in the local lime juice); grilled – then flambéed – bananas are to die for. Live entertainment is provided by a local band on a Friday evening after the market closes. Well-priced venue.

• St-Paul and St-Gilles-les-Hauts

Around US$15

Table d'hôte Ramassamy, 100 chemin des Roses, St-Gilles-les-Hauts. ☎ 55 55 06 (book in advance). 5min from the Domaine du Villèle. Tasty guinea-fowl, vegetable 'au gratin', Creole curries. Informal atmosphere.

• Boucan Canot

Under US$15

Les Boucaniers, 1st mobile snack bar on the left as you reach Boucan Canot, on the road from the beach (one-way). Very good salads, delicious 'cari', glorious fresh guava juice.

Case Bambou, Le Bambou Bar, Plage de Boucan Canot, ☎ 24 59 29 CC All day; closed Mondays. Opposite the beach, the combined Bambou Bar and the Case Bambou establishment is the "in" snack bar-restaurant of Boucan. The snack bar is full every weekday lunchtime. The cooking is good and the boss has cleverly taken advantage of the increase in tourism to raise prices without running the risk of losing clientele. Pleasant setting, luxurious vegetation.

US$30-45

Le Grand Hunier, Hôtel St-Alexis, 44 rue du Boucan Canot. ☎ 24 42 04. Lunch and dinner. Gastronomic restaurant at one of the most luxurious hotels on the island. Original and refined cuisine.

• St-Gilles-les-Bains

US$7-15

Cap Ouest, Port de Plaisance, ☎ 33 21 56 CC Situated near the Alpha fishing centre, this bar-restaurant is on its way to becoming one of St-Gilles' most popular places. During the day, you can enjoy an Ocean Salad in a relaxed atmosphere opposite the sea. At night-time, the bar gets busy and would appear to be the place to go before going out nightclubbing.

Les Tipaniers chez Dante, 58 rue du Général de Gaulle. ☎ 24 44 87. Lunch and dinner; closed Tuesdays. Provençal/Marseillais restaurant specialising in seafood – notably shark and swordfish. Epicures should try the two-chocolate mousse. Terrace opens out onto the main street of St-Gilles.

La Bobine, plage de l'Hermitage ☎ 33 94 36. Lunch and dinner. The terrace is arranged with rustic tables facing onto the lagoon to provide an ideal spot from which to watch the sun go down. Slightly cramped, but atmospheric venue. Simple but flavoursome cooking: local 'caris', selection of grilled meat and fish (subject to what the fishermen have brought in).

US$15-30

Le Manta, 18 boulevard Leconte de Lisle, Les Filaos. ☎ 33 82 44. Lunch and dinner. This civilised restaurant, situated right by the beach at l'Hermitage, is pleasantly informal. The terrace has a beamed roof covered, on the outside, with thatch. House delicacies include fine slices of red tuna marinated in lemon juice and olive oil, grilled dorado with herbs, with a chocolate fondant for desert. Most dishes comprise simply prepared good-quality fresh produce. To round off your meal, sit back and enjoy a shot of rum.

Centre de pêche alpha, on the harbour front. ☎ 24 02 02. Lunch and dinner; closed all day Monday and Tuesday lunchtime. Mr Benattar – Benett for short – is both an ardent fisherman and restaurateur, so his menus always list a selection of freshly caught fish: swordfish carpaccio (finely sliced raw fish drizzled with lemon juice and olive oil), tuna fish 'tartare', not to mention the overwhelming array of other kinds available. For desert, let yourself be tempted by a 'fondu de chocolat' with fresh fruit. The dining area overlooks the harbour filled with bobbing skiffs belonging to the local fishing fleet.

Native, place du Marché, ☎ 33 19 34 CC Lunch and dinner; closed Tuesdays. In a tasteful intimate décor with art deco rattan and wood chairs, this restaurant offers good French cooking and fish specialities. Young, friendly staff and relaxed atmosphere. If either the lamps or the tables are to your taste, all the furniture is on sale in the store nextdoor to the restaurant.

• Around St-Leu

From US$7

Le Souffleur, RN1, Bois Blanc (between St-Leu and L'Étang-Salé). ☎ 26 61 13. Lunch and dinner; closed all day Monday, as well as Thursday and Sunday evenings. Tables are available inside the tin-roofed, rather basic fisherman's shack decorated with fish and knick-knacks, or on the terrace outside. The view extends over the golden savannah all around, and when the sea is rough, you can occasionally see the spray pushed up through the blowhole. The food here is typically Creole: stewed zourite (octopus), curried crab, sausages with onions and tomato.

Le Stella, Stella Matutina museum (no charge for access to the restaurant). ☎ 34 07 15. Lunch Tuesday to Sunday; closed Monday. An excellent place to stop and eat after visiting the museum. Light Creole dishes: smoked marlin, oven-baked papaya. Good view over the bay of St-Leu.

• St-Leu and Avirons-les-Hauts

US$12-20

La Varangue, 36 rue du Lagon, ☎ 34 79 26. CC Lunch and dinner; closed Sunday, Monday and Tuesday evenings. A quiet restaurant on the way into St-Leu with a magical feel to it. Meals are served on the seafront overlooking the lagoon. Don't miss the kangaroo civet with guava.

O'Jacaré, 55 rue du Général Lambert, ☎ 34 88 88. CC Lunch and dinner; closed Sundays. This roadside restaurant may be a bit noisy, but it is still a nice place to stop for a salad or grilled meat dish. Colourful décor and very reasonable prices.

Auberge les Fougères, 53 route des merles, Le Tévelave. ☎ 38 32 96 (reserve in advance). Lunch and dinner; closed Monday lunchtime and Sunday evenings. Traditional Creole food cooked over a wood fire. Pleasant and unpretentious. A good excuse for going walking in the hills.

• Trois Bassins

US$25-45

Domaine Gastronomique de Piveteau, Chemin Piveteau, L'Étang-Salé-les-Hauts, ☎ 24 74 14. CC Lunch and dinner (reservations only); closed Sunday evenings and Mondays. Getting to this restaurant requires quite a drive up into the mountains and a search through the cane fields. However it's more than worth the effort. Once there, you will be amazed by the magnificent panoramic view over the sea and the west coast, from the bay of St-Paul to the bay of St-Leu. Excellent cuisine, friendly service. Well worth the trip.

• L'Étang-Salé-les-Bains

US$5-18

L'Été Indien, RN1 ☎ 26 67 33. Lunch and dinner. Closed Mondays. Striped blinds shut out the bustle of the village high street outside, leaving you to concentrate on enjoying a plate of mixed salads, stuffed pancakes, crunchy pizzas, a mixed grill or other typically local dish. Reserve a enough space for one of the many varieties of home-made ice creams on offer. Attentive service.

• L'Étang-Salé-les-Hauts

US$15-25

Chez Mme Sergine Hoareau, 231 route du Maniron, L'Etang-Salé-les-Hauts, ☎ 26 41 07. Lunch and dinner (reservations only). Take a seat on the veranda of this pretty Creole case and enjoy the splendid coastal view, while you savour the house's sophisticated and delicious Creole cuisine. Their meat rolls with green banana, cod manioc bredes or chicken cari with bredes will be one of the culinary high-spots of your stay in Réunion. Very friendly welcome. Perhaps the best table d'hôte on the island.

Having a drink

Bars and ice creams – *La Siesta*, rue Eugène Dayot, St-Paul. ☎ 22 55 72. Monday to Saturday, 4pm-12midnight; closed Sundays. Good place for an informal drink.

Loïk Olivier, 15 rue de la Plage, St-Gilles-les-Bains ☎ 24 33 73. Delicious assortment of ice creams, cakes and chocolates to eat in or take away.

La Rhumerie, high street, St-Gilles-les-Bains. ☎ 24 55 99. Open-air seating area ideal for soaking up the local atmosphere and watching the world go by.

Chez nous (les supporters de l'OM), 122 rue du Général de Gaulle, St-Gilles-les-Bains ☎ 24 08 08. Classic bar run by a Marseillais who does wonders to soothe many a homesick Frenchman.

Jungle Village, rue Général de Gaulle, St-Gilles-les-Bains, ☎ 33 21 93. Located opposite Chez Nous, to the south of the village, this establishment is combines a beach bar feel with rock music. Always packed at weekends. If you get bored, take your drink to the bar, which is no less than a giant aquarium.

Nightclubs – *Le Moulin du Tango*, St-Gilles-les-Bains ☎ 24 53 90. Popular retro-evenings on Wednesday, Friday and Saturday nights.

Le Circus, l'Hermitage ☎ 33 84 84. Open from 10pm; closed Mondays, Wednesdays and Sundays. Entrance fee charged. Habitués essentially from the French mainland. Good for dancing by the sea.

Le Pussycat, 1 rue des Îles Éparses, St-Gilles-les-Bains ☎ 24 05 11. Friday and Saturday nights only. Mainly French.

Le Privé, 1 rue Général de Gaulle, on the left as you enter St-Gilles-les-Bains, ☎ 24 04 17/24 49 16. Somewhat less "teenagerish" than most of the town's other nightclubs. Caters more for the 25-30 age bracket.

Sports and pastimes

Beaches – *Relax Beach location* ☎ 33 90 66. Supervised beach where you can hire mattresses, parasols, beach towels and lockers (10FF per hour; 60FF per day). The beach is raked clean every morning and prices include a free drink. Additional facilities provided for children.

Scuba diving – *Gloria Maris*, opposite open water mooring area, St-Gilles-les-Bains ☎ 24 34 11. Reputable diving club. Initial lesson 150FF.

CEREPS, St-Gilles-les-Bains harbour ☎ 24 40 12. Respected club for the more experienced divers.
Bleu Marine Réunion, opposite open water mooring area, St-Gilles-les-Bains ☎ 24 22 00.
Manta Plongée, plages des Brisants, opposite the Roches Noires beach, St-Gilles-les-Bains ☎ 24 37 10.
Korrigan Ar Mor, routes des Colimaçons, St-Leu activity centre ☎ 34 77 47. Initial lesson 160FF. Attractive diving site, quite different from the one at St-Gilles. Good vibes.

Deep-sea fishing – Allow at least 350-450FF for half -day's fishing (two-four people).
Centre de Pêche Europa, St-Gilles-les-Bains harbour ☎ 24 45 96.
Marlin Club de la Réunion, La Possession. Reservations ☎ 24 56 78.
Centre de Pêche alpha, St-Gilles-les-Bains harbour ☎ 24 02 02.

Other water sports – ***Ski-Club de St-Paul***, Étang-de-St-Paul ☎ 85 14 96. Approx 85F per circuit.
Club nautique de Bourbon, rue des Brisants, St-Gilles-les-Bains ☎ 24 30 75. Dinghy-sailing instruction for children and adults.

Helicopter flights – See the island from the air and enjoy a gastronomic meal on Mafate. ***Hélilagon***, l'Éperon helipad, St-Paul ☎ 55 55 55.
Héliréunion, St-Gilles heliport ☎ 24 00 00. Around US$200 per person for 45min flight.

Microlight flights – ***Félix ULM RUN***, base ULM du Port ☎ 43 02 59. Catch a bird's-eye view of the island scenery from above by going up with a member of the dynamic flying team. Given the choice, opt for the "pendulaire" over the "trois-axes". Guaranteed thrill. Broad range of circuits. Budget 150FF (initial flight) to 1 200FF (flight inland over the volcano).

Paragliding and hang-gliding – ***Parapente Réunion***, 4CD 12 Montée des Colimaçons ☎ 24 87 84. You can trust this professional organisation to show you how to master the warm updrafts in complete safety and try out various free-flights over different parts of the island (introductory session and courses). Friendly outfit.
Azurtech, Ravine de la Souris Chaude, La Saline ☎ 85 04 00. Maiden flights and courses in paragliding and motorised hang-gliders. Fred can also take you flying out over the lagoon in search of dolphins, while hanging off his delta-plane.

Hiking – ***Magma Rando***, see p 81.

Horse-riding – ***Centre Équestre du Maïdo***, route du Maïdo, St-Paul ☎ 32 49 15.
Crinière Réunion, Chemin Lautret-Bernica, St-Gilles ☎ 55 54 29.

Golf – ***Golf-club du Bassin Bleu***, Villèle, St-Gilles-les-Hauts ☎ 55 53 58.
Golf-club de Bourbon, L'Étang-Salé-les-Hauts, Les Sables ☎ 26 33 39.

Cross-country biking – ***VTT Découverte***, place P-J Bénard, St-Gilles ☎ 24 55 56.

SHOPPING

Marché St-Paul see p 108.
Village artisanal de l'Éperon, St-Gilles-les-Hauts (D10). 8.30am-12noon /1.30pm-6pm. Pottery and other hand-made objects.

Crafts – ***Native***, place du Marché, St-Gilles-les-Bains, ☎ 24 33 00. A very attractive art deco store. Indonesian furniture and knick-knacks. Young, friendly efficient staff.

ART GALLERY

Art'Senik, Ravine des Sables, St-Leu ☎ 34 12 56. Open daily. Sculpture, theatre and music workshop. Permanent exhibition.

The Southeast★★

St-Pierre to St-Benoît

Approx 85km by the coast road (without excursions)
Allow 2 days
See map p 130-131

Not to be missed
A picnic on the beach at Grande Anse.
A visit to the spice garden at St-Philippe.
A drive along the side of Grand Brûlé.

And remember...
Make a reservation to visit the spice garden.

The exposed southeastern side of the island is often referred to as **"la côte au vent"** as it is subjected to extreme weather conditions, partly as a result of perturbations in the Indian Ocean. All year round, strong trade winds propel powerful currents and heavy showers accompanied by cooler temperatures from across the vast expanse of sea. In time, both the local population and the flora have learnt to adapt to the climate. By comparison to the more developed regions of Réunion, the southeastern part remains somewhat wild and unspoilt. The small Creole houses would be lost among the luxuriant and dense vegetation if they were not painted in strong vibrant colours. By resisting change, however, the people here are missing out on the economic benefits of tourism. Instead, the curious visitor will find great variety and generous contrasts among the species of plants, between lava flows and a coastline eroded by a constant assault from the foaming sea. The scenery in the hills of the hinterland is different again, for up there in the remoter villages, the people appear to be living in a forgotten era and the exuberant tropical flora has been allowed to flourish unchecked.

Turn off the road at the first exit after the bridge across the Rivière St-Étienne, following the D26 towards l'Entre-Deux. At the roundabout, turn left and continue into the industrial estate.

■ **L'usine sucrière de Pierrefonds** – *Allow 10min. No charge.* Visitors are free to wander around the precincts of the former sugar refinery (1830-1960) and see the steam-driven hydraulic water-powered machinery from the St-Étienne canal.

Go back to the D26 and turn left. At the first crossroads, follow signs for l'Entre-Deux.

■ **L'Entre-Deux★** – The road picks its way along the broad bed of the **St-Étienne River** through an area dotted with old sugar refinery chimneys. In the distance, a great stone cliff dominates the skyline, sculpted by the wind and rain. After crossing over a metal bridge, the road snakes its way round several tight bends before reaching the pretty village of l'Entre-Deux that was already well-established in the 18C. For a long time, the local economy depended completely on the cultivation of coffee. When a fungus began spreading through the plantations and destroying large numbers of bushes, land-owners switched to sugarcane. This, together with market gardening and tourism, comprises the region's present sources of revenue. A short walk through the streets will allow you to discover various **cases Créoles**, each one more endearing than the next.

Hiking up around le Dimitile*

Book a night in a gîte (see Where to stay) and then drive up in a 4WD vehicle (available through special agents). Le Dimitile is named after a slave who found refuge on this remote mountainside. Three splendid tracks lead up to it *(sign-posted in the village)*, each one gaining a ridge from where grandiose **views** may be had over the Plaine des Cafres and the coast.

From even further up, a great **panorama**** unfurls to include Cilaos and its Lilliputian scale *îlets* (remote villages).
The **Sentier de Bayonne** is the perhaps the most spectacular route, although it is also the most vertiginous and demanding *(20km, 9hr there and back, 1 500m rough ground. Very arduous).*
The alternatives – **Sentier du Zèbre** and the **Sentier de la Grande Jument** – both come out at the same viewpoint *(15.5km, 7.5hr there and back, 1 400m rough ground. Difficult).*

Back at l'Entre-Deux, take the N1 to St-Pierre. Turn right following signs for "St-Joseph, front de mer" and then turn down rue de la Poudrière before the first roundabout, down to the sea.

■ St-Pierre*

The colonists who settled in St-Pierre in the 18C allocated themselves land-holdings that were defined by the natural contours of the landscape: hence the origins of such demarcations as "Ligne-de-Bambous" and "Les Quatre Cents". The peaceful seaside town of St-Pierre (Pop 59 000) preserves a certain charm imparted by its run-down appearance and old-fashioned feel. The busy streets lined with buildings from a different age, the harbour and the beach are certainly worthy of a few hours' visit.

Slow beginnings

A wooden chapel dedicated to St Peter in honour of the then governor, **Pierre Benoît Dumas**, was built on the edge of the River d'Abord in 1731. A few years later, the French East India Company opened a series of shops nearby and the town began to grow. But development and expansion was severely affected by the lack of water until the **St-Étienne canal** was completed in or around 1826. Once that fundamental problem was resolved, work began on various new facilities. The first major project – the construction of a proper harbour – was launched in 1854; but 32 eventful years later, the initiative was declared a failure and St-Pierre narrowly escaped bankruptcy. Not only was the designated area found to be too small for any reasonably sized vessel to manoeuvre, the enclave was constantly silting up so that, before long, only fishing smacks and sailing boats could be accommodated. In a frantic effort to resolve the financial crisis, entrepreneurs poured their investments into sugar-refining and slowly the town's economy was revived. Since then, St-Pierre has been elevated to the status of the island's sub-prefecture and principal financial centre of the south, and continues to thrive.

Town

Continue past the open harbour area to the roundabout and take the second exit; 200m further on, turn left down the slip road.

A slight diversion to Ravine Blanche will take you to the eclectic **Narasinga Péroumal Kovil Tamil Temple** *(religious ceremonies almost every Saturday. Please respect the rules listed at the entrance. Allow 10min for a visit, much longer if a service is*

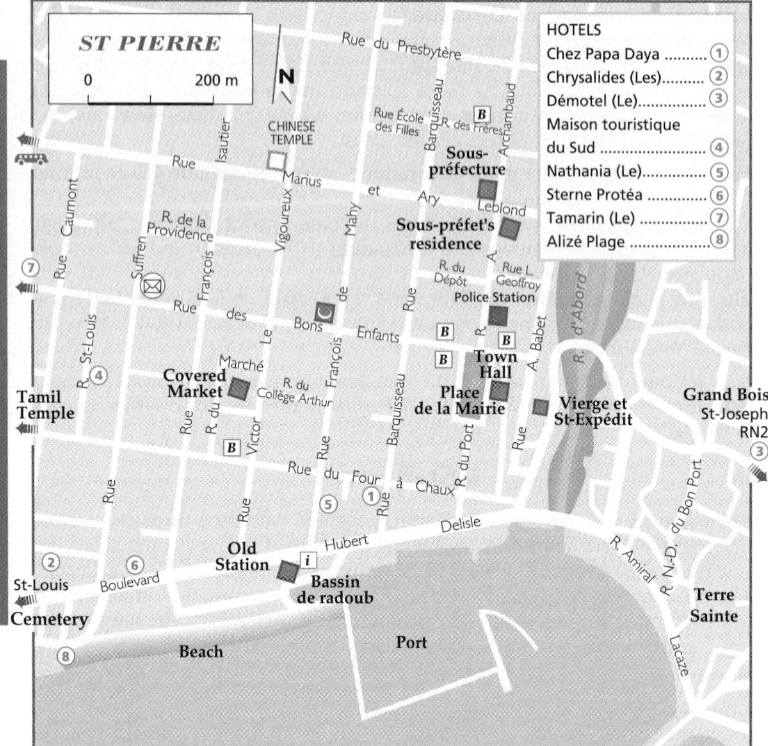

being held) painted in pale shades of various hues. The temple attracts visitors of all kinds throughout the day, although it assumes a most distinctive atmosphere when large gatherings are held. If you are lucky, you may be privileged to see the place bedecked in flowers and garlands for one of the major annual Tamil festivals *(see p 75 Religious festivals and p 48 Hindu festivals)*.

On the seafront, on the left-hand side, beyond the police station.

Cimetière – The cemetery *(daily, May to September, 7am-5pm; October to April, 6am-6pm. Allow 15min)*, which dates from 1729, is a happy place full of colour and flowers.

The principal point of interest set among the bright white gravestones is the vermilion-coloured **tomb of Sitarane**⋆. *Turn left about halfway along the main avenue, behind the main Monument to the Dead and make your way to the outer wall.* Here you are likely to find a variety of strange tokens bearing a scrawled prayer, a glass or two of rum and half-smoked cigarettes left as offerings.

To get a taste of how easy life in St-Pierre can be, you need go no further than the **sea front**⋆ where the good people of the town come together for a stroll along the **harbour** wall or to sunbathe on the **beach**. Others will congregate with friends and families around one of the many mobile snack bars, to share a drink and a gossip or play cards under the Indian almond trees. The **ancienne gare**, a former

Sitarane

In the early part of the 20C, an elusive band of thieves carried out a series of burglaries across the south of the island, inciting both fear and suspicion among the local population. Each crime precipitated a wave of new mystery that was quickly attributed to witchcraft, justifying why no dog barked or why the victim did not wake up. For years, the outlaws limited themselves to stealing, then a murder was committed, and terror ensued. At last, in 1909, ten or so men were arrested and the ring-leaders were condemned to death although Calendrin, nicknamed St Ange despite his reputation as a sorcerer and conjurer, was spared for not having actually killed anybody. Instead, Sitarane, a proud and strongly-built Mozambican, was implicated by his naïvety and publicly executed in 1911.

station on Hubert Delisle Street, provides an alternative meeting place since it was restored and transformed into a restaurant. The surfers, meanwhile, walk the length of the harbour pontoons to catch a wave coming in from the open sea. It is also worth venturing out to the **bassin de radoub** where the colourful fishing boats are moored.

Walk up the rue du Port to the place de la Mairie.

A tour of the old town should begin with the shaded square overlooked by the town hall, or **Hôtel de Ville** *(no charge)*, which was built c 1740 by the French East India Company as a grain-depot. Upriver from the square runs the town's main shopping street – **Rue des Bons Enfants** – where the southern islanders come to shop. A little further on the left *(200m)*, you will come to rue Victor Le Vigoureux, which leads to the fully renovated **covered market*** *(marché couvert, Monday to Saturday, 7.30am-6pm; Sunday, 7.30am-12noon)*, around which pervades an intoxicating smell of spices.

Continue up rue Victor Le Vigoureux to rue Marius et Ary Leblond and turn right.

The rue Marius et Ary Leblond *preserves* a number of superb Creole townhouses with white lace-like fretwork decoration, notably the **sous-prefecture*** (n° 18) and the **sous-préfet's residence** (n° 28).

At the bottom of the street, turn down rue A Babet which turns sharply round to the left before opening out onto the River d'Abord.

There you will be greeted by a strange sight: a place of prayer, graced with a white niche harbouring a statue of the **Virgin Mary** and another brightly-coloured – but predominantly red – figure representing **St Expédit**.

Continue over the river and across the junction to rue Amiral Lacaze opposite.

■ **Terre Sainte** – It is well worth driving through this lovely village, whose name translates as the Holy Land, in the morning when the fishermen are unloading their catch. You might also like to laze idly on the beach in the shade of the large banyan trees with a picnic or watch the locals engage in a lively game of cards or dominoes.

Head for St-Joseph along the N2.

■ **Grand Bois** – The topological name "big wood" refers to the dense forest that covered this region less than a century ago, but which was ruthlessly cut down to make way for sugarcane plantations. The **sugar refinery** and **planter's house** *(maison de maître)*, although closed to the public, provide some indication of the island's architectural and historic heritage. The **chimney** stands on the far side of the road, while the industrial **scales** in the back yard continue to be used for weighing out the sugarcane.

Continue along the N2.

The wild South★★

Approx 80km from Petite Île to St-Benoît. Allow a whole day.

As the N2 reaches the top of the hill, turn right down the D30. Some 300m further on, take the road on the right for Grande Anse.

■ **Grande Anse** – The landscape is dominated by the great green land mass known as the **Piton de Grande Anse**★, which plunges down into metallic blue sea. The bay is skirted by a superb **beach**★★ of fine white sand and shaded by rows of coconut palms. This is France's southernmost beach, and amongst its most beautiful, remote and wild. Bathing, however, is prohibited here as the currents are treacherous and sharks are known to roam in the coastal waters. Be warned: a number of people have drowned off this beach over the years as the crosses at the end of the beach will testify. Stick to swimming in the sheltered waters on the left of the beach.
If you see a crowd of people milling in the parking area, it is likely that formal marriage photographs are being posed for by the old **lime kiln**. From the top of the headland, high above the cliffs *(40min there and back on foot)*, you can watch the sea birds – notably the lovely white-tailed tropic bird – gliding over the water.

Come back onto the RN2 and continue left. About 1.5km after the ravine, turn right twice following directions for Manapany. Walk the last 500m from the parking area.

■ **Manapany les Bains**★ – Enjoy a swim among the rocks of this lovely and peaceful bay before continuing on to the **old docks**★ *(level with the parking area)*, where sugar, refined in the local Manapany factory, was loaded onto special boats and ferried across the perilous reef to the larger trade-ships anchored offshore. If you venture down to the pandanus trees, keep an eye out for the rare and protected **Manapany green lizard**.

Go back to the N2 and turn right to St-Joseph.

■ **St-Joseph** – The slow and arduous colonisation of this southern region, begun in 1785, progressed largely as a

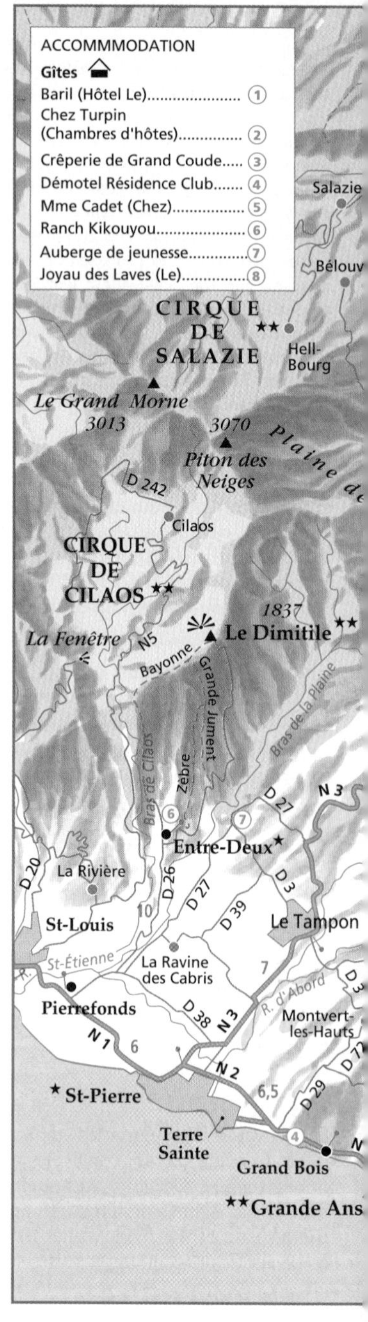

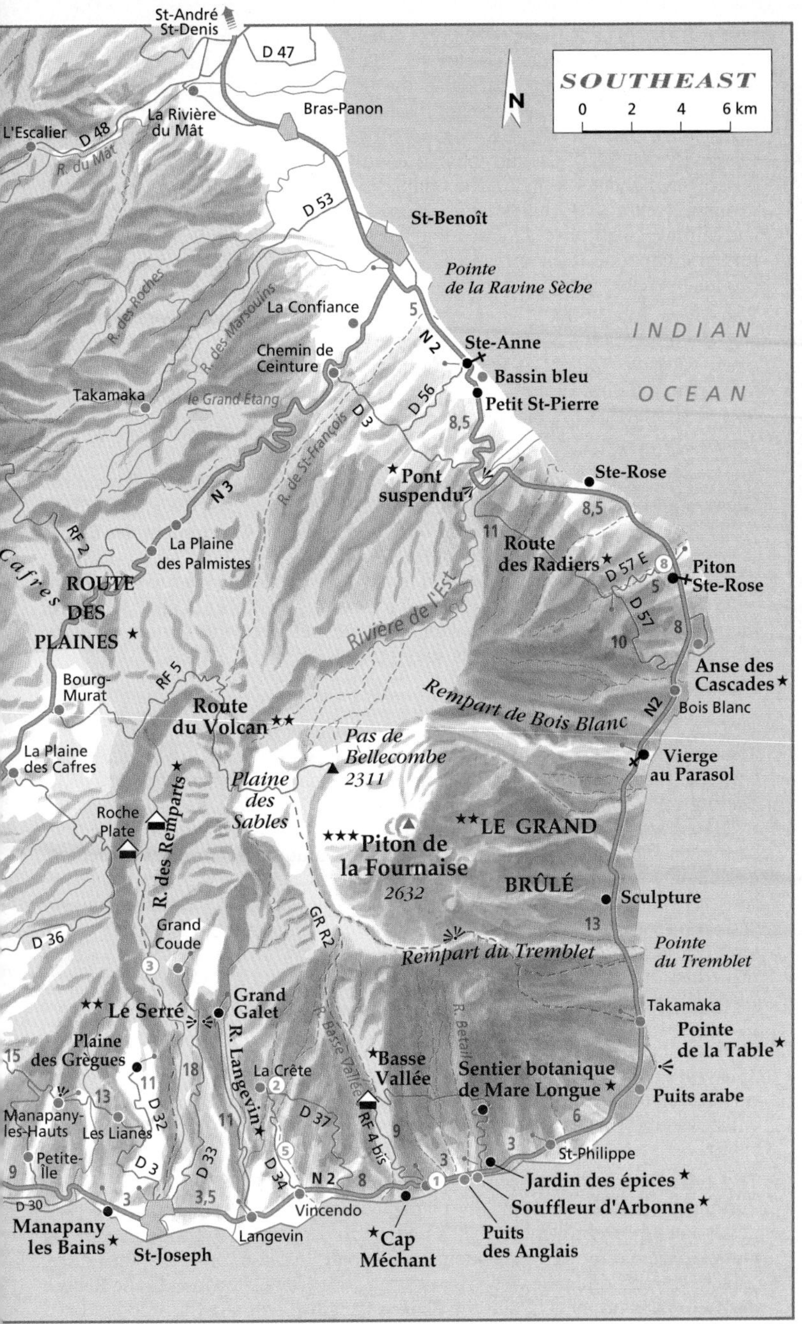
SOUTHEAST
0 2 4 6 km
N
St-André
St-Denis
D 47
Bras-Panon
L'Escalier
D 48
La Rivière du Mât
R. du Mât
D 53
St-Benoît
Pointe de la Ravine Sèche
La Confiance
R. des Roches
R. des Marsouins
Chemin de Ceinture
N 2
Ste-Anne
Bassin bleu
Petit St-Pierre
INDIAN
OCEAN
Takamaka
le Grand Étang
D 56
D 3
R. de St-François
Pont suspendu
Ste-Rose
N 3
La Plaine des Palmistes
RF 2
Cafres
ROUTE DES PLAINES
Route des Radiers
D 57 E
Piton Ste-Rose
D 57
Rivière de l'Est
Anse des Cascades
Bois Blanc
Bourg-Murat
RF 5
Rempart de Bois Blanc
Route du Volcan
Pas de Bellecombe 2311
La Plaine des Cafres
Vierge au Parasol
Plaine des Sables
R. des Remparts
Roche Plate
LE GRAND BRÛLÉ
Piton de la Fournaise 2632
Sculpture
GR R2
Grand Coude
D 36
Rempart du Tremblet
Pointe du Tremblet
Le Serré
Grand Galet
R. Langevin
R. Basse Vallée
R. Bétail
Takamaka
Pointe de la Table
Plaine des Grègues
Basse Vallée
La Crête
Sentier botanique de Mare Longue
Puits arabe
D 32
D 37
RF 4 bis
Manapany-les-Hauts
Les Lianes
D 33
Petite-Île
D 3
D 34
N 2
St-Philippe
Jardin des épices
D 30
Vincendo
Souffleur d'Arbonne
Manapany les Bains
St-Joseph
Langevin
Cap Méchant
Puits des Anglais

result of the botanist **Joseph Hubert**, a self-taught and ardent amateur of "all things living and natural". Hubert set about cultivating spices, concentrating especially on cloves and nutmeg, in the hope of encouraging, by example, a group of lower-middle class Whites to settle there and bring some kind of prosperity to the place. In the 19C, sugarcane became the mainstay of the area, with *vetiver* (lemon-grass), tea and tobacco contributing their share to the economy of the town and its vicinity. The emphasis attached by Hubert to agricultural diversity continues to influence the crops grown there today: although cloves and nutmeg may have all but disappeared, a little *vetiver* (lemon-grass) and turmeric continue to be grown in the Upland reaches and the market-garden produce is renowned for its quality.

The town (Pop 25 000), which has grown up around a single axis, has few, if any, distinguishing features. A little street (100m after the church on the right when walking towards St-Philippe) leads to the tomb of **Raphaël Babet** (a former mayor of St-Joseph) and **Piton Saladin**, from the top of which a fabulous view stretches out across the sea.

Head north out of town on the D3, and then turn right along the D32.

The road picks its winding way through the fine scenery between Ravine des Grègues and Rivière du Rampart to the village of **Plaine des Grègues** *(estimate 90min there and back)*. There you will find the **Maison du Curcuma et des Épices** *(14 chemin du Rond, Plaine des Grègues. Daily, 9am-12noon/2pm-5pm. No charge)* which provides detailed information on and about what the locals refer to as "saffran" – but which in fact is turmeric *(curcuma)* – as well as a number of other flavourful ingredients added to Creole cooking. Facilities also provide visitors with the opportunity of tasting the various spices that are available for sale.

Continue to Tampon along the D3.

Route Hubert Delisle

The road from St-Joseph to Tampon *(approx 28km; 1hr one way)* twists and turns between the disparate villages scattered through the changing countryside, offering open views over the coast.

At **Manapany-les-Hauts**, there is a **vetiver distillery**, which processes the delicate green-leafed crop grown in the fields surrounding **Montvert-les-Hauts** and **Les Lianes**. Lemon-grass oil has been distilled from the root of the plant *cymbopogon citratus* (formerly known as *andropogon schoenanthus*) for use in perfumery and soap since the 18C. Today, the 72-hour extraction process is the same. The long dry leaves, once used to thatch roofs, are now woven by the women to make hats and baskets.

Go back to St-Joseph and head for Grand Coude along the D33.

Rivière des Remparts*

Allow 1hr round trip by car. This excursion takes you down the broad river, which runs down its deeply cut valley eroded over time – and which, in the 18C, provided fleeing slaves with a safe hideaway – to enjoy a succession of spectacular views.

The itinerary takes you between the houses and past their exuberant gardens. Further up, you come upon the plantations of sugarcane. Although the road deteriorates into a broken track, it is well worth persevering to the **Serré viewing platform****. From this exceptional viewpoint, located on the 60m ridge, stretches a most dramatic view over the two great rivers of St-Joseph: the **Rivière des Remparts** on the left, and the **Rivière Langevin** on the right, leading down to the village of Grand Galet. If you continue another dozen or so kilometres uphill, you reach a small plateau, that once was thickly wooded, on which sits the village of **Grand Coude**. Blessed with fertile soil and cool temperatures, the 500 local inhabitants are able to sustain a living from growing seasonal vegetables and keeping livestock.

Return to the N2 coastal road and after crossing the bridge over the Ravine Langevin, turn left along a minor road leading back up into the hills.

Rivière Langevin*

Approx 45min by car there and back. Avoid weekends. The road, lined with avocado and lychee trees shadows the route taken by the river. **Pools** of cool water along the way seem laid on for a refreshing dip. At last, you will come to **Grand Galet**, a serene-seeming village made up of weatherboarded houses and a chapel, where all sounds are drowned out by the roar of the great **waterfall**. From here, one can hike up to the **Plaine des Sables** *(see p 160)*.

Grand Brûlé region**

Approx 32km – allow 2hr.

On 20 March 1986, **Piton de la Fournaise** erupted: great rivers of red-hot lava flowed down from the crater of Piton de Takamaka, 1 000m above sea-level. A few hours later, the first lava flow halted some 600m from the coast, while a second tumbled down into the sea, causing the ocean to bubble furiously and the sky to be filled with large clouds of steam. Three days later, a rare phenomena ensued, as additional cooling magma was forced from a narrow crack a few hundred metres from the coast. This new lava flow solidified in the sea to form "Pointe de la Table" *(see p 135)*. Thankfully, there were no casualties despite the moving lava obliterating some eight houses that happened to be in its path.

Inevitably, as a result of this memorable volcanic eruption, the landscape of the eastern coast was indelibly transformed. It remains, however, a wild place covered in thick forest or, where this has been burnt out, a barren land of exposed black rocks that occasionally glisten in the burning bright sunlight. The locals survive on exercising their traditional crafts using pandanus leaves, as well as from cultivating vanilla and sugarcane.

Turn right off the N2 immediately after crossing the bridge over the Ravine Basse Vallée; then turn right after the sports centre.

Cap Méchant*, a jagged headland of dark rock, is relentlessly pounded by the sea. Its remarkable texture however, is slowly being refashioned by the waves, which can be tempestuously strong in these parts, and refined as small chips of basalt are gradually flaked away to leave flashes of pink stone.

The **Puits des Français** – a well built by the French to supply the needs of the local population before the modern water distribution system was built – is to be found below and left of the parking area.

Return to and continue along the N2 for 150m and turn left for the gîte de Basse Vallée. Follow the RF4bis.

Basse Vallée*

The forestry track cuts through the **Forêt de St-Philippe***, the island's most extensive nature reserve, stretching from the coast to the top of the volcano and including most of the recent lava-flows, where various species of coloured wood have established themselves.

The hostel (gîte de Basse Vallée) provides the starting point for two major **hikes**: one track winds its way through the forest for 16km before continuing down to **Mare Longue** across the nature reserve *(see below)*; the other leads to the edge of the ravine de Basse Vallée before climbing up to the Plaine des Sables and the **Volcano** *(17.5km to the gîte du Volcan; 7hr one-way; 1 700m rise in altitude; very arduous)*.

Once back on the N2, turn right onto a minor road after Le Baril (signposted).

The **Puits des Anglais** – a well built in 1822 to ease the shortage of water in an area of high rainfall but with porous soil – is a fine piece of stonework. Needless to say, the place is steeped in mystery as legends tell of a treasure being hidden there.

When you get to the pandanus trees on the right of the RN2, a short distance beyond the well, stop the car and take a look at the **Souffleur d'Arbonne*** *(caution advised)* and the curiously twisted formations in the petrified lava. When the sea is rough, you can watch the water being forced into the empty space and the spray of foam being expelled up through the blowhole like a geyser.

At this point, you will see a forestry track leading off to the left: follow it for 3km to the carpark.

■ **Le Sentier Botanique de Mare Longue*** – Two way-marked footpaths have been carefully designed to take visitors into and around the Hauts de St-Philippe *(60min round trip for either one)*. An additional 13km of easy and enjoyable walking will bring you out onto the upper section of the Basse Vallée forestry track and the gîte *(see above)*. The most dramatic scenery is to be found in the heart of the prime forest area among the trees, many several hundred years old, that have colonised the successive lava flows. Ground cover is provides by luxuriant species of delicate fern and epiphytes. Happily, many of the varieties are tagged with labels bearing descriptive names like *Joli Cœur* (Happy Heart), *Bois de Pomme* (Apple Wood) *Bois de Prune* (Plum Wood) and *Bois de Corail* (Coral Wood).

The second circuit takes you to a more recently forested area where the undergrowth is less dense and so varieties of plant can be more easily approached and studied in detail.

Approximately 600m after the Souffleur d'Arbonne, a forest track forks left off the N2.

■ **Jardin des épices et des parfums*** – *Tuesday to Sunday for guided tours at 10.30am and 2.30pm, subject to reservations made through the St-Philippe Tourist Office ☎ 37 10 43; closed Mondays). Allow 2hr. Entrance fee. Take insect repellent. Set meal available if booked in advance.*

A stop at the Spice Garden in the middle of the primary forest is sure to beguile all the senses and acquaint enthusiasts with various different species, including some of Réunion's endemic flora. The local guide is happy to share his passion and knowledge of the forest, its strange fruits, voracious creepers and delicate orchids, by letting you taste and smell the more common varieties of spice tree.

Return to the N2 and continue for 5km before turning right along the RF3.

March 1986 lava flows*

Along the footpath that leads down to the sea, wild **vanilla** *(illustration p 29)* grows up and around the pandanus and casuarina trees. A little further down on the left, you will come across the **Puits Arabe** – so called because the well dug from the lava resembles those found in the Middle East and baffled historians for so long. A track *(4km)* leaves the parking area to cut through a section wooded with pandanus trees, before coming out at **Pointe de la Table***. It is almost incredible to think that this vast (30ha) basalt lava plateau surrounded by sea was formed as a result of a single volcanic eruption, over a period of six days.

A few hundred metres further along, the N2 passes two other places where separate lava flows have scarred the landscape. Like two gushing torrents petrified in time, these two stone rivers seem to pour themselves through the forest and across the coastal road, cutting it in two places 2km apart. Gently, the invasive black basalt mass is being tempered by nature and the growing colonies of silvery grey lichens.

From the spot known as **Takamaka**, there is a footpath up to the **Abri du Tremblet** *(15km there and back; 7hr; 1 100m rise in altitude; arduous)* and the **Gîte du Volcan** *(see p 165)* further on. This follows the lava flow up to the **crater**. Rather than continuing back along the way you came, it is possible to complete the circuit by going down to the sea and coming out at **Pointe du Tremblet**, joining up with the GR R2 and walking through a stretch of forest populated with trees of coloured woods.

Continue north along the N2.

A little further on, the lava flow of 1998 has left its trace, avoiding the road by just a few metres. It's possible to walk up the lava flow, in order to get an impressive view of this block of lava.

Grand Brûlé**

The eastern flank of the volcano is defined in the south by Rempart du Tremblet, and in the north by Rempart de Bois Blanc. Over time, this area has been subjected to a number of eruptions and lava flows that on occasion have run down to the sea.

La Vierge au Parasol

E. Valentin/HOA QUI

From **Rempart du Tremblet**, an extensive **panorama***** opens out over the Grandes Pentes, a somewhat desolate yet beautiful forest landscape that has been abruptly arrested by the outpourings of sparkling black basalt.

Some 3km beyond the entrance to Grand Brûlé, turn left off the N2 along a rough track. Park the car in the designated area and continue 300m on foot.

A platform on the edge of the lava flow – installed for a scientific survey into geothermal activity – provides a podium for a sculpture by the artist Mayo entitled "**Symbiosis for Volcano and Birds**". Be advised that this composite basalt arrangement does not incite a profound emotional reaction in everyone. A very different attraction is to be found in the far northern reaches of Grand Brûlé, and that is the **Vierge au Parasol**. Each year, for the Feast of the Assumption (**15 August**), thousands of pilgrims flock to this figure of the Virgin with a parasol and deposit at her feet an offering in the form of flowers or an ex-voto. The origins of such veneration date back to the early 20C when a river of lava flowed down through the immediate area without even touching her. Thenceforth, she was entreated as the guardian of the region against the wrath of the volcano. In reality, the figure that stands there now, symbolically protected from the sun and rain, is a substitute for the original that was swept away following the eruption in 1961.

Return to the N2 and continue to Bois Blanc. Then after a further 3km, turn right up Chemin des Cascades.

■ **L'Anse des Cascades*** – At the top of this road there is an fabulous grove of *palmiste* palms *(Deckenia nobilis)* complete with its own restaurant where visitors can taste the famous palm-heart, served in a "Millionaire's Salad" or baked in the oven. Normally, this is a haven of peace and quiet, although after heavy rain, the place thunders with the roar of the **waterfalls**. Nonetheless, as temperatures always remain cool and fresh, this a pleasant place to come and enjoy the sight of the coloured fishing boats drawn up the **landing stage**.

Go back to the N2: either head back towards Bois Blanc and turn right up the D57, or continue to Piton St-Rose and turn up the D57E.

Route des Radiers*

This excursion to the Uplands *(16km, 45min)* takes you across a number of concrete fords, but offers a number of wonderful opportunities to survey the sea and the mountains. The most dramatic sight is provided by the **1977 lava flow**, as here you can clearly see how the molten magma has twisted its way downhill to the church at Piton Ste-Rose and beyond to the sea.

Drive on to Piton Ste-Rose along the N2 or the D57E.

■ **Piton Ste-Rose** – The small coastal settlement was subjected to the most terrifying event in its history in April 1977 when, over a period of four days, two red-hot rivers of molten magma coursed through the village and ran into the sea raising a deafening noise on impact. Fortunately, there were no casualties, although a number of houses were obliterated. However, at one point, the lava completely surrounded the church – which thereafter became known as **Notre-Dame des Laves***. None of it managed to reach the interior, probably because as the molten mass seeped slowly forwards it cooled and solidified, blocking the narrow entrance. The sight of this glassy black petrified magma is quite intriguing.

R. Mazin/DIAF

The tricky crossing of a ford in spate

Walk round the church towards the sea; at the crossroads turn right and continue to the bridge.

A path picks its way along the lava flow between the rough basalt outcrops. Walk down to **Pointe Lacrois*** and its small glistening bronze-black sand **beach**. If you let the sand run through your fingers, you will notice how it is made up of the same olive-green **olivine** crystals found encrusted in the basalt boulders.

Head onwards to St-Rose by means of the N2 and turn right by the church.

▪ **Ste-Rose –** In 1809, at the height of the Franco-British war being waged in the Indian Ocean, part of the British fleet attacked the village before taking shelter in a secluded creek and coming ashore at **la Marine***. There, they remained encamped for a month until, at last, they were expelled. All that remains of their stay is a **monument to a Captain Corbett**, who was apparently killed at sea in 1810 and whose body was later repatriated by his shipmates. From there, a pleasant walk along a footpath can lead you along the seashore, where you are bound to meet a few local fishermen.

Ste-Rose to St-Benoît

18km – Approx 1hr

Head north along the N2.

The **Rivière de l'Est** has always been prone to breaking its banks after torrential storms, and, over the years, several bridges has been swept away by cataclysmic flooding. The present **suspension bridge***, with its great stone arches on either side of the watercourse, has a headroom of 50m and must surely rank among the finest man-made monuments to grace the island. For those with the stamina, it is possible to bungee-jump off the bridge (*see p 143*).

On the other side, the road crosses the delightful little village of **Petit St-Pierre**, with its colourful array of houses and gardens.

Turn up the first street on the right, and then down the Vieux Chemin on the left. The road crosses the mouth of the Petit St-Pierre Ravine passing the **Bassin Bleu**, where you can stop for a deliciously refreshing swim before continuing along the coast road. Further on, to your right, a flight of steps leads to an altar devoted to the Virgin Mary, set into a cliff face. Called the Lourdes Cave (no less!), it is a meeting point for many pilgrims and continues to be popular amongst the locals.

▪ **Ste-Anne** – The village is only really renowned for its curious **church***, which was largely the work of **Père Dobemberger**, because it was featured in a film directed by François Truffaut entitled *La Sirène du Mississippi*. Father Dobemberger, the son of an architect of Alsatian extraction, set about remodelling the church (1926-50) with the help of his pupils studying for their catechisms, by encrusting the chapel and church front with all kinds of ornamentation – predominantly fruit and flowers – moulded in cement.

As the N2 approaches St-Benoît, it becomes very narrow in places.

The road cuts through a series of immense sugarcane plantations rustled by the wind or along stretches of coastline skirted with pebble beaches. Beyond the main roundabout, the N3 continues inland to return to St-Pierre *(see p 152)*.

Making the most of the Southeast

Getting there

By bus – A regular service connects all the main towns and villages along the coast. In most cases, the bus stations are located near the town centre: at St-Pierre in rue Luc Lorian; in St-Joseph at 2 avenue du Général de Gaulle. A few buses and shared taxis provide access to the hinterland.

By car – With an independent means of transport, you can stop where and when you like to admire the view or explore the remotest backwaters. Do be wary of driving during heavy storms: the roads are prone to flash flooding and can be treacherously slippery. If caught unexpectedly, it is worth stopping on the side of the road and waiting for the shower to pass.

Address book

Tourist Information – ***Office du Tourisme de St-Pierre***, 17 boulevard Delisle ☎ 25 02 36, Fax 25 82 76. Monday-Friday, 8.30am-5.15pm (summer)/ 9am-5.45pm (winter), Saturdays, 9am-3.45pm.
Syndicat d'initiative de l'Entre-Deux, Dimitile Accueil, rue Fortuné Hoareau ☎ 69 69 80, Fax 39 69 83.
Pays d'accueil du Sud sauvage, 69 rue Babet, St-Joseph ☎ 56 00 29. Information on white-water rafting.
Office du tourisme de St-Phillipe, 64 rue Leconte Delisle ☎ 37 10 43, Fax 37 10 97. Monday-Saturday, 9am-5pm ; Sundays, 9am-2.30pm. Bookings for tours of the Spice Garden.
Office du tourisme de Ste-Rose, ☎ 50 21 29. Information on long-distance footpaths and cross-country routes.

Banks – There are branches of various banks at St-Pierre. There are very few ATM / cashpoints between St-Pierre and St-Benoît: ensure you have sufficient cash.

Post Offices – Main post office at St-Pierre, 108 rue des Bons Enfants. At St-Joseph, St-Phillipe and St-Rose, the post office is situated in the high street.

Telephone – There are a few public phone boxes at St-Pierre, especially along the seafront, but almost none elsewhere until you get to St-Benoît.

Car rental – Agents are located at St-Pierre.

Medical emergencies – Most towns have one or more pharmacies, doctors and dentists.

Centre hospitalier général de St-Pierre Le Tampon, RN2, Terre Sainte ☎ 35 90 00.

WHERE TO STAY

Prices given here are based on the cost of a double room with breakfast for two.

• L'Entre-Deux

Under US$15

Auberge de Jeunesse (Youth Hostel), Chemin Defaud, Ravine des Citrons (a bus leaving l'Entre-Deux stops in front of the hostel), ☎ 39 69 60, Fax 39 59 20 – 29 rm Quite a distance from l'Entre-Deux, the hostel's comfort is pretty basic, but the rooms are impeccable, the welcome friendly and the prices unbeatable. Ideal for groups and large families on small budgets.

US$25-30

Ranch Kikouyou, Centre de tourisme equestre, 4 rue Cinaire, Grand Fond ☎ 39 60 62 – 12 beds. ✕ Dinner, bed and breakfast establishment, run alongside a stable, with plenty of character: four-poster beds or rosewood sleigh-beds with private bathroom. Alternatively, you can opt for the self-catering/dormitory facility. Eat breakfast on the open sun-drenched terrace and watch the horses being taken out for exercise. Set dinner comprises freshly cooked dishes using locally grown fare. Endearing in its charm.

• St-Pierre

US$25-30

Chez Papa Daya, 27 rue du Four à Chaux ☎ 25 64 87/25 11 34, Fax 25 64 87 (evenings) – 16rm Private/shared shower-room and toilet depending on room. Picturesque establishment, brightly painted and cluttered with figurative ornaments and colourful Indian paintings. All rooms are clean and spacious. Communal kitchen facilities and pleasant open seating-area. Near to the beach. Reasonably priced.

Maison touristique du Sud, 24 rue St-Louis ☎ 25 35 81 – 8rm Family-run boarding-house in a terraced-roofed villa built in the 1970s. The simply furnished and peaceful bedrooms overlook a quiet street, 600m from the beach. Other facilities include two small well-equipped kitchens and a welcoming TV/sitting area.

Hôtel le Tamarin, 64 rue du Père Favron, Ravine Blanche, ☎ 25 30 60, Fax 25 06 82 – 13 rm TV CC Small unpretentious establishment in a residential neighbourhood, 200m from the seashore. Clean, rather nondescript rooms.

US$45-60

Les Chrysalides, 6 rue Caumont ☎ 25 75 64, Fax 25 22 19 – 16rm TV CC The main reason for choosing this white-washed, modern and modest hotel is its proximity to the sea. Some of the rooms at the front have a view of the cemetery in the distance and the sea on the left. What a pity that the sitting-cum-breakfast area is squeezed into a long narrow chamber between the reception and the front hall.

Alizé Plage, St-Pierre beach, ☎ 35 22 21, Fax 25 80 63 – 6 rm TV ✕ CC Set right on the beach of St-Pierre, this hotel provides excellent value for money. The recently built rooms are comfortable and almost all have a terrace. The ones overlooking the sea are the most pleasant. Very decent restaurant.

US$70-85

Le Nathania, 12 rue François de Mahy ☎ 25 04 57, Fax 35 27 05 – 9rm TV ✕ CC Right in the centre of town. The front entrance is marked by a pretty gate and a row of trees under which are arranged various tables. It is a shame that the welcome is so cool and that the sitting room, shoe-horned between the entrance and the bar, lacks in atmosphere. The bedrooms, furnished with wooden furniture, are quiet, spacious and comfortable. Evening meals are served outside when the air is cool and the lanterns burn bright. Very peaceful.

Démotel Résidence Club, 8 allée des Lataniers, Grands Bois (5km from St-Pierre along N2 towards St-Joseph) ☎ 31 11 60, Fax 31 17 51 – 30rm Highly accessible, yet set back from the N2. Warm and friendly reception on arrival. Two separate sets of bungalows, each comprising several bedrooms, are arranged in a mature garden on opposite sides of the well-sheltered swimming pool in the middle of which grows a traveller's palm. Each room is equipped with a small kitchen. One corner is given over to a barbecue area with a wondrous view of the sea. This lovely place set in a rugged part of the coast may give you the impression of living on the very edge of the world.

Over US$90

Le Sterne Protea Hotel, bd Hubert de Lisle, ☎ 25 70 00, Fax 35 01 41, sterne@guetali.fr – 50 rm Set on the shorefront, the Sterne Hotel is St-Pierre's grandest hotel. Modern, well-equipped rooms and a pleasant first floor swimming pool. 10min from the 18-hole Bourbon Golf Club. Reasonably priced, stylish with courteous service.

• St-Joseph

Under US$15

Le Malmany, Le Dimitile, Roche Plate, ☎ 56 40 59 – 3 rm The Malmany's mountain lodge style rooms and dormitories are clean, and the owner's warm welcome more than makes up for the somewhat basic comfort. Don't miss the visit to the trout farm. What's more, the trout served in the restaurant are the best to be had on the island.

US$25-30

Gîte de Roche Plate (Madame Bègue), Rivière des Remparts, accessible by four-wheel drive vehicle or on foot (see p 165 or 132) ☎ 59 13 94 (or book through the Maison de la Montagne) – 31 beds (rooms or dormitories). Warm and genuine welcome extended from both charming Creole bungalows built in wood. Extraordinary situation. Compulsory overnight stop on the Nez-de-Bœuf to St-Joseph cross-country hike. Excellent meals with specialities based on guava.

Crêperie de Grand Coude, Grand Coude ☎ 56 25 90 – 1rm Heating (50FF supplement). Bungalow sleeping two or three people, surrounded by lovely garden. Particularly pleasant and agreeable atmosphere.

Chambres et table d'hôtes Chez Turpin, La Crête (follow the D34 from Vincendo for 8km) ☎ 37 40 62/ 37 40 39 (reservation recommended) – 5rm Pleasant house surrounded by lush greenery. Spacious and spotlessly clean rooms. Perfect Upland haven for fresh-air fanatics keen on their food. Excellent banana combinations concocted by Mme Turpin: in fruit punches, baked, or curried (cari baba figue made with banana flowers). Engaging reception. Reasonably priced.

Auberge des Salaganes, chez Mme Cadet, Bel Air (9km inland from St-Joseph) ☎ 37 50 78 – 4rm Right in the heart of olde worlde Réunion, the charm and originality of this gîte surrounded by straw cases, built in the 19C style, delights all visitors. All the prettily arranged, cosy rooms are named after local spices: curcuma, vetiver, vanilla, geranium, etc. Mrs Cadet's welcome is irresistible.

• St-Phillipe

US$15-30

Gîte de Basse-Vallée ☎ 37 00 75 (reservation through the St-Philippe Tourist Office ☎ 37 10 43, Fax 37 10 97) – 28 beds in dormitories Fine mountain hostel, recently modernised and convivial atmosphere, set in the wonderful wild forests region in the Uplands of St-Phillipe.

US$30-45

Hôtel Le Baril, RN2 (approx 5km west of St-Phillipe) ☎ 37 01 04, Fax 37 07 62 – 13rm . Cross-country bikes available. The hotel can become extremely damp when the sea is rough. Depending on the weather, it is worth asking for a room with a private balcony overlooking the sea or a small bungalow in the garden, set amongst the vegetation and less susceptible to the ocean mists. Variable reception.

• **Piton Ste-Rose**

US$30-60

Le Joyau des Laves, Piton Cascade, ☎ 47 34 00, Fax 47 29 63 – 3 rm CC This recently opened roadside establishment has rooms at a wide range of prices, from the most basic to practically luxurious. Friendly hosts who love to treat their guests to local farm produce. Possibility of visiting the farm.

WHERE TO EAT

• **St-Pierre**

US$7-15

Restaurant Thai, 54 rue Caumont ☎ 35 30 95. Lunch and dinner; closed all day Monday. Good Thai staple dishes reasonably priced. The owner extends an especially affable welcome to all customers.

Chez Gros Louis, 4 rue François Isautier, ☎ 25 66 77. Lunch and dinner. Good Creole family-cooking at reasonable prices, right in the heart of the city, in a somewhat characterless room. Traditional well-cooked dishes (chicken cari, massalé cabri, etc.).

L'Utopia, 6-8 rue Marius et Ary leblond ☎ 35 15 83. Lunch and dinner; closed all day Sunday. Large restored Creole townhouse. À la carte menu lists a choice of cheap simple dishes, more elaborate and sophisticated gastronomic delicacies (chicken thighs stuffed with crayfish) as well as a range of more expensive specialities from southwestern France (as the owner is from Bordeaux).

Le Flamboyant, corner of rue Désiré Barquisseau and rue Four à Chaux, ☎ 35 02 15. Lunch and dinner. CC Choice of decent Creole and French cooking, served in a relatively ordinary Creole style house. It's possible to eat on the terrace, but during the day it's better not to because the street's very noisy.

L'Aquarhum, 18 petit boulevard du front de mer, ☎ 35 25 02 Lunch and dinner; closed Sunday lunchtime. Original small Creole townhouse with original fixtures. Warm reception. Salads and chef's special changes daily: tasty and generous portions at a reasonable price. Gastronomic evenings on a particular theme. Bar and live music attract a younger set from the local population.

US$15-30

Le Bistroquet, 87 boulevard Hubert Delisle ☎ 25 04 67. Lunch and dinner; closed Wednesdays. This fine Creole yellow and orange townhouse enjoys a prime site facing the sea. The house specialities are both delicious and unusual - like ostrich steak Bourbon-style, duck breast flavoured with vanilla and aged rum, or a filet of beef with onion and ginger chutney.

Alizé Plage, boulevard Huberst-Delisle ☎ 35 22 21. Lunch and dinner. A second option on the seafront, this time overlooking the beach. Specialities include cari and fresh fish.

Le Soubise, 17 rue Caumont, ☎ 25 40 50. Lunch and dinner, closed Sunday evenings. CC This restaurant offers a "nouvelle cuisine Creole", inspired by the best of local and French traditions, creating a combination of original flavours and exotic dishes (toasted chouchou with curcuma, pepper entrecote steak). Polite service.

• **St-Joseph**

Under US$2

Les Vrais Samoussas, 69 rue Raphaël Babet, ☎ 56 33 48. Open all day long. A little snack bar reputed to make the best samoussas on the island. Go and see what you think. The boss, a jovial appealing "Z'arabe chiite", takes great pleasure explaining all the medicinal virtues of each spice while you bite into his samoussas.

Under US$15

Snack Chez Joe, boulevard de l'Océan, Manapany-les-Bains, ☎ 31 48 83. Small snack bar serving good quality food at reasonable prices. The octopus chop-suey (35FF) is especially recommended!

L'Hirondelle, rue Raphael Babet ☎ 56 17 88. Lunch and dinner; closed Mondays. The establishment itself is rather cold, although the delicious caris more than make up for the decor. Those not keen on overly spicy food are advised to request "sans piment".

US$15-30

Chez Mme Grondin, 24 chemin de la Croisure, Grand Coude, ☎ 56 39 48. Lunch and dinner (reservations). A distinguished table d'hôte with impeccable service and excellent cuisine, prepared only with local farm produce. The Ti'-Jacques andouillette cari and the guava coulis with fresh cream are more than worth the trip. The menu, which includes six dishes and wine, is excellent value for money.

La Case, 31 rue Leconte de Lisle, ☎ 59 41 66. Lunch and dinner, closed Sundays and Monday evenings. CC A flight of steps leads up to this superb, fully renovated Creole case, beautifully enhanced by lighting in the evenings. Inside the wood panelling adds an inimitable touch of distinction. The cuisine is in keeping with the setting: traditional (excellent chicken cari) and distinctive (fillet of piveteau with combava). It will delight all amateurs of fine food. One of the island's best restaurants.

• St-Philippe

Around US$15

Table d'hôte Chez Guimard, 4 route Forestière, Mare Longue (between Le Baril and St-Philippe) ☎ 37 07 58 (advance booking essential). Lunch and dinner; closed Sunday evenings and all day Monday. An excellent place to eat after visiting the Spice Garden next door. Wonderful country cooking, generous portions and good wine list. The surroundings are great and the atmosphere improves as the food is enjoyed.

• Ste-Rose

US$10-20

L'Anse des Cascades, 6 chemin Anse des Cascades, Piton St-Rose, ☎ 47 20 42. Lunch only; closed Wednesdays. Traditional Creole cooking served in an unusual setting in a cool and shady glade of trees. View over the sea and the marina where various coloured fishing boats are moored. Sundays tend to be very overcrowded.

• Ste-Anne

US$15-30

L'Auberge Créole, 1 rue du Case ☎ 51 10 10. Lunch and dinner; closed Wednesdays. Creole and French cuisine. Specialities include prawns and fish fry, good "caris", pizzas, etc. The service is attentive, whether you are served in the dining room or on the terrace outside; and the decor of the place, close to the sea, is more than satisfactory.

Out for a drink

Bars – *L'Aquarhum*, St-Pierre: see above: Where to eat.

Alizé Plage, bd Hubert-Delisle. Closed Mondays. A good place for a drink, in a young, relaxed, fun atmosphere. Music.

Le Malone's, 8 boulevard Hubert-Delisle, St-Pierre ☎ 25 81 41. Trendy drinking/eating place on the waterfront. Lively, popular establishment to while away an evening listening to funky local music and mellow jazz. Live bands perform once a week, usually on Saturdays.

Nightclubs – *Le Refuge*, 126 allée des Bois Noirs, Ravine des Cabris, St-Pierre ☎ 49 56 32. Friday and Saturday nights from 10pm, and from 2pm on Sundays during the Réunion school holidays. Creole clientele, especially on Sunday afternoons. Entrance charge. Depending on your mood, you can switch from "club retro" to "club exotique". Premises also host fashion shows, live concerts, and all kinds of other entertainments on a regular basis.

Le Chapiteau, Ravine des Cafres, Montvert-les-Bas (8km from St-Pierre on the road to St-Joseph) ☎ 31 00 81. Saturdays and the evenings before a public holiday from 9.30pm. Entrance charge. This is one of the island's veritable institutions: not only is this disco the largest, it is also the most famous. All four dance floors attract crowds of people, including some from St-Denis. Mixed clientele drawn from residents, ex-pats and tourists all ready to dance to sega, zouk, techno, rock, waltz, tango and even the cha-cha-cha. Great atmosphere and well worth a visit.

Live shows – *Le Bato Fou*, 15 rue de la République, St-Pierre ☎ 25 65 61. Friday nights. This is the only such establishment in the south of the island, and so live shows include performances by local groups as well as touring international stars. The bar, which has been tastefully refurbished, serves a selection of excellent cocktails. Although it can get a bit stuffy and the acoustics are not very good, you are guaranteed an enjoyable evening out.

Sports and pastimes

Horse-riding – *Ranch Kikouyou*, 4 rue Curaire, Grand Fond, L'Entre-Deux ☎ 39 60 62. Excursions to Bras Long (85FF per hr or 150FF per 2hr), Argamasse (250FF per half-day). Helpful staff. Accommodation available (see above, Where to stay).

Various – *Alizés Plage*, boulevard Hubert-Delisle, St-Pierre ☎ 35 22 21. Masks and snorkels for hire; canoeing, canyoning and cross-country biking facilities.

Elastic Jump ☎ 31 71 71. Bungee-jumping from the bridge over Rivière de l'Est.

Shopping

St-Pierre market, boulevard Hubert-Delisle (alongside the CORA supermarket). Saturday mornings. The largest weekly market in the southern region takes place on the waterfront: fruit, vegetables and other perishable items, flowers, medicinal herbs, jams and preserves, as well as hand-made goods from Réunion, Madagascar and Indonesia.

St-Pierre covered market, rue Victor Le Vigoureux. Open Monday to Saturday, 7.30am-6pm; Sunday, 7.30am-12noon. Fruit, vegetables and handicraft.

Association Les Chocafils, Ravine Citron, L'Entre-Deux ☎ 39 52 59. Co-operative of artisans making and selling a variety of things using choca (macramé, braids, string bags).

Association Cass'le coin, Basse Vallée, St-Philippe ☎ 37 09 61. All kinds of basketware made from the local vacoa: baskets, trays, hats and a miscellany of decorative mats.

THE NORTHEAST
ST-BENOÎT TO STE-MARIE

Approx 35km (without excursions)
Set aside a whole day for exploring the Uplands

Not to be missed
A swim at Bassin La Paix.
A visit to the Maison de la Vanille.

And remember
Take waterproofs.

The northeast of the **"côte au vent"**, or windward side, of the island is an area of vivid contrasts in colour, with its dark red earth, pale green sugarcane fields and steely blue sea. The lushness of the coastal region is entirely due to the great quantities of rain it receives, brought in by the trade winds from across the ocean. The result is that the landscape has been transformed into what appears to be one vast sugarcane plantation, bisected here and there by long farm tracks lined with coconut trees leading to and from the large farm holdings. As you explore the plain, you will come across a series of Tamil temples scattered among the fields and be reminded of just how important the Indian community is, especially since 1848 when slavery was formally abolished.

The Uplands – Les Hauts – boasts one of the island's best primary forests. The relief is carved up by deep ravines, in which are contained a great number of secluded rock-pools and dramatic waterfalls: a perfect spot for a quick dip or a sobering shower. This part of Réunion, which lies outside most tourists' itineraries, also holds the key to the secret mysteries of vanilla.

The plain of plenty

Since the 18C, this region was recognised as being highly fertile and a source of great prosperity for the locals as well as for the island's economy as a whole. The early planters grew rice, wheat and tobacco; then maize, manioc (a type of cassava), fruit and flowers, coffee and vanilla were introduced, not to mention the precious exotic spices (notably cinnamon, cloves and nutmeg) planted by the botanist **Joseph Hubert** in the area around St-Benoît. Early in the 19C, the majority of these fragile plantations were destroyed by two successive cyclones, and so, in desperation, farmers turned to sugarcane, a highly lucrative cash-crop. As the demands for coffee dwindled, the management practices that for so long had been applied to farming in the northeast were reformed; while some abandoned the land, others expanded their properties to form large estates. Indeed, little remains of the many sugarrefineries that once operated there, save the odd empty building and stone chimney standing tall in the cane fields.

■ **St-Benoît** – For a long time, the town at the extreme end of the route des Plaines was forced to endure its isolation on account of its inaccessibility. Today, it is a dynamic commercial centre, the economic metropolis of the eastern region, raised to the ranks of a sub-prefecture of Réunion. Although the old **town centre** was essentially destroyed by a great fire in 1950, a few simple little shops, known as **cases-boutiques,** survive.

Follow the N2 as it bypasses St-Benoît and turn off into the cane fields when it comes into the district called Beaulieu: continue to the parking area (3km).

■ Bethléem

A track *(1km one way, 20min of easy walking. Reserve a bed if you wish to spend the night at the gîte)* lined with bamboo and *longanes* (delicious little brown fruit) leads the way to a clearing shaded by a magnificent lychee tree. Down by the **Rivière des Marsouins**, which runs below the basalt chapel dedicated to Notre-Dame de Fatima, you will find a heavenly spot for swim.

Go back the way you came and turn down the first small road on the left which returns to the D53; follow it for 15km. This pretty, narrow and winding road leads to a parking area.

■ Takamaka*

Leave early in the morning to avoid cloud and rain: there is an annual rainfall of about 7m! Continue along the road on foot for a 100m or so to where you can marvel at the wild and magnificent scenery with water tumbling in great **falls** over lofty precipices and tapering rocks emerging from the thick, damp undergrowth.

On the right, a **footpath** (very steep in places) passes under the overhead cables of an abandoned cable-car on its way to the Bébour forest.

Return to the N2. At Beauvallon, turn left along the Chemin La Paix; park the car, cross the bridge on foot, and follow the signposted path on the right.

Rivière des Roches rock pools*

30min to Bassin La Paix and back; 1hr to Bassin La Mer and back. Avoid weekends. Walk down the 182 steps through the lush vegetation to **Bassin La Paix*** where you can bathe with care, as the wonderful **waterfall** gushes down from a height of 10m with considerable force. Note on the right, the unusual **geological formation** of the basalt as it has cooled.

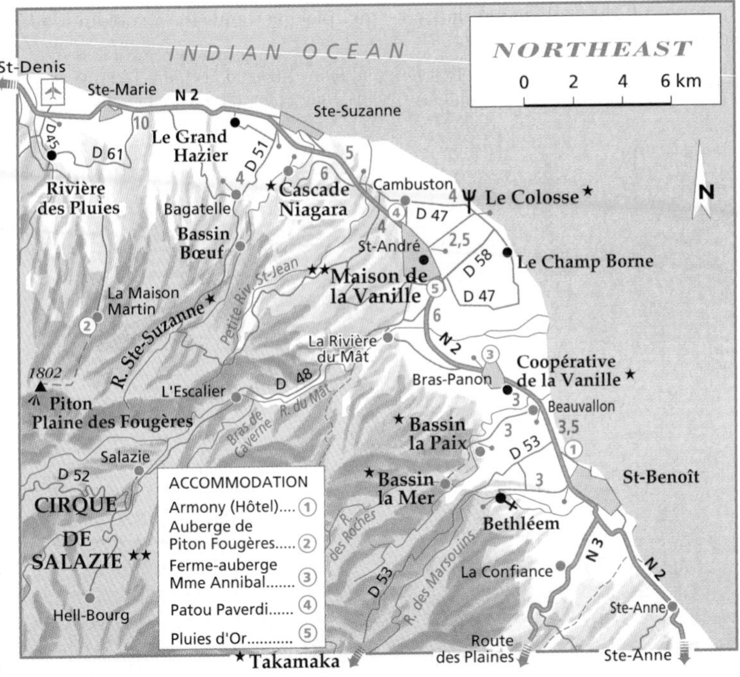

Retrace your steps up to the path that continues along the right side of the river. After 15min, you will come to **Bassin la Mer*** – a far less frequented spot, despite its superb waterfalls and unspoilt natural beauty.

Head north along the N2 towards Bras-Panon.

On crossing the **Pont de la Rivière des Roches** in summer, you may see a group of people jostling down by the mouth of the river clutching nets, **fishing for young fry** *(bichiques)*. For there are several species of fresh-water fish that, like salmon, lay their eggs in the sea. Then, at a specific point in the moon's cycle, the elver-like spawn have to make their way back upriver, past the fishermen lying in wait for them with specially designed hooped nets *(vouves)* at the ready. This seasonal delicacy is considered to be the local equivalent of caviar and sells for up to 200F a kilo when sold from improvised stalls along the side of the road – sometimes causing horrendous traffic jams in the process.

■ **Bras-Panon** – The town's main attraction is the **Vanilla Cooperative*** *(21 Route Nationale. Monday to Friday, 8am-11.15am / 1.30pm-4.15pm; Saturday, 9am-11.15am / 1.30pm-4.15pm; closed Sunday. Entrance fee for adults. Guided tours every 30min)*. Vanilla is a seasonal crop and so the "factory" only operates between May/June and November. At other times, the place may appear rather desolate. The cooperative was formed in 1950 in an attempt to reduce the costs of production and improve distribution. Today, it markets its quality product under the label **Vanille Bourbon** and is responsible for 75 % of the island's total output. A basic introduction is presented in the form of a video, then a guide takes visitors through the painstaking procedures involved in the commercial production of vanilla – the world's second most expensive spice (after saffron). This begins with the planting of the climbing herb, the assisted pollination of the ephemeral flowers, the picking, and the "cooking" and fermentation of the seed pods.

Back on the N2, continue to the first fork and follow signs to St-André (centre) on the right. Pass down under the N2 and bear gently right along the rue de la Gare.

Fishing for fry

C. Vaisse/HOA QUI

Vanilla
The vanilla orchid (Vanilla planifolia) was introduced to Réunion from South America in 1819 as an ornamental exotic. In 1841, a slave named Edmond Albius developed a way of tearing the membrane that isolates the ovary from the pollen with a needle, thereby pollinating the flower artificially – a procedure which otherwise fell to humming birds or insects. Since then, throughout September, when the flowers open for a couple of hours only, specially skilled "matchmakers" pollinate over a 1 000 flowers each by hand between 6am and 1pm. The green fruits are picked during April; these are immersed in water and heated to 65°C, drained, dried in the sun and then in ovens, before being sealed into airtight containers for eight months to ferment. This brings out the vanillin and intensifies the flavour.

■ **St-André** – Despite its recent modernisation, St-André retains elements from its rural past. The main square, dominated by the **town hall**, is shaded by ficus trees and so attracts locals, during the hottest hours of the day, to discuss the general state of affairs and engage in a noisy game of cards or dominoes. Otherwise, the buildings are rather ordinary: neither the odd traditional **townhouse** nor the **boutiques** will detain you long.

The profusion of **Malabar Temples**, however, serve to emphasise the importance of Tamil culture in the region. For the most part, this great Tamil community, descended from the Indian workers recruited to toil in the cane fields after the abolition of slavery in 1848, appears happy to explain to visitors the various rituals and practices involved in their religious celebrations, even allowing them to participate in their festivals. *(Information and dates available from the Tourist Information Centre at 68 rue de la République, ☎ 46 91 63. Tuesday to Saturday, 8.30am-12noon/1.30pm-5.30pm, until 4.30pm on Saturdays; closed Sundays and Mondays.)* You may be there to witness the **walking over hot coals**, which takes place at the end of December and during January, or watch the **Cavadee procession** around February/March *(see p 48 Hindu festivals)*.

The **Maison de la Vanille**** *(466 Rue de la Gare, ☎ 46 00 14. Tuesday to Sunday, 9am-12noon / 2pm-6pm; closed Mondays. Entrance charge. Guided tour available)* is a family-run concern that operates on a private estate belonging to the Floris family associated with the French perfume house of the same name. Here, it is possible to see how the pods have been carefully processed by hand in the traditional way since the 19C. As with visits to the Bras-Panon cooperative, it is only worth coming here between May/June and November, when the vanilla is being prepared for its fermentation. Unfortunately, the lovely Creole house and its outbuildings are not open to visitors.

At St-André, you will find signs for the **cirque de Salazie**** *(see p 166)*.

At the end of rue de la Gare, turn right down chemin Lagourgue passing beneath the four-lane road bridge. After 200m, turn left up the narrow drive way.

The palm-lined track leads up to **Maison Martin-Valliamé*** *(presently closed)*, a classified historic monument, which effectively demonstrates how Eastern and Western elements were combined to make a distinctive Réunion style. In this case, the country house is a typical example of Indo-Mauritian colonial architecture, with the addition of art deco details brought from Europe.

Make your way back to chemin Lagourgue, and turn left down to the sea.

■ **Le Champ Borne** – The rugged coastline is a fusion of contrasting colours. The beach is lined with sea-worn pebbles, and the rocks are scarred by the relentless assaults of the elements. In 1962, **Cyclone Jenny** ripped the roof off the **church** and destroyed the bell tower. Today it remains abandoned.

JF Galmiche

La Maison de la Vanille

Head north along the D47 coastal road for about 1.5km.

On the left-hand side of the road, stands the **Colosse***: one of the island's largest Tamil temples. Enclosed within a protective wire-fence, it comprises one long main building covered with ornate and brightly-painted sculpture. In Réunion between the end of December and mid-January, you may like to witness **walking over hot coals**. Towards the middle of July the festival of **Kali** is celebrated, during which goats and cockerels are sacrificed.

Stay on the D47 and go through Cambuston village, then follow the signs to Bois-Rouge.

The sugar factory of Bois-Rouge, one of the remaining two still in operation in Réunion, can be visited (*to reserve contact the Tourist Office of St-André for guided visits on Wednesdays and Saturdays*).

Go back onto the D47 and through Quartier Français village. After the St-Anne river bridge, follow the signs to Cascade Niagara.

Rivière Ste-Suzanne*

A number of freshwater pools lie alongside the river course, and, for the most part, these are fairly accessible. Furthermore, being more remote than those in the Ravine St-Gilles to the west (*see p 111*), they tend to be less crowded. The famous waterfall, known as the **cascade Niagara***, which features in so many holiday brochures, nestles in a truly enchanting landscape. It is also a favourite Sunday picnic spot among the islanders. A footpath leads to the top of the stone cliff. If you feel like a quiet swim, head upstream to a more secluded pool.

Go back down to Ste- Suzanne and head inland along the D51: at Bagatelle, turn left opposite the church. Ask for directions to the hidden pools lost among the dense wild vegetation known as **bassins Nicole**, **Bœuf** and **Grondin**.

Return to Bagatelle (D51), but fork left before StSuzanne, following signs for Grand Hazier.

■ **Le Grand Hazier** – *Ring Mr Chassagne to arrange a visit ☎ 52 32 81. Entrance fee.* To visit the **estate**, you have to drive up a long avenue of coconut palms. There you will be met by the present owner, who is happy to regale visitors with the history of the land conceded in 1690 for the cultivation of coffee, maize, tobacco and cloves over an area that at one time extended nigh on 60ha. A tour of the house, built of sideroxylon and tamarind, is followed by a walk around the **orchard** where bananas, cocoa, spices and medicinal plants are grown.

Drive to the N2 and continue towards St-Denis. Come off at the exit for the airport and follow the D45 all the way to Rivière des Pluies. Park in front of the village church.

■ **Rivière des Pluies** – To the left of the village church, a wonderful array of flowers surrounds the **Sanctuary of the Black Virgin**★. This shrine attracts pilgrims all year round, but on 15 August thousands gather here to celebrate the Feast of the Assumption.

The Legendary Black Virgin

Once upon a time, many moons ago, a young coloured slave miraculously managed to escape from a group of Whites. As he knelt and implored the little ebony figure of the Virgin he had placed in a flowering grotto, the spiny branches of a bougainvillaea seemed to grow outwards and block the path of his assailants, who by then were on the point of capturing him. The slave died a free man, and the miraculous bougainvillaea continues to flourish at the foot of the effigy of the sacred Black Virgin.

Drive on towards Grande Montée, Beaumont-les-Hauts, Maison Martin.

From there, a wonderful footpath leads up to **Piton Plaine des Fougères**, 1 802m above sea level. *(5hr there and back; medium difficulty; start and finish signposted near Maison Martin.)* As the track climbs upwards, it meanders through the tree-ferns and lichens to reach a **viewing platform** overlooking the Cirque de Salazie.

Making the most of the Northeast

Getting there

By bus – Most of the towns in the northeastern region are served by buses from the bus station in St-Denis. In all cases, the bus stations are located in or near the town centre as at St-Benoît (☎ 50 10 69) and St-André (☎ 46 80 00). Minibuses and shared taxis also stop here before departing for the Uplands.

By car – The only way of exploring the region at will is by private means. Do be careful if driving after heavy rain as the roads can be very slippery.

Address book

Office du tourisme de Bras-Panon, place de la mairie ☎ 51 50 62. Monday to Friday, 8am-12noon / 1.15pm-5pm; closed Saturday and Sunday. Day-long excursions to the Uplands including a visit to the Vanilla Cooperative, a drive through the region and a gastronomic meal.

Office municipal du tourisme de St-André, 68 Centre commercial ☎ 46 91 63. Tuesday to Saturday, 8.30am-12noon/1.30pm-5.30pm (until 4.30pm Saturday); closed Sunday and Monday. Art gallery, display and sale of local craft-work. Information on Tamil festivities.

ADRP (Association Découverte Réunion Profonde), 1066 chemin du Centre, St-André ☎ /Fax 58 02 50. Organisation arranging thematic (fascinating and highly original) excursions, orientated towards a single cultural or religious element pertinent to the island. Unusual way of gaining a different perspective on the local population.

WHERE TO STAY

Prices given here are based on the cost of a double room with breakfast for two.

• St-Benoît

US$45-60

Hôtel Armony, 204 RN2, La Marine ☎ 50 86 50, Fax 50 86 60, armony@la-reunion.com – 50rm Modern setting, comfortable and relaxing facilities. All the rooms are spacious, are tastefully furnished with green woodwork, and have use of a kitchenette. Professionally trained staff ensure the smooth running of your stay. Ask for one of the bungalows by the pool with view over the sea.

• Bras-Panon

US$15-30

Ferme-auberge de Mme Annibal, 6 chemin Rivière du Mât (at the entrance of Bras-Panon if coming from StDenis; turn left up rue des Limites to Rivière du Mât and then right towards the riding centre). ☎ 51 53 76 – 4rm The rooms are housed in a small and unpretentious building, 200m from the farmhouse. Shared bathroom and toilet facilities. Meals served – see below Where to eat.

• St-André

US$30-45

Pluies d'Or, 3 allée des Sapotilles, La Cressonière (as you leave St-André, go under the bridge and turn right into chemin des Bougainvillées), ☎/Fax 46 18 16/46 57 26, pluiedor@oceanes.fr – 13rm This spacious Creole residence houses a very cheap, somewhat hippy-like establishment where guests feel at home right away. The rooms are basic and clean. There is also a TV room (with cable TV) and an internet connection. Rates can be negotiated depending on the length of your stay. Meals are served in the evening, on request, at very moderate prices. Reservations are recommended.

Chez Patou Paverdi, 460 ruelle Virapatrin (as you enter St-André, follow the signs to Cambuston), ☎ 46 46 07 – 3rm Indian-style, comfortable rooms are located in a small building set opposite the owners' very beautiful Creole house. The welcome is always warm and friendly and your hostess will be delighted to show you around her exceptional garden while she explains all the secrets of its lush vegetation. The cooking is also excellent and depending on the evening, you'll be able to taste beignet de songe (savoury fritters), camaraon or chicken cari. Classic, but very good.

• Ste-Marie

US$15-30

Auberge de Piton Fougères, follow directions to La Ressource, then Terrain Elisa and Plaine des Fougères (45min from St-Denis) ☎ 53 88 04 – 6rm This country retreat is perfect for those wishing to explore the high area above Ste-Marie. The genuine welcome and natural simplicity are appreciated by all.

WHERE TO EAT

• St-Benoît

US$30-45

Le Bouvet, 75 rue de l'Amiral Bouvet ☎ 50 14 96 / 50 17 27. Lunch and dinner; closed Sunday evening. You enter an impressive white Creole house via a luminous veranda that still boasts the original tiles. In the dining room, the decoration may at first appear somewhat bland, but the establishment soon compensates for any lack of warmth in its decoration with its excellent cooking: red fish cari, zourite cari or a mouth-watering eel cari. In addition to the traditional Creole dishes, the restaurant also serves chicken with fresh palm or veal escalope with palm. Try the chocolate charlotte dessert or the guava mousse and coulis to finish off your meal perfectly.

• Bras-Panon

Under US$15

Le Vanilla, 21 route nationale 2 (next to the Vanilla Cooperative), ☎ 51 56 58. Lunch only; closed Saturdays. A tasteful little restaurant located in a typical Creole case. Paintings, most of which depict daily Réunion life, add colour to the establishment and a certain charm. Of course, vanilla is present in all the dishes, whether chicken fricassee, duck, crème caramel, banana pie or even coffee. Not at all cloying, everything is good and tasty and the service is efficient and discreet.

US$12-20

Ferme-auberge de Mme Annibal, 6 chemin Rivière du Mât (at the entrance of Bras-Panon if coming from St-Denis; turn left up rue des Limites to Rivière du Mât and then right towards the riding centre). ☎ 51 53 76 (advance booking essential). Lunch and dinner; closed Sunday evenings. One of the very best meals of its kind in Réunion. Long parallel tables, covered with waxed cloths, make this venue extremely informal, although both the food and the conviviality of the place are reputed far and wide. Start with a glass of fruit punch or rum cocktail to put you in the mood for a serious meal! Before tasting that famous duck and vanilla dish, you will be served an appetiser in the form of a baked seasonal vegetable like chouchou or jackfruit/tijack from the garden, and then a serving of fish cari. To finish, why not select a light and refreshing home-made sorbet – papaya or star-fruit ("carambole").

• **St-André**

US$12-25

Le Beau Rivage, Champ Borne, ☎ 46 08 66 / 46 07 07. Lunch and dinner; closed Sunday evenings and Mondays. Located in an attractive wood and glass Creole house, wedged in between the sea and the roadside, this restaurant serves good French cooking, sometimes adapted to local tastes, together with a few traditional Creole recipes. Ask for a table with a view of the sea and tuck into some delicious sweetbread à l'ancienne or a jugged 'country' duck, while savouring an excellent South African wine. A nice place to stop on the way out to the east coast with very reasonable prices.

La Coupole, Centre commercial "Les Cocoteraires", ☎ 46 94 77. Lunch and dinner; closed Sunday evenings and Mondays. One of the island's best Chinese restaurants, rumoured to bring its cooks over directly from China. Despite a somewhat ordinary setting, the food is both unusual and innovative. Not to be missed, with something for every budget.

• **Ste-Suzanne**

US$12-18

Table d'hôte Caladema, Ste-Vivienne (at Quartier Français, follow signs for Ste-Vivienne: stop by the fourth house after the church along the road to Bras des Chevrettes) ☎ 46 11 43 (reservation advised). Closed Mondays. The Indian owners are Tamils from a predominantly Christian area, and they will serve you a generous range of delicious goodies ranging from samossas, baked dishes, caris or spicy curries to various desserts made entirely from home-grown produce. Simple cooking, attentive service. The large open dining room is a little dark, but the atmosphere more than makes up for the decor.

SPORTS AND PASTIMES

Kalonoro, Bras-Panon ☎ 50 74 75. Canyoning, canoeing, river-swimming, you will be taken deep into the wildest countryside. High degree of professionalism, serious but good-natured team of qualified and approved instructors.

Centre hippique de l'Est, chemin Rivière du Mât, Bras-Panon ☎ 51 50 49 (reservation recommended). Proficient horsemen/women can go on excursions, accompanied by a guide, through the cane fields to the steep and wild cliffs on the eastern coast. Treks mainly organised on Saturdays at 9.30am or 2pm (150FF for 2hr; 400FF per day).

SHOPPING

Le Pandanus, RN2, Bras-Panon (place de la mairie). Monday to Friday, 8am-4pm; closed Saturday and Sunday. Hand-made goods crafted using plaited and woven vacoa leaves (baskets, wallets, mats, etc).

Parfum Vanille, coopérative Vanille de Bras Panon, 21 RN2. Monday to Saturday, 9am-12noon / 1pm-5pm; Sunday 10am-5pm. Vanilla in all its forms: pods, essence, plaits, powder, liqueur, and other tourist souvenirs (post cards, jams, alcohol).

ADAR, Champ Borne (opposite the church). 8am-12.30pm; closed Saturday. Craft centre for all things connected to the working of vacoa.

Kamala, 629 avenue Bourbon, StAndré, 6am-7pm; closed weekends. Stocks a wide range of Indian arts and crafts.

Route des Plaines★

St-Pierre to St-Benoît

Approx 60km drive
Allow a whole day
Be prepared for cool and damp weather

Not to be missed
Visit the Maison du Volcan.
Admire the view over Grand Bassin from Bois Court.
A walk in the forest of Bébour-Bélouve.

And remember
Take care on the windy stretches of the N3, shrouded in mist and often slippery.
Make a reservation at the Maison de la Montagne to spend the night at Grand Bassin.
Spend at least one night in Les Plaines or thereabouts.

Extreme conditions: hot and humid to cool and windy

The Route des Plaines cuts right across the island, taking you through extremes of climate, scenery and vegetation. The RN3, which relays St-Pierre on the south coast to St-Benoît on the northeast coast, snakes its way between Réunion's two largest mountain ranges: Piton des Neiges and Piton de la Fournaise. A rugged saddle of land with a pass at an altitude of 1 600m separates the Plaine des Palmistes from the Plaine des Cafres. In winter, the desolate plateau, which is covered with natural pasture and wild moorland dotted with clumps of heather, gorse and St-John's Wort, is often blanketed in thick cloud and mist. Temperature can fall to below zero at night, but, before long, the early-morning frosts are melted away by the first rays of sunshine. The hamlets in this remote region consist of a different style of simple home, with a fireplace or a wood-burning stove, and it is not unusual to find the windows left wide open during the day in an attempt to banish the lingering damp.

These highland plains remained uninhabited until the middle of the 19C for several reasons – their isolation, difficulty of access, harsh weather conditions, and the many coloured slaves (referred to as *Cafres*, which means Kaffirs, hence the Plaine des Cafres), who found refuge there from their former employers. Since the road was completed, a number of villages and small towns have grown with the influx of wealthy residents from the coastal regions in search of the fresh mountain air.

St-Pierre to Plaine des Cafres

30km – Allow 30min without excursions.

Route du Tampon

The dual carriageway (N3) between St-Pierre and Tampon runs past a succession of hillsides planted with sugarcane, interrupted here and there by powerful sprays that glint in the sunlight. The green expanse of the Tampon plateau is dotted with a multitude of simple shacks surrounded with colourful flower-filled gardens. It was only in 1830, that **Count Gabriel Kerveguen** managed to secure great swathes of this sparsely populated countryside. It was he who, in or around 1859, introduced obsolete German coins called *kreutzer* or *kerveguen* to Réunion that were only withdrawn from general circulation in 1880.

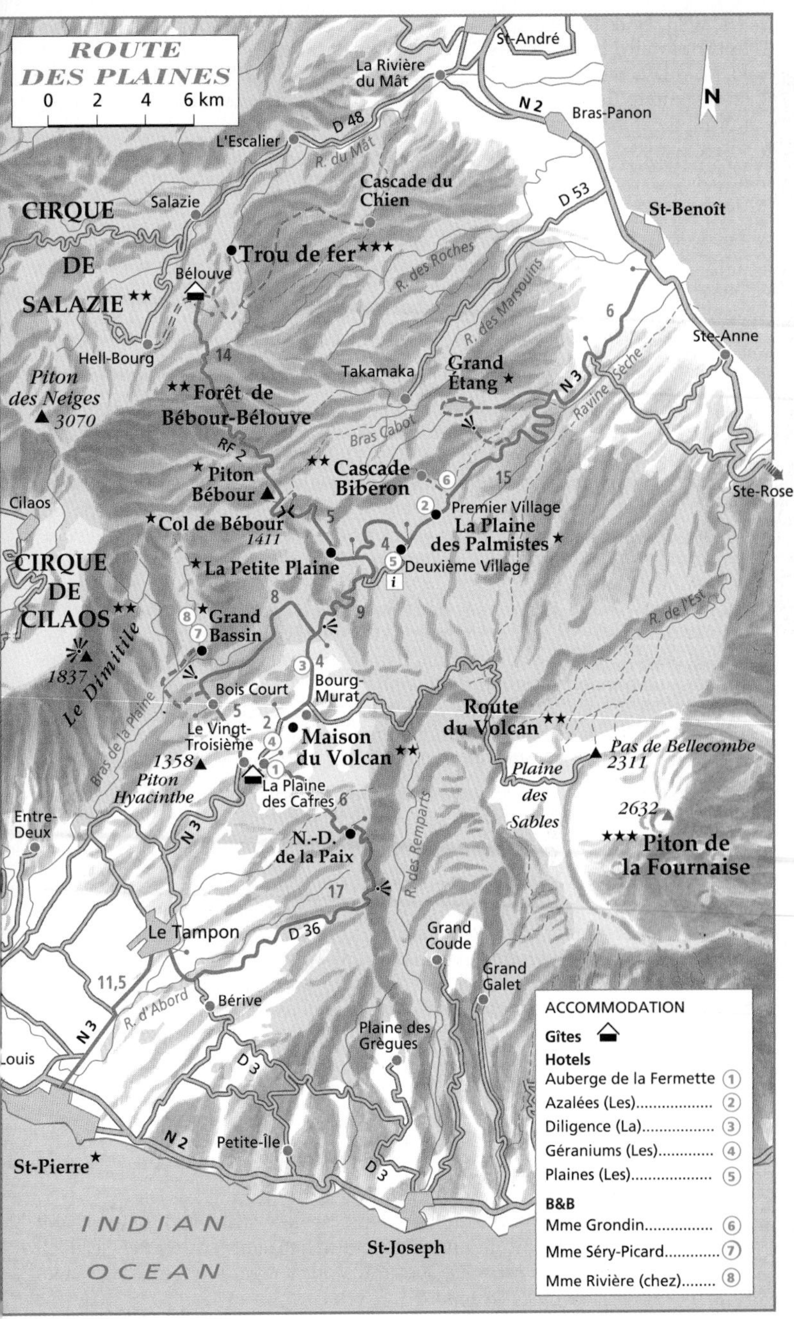
ROUTE DES PLAINES
0 2 4 6 km
N
St-André
La Rivière du Mât
N 2
Bras-Panon
D 48
L'Escalier
R. du Mât
Cascade du Chien
D 53
St-Benoît
CIRQUE DE SALAZIE ★★
Salazie
Trou de fer ★★★
Bélouve
R. des Roches
R. des Marsouins
Hell-Bourg
14
Ste-Anne
Piton des Neiges
3070
★★ Forêt de Bébour-Bélouve
Takamaka
Grand Étang ★
N 3
Ravine Sèche
Bras Cabot
RF 2
★ Piton Bébour
★★ Cascade Biberon
15
Ste-Rose
Cilaos
★ Col de Bébour
1411
Premier Village
La Plaine des Palmistes ★
Deuxième Village
CIRQUE DE CILAOS ★★
★ La Petite Plaine
★ Grand Bassin
R. de l'Est
Le Dimitile
1837
Bois Court
Bourg-Murat
Route du Volcan ★★
Le Vingt-Troisième
Maison du Volcan ★★
Pas de Bellecombe
2311
1358
Piton Hyacinthe
Bras de la Plaine
La Plaine des Cafres
Plaine des Sables
Entre-Deux
2632
★★★ Piton de la Fournaise
N.-D. de la Paix
R. des Remparts
17
Le Tampon
D 36
Grand Coude
Grand Galet
11,5
Bérive
R. d'Abord
Plaine des Grègues
Louis
D 3
N 2
Petite-Île
St-Pierre ★
INDIAN OCEAN
St-Joseph
ACCOMMODATION
Gîtes
Hotels
Auberge de la Fermette (1)
Azalées (Les).................. (2)
Diligence (La)................. (3)
Géraniums (Les)............. (4)
Plaines (Les)................... (5)
B&B
Mme Grondin................ (6)
Mme Séry-Picard............ (7)
Mme Rivière (chez)........ (8)

The RN3 winds its way up to the high plateaux passing through small villages, known locally as **bourgades**, denoted by their distance in kilometres from St-Pierre – hence Onzième (11th), Douzième (12th), Dix-Neuvième (19th), and so on. Along the way, there are various lay-bys and stopping places for admiring the view of the coast below.

As you reach Tampon, the dual-carriageway comes to an end, turn right at the first traffic-lights along the D3 (direction Bérive), and continue for 2.5km: at the fork, go left (D36).

The D36 is a pleasant little road that leads to **Notre-Dame de la Paix** and on up to the Plaine des Cafres. Just before Notre-Dame de la Paix, it provides a superb **viewpoint**** for looking out over the Rivière des Remparts. Coming this way, you will also glimpse a different landscape of pineapples and strawberries and fields of flowers destined to be cut for market.

At the centre of the village at the 23rd km, follow signs for D70 and Bois Court (5.5km).

The road terminates at **Bois Court**, where there is a special **viewpoint**** from which to survey the valley and Grand Bassin *îslet* (hill village) some 700m below, its tin roofs glinting in the sun. Only a winch – assuring the daily delivery of absolute necessities – and a steep path provide access to this lonely hamlet. When **walking** this way *(return to the road and turn right before the discotheque: parking area 500m further on. 8km, 4hr round trip. 650m rise in altitude; medium difficulty. Accommodation available at the gîte, subject to reservation in advance through the Maison de la Montagne, or at a local B&B)*, you are bound to meet people from **Grand Bassin*** as, each Sunday evening, the children take this path to get to school in the Uplands, returning home as often as not the following Saturday. In the village itself, narrow tracks lead up to the simple little houses, surrounded by stone walls, only a few of which benefit from having electricity. You may like to take advantage of the refreshing waterfall, known locally as **Voile de la Mariée** (although the real "bridal veil" is at Salazie, and visible from the D48), and its inviting pools hidden among the vegetation.

From the Bois Court viewpoint, drive 250m to the left before turning down the road to Piton Bleu. This takes you across the sparsely populated heathland and back to the N3: turn right towards Bourg-Murat.

▪ **La Maison du Volcan**** – *27th km, Bourg-Murat,* ☎ *59 00 26. 9.30am-5.30pm; closed Mondays. Entrance fee. Guided tours by arrangement. Allow 1hr-2hr.* The building has been designed to reflect the forms of the volcano. Inside, the museum presents explanatory information about volcanic activity and the earth's genesis, both scientifically and amusingly. **Piton de la Fournaise**, of course, is given centre-stage and all its secrets are unfurled. Concentration is sharpened by the subdued lighting, and didactic show-cards, fascinating videos, interactive sites and models of volcanoes leave visitors free to discover the museum at their own pace. At Bourg-Murat starts the **route du Volcan** (RF5): see p 160.

La Plaine des Cafres to St-Benoît

32km – Allow about 3hr, without excursions.

In the middle of the plateau, the N3 intersects the waymarked footpath (GR R2) that crosses the island. In one direction, this magnificent **track**** leads to the volcano *(6hr, 17.5km one way)*, and in the other it goes to Piton des Neiges *(Caverne Dufour, 5hr, 15km one way)*.

Route de la Plaine des Palmistes*

The Col de Bellevue marks the abrupt end of the Plaine des Cafres, at the point where a jagged cliff – the **Rempart de la Grande Montée** – towers skywards over the Plaine des Palmistes. The sudden change in the landscape is accompanied by a radical variation in the now very humid weather and vegetation. Specially conceived lay-bys accommodated in the hairpin-bends provide excellent **vantage points** from which to survey the scenery falling down towards the sea.

On reaching the base of the cliff, turn left off the N3 towards Petite Plaine; then fork left again onto the RF2 and continue for about 1.5km.

▪ **La Forêt de Bébour-Bélouve**** – The road begins in a forest of Japanese *cryptomerias*. An excellent introduction to the highlands' flora is to take the time to walk the nature trail along which the species are all labelled and identified: **Sentier Botanique de la Petite Plaine*** *(1hr circuit; leaflets and information from ONF ☎ 90 48 00)*. Some way beyond, the road slices through orchards of guava which, in June, are laden with the little red fruit that are so delectably sweet and sour *("pick your own" open to all, subject to entrance charge)*. Little by little, the vegetation appears to become wilder and the road leads into a splendid endemic **primary forest*** (*bois de fer*, *bois de pintade*, *bois de demoiselle,etc*). Foot paths proliferate in every direction. These are as suitable for an afternoon stroll as for a two-day hike through tree-ferns, lichens, arum lilies and *fahams* (white orchids), large tamarind trees and other aged specimens *(see illustration p 16-17)*. At the weekend, you will encounter crowds of Creole families who have settled in the shaded undergrowth for their ritual picnics.
After the **Col de Bébour***, the road passes yet more cryptomerias before plunging back into primary forest once more, until it emerges 13km later at the **Gîte de Bélouve** (*see below* Where To Stay).

Just after the **Bras Cabot** ford, a path branches left and heads up around **Piton Bébour*** *(circuit 90min)*, a magical place that is both cool and humid, fragrant with the smell of damp forest vegetation, thick with lush intertwined greenery and home to the noisy bulbul.

Return to the road and continue to the Gîte de Bélouve. At the weekend, all vehicles must stop 3km before the gîte.

From the gîte, there is one footpath in particular, the one for the Trou de Fer *(3hr there and back; easy)*, that is especially lovely as it meanders among the tamarinds and ferns before coming out at a **waterfall**. The actual **Trou de Fer*****, a highly impressive canyon, is only accessible by abseiling down the cliffs or, from above, by helicopter. Such a flight makes for an unforgettable experience and, if you find it within your budget, not to be missed! (*see below* Activities). Halfway along the track, you will come to a fork with another path that leads to the Hauts de Bras Panon and the **cascade du Chien** *(8hr one way; 900m rise in altitude; arduous)*. This no less spectacular hike takes you through the different bands of forest vegetation.

Make way back to Petite Plaine, and turn left (D55).

▪ **Plaine des Palmistes*** – The road to the village of Plaine des Palmistes is lined with hydrangeas, bamboo and plane trees – which are very rare for a tropical island. The village takes its name from the immense forest of *palmiste* palms that once covered the area but has now all but disappeared. One attraction is the particularly fine old planter's houses – among the best on the island – which are to be found here such as the restored **Villa des Tourelles*** at the entrance to Premier Village on the left. Built in 1927 by Alexis Jean de

Villeneuve, one of the main landowners of St-Benoît, this fine residence now houses the **Pays d'Accueil des Hautes Plaines** (☎ *51 39 92. Monday-Friday, 8.30am-5pm, weekends and bank holidays 10am-5pm)*.

Coloured awnings, **decorative woodwork**, **airy verandahs** and flower-filled gardens all help to recapture some of the charm of former times, while the warm reception of the locals more than compensates for the inclement weather. It is well worth sampling the local cheeses seasoned with herbs and spices. Every year, in the last week of June, the village hosts the **Guava Festival**, complete with its merry-go-round, raffles, tastings and sales of delicious home-made jams, pickles, sauces and such like.

In Premier Village, continue 1km past the town hall: at the fork, go left for 100m.

A small path *(90min. Beware! Conditions can be treacherously slippery after heavy rain)* leads to the base of the **Cascade Biberon****. Here, beside the lofty waterfall, you can swim and enjoy a picnic. In winter, the track is lined with fruiting guava-plants, which is an added bonus!

Head back to the N3 and turn left 5km after the village's administrative centre.

Cutting through the luxuriant undergrowth comprising tree-ferns and tamarinds, a path takes one on foot *(3hr round trip; gentle gradients; easy)*, to the top of a rocky ledge over 400m high, overlooking **Grand Étang**.

Cross the bridge over Ravine Sèche and turn left onto the Grand Étang forest road (2.5km to the car park).

■ **Grand Étang*** – The water level of the lake – formed as a result of a massive landslide – varies according to the season's rainfall. On all sides, exuberant vegetation claws its way up the steep rock faces. A path *(6km, 2hr, easy-going)* runs right around the enclave past trees of different coloured woods, guavas and *jamerosiers* (delicious yellowish-pink fruit tasting of roses). Halfway round, a track leads off *(40min circuit)* to the **waterfalls** that feed the lake.

The N3 descends gently down towards **St-Benoît**, across acres of sugarcane that gently sway at the whim of the trade winds, and often cower beneath violent squalls coming in from the sea.

Making the most of the Route des Plaines

Getting there

By bus – Public buses operated by ***Les Cars Jaunes*** operate along the N3 between St-Pierre and St-Benoît. Shared taxis also run regularly along the same route.

By car – The road is pocketed with rather nasty potholes, so do drive carefully. There are three fuel stations along the way, at Plaine des Cafres, Bourg-Murat and Plaine des Palmistes. Thick bands of fog often appear unexpectedly up in the hills, so do take care when out driving.

Address book

Tourist information – ***Pays d'Accueil des Hautes Plaines***, Domaine des Tourelles, rue de la République, Plaine des Palmistes, second village, ☎ 51 39 92, Fax 51 45 33. Puts on temporary exhibitions of local artists' work. For activities, contact ***Association des Amis du Jardin Capricorne***, rue Arums, ☎ 51 48 14.

Banks – The last bank with ATM/cashdispenser before StBenoît can be found at Plaine des Cafres. There is also an ATM dispenser at Plaine des Palmistes Post Office.

Y. Arthus-Bertrand/ALTITUDE

Low-level in the Trou de Fer

Route des Plaines

Post Office – Both Plaine des Cafres and Plaine des Palmistes have post offices that are open Monday to Saturday, 8am to 12noon / 1pm-4pm; closed Sundays.

Telephone – Card-operated public telephones are to be found in most town centres.

Vehicle rentals – Agencies at St-Pierre, Le Tampon, and St-Benoît.

Medical services – Pharmacies and doctors in the villages of Plaine de la Cafres and Plaine des Palmistes.

WHERE TO STAY

Prices given here are based on the cost of a double room with breakfast for two unless otherwise indicated.

• Plaine des Cafres

US$30-45

Auberge de la Fermette, 48 rue du Bois Court, La Plaine des Cafres ☎ 27 50 08, Fax 27 53 78 – 10rm The draw of this simple but convivial hotel is its fresh and peaceful situation in the heart of the countryside. All the rooms are accommodated in an annexe overlooking the garden. Dinner (except Wednesdays).

La Grande Ferme, 44 village de la Grande Ferme, ☎ 59 28 07 – 4rm Located in a modern Creole house, 3km from the Maison du Volcan, this gîte provides comfortable, pleasant accommodation. Ask for a room with a view of the Piton des Neiges.

US$45-60

Hôtel La Diligence, 28th km ☎ 59 10 10, Fax 59 11 81 – 27rm Accommodation consists of a series of small clean, but quite ordinary, chalets set among the greenery. Warm and efficient reception, helpful in arranging sporting activities like pony-trekking, tennis, cross-country biking. Welcoming dining room with open fire.

US$60-75

Hôtel Les Géraniums, 24th km ☎ 59 11 06, Fax 59 21 83 – 16rm You may get the opportunity of seeing the geraniumstill functioning by the entrance. To take maximum advantage of this pleasant and warm hotel, ask for a room with a view of the Piton des Neiges. Private use of a television in the room on request. Good restaurant: see below Where to eat.

• Grand Bassin

Under US$30/person half-board

Chambres d'hôtes de Mme Séry-Picard, ☎ 27 51 02 Guests are warmly welcomed into the family home, so, before long, they have the chance of becoming involved with the activities going on in this remote village.

La Paille en Queue, chez Mme Rivière, ☎ 59 03 66 / 59 20 08 – 3rm The authentic charm of this adorable, prettily decorated little Creole house and its magnificent flower garden is undeniable. Friendly welcome and excellent cooking: gratin de chouchou, cari baba figue and sanquette are a delight. It's also possible to reserve a table d'hôte if you're not actually staying there.

• Bébour-Bélouve

US$15-30

Gîte de Bélouve ☎ 41 21 23 (book overnight stays through the Maison de la Montagne, and arrange meals with the gîte) – 37 beds Ideal for those wishing to make the most of the forest location and spend the day hiking.

• Plaines des Palmistes

US$15-30

Chambres d'hôtes de Mme Grondin, 17 rue Dureau, Premier Village ☎ 51 33 79 – 3rm Excellent place to stay. Guests are given a warm welcome in a large Creole house, just outside the village, and therefore nice and quiet. Rooms are in an annexe set in the garden. Reputed to be one of the best places to eat too.

US$45-60

Les Azalées, 80 rue de la République, Premier Village ☎ 51 34 24, Fax 51 39 89 – 42rm All the rooms are arranged in large bungalows, dotted around the garden. This rather mundane establishment does boast a most spectacular view of the Cascade Biberon spilling out of the bedrock.

US$60-75

Hôtel des Plaines, Deuxième Village ☎ 51 31 97 / 51 36 59, Fax 51 45 70 – 14rm Attractive Creole house with verandah facing onto the street. Rooms are spacious and comfortable. Open fire in the dining room (see Where to eat).

Where to eat

• Plaine des Cafres

US$15-30

Auberge du 24ème, 36 rue du Père Favron, 24th km ☎ 59 08 60. Lunch and dinner. Menu to suit all appetites and wallets: baked chouchou or fresh palmiste salad, swordfish cari or camaron (large prawns) and home-made dessert to follow. Book in advance especially if you fancy the à la carte menu listing duck-breast with geranium mushrooms. The dining room has a good atmosphere and is well heated in winter.

Hôtel Les Géraniums (see above Where to stay). Lunch and dinner. The menu includes à la carte dishes. Large wood-panelled dining area decorated with pictures of the scenes from daily life in Réunion, wonderful great fireplace and superb view to the Dimitile Ridge. Outdoor barbecues can also be arranged, in full view of the mountain.

• Plaine des Palmistes

US$15-30

Table d'hôtes de Mme Grondin (see above Where to stay). Reservation advised. Excellent "cari baba figue" (banana flowers) and "cari ti jacques" gently cooked over an open fire.

Ferme Auberge le Pommeau, rue de Peindray d'Ambelle, ☎ 51 40 70. Lunch and dinner. This inn belongs to the new generation of accommodation currently under development in the High Plains. Tastefully decorated, it provides good traditional Creole dishes at very reasonable prices (amazing gratin de chouchou). Seated around an open fire in the middle of the room, taste one of the house punches and enjoy the warm, friendly welcome.

Auberge des Goyaviers, 63bis rue H Pignolet, tourist route to Petite Plaine ☎ 51 30 26. Lunch and dinner; closed Wednesdays. The owner won a special prize in 1996 for his guava-based recipe for a dish combining foie gras with lobster. Other unique combinations include kangaroo filet with guava wine. Fine view of the coast, together with carefully contrived decor, combine to enhance the delicious cooking and its conscientious presentation.

Hôtel des Plaines (see above Where to stay). Lunch and dinner. Sophisticated food prepared with locally produced seasonal ingredients. Besides such classic dishes as fresh and baked palm-heart, you can elect to have glazed duck confit in its unctuous vanilla-flavoured sauce. Delicious lime mousse with guava coulis. Impeccable service. Formal decor.

Shopping

Roadside stalls along the RN3 offer seasonal produce and home-made goodies for sale: cheeses, fruit and vegetables, honey, duck confit, jams and pickles.

Comptoir Austral, 207 RN3, PK 27, Bourg-Murat, Plaine des Cafres ☎ 59 09 45. Attractively packaged home-made products using lemongrass, coconut, soaps, sweet-smelling wood, hand-crafted objects.

Péïdéo, 10 rue de la Fournaise, Bourg Murat, La Plaine des Cafres, ☎ 51 10 29. Popular art gallery, literary centre and traditional music concert hall all in one, Péïdéo sets out to demonstrate and promote 'Creole' and 'Réunion' arts above all. Located in a colourful case, the place is very appealing. Everything's for sale, except the walls themselves.

Alandroso-Tsara, 262 rue de la République, La Plaine des Palmistes, ☎ 51 48 32. Lovers of Madagascan art will fall in love with this Ali Baba's cave with a little of everything in all ranges of prices.

Sports and pastimes

Hiking – ***Magma Rando***, see Sports and Pastimes, p 81.

Horse-riding – ***La Diligence***, 28th km, Bourg-Murat, La Plaine des Cafres ☎ 59 10 10. Pony trekking, carriage rides (100FF/hr; 600FF/day). Accommodation: see above Where to stay.

Centre équestre de Pont Payet, Grand Étang ☎ 50 90 03. Pony trekking, as well as tour of the botanical garden, arranged by Luco Noury, who is happy to share his love and knowledge of medicinal plants (40FF/person).

Cross-country biking – ***Rando Bike***, 100 route du Volcan, Plaine des Cafres ☎ 59 15 88.

Le Volcan★★★

57km from St-Pierre – 64km from St-Benoît
Allow at least a day
Altitude: 2 632m
Gîte accommodation available – Map p 162-163

Not to be missed
The route du Volcan.
A hike to Nez Coupé de Ste-Rose.

And remember
Take warm clothing, particularly in winter.
Follow safety advice when out hiking.
Wear sturdy walking boots with thick soles and a good tread.
Leave in the early hours so as to make the most of the day before the mist descends.

Three million years ago, the volcanic island of Réunion arose from 4 000m below the sea. **Piton des Neiges** became extinct 20 000 years ago but **Piton de la Fournaise** (known everywhere simply as "le volcan") remains active to this day (*illustration p 26*).
When the volcano is dormant, it is difficult to imagine that you are roaming freely over what may one day be covered by molten magma. The area has become so familiar that it is enjoyed by all and sundry for picnics, walks, to show to new visitors, to photograph and so on. Nonetheless, it remains a curiosity of nature and it is difficult to resist its powers of attraction and the awe it inspires.

Follow the RN3 to Bourg-Murat, then turn onto the RF5.

Route du Volcan★★

30km, approx 45min by car without stopping.

The unique scenery, its combinations of colour, smell and atmosphere are unequalled. The road crosses a plateau with a scattering of farm buildings and open pasture before engaging in the climb, gentle at first but soon involving a series of tight hairpin bends. Here and there, you are allowed to glimpse the plains below, the coastline and the island's tallest peaks. To appreciate the full impact, try to undertake this excursion at sunrise, or, even better, at sunset.

Continue up to **Nez de Bœuf**★★★ which provides the most complete view of **Rivière des Ramparts**. There you will find a number of purpose-built shelters for picnicking or for camping.
Further along on the right-hand side of the road, you come to the gaping red crater – the **cratère Commerson**★★ – ever open to erosion from the elements. Beyond the **Plaine des Remparts**, the **Plaine des Sables**★★★ suddenly appears below: a vast reddish and bronze-tinted lunar landscape, interrupted by great clefts in which rivers run and by two rather unusual-looking conical outcrops. To the right of the road, at **Pas des Sables** (before reaching the Plaine des Sables at the bottom), you will find a schematic drawing that identifies the various features.
The road continues to pick its way through an area strewn with basalt boulders and comes out at **Pas de Bellcombe**★★★. Straight ahead stands the volcano, majestic and proud, its flanks streaked with brown and grey.

Rivière des Ramparts from Nez de Bœuf

▪ Piton de la Fournaise***

Since the 17C, accounts have referred to the existence of a "Mountain of Fire" in the southeastern part of the island. But it was only a century later that anyone seems to have transcribed their experiences of climbing the volcano, the most famous being the descriptions by Donnelet, Commerson and Bory de Saint-Vincent.

Although the peak is easily accessible today, it still ranks among the most active volcanoes in the world. Even if it does not pose any immediate danger, it regularly makes its presence felt by venting its smouldering fury in full view of the islanders. Should the volcano or any of its neighbouring craters show signs of erupting during your stay in Réunion, the sheer cliffs provide completely safe observation points from which to watch the action.

An eye-witness account of the 1989 eruption

"3pm: we reach the scene of the eruption. A long fissure has opened up and fountains of solidifying lava spout from three small craters. The overall effect is quite spectacular. Night falls, and with it comes the rain. The clouds are low and the sky is a smouldering red. We warm ourselves beside the cooling lava-flows, while keeping an eye on the glowing molten mass edging its way towards us. At daybreak, we quickly cross the fissure, which, in the meantime, has healed up to leave a steel grey scar, in order to approach and inspect the magma still pouring from the two or three active craters. An indescribable low rumble emanates from within. Billowing clouds of sulphurous fumes force us to recoil. After a few hours, we regretfully leave this magnificent display which continues for a few days..."

An excellent booklet produced by the ONF (Office National des Forêts) lists the varied hiking trails around the volcano with explicit directions illustrated on magnificent aerial photographs.

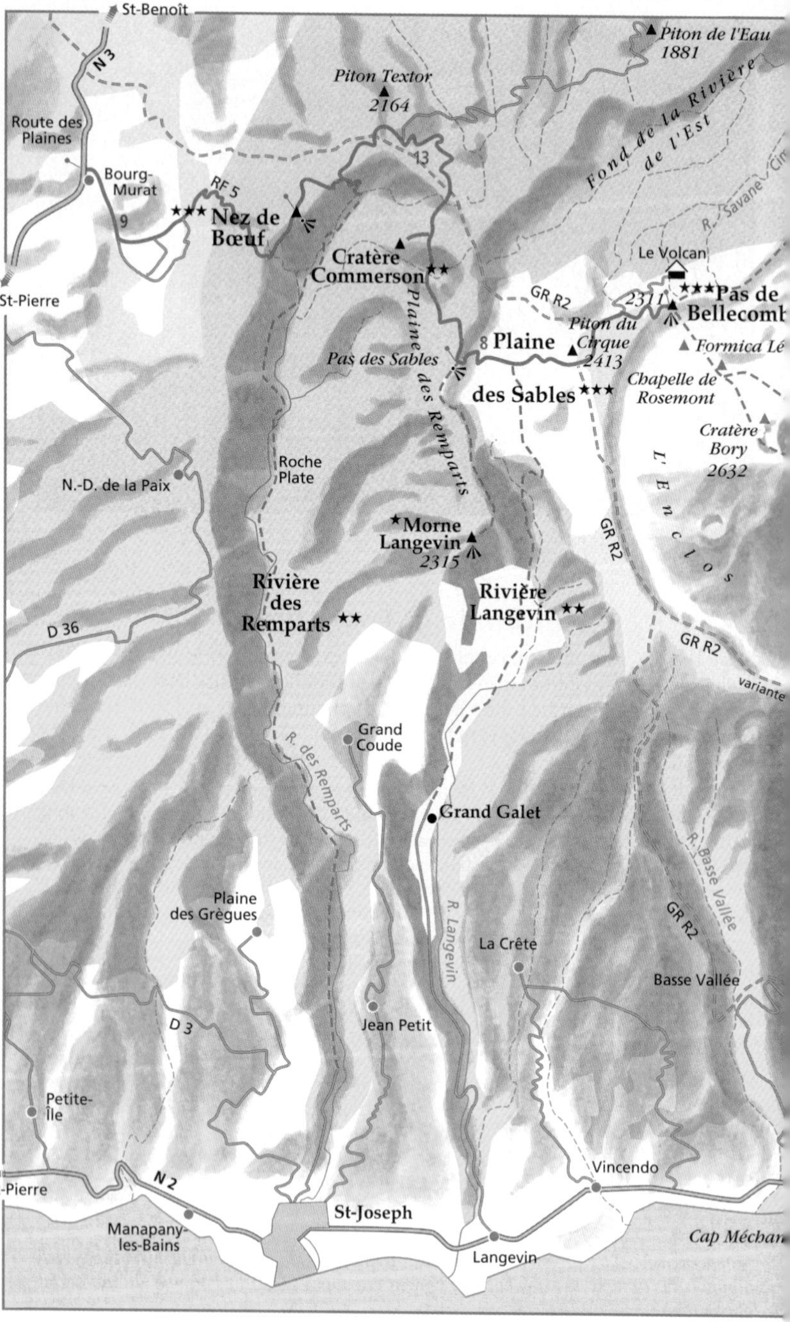

St-Benoît
N 3
Route des Plaines
Bourg-Murat
RF 5
9
★★★ Nez de Bœuf
St-Pierre
Piton Textor 2164
13
Piton de l'Eau 1881
Fond de la Rivière de l'Est
R. Savane Cimetière
Cratère Commerson ★★
Le Volcan
GR R2
2311
★★★ Pas de Bellecombe
Piton du Cirque 2413
8 Plaine des Sables ★★★
Formica Léo
Pas des Sables
Plaine des Remparts
Chapelle de Rosemont
Cratère Bory 2632
L'Enclos
Roche Plate
N.-D. de la Paix
★ Morne Langevin 2315
GR R2
Rivière des Remparts ★★
Rivière Langevin ★★
D 36
GR R2
variante
Grand Coude
R. des Remparts
Grand Galet
R. Basse Vallée
Plaine des Grègues
R. Langevin
La Crête
GR R2
Basse Vallée
D 3
Jean Petit
Petite-Île
Vincendo
St-Pierre
N 2
St-Joseph
Manapany-les-Bains
Langevin
Cap Méchant

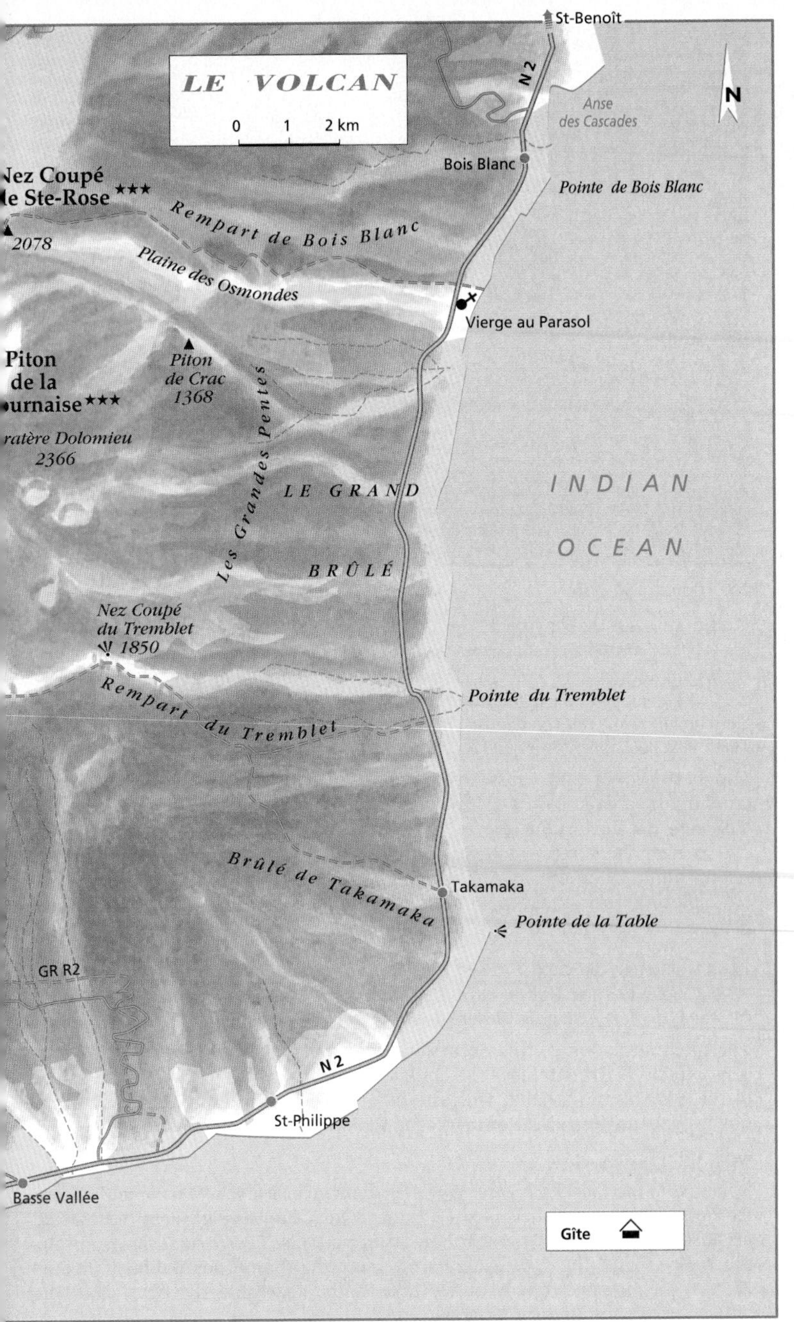
LE VOLCAN
0 1 2 km
St-Benoît
N 2
N
Anse des Cascades
Bois Blanc
Pointe de Bois Blanc
Nez Coupé de Ste-Rose ★★★
Rempart de Bois Blanc
2078
Plaine des Osmondes
Vierge au Parasol
Piton de la Fournaise ★★★
Piton de Crac 1368
Cratère Dolomieu 2366
Les Grandes Pentes
LE GRAND BRÛLÉ
INDIAN OCEAN
Nez Coupé du Tremblet 1850
Rempart du Tremblet
Pointe du Tremblet
Brûlé de Takamaka
Takamaka
Pointe de la Table
GR R2
N 2
St-Philippe
Basse Vallée
Gîte

Y. Arthus-Bertrand/ALTITUDE

The Formica Léo crater

Tour of the volcano★★★

The track begins 600m from the gîte and undertakes a 13km circuit; allow 4.5hr; 430m rise in altitude; medium difficulty. The easier option is to walk up from La Soufrière. It is essential that you take appropriate clothing to protect you from the crippling cold and the scorching sun. You should also carry plenty of water. Keep to the track at all times. Thick mist can come down quickly and the sides of the craters are unstable.

The best-known and most striking hike leaves from **Pas de Bellcombe**, crossing the area known as **L'Enclos** where the two craters, **Formica Léo** and **Chapelle du Rosemont**, are to be found. It then proceeds up two further craters near the summit, known as the **Bory** and the **Dolomieu,** from which strong fumes often emanate. This splendid walk provides a rare opportunity of exploring the landscape for oneself and learning how to differentiate between the different forms of volcanic lava.

Nez Coupé de Ste-Rose★★★

4.3km; 4.5hr there and back; easy. Departure from Pas de Bellecombe. Possibility of extending the hike along the Rivière de L'Est (1hr) or continuing to Bois Blanc (9hr).

The main attraction of this excursion is the phenomenal **view★★★** at the end of the track. Below stretches the contained area known as L'Enclos, the flanks of the the volcano striated with the different petrified flows of lava running down over the **Grandes Pentes** to the **Plaine des Osmondes**.

Morne Langevin★

3.5km; 3.5hr there and back; easy going. Departure from the right of the car park, before the Pas des Sables orientation table. Do not stray from the main path along the Rempart des Sables as the rock may crumble away on the side of the Rivière des Remparts. From the rocky ledge, the view extends out over the **Plaine des Sables**. Once at Morne, the prospect opens out to take in the coast and the deep valley in which nestles the **Rivière Langevin**.

Rivière Langevin**

13km; 6hr one-way; 1 700m rise in altitude; medium difficulty. Departure from the Plaine des Sables. For the return see below: Coming and going.

This magnificent hike follows River Langevin. After crossing the **Plaine des Sables*****, the footpath winds its way into the narrow valley of **Grand Sable** before leading into the broader gorge of **Grand Pays**, where fine views open out over the lush vegetation. At last, the track comes to the village of **Grand Galet**.

Rivière des Remparts**

23km; 6.5hr one-way; 2 000m rise in altitude; medium difficulty. Departure from Nez du Bœuf, a short distance beyond the 8.5km marker.

The descent into the valley of the Rivière des Remparts is beautiful, much longer and far more gradual than the way down to the Langevin River. The most interesting part falls between **Nez de Bœuf** and the **Mahavel** dam, an area in which an especially diverse and unique range of plants are to be found. In winter, hikers can revive their energy levels by plucking and eating guavas along the way in and around the village of **Roche Plate**. A **nearby gîte** provides accommodation for an overnight stay. The protracted descent to St-Joseph continues alongside the sunken stony river bed.

Making the most of Le Volcan

COMING AND GOING

It is important to note that when an eruption is expected to occur in the Enclos region, all access is sealed off. It is still possible, however, to go and watch the volcanic activity from the safety of the cliffs reached by footpath between Nez Coupé de Ste-Rose and Nez Coupé du Tremblet.

By bus – There are no regular bus services to the region. For further advice, check with specialised travel operators and excursion organisers.

By car – The road is well marked. Be careful of thick bands of fog. The last fuel station on the way up is situated at Bourg-Murat. In some cases, it is too complicated and time-consuming to walk back to the point where you have left your vehicle. It is, therefore, advisable to check with a local agent or driver whether you can be met and then driven back to your starting point (further information from the Maison de la Montagne and local tourist information centres).

ADDRESS BOOK

Tourist Information – ***La maison du Volcan***, RN3, Bourg-Murat ☎ 59 00 26.

Banks – Remember to take sufficient amounts of cash.

Post Office – The nearest post offices are situated at Plaine des Cafres and Plaine des Palmistes.

Telephone – The nearest public payphone is in Bourg-Murat. It may also be possible to use the telephone in the gîte du Volcan.

Medical services – see p 158.

Hiking – ***Magma Rando***, Fleurimont, St-Gilles-les-Hauts ☎ 55 72 22/85 94 92. Geneviève Planchard Brave, an exceptionally knowledgeable guide to these parts, takes people around the volcanic area and beyond, in search of the local basalt formations and other interesting geological features.

WHERE TO STAY – WHERE TO EAT

80FF per person per night – 90FF per meal

Gîte du Volcan ☎ 21 28 96 – 60beds ✕ Reservations through La Maison de la Montagne. The gîte is situated on the main road (turn off just before Pas de Bellecombe onto the forestry road on the left). 4-12 bed dormitories, cold showers, but splendid location. Good friendly atmosphere, especially in the groups huddled around the roaring fire in the dining room. The place also provides a good spot for a hearty breakfast while waiting for the weather to clear or for the thick mist to disperse from around the mountain.

LES CIRQUES★★★

SALAZIE – CILAOS – MAFATE

Map p 168-169

Not to be missed

A stroll through Hell-Bourg and a visit to the villa Folio (Salazie).
A drive along the Bélier (Salazie) and Cilaos roads.
An ascent of Piton des Neiges.
A night at La Nouvelle – See the Gouffre des Trois Roches (Mafate).

And remember

Make reservations for staying at a mountain gîte through the Maison de la Montagne, St-Denis.
Enquire after the state of the footpaths.
Be wary of rockfalls along the mountain roads during or after heavy rain.

Standing anywhere on the coast, it is difficult to imagine just how extraordinary are the geological features of the island interior. Only the deep gorges bearing torrential watercourses down to the gently contoured coastline might hint at what lies beyond: lofty cliffs, precipitous ridges, minute and intricate platforms of land so inaccessible as to be unspoilt by man and beast – all preserving a natural wild beauty of their own. Instead of the familiar, saintly names given to the coastal towns, these remote parts have epithets borrowed from Madagascan and African dialects that were brought here by slaves. After the abolition of slavery, the *P'tits Blancs* of modest means migrated to the circus region, intent on rebuilding their lives and enjoying the freedom of self-sufficiency. Nowadays, Mafate is supplied with essential goods by helicopter, and Cilaos has a cinema. Despite this, the local population preserves its own individual identity and the majestic space, the mysterious rivers of Mafate, Salazie and Cilaos are there to be explored in all their splendour on foot, by river or from the air.

CIRQUE DE SALAZIE★★

Allow at least one whole day.

The Cirque de Salazie claims to have registered the largest rainfall in the world: with up to 1 170mm falling in 12 hours, and more than 3m in 72 hours during violent cyclones. This explains the extensive erosion that continuously reshapes the amphitheatre, nurtures the profuse luxuriant vegetation and feeds the great numbers of waterfalls. There are regular downpours throughout the year that sustain the rivers, but towards the end of the wet season they assume truly impressive proportions. In addition to the abundant rain, this amphitheatre receives plenty of sun, making it the greenest of the three circuses and one of the most fruitful.

From the coast, follow the road inland from St-André for 17km to the village of Salazie; a good hour's drive. Coming from St-Denis, turn off the N2 at the 3rd exit on the right (D48).

Route de Salazie★

The Salazie amphitheatre is the most accessible, as the road follows the course of the **Rivière du Mât** through sugarcane plantations and orchards. Then, suddenly, the countryside changes and the cliffs seem to loom forwards, rising to ever loftier heights. The light somehow becomes softer and exaggerates the scale of the relief. A break in the skyline marks the entrance to **Bras de Caverne** from which flows a thundering great waterfall that feeds into the river.

There is little to indicate the entrance to **L'Escalier** save a line of roadside stalls stacked with a selection of mixed fruit and vegetables. After the bridge, the gorges broaden out to reveal the first signs of the circus beyond. In the distance sits **Piton d'Enchaing**, with **Piton des Neiges** breaking the skyline of the far horizon. The road passes rows of fruit trees before snaking its way among small houses and flowering gardens to reach the village of **Salazie**. Continue through the village for an additional 1.5km or so and pull into the lay-by to contemplate the **Voile de la Mariée** ("veil of the bride"). Several **waterfalls** swollen after heavy rains plunge down the sheer rock faces, encouraging the luxuriant vegetation, before disappearing among gardens planted with trellises of *chouchou*.

At the crossroads, continue along the D48 to Hell-Bourg.

■ **Hell-Bourg**★★ – A short distance beyond **Mare à Poule d'Eau**, the road leads up to a village that became famous for its picturesque situation, its climate and its thermal springs – discovered in 1832 and developed in 1852. Before long, residents enjoyed prosperity, and attractive houses mushroomed here and there along the ordered streets. Many of these have weathered well and preserve a somewhat charming old-fashioned look. Little, however, remains of the spa which was largely obliterated by a landslide during a cyclone in 1948. Today, the village continues to attract people in search of the cool mountain air, its serenity and its restfulness.

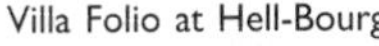

Villa Folio at Hell-Bourg

S. Grandadam/HOA QUI

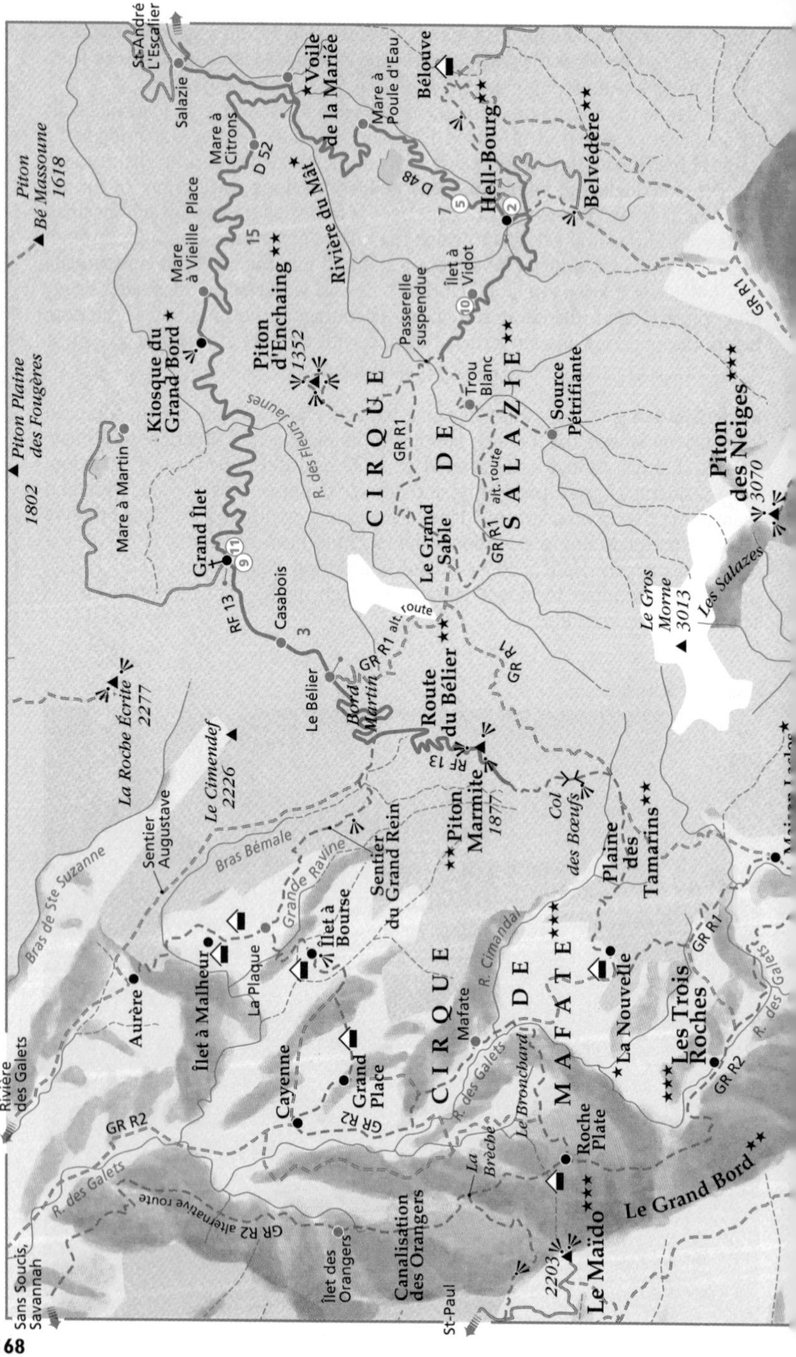

St-André
L'Escalier
Salazie
Voile de la Mariée
Mare à Poule d'Eau
Bélouve
Hell-Bourg
Belvédère
Mare à Citrons
D 52
Rivière du Mât
D 48
Piton Bé Massoune 1618
Mare à Vieille Place
Piton d'Enchaing 1352
Îlet à Vidot
Passerelle suspendue
Kiosque du Grand Bord
Piton Plaine des Fougères 1802
R. des Fleurs Jaunes
CIRQUE DE SALAZIE
Trou Blanc
Source Pétrifiante
GR R1
Piton des Neiges 3070
Mare à Martin
Grand Îlet
Le Grand Sable
alt. route
Casabois
RF 13
Le Gros Morne 3013
Les Salazes
Le Bélier
Bord Martin
Route du Bélier
La Roche Écrite 2277
Le Cimendef 2226
Piton Marmite 1877
Col des Bœufs
Sentier Augustave
Bras Bémale
Sentier du Grand Rein
Plaine des Tamarins
Bras de Ste Suzanne
Grande Ravine
Îlet à Bourse
La Plaque
Îlet à Malheur
Aurère
CIRQUE DE MAFATE
Mafate
R. Cimandal
La Nouvelle
Les Trois Roches
R. des Galets
GR R2
Cayenne
Grand Place
Le Bronchard
La Brèche
Roche Plate
Le Grand Bord
Dos d'Âne, Rivière des Galets
GR R2 alternative route
Canalisation des Orangers
Îlet des Orangers
Le Maïdo 2203
Sans Soucis, Savannah
St-Paul

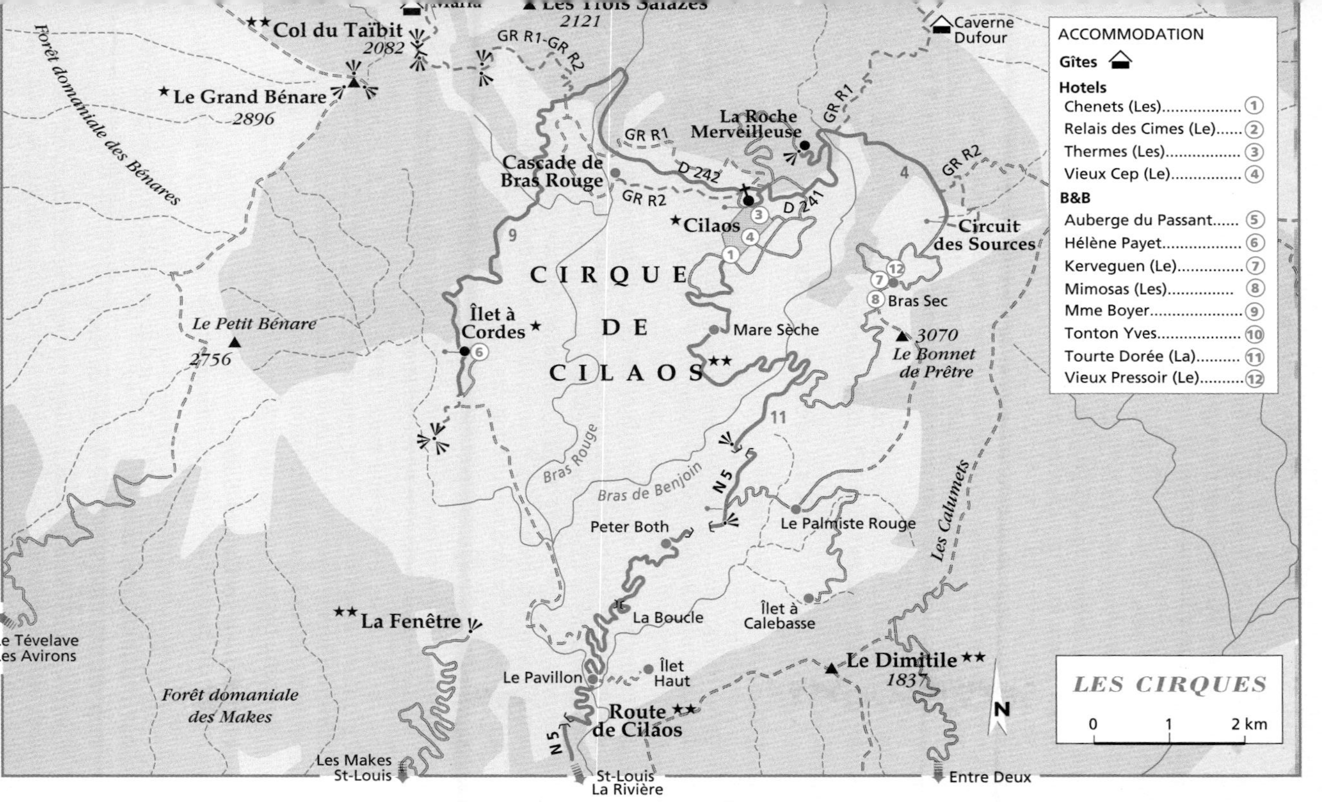
Col du Taïbit
2082
Les Trois Salazes
2121
GR R1-GR R2
Caverne Dufour
Le Grand Bénare
2896
Forêt domaniale des Bénares
Cascade de Bras Rouge
GR R1
GR R2
D 242
D 241
La Roche Merveilleuse
Cilaos
Circuit des Sources
Bras Sec
3070
Le Bonnet de Prêtre
CIRQUE DE CILAOS
Îlet à Cordes
Mare Sèche
Le Petit Bénare
2756
Bras Rouge
Bras de Benjoin
N 5
Peter Both
Le Palmiste Rouge
Les Calumets
La Boucle
Îlet à Calebasse
La Fenêtre
Le Tévelave
Les Avirons
Le Pavillon
Îlet Haut
Le Dimitile
1837
Route de Cilaos
Forêt domaniale des Makes
Les Makes
St-Louis
St-Louis
La Rivière
Entre Deux
N
ACCOMMODATION
Gîtes
Hotels
Chenets (Les) 1
Relais des Cimes (Le) 2
Thermes (Les) 3
Vieux Cep (Le) 4
B&B
Auberge du Passant 5
Hélène Payet 6
Kerveguen (Le) 7
Mimosas (Les) 8
Mme Boyer 9
Tonton Yves 10
Tourte Dorée (La) 11
Vieux Pressoir (Le) 12
LES CIRQUES
0
1
2 km

Each May, the village hosts the **fête du chouchou** a country fete celebrating the rather bland type of gourd that is grown so profusely thereabouts as to become the locality's emblem. A full range of entertainments are laid on, including fun-fair amusements, a merry-go-round, raffles and lucky-dips for children, and large quantities of *chouchou* curry, *chouchou* gratin, *chouchou* salad, *brèdes chouchou* are cooked,up to feed all and sundry. Other *chouchou* by-products – hats, baskets and mats – are also available for sale.

Villa Folio** *(5 rue Amiral Lacaze, opposite the church.* ☎ 47 80 98 *Visits by appointment, 9am-12noon / 2pm-5.30pm. Entrance fee. Allow 60-90min)*, or **Villa des Châtaigniers** as it is also referred to, nestles in a rather overgrown and ramshackle garden full of orchids, camellias, *anthuriums* and azaleas. The owner is only too happy to take visitors around and indulge his passion; you may even be offered a taste of his home-grown citrus fruits at certain times of year. The interior of the house is furnished with a selection of Creole furniture. Outside, an elegant summer house-cum-pavilion houses a collection of traditional musical instruments.
If you continue to the far end of rue Charles de Gaulle, on the left you will see the lovely **guetali** (summer house) belonging to the **Villa Lucilly**.

A choice of walks

Hell-Bourg to Bélouve*

In Hell-Bourg, continue to the top of the main street and turn down the last road on the left; go past the school and take the second left turn, cross the bridge and go left again. The path (10km; 3hr there and back; 580m rise in altitude; medium difficulty) leaves from the designated picnic area.

The footpath follows along the side of the cliff, rising through several bands of vegetation before reaching the forest comprising trees of different coloured woods. A series of kaleidoscopic views punctuate the climb up to the gîte de Bélouve *(see below* Where to stay), although for the prime sight of the amphitheatre you have to walk on up to the **belvedere****, 15min south of Hell-Bourg (in the direction of Piton des Neiges).

Hell-Bourg to Source Pétrifiante*

Follow the asphalt road out of Hell-Bourg to Îlet à Vidot and park the car there. 6km trail; 5hr there and back; 200m up rise in altitude; medium difficulty.

Set out from **Îlet à Vidot** and make for the path on the left heading off to Trou Blanc. When you reach the junction with the GR R1, fork left. To reach the actual spring, which lies hidden within an underground cave, you have to lie on the ground and squeeze through a narrow gap. Once inside, make for the reddish concretions left by the water as it oozes through the rock.

Hell-Bourg to Grand Sable*

Depart from Îlet à Vidot (see above). 18km circuit; 6hr; 300m rise in altitude; medium difficulty.

Continue straight along the track at the end of the asphalt road, turning down the second footpath on the left. The first challenge is to make it across the suspended footbridge over the **Rivière du Mât***.

This takes you to **Grand Sable**, a village that was tragically engulfed, complete with its local residents when part of Gros Morne collapsed. At this point, you have the choice of continuing along the GR R1 southwest *(4-5hr; fairly difficult)* to the Cirque de Mafate and **La Nouvelle**, or northwest along the GR R1 *(2hr)* to **Bélier**. Alternatively, you can simply return to Hell-Bourg by completing the Grand Sable circuit via **Trou Blanc**.

Piton d'Enchaing*

Leave from Îlet à Vidot (see above). Cross the footbridge; at the junction, turn right along the GR R1 (10km; 4-5hr; 760m rise in altitude; medium difficulty). The track winds its way up through mature casuarinas which, as the climb becomes progressively steeper, give way to indigenous hardwoods. From the flat clearing at the top, a fabulous **panorama**** pans through 360° to embrace the whole circus-bowl and the surrounding ridge of peaks, masked here and there by the encroaching dense vegetation.

Freeman Enchaing

Piton d'Enchaing is named after a runaway slave, who, with his wife, fled to the mountain after managing to escape exploitation by his cruel masters. Up there, where he could keep a lookout without being seen, he was able to live with his partner and their numerous children for nigh on 25 years, until a slave-hunter succeeded in flushing the family out. Nobody will ever know with certainty what befell Enchaing. According to hearsay, he was transformed into a bird that disappeared over the horizon to sunnier climes.

Head along the D48 leaving Hell-Bourg behind and fork left along the D52.

Route de Grand Îlet*

On the far side of Mare à Vieille Place, there is a designated area by the **Kiosk du Grand Bord*** from which one can contemplate the great **ridge above the Plaine des Fougères** that encloses the amphitheatre on the northern side. A succession of peaks extends into the far distance, on which sits the imposing mass of **Roche Écrite**. The view east bristles with lines of hills that lead the eye towards Mafate, beyond the distinctively pointed form of **Cimendef**. After leading over the **Rivière des Fleurs Jaunes**, the road wends its sinuous way to the very heart of **Grand Îlet**, a large village populated essentially by stock farmers, centred around the striking wood-boarded **Church of St-Martin***.

Make your way back to the RF13 at the entrance to Grand Îlet, on the left.

Route du Bélier**

This itinerary cuts through the villages of Casabois and Bélier follows along the edge of Bord Martin to arrive at **Piton Marmite**, the highest point on the ridge separating Salazie from Mafate. The badly potholed, stone-covered track is hard work, although the **extensive views**** it provides are quite extraordinary: in certain places, the prospect embraces both amphitheatres. An **orientation table** beside the car park identifies the main elements making up the relief before it. From this point, it is possible to walk through the **Col des Bœufs** and all the way to the village of **La Nouvelle**, which nestles in the Cirque de Mafate: this is in fact the easiest way into Mafate *(see p 175)*.

CIRQUE DE CILAOS**

Allow at least one whole day.

Cilaos is blessed with all the attributes that inspire poets and painters: a dramatic skyline, vertiginous cliffs, subtle light, great space and awe-inspiring scenery. Furthermore, the local population courteously welcomes strangers curious enough to seek out the traditional attributes of the region – lentils, wine and embroidery – or partake of the invigorating spa waters.

A haven from persecution

The first people to settle in the circus were runaway slaves in need of a secluded and remote sanctuary where they might settle with their wives and children. There, they formed individual communities and survived on hunting and growing their own food. Occasionally, they might venture down to the lowland plains to collect seed and other staple necessities or to steal tools and timber. Each village became quite extensive, comprising some fifty or sixty families, and, being extremely close-knit, all other settlers were repudiated. At last, in the mid-18C, various brutal mercenaries were charged with rounding up the rebels: an operation which resulted in the extermination of several hundred former slaves. The area, having been "cleared", attracted a small band of *P'tits Blancs,* who set about completing three decisive projects: to drain the Cilaos plateau, to develop the potential offered by the natural springs and to build a major means of access.

Leave the coast at St-Louis and head inland (north) along the N5: 36km; allow 90min-2hr.

Route de Cilaos★★

The road to Cilaos, which opened in 1932, is a great technical feat of engineering as the relatively short stretch (30km) between Rivière St-Louis and the village of Cilaos (1 200m above sea level) includes some 350 bends. Do exercise great care when driving: use the horn before blind corners, approach narrow sections slowly, and keep a look out for fallen scree and other debris littering the road. Les Hauts de St-Louis marks the entrance to the **Bras de Cilaos**, a deep valley lined with rock cliffs that loom ever higher as one approaches the circus. On emerging from the second tunnel, you find yourself mid-way up the rock face with a fine **view★** to the Calumets ridge opposite.

The road enters one last tunnel before coming out at the very heart of the amphitheatre in the middle of the most staggering landscape. Below runs the sunken course of the **Bras de Benjoin**; on the left, rise the serrated hills masking **Îlet à Cordes**; straight ahead stretches the **Mare Sèche** plateau overlooked by the proud mass of **Piton des Neiges**.

A short while later, you reach the village of Cilaos.

■ **Cilaos★** – The inhospitable nature of the region, exacerbated by the great quantities of stagnating rainwater that collected there, forced the first inhabitants to settle on the periphery of the plateau. It was not until much later that the marshy site was successfully drained and rendered fit for habitation. Slowly, the village began to take shape and acquire a favourable reputation due to its clean air, cool climate during the scorching summer months, and spring-water. The amenities for taking the waters remained primitive in the extreme until 1897, when a **Doctor Mac Auliffe** opened a new spa complete with proper facilities. The doctor continued thereafter to play an important role in further developing Cilaos.

The **high street**, leading straight to the spa, is the busiest part of town, where the nicest shops, a scattering of hotels and restaurants and the tourist office are to be found.

It is well worth stopping at the **thermal baths** *(8bis route de Bras Sec ☎ 31 72 27, Fax 31 76 57. Appointment essential. Daily, 8am-12noon/2pm-6pmSunday, 9am-5pm; closed Wednesday afternoons)*. There is nothing like a relaxing bit of pampering after a good hydro-massage and/or sauna to relieve those aching joints!

J.-F. Galmiche

The Petit Séminaire, Cilaos

Further on sits the **church** overlooking part of the plateau and the **Petit Séminaire** tucked in behind. The small seminary is a wholly Creole institution, built entirely of wood and ornamented with turrets and decorative details. Although now deserted, it was long used as a college for educating priests and the children of privileged families. Former French Prime Minister, Raymond Barre, was once a pupil here.

The **Maison de la Broderie*** *(4 rue des Écoles ☎ 31 77 48. Open Monday to Saturday, 9am-12noon / 2pm-5pm; Sundays and holidays, 9.30am-12noon. Entrance fee)* collects and displays the traditional embroidery of the area known as **"Jours de Cilaos"**: a meticulous craft introduced to the community by the doctor's daughter, Adèle Mac Auliffe. Prices are indicative of the time taken to make it: a sheet, for example, might involve one to two months of work.

The other local highly regarded speciality, the wine of Cilaos, can be tasted at the **Maison du Vin** *(34 rue des Glycines ☎ 31 71 69. Daily, 8am-12noon / 2pm-4pm except Sunday afternoons when it closes at 12noon. Entry charge includes tasting. Tour of the cellars: enquire at the Cilaos information centre ☎ 31 73 06)*. Until recently, wine was produced on a small scale using grapes from a variety called **Isabelle**; now it is a major speciality in the Cirque. Popular belief used to claim it addled the brain, but try a glass anyway, out of curiosity. Growers have recently planted better quality vines, which now produce much better-tasting wines.

At the crossroads before the baths, turn left along the D242.

■ **Îlet à Cordes** – *Allow about 90min to get there along the tortuous road, completed in 1972, which should not be used during heavy rain.*

The land around this tiny hill village was conceded in the 19C to a freed slave. Since then the locals have grown and marketed their **Cilaos lentils**. From the southern-most edge of the village, splendid **views**** extend over the whole amphitheatre.

A choice of walks

The Cirque de Cilaos is open to walkers of all calibres. You can complete a hike that takes in all the villages and then return by bus (details and timetables available from the tourist office). During the rainy season, it is best to avoid itineraries with fords across streams and rivers. Although the water in the various secluded pools along the way tends to be rather cold, you may like to take a swimming costume in case you are tempted to swim. The list of hikes below is far from exhaustive.

Cascade de Bras Rouge*

The track departs from the Maison de la Montagne de Cilaos (GR R2; 4km; 2.5hr there and back; 150m rise in altitude; fairly easy).

At one time, this was the path the porters used to take to the **old baths** *(anciens thermes)*, where it is still possible to bathe and unwind in the hot, iron-rich water. If you continue along the track, you come to a lovely spot with a **waterfall**, where it is dangerous to swim.

Col du Taïbit**

Follow the road to Îlet à Codes (D242) from Cilaos for 5km and park the car beside the designated picnic area. The footpath is signposted, leading off to the right (GR R1-GR R2; 8km; 4hr there and back; 800m rise in altitude; medium difficulty). Be warned, it is extremely windy at the top.

The first uphill section is shaded by trees of different coloured hardwood that soon give way to a forest of pines and eucalyptus. A flat clearing with a little stream provides a convenient place for a pause. The track then climbs even steeper than before to take you to the **Plaine des Fraises,** from where a wonderful broad **view**** opens out on Cilaos on the one side and to Trois Salazes on the other. A final haul brings you to the **Col du Taïbit** pass. From here, the **panorama**** unfurls. To the south lies Îlet à Cordes, the Cirque de Cilaos with its narrow entrance and then in the far distance, the sea. Northwards the view sweeps down across the Cirque de Mafate to which it is possible to walk down a fairly steep slope through sweet-smelling mimosas *(approx 45min to Marla;* *see p 176**).*

Piton des Neiges***

Head out of Cilaos towards Bras Sec along the D241, and leave the car in the car park. 8km (GR R1); 8hr there and back; 1 700m rise in altitude; difficult.

This highly popular excursion on foot – coupled with the one to Piton de la Fournaise – provide particularly marvellous **viewpoints***** from which to survey the scenery. The overall experience is further heightened if you manage to make it to the summit in time to watch the sun rise, and watch the landscape gently shake itself awake in the magical morning light that is so clear at this altitude.

The hike is completed in two stages. The first more arduous section *(so allow 4hr)*, involves a climb of 1 100m over the short distance between the Bras Sec road to the **Caverne Dufour** *(gîte, see below:* Where to stay). As you climb in altitude, the trees thin out and the vegetation becomes more sparse and scraggly. The second stage to **Piton des Neiges** is less steep (590m change in height) but nonetheless quite tough given that much of the pull is up loose volcanic rubble and **scoria**. The vegetation peters out altogether and the landscape assumes a bleak austerity relieved in part by the changing hues among the black, brown and orange volcanic rocks. In the depth of winter, all the surfaces are further encased in a fragile layer of ice crystals. From the island's tallest point, a **panoramic view***** spans 360° across the most wonderful, varied and unique prospect.

Circuit des Sources

After the baths, turn down the D241 and leave Cilaos behind you. Just before the village of Bras Sec, turn left. Leave the car by the sports centre and follow the footpath on the left (2.5km circuit; 90min; 50m rise in altitude; easy walking).

Before long, the *cryptomeria* trees give way to a rich variety of coloured hardwoods. **Water** tumbling down the rocks makes the place pleasantly cool. Gaps in the thick undergrowth allow one a fleeting glimpse of the amphitheatre beyond. At the junction with the GR R2, turn left. This takes you back through the cryptomerias and down to the main road (D241).

Cirque de Mafate★★★

Allow a minimum of 2-3 days.

The first people to come to live in Mafate arrived in and around 1783 and settled in the region of **Aurère**. Before long, the new residents fell foul of the **Office National des Forêts** (National Forestry Commission), which intended to preserve the area from the systematic deforestation being wrought elsewhere. These conflicts continued until the 1950s, when efforts were streamlined into safeguarding the natural environment and developing its potential in parallel with subsidising improvements in local living conditions. The principal sources of income are today derived from farming (arable and stock); a proportion of the residents, ironically, work for the ONF! In recent years, investments have been underpinning the infrastructure for various mountain and leisure activities, as the proliferation of tourism-related buildings would indicate. Despite such initiatives, this isolated natural enclave, only accessible by helicopter or on foot, continues to be wracked by major financial and social problems.

A hiker's paradise

Mafate remains a perfectly preserved haven for all those who enjoy walking the 180km of well-maintained footpaths. The locals are natural walkers and are to be seen either barefoot or wearing ropy old shoes, carrying huge loads on their back, scampering up even the challenging slopes without hesitation, gently mocking the slow progress of another in his/her passing.

Solar-powered telephone at La Nouvelle

M. Lemerle/MICHELIN

The first impression of Mafate will depend entirely on whether it is approached from the east or from the west. Interestingly enough, the circus can claim to have two microclimates separated by an imaginary north-south dividing line running between **Bras de Ste-Suzanne** and **Col du Taïbit**. The eastern side is well watered and so is covered with luxuriant vegetation and forest. The west, meanwhile, consists of arid slopes tufted with low-lying scrub, deeply scarred by erosion. There are seven "gateways" into Mafate and twenty or so itineraries detailed in the excellent ONF guide *(Cirque de Mafate – Découverte et Randonnées,* Encrages Édition). Only a small selection of the more popular excursions will be listed here.

You must reserve overnight accommodation and meals through La Maison de la Montagne several days before setting out. You will find grocery / general stores in almost all villages.

Col des Bœufs to La Nouvelle**

Drive up through the Cirque de Salazie following directions for Grand Îlet (D52), and Bélier (see p 171). Thereafter, continue along the RF13 to the last car park from where the path leaves. 8km; 4hr there and back; 400m rise in altitude; easy.

This option is the most direct (shortest and easiest) route to Mafate. A track climbs (1.5km) to the **Col des Bœufs**, the so-called frontier between Salazie and Mafate. From the far side of the pass, a fine **view*** stretches towards Mafate and the lofty Maïdo cliff face. The track then snakes its way down through the huge forest of the **Plaine des Tamarins****. See how the trees have grown twisted trunks in their attempts to reach the light. The hair-like moss – known as St Antony's beard – hanging from the tall branches add to the fantastical nature of the place. You half expect the mist to swirl down and elves to jump out. Instead, all you hear is the crunching sound of a few reddish cows grazing peaceably nearby.

■ **La Nouvelle*** – The largest community in the Mafate region founded its village on a vast plateau of land in the second half of the 19C. For more than a century, its inhabitants subsisted on home-grown produce, almost entirely cut-off from the outside world, save a handful of ONF employees. In 1848 a school was set up; in 1976 a chapel was built. At the close of the 20C, the thirty or so families living there rely on regular supplies delivered by helicopter. Every need is provided, for the village boasts a number of gîtes and small restaurants, various general stores, a bakery and a small timber-boarded **chapel**. There is even an incongruous-looking solar-powered public **telephone**! All the while, the perspective of this Surrealist scene is dramatically foreshortened by the massive bulk of the **Grand Bénare** and the **Maïdo** looming behind.

La Nouvelle to Marla*

GR R1; 5.2km; approx 2hr one way; deceptively flat; easy going. The footpath heads out from south of the village, runs downhill and into a glade of casuarinas. At the intersection, fork left and carry on across the **Rivière des Galets** *(footbridge)*. Eventually you come upon a lovely spot known as **Maison Laclos*** in its pastoral setting close to the **Ravine Kerval** and **Ravine de Marla**, where you might be tempted to swim. From there, a short *(30min)* uphill stretch takes you up to Marla.

J. du Boisberranger/HEMISPHERES

Cirque de Mafate

■ **Marla** – The population of the village has now dwindled to some ten or so households eking their living from growing lentils and grazing stock. It the past, however, this – the highest village in the region (1 6454m) – ranked among the area's more important communities. On the western side looms the tall mass of **Grand Bénare** (2 896m). To the east, meanwhile, rises the ridge bristling with the three huge basalt outcrops (laid bare by erosion) called the **Trois Salazes**** that mark the boundary between the Cirque de Mafate and the Cirque de Cilaos. Watch them as the sun goes down, glinting in the evening light as if they were made of burnished bronze.

Marla to Col du Taïbit*

2.5km; 1hr one way; 500m rise in altitude (see p 174).

Marla to Roche Plate**

GR R2, 11km, 4hr, fairly easy. The track from the gîte heads northwestwards across the Marla plateau before dropping down over a section of scoria to the **Rivière des Galets**. Wade across the ford and turn down along the river to **Trois Roches*****. The splendid chasm down which the water gushes is so called because of the three rocks counterbalanced on the bank *(beware of slipping over the wet stones)*. The path continues to lead from one ravine to the next, ducking and diving towards and then away from the **Rempart de Grand Bord****, before gently descending down towards the *îlet* of **Roche Plate**, clinging tentatively to the steep scree and rubble fallen from the Maïdo escarpment anchored to firmer soil by casuarinas. The conditions on this side of the circus are dry and arid, as the stunted and scraggly vegetation will testify.

Only twenty or so families live here now, supported by small-scale market-gardening, a small collection of animals and tourism.

Route du Maïdo to Roche Plate*

Accessible by car from the west coast. Follow directions along the Maido road (see p 109) to the PR11, parking the car shortly after the ravine Divon. Take the track that leads left (7.5km; 2.5hr; 750m rise in altitude; medium difficulty).

This rather steep and therefore fairly arduous route up to Mafate is rewarded by the wonderful panoramic **view**** from the top. The track starts off by entering a forest of tamarind trees and continues across scrubland covered with gorse. 500m further on, the track comes to an abrupt end at the edge of a gaping abyss. Thereafter, you make your way carefully down the length of the dry escarpment to arrive at **Brèche**. Before venturing further, turn right and continue through the cultivated fields to Roche Plate.

Canalisation des Orangers

Accessible by car from the west coast. Follow the dual carriageway out of St-Paul (see p 106), turning off at Savannah and continuing along the RD4 towards La Plaine. Pick up directions for Sans Souci. The path is signposted left (GR R2 alternative; 22km to Roche Plate; 7hr; false ridge, easy).

This footpath, running along a narrow ledge cut into the Rivière des Galets cliffside, provides a dramatic perspective over the tortured relief of the landscape around the circus. Although long, this route makes for a pleasant walk.

Roche Plate to Cayenne*

GR R2; 9km; 4hr; 450m drop followed by 450m rise in altitude; difficult, with some stretches requiring particular care: check the conditions of the path before setting out.

At first, this route promises to be easy going, but soon the track tips steeply down the **Rempart du Bronchard**, to the point of being precarious in places, down into a great **canyon****. Here, the **Rivière des Galets** runs its course along a narrow gully where it has managed to erode away the bedrock. In the area of **Mafate**, a number of ruins mark the site of some former spa complex. Once again, the path loses itself in the canyon, crossing the river in two places before winding alongside an escarpment and reaching **Cayenne**.
The one-time fashion for "taking the waters" at Mafate, despite their sulphurous content, secured the fame and fortune of the village. Once easy access to the springs had been assured, the village expanded and became increasingly popular. Today, it continues to be one of the largest and most populated villages in the region.

From Cayenne, a path leads to Grand Place.

Grand Place to Aurère**

10km; approx 5hr; 200m rise in altitude; medium difficulty. This hike, probably more than any other, shows up the radical differences between the two sides of the amphitheatre in terms of landscape and vegetation. The greatest contrast is apparent from the small ridge overlooking Grand Place, when the relief becomes less jagged and the flora more luxuriant. The next village, **Îlet à Bourse,** an attractively green place, also enjoys splendid **views**** over the circus. The footpath then heads steeply down into the **Grand Ravine** and up the other side before levelling out again as it heads towards the unfortunate-sounding **Îlet à Malheur**, which was so named after a bloody episode in the hunt for fugitive slaves. A last pull takes you up to the village of **Aurère** that sits at an altitude of over 900m.

From Aurère, one can walk all the way to the western coast by following the course of the **Rivière des Galets** *(16km; approx 5.5hr. 250m drop in altitude; reasonably straight forward).*

Aurère to Salazie**

From Aurère, head southwards towards Îlet à Malheur. On reaching the intersection at La Plaque, turn down the track on the left known as the **sentier du Grand Rein**, or **sentier Scout**, which continues to Bord Martin *(6km; approx 3hr; 200m change in altitude; fairly easy)*. The only challenge on this hike is the 600m climb at the beginning. After that, you emerge on the Grand Rein ridge from where there is an expansive **view**** over the amphitheatre with, in the far distance and through the gap, the town of Le Port. The path continues down towards **Bras Bémale**, and up through thick undergrowth to come out at **Bord Martin** on the border with the Cirque de Salazie.

Making the most of Les Cirques

Getting there

By car – There are only two fuel stations, at Salazie and Cilaos. If you plan to walk to Mafate via Salazie and the Col des Boeufs, do not leave your vehicle for more than a day in a car park. Entrust it rather to Mr Noury, ***"Chez Titine"*** in Bélier ☎ 47 71 84. Estimate US$7 per night per vehicle – this includes a lift up to the pass. Cost of transfer there and back for 5-8 persons: US$40.

By bus – Services in operation to Salazie from the bus station at St-André (☎ 46 80 00): Monday to Saturday, 7 departures between 6.10am-5.45pm; Sundays and public holidays, 3 departures. 30min journey time.
Services to Cilaos from the bus station in St-Pierre (☎ 35 67 28): Monday to Saturday, 8 departures between 8am-5.15pm; Sundays and public holidays, 4 departures. 1hr 40min journey time. 8 services also out of St-Louis.
Within the circus localities: buses from Salazie to Hell-Bourg and Grand Îlet; from Cilaos to Bars Sec and Palmiste Rouge.

Private minibus – ***Rando Trans*** ☎ 55 52 66. 8-seater minibus shuttles to St-Gilles-les-Bains. Expensive (US$130 for Cilaos, US$155 for Salazie).

On foot – Access to Salazie: from Mafate via the Col des Bœufs or Bord Martin; from Cilaos via Caverne Dufour (GR R1); from Roche Écrite.
Access to Cilaos: from Mafate by the Col du Taïbit.
Access to Mafate: from Salazie by the Col des Bœufs or Bord Martin; from Cilaos by the Col du Taïbit; from St-Paul by the Canalisation des Orangers (Sans Souci) or by the Maïdo.

Address book

Tourist information – ***Syndicat d'initiative de Salazie***, CD48, Pont de l'Escalier, ☎ 47 50 14, Fax 47 60 07. Tuesday-Friday, 9am-3pm; Sunday 9am-11am. Information on hiking and accommodation.
Pays d'Accueil de Salazie, Hell-bourg Craft Centre, rue du Général de Gaulle, Hell-bourg, ☎ 47 89 89, Fax 47 88 67. Monday-Friday, 8am-4pm, weekends, 9.30am-12noon/2pm-3.30pm. Information and a few exhibitions.
Office du tourisme de Cilaos, 2bis rue Mac Auliffe, Cilaos ☎ 31 78 03. Open Monday to Saturday, 8.30am-12.30pm/1.30pm-5.30pm; Sunday and public holidays, 9am-1pm.
Maison de la montagne de Cilaos, same address as above ☎ 31 71 71. Monday-Saturday, 8.30am-12.30pm/1.30pm-5.30pm, Sundays and bank holidays, 9am-1pm. All available information on footpaths and other outdoor activities, booking service and advice on accommodation / board.
Pays d'accueil de Cilaos ☎ 31 73 06. Organises "introductory" sessions for visitors with an excursion on foot to Roche Merveilleuse, a visit to the hot springs, the Maison de la Broderie and the Cilaos wine-cellars (50FF per person).

Banks and money – Take sufficient amounts of cash with you: few if any hotels/restaurants accept payment by creditcard. There are no banks at Salazie nor at Mafate; there is one bank and a cash-dispenser/ATM at the post office in the village of Cilaos.

Post office – 59 rue Georges Pompidou, Salazie; 31 rue du Général de Gaulle, Hell-Bourg; 76 rue du Père Boiteau, Cilaos.

Telephone – Facilities also available at a number of hostels. A few public call-boxes (taking phone cards) at Salazie, Hell-Bourg and Cilaos. In the Cirque de Mafate, you will find a solar-powered public telephone at La Nouvelle.

Bicycle hire – ***Mountain Bike***, 48 rue du Père Boiteau, Cilaos ☎ 31 81 95.

Medical services – ***Chemists***: 73 rue Georges Pompidou, Salazie ☎ 47 50 82; rue du Général de Gaulle, Hell-Bourg ☎ 47 80 31; Chemin Départemental de Grand Îlet, Grand Îlet ☎ 47 72 13; 47 and 58 rue du Père Boiteau, Cilaos ☎ 31 77 56 / 31 70 41.
Doctors: Dr Corre (☎ 31 71 72); Dr Jarre (☎ 31 82 18), Dr Techner (☎ 31 71 30) at Cilaos. Dr Rakotovelo (☎ 47 54 04) at Salazie. Surgery at Hell-Bourg (☎ 47 80 51) and at Salazie (☎ 47 53 74).

Where to stay

Unless stated otherwise (in the case for hostels and gîtes), the prices listed are calculated on the basis of two people in a double room with breakfast.

• Cirque de Salazie

US$15-30

Chambres d'hôtes chez Mme Boyer, Chemin de Camp Pierrot, Grand Îlet ☎ 47 71 62, Fax 47 73 34 – 5rm Creole-style house overlooking Grand Îlet. All modern conveniences and spotlessly clean. Informal welcome, meals on request. Excellent value for money.

Chambres d'hôtes la Tourte Dorée, chez Mme Grondin, rue du Père Joanno, Grand Îlet ☎ 47 70 51 (advance booking recommended) – 6rm This large house offers two standards of room. Opt for the simply furnished, more spacious rooms upstairs with private bathrooms rather than the sad and gloomy but cheaper rooms on the ground floor. Pleasant setting in a colourful garden with view of the mountains. Nice welcome. Excellent food (see below: Where to eat).

US$30-45

Chez Tonton Yves, Îlet at Vidot, Hell-bourg, ☎ 47 84 22 – 3rm This recent, slightly elevated house offers cosy, comfortable rooms. The cooking is creative, original and excellent: boudin Creole, rabbit escalope, duck in orange, chicken cari and dessert etc, all at very reasonable prices.

Auberge du Passant, Chez Mme Grondin, rue du Stade, Hell-bourg, ☎ 47 86 28 – 3rm The rooms are located in the main house and in a much prettier little Creole case, which is more secluded and quieter. The owner's enthusiasm and warmth rarely fails to win over guests.

US$45-60

Le Relais des Cimes, rue du Général de Gaulle, Hell-Bourg ☎ 47 81 58, Fax 47 82 11 – 17rm TV CC Sauna. Choose between staying in the comfortable rooms in the annexe or in the noisier but ever so charming rooms in the main house. Excellent food (see below: Where to eat).

• Cirque de Cilaos

US$15-30

Gîte de la Caverne Dufour ☎ 51 15 26 (book in advance). This far from spotless hostel only has the most basic facilities – no running water or toilets. Its one redeeming feature is its situation, providing a convenient place for a kip during your climb to the top of Roche Écrite early the next morning in time to watch the sun rise.

Chambres d'hôtes le Kerveguen, chez Doris Flavie, 8 chemin Matharum, Bras Sec ☎ 31 71 23 – 2rm (evening meals only, by prior arrangement). 1.5km from Cilaos. This newly built house perches on the side of the mountain and so enjoys fine views over the valley below. Immaculately kept rooms. Shared toilet facilities. Particularly warm welcome extended by your host who will be only too pleased to recommend what to see and where to walk in the circus. Excellent food cooked over a woodfire.

Les Mimosas, chez Jean-Paul Benoît and Mimose Dijoux, 29 Chemin Saùl, Bras Sec, ☎ 25 31 72 – 4rm This flowery Creole case, covered in orchids out of the garden of Eden, is a very pleasant halting place. Classical, clean, calm rooms. The cooking is done in the next-door 'boucan' (shed): goose stew or pork and chouchou cari. Traditional and excellent.

Chambres d'hôtes Le Vieux Pressoir, chez Christian Dijoux, 40 chemin Saul, Bras Sec ☎ 25 56 64 – 5rm Small modern country house in a peaceful setting 6km north of Cilaos. Genuine welcome on arrival from owner, who is happy to provide tours and tastings of his wine-making operation. Good home-cooked food.

Chambres d'hôtes chez Hélène Payet, 13 chemin Terre Fine, Îlet à Cordes ☎ 35 18 13 – 2rm Small and well-cared-for Creole house with verandah in a fabulous location, within a remote little hamlet, 12km northwest of the village of Cilaos. Small but comfortable rooms. Warm and convivial atmosphere. Good local cooking (see below: Where to eat).

US$45-60

Le Vieux Cep, 2 rue des Trois Mares, Cilaos ☎ 31 71 89, Fax 31 77 68 – 55rm TV CC This newly built establishment benefits from a tranquil setting, surrounded by greenery. Architecturally designed in the vernacular style, all facilities are essentially arranged around the swimming pool. Some rooms, complete with private balcony, benefit from a lovely view over the mountains, notably Piton des Neiges. Obliging staff eager to ensure guests enjoy their stay.

Over US$75
Hôtel des Thermes, 8 rue des Sources, Cilaos ☎ 31 89 00, Fax 31 74 73 – 28rm This rather old-fashioned hotel overlooks the Cilaos plateau. Courteous staff. Rooms are spacious and comfortable, those situated at the front of the building enjoy fine views over the whole town. The interior decoration dates from the 1970s and could do with freshening up. Nonetheless, the place exudes an endearingly civilised atmosphere.
Les Chenets, 40 E Chemin des Trois Mares, ☎ 31 85 85, Fax 31 87 17 – 17rm The first grand hotel of the Upper Plains region, with piano-bar, hammam, sauna, internet and conference room. The colourful rooms with design furniture are each individually decorated and the service is impeccable. Ideal to relax in the mountains, whilst enjoying the comfort of a prestigious establishment.

• Cirque de Mafate

Reserve your overnight stays in the mountain hostels through the Maison de la Montagne at St-Denis (☎ 90 78 78, Fax 41 84 29) or at Cilaos (☎ 31 71 71). Meals should be arranged directly with the gîte concerned. Irrespective of which hostel you choose, budget between US$7-15 per person per night, plus US$3-5 per person for breakfast, and US$10-15 per person for dinner. Enquire about staying with a local family as a paying guest.
Maxime Oréo, La Nouvelle ☎ 43 58 57 – 14 beds Attractive private hostel, open fires and candle-lighting. Excellent cari and warm reception.
L'Arbre du Voyageur, La Plaque, ☎ 43 50 60/34 87 70 – 6rm Reservations only. Only recently opened, this establishment is composed of several little kiosks built in a large park. The rooms, that can sleep six people, are very clean. Tents can be rented or you can pitch your own for a moderate price. The owner, known as the Hermit, is one of the region's characters and is well worth getting to know. Meals are prepared on request. Library available.
Hoareau Expedit, Marla ☎ 43 78 31 – 19 beds Very hospitable private hostel. Good food.
Gîte Giroday, Marla ☎ 43 83 13 – 32 beds Private hostel with complement of facilities, including cold showers and exterior toilets.
Gîte de M Thiburce, Roche Plate ☎ 43 60 01 – 24 beds Private hostel. Dining hall 10min walk away. No alcohol.
Chez M Guy Libel, Îlet à Malheur ☎ 43 56 96 – 20 beds Fabulous private gîte: brand new, well designed and comfortable.
Gîte de montagne, Cayenne-Grand-Place ☎ 43 85 42 – 16 beds Fine, bright hostel situated on a tongue of land, with good prospect over circus and Rivière des Galets. Good meals.
Gite de montagne, Îlet à Bourse ☎ 43 43 93 – 16 beds Comfortable, convivial atmosphere.

WHERE TO EAT

• Cirque de Salazie

US$7-15
Les Lilas, 9 rue Georges Pompidou, Salazie ☎ 47 52 04. Lunch; dinner by arrangement. Attractive Creole house situated in the village itself. Warm welcome. The owner will not fail to have you tasting his home-cured charcuterie.
Ferme-auberge la Tourte dorée, chez Mme Grondin, rue du Père Jouanno, Grand Îlet ☎ 47 70 51 (book in advance). Lunch and dinner. Closed Wednesday lunchtimes and Sunday evening. Wonderful range of house delicacies prepared exclusively using home-produced ingredients. Definitely worth investigating. An excellent recommendation.
Chez Alice, chemin Sanglier, Hell-Bourg ☎ 47 86 24. Lunch and dinner; closed Thursday evenings and all day Mondays. Mouth-watering house specialities include locally fished trout. Informal family meals.
Chez Cocotier, Centre artisanal, rue du Général de Gaulle, Hell-Bourg ☎ 47 84 01. Lunch and dinner; closed all day Wednesdays. Large basic dining room. Good atmosphere. Varied menu listing original dishes. Generous portions. Excellent "house" trout.

US$15-30
Le Relais des Cimes, rue du Général de Gaulle, Hell-Bourg ☎ 47 81 58. Lunch and dinner. Wonderful wood-boarded Creole house. Convivial atmosphere pervades fine dining room. Conscientious service. Original and varied Creole cooking prepared with seasonal local produce. Highly civilised establishment.

• Cirque de Cilaos

US$7-15

Chez Noé, 41 rue du Père Boiteau, Cilaos ☎ 31 79 93. Lunch and dinner; closed all day Monday. Charming little painted wood Creole house with terrace. Warm reception. Good straightforward food, be it a sandwich, salad, steak or a delicious dish of smoked (boucané) palm-heart. Menu to suit all tastes, hungers and purses! Good value for money.

Chez Hélène Payet, 13 chemin Terre Fine, Îlet à Cordes ☎ 35 18 13 (reservation advised). A single table with seating for up to a dozen people. Civilised range of dishes, copious portions (deep-fried bringelles, chouchou leaves stuffed with smoked meat, duck, excellent chicken caris, delicious orange cake). Wine and rum cocktail included in price. All in all, an unexpected port of call in the back of beyond, beloved by walkers / hikers gladdened by the colour and sociable informality of the place.

US$15-30

Chez Yahameti, Îlet Haut, ☎ 25 69 80 (reservation mandatory). Allow about an hour to get there on foot; easy walking. Delicious locally produced duck breasts. Cards and music added to the presiding atmosphere and the rum cocktails, combine to guarantee an evening to remember. Its remote mountain situation, however, necessitates a stay in the rather basic hostel on site.

Le Vieux Cep, 2 rue des Trois Mares, Cilaos ☎ 31 71 89. Lunch and dinner. Welcoming atmosphere kindled by open fire, overlooking the hotel swimming pool. Good regional cooking from Cilaos: smoked pork with lentils, cari chicken with sweet-corn, as well as a choice of traditional French dishes.

• Cirque de Mafate

See the gîte listed above under Where to stay.

SPORTS AND PASTIMES

Long walks and cold rivers – ***Réunion Sensations***, 2 rue Mac Auliffe, Cilaos ☎ 31 71 71. Organisation founded by an official canyon guide. Programme of activities including canyoning, helicanyoning, rock-climbing, ridge-walking and cross-country motorcycling. All calibres catered for. Check for discounts available on course sessions.

Maham, Cascade des Demoiselles, Hell-Bourg, Salazie ☎ 47 82 82. Tailor-made programmes for cross-country cycling, canyoning, walks and climbs. State-registered guides assure approved standards of safety. Relaxing and sociable pursuits to suit everyone. Cross-country hiking and cultural tours.

Réunion Nature Sauvage ☎ 94 30 66. Minibus (seven-seater) excursions to Cilaos, Salazie, Bélouve, Le Volcan including gastronomic picnic, cultural attractions, nature trails and talks about local flora and fauna, etc. Estimate 320FF per day.

Cross-country biking – ***Vélo des Cimes***, Station Caltex ☎ 21 35 11. Budget 100FF per day.

Le Mountain Bike, 48 rue du Père Boiteau, Cilaos ☎ 31 81 95. 110FF per day.

Parc piscicole, Hell-Bourg ☎ 47 80 16. Open daily, 7.30am-6pm. Children will be delighted to hook their own fish at this fish-farm. Giggles assured. Take your catch home for 75FF per kg.

Centre thermal Irénée Accot, Route de Bras-Sec, Cilaos ☎ 31 72 27 (by prior arrangement). Beauty treatments and/or longer stays (prices vary from 150FF-500FF).

SHOPPING

• Cirque de Salazie

Case Mémé ☎ 47 81 22. On the road to Hell-Bourg. 9am-12noon/1pm-6pm; closed Tuesday. Exhibition area displaying array of historical artefacts and shop selling goods made locally.

Tresses des Salazes, Salazie (near the town hall). Open during festivals and other special occasions. Hats and other things made from dried chouchou.

Artisanat bambou, Hell-Bourg ☎ 47 84 90. Daily 9.30am-12.30pm/1.30pm-5.30pm. Assortment of goods made of bamboo: vases, ash-trays, boxes, lamps etc.

La Cazanou, rue du Général de Gaulle, Hell-Bourg ☎ 47 88 . Daily, 9am-12.30pm/1.30pm-6.30pm. Newspapers, local produce and handmade goods: straw hats, jams and pickles (delicious with a pre-dinner drink or with meat), jewellery.

MAURITIUS

Official Name: Republic of Mauritius
Area: 2 040sqkm
Population: 1 150 000
Capital: Port Louis
Currency: Mauritian rupee (Rs)

Setting the scene

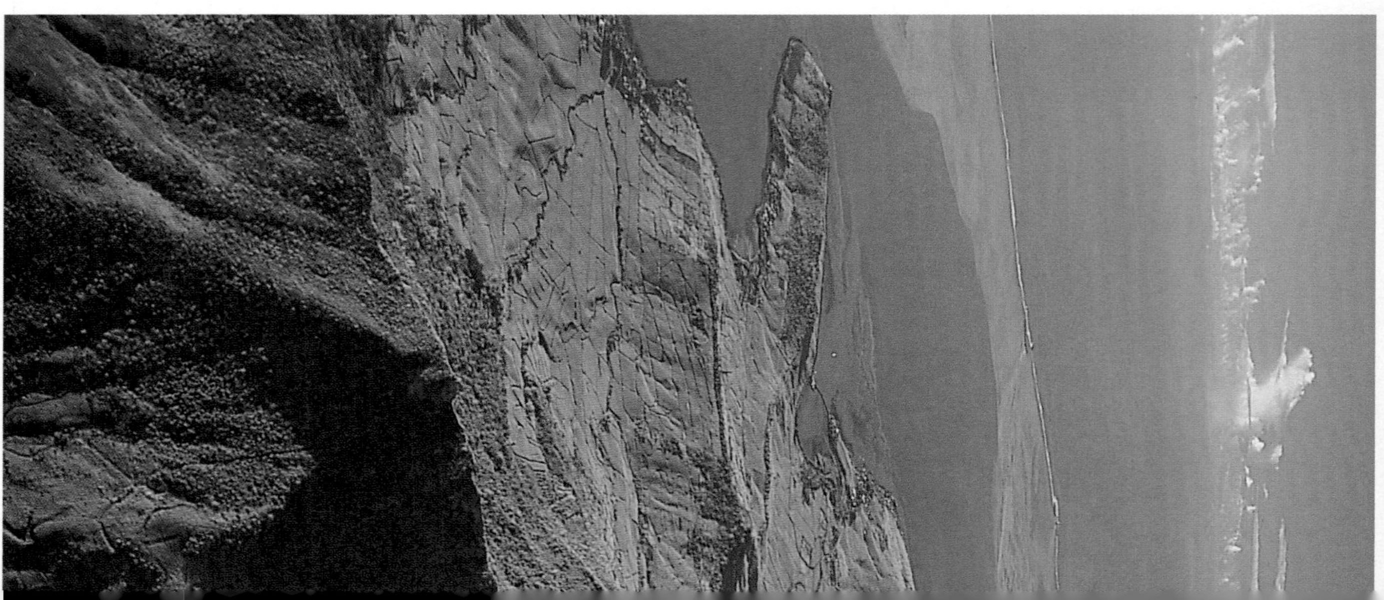

C. Pavard/HOA QUI

Lion Mountain overlooking the southeastern lagoon

Star of and Key to the Indian Seas

"God created Mauritius, and then heaven in its image", Mark Twain
"Golden, azure and emerald isle", Malcolm de Chazal
This tropical island rising out of the Indian Ocean has always been an image of paradise.

Mascarene Archipelago

Mauritius lies at the heart of the Indian Ocean at 20° Latitude South and 57° Longitude East; 220km northeast of Reunion and 900km east of Madagascar. On a broader level, the substantial land-mass – most of which is submerged by the sea – forms part of a chain of volcanic outcrops that include the Seychelles and Reunion. With its neighbours Reunion and Rodrigues – the small island 563km northeast of Mauritius – the group is known as the Mascarene Archipelago.
The Island of Mauritius measures about 63km from top to toe and 47km at its widest point across the beam, with a surface area of 1 865sqkm.
For much of its history, the island has been considered to be strategically important, initially as a port of call on the long and arduous trade routes to the Indies, and then more recently for the oil-tankers plying their way across the world. The Republic of Mauritius meanwhile, includes the Island of Rodrigues, the Cargados Garayos Archipelago (St-Brandon) which lies 400km offshore in the northeast, and the Agalega Islands (1 000km north).

Volcanic beginnings

Coral reefs surround almost all 160km of Mauritius' coastline, protecting it from the onslaughts of the ocean and providing a series of tranquil lagoons lined with long stretches of white sand interrupted, here and there by volcanic outcrops of black basalt rocks. These volcanic origins are also evident in the island's relief. Unlike its younger neighbour Reunion, Mauritius – formed 8 million years ago – is less mountainous and completely inert.
The central region consists essentially of a **huge plateau** that reaches to heights of 600m, crisscrossed by a number of densely overgrown gorges filled with rivers that flood easily after heavy rain and tumble through tumultuous waterfalls (Chutes de Tamarin or La Rivière Noire). Elsewhere, the bed-rock is pockmarked by volcanic craters that have naturally been transformed into lakes (Grand Bassin, Bassin Blanc, Trou aux Cerfs, Trou Kanaka). All around this lush and densely populated area rise a succession of **basalt peeks** that taper to sharp points: the Moka chain of mountains encircle the capital Port Louis, the Bambous range reaches down to the east coast, the Rivière Noire and Savanne massifs – clad in fabulous virgin forest – stretch out towards the southeast, while Le Rempart and Les Trois Mamelles overlook the west coast, and Morne Brabant sits alone off the southwest peninsula. The tallest of them all is Piton de la Rivière Noire (828m) which, coupled with Pieter Both (823m) and Pouce (812m) stands proudly over the **coastal plains** that make up a large part of the island. Much of the fertile basalt land is dedicated to growing sugarcane, the island's principal crop. Every so often, the fields are interspersed with "Creole pyramids" built of lava stones collected from the fields as they are being ploughed, so called because they are reminiscent of the Aztec temples.
The majority of the working population commutes to Port Louis from their homes on the central plateau in the sprawling conurbation of Curepipe, Rose

C Vaisse/HOA QUI

Morne Brabant

Hill, Beau Bassin, Vacoas, Phoenix and Quatre Bornes. The only other large town is Mahébourg, situated in the southwest of the island. In between, small rural communities with evocative names dot the coastline and the more remote hinterland. There are only two breaches in the offshore barrier reef substantial enough to allow large vessels to pass into the sheltered lagoon, and these are opposite the large commercial (and natural) harbour at Port Louis, and the now abandoned Grand Port in the southeast.

Temperate tropical climate

The tropical climate enjoyed by Mauritius is tempered by cool ocean breezes and strong **trade winds** blowing in from the southeast that bring heavy rains (1 500mm annual rainfall). The high peaks of the central plateau are shrouded in cloud all year round and it is here that the largest amounts of precipitation are released (4 500mm rainfall) while the northern and western corners of the island regularly suffer drought (900mm rainfall).

Each year, this part of the Indian Ocean is subjected to **cyclones**, particularly in January and February. As both Mauritius and Rodrigues lie in the paths of these violent storms, they suffer the consequences to differing degrees. Some years, this might be limited to heavy rains, while other years the winds can cause considerable devastation, tearing down buildings and vegetation. (*See p 69* Cyclone Alert).

Flora at Risk

Indigenous and imported species

Mauritius' hot and humid climatic conditions allow the tropical vegetation to flourish. The indigenous species encountered by the first settlers on arrival were established there by means of seeds probably borne by wind, sea and migratory birds over the millennia. Some plants gradually mutated in their new environment to become endemic species. (*see p* 27 Some Definitions).

Tragically, less than 1 % of the indigenous forest that once covered the island survives. For shortly after the first colonists – Dutch and then French – had settled there, they began clearing the woodland in order to capitalise on the rare hardwoods like teak, purple wood and ebony, so highly prized in furniture-making at home or for export markets. Instead of allowing these areas to replenish naturally, the land was irrevocably turned over to the cultivation of sugarcane.

What is left of the indigenous forest – like the patch at Gorges de la Rivière Noire, and offshore on Île Ronde and Île aux Aigrettes – is now subject to strict protection orders and conservation measures.

Some areas of Mauritius have been reforested with woodland, comprising essentially of conifers, eucalyptus, camphor and mahogany, whereas elsewhere, warm and humid conditions in the centre of the island allow **tree-ferns**, creepers and bamboo to proliferate.

Trees

Among the more common kinds of tree, there are several highly distinctive ones: the **casuarina** (*Casuarina equisetifolia*, locally known as *filao, cedre* or whistling pine) is a tall, tapering pine tree with fine needles and tiny cones (spiky if you are out walking barefoot) often planted along the coast to safeguard against erosion and shifting sands; the **banyan** (*Ficus benghalensis*, known as *multipliant*) which grows a multitude of offshoots that then take root, sometimes forming an extensive complex of shaded tunnels and the **traveller's palm** (*Ravenala madagacariensis* or *arbre du voyageur*) with its proud sheaf of leaves radiating outwards in a great fan – so named because of its usefulness to man as a source of thatch or roof covering, and as a source of drinkable sap collected at the base of the leaf stem. Others to look out for include the Indian almond (*Terminalia catappa* or *badamier*) which produces edible nuts, the Alexandrian laurel (*Calophyllum inophyllum* or *takamaka*), various types of palm trees – coconut palms and **vacoa** (*Pandanus*) whose fibres are used in basketwork – and clumps of mangroves whose invasive aerial roots are overtaking some of the sandy beaches on the east and west coasts.

Flowers

The wealth of colour and variation that pervades life in Mauritius is also apparent in the great diversity of flowering species that grow so profusely everywhere, especially in the coastal areas: mauve *jacaranda*, yellow **allamanda**, oleander, sweetly scented **frangipani**, lilies, startlingly bright **bougainvillea**, all sorts of **hibiscus**, various orchids, red and white **anthuriums** (sometimes called the flamingo flower), red and green **poinsettias** and bright red **flamboyants** (in December and January).

Fruit

The climate also encourages a broad variety of tropical fruits to flourish. Some – bananas, pineapples, papayas, coconuts to name a few – can be harvested all the year round. However, the more succulent fruits – lychee, *longan*, mango, soursop (*Annona muricata* or *corossol*), avocado, jackfruit, guava and star-fruit (*Averrhoa carambola*) – only ripen during the summer (December/January).

FAUNA UNDER THREAT

Birds

Species in bold are illustrated p 14-15

The emblem of Mauritius is the *dodo*: a large, flightless bird with a hooked beak that was hunted to extinction by Dutch colonists and predators in around 1692. Its cousin, the *solitaire* which once roamed the Island of Rodrigues, suffered the same fate. A plausible interpretation of the available factual and scientific data has been used to conceive how the extinct *dodo* must have appeared, and this displayed at the Mauritius Institute in Port Louis *(see p 257)*.

The few indigenous birds to have survived the process of colonisation and changes in land-management are to be found nestling in the Domaine du Chasseur and the Macchabée-Bel Ombre Nature Reserve. Several threatened species owe their narrow escape from obliteration to various initiatives instituted by international conservation pressure groups in collaboration with local government and the national nature protection agency. In some cases, these birds have been saved by successful "breeding in captivity" programmes undertaken abroad (at Jersey Zoo in the Channel Islands for example). With patience and luck, bird-watching enthusiasts can now be treated to a view of the **Mauritius kestrel**, pink pigeon, Mauritius fody (affectionately known locally as *zozo banane*, the male has a bright red head and an olive breast), cuckoo shrike, Mauritian bulbul and the echo parakeet (*catau verte*) – alive and well in their natural habitat.

Many of the more common birds, meanwhile, were introduced to Mauritius by the colonists: these include the common sparrow, the Mauritius grey white-eye (*zozo manioc* or *picpic*, the **Madagascan cardinal** (or red fody), the yellow weaver, the common **mynah**, the **red whiskered bulbul** (or *condé* with its dark crest, white chest, red patches behind the eye and under the tail, who is cheeky enough to come and peck from a dinner plate) and the yellow-eyed **canary**.
The most eye-catching species are probably the sea-birds that may be seen gracefully wheeling through the skies above the coast: among these, there are elegant **white-tailed tropic birds** *(paille-en-queue)*, various gulls and terns *(goelettes)*, wedge-tailed shearwaters *(fouquets)*, boobies, *mariannes*, swallows and *corbigeaux*. The majority, however, are migrants that come to Mauritius in search of warmer weather sometime in October. The best places for bird-watching are in and among the small offshore islands.

Land fauna

The only indigenous mammal is the Mauritius fruit bat (or flying fox/*renard volant*). Other creatures were introduced from abroad in the course of the 17C by the Dutch: the Java deer, for example, that is so prized for its meat, is still bred for hunting; as are wild boar and hares. Exceptions to this rule include the colonies of monkeys living in the forest that were brought by the Portuguese, and the mongoose - introduced from India at the beginning of the 20C – for curbing the rats that were devastating the fields of sugarcane.

Mauritius can claim to have fifteen indigenous species of reptile, of which eight are endemic to Île Ronde. None, however, are venomous and the only snakes are either grass-snakes or boas. The giant land tortoises and sea turtles, culled for their meat, have disappeared from Mauritius and from Rodrigues – where for a long time they continued to flourish. The specimens there now all come from the Seychelles.

Over 3 000 different species of insect are found in Mauritius, including a selection of gorgeous butterflies and beautiful damselflies. The only pests really to trouble visitors to the island are the wasps, flies and mosquitoes.

Sea life

Species in bold are illustrated on p 11 to 13.

The marine life that once abounded in these waters has been severely affected by the boom in tourism and the tragic consequences of using fine-mesh dragnets – despite the strict laws imposed by government forbidding their use – to plunder fish stocks, gather sea-shells and damage the banks of living coral beyond redemption. The situation is now quite dire and the offshore barrier reef that protects the coastline of Mauritius is dying. Given that it takes almost a year for the coral to "grow" one centimetre, the hope of a speedy recovery is simply unrealistic, especially as the demand from scuba-diving enthusiasts focuses ever-growing pressure on a dwindling number of living colonies. (*see p 361* Living coral).
At last, the government is finally showing signs of responding to the demands of the different ecologically-minded organisations to do something about arresting the further degradation of marine habitats. To date, preservation orders have been applied to several of the offshore islets, and their waters have been declared nature reserves.

Meanwhile, in the lee of the barrier reef, fantastic arrays of colourful fish continue to thrive in the calm and warm waters of the lagoons – much to the delight of snorkellers and owners of glass-bottomed boats. Common species include **parrot-fish**, squirrel-fish, **lion-fish** (with a painful sting), stone-fish (dangerous), **trumpet-fish**, clown-fish, **emperor angelfish**, pyjama-fish, surgeon fish, etc. There are few edible species left in the lagoons as these have been over-exploited over the years.

The really big game fish for which Mauritius has become renowned continue to thrive in the deep waters beyond the barrier reef, for the time being at least. It is difficult though to ascertain just how large the stocks are of such prize fish as the blue, black or striped marlin, yellow-fin tuna, bonito, *wahoo*, barracuda, swordfish, bream and sharks (blue, hammerhead, tiger, black and, the most feared – white).

Besides the fish, many textured sponges, corals, anemones, gorgons, worms, starfish, octopus, sea urchins and sea slugs, there are some beautiful shells to look out for: white, striped, ridged or speckled **cowries**, **helmet shells**, pink or mauve spider shells, tritons and several species of **mitre** – papal, episcopal or pontifical. Among the different **cone shells** some are venomous.

A YOUNG NATION

10C	Arabs landed at **Dinarobin**.
1507	Portuguese seafarers rediscovered **Ilha do Cirne**.
1598	The Dutch settled in **Mauritius**.
1715	The French took possession of the **Île de France**.
1735	**Mahé de La Bourdonnais** was declared Governor.
1764	The island's administration passed from the French East India Company to the French Crown.
1790	Revolutionary autonomy.
1810	Napoleonic victory over the British at Grand Port British victory at Cap Malheureux.
1814	**Mauritius** became a British colony.
1835	Abolition of slavery in all British Colonies.
1968	Independence. Mauritius became a monarchy under the reign of Elizabeth II. Rodrigues was the 21st district of the State of Mauritius.
1992	Institution of the Republic of Mauritius. Cassam Uteem was elected President of Mauritius.
1995	Navin Rangoolam, son of Seewoosagur, became Prime Minister.
1999	Rioting following the death, while imprisoned, of the Creole minority singer, Kaya.

Discovery

The island's strategic situation in the Indian Ocean meant that vessels sailing with the trade winds with each monsoon could stop there and replenish their supplies of fresh water and food. By the 10C the **Arabs** were familiar with it and referred to it as Dinarobin (Silver Island). In 1505, it was "discovered" by the Portuguese navigator **Pedro Mascarenhas** (after whom the Mascarene archipelago is named), and called Ilha do Cirne (Swan Island). In time, the island became increasingly used by trading ships as a port of call, and pirates continued to use it as a place of refuge. The Portuguese never actually colonised the island as resources were primarily concentrated on developing their interests in the Far East.

Dutch occupation

In 1598, Dutch admiral **Van Warwyck** landed on the south-east coast of the island on his way to the Orient in search of silks and spices and named the island **Mauritius**, in honour of Maurice of Nassau, Prince of Orange. A contingent of Dutch colonists from South Africa then arrived and settled in the region of Vieux Grand Port, near Mahébourg, where the community thrived until 1710. Unlike the previous visitors, these men set about colonising the island. They had bands of men condemned to a lifetime of forced labour sent out from the Dutch spice island colonies in Indonesia and acquired teams of African and Madagascan slaves to serve as agricultural workers. Soon the population of 25 had increased to more than 500.

To feed their workforce, the Dutch were forced to import a ready source of food. Hence the introduction of Java deer, bananas and most significantly, sugarcane. Meanwhile, the natural resources were plundered for food and timber. Great swathes of indigenous forest were cleared, and many endemic species of flora and fauna were destroyed in the process. As many mature ebony trees as could be found were felled and the dodo was hunted to extinction.

At last, in 1658, after the island had been ravaged by cyclones, drought, disease, shipwreck, pirates and runaway slaves, the Dutch gave up any hope of colonising this hostile Garden of Eden. In 1664, they made a second attempt at imposing some kind of order on the place. After all Mauritius was an extremely strategic colony to have; but a similar succession of troubles gradually undermined the cause and all was abandoned in 1710.

French colonisation

In 1715, the French arrived from Île Bourbon (modern day Réunion) aboard *Le Chasseur*, a French East India Company vessel captained by **Guillaume Dufresne d'Arsel**. First they took possession of the island, then they renamed it **Île de France** and finally they declared it a monopoly of the French East India Company; only in 1721 was it properly settled by colonists. Establishing control was impeded by cyclones, rats and runaway slaves.

1735 marked an important turning point in the history of the territory when King Louis XV nominated **Bertrand François Mahé de La Bourdonnais**, a captain of the East India Company, as "Governor of the Islands of Bourbon and France". The "Father of the Island" – as he came to be known later – landed at Port Nord-Ouest. Without delay, he set about building a new capital there complete with a harbour (to the detriment of Grand Port which was proving too exposed to the south-east trade winds). And so Port Louis came into being. Next he founded a boat-building yard and charged it with supplying him with a considerable fleet of ships designed for commercial trade and for battle. A number of major building projects were completed including a hospital, the first sugar refinery (at Pamplemousses), fortifications and a road network. Wheat and cotton were introduced to supplement sugarcane. Slaves were imported from Madagascar and Mozambique by the French to man the sugarcane plantations that now were operating on an industrial scale. As the regeneration proceeded, increased numbers of immigrants flooded in from France swelling the population to 60 000. As the large landowners tasted prosperity, they built themselves sumptuous homesteads and improved sugar production plants, of which there are scant remains.

C. Pavard/HOA QUI

Mahé de La Bourdonnais

A Young Nation

Mahé de La Bourdonnais died in France in 1753, after being subjected to streams of accusations, humiliation and imprisonment. Nevertheless, it was largely due to his determination and vision that Mauritius was transformed from a wild deserted island into a prosperous French colony.

Franco-British rivalry

Following his nation's setbacks in India, the **French king** became anxious about reasserting his people's naval superiority in the Indian Ocean over that of the British. In 1764, he bought **Mascarenes** back from the French East India Company, which was on the decline following the ongoing wars and their repercussions on trade. As a result, large numbers of reinforcement troops and seamen were stationed on the island. Meanwhile, the French intervention in the American War of Independence further reinforced the already deep-rooted British mistrust for the French.

Mauritius lay at the very heart of the Franco-British rivalry for supremacy over the trade routes with India and the control of the Seychelles Islands. Now a third player entered the fray, for Mauritius was also a refuge for marauding pirates and mercenaries. During the 18C, they were able to trade off immunity from prosecution by the French if they concentrated on attacking and plundering the British ships that sailed between Africa and the East. Port Louis became the notorious haunt of mercenaries, a place where they could off-load and sell their valuable booty; business flourished there. When the British put a price on the head of the "King of the Corsairs" **Robert Surcouf**, he quickly found support and favour among the businessmen of Port Louis and, being a "friend" of Napoleon, he was offered official protection by the French government.

The repercussions of the French Revolution were felt in Mauritius in 1790 when a band of colonists rose up, revoked the power of the Crown Royal and secured a mandate for self-rule that was to last 13 years. Tensions grew and then erupted in 1794 when Paris decreed that slavery should be abolished and the Mauritian land-owners refused to obey. Finally, the measure was repealed by **Napoleon Bonaparte** so that order could be reinstated, and a new governor was sent to oversee law and order.

After over a century spent fighting the French, and the consistent loss of valuable assets to the pirates, the British decided to seize possession of this strategic territory for themselves and consolidate their colonial interests in India.

In 1810, a crucial event occurred. In August of that year, Napoleon won the only naval battle of his reign (commemorated by the Arc de Triomphe in Paris) at **Grand Port**, in the south-east corner of the island. The defeated British retreated to the island of Rodrigues, where they had already been entrenched for a year, to consolidate and plan their revenge. Then a few months later they made a surprise landing on Cap Malheureux, the northerly tip of Mauritius, and proceeded to take hold of the whole island.

British rule

The **Treaty of Paris** officially ceded Mauritius, Rodrigues and the Seychelles to the British in 1814. Réunion was allocated to the French.

Île de France – now a British colony – reverted to being called **Mauritius**. The penal system of law and order laid out by the **Napoleonic Code** remained in place and little, with regards to civic administration and procedure, was changed. The Franco-Mauritian people were free to practise their customs, language and religion (Catholicism) as before, and retain all rights to their properties and interests in the sugar business. It is ironic therefore that it was

C Pavard/HOA QUI

The arrival of immigrant slave workers c1850

the small British contingent, and the first of His Majesty's appointed governors **Robert Farquhar** in particular, who ensured that French culture survived in Mauritius as it does today.

During the 19C, new roads were laid out; free trade out of Port Louis was encouraged and developed. More importantly, Farquhar supervised the building up of the local economy on the production and refining of sugar. By the middle of the century, there were 250 sugar refineries in operation on the island.

When slavery was abolished in 1835 – a momentous event in the history of Mauritius – the slaves, predominantly from Africa and Madagascar, accounted for some two-thirds of the population. Their emancipation therefore spelled major problems for all forms of labour-intensive industry. In an attempt to contain the dangerous repercussions, the British decided to offer to take on a new **"immigrant labour"** force from Southern India. By 1907, the number of people recruited amounted to 450 000.

During the early years, these workers were exploited as slaves, and conditions towards the close of the 19C remained arduous as the economy of the island reeled from the consequences of fluctuating prices for raw sugar on the international markets, destructive cyclones, devastating fires, and a malaria epidemic. Despite this, the Indian community gradually managed to diversify into other commercial sectors; by the mid-20C they were completely integrated into all socio-economic groups and taking an active role in political life.

Quest for independence

Mauritius attained her independence on 12 March 1968. It was only really after World War II that the process of de-colonisation took off in earnest and the island replaced the status of colony for that of a sovereign state.

During those twenty years of evolution, five successive Constitutions were sworn-in. From these, several radical and fundamental issues were resolved: in 1958 it was universal suffrage and ministerial responsibility; in 1964 specifications for a

Sir Seewoosagur Ramgoolam (1900-85)
After excelling at his studies in England, the young Hindu embarked on a long political career in Mauritius. He joined the Labour Party in 1948, and soon rose to be its leader. From the outset, he played a vital role in the island's move towards independence. It seems appropriate that in 1965 he was chosen to represent his party at a constitutional conference in London and lobby for the cause. As had been hoped, delegates voted for Mauritius to be accorded her independence. In 1968, Ramgoolam was made Prime Minister – a key position he was to enjoy for 13 years until 1982, when he was defeated politically for the first time and forced to stand down for Aneerood Jugnauth of the Mouvement Militant Mauricien (MMM). In 1983 he was made Governor-General, thereby renewing his participation in government in 1985, the year of his death. Generally acknowledged as the father of the Mauritius nation, his name lives on as a street name, appended to a public building and other important institutions like the airport and the Pamplemousses Botanic Garden.

Council of Ministers and Legislative Assembly were established. In 1967, internal self-government was achieved as a prelude to complete independence. Throughout this period, the Hindus – by far the largest ethnic majority – wielded considerable power in deciding policy while many other Mauritians remained reticent about change. Since 1948, the political parties have been a fair reflection of opinion among the racially diverse and multi-faith population. For a long time, politics have been dominated by the socialist **Parti Travailliste** which is the party favoured by the Hindu majority. Since 1958 or thereabouts, opposition has been provided by the likes of the **Parti Mauricien Social Démocrate** (PMSD) that is supported by Franco-Mauritians and Creoles and the **Comité d'Action Musulman** which represents Moslem interests.

Over the years the parties have formed a succession of coalitions. The Hindus united with the Muslims in 1965 to fight for independence in opposition to the PMSD led by Gaétan Duval; at the 1967 election, the socialists were voted in and S S Ramgoolam was made Prime Minister in 1968.

The **Constitution** that was sworn in on 12 March 1968 was formulated according to the same principles adopted by other Commonwealth countries. Mauritius is a confirmed member of the British Commonwealth and as such recognises the British sovereign Elizabeth II, Queen of the United Kingdom and Mauritius, as their Head of State, represented on the island by the Governor-General and a High-Commissioner. At the same time, Rodrigues was constituted as the 21st district of the State of Mauritius.

The Republic of Mauritius

In 1969 the **Mouvement Militant Mauricien** (MMM) was formed by a coalition, led by the Labour party, of parties with militant tendencies, led by the Franco-Mauritian Paul Bérenger. The MMM, which was to amass a considerable following during the 1970s, was founded on the basis that a political party should not represent a single racial community as had been the norm to date, but aspire to being multi-ethnic and Marxist-Socialist in doctrine.

After a few turbulent years, the MMM came to power following the 1976 elections without a majority, and Prime Minister Ramgoolam was obliged to form a coalition government with the MMM in association with the Labour party and PMSD, to prevent the MMM from wielding any power.

The collaboration of the MMM with the newly formed **Parti Socialiste Mauricien** (PSM) secured them a great majority at the 1982 elections. Under the new regime, Aneerood Jugnauth (leader of the MMM) became Prime Minister, Paul Bérenger assumed the role of Finance Minister, while Gaétan Duval was made Leader of the Opposition.

Personal and political dissension between the two men finally reached crisis point in 1983. The collaboration finally collapsed when Paul Bérenger resigned from his position, and set himself up as leader of the opposition with the support of more than half of the former government ministers.

Prime Minister Jugnauth was thus forced to create a new party: **The Militant Socialist Movement** (MSM). Later in the same year, the elections were won by a 5-party coalition opposed to Bérenger's the MMM.

The in-fighting between men and ministers continued throughout 1983-87. It was not until 1990 that a new political arrangement was arrived at and a resounding majority for a coalition of the two main parties, the MMM (Bérenger) and the MSM (Jugnauth), was declared at the legislative elections in 1991. This put an end to the polarisation of Mauritian politics and allowed government to concentrate on attaining its independent status. At last, on **12 March 1992**, Mauritius was officially proclaimed a republic.

Mauritius today

The **President of the Republic** is elected for a 5-year term. Despite there no longer being a Governor-General appointed by HM The Queen, the organisation and running of public affairs have not radically changed since Mauritius became a republic. Executive power is exercised – much as it is in Britain – by a cabinet of 25 ministers appointed and headed by the Prime Minister, leader of the party with a majority in Parliament.

The **National Assembly** is the legislative body, made up of 62 elected members and 8 additional members, with each of the twenty island districts being represented by three elected members and the island of Rodrigues by two. The extra eight delegates are those runners-up with the second largest number of votes. This is designed to counterbalance any bias towards a single party and maintain a good cross-section of ethnic interests. A relative majority is sufficient to be elected. However as this is usually achieved only with the co-operation of the minority parties, Mauritius politics are not overly dominated by the two principle factions. It is easy to see, therefore, how racial tension among the minority groups pressurised the first president Veerasamy Ringadoo – a Hindu and representative of by far the largest ethnic group – to resign in favour of the Moslem **Cassam Uteem**.

The last decisive political coup occurred in 1995. In retrospect, the 13 years of government under Jugnauth had been essentially positive for Mauritius and the economy was in better shape than ever before, but the electorate was disenchanted with the ongoing political intrigues and financial shenanigans that had long beset the party, and demonstrated their discontent by overwhelmingly voting for the opposition alliance of the Labour Party under **Navin Ramgoolam** (son of Sir Seewoosagur) and the MMM party led by Paul Bérenger. More recently, the death while in prison, of a reggae singer and member of the Creole minority, Kaya, caused rioting. The **judiciary,** which is guaranteed independence from the executive by the Constitution, is drawn from both the French and English legal systems. Mauritius is divided into **ten administrative districts**. Given its geographical situation and its status as a parliamentary democracy, Mauritius constitutes a major player in **international relations**. It takes an active role in over 20 international organisations, and maintains relations with all the leading countries, with particular emphasis on economic, cultural and scientific co-operation. Mauritius is home to the HQ of several of the region's largest cooperation organisations, the **Indian Ocean Commission** (IOC), the **Indian Ocean Rim** (IOR/ARC) and the **Southern Africa Development Community** (SADC), thereby ensuring it an active role in international relations.

A Booming Economy

Sugarcane

Sugarcane was introduced by the Dutch from the Indonesian island of Java in 1639, and found to be well-suited to conditions in Mauritius. In the early days, the crop was grown for making the alcoholic drink **arak**; it was only later that the islanders turned to refining the cane sap into sugar. Under the French, planters remained cautious about its cultivation, but during the British administration, things radically changed. Before long, sugar had become the **prime export** commodity; by the 19C plantations occupied some 80 % of the entire island's available agricultural land and the economy fluctuated with every rise or fall in price on the international markets.

The reason that so much cane is grown is in part due to its ability to withstand the ravages of cyclones. In any event, it continues to be cultivated on an industrial scale to this day and to constitute a key element in the country's economy. To ensure against the risk of the market collapsing, Mauritius has managed to secure long-term concessions for sugar futures with countries of the EC and the Commonwealth.

The large cane plantations still tend to be owned by members of the white Franco-Mauritian "gentry", who live in sumptuous colonial homesteads surrounded by fields, while the workforce lives in small communities on the periphery. Since the 19C, the number of small land-owners has mushroomed. In some cases, the large colonial estates have been sold off in parts with a small parcel of agricultural land being acquired by the second-generation of Indians.

The cane is still usually harvested by hand, although the process is becoming increasingly mechanised. In the old days, the women cleared the cane fields of weeds and dried grass before they were harvested; nowadays the undergrowth is simply set alight. This technique also heightens the cane's sugar content as moisture is evaporated off before the cane is cut.

Sugarcane is harvested once a year between June and September when the plant has reached full maturity, and while it is in flower. Then, during the two to three months before replanting, the fields are used to cultivate **secondary crops** like maize, groundnuts and potatoes. But the yield from these crops is not enough to allow the islanders to be self-sufficient. Despite the high annual rainfall, the permeable nature of the soil and the high temperatures usually necessitate some degree of irrigation.

Since independence, the government has been trying to encourage land-owners to diversify in the hope of safeguarding against disease or cyclones devastating the island's entire crop, and against a severe fall in the price of sugar. To this end, tea, tobacco, exotic fruits and tropical cut flowers (especially *anthuriums*) are being grown for export.

Mauritius Export Processing Zone

The huge industrial zone was started in 1970 so as to encourage local investors and foreign entrepreneurs away from the sugar industry and into new industries that could provide jobs for the growing population. During the 1980s, efforts were focused on the diversification of light-industry and the improvement of technological capabilities. An area dedicated to the service industry was also created. With favourable rates of exchange, low duty, abundant supplies of cheap labour and a reassuringly stable period of government have all helped to make this initiative a great success. There are now over 600 manufacturing businesses operating under the scheme, accounting for 65 % of the output for the country with a variety of goods ranging from electronic products, toys, jewellery, clocks and watches and **textiles** (cotton and wool) as well as banking services. More and more well-known French and English designer clothes are manufactured in Mauritius. Indeed, this industry has now overtaken sugar as the prime source of income for the country, work in a mill or in a clothes factory is considered far more desirable than a job in the cane fields.

Tourism

To coincide with the inauguration of the "Export Processing Zone", the government launched a major initiative aimed at developing tourism. The economic boom of the 1980s that swept through the western world allowed Mauritius to establish itself as a major holiday destination. Over the past 15 years, the tourist industry has shown an annual increase in turnover of 10-15 %. In 1998, some 590 000 visitors came to the island, bringing in nearly US$17 000 million to the country.

In order to take advantage of this incredible growth, hotels and dependent facilities are constantly being developed, and providing ever greater opportunities for foreign investors, notably from South Africa.

Although the industry recognises that it has to adapt to the demands of mass tourism, the government is keen to preserve Mauritius as an exclusive destination and so all forms of charter flight are excluded. Almost 30 % of tourists come from Réunion, followed by the South-Africans, French, English, Germans, Australians and Italians.

Clothes factory

J L Drouin/DIAF

Tourism generates the third largest share of the national economy. Furthermore it brings in considerable amounts of **foreign currency**. The local population also benefits from the number of extra **jobs** created: in hotels, restaurants, transport services, as well as in the making of model boats, selling sarongs, jewellery and shells on the beach.

The downside of tourism is its detrimental effect on the environment. Because of the viability of property development it is increasingly encroaching upon green field sites and agricultural land, for the urban areas are already saturated with high population densities of more than 600 people per square kilometre. Elsewhere, the local population is forced to accept an altered way of life as hotels are put up along the coasts, the beaches are usurped by foreigners, the sea is overrun with leisure craft and sporting activities, and the peace of the night is disturbed by blaring music and garish lights.

Altered socio-economic climate

Industrialisation and technological advances have increased output and reduced the number of jobs available in the sugar industry. This is balanced out by the workforce required by the industrial estates right across the island, and by tourism in the seaside resorts. In between, there remain pockets of land where rural life can continue at its usual pace. Thus due to the growth of investments and trade with Madagascar and East Africa, the tax free port zone has increased considerably since 1998. Furthermore the island has been developing "offshore" financial services in which area it is very competitive.

Looking to the future, the prospects for the economy are set to continue to flourish. The country's balance of payments is making progress and global inflation is in check. To add to this, unemployment is so low that since 1990, Mauritius has had to turn to other countries (mainly Madagascar) to recruit additional labour.

Meeting the people

E. Valentin/HOA QUI

18th anniversary
of Independence

A FUSION OF CULTURES

Population explosion

Over the past years, the population of Mauritius has not stopped growing, as a result of improved healthcare and diet, and better provision of drinking water. The situation has been further exacerbated by the tightening-up of immigration controls in such countries as Britain, France, parts of Africa, and to a lesser extent Canada and Australia. Today the population is estimated at around 1 150 000 which, given the size of Mauritius, gives the territory one of the highest population densities in the world with nearly 540 inhabitants per square kilometre. This seems incredible if the coastal plains are anything to go by as these areas appear to consist of vast expanses of sugarcane dotted with little hamlets. If you drive up across the central plateau, however, the towns are lost in a great suburban sprawl as far as the eye can see. The great exodus from Port Louis in 1860 was prompted by a malaria epidemic – since then, people have naturally congregated in the more salubrious areas, preferably those least affected by cyclones and disease – hence the predilection for the central plateau where the climate is cooler. When the railway was completed, this region became even more readily accessible, so the working population came in droves to settle there.

During the 1970s, efforts at slowing down the population explosion were directed at promoting family planning measures, setting new social values and encouraging people back into work.

A cultural melting-pot

The geographical situation of Mauritius at the cross-roads of Africa, Asia and Europe, is reflected in its cultural make-up, with additional colour and variety being injected by minority groups and castes.

Franco-Mauritians

The white population, which in the main is descended from French colonists and settlers, has preserved its strong cultural identity over the centuries. To this day, almost all the plantations and sugar refineries, as well as the finest colonial homesteads remain in their possession.

Their inherited wealth has also allowed the more enterprising among them to invest in new industries and holiday resort developments. This Mauritian "aristocracy" is dwindling, however, and accounts now for a mere 2% of the population. Many have gradually drifted back to France, Britain or South Africa and the decline in numbers is having dire consequences on the birth-rate, especially as most are reluctant to intermarry with other social groups.

Few are inclined to be involved in national politics, but are happy to wield their influence in matters of business and exert pressure on the local economy indirectly by means of their activities in key areas and associations with important people abroad.

Creoles

The collective term "Creole" is an ambiguous one for at the outset it was used to denote those people who were descended from the slaves recruited by the early settlers from Madagascar and East Africa. Over the years, the term has come to allude to a larger community of mixed race.

The original and principal components of the **"general population"** are the Franco-Mauritians and the Creoles. Both share a faith in the Catholic religion and neither is rooted in Asian culture. Otherwise, the Creoles come from all social classes, from the wealthiest families of planters and landowners to the humblest of fishermen and menial labourers with African or Madagascan forefathers.

Indo-Mauritians

The largest ethnic group is descended from the people who were recruited from Southern India post-1835, to work on the sugar plantations after the abolition of slavery. The predominant communities making up the Indo-Mauritian sector is the large Hindu group – including a considerable number of Tamils – and the Moslems.

Among the **Tamils**, those who arrived in Mauritius from Southern India (Tamil-Nadu) way back in the times of Mahé de la Bourdonnais tend to be traditional craftsmen and as such have been completely integrated into the mixed societies of the urban areas. While the **Hindu** descendants of immigrant workers from Northern India have preferred to continue to work the land and eventually buy it in somewhat isolated areas in the hinterland. These rather rural communities continue to respect the precepts of the ancient Indian caste system, with a little more flexibility and tolerance than in the motherland.

At the top of the pyramid sit the caste of the Brahmin priests (known as the *Maraze* in Mauritius); next come the warriors or *Khastriyas* (*Baboudji* in Mauritius), the land-owners, shopkeepers or *Vaishya* (*Vaish* in Mauritius), and the more menial workers or *Sudras*; at the bottom come the untouchables or *Pariahs*, who are considered impure.

As is often the case with a class system, the top two castes form a minority that will socialise together at weddings and elections. The "middle class" forms the largest social group and as such is the most representative of Hindu interests across the board, and plays a central role in national politics. In fact a tacit rule exists whereby the prime minister and leader of the opposition should be from this particular caste.

In the main it is the Hindus who have dominated and shaped the country. For in a democratic country where people are asked to vote for

An Indo-Mauritian Moslem

E.Valentin/HOA QUI

A cultural melting-pot

a party that best reflects their own social and religious interests, the largest community will inevitably cast the majority of votes. So, as long as the Hindu community remains the largest, they will retain the upper hand in politics. Furthermore, Hindus have penetrated all the economic sectors and so they have a major hold on business as well.

The **Moslems,** meanwhile, are one of the Indian minority groups, including descendants who came to Mauritius from Northern India (Bengal and Bihar) in the hope of making their fortunes as farm labourers, as well as the traders originally from Gujurat in Western India who came to increase theirs. Today, many of these people are to be found living in and around the capital Port Louis, involved in textiles or the financial sector.

Chinese-Mauritians

Most of the Chinese immigrants who came to Mauritius in the 19C were entrepreneurs. Although a minority in terms of numbers, this community is extremely dynamic and hard-working especially when it comes to business and commerce. Indeed almost half of the doctors, architects, engineers and accountants in Mauritius are Chinese in origin. The only distinctive factions within this social group depend on whether the family originated from **Canton** or from **Hakka**, both of which are in southeast China.

Distillation of a national identity

From the outside, the Mauritian people seems an exceptional example of inter-racial harmony and integration. The image is reinforced by the brochures addressed to tourists and confirmed by a short stay on the island. The reality, however, is a great deal more complex. Even if the various communities appear to coexist peacefully, all are rent by internal tensions and disputes over ethnic and social issues. These differences encourage a certain amount of partitioning within the various subgroups, and as mixed marriages remain fairly rare, prejudices and intolerance are perpetrated alongside traditional practices and beliefs.

But rather than opting for sectarianism, the people of Mauritius recognise that they are in fact united by a common culture that has been distilled out of cultural diversity and that they should in fact celebrate their eclectic heritage. Even if history and origin have discriminated against groups in the past, the population is united in its aspirations for the future.

It was the slaves from Africa and Madagascar who gave birth to Creole, now the common language across Mauritius, and who formulated the musical sounds and dancing rhythms of *séga*. The legacy of the French and English colonials has been to provide the islanders with the languages required for international relations and negotiations. Mauritius has also benefited from parliamentary and legal systems that had been tried and tested long before being instituted by the British. The Indians who came as recruited workers have contributed their hard-work ethic to the melting pot, whereas the Chinese have injected their spirit of enterprise and astute business-sense to it.

The result has produced a distinctively Mauritian Creole form of language and culture, similar yet different to the Creole cultures of the islands of neighbouring archipelagos. This specificity has provided the nation, over and above ethnic, linguistic or religious differences with a form of unity and communication that has led to a common identity and references.

Religious blends

Religion is often allied to ethnicity, and this is more than apparent in Mauritius. Differences of creed on the whole are respected, but rivalries and tensions within a sect or faction do sometimes undermine the common ground of tolerance and peaceful cohabitation.

For despite the distances that separate the Mauritians from the homeland of their forebears, each ethnic group remains faithful to its original beliefs and religious practices. And so it is that all the great religions are represented here, albeit in a rather eclectic form. Indeed, all kinds of ancestral rituals and modern customs, Islamic fundamentalists and less sectarian Moslems, Hindu patriarchs and westernised youth, urgent birth control and strict Catholicism live side by side. As a result, the population participates in the celebrations of all cults and enjoys the benefits of a blended spirituality. This mix has added a unique, special touch to the Mauritian cultural kaleidoscope.

Hinduism

More than 50 % of Mauritians are Hindus, and their observance of the faith is a good deal more flexible than in India. Having evolved from ancient scriptures known as Vedas, Hinduism cannot be divorced from Indian history, tradition and social ethics. Religion dictates the means by which the community is ordered into castes and ensures that adherents live their lives according to Hindu precepts and values. Needless to say the system is a great deal more tempered than in India. Nonetheless, Hinduism has profoundly influenced Mauritius by conferring a markedly Indian character to it.

The three fundamental principles of Hinduism are a belief in *maya* (the illusory nature of the world), *karma* (the effect of deeds in one life influences destiny in the next life) and *samsara* (the cycle of birth, death and rebirth or reincarnation).

The three main deities, who together represent the Hindu Trinity or Trimurti, are the Creator **Brahma,** the One Absolute Reality, the Destroyer **Shiva,** the god of destruction and rebirth, and the Preserver **Vishnu,** who restores the balance of the world. In other words, these three represent three distinctive aspects of the same god.

GJ Galmiche

Hindu altar at the top of Piton Grand Bassin

E Valentin/HOA QUI

Devout prayer

Each deity conveys its power to mortal man through the primordial feminine power of the universe: *Shakti* or Devi. A myriad of secondary deities completes the Hindu pantheon, each capable of being incarnated on earth and being idolised. Furthermore, qualities and attributes can be venerated in the form of animals, such as cows which have been held sacred since Vedic Antiquity, and natural phenomena, such as rivers which symbolise the course of life and its renewal. Thus, the primordial importance of India's sacred river: the Ganges.

There is no clear distinction between the rituals of daily life and the practice of the Hindu religion, and philosophy plays its part as much as do the diverse divinities and animistic personifications. Hinduism is more a prescription of life-style and attitude than a matter of doctrine or dogmatic belief. A commonly held idea is of God evolving as a transcendental entity whose visible aspects show themselves in the ever changing world. Hence the acceptance of the divine principle of eternity embodied in every living thing on earth. Images of the deity in all its personifications help people to remain aware of their relationship both with the world as it appears around them and with the superior entities beyond reach. In this way, cosmic order is maintained.

Hindu pantheon – The Universal Creator, **Brahma**, reigns supreme over the trinity. He is often shown with four heads turned towards the four corners of the earth, and four arms holding a lotus flower, a conch shell, a discus and the sacred texts, or Vedas, which contain eternal knowledge. **Shiva** is usually represented astride a bull, surveying the world at large, and with a *lingam* (or phallus), for the guru of the gods is both a creator and a destroyer. Other symbolic attributes include the trident, fire, a crescent moon in his hair, an axe, the waters of the Ganges, a small bell and an antelope. His mount is the bull **Nandi** which represents the earthly forces and procreation. **Vishnu**, the Sun God, is regarded as the preserver of the world and, as such, is immobile and often in opposition to Shiva. Alternatively, Vishnu combines with Shiva to form a single deity, Hari-Hara. He, in turn, is sometimes accompanied by **Parvati**, the wife of Shiva, together with their eldest son Ganesh who has the head of an elephant. For Shiva cut off his son's head by accident, and then promptly replaced it with the head of the next creature that came along. **Ganesh** is the God of wisdom and goodwill. He makes anything possible and is always invoked before a ceremony. **Muruga** is the Tamil God of youth, beauty and war; chief of the celestial army; army instructor; the destroyer of demons though a demon himself. His attribute is the cobra, and he is often depicted riding a peacock with its tail feathers fanned out, and armed with a lance and a bow. The black goddess **Kali**, also known as Durga, is the consort of Shiva and symbolises judgement and death.

Islam
The Moslems of Mauritius are rather more moderate than Arabic Moslems (alcohol is sold everywhere). Despite this, they respect the same fundamental rules or Five Pillars of Islam: there is no God but Allah, the importance of regular prayer, the giving of alms, the observance of fasting during Ramadan and, if possible, the completion of a pilgrimage to Mecca. To this end, the faithful congregate in the mosque each Friday to listen to the Imam and pray together. The largest faction in the Moslem community is **Sunni**, whereas the **Shiites** form a minority.

Catholicism
Roman Catholicism, as prescribed by the original French settlers, is practised by the white Franco-Mauritians and the Creoles. There are also a considerable number of converts of Chinese descent.

Buddhism
For the most part, the Chinese Mauritians are Buddhists although their rites and aspirations have been tempered by the cult of ancestors and the honouring of the dead, and the influence of the moral philosophy of Confucius. The teachings of Buddha are rooted in Brahmanism for they focus on the reasons behind human suffering and how men and women can free themselves from this yoke. Based on the beliefs Buddha taught his early disciples, the Three Truths are the foundation of this religion. The first is a pessimistic concept of life, where all is suffering because ephemeral. The second attributes unhappiness to the desires created by this temporary state of suffering and the third explains how suffering can be abolished by suppressing their cause, desire.
The cycle of reincarnations (*samsara*) will lead to Nirvana, a state of total beauty and complete calm, in which all desires are extinguished.

Holy days for all

Just about all the public holidays in the Mauritian calendar mark some form of religious festival, and as such they reflect the diversity and intensity of the island's religious beliefs.

Hindu festivals
All the Hindu festivals attract great gatherings of people, with crowds of several hundred thousand in attendance. They are lively events involving acts of devotion, sometimes entailing the endurance of great suffering, the significance of which might easily elude the foreign visitor. Despite this, everyone is welcome to participate in the colour, the joy and the celebrations, the dressing-up, the decorations of flowers and lights, the music and the merrymaking.

Probably the most popular annual festival is **Maha Shivaratri** (which literally means "The Great Night of Shiva"). This celebrates Shiva's victory over Brahma and Vishnu and takes place in February or March over five consecutive days. Over the years it has established itself as the biggest Hindu festival to be held outside India.

First the faithful, all dressed in white, gather for an all-night vigil. Then as day breaks they go in a procession to the lake at Grand Bassin to make their ablutions in the purifying water, as if it were one with the sacred River Ganges. Each *kanvar* – a bamboo edifice covered in flowers, ribbons and mirrors representing one of Shiva's temples – is borne by several men. As they complete their arduous journey to the lake, the pilgrims make offerings of food, immersing themselves in the sacred water and pouring it over the phallic *lingam* at the entrance to the temple which symbolises Nature, the universe, the power and creative energy of Shiva.

Divali or **Diapavali** which is held in October or November, celebrates the victory of Rama (Vishnu's incarnation as a sun god representing cosmic law) over the demon Ravana who had abducted his wife Lakhsmi, the goddess of multiplicity and good fortune.

As a moon-less night begins, the faithful light their houses with candles, oil lamps and electric bulbs; then leaving all the doors and windows of the house wide open, they pray for riches, plenty and success, and hope that the good luck has entered into their homes. Great offerings of fruit and flowers are made to Lakhsmi. Divali also celebrates generosity, and so cakes and sweetmeats are shared among the crowd. Fireworks and firecrackers to ward off bad luck add to the general gaiety of the occasion and the party atmosphere.

This "festival of light" is also marked and celebrated across the island by the various other communities in their own special way.

Holi, the joyous Hindu festival of fire and colour, celebrates the cult of fertility and regeneration. It takes place around the time of the spring equinox on a night with a full moon in February or March. On the chosen day, everyone goes outside to sprinkle the ground with water and powdered colour, and exchange good wishes. The red powder symbolises amorous desire and the new life-giving blood that courses through the veins. The festivities end with a bonfire on which cakes are burnt, along with a straw effigy of the demon Holika, symbol of the forces of evil. Should you find yourself in Mauritius at this time, put on some old clothes for the occasion and join in the fun.

Ganga Asna is marked in India in October or November with people immersing themselves in the Ganges. In Mauritius, the Hindus go to the beach, present their offerings and then bathe in the sea in an act of purification as if it were the waters of the scared Indian river.

The Tamil festival of **Cavadee** (or *Thai Poosam*) takes place in January or February depending on the year. The specific date and hour of the ceremony are of great consequence and are chosen by the *swami* or priest to coincide with a particular phase in the lunar cycle. During this festival of purification, the faithful perform acts of penitence to rid themselves of sin and free their soul from evil. According to legend, they do this in honour of Muruga, head of the celestial armies who delivered the sage Idoumban from a demon. Before the festival therefore, adherents are required to pray, fast and practise self-restraint for ten days.

C Pavard/ HOA QUI

Tamils celebrating Cavadee

On the actual day of the festival, the faithful seek to purify themselves in the river at dawn. Some will then atone for their sins by painful self-mutilation by threading needles and hooks through the flesh on their back, torso or neck and then attaching lemons to them. Alternatively, they might pierce their tongue and cheeks with skewers. Others walk on soles bristling with nails. Already weakened by their long fast, these people proceed in a feverish trance, carrying the *cavadee* high on their shoulders. This is a wooden contraption designed to represent Muruga's temple and containing an effigy of the god. At each extremity is balanced a bronze pot (or *sambo*) of milk (sacred liquid), and decoration is provided by flowers and palm fronds. Women, meanwhile, usually carry a large copper vessel full of milk instead of the *cavadee*. The lengthy procession on foot leads to the temple where the milk is presented to the deity during a ceremony conducted by the *swami*. It must be said that certain Hindus join in the celebration without doing the ritual of penitence, preferring simply to pray and make offerings on a copper tray such as a coconut with its milk, three bananas, some flowers, camphor and incense.

Ganesh Chaturti, sometime in August or September, celebrates the birth of Ganesh, the God of travellers, merchants and shopkeepers, thieves and scholars. Ganesh has the power to remove obstacles and to bestow immortality on the faithful. He is the son of Shiva and Parvati, and is represented with a human body and the head of an elephant, because his own was cut off by Shiva in a fit of rage. For this holy day, replicas of Ganesh are modelled out of clay and prayers are offered up to them over the ensuing days until, finally, they are carried in a procession to the sea and allowed to melt in the sacred water.

The most astonishing practices, however, are the remarkable feats of **walking on hot coals** that usually take place in December and February during the Tamil festival of **Teemeedee**. First the participants must devote a specific period of time to fasting, praying, abstinence from just about everything and meditation; then they must go in a procession together to the river nearest to their local temple and cleanse themselves in the water. At last, the men, women and children gather before the temple in clouds of burning incense and prepare to undertake the slow walk across the long pit of red-hot coals, encouraged by the doleful beat of drums. Finally they are able to plunge their feet in a bowl of milk to soothe the burns. This extraordinary ritual is enacted to atone for sin, to seek favour with the Gods, and to prove the power of mind over matter.

The Tamils celebrate **Thai Pongal** in January or February by offering food to the Gods.

Moslem festivals

Moslem holy days tend to be quite different to the public displays and spectacular celebrations of the Hindus. Instead, they consist of collective prayer meetings in the mosque followed by a gathering of the family for a special meal accompanied by games, music and song; donations are made to charity and, good wishes, sometimes presents, are exchanged.

Yamun Nabi commemorates the birth of the Prophet Mohammed. On that day, the faithful gather to listen to a eulogy of Mohammed and an account of his life.

Id-El-Adha celebrates the time when Abraham prepared to sacrifice his son Ismael, and God told him to kill the ram caught in a thicket nearby instead. To mark this auspicious day, people go to the mosque and pray and then go home to kill a sheep, goat or cow. In accordance with tradition, the animal is divided into three parts with two thirds being given to the poor and distant relatives, and one third being eaten by the immediate family.

Id-El-Fitr marks the end of Ramadan, the month of fasting, and so celebrations culminate with a huge gathering and much joy. First the believers will have a bath and change into clean clothes; then they go to the mosque to pray and give thanks to God for helping them to endure the rigours of Ramadan. Finally, they are free to pay visits to friends and family, exchange goods, wishes and gifts, and give alms to the poor. This is a truly special day when goodwill prevails, offenders are pardoned, scores are settled and quarrels are patched up.

Ghoons is marked annually by the small Shiite community in honour of the martyr Imam Hussein, a descendant of the Prophet. The one and only procession makes its way through Port Louis. In some ways it resembles the Hindu festival of Cavadee, with a *ghoon* – like the *cavadee* – built of bamboo and decorated with flowers carried through the streets. As with the Tamil festival, the Moslem penitents inflict pain on themselves by piercing their bodies with needles as expiation for their sins.

Christian feast days

See p 47 Christian Festivals

The most celebrated day of the Catholic calendar in Mauritius is the **Fête du Bienheureux Jacques Désiré Laval** which takes place annually on 9 September, the anniversary of Laval's death in 1864. Laval was a French doctor turned missionary who converted many of the liberated slaves to Christianity, and is considered by many to have miraculous healing powers. Long after his death he continued to be regarded as a saint and was eventually beatified by Pope John-Paul in 1979.

For more than a century, Mauritians of all denominations have gathered at the tomb of Father Laval – whom they have adopted as the rightful patron saint of Mauritius – at Ste-Croix, on the outskirts of Port Louis *(see p 264)*. To mark his feast day, several thousand people of every religious inclination and ethnic background gather in a great procession, and masses are said every hour for about two days.

Chinese festivals

The **Chinese Spring Festival** corresponds to the Chinese New Year (in January or February depending on the lunar calendar). Before New Year's Day, each family completes a series of rites designed to chase away the evil spirits of winter. The Spirit of Food is also honoured and encouraged to go to heaven for a week every year to report to the Celestial Emperor on each family. To mollify him, the Chinese traditionally make generous offerings of rice and honey cakes at his altar.

During and about the time of the festival, particular efforts are made towards remembering ancestors and forebears. To do this, the head of the family invites the departed to share in the joy of renewal with their descendants. Members of the family are then required to recount the events of the past year and ask for blessings for the coming year. Throughout the period when the ancestors are called to the family, their altars are laden with food offerings and burning incense. The delicately prepared dishes are then eaten by the family.

In the weeks leading up to New Year, everyone tries to settle any unpleasant business in order to be able to begin the new year auspiciously with a clean conscience. The festive season is a time when people call upon parents and fellows to acknowledge the bonds of friendship and kindness shown. It also is a time for individuals to confer good wishes for good health and prosperity on those they love and admire, and exchange gifts with them.

Each year, every family sets about spring-cleaning – and sometimes repainting – their house. To mark the occasion, almost everything is painted red, the colour of happiness. Banners and scrolls inscribed with good wishes bedeck the houses. Traditional dishes of all kind are prepared so that food might be plentiful in the ensuing year. Plants with colourful foliage, fruit and spring flowers form a vital part in the festivities, and firecrackers are exploded everywhere to chase away the spirits of evil. Finally, all the Chinese, dressed in brand new clothes for the occasion, settle down to the best meal of the year with all the family.

If you happen to be in Port Louis at that time, pay a visit to one of the pagodas to see the faithful making their offerings to Buddha, burning texts or images of the household god and honouring ancestors, lost in the fog of burning incense.

The Dragon or **Lantern Festival** is held a fortnight after New Year, to celebrate the victory of Buddha's wisdom and knowledge over evil, symbolised by the cruel dragon. That night, everyone goes outside with glowing paper lanterns of all shapes and colours. Costumed parades and dragon dances complete the festivities, and ensure that the ancient art of making brightly-coloured traditional masks and costumes lives on with future generations.

The **Festival of Ching Ming** is a private festival devoted to the cult of ancestors. For this, Chinese Mauritians take flowers and food to the dead and burn incense on their graves by candlelight.

DAILY LIFE

Endangered architecture

Traditional examples of Mauritian architecture are fast being replaced by modern constructions – largely for economic reasons. Over the past decades, the fragments from the distant past have been lost beneath new developments, as in Port Louis for example, where land is at a premium and developers are keen to capitalise on their investments.
To make matters worse, the old timber and corrugated-iron Creole buildings and magnificent colonial homesteads are expensive to maintain and have suffered over the years from neglect and a lack of funds, and are vulnerable to both cyclones and termites.
Local authorities encourage architects to design new buildings in the traditional Creole style with modern materials such as concrete, fibreglass and specially-treated wood. In the meantime, it is vital that investment is aimed at preserving and restoring what remains of the island's building heritage, notably the houses dating from the 18C and listing more houses as monuments.
The first fine houses, symbols of a certain "art de vivre", were built in the 18C, during French colonial times under the aegis of the governor Mahé de La Bourdonnais. Under the guidance of French craftsmen, slaves and ship carpenters were set to work at constructing elegant country houses and built colonial towns.
Over the years, the style of buildings assimilated new elements that reflected the tastes of the different ethnic communities. Then, in the 19C, the colonists realised that their buildings should be adapted to cope with the specific characteristics of the island's climate, and this could be done by restricting or increasing the use of certain materials. It was particularly during the British era between 1860 and 1930, that elements of French and British architecture became integrated into the Mauritian style of buildings.

See illustrations p 18-19.

Colonial townships

Most towns are laid out on a grid system. The sober-looking public buildings are constructed in the more permanent materials like stone, and have survived the ravages both of time and cyclones. Examples of this type include the government building in Port Louis, the town hall in Curepipe and the Château du Réduit.
In contrast, remarkably few of the large two-storey Creole townhouses built in wood with a fine wrought-iron balustrade on the first floor have been well-preserved. For at one time, the merchant families had large and spacious shops with storage facilities on the ground floor, and a fine family apartment above. The odd one survives in Port Louis and in Curepipe.
Dotted about town, there is a dwindling number of little Creole houses. These, built for the workers, have often suffered from complete abandon and stand somewhat at odds with their ugly and faceless high-rise neighbours. Fortunately, originality and character are preserved in the Chinese Mauritian homes and in Indo-Muslim style buildings ornamented with oriental curlicues and serpentine lines. These often modest yet comfortable family homes line the streets, sheltered behind solid walls and an iron gate or **baro**.

Country houses

If the old townhouses have been pulled down for economic reasons, those in more rural areas have suffered from the ravages of time.

The **planter's house** consists essentially of a wooden villa with a steeply pitched roof covered with wooden tiles **(bardeaux)** painted bluish-grey or dark-grey and a decorative ridge, surrounded by endless fields of sugarcane. In the beginning, it was designed largely on French colonial lines as found in the East Indies. Later, it came to reflect the taste for neo-classical simplicity that was all the rage in France in the early 19C.

The second distinctive feature after the roof is the Creole **varangue**, a veranda – flat-roofed and covered in *argamasse* (water-resistant mortar made with lime, egg and sugar) – up a few steps from the garden and leading into the house. Alternatively, this terrace area might run like a gallery right around the house; support is provided by a series of columns and a decorative balustrade. It might be glazed like an English bay-window or shuttered (with cane or palm-leaf blinds) to keep out the sun, wind or rain depending on the season, or simply to provide privacy from prying eyes.

The veranda is the heart of the Mauritian home. It is the one place in the house that is never too hot nor too cold, where the family can gather with friends and neighbours, or where members can relax, work, eat or snooze in complete comfort.

Later, various fancy elements started appearing in Mauritian architecture. Roofs sprouted decorative little multifaceted turrets, for example, sometimes with gables as well. The door and window canopies assumed decorative lace-like fret-work edging, or **lambrequins,** cut from the wood or corrugated iron.

Inside, the living room, dining room and bedrooms are inter-connected so as to make the most of a ventilating through-draught.

Separated from the main house, small shacks were built to accommodate the family bathroom and kitchen (*boucan*) to minimise the risk of fire.

Today these lovely and spacious houses are owned by wealthy Mauritians, descended from the prosperous French planters in the main, who like to retreat into their homes behind overgrown gardens at the end of great wooded avenues and tall bamboo hedges. So little is visible from the outside. A few are listed in the descriptive text, but many are left to be discovered by the inquisitive visitors.

Workers' houses are conceived along the same practical lines as the planter's homesteads, but they are more modest in scale and often painted in somewhat garish colours as compared to the sober shades of the gentrified villas.

The internal space is divided into two areas that serve as the sleeping quarters and the dining room. An additional room is provided by the veranda-cum-living room decorated on the outside with the traditional *lambrequin* over the porch. Originally, these houses would have been thatched with pandanus leaves, dried cane or wooden strips. Now they tend to be covered in and fronted by sheets of undulating corrugated iron.

In the 19C, the **campements** provided the wealthy middle classes with a secondary home by the sea. As such they were conceived for temporary use during the winter when temperatures on the central plateau dropped below comfortable levels. They were built out of traveller's palms and roofed with straw. When the household moved down from the main house, it brought along all the furniture and furnishings required to make the place habitable. These days, the one-time temporary holiday homes strung along the coastal roads are built of concrete. The few that are roofed with *ravenala* palm fronds combine the best of new and old – solidity with aesthetic appeal.

Religious buildings

The island is dotted with religious monuments, such as white-domed Tamil temples and Hindu temples painted in distinctive candy shades of colour. The odd Chinese pagoda, meanwhile, verges towards the reddish, the mosque minarets are green and white, whereas the small iron-roofed Christian churches feature a dark grey stone.

Education

Education is free but not compulsory, more than 90 % of children, however, attend **school**.

During your stay it is inevitable that you will see clusters of schoolchildren dressed in their two-colour uniform which vary from one institution to the next. In order to ensure that all children theoretically grow-up bilingual, key subjects are taught in French and English from primary level onwards. More and more pupils then graduate to the college at Réduit, the island's largest university. The more fortunate leave to study in France or England.
This small and isolated territory in the middle of the ocean, endowed with little to no natural resources save for its acres of sugarcane, does not require its youngsters to do **military service**. Instead, the island militia is made up of some 5 000 or so volunteers, who also assume the responsibility of policing the island. It is rare for young people over the age of 24-25 to be single. As is common practice in India, the Hindus organise **arranged marriages** for their children. Traditionally, the parents must first negotiate terms. Eventually the intended are allowed to meet each other one week before the designated wedding day, and permitted to consummate their marriage only three days after the wedding. Whatever the background and ethnic origins of the couple, nuptials are always occasions for religious rites and colourful celebrations.

Dress

For Indo-Mauritians, Hindu or Moslem, culture and religion go hand in hand, and they regard dress as fundamental to their cultural identity. Hindu women wear saris which comprise a cropped shirt and a single length of beautiful coloured Indian cloth (preferably silk). Conversely, although the teachings of the Koran are quite flexible in Mauritius, Moslem women are encouraged to cover their heads with a veil and attire themselves in wide trousers and long straight tunics down to the ankle.

Just about everybody else chooses western forms of dress. Jeans and T-shirts are especially popular, possibly because many different styles and foreign designer labels are readily available from the local clothes factories or back-street markets. In Port Louis, businessmen and office workers wear conventional suits and ties as they would in any other capital city.

C Pavard/HOA QUI

Tamil Temple (detail)

C Vaisse/HOA QUI

The corner video-club shop

Pastimes

Football is considered by many as the national sport, especially since international matches have been screened on television. Not only do Mauritians follow the sport assiduously, they will be out kicking a ball whenever they have the chance, after work and at weekends. Clubs are often proudly named after English soccer teams.

On the beach, basket-ball and volley-ball are extremely popular.

Port Louis' race track, the Champ de Mars, regularly attracts a large and rowdy crowd during the **horse racing season** *(see The Champ de Mars p 259)* between May and October.

Gambling at the casino, and the local version of bingo, are both widely enjoyed.

Mauritians are also keen on watching films. As the number of families with video recorders grows, **video** shops have sprung up to satisfy demand and cinema audiences have fallen.

Art and Folklore

Music and dance

Mauritians have an innate sense of rhythm and will break into song or dance at every available opportunity.

Séga

Séga still rings with the sounds and rhythms once improvised by African slaves grouped around a fire on the beach at nightfall. After a hard day's work in the cane fields, the men would warm the *ravane* (a large flat drum) over the flames to make the goatskin taught, and swig rum. Before long they were in the mood for airing their feelings, and the songs would ring through the night air, speaking of unrequited loves, the trials and tribulations of growing old and the hardships they had to endure as slaves. The improvised lyrics were always touched with humour, often involving expressions in Creole with double meanings that veiled the underlying mockery. Gradually the rhythms provided by short, light beats became more insistent, coaxing both men and women to join in the dance one by one. As they came to shed all inhibitions and gave themselves up to the dancing, ample skirts brushed provocatively against cropped trousers, teasing the participants to a frenzy of desire, but couples never actually touched. For the seductive sensuality of the dance lay in flirting with propriety.

Nowadays, people are not bound by the same constraints of slavery and so inevitably, the exciting spontaneity of *séga* has long gone. Indeed the modern forms are a pale imitation of the original dance; and traditional instruments – the **ravane**, **maravane** (hollow gourd full of dried seeds or beans) and the **triangle** – have all but died out. The *séga* performed at the hotel pool-side or on the beach is now far removed from its traditional form.

A variation of *séga* evolved during the 1980s, when a Rastafarian group experimented with mixing sounds of Jamaican reggae into the Creole dance. They called the outcome **seggae**.

Cosmopolitan music

In towns and villages across the island, the strains of high-pitched **Indian music,** most often borrowed from a popular film soundtrack, add a joyful note to the urban environment. Besides the rich local tradition of music-making, the youth are avid followers of **western pop music** which sets the beat in the discotheques and invites the younger generations to dance.

Painting comes into its own

In the 19C, local artists were restricted to painting commissioned portraits of governors and other dignitaries. Things changed radically in the course of the 20C when painters like Xavier Le Juge de Segrais and Max Boullé, picked up their brushes and responded to the clear light and strong colours around them, and set to painting island life as they found it. Malcolm de Chazal on the other hand, tended towards the Primitive, influenced perhaps by Surrealism. Among them, only Hervé Masson has truly attained international renown.

The art galleries at Rose Hill and Port Louis display artworks of vastly varying quality, possibly with greater commercial interest than artistic merit.

It is now the contemporary artists – Véronique Le Clézio, Hervé Decotter, Henri Khoombes and Khalid Nazroo – who must ensure that painting continues to thrive.

Scant craftsmanship

Contrary to what one might expect, this diverse island population has a somewhat poor craft tradition, and those goods that are produced are destined entirely for the tourist market. Indeed a large proportion of hand-made leather items, basketry or woodwork comes from Madagascar. You may find the odd striking length of Indian fabric, a hat or a basket from Rodrigues to your taste. The most original and truly Mauritian examples of quality craftsmanship are the **model boats** made by both men and women. While the former whittle the wooden components, the latter assemble the models, adding the sails – dipped in tea to heighten the effect, the rigging and the ropes.
This trade only really took off in the 1970s after a series of historical boat replicas made by artisan José Ramart were displayed in an exhibition. There are now a hundred or so workshops across the island producing scale models from archive drawings. The fleet comprises galleys, frigates, galleons, schooners and other French and English vessels – bearing famous names like *Le Saint-Géran*, *L'Étoile*, *La Boudeuse*, *L'Astrolabe*, *La Boussole*, *Le Revenant*, *The Titanic* and *The Bounty*.

Literary creation and heritage

Mauritius has a unique oral tradition. For over the centuries, the stories that were originally imported by European colonists have been "Creolised" and adapted into tales that might be more pertinent to life in a different land. As a result, the stories were fused with African, Madagascan and Indian myths and legends, and coloured with vernacular details and superstition. Riddles, known as *Sirandanes*, are a fair representation of the Mauritian cultural diversity.
These have been transmitted orally from one generation to another. In each case, the definition required a single word as a solution:

"Dileau en pendant" (hanging water)?	a coconut
"Dileau diboute" (water standing up)?	sugarcane
"Cote mo allé li sivré moi" (wherever I go it follows me)?	my shadow
"Mouce dans di lait" (a fly in the milk)?	a black person dressed in white
"Nenez Madame angles en bas la terre" (an English lady's nose in the ground)?	a radish
"Ptit batt mamman" (a child hits its mother)	a bell
"Baionette pas dérière" (rear-loaded bayonet)?	a wasp
"Ptit bonhomme, grand capeau" (small man, big hat)?	a mushroom

Vernacular literature underwent a major renaissance in the 19C in response to influences from **France** where important movements were flourishing and evolving: Romanticism, Parnassian poetry, Symbolism and Surrealism. Indeed, some writers, such as Malcolm de Chazal and Loys Masson lived for a time in Paris. Back in Mauritius, the prime concern was a fear of conflict between the island's different ethnic groups – and that theme pervades all forms of literature throughout this period. In the 20C, writers have also sought inspiration in **Indian** and **African** cultures, and more recently, have found expression in **English** and **Hindi**. Since the 1970s, authors have chosen to write in **Creole** although this literature has not rallied much of a following. Mauritius has not only inspired local writers, such as Robert E Hart, Loys Masson, Macolm de Chazal, JMG Le Clézio, it has also motivated some very famous non-Mauritian authors, such as Mark Twain, Joseph Conrad, Bernardin de Saint-Pierre, Charles Baudelaire and Alexandre Dumas.

SOCIAL ETIQUETTE

How to mix with the locals

There are hundreds of ways to discover all the different faces of the island's best-kept secrets. First and foremost, almost all Mauritians speak English, some more fluently than others, but relationships are easily made. The resort hotels and seaside complexes provide all the facilities and services one could possibly wish for to have a pleasant and restful holiday, but the impression they give of Mauritius itself is distorted, or at least incomplete. Indeed, however amenable the staff and employees you will meet there, dealings with them will always remain somewhat artificial.

- For a more authentic experience and an insight into daily life, stay in a small hotel or guesthouse and eat in the cheap and cheerful village restaurants or in the markets.
- Venture out to the remote little hamlets that are devoid of so-called tourist attractions. Here, in stark contrast with the seaside resorts, you will encounter the local fishermen and shop-keepers who, more often than not, see life from a wholly different perspective.
- Linger around the temples, mosques and churches where people gather after prayers at the end of the day or at weekends, and absorb the atmosphere.
- Find out when and where the local festivals are held and try to attend, showing discretion and respect for the different religious practices.
- Explore the sparsely populated regions, and you might be lucky enough to be invited inside a house for a cup of tea and a chat.
- Wherever possible, hop on a bus and engage in conversation with fellow passengers. If you can manage to squeeze onto a packed bus in the capital bound for the towns of the central plateau at rush-hour, you will get a true taste of what Mauritian commuters have to contend with on a daily basis. You can then continue on a circuit through the residential quarters for a more complete picture of how people live.

If you cannot deal with the crowds, opt for one of the less popular bus routes heading out along the east coast for example, where there may be time to chat with a fellow passenger in a sari or wearing a skullcap.

A ready smile and a pleasant disposition are professional requisites in the tourist resorts, but outside these places, Mauritians may not always seem quite so affable at first; indeed, they may seem a little cold and distant. You might even discern a certain lassitude and weariness with tourism, and a marked lack of interest unless there is a chance of making a profit. But should you persevere with enquiring about genuine issues like politics, sport and religious rituals, you will discover the open and friendly personality of these naturally curious people.

- You will often be asked for your impressions of their "Paradise" island and whether you have visited a particular area or enjoyed a special beauty spot.
- Many a Mauritian will want to know about where you come from, and share their dreams of visiting the countries that lie beyond their own horizons and that had so much influence on their nation. Indeed many already have relations living far away.

Besides an historic or affective attachment to a country, the idea of foreign lands widens most people's horizons. Even though many Mauritians are descended from immigrants from developing countries like India or China, most of them have never travelled beyond the shores of Mauritius. An insular life can be rather restricting, and meeting visitors makes dreams of travelling come to life. Despite improvement in the island's economy, many things portrayed by television, remain outside the reach of most Mauritians.

Forewarned is forearmed

• Mauritians have an innate sense of fun and love jokes. They are easy-going by nature and enjoy teasing people around them: so do feel free to join in and share in their laughter.

• You will always be made to feel welcome if attending a celebration (like a wedding), and your host will be delighted to see you join in the dancing rather than just watching the action.

• Remember to remove shoes before entering a mosque or a Hindu temple. It is also important to dress appropriately keeping shoulders and knees covered, and avoiding plunging necklines. Ensure that you are not wearing anything made of leather (belts, bags) in a Hindu temple as it is considered impure.

• Mauritius forbids nudism. Topless women are tolerated on hotel beaches, but may cause offence on public beaches. It should be noted that most Mauritians wear one-piece swimsuits and that there are still some Indo-Mauritian women who bathe in the sea fully clothed. Being seen walking anywhere but along the beach in a swimming costume or with a bare chest is liable to provoke unwarranted attention, shock and titters of embarrassment from the locals.

• On the whole, Mauritians never argue or lose their cool in public, and so they are likely to view a ranting tourist with a disconcerted eye.

• Mauritians are generally happy to pose for photographs, but you should nevertheless seek their permission first as a matter of courtesy. Indian women will sometimes turn their head away if they catch a lens being focused on them. In stark contrast, young children will jostle for attention. This inevitably makes it a challenge to catch them looking spontaneous.

• Mauritians might refer to racial communities other than their own as *Malbars* or *Malabars* (Hindus), *Madras* (Tamils) or *Lascars* (Moslems): these terms – considered pejorative – should not be used by westerners as they may be interpreted as derogatory and insulting.

• When requesting directions or information, it is well worth asking several other people for verification. Rather than admitting ignorance, locals might prefer to be seen as trying to be helpful by giving incorrect advice.

• In Indian restaurants, do not think the waiter is being too familiar if he spreads out your napkin on your knee.

EATING AND DRINKING

Mauritian cuisine is as varied and diverse as its cosmopolitan population, with a broad choice of dishes reflecting Indian, Chinese, European and Creole origins. Rice is the common staple and it should be the first thing to be spooned onto the plate. Only then is the fish or meat stew, which has been simmered and flavoured with spices, ladled out. This is accompanied by a variety of local vegetables such as *chouchou* (*chayote* or *choko*), *giraumon* (red pumpkin), squash (*pâtisson*), aubergine, *brèdes* (greens) or *achards* (a vegetable pickle).

Creole cuisine

The most common dishes are those made with locally-found ingredients. The favourites have been combined from a variety of traditions, with an inevitable bias towards the Indian.

Cari comes in various forms (fish, fowl, red meat) and comprises onions, ginger, garlic, herbs and spices (coriander, cumin and turmeric), tomatoes or coconut milk, with a portion of lentils, pulses or beans on the side. **Rougail** consists of meat, sausages or fish which has been simmered with cherry tomatoes (known locally as *pomme d'amour*), onions, garlic, ginger, herbs and chilli peppers. **Vindaye** is prepared with fish or venison that has been marinated in a mixture of vinegar, mustard seeds, turmeric, lightly fried onions, ginger and garlic. To accompany the main dish, a bland or plain vegetable like steamed or boiled *chouchou* or *brèdes* is served. Alternatively, there may be a relish or some *achards* (grated vegetables, shredded green mango or lemon, seasoned with mixed spices and oil) or a form of chutney (onion, garlic, spices, herbs, and usually tomatoes pickled in vinegar).

Mauritians eat all kinds of fish, the most prized being *capitaine*, *sacrechien*, *vieille rouge*, *cordonnier* and tuna They also love seafood delicacies like squid, prawns, crab and lobster cooked simply over a grill and served with a squeeze of fresh lime. Large fish, such as marlin, are often smoked or eaten raw Japanese-style. Another favourite way of eating fish is in soup.

The ultimate speciality is **"Millionaire's Salad"**, a simple dish comprising the

Preparing rice

Pratt-Priest / DIAF

growing shoot of a *palmiste* palm that has been tenderised in milk. The reason for its name hinges on the fact that it takes the tree several years to grow and each "heart" only yields 600g of edible flesh.

Deer, introduced by the Dutch in the 16C, are still farmed. During the hunting season (June to September), venison curry is widely available.
It is also well worth sampling the fritters and doughnuts sold along the beach, on street corners and in the market: **gateaux piment** (small round spicy fritters), *bringelles* (aubergine/egg-plant fritters), **samossas** (deep-fried triangular pastries filled with meat, fish or spicy vegetables), *gateaux patates* (sweet potato dumplings with added sugar and grated coconut), **dhal puri** (lentil flour pancakes with a delicious curry sauce).

Indian cuisine

Indian food is known to be highly flavoured by blends of spices and can be very hot. The standard – and equally delicious – dishes are **curry** and **biriyani** and both vary from place to place as every housewife has her own favourite recipe. With curry, the rice is cooked separately from the meat, fish and vegetables, whereas in biryani the rice is layered with vegetables, meat, fish or eggs, infused with spices, and then baked. A simple version of this one-dish casserole is eaten on a daily basis, whereas more complex and lavish versions are the preserve of banquets and Moslem celebrations.
Variation is also imparted by particular sects, for some foods are forbidden by religion. The Koran prevents Moslems from eating pork because it is "unclean", whereas Tamils refuse to eat beef as they consider the cow sacred.

Chinese cuisine

Chinese food is by far the most delicate and refined form of cooking in Mauritius because the restaurants go to great lengths (and expense) to coax their chefs away from China, and pride themselves in the integrity of their food. In most instances, the vegetables, bean curd, bamboo shoots and mushrooms are lightly fried in a wok (large round metal pan heated by a bare flame). Then, before they lose their crunchiness, shredded pork, beef, shrimps or fish are added along with a seasoning of ginger, lime, lemon grass, fresh coriander, and soy, shrimp or oyster sauce. If you are unfamiliar with Chinese food, try the **mine frit** – a popular dish of sautéed noodles – from street-stalls or restaurants anywhere.

Spices

In each case, Mauritian food is prepared with a careful combination of spices including saffron, turmeric, cloves, nutmeg, cumin, coriander, cinnamon, cayenne pepper, cardamom, ginger and pepper often imported from India, the Dutch East Indies or the Far East.

Mauritian drinks

Mauritians like to drink **Bois Chéri tea** and **Chamarel coffee**, sometimes flavoured with vanilla, with milk and sugar (if you prefer it served in any other way, you should say so). Alternatively, when out on the town, they might opt for a fizzy drink or a (sweet or salty) yoghurt *lassi* from a street-vendor. Sunday lunches, however, would not be complete without ample supplies of local beers: *Phoenix, Blue Marline* and *Stella* and *Green Island rum*.
In restaurants, you will find a range of reasonably priced South African wines, and a restricted selection of more expensive French wines that have rarely been stored properly. Bottled mineral water is widely available everywhere, and the tap water is completely safe to drink.

LANGUAGE

Mauritian Creole is not officially recognised and therefore it is not taught in schools. Despite this, it is the common language spoken by all the different communities everyday and in all walks of life.
This popular dialect evolved in the 18C out of a need for slaves from various parts of the world to communicate with each other, and with their colonial masters.
The origins therefore are rooted in colloquial French, and the structure is provided by phonetics. As a result, everything is reduced to its most fundamental basics: pronouns are dispensed with, tenses are limited to the present etc. Then over time, other words of African and Madagascan, English, Hindi and Chinese derivation were assimilated.
To date, Creole has been an oral language, peppered with the vivid use of imagery. It is only very recently that efforts have been directed at formalising it and setting a single standard for grammar and spelling. One should remember that for generations, babies have been growing up surrounded by and speaking their mother tongue; only as young children have they then learnt to speak Creole and gone out into the wider community.
The Creole spoken by Mauritians is specific to Mauritius. Although similar to the versions found in the Seychelles Islands and Rodrigues, it differs quite considerably to the dialect in Réunion. Having said this, the basics of Creole are common to all the Indian Ocean islanders, so everyone is at least able to make himself understood.

The official language is **English.** Not only is it taught at school from a young age, it is the universal language of administration, politics and business. Few people, however, tend to use English outside their working environment, preferring instead to speak **French** among themselves. French is also increasingly used by the media.

The ethnic communities meanwhile preserve their own languages for use in the family home and for religious practices. Indo-Mauritians speak Hindi (particularly in the media), Urdu (which is written with the Arab alphabet), *Bhojpuri* (from north India) or Tamil, *Telugu*, *Marathi* or *Gujarati*. Chinese-Mauritians speak Mandarin, *Cantonese* or *Hakka*.

A lexicon of Creole phrases

Pronunciation

See p 62

Everyday expressions

Bonswar	Good evening
Bonzour	Good morning
Correc	Agreed, that's fine/OK
Ena	There are
Ki manière?/Koman ou ete?	How are you?/How's it going?

Ki mo pou faire?	What can I do?
Ki ou non?	What's your name?
Kombyen sa?	How much is that?
Koté cabiné	Where is the toilet / WC?
Koté capave téléfoné	Where is the phone?
Li	He or she
Mo content	I like
Mo oulé	I want / I'd like
Mo pas comprend	I do not understand
Mo soif	I'm thirsty
Na pas tracas	Don't worry
Orevar	Good bye
Ou ena...?	Do you have...?
Pas correc	Not agreed/ not OK
Sa li byen zoli	It's very beautiful
Silvouplé	Please
Tapeta!	Cheers!

A few useful phrases

Achards	Hot spicy grated vegetables in saffron oil
Arak	Alcohol distilled from fermented sugarcane
Auvent	Little roof jutting out over a door or window
Bagasse	Waste sugarcane pulp dried and burnt as fuel
Bardeau	Wooden roof slat
Bazar	Market
Bonbon	Sweet fritter or patty
Brèdes	Greens used in soup or stews
Bringelle	Aubergine/egg-plant
Cabri	Goat (for spicy Tamil dish)
Camaron	Large prawn
Campagne	Large wooden house surrounded by land. Few remain because of encroaching farms and houses
Campement	Traditional beach house
Cari	Creole dish (originally from India)
Case	Corrugated-iron or breeze-block shack. Only really grand houses are called "châteaux"
Chouchou	Gourd-like green vegetable known as chayote, christophine or choko
Cour	Colloquial word for a garden
Dholl puri	Indian pancake made with pulse flour and served with spicy sauce
Gâteau Piment	Lightly spiced savoury fritter made from pulses
Giraumon	Red pumpkin
Lambrequins	Decorative fretwork ornamenting wooden or iron underside of roofs or veranda
Limon	Green lime
Malabar/Malbar	Indian from the Malabar coast of southwest India
Marron	Literally means "brown" but used to mean fugitive, wild, illicit, clandestine; hence the allusion to a run-away slave, wild animal or prolific weed.

Massala	Mixture of Indian spices
Mine frit	Fried noodles
Morne	Small, isolated round mountain rising above a denuded plain
Pistache	Peanut
Ravanela	Traveller's palm, formerly used to roof houses
Rhum préparé	Rum in which fruit and spices have been steeped for several months
Roche cari	Stone used to crush spices
Rougaille	Prepared with tomatoes, onions, herbs and garlic
Samossa/Samoussa	Indian savoury fried pastry stuffed with meat, fish or spicy vegetables
Sari	Length of draped material traditionally worn by Indian women
Tabagie	Tobacconist
Varangue	Creole veranda across one or more sides of the house, closed or open
Vindaye	Fish or venison steeped in a flavoured marinade

Practical Information

P. Desclos/SCOPE

Mauritian crossroads

Before Going

• Local Time

Mauritius is 4hr ahead of London in the winter and 3hr in the summer and 9 hours ahead of Eastern Standard Time (EST). When it is 9am in Britain, it is either 12noon or 1pm in Mauritius, depending on the season, and when it is 9am in New York and Toronto, it is 6pm or 7pm in Mauritius, depending on the season.

• How to Call Mauritius

Dial international + 230 + the number you wish to call.

• When to go

Although the temperatures are relatively pleasant all year round and the chances of rain are equally spread out, the best times to go to Mauritius and Rodrigues, and to Réunion, are **April-June** and **September-November.**
The region's climate varies greatly but does nonetheless have two main seasons. However, contrary to the idyllic image conveyed by travel agencies, the Mauritian sky is more often grey than blue and sunny. As it is situated in the southern hemisphere, summer and winter are the opposite of our European and North American climates.

Southern summertime

The weather is hot and humid **from November to April**, with temperatures varying between 25 and 33°C; the highest temperatures being in January. It is a very rainy season, especially in the heart of the island, with the heaviest rainfalls between January and March. Daylight is from 5.30am to around 7pm. This is the best time for diving (December to March) and fishing (September to March). The **cyclone** season runs from January to April. Some years cyclones completely miss the islands, or affect them only lightly; other years they can cause devastation to crops and buildings. Do not worry, though, all the hotels are built and equipped to deal with these natural catastrophes.
The busiest periods are Christmas and the New Year (prices rocket during this festive season) and during the European and Réunion summer school vacations (primarily July and August).

Southern wintertime

The weather is, theoretically, coolest and driest during the **May to October** period, with temperatures dropping to between 14° to 25°C, the lowest temperatures of which are recorded in August. Rain can be a feature at anytime though, ranging from brief, heavy showers to a more lasting, fine drizzle. Daylight from around 6.45am to 5.45pm. This is the best time for surfing (June to August).
In the **Central Plateau region**, temperatures can be at least a 5°C lower compared to the coast. The **west and north coasts** are warmer and less rainy than the **east and south coasts**, where southeast winds bring in rain and cooler temperatures off the ocean.

• Packing List

Take lightweight, casual clothes and a swimsuit.
A pair of easily removable shoes is a good idea for visiting temples and mosques, together with clothes which cover shoulders and legs (no shorts or sleeveless t-shirts). Pareos, which you can find on the island very cheaply, may often prove

to be a useful buy. Plastic footwear will be useful protection against sea urchins, stone-fish and coral. You may also want to take along your snorkelling gear, because the local equipment is often of rather poor quality. Do not forget a pair of trousers and a pullover for the cool, (even downright cold in the winter) evenings, and to protect against mosquitoes in the summer.
Do not forget your sunglasses.
A light raincoat or umbrella often prove useful, even though it rarely rains for very long.

• A trip for everyone

Travelling with children

Mauritius is a family destination where everything possible is organised around children. The large hotels often have a Kid's Club, where parents can leave their children during the day and babysitting facilities are widely available for evenings out. Special family rates are available in most hotels.

Women travelling alone

A woman travelling alone will surprise, attract attention, may be pestered, but is unlikely to run any real risk.

Elderly people

Travelling to Mauritius presents absolutely no difficulty. The quality of the transport, accommodation and hygiene is such that elderly people can travel without qualms, providing of course they are prudent regarding the sun.

Disabled persons

The island's best hotels are well-equipped to cater for handicapped visitors.

Pets

All pets are subjected to a quarantine period of 6 months before being admitted to the island.

• Address book

Tourist Information Offices

United Kingdom – Mauritius High Commission, 32-33 Elvaston Place, London, SW7 5NW ☎ (171) 584 3666, Fax (171) 225 1135, mtpa@btinternet.com
USA – Information can be obtained from either of the embassies listed below.

Web Sites

www.mauritius.net
www.intnet.mu
www.travelocity.com

Embassies and Consulates

Australia – 2 Beale Crescent, Deakin, Canberra, ACT 2600, ☎ (26) 281 1203, Fax (26) 282 3235

Canada – 606 Cathcart Street, Office 200, Montreal, Quebec H3B IK9, ☎ (514)393 95 00, Fax 393 93 24

United Kingdom – Mauritius High Commission, 32-33 Elvaston Place, London, SW7 5NW ☎ (171) 581 0294, Fax (171) 823 8437

USA – New York: 211 East 43rd St, 1502-NY, NW10017, ☎ (212)949 0190, Fax (212) 697 3829

Washington DC: Suite 441, Van Ness Centre, 4301 Connecticut Ave NW, Washington DC, 20008 ☎ (202) 244 1491, Fax (202) 966 0983

• Formalities

Identity Papers

Nationals from Australia, Canada, the European Community and the USA can enter Mauritius with a passport, valid at least 6 months after the return date, and a return or onward ticket. Visitors must also be able to prove that they have enough to live on for the duration of their stay. A visa, valid for 3 months, is delivered free of charge on arrival.

If you wish to extend your visa (maximum 3 months), contact the **Passport and Immigration Office**, Line Barracks, Kirchner St, Port Louis ☎ 208 1212, Fax 212 2398. A return or onward ticket, current passport and proof of sufficient funds (a photocopy of your credit card may suffice) will be required.

Customs

There are n° restrictions on importing foreign currencies into Mauritius.

Visitors aged 16 years and over, can bring in 200 cigarettes, 50 cigars or 250g of tobacco, 1 litre of spirits and 2 litres of wine or beer, 25cl of eau de toilette or 10cl of perfume.

Possession of drugs is liable to the death penalty.

Sanitary regulations

A permit, issued by the Ministry of Agriculture after a six-month quarantine period, is required to import plants, fruit or animals.

Vaccinations

No particular vaccinations are required, but proof of vaccination against yellow fever must be given by all visitors who have spent time in an infected area.

Driving licence

Anyone wishing to rent a car must be aged 23 years or over and have had a driving licence for over a year. An international driving licence will sometimes be requested for visitors staying over a month.

• Currency

Cash

The national currency in Mauritius is the Mauritian Rupee (MRs or Rs), US$1 = Rs24. The rupee is divided into 100 cents and is a relatively stable currency.

Money Exchange

Although the Mauritian Rupee can only be purchased in Mauritius, changing money poses n° problem. Banks and foreign exchange offices can be found at the airport on arrival or departure of international flights, in all tourist sites, in the larger villages and towns and in most hotels. Most foreign currencies are accepted.

The exchange rate, fixed daily by the government, is identical everywhere and there is no black market in Mauritius.

Travellers' Cheques

You can exchange your travellers' cheques practically everywhere. The rate is better than for foreign currency, but a commission is taken on each exchange.

Credit Cards

Most hotels, restaurants, souvenir shops and banks accept American Express, Diner's Club, Master Card and Visa.

There are also a few cash dispensers in Port Louis and it is possible to withdraw cash with a Visa card in certain banks in the main towns and tourist locations.

• Spending money

The government is currently developing more upmarket tourism and prices are fairly high. The cost of living in Mauritius is nonetheless lower than in the Seychelles or in Réunion.

That said, prices can double depending on the season and practically all prices increase by 20 to 30 % between 15 December and 15 January. It must also be remembered that a 12 % **government tax** is added to all hotel and restaurant bills.

For two people travelling together, you can find a hotel for less than US$10 per day and per person and eat out for around US$3 per meal. More upmarket accommodation and restaurants, without being luxurious, will cost around US$30 per day per person including meals. Travelling by bus is by far the cheapest, but not the most convenient, form of transport. It will cost around US$40 a day to rent a car or a taxi.

For more details, see the transport, accommodation and restaurant sections in this chapter.

• Booking in advance

If you wish to plan your trip ahead, you will need to book between several weeks or months in advance depending on the season.

Hotel rates are often much cheaper if booked through a travel agency. Do beware of misleading descriptions or photos in some glossy brochures.

The number of hotel beds is such that it is always possible to find a room, albeit not perhaps the room of your dreams, if you prefer to book when you arrive. During the Christmas/New Year season, it is advisable to book in advance, especially for the better addresses.

Similarly, during the Christmas/New Year and summer months, if you decide to rent a car, it would also be better to book in advance.

If you intend to visit Rodrigues during your stay, make sure you book a return ticket between the islands *(see Getting there, p 234-235)*.

• Repatriation insurance

Remember to take out repatriation insurance. This can often be done through one's bank: some bank cards include special insurance policies. If booking through a tour operator, emergency/repatriation insurance is often included in the price of trips. The following may however prove useful.

Travel Insurance Agency, Suite 2, Percy Mews, 755B High Rd, North Finchley, London NI2 8JY, UK, ☎ (181) 446 5414, Fax (181) 446 5417, info@travelinsurers.com

Travel Insurance Services, 2930 Camino Diablo, Suite 200, PO Box 299, Walnut Creek, CA94596, USA, ☎ (800) 937 1387, Fax (925) 932 0442, webinfo@travelinsure.com

• Gifts to offer

If you want to take a gift to friends or for possible new acquaintances, you could take souvenirs of your city and country, photos of your family and home. As the Mauritians are keen soccer fans, you might also take a t-shirt or badge of your favourite local team (soccer or baseball)! Women may well prefer more traditionally feminine gifts, such as flowers or perfume.

GETTING THERE

• By air

Scheduled flights

You can fly direct to Mauritius from London (12hr), from Perth (8hr) and from Johannesburg (4hr20). Visitors travelling from the United States or Canada will need to stop in Europe or South Africa for a connecting flight.

Air Mauritius, the national airline, flies from London twice a week. Head Office: Air Mauritius Centre, 5 Pres. J.F. Kennedy St, Port Louis, Mauritius, ☎ 230 207 7070, Fax 230 208 8331, www.airmauritius.com

British Airways operates four flights a week from London, via Paris with **Air Liberté**. Information: callers within the UK ☎ 0345 222 111, callers outside the UK ☎ 44 141 222 2222, www.britishairways.com

Air France, operates five regular flights per week between Paris and Mauritius. Information: callers within France ☎ 0802 802 802, callers outside France ☎ 33 0802 802 802, www.airfrance.fr

Air Madagascar, South African Airways, Singapore Airlines and **Condor Airlines** also fly to Mauritius.

Charter flights

Whereas there are n° charter flights to Mauritius, many travel agencies and airlines offer highly interesting promotional rates on regular flights.

Flights between Mauritius, Rodrigues, Réunion and Seychelles

Air Mauritius, operates several daily flights between Réunion and Mauritius (40min) and two-four daily flights between Rodrigues and Mauritius (90min). It is perhaps worth remembering that the ticket is much more expensive when leaving from Réunion than when leaving from Mauritius (US$180 compared to US$110).

Mauritius – Roger's House, 5 President John F. Kennedy St, Port Louis, ☎ 207 7070 (Reservations/confirmations: ☎ 207 7575. Information also from Air Mauritius Center, Bille en Queue Court, Pres John F Kennedy St, Port Louis.
Réunion – 13 Rue Charles Gounod, 97400 St-Denis, ☎ 94 83 83.
Rodrigues – Douglas St, Port Mathurin, ☎ 831 1558
Seychelles – Kingsgate House, PO Box, Victoria, Mahé, ☎ 32 24 14

Air Austral operates daily Réunion-Mauritius flights and two-weekly Réunion-Seychelles flight.

Mauritius – Roger's House, 5 President John F. Kennedy St, Port Louis, ☎ 212 2666, Réunion – 7 rue de Nice, St-Denis, ☎ 90 90 90
Seychelles – Victoria House, Victoria, Mahé ☎ 22 51 59, Fax 38 13 00

Air France has three regular Mauritius-Seychelles flights and two regular Mauritius-Réunion flights per week.

Mauritius - Roger's House, 5 President John F. Kennedy St, Port Louis, ☎ 208 6820
Réunion – 7 av de la Victoire, 97477 St-Denis, ☎ 40 38 38
Seychelles – Independence Av., Victoria, Mahé.

Air Seychelles flies twice weekly to Mauritius and once a week to Réunion from Seychelles.

Mauritius – Roger's House, 5 President John F. Kennedy St, Port Louis, ☎ 208 6801, Fax 208 3646
Réunion – Air France, 7 av de la Victoire, St-Denis, ☎ 40 38 38
Seychelles – Victoria House, PO Box 386, Mahé ☎ 38 10 00, Fax 22 59 33

Sir Seewoosagur Ramgoolam International Airport

Mauritius Airport (☎ 603 3030/637 3552) is at Plaisance, 4km out of Mahébourg, in the southeast of the island, 48km from Port Louis. A few duty-free stores, bars, a restaurant, a tourist office, banks to change money and a post office, as well as counters of the main car rental agencies, will, in theory, all be open on the arrival of international flights.

Taxis await the arrival of each flight. It is quite acceptable to negotiate the price of the fare. Public transport buses stop by the airport roughly every half hour, between 6am and 6pm, behind the airport car park. They take visitors to Port Louis from Mahébourg, via Curepipe.

Confirmation

It is highly recommended to reconfirm your return flight if possible, and at the very latest 72hr before your return flight, at the Air Mauritius counter in the airport arrival hall. When leaving Mauritius, it is best to arrive 2hr before the scheduled departure time because overbooking is frequent.

Airport tax

Make sure you keep Rs300 to pay the airport tax leaving Mauritius.

Package deals

Travel agencies offer a wide range of packages for stays on Mauritius. It is becoming more and more advantageous to purchase deals which include an air ticket, full board and accommodation and even a rental car than to organise your trip yourself. *See the list of specialised tour operators, p 72-73.*

By boat

The cargo-ship, *Mauritius Pride*, leaves Mauritius for Rodrigues roughly three times a month depending on the season (between 24 and 30hr per crossing depending on the direction) and much more irregularly for Réunion, depending mainly on traffic (the crossing lasts between 10 and 12hr and will cost between US$120 and US$200 return depending on the season and class).

Mauritius Shipping Corporation, Nova Building, 1 route Militaire, Port Louis, Mauritius, ☎ 242 5255, Fax 242 5245.

Islands' Service, Port Mathurin, Rodrigues, ☎ 831 1555, Fax 831 2089.

SCOAM, 47 rue Evariste-de-Parny, 94720 Le Port, Réunion, ☎ 42 19 45, Fax 43 25 47.

Another boat, *l'Alinhoa*, does the crossing in 6hr .

Mr Ocean Line Co Ltd, rue Sir William Newton, 2nd floor, Orchid Tower, Port-Louis, Mauritius, ☎ 210 7104, Fax 210 6961.

Blue Line Shipping, rue St-Paul, Le Port, Réunion, ☎ 55 23 25.

THE BASICS

• Address Book

A selection of magazines in English and French (What's on in Mauritius, etc) with tourist information are distributed free at the tourist information office and in most of the hotels and stores. The Tourist Office edits its own, informative "Practical Guide to Mauritius and Rodrigues". They contain all sorts of useful information and addresses.

Tourist Information

Mauritius Government Tourist Office, Port Louis Waterfront, Port Louis, ☎ 208 63 97, Fax 212 5142. Few brochures are available, but the staff is very happy to answer your questions.

Embassies and Consulates

Australia – Rogers House, President John F. Kennedy St, Port Louis, ☎ 208 1700, Fax 208 8878.

Canada – C/O Blance Birger Company Ltd, 18 Jules Koenig Street, Port Louis, ☎ 208 0821.

United Kingdom – Les Cascades building, Edith Cavell Street, Port Louis, ☎ 211 1361, Fax 211 1369/8470

USA – Rogers House, 5 President John F Kennedy Street, Port Louis, ☎ 208 9764-69, Fax 208 9534

• Opening and closing times

Opening hours vary widely from one place to another and the following are given purely as a guideline.

Banks

Monday to Friday, 9am-3pm; Saturdays, 9am-12noon. Banks are, however, open later in the more touristy villages or towns.

Post Offices

Post offices are open Monday to Friday, 9am-4pm; Saturdays, 9am-12noon.

Shops

At Port Louis, stores are open Monday to Friday, 8.30am-5pm; Saturdays, 9am-12noon.

Stores in the Central Plateau and in the main villages are open Monday to Wednesday and on Fridays and Saturdays from 9am to 6pm. On Thursdays and Sundays, they are open 9am-12noon.

Markets

Monday to Saturday, 7am-5pm; Sundays, 6am-11.30am.

Restaurants

Opening days and hours vary from one establishment to another.

Offices

Office opening hours are Monday to Friday, 8/9am-4pm and 9am-12noon on Saturdays.

• Museums and gardens

Hours

Most are state run and museums generally open from 9am to 4pm, from Monday to Friday and from 9am to 12noon at the weekends. Private places of visit operate varying opening hours.

Entrance fees

For museums and gardens which are state run, entrance is free. The others charge from between US$3 and US$5. Reductions are often available for children.

• Postal service

There are post offices in most of the main villages and towns and the postal service operates well, but it is preferable to post any mail from your hotel or post office, rather than from an isolated post box.

Stamps can only be purchased from post offices, but most hotels have stamps available for residents.

It is possible to air-mail packages at a cost of around US$15 for the first kilogram and US$1.5 for each additional kilogram.

• Phone and fax

Mauritius' recently modernised automatic network now covers the whole island. Phone boxes can be found in towns, near police stations and supermarkets and close to most of the main public beaches. They work with cards that can be bought from supermarkets, some fuel stations and occasionally with a Visa card. Telephoning from hotels is much more expensive and residents are often billed for a minimum of 3 minutes.

International calls

You can call from a **Telecom** telephone centre or from hotels. Rates are lower from Saturday afternoon through to Sunday midnight.

Codes and rates

To call abroad from Mauritius, first dial 00 + country code + phone number.

To call Rodrigues from Mauritius, dial 00 + 095 + phone number.

No code is necessary from Rodrigues to Mauritius.

Codes of other countries United Kingdom: 44; USA/Canada: 1; Australia: 61

Directory enquiries

Local directory enquiries : dial 90.

International directory enquiries: dial 100 90.

• Public holidays

The ethnic and religious complexity of Mauritius results in a total of 13 official public holidays. For the meaning and description of some of the holidays, *see Religious blends, p 207-213.*

Fixed dates

1 & 2 January	New Year
12 March	Independence and Republic Day (speech and celebrations at Champ de Mars in Port Louis)
1 May	Labour Day
1 November	All Saints' Day
25 December	Christmas Day

Variable holidays

These holidays vary according to the moon. Official calendars are available at the Tourist Office in Port Louis.

January-February	Cavadee
January-February	Spring holiday (Chinese New Year)
February-March	Maha Shivaratree and Holi
March	Ougadi
May-June	Id-al-Fitr
September	Ganesha Chathurti
October-November	Divali

The Basics

GETTING AROUND

• By car

Before renting a car, you may like to know that it can often be more interesting, less expensive and less tiring, to rent a taxi for a day to go on an excursion. Ask at your hotel. Driving on the left is not always easy if you are not used to it and driving Mauritian style can be quite a feat!

Car rental

To rent a car you must be aged 23 or over and have had a current driving licence for over a year.

The main car rental companies (Avis, Hertz, Europcar etc) are represented at the airport and in hotels. The smaller car rental firms offer very attractive prices, but it is worth checking the condition of the vehicle (brakes, headlights, windscreen wipers) and the insurance terms very carefully prior to renting. To avoid any problems, only rent official rental vehicles, easily recognisable by their yellow number plates.

Car rental costs between US$30-75a day.

Road network

A network of over 1 800km of surfaced roads, most in good condition, covers the island. A motorway runs between Plaisance and Port Louis, passing through the towns in the Central Plateau, through to Grand Baie. Another major highroad runs from Grand Baie to Pamplemousses. An additional road links Plaisance to Port Louis, by-passing the central towns, whereas the older Royal Road passes through them.

Signposting is irregular and distances are indicated sometimes in kilometres and sometimes in miles.

Driving

You must drive on the left side of the road and, in theory, give way to vehicles coming from the right. However the locals drive very fast, and giving way to vehicles coming from the right mainly seems to be a case of who honks loudest and longest. Speeds are limited to 50km/hr in towns and 80km/hr on the open road. Roads are not lit at night. Drivers should also watch out for children on the roadsides, as well as large numbers of stray dogs.

Fuel

There are fuel stations practically everywhere, most of which close at around 7pm.

Parking

Paying parking areas are available in Port Louis, Rose Hill, Quatre Bornes and Curepipe.

• Taxis

The island is well equipped with taxis, distinguishable by their black-on-white background number plates, as opposed to private vehicles, which are white-on-black. In theory, meters are compulsory, but few drivers use them and it is best to negotiate the fare before leaving. Drivers will offer their services for daily excursions round the island (between US$30 and 45 depending on the season and the distance). Some are excellent tourist guides. Watch out for stores or restaurants where they will insist on taking you in order to get a commission. Taxis can be found in front of most hotels.

J. F. Galmiche

Getting Around

• Group taxis

Some taxis run, in parallel with public transport, regular services between villages, with as many passengers as possible. These "taxi-trains" will often stop and propose their services if they see you walking on the roadside, but they are not easily identifiable. Prices are roughly equivalent to those of public transport.

• By bus

The island has a good public transport network, but it does not cover all the tourist sites. Long trips will often involve changing at Port Louis, Quatre Bornes or Curepipe. Normal buses stop everywhere and are often extremely slow.
Express buses are in theory direct and twice as fast They run between 6am and 6pm in towns and 6.30am and 6.30pm between the villages (no buses at the weekend). A night service exists up until 11pm between Port Louis and Rose Hill, Quatre Bornes and Curepipe. Tickets are bought on the bus and are extremely cheap (around US$0.50).
For more details on routes and times, ask for the *Mauritius Island Practical Guide* at the Tourist Office.

• Organised tours and excursions

Travel agencies organise transfers and excursions around the island. They have offices in the main towns, the airport and most of the hotels An excursion costs between US$25 and 50 per day with meals.
Mauritius Travel & Tourist Bureau (MTTB), corner of Royal St and Sir W. Newton St, Port Louis ☎ 208 2041.
Grand Baie Travel and Tours (GBTT), ☎ 263 8771 or 263 8273, Fax 263 8274
Mauritours 5 Venkatasananda St, Port Louis ☎ 454 1666, Fax 454 1682.
10 Sir W. Newton St, Port Louis ☎ 208 5241.
White Sand Tour, La Chaussée, Rose Hill ☎ 212 6092 or 212 3712.

• Renting a bike or a moped

Can be rented per day at reasonable rates. US$5 a day for a bicycle or US$10 for a moped, US$15 for a motorbike.
Most of the rental firms are located in the north west of the island, mainly at Grand Baie. Helmets are compulsory on motorbikes (under 70cc) or mopeds.

• Flights between Mauritius and Rodrigues

Air Mauritius has two-four daily flights (depending on the season) between Mauritius and Rodrigues on a 46-seater ATR 42. The flight lasts 90min and baggage is limited to 15kg. Confirm your return flight on arrival at Plaine Corail. A return ticket costs around US$150 and as seats are limited, it is best to book in advance.

• Sea crossings between Mauritius and Rodrigues

"*Mauritius Pride*", a cargo ship, leaves for Rodrigues on average twice a month (the crossing lasts between 24 and 30hr depending on the direction and weather conditions). In addition to containers and cattle, it also carries 264 passengers, 16 in first-class cabins (US$190 return ticket); the other passengers are seated as if in an aeroplane (US$90).
Mauritius Shipping Corporation, Nova Building, 1 route Militaire, Port Louis, Mauritius, ☎ 242 5255/241 2550/242 2912, Fax 242 5245.
Islands' Service, Port Mathurin, Rodrigues, ☎ 831 1555, Fax 831 2089.

BED AND BOARD

• Where to stay

The size of the island is such that you can stay in the same place throughout your visit, taking day trips to visit the rest of the island. This enables tourists to choose their location depending on taste, budget, as well as climate and season. It all depends on whether you are looking for a rest, the beach and sun, sports, night-life, a change of scene, immersion in local life.
Depending on the region chosen, your impression of the island will be vastly different: tourist seaside resorts in the northwest, small peaceful villages like Tamarin, residential areas in Mahébourg or wild landscapes in the south or east of the island.
Alternatively, you could opt to travel round the island, getting to know all its different regions. Have a look at the detailed descriptions of each coast in the *Exploring Mauritius* section.
There are small, often cheap and poorly-equipped hotels in all the towns, but there is absolutely n° reason for staying in them, because of the variety and quality of the coastal hotels.

• Various categories

Mauritius has a wide selection of accommodation with prices for all budgets. A complete list can be obtained from the Tourist Office in Port Louis.
In most hotels, prices decrease if you stay several nights. Prices also vary depending on the season, dropping by around 20 % during the colder season (June to September) and rising by 30-50 % at Christmas and the New Year. A 15 % government tax is added to all hotel and restaurant bills, but most establishments already include this in their rates.
As prices can increase twofold depending on the season and the room, the range of prices given in the practical information sections of this guide is for a standard double room with breakfast for two people, mid-season. Whenever half-board is compulsory in a hotel, this is indicated. Rates for studios or flats which do not include board are also indicated. In both cases, the classification is based on a flat rate calculated by subtracting either the approximate value of a meal or by adding that of a breakfast
It is clear that a four / six person bungalow will cost proportionately less than a studio flat for two and thus change price range. Likewise, a single room will cost proportionately much more than a double room.

Camping

Camping is permitted on the island, which does not, however, have a single official camp site, primarily due to the lack of enthusiasm among the locals.

Guesthouses

A broad term that can include the best and the worst: from dirty, sinister, little hotels to simple, but clean and welcoming, guesthouses. Some guesthouses may constitute an interesting alternative for those on limited budgets or for those who would prefer to experience a cosy family welcome rather than that of the more sophisticated hotels.

Hotels

Whether a small, simple hotel or a luxury palace, whether on the seashore or the roadside, Mauritius has excellent hotel facilities to suit all budgets.

Apartment rental

Visitors can choose between a large choice of rooms, studios, flats, bungalows or villas for rent. It is generally a cheaper form of accommodation, especially for those travelling with children or a group of friends. If you rent a flat or a house, it is worthwhile checking that a main road does not flank the house or that the dream beach so extolled by the brochure really is a stone's throw away, etc. House cleaning and cooking can be organised at very reasonable rates. It must however be noted that isolated rentals have become a prime target for thieves, particularly in the northeast tourist area. We recommend steering clear of the numerous "rooms for rent" signs on the roadsides in the Grand Baie region and would advise visitors to opt rather for a supervised hotel residence rental. What is more, these generally offer a range of additional services: swimming pool, cleaning, car or bicycle rental, some water sports, excursions, etc.

• Eating out

In hotels

Most of the larger hotels have a restaurant and half-board is compulsory, particularly during the 15 December – 15 January period. They primarily serve a bland international-style cuisine or an adulterated local cuisine, adapted to tourist "tastes". Most however also do feature more authentic, and sometimes much better, dishes on their à la carte menu. Most hotels also organise Creole buffet evenings, followed by a séga demonstration at least once a week. Some establishments have adopted the buffet formula for all meals and organise corresponding theme evenings. A meal, in half-board, costs on average, depending on the hotel's category, between US$3 and 12.

In restaurants

Whether Chinese, Indian, Creole, French or Italian, you will be lost for choice in Mauritius. A combination of the island and tourist demographics means that the best restaurants are concentrated in the Central Plateau towns and the majority of restaurants in the north and in other tourist zones are on the whole mediocre. Mauritians enjoy eating out, whether in couples or with the family, on Friday and Saturday evenings. It is not rare to find good Chinese or Indian restaurants reserved for a wedding or other celebration. It is therefore recommended to book a table in the better, more well-known establishments. A meal including a starter, main course and dessert, depending on the restaurant's category, will cost between US$5 and 15.

In the street

At lunchtime in the towns and next to the beaches, street sellers offer what can be very tasty *samossas*, *dholl puri*, *mine frits*, savoury fritters and sometimes even soup or *cari*. It is a chance to try a taste of local cuisine at unbeatable prices, but is not available everywhere.

Drinks

Tap water is in theory drinkable but it is better to stick to bottled mineral water. Soft, fizzy drinks, which the Mauritians love, can be found everywhere, together with fruit juices and the cheap, very pleasant local beer (*Phoenix, Blue Marlin, Stella*).

Most hotels serve wine, imported generally from South Africa at great expense. The famous punch brand, *Châtel*, has a production unit on the island. Rum is a very popular drink on the island. Some restaurants also have French wine, but it is generally at exorbitant prices and often badly stored. Mauritius produces its own tea (at Bois Chéri) and coffee (at Chamarel), both of which can be vanilla-flavoured or not, and most often served with milk and sugar (it is best to say if you would rather drink it "black").

SPORTS AND PASTIMES

• The sea

Although all the beaches in Mauritius are officially public, more and more hotels are appropriating beaches which they have 'guarded' to dissuade outside visitors. With the exception of shell and pareo sellers, you will paradoxically meet very few Mauritians on the beach (except at the weekends). The beaches mentioned in this guide are "public" beaches which are as yet free of hotel surveillance and open to all.
In most hotels, water sports are generally included in the price of the room, with the exception of diving, deep-sea fishing and occasionally water skiing, for which there is a supplement.
Swimming, with or without snorkelling gear (make sure you have plastic sandals to protect against sea urchins and coral and a t-shirt against sun burn), **windsurfing**, **water-skiing**, **dinghy sailing**, **canoeing** or renting a **pedal boat** is possible all over the island.
The west and north coast lagoon is calmer and warmer. Snorkelling and sailing amateurs will however prefer the east coast.
Under-water hunting or collecting of shells and coral is strictly prohibited.

Surfing

The west coast bay of Tamarin, especially during the June-August period, has the best waves. Boards can be rented here.

Deep-sea fishing

Mauritius is famous for the quality of its fish. From **October to March**, extremely large fish (blue or black marlin, tiger and black and white fin shark, bonito, yellowfin tuna, bream, swordfish, barracuda, wahoo) come prowling and hunting off the coast of Mauritius, often close to the coral reef and sometimes close to the shore. The best currents and tides are found on the **west coast**.
A lot of hotels own modern boats equipped for deep-sea fishing. They organise outings (maximum five persons) beyond the coral reef for a day's (or half-day) fishing (approx. Rs9000 per day). Deep-sea fishing clubs are located at Rivière Noire, Morne, Flic en Flac, Wolmar, Trou aux Biches, Grand Baie and Anse Jonchée: see the corresponding practical information sections.

Sailing

Excellent sailing conditions make day trips around the lagoon's islands extremely pleasant. Lunchtime barbecues are generally organised on a beach. Catamarans can also be hired for several days with a skipper.
The main sailing organisations are located at Grand Baie, Cap Malheureux, Riche en Eau and Trou d'Eau Douce: see the corresponding practical information sections.
The east coast lagoon, full of little coastal islands and a historic past, is without doubt one of the most beautiful and interesting.

Scuba diving

The Mauritian sea bed has been greatly damaged by dynamite fishing techniques and the discharge of fabric textile dies and fertilisers into the sea. Almost 95 % of the coral reefs have been destroyed (except to the southeast of the island) and many species of fish have disappeared from the lagoon. Under-water fishing of fish, shells or coral is strictly prohibited due to the threat still facing so many species. Some scuba diving sites can still however provide visitors with interesting explorations off the coast of Flic en Flac, Morne Brabant, Blue Bay or near Ronde Island. Many hotels offer scuba diving initiation in swimming pools for beginners or sea excursions for confirmed divers.

An outing costs around Rs700-800 for a dive, including equipment.

Information: **Mauritian Scuba Diving Association**, Beau Bassin, ☎/Fax 454 00 11.

Mauritius Underwater Group, Vacoas, ☎ 696 5368.

The most reputable clubs are located at Rivière Noire, Villas Caroline Hotel in Flic en Flac and Pirogue Sun Hotel at Wolmar (see the appropriate practical information pages).

Under-water walking

If scuba diving is not really an option, under-water walking may well constitute a good alternative. Open to all ages from seven years upwards, you do not even have to know how to swim to enjoy this fun experience (Rs650 for an hour's walk). A boat takes walkers out to a platform, from which you descend via a ladder, weighted down by a lead belt, into a depth of two to five metres. Walkers are fitted with large helmets, supplied with oxygen, can thus walk about freely and safely on the sea bed.

Information from **Undersea walk**, Grand Baie (☎ 423 8822 or 263 7820) and **Alpha 2** at Grand Baie (☎ 263 9036) or Belle Mare (☎ 422 7953).

Glass-bottomed boats

An excursion in a glass-bottomed boat is another way to explore the sea bed, this time without getting wet. Most of the beaches offer this type of outing, but for maximum visibility, choose a sunny, windless day and a calm sea

Sports and Pastimes

to make sure of getting over the coral reef. In the lagoon, the boat's engine scares away most of the fish and all the coral is dead. Also, do not forget to take a quick look at the "glass-bottom", because they are often scratched or cracked.

• Other activities

Riding

The **Domaine les Pailles** riding stables (☎ 212 4225) organises riding in the park (see p 261). Some of the larger hotels also organise outings on the beach.

Tennis

Most hotels are equipped with a tennis court, sometimes open to non-residents for a fee.

Golf

Several hotels have nine-hole practice courses. There are also 18-hole courses at Morne Brabant and Belle Mare. Most courses are open to non-residents.

• Helicopter

Air Mauritius Helicopter Serves, ☎ 637 3552, organises flights over the island. A 20-minute flight costs around Rs4000.

• Night-life

Night-life is virtually nonexistent in Mauritius and is centred almost entirely around the hotels to keep pace with night-loving tourists.

Concerts and dancing shows

At least once a week the majority of hotels organise *séga* evenings. Created for tourists, these shows, of irregular quality, do not have a lot in common with traditional dancing and are often sorely lacking in enthusiasm. The Tourist Office in Port Louis publishes a list of hotel *sega* evenings. Jazz evenings take place every Friday at **Domaine les Pailles**.

Theatre

The programme of the island's two theatres, in Port Louis and Rose Hill, is available from the tourist office. With a little luck, you might be able to see an original, Indian or Chinese, performance.

Cinema

Although videos have largely replaced the movie screen, Mauritians still enjoy going to the cinema. Port Louis movie halls have attempted to diversify the choice available in recent years, leading primarily to a majority of Indian and American movies.

Casino

More and more hotels are opening casinos within their premises, with roulette, black jack or baccarat tables. Such hotels include St Géran and Belle Mare beach hotels at Poste de Flaq, the Paradis and Beraya hotels at Morne Brabant or La Pirogue Hotel at Wolmar (for more information see the practical information sections).

Night clubs

Mauritians love to go out dancing, but most of the hotel night clubs are only frequented by tourists. Those looking for more "local colour" will have to go the Central Plateau towns.

SHOPPING

• What's on offer

Clothes

Mauritius is reputed for its low-price textiles and clothing, available from the many stores, primarily in Port Louis, but also in the Central Plateau towns.

Indian fabrics and crafts

The town markets and stores all sell silk or cotton fabric by the yard, clothes, saris and other Indian textiles. When you buy fabric by the yard, you can have your clothes made to measure by one of the numerous well-established local tailors (mainly in Mahébourg and Port Louis).

Model ships

A speciality of the Mauritian craft trade, model ships are on offer more or less everywhere, but the main workshops are in the Curepipe area. Models are available at a wide range of prices, from Rs500 to Rs50 000, depending on the materials used, size, quality and finishing. They will be wrapped in special air-transport packages. Keep any bills carefully: the customs may well demand to see them on leaving the country.

Gold and diamonds

Mauritius is famous for the size of its diamonds. The island's several gold and diamond boutiques sell jewellery at extremely competitive duty-free prices.

Flowers

Taking home flowers will require a permit from the Plant Department of the Ministry of Agriculture. There is however a stand at the airport, open during the departure of international flights, that sells *anthuriums*, ready to take on the plane without a permit.

Spices

The Mauritian markets are a feast for the eyes and the nose. You will find a wide variety of Mauritian-produced vanilla-flavoured tea and coffee and all sorts, colours and flavours of Indian spices, to take home and let you try your hand at delicious *caris*.

Rum

Mauritius produces white rum, the best known of which is "Green Island". There is also a particularly delicious spicy variety. Although very cheap on the island, it is still better to buy it duty-free at the airport.

• Where to shop

Markets

The main markets are held at Port Louis, Rose Hill, Curepipe and Mahébourg. In addition to fruit and vegetables, they also offer a selection of spices, fabrics, pareos, baskets, Madagascan embroidered table cloths, etc.

Stores

Most of the stores of likely interest (clothes, souvenirs, models, jewellery, etc) are in Port Louis, Curepipe, Rose Hill and Grand Baie.

Duty-free boutiques

Tourists should be aware that the duty-free concept occasionally suffers from a tendency to misappropriation. The two main boutiques, **Adamas** (at Floreal) and **Poncini** (at Port Louis or Curepipe) sell gold jewellery, unset diamonds, precious stones and pearls, according to government imposed regulations. Duty-free purchases require an airline ticket and passport. Payment is by banker's card or in foreign currency.

• Bartering

See p 247.

• Taxes and regulations on certain articles

Exports of plants, fruit or flowers require an authorisation issued by the Plant Department of the Ministry of Agriculture.

HEALTH AND SAFETY

• Precautions

Mauritius and Rodrigues have no tropical illnesses; the only dangers are from the sun or the sea.

• Medical kit

Take an extra-strong protective sun cream and an anti-mosquito lotion. If prone to upset stomachs, also bring anti-diarrhoea pills.

• Health services

First Aid

The larger hotels are equipped with an infirmary and they can contact a doctor if necessary.

Hospitals

Mauritius has several free, public hospitals, but these are not always a good choice. The private clinics, relatively cheap and less over-crowded, are on the whole better.

Clinique Darné, G. Guibert St, Floréal, ☎ 686 1477. The island's best medical establishment.

Sir Seewoosagur Ramgoolam Hospital, Pamplemousses, ☎ 243 3661.

In the case of any serious illness, it is best to go to Réunion.

Pharmacies

Most of the villages have a small pharmacy, but the best-stocked ones are in the towns and at Grand Baie.

Dentists

There are quite a few dentist surgeries dotted around the island. Contact your embassy or ask at your hotel. One reputable address:

Dr Audibert, 17 Lees St, Curepipe, ☎ 676 1495.

• Emergencies

Call ☎ 999 and ask for the required service (police, fire brigade, ambulances).

FROM A TO Z

• Bartering

Very commonplace in a wide variety of circumstances. Do not think twice before negotiating a 20 to 30 % reduction on hotel rates if staying more than a week, and especially during the low season. Negotiating taxi fares is generally de rigueur and will demand a certain degree of enthusiasm, you can also negotiate rental or bicycle rentals if for several days.

• Conversion

Mauritius has adopted the metric system, but the old Anglo-Saxon system is constantly popping up. *See Units of Measurement p 248.*

• Drinking water

The chemically-treated tap water is in theory drinkable on Mauritius, but drinking bottled mineral water is recommended – this is available everywhere. On Rodrigues, the tap water is not drinkable.

• Electricity

Electricity is 220 volts. Most rooms are equipped with either British three-point or French two-point sockets, so taking an international adapter is advisable.

• Laundry service

All the hotels offer cheap, fast laundry services.

• Newspapers

Foreign newspapers can be found in most hotels and on newspaper stands in tourist areas, usually a few days late.

• Photography

A relatively good choice of films is available which you can have developed in some tourist areas and towns.

• Radio and television

Programmes are primarily broadcast in French, and less frequently in English or Creole.

• Smoking

Cigarettes are expensive in Mauritius. It is best to buy any tobacco products at the duty-free store at the airport.

• Thefts

Thefts have been reported from unguarded rental villas, primarily in the Grand Baie region. It is best not to leave any valuables unattended on the beach or in your car.

• Tipping/gratuities

Service is generally included and tips are at the customer's discretion. Mauritians however have progressively grown to expect a tip.

• Weather forecasts

Call ☎ 96.

• Units of Measurement

Distances in this guide are given in kilometres. As a rule of thumb, one kilometre is five-eighths of a mile: 5 miles is therefore about 8 kilometres, 10 miles is about 16 kilometres and 20 miles is about 32 kilometres.

Consult the table below for other useful metric equivalents:

Degrees Celsius	35°	30°	25°	20°	15°	10°	5°	0°	-5°	-10°
Degrees Fahrenheit	95°	86°	77°	68°	59°	50°	41°	32°	23°	15°

1 centimetre (cm) = 0.4 inch
1 metre (m) = 3.3 feet
1 metre (m) = 1.09 yards
1 litre = 1.06 quart
1 litre = 0.22 gallon
1 kilogram (kg) = 2.2 pounds

LOOK AND LEARN

• Architecture

GAJEELEE, RAJENDRADEY, ***National Monuments of Mauritius***; ***Port Louis District***, Editions de l'Océan Indien, 1992.

• General

BENNETT Pramila Ramgulam, ***Mauritius***, Clio Publishing, 1992. Bibliography.
DOMMEN Edward and Bridget, ***Mauritius: An Island of Success***, James Currey, 1999.

DORMANN Genevieve, ***Mauritius from the air***, Southern Book Publishers, S. Africa, 1993.

GEORGES Eliane, ***The Indian Ocean***, B Taschen Verlag, Germany, 1998. Coffee table book.

• Children's books

PENNY Malcolm, ***The Indian Ocean***, Raintree Publications, 1997. Children's nature guide.

• Fauna and flora

HALL TR, ***Fishes of the Indian Ocean***, Calypso Publications, 1998
LIESKE Ewald, ***Coral Reef Fishes, Caribbean, Indian Ocean and Pacific Ocean***, Princeton University Press, 1999.

MICHEL Claude, ***Birds of Mauritius***, Editions de l'Océan Indien, 1996.

MICHEL Claude, ***Marine Molluscs of Mauritius***, Editions de l'Océan Indien, 1992.

QASIM S Z, ***Glimpses of the Indian Ocean***, Sangam Books, 1998.

SINCLAIR Ian, ***Chamberlain's Guide to the Birds of the Indian Ocean Islands***, C. Struik, South Africa, 1998.

• Fiction

CONRAD Joseph, ***T'wixt Land and Sea***, available in Penguin. A trilogy of 3 tales, all of which take place on Mauritius.
O'BRIAN Patrick, ***The Mauritius Command***, Harper Collins, 1996. The captain of a frigate has to take Réunion and Mauritius, which served as a naval base for Bonaparte, and "hampered" the India Route, from the French.

ST-PIERRE Bernardin de, ***Paul et Virginie***, 1788. Set in Mauritius, a great classic if you are up to the French.

• Food

FELIX Guy, ***Genuine Cuisine of Mauritius***, Editions de l'Océan Indien, 1992.

• History

CARTER ***Marina, Servants, Sirdars*** and ***Settlers; Indians in Mauritius, 1834-74***, Oxford UP (India), 1995.
COOMBES Alfred North-, ***History of Sugar Production in Mauritius***, Editions de l'Océan Indien, 1993.
DOMMEN Edward, ***Mauritius; An Island of Success – A retrospective study, 1960-93***, Cambridge UP, 1999.
MACPHERSON Ken, ***Indian Ocean; A history of people and the sea***, Oxford UP, India, 1998
MOREE PJ, ***Concise History of Dutch Mauritius, 1598-1710***, Kegan Paul Intl, 1998.
PITRAY Alfred S De, ***"Post Office Mauritius" and Its Legend***, Editions de l'Océan Indien, 1992.
RIVIERE Lindsay, ***The Historical Dictionary of Mauritius***, Scarecrow Publishing, 1992.

• Language

LEE Jacques K, ***Mauritius; its Creole language – The Ultimate Creole Phrase Book and Dictionary***, Nautilus Publishing Co, 1999.

• Maps

IGN Map, ***Mauritius Island***, 1:100 000. THE REFERENCE.
Macmillan Map, ***Mauritius Traveller's Map***.
Globetrotter Map, ***Mauritius Island***, Less detailed, but interesting relief detail.
Ordinance Survey Maps, ***Mauritius***, 25:000 000. Mauritius Island covered by 13 highly detailed maps.
On arrival, you will also find many other maps of the island, Port Louis and Rodrigues in shops and bookstores.

• People and Culture

CHANDRASEKHAR S, ***Population of*** Mauritius***; Facts, Problems, Policy***, Indus Publishing Company, 1997.
ERIKSEN Thomas, ***Common Denominators; Ethnicity, Nation-building and Compromise in Mauritius***, Berg Publishers, 1998.
LUM Roseline, ***Mauritius; A Guide to Customs and Etiquette***, Kuperard, 1997.
RAMDOYAL Ramesh, ***Festivals of Mauritius***, Editions de l'Océan Indien, 1992.
Beyond Inequalities; Women in Mauritius, Southern African R&D Centre, Zimbabwe, 1998.

• Religion

PARKIN David, ***Islamic Prayer along the Indian Ocean Littoral***, Curzon Press, 1999.

• Sport

HEIKELL Rod, ***Indian Ocean Cruising Guide***, Imray, 1999.
JACKSON Jack, ***Diving in the Indian Ocean***, Rizzoli Publications, 1999.
MOUNTAIN Alan, ***Dive Sites of Mauritius***, NTC Publishing Group, 1997.
VENTER, Al J, ***Underwater Mauritius***, Ashanti Publishing, Gibraltar, 1990.

Exploring Mauritius

E. Valentin/HOA QUI

Sugarcane
in blossom

Port Louis★

Port and capital of the island of Mauritius
About 230 000 people work there, of whom 160 000 are residents
Hot and humid climate – Map p 254-255

Not to be missed
The morning market.
A stroll in the Chinese quarter.
A drink on the shady terrace of the Vieux Conseil Café.
Horse racing at Champ de Mars.

And remember...
Port Louis is cooler and more animated in the morning.
Avoid the rush-hours between 7.30am-10am / 4pm-6pm.
Mondays and Tuesdays are the best days to visit the town.

At first sight, Port Louis does not seem particularly alluring. The streets are throttled by traffic jams, parking spaces are scarce, the narrow pavements are crowded with pedestrians, gutters are awash with debris after tropical downpours, and a simple act such as crossing the roads becomes a hazardous feat given the chaotic way drivers handle their simple or motorised two-wheelers. To make matters worse, the place is hot and humid, the pollution is suffocating and the noisy, overcrowded streets are dirty with litter. Despite this, Port Louis is not without charm

It is a town that needs to be explored nonchalantly and unhurriedly rather than formally visited with a guidebook in hand. It is the nerve-centre and soul of the island, where memories of the past mingle with aspirations for the future. Colonial buildings testify to the island's history, places of worship to suit every creed reflect the ethnic mix of the island population, whereas modern shops and sky-scrapers suggest that the country is progressing rapidly.

After the hectic bustle of the day, a sudden languor pervades the town: the offices are silent and the streets are empty. As night falls, only the Chinese quarter shows signs of wakefulness, its smoky gaming rooms filled with sailors from all over the world.

Capital of Île de France: transit post on the route to India

Almost as soon as François Mahé de La Bourdonnais, Governor General of the Mascarenes, landed on the Île de Bertrand in 1735, his plans to build a town began to be implemented. Not only did he intend to make Port Louis a maritime trading post on the Indies route, he wished to construct a town worthy of becoming the capital of Île de France – which in time was to become the most important town in the Indian Ocean. He swiftly endowed it with municipal buildings dedicated to his administration, a hospital and a church. Fortifications were erected around the new capital to safeguard it from attack by the British. Only then did the town assume the name Port Louis in honour of the reigning French monarch Louis XV. Later, this title was to change several times in accordance with the course of French history. At the beginning of the French Revolution it became "Port Nord-Ouest", then under the Empire, "Port Napoléon"; finally, the original name was restored by the British in 1810 after they assumed power.

The capital was quick to blossom; up until 1865, when a malaria epidemic swept through the region, the majority of the island's population was concentrated there. Malarial mosquitoes, probably accompanying a large wave of immigrants from India in 1835, found the perfect breeding conditions in Port Louis's warm, damp climate. The wealthy townsfolk left the capital in droves in search of cooler climes on the high central plateaux (around Curepipe), taking with them all their worldly goods – including, in some cases, their houses which they then conscientiously reassembled.

In 1865 life in Port Louis was boosted by the completion of a railway line to Mahébourg, although the town never regained anything resembling its former splendour. The reason for choosing this particular spot is self-explanatory. The town is strategically set facing a deep, well-sheltered bay and protected by a ring of peaks belonging to the Moka mountain chain (Pouce, Pieter Both and Montagne des Signaux). This site between the sea and the mountains, which once was so judiciously chosen by the French East India Company for their new colony's capital, is now too small for the town, especially as it succumbs to economic expansion and population explosion.

A walk about town

Allow a day.

The populous and traffic-filled town of Port Louis is best visited on foot. It is easy to find your way around the grid-pattern of streets thanks to the citadel boldly silhouetted on the skyline or the modern mosque's minaret rising proudly above the town centre. Street names are inconsistently written in French or English, sometimes in both; moreover, you may find streets which were renamed in 1968 after the Island was granted independence, marked up with their original name as well.

Whether visitors come into town by car, bus or taxi, the logical place to start from is the **port** (A1) for this is the nerve-centre of the town and the island as a whole. For security reasons, the main docks are not accessible to the general public, so one must be content to watch from afar the large container ships attracted here from across the seas by the tax-free zone.

The striking colonial-style white and grey stone-fronted central **post office** (B1) is the first major anachronism along the main road into the capital, overlooking the modern harbour. Next door stands the little **Musée de la Poste** *(open Monday to Friday, 9am-3pm; Saturdays 9am-11.30am; closed Sundays)*, which houses a substantial collection of Mauritius stamps – including a copy of the famous blue stamp – that appeals essentially to stamp-collectors and philatelists. Other associated artefacts include franking equipment, rubber stamps, weighing-scales etc.

The area opposite the harbour is the **business quarter** which progressively continues to be developed upwards given the lack of space to expand sideways. Unfortunately, the recent economic boom enjoyed by Mauritius has prompted the construction of rather ugly utilitarian high-rise buildings that do not inspire confidence for future developments (notable eyesores include the enormous **MCB** headquarters in the town centre. **Le Caudan**, a quite honourable replica of Cape Town's Waterfront in South Africa, is comprised of two colourful, well-designed, modern buildings that give Port Louis a slightly seaside resort air. It teems with bars and some excellent restaurants and is also the only place on the island where recent European, Indian or American movies are shown.

Opposite the central post office: bounded by Queen Street, Corderie Street, Sir W Newton Street and the trunk road (M2).

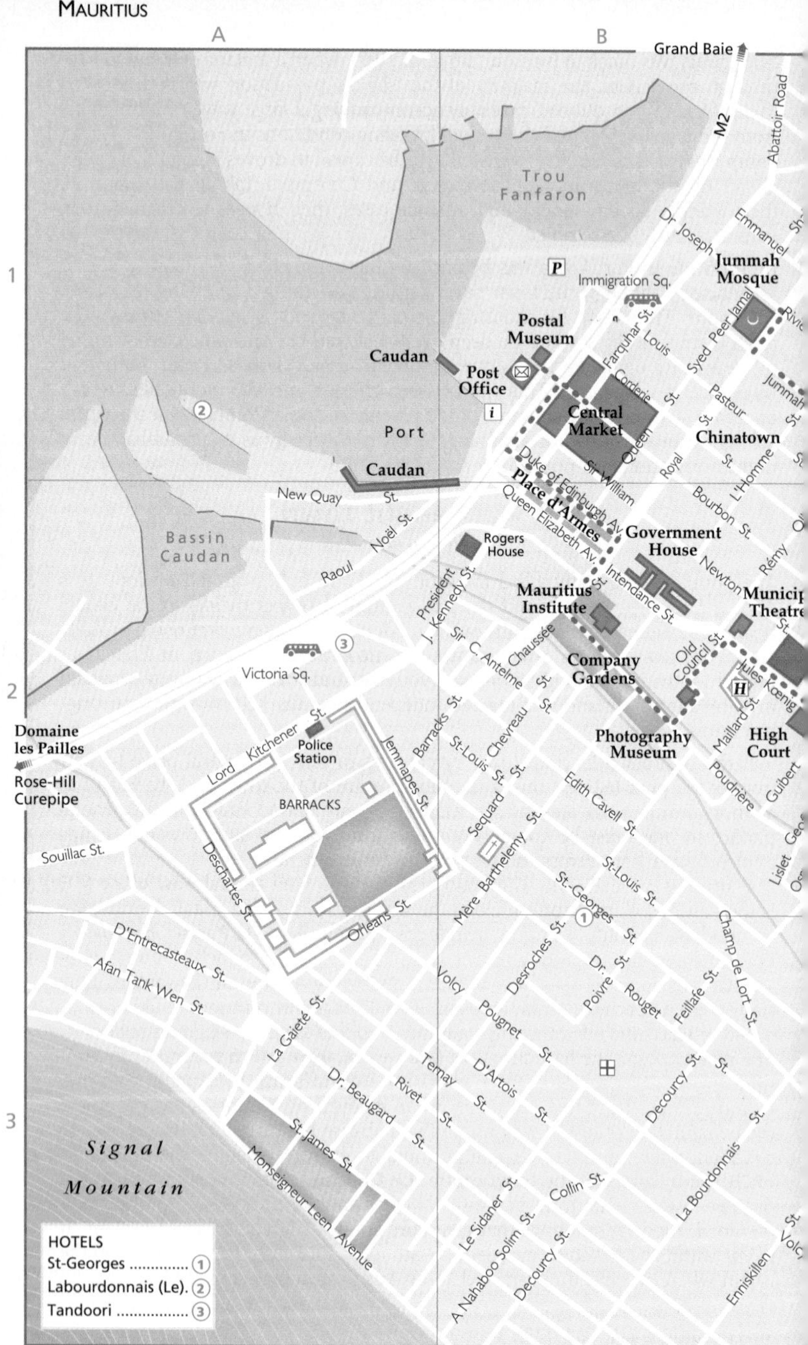
A
B
1
2
3
Grand Baie
M2
Abattoir Road
Trou Fanfaron
Dr Joseph
Emmanuel
Jummah Mosque
Immigration Sq.
Postal Museum
Farquhar St.
Louis
Syed Peer Jamal
Caudan
Post Office
Corderie
St.
Pasteur
Jummah
Central Market
Queen
Royal
St.
Port
Caudan
Chinatown
L'Homme
Duke of Edinburgh Av.
Sir William
Place d'Armes
Queen Elizabeth Av.
New Quay
St.
Noël St.
Bourbon St.
Bassin Caudan
Rogers House
Government House
Raoul
Rémy
President J. Kennedy St.
Mauritius Institute
Intendance St.
Newton
Theatre
Sir C. Antelme
Chaussée
Old Council St.
Company Gardens
Victoria Sq.
Jules Koenig
Domaine les Pailles
Kitchener St.
Barracks St.
St.-Louis St.
Chevreau St.
Photography Museum
Maillard St.
High Court
Police Station
Jemmapes St.
Rose-Hill
Curepipe
Lord
BARRACKS
Edith Cavell St.
Poudrière
Guibert
Sequard St.
Souillac St.
Descharte St.
Mère Barthelemy St.
St-Louis St.
Lislet
St.-Georges St.
Orleans St.
Champ de Lort St.
D'Entrecasteaux St.
Desroches St.
Dr. Poivre St.
Afan Tank Wen St.
Volcy
Rouget
Feillafe St.
La Gaieté St.
Pougnet St.
Temay St.
D'Artois St.
Dr. Beaugard
Rivet
St.
Decourcy St.
St.
St. James St.
Signal Mountain
Monseigneur Leen Avenue
Le Sidaner St.
Collin St.
La Bourdonnais
A Nahaboo Solim St.
Decourcy St.
Enniskillen
HOTELS
St-Georges .... ①
Labourdonnais (Le). ②
Tandoori .... ③

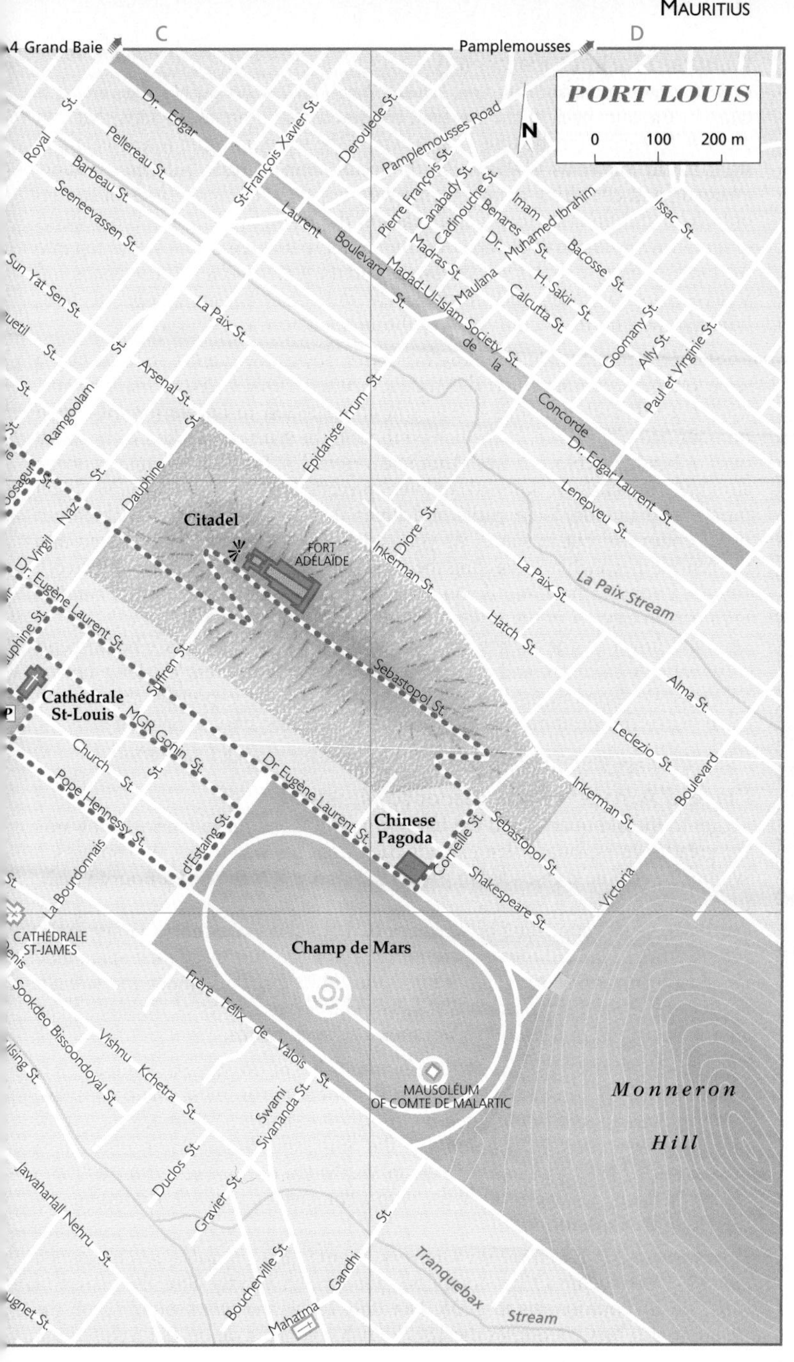
PORT LOUIS
0 100 200 m
N
C
D
A4 Grand Baie
Pamplemousses
Citadel
FORT ADÉLAÏDE
Cathédrale St-Louis
CATHÉDRALE ST-JAMES
Chinese Pagoda
Champ de Mars
MAUSOLÉUM OF COMTE DE MALARTIC
Monneron Hill
La Paix Stream
Tranquebax Stream
Dr. Edgar Laurent Boulevard
St-François Xavier St.
Deroulede St.
Pamplemousses Road
Pierre François St.
Canabady St.
Cadinouche St.
Benares St.
Imam St.
Dr. Muhamed Ibrahim St.
Issac St.
Bacosse St.
Madras St.
Maulana St.
H. Sakir St.
Calcutta St.
Madad-Ul-Islam Society St.
de la Concorde
Dr. Edgar Laurent St.
Goomany St.
Ally St.
Paul et Virginie St.
Royal St.
Pellereau St.
Barbeau St.
Seeneevassen St.
Sun Yat Sen St.
La Paix St.
Arsenal St.
Ramgoolam St.
Epidariste Trum St.
Dauphine St.
Naz St.
Dr. Virgil
Dr. Eugène Laurent St.
Diore St.
Inkerman St.
Lenepveu St.
Hatch St.
Sebastopol St.
Alma St.
Leclezio St.
Boulevard
Victoria
Suffren St.
MGR Gonin St.
Church St.
Pope Hennessy St.
d'Estaing St.
Dr Eugène Laurent St.
Corneille St.
Shakespeare St.
La Bourdonnais St.
Sookdeo Bissoondoyal St.
Vishnu Kchetra St.
Frère Félix de Valois St.
Swami Sivananda St.
Duclos St.
Gravier St.
Jawaharlall Nehru St.
Boucherville St.
Mahatma Gandhi St.

Central Market* (Bazar) (B1)

Open Monday to Saturday, 6am-5pm; Sundays, 7am-11.30am. Beware of pickpockets. It is here, in the four halls of the **covered market** at the heart of the city, that you are sure to encounter the true atmosphere of the town and gain a real feeling of what life in Mauritius is about. All the locals seem to hang out here, jostling, elbowing and chattering among themselves, unperturbed by the gaze of foreign onlookers and immune to the shrill calls of the market sellers' and the hubbub of muttering housewives picking over the fresh produce. As soon as you step into the maze of narrow streets you are swept into the active melee of pedestrians and street-vendors weaving their carts laden with chattels, sweetmeats or fruit, honking their horns to clear the way through loiterers and beggars.

To the right of the **main doorway** on Queen Street, the market stalls display a selection of goods aimed at the tourist market: clothes, spices, basket-ware, leather goods and souvenirs – that you are expected to haggle for with good humour and persistence. In the hall on the left, the stalls are stacked with careful piles of beautiful coloured fresh fruit and vegetables: handfuls of chilli-peppers, attractive bunches of knotted onions, precariously arranged *chouchous*, tall pumpkin pyramids, loose garlic and limes (locally called *limons*) packed into paper cones laid out in stars... As you come out of this building and step into the central thoroughfare bisecting the market complex in two (Farquhar Street), you are bound to be asked if you fancy trying a special concoction of curative herb teas to ease away the aches and pains of the mind and body.

Few will linger in the section set aside for the meat-merchants who suspend their various carcasses and weighing scales from the rafters on long hooks. Whereas the fishmongers' hall can be a feast to the eye, especially after a good catch, when the gleaming fresh fish display a complete array of rainbow colours.

Come out of the market and on the waterfront, turn left to walk some 100m.

Place d'Armes* (Place Bissoondoyal) (B1-B2)

To get to the old quarter and the historic part of town, make your way towards the great open esplanade that extends back from the waterfront. As you pass, a symbolic welcome is extended to you by the **statue of Mahé de La Bourdonnais**, the town's founder.

This great square stretching between the harbour and Government House is the main feature of the old town where people come to while away their spare time among the upturned cannons, statues and white benches under the straight avenues of Royal Palms, especially during the hottest hours of the day for an afternoon snooze or a lively conversation between friends.

The left side of the square is marked by the **Duke of Edinburgh Avenue**, overlooked by a long row of old Creole houses now overrun by airline companies. The parallel southern side is lined by the **Queen Elizabeth Avenue** whose proportions have been interrupted by the imposing **State Bank** built in a post-classic style that was all the rage in Manhattan during the 1980s. Its more discreet neighbour, an elegant house with a colonnaded veranda, is occupied by the **Hong Kong Bank**.

Government House/Hôtel du Gouvernement* (B2) (*no public access*), which closes off the square to the southeast, was erected shortly after the arrival of Mahé de La Bourdonnais in 1735. Not only is this the oldest building on the island, it also best epitomises the 18C French colonial style of architecture built of wood and dressed stone, topped with a wooden slat roof and fronted with a three-tier colonnaded open white veranda. Having served as the Governor's town residence, the house was used for streams of parties and formal functions attended by the successive representatives of the East India Company, the kings of France, the Republic, the Empire and Britain and her empire. To some, the severe gaze of **Queen Victoria** whose statue overlooks all proceedings from the entrance, will inspire some idea of what the place must have been like at the turn of the 20C, when, attired in its past splendour, extravagant receptions were hosted here by the wife of the governor for two hundred guests or more – including officers and dignitaries with beautiful Creole ladies in attendance – in the drawing rooms full of rare exotic wood furniture supplied by the East India Company. The illuminated **courtyard** opened directly onto Port Louis's natural harbour where sailing ships pitched with the winds and tide.

Few such occasions survive from that magnanimous era, save for the annual state opening of the new legislative session which is marked with great pomp by a solemn ceremony and the formal inspection of the Guard of Honour by the Governor-General.

Cross Intendance Street to the right of Government House and turn down Chaussée Street.

A short distance along stands the **Mauritius Institute** (B2) *(Open Monday-Tuesday, Thursday-Friday, 9am-4pm; Saturdays and Sundays, 9am-12noon. Closed Wednesdays. No charge)*, a natural history museum founded in 1831 with a model of the famous **dodo**, the clumsy bird often used as an emblem of the island, as well as various other birds, shells and fish. Displays are presented in a scholarly way but the cabinets are rather in need of rearrangement.

On leaving the museum, turn left along Poudrière Street.

Company Gardens/Jardin de la Compagnie (B2) retain their name from the time when they were owned and managed by the former French East India Company and included from 1776 onwards Port Louis's first theatre, where works by the likes of Molière and Racine were staged. Although much of its original charm has faded, the gardens provide a pleasant place to while away the hot hours of the day in the shade of the Banyan trees, but you will not be the only one, for the place is often crowded at lunchtime with office workers and street sellers hawking *mine frit*, cakes and brightly-coloured drinks.

Jules Kœnig Street to Champ de Mars★ (B2-C2)

This busy quarter comprises a motley assortment of modern concrete buildings – like the Town Hall and Ministry Offices – and a range of historic constructions in wood or stone. Together, these house Mauritius's political and administrative infrastructure.

Step out of the Jardin de la Compagnie and into Poudrière Street before turning down the second street on the left.

Old Council Street/Rue du Vieux Conseil (B2) at one time was where the island's High Court held its assizes. Today, the attractive paved street lined with wooden houses and picturesque street-lamps reminiscent of a stage set is the preserve of pedestrians. It is somewhat appropriate therefore, to find a **Photography Museum/Musée de la Photographie** *(Open, Monday to Friday, 10am-12noon/1pm-3pm. Entrance fee)* located here, displaying old-fashioned camera equipment and a selection of archive photographs showing what Port Louis was like in its heyday.

Note that the museum does not conform to the advertised opening times, but with a little perseverance you will probably manage to gain access. Should you find the place closed, you might like to seek consolation from the tiny **"Patisserie Idéale"** *(see below:* Where to eat) by trying out one of their delicious banana tarts.

Follow Old Council Street to Jules Kœnig Street.

The yellow classical **Municipal Theatre** (B2), which was designed by a French architect and completed in 1822, was tremendously popular up until the Second World War, especially during the Mauritian winter months when it hosted a season of performances put on by actors from the Comédie Française in Paris. The programme enticed many of the established land-owning families back to their townhouses in Port Louis, in order to join in the endless circuit of society gatherings, horse racing events, nights out at the theatre and dances hosted by the Governor. Nowadays, these families move to their seaside villa for a change of scenery.

Since 1940-50, the theatre has been used only very rarely, and then it is more likely to be hired out for a political party conference or a trade union debate than for a theatrical evening's entertainment. Occasionally, it stages Chinese and Indian ballets or small-scale Creole productions.

Continue along Jules Kœnig Street past the police station, and on the right.

Set back from the street, at the far end of a formal garden planted with mature trees, sits a fine colonial-style building housing the **Supreme Court/Cour Suprême** (B2). Trials are open to the public, and watching proceedings involving various be-wigged judges and court officials addressing each other as "Your Lordship" while considering the fate of a chicken thief can appear somewhat incongruous.

Immediately after the court-house on the left.

The grey stone **Cathédrale St-Louis** (C2) dates from 1770, otherwise it is of little particular interest. Inside, you will find the entombed remains of **Madame Mahé de La Bourdonnais** and her son, transferred with great pomp after their discovery in 1829 in the former Government House chapel.

Jules Kœnig Street extends between the cathedral and the Champ de Mars to become **Pope-Hennessy Street** (C2) in which you will find a number of Port Louis' best-preserved wooden colonial townhouses. Among the most remarkable is Chinese-style **no 29** decorated with yellow and red ideograms.

The **Champ de Mars** (C2-C3) at the end of Pope-Hennessy Street was conceived by the French in 1740 as a parade ground where the military could exercise and display arms. In the days of Mahé de La Bourdonnais, the area was used as a duelling-ground; later, the "sans-culottes" celebrated the outcome of the Revolution here. When the British arrived, great crowds drawn from High Society came to watch the highly regimented troops marching in formation to the sound of the military bands. In 1812 the area was transformed into a hippodrome.

Indeed, if you visit the island between June and November, you may like to go down there on a Saturday afternoon to watch the **horse racing:** the betting goes apace and a terrific atmosphere reverberates through the packed stands. The action draws a mixed and friendly crowd of spectators irrespective of social class or creed, with adults and children participating in the action clutching paper flowers and multicoloured balloons especially sold for the occasion.

Besides the vast race track overlooked by the magnificent ring of mountains, the complex comprises a sports stadium, a children's play area, a large parking lot and a rostrum for political or religious meetings. Additional landmarks include a **statue** of King Edward VII of England and the **mausoleum** of Comte de Malartic, the French governor of Mauritius who died in 1800.

C. Pavard/HOA QUI

Racing at Champ de Mars

Turn down the second street on the left off d'Estaing Street.

If you enjoy looking at the Creole townhouses, you may like to make a detour by **MGR Gonin Street** (C2): at **no 18** you will find a house with a fine veranda, whereas the handsome colonial house with a colonnade situated behind the cathedral, is the official residence of the **Port Louis Bishopric**. You may like to go down **Dr Eugène Laurent Street** (C2) while you are in the vicinity, and admire **no 43 & 45**; look out for the attractive little **Chinese pagoda** on the corner with Corneille Street.

From Dr Eugène Laurent Street, turn left past the Chinese pagoda and go up Corneille Street to Sebastopol Street. Turn left and continue to the top.

Climbing up to enjoy the **view** from the **Citadel/Citadelle** (Fort Adélaide) (C2-D2) built by the British in 1835 requires both time and stamina. From the top there is a good view out over the town laid out with its grid-street pattern in the lee of the cannon-fire, the harbour and the neighbouring mountains.

Your visit may coincide with a **Son et lumière** show *(enquire for information and dates from the Tourist Office)*.

Walk down the road from the citadel making for the sea or take the steps down to Jummah Mosque Street. Alternatively, go back to the Champ de Mars, and proceed to the Chinese quarter between Sir S Ramgoolam Street and Royal Street.

Chinese Quarter/Quartier chinois★ (B1-2 C1)

This is undoubtedly the town's most picturesque commercial quarter and a fine place for a casual stroll among the modern and old – perhaps rather shabby and dilapidated – houses with wrought-iron balconies decked with flowering pot-plants upstairs and colourfully cluttered shops at ground level.

G. Boutin/HOA QUI

A hardware store on the pavement of Port Louis

From each cluttered shop the merchandise spills onto the pavement: white-metal utensils and plastic receptacles, dried fish stiff with salt and sacks of rice. Anything and everything one can imagine is available from these little treasure-trove stores: calligraphy paint-brushes; Chinese medicines; intoxicating perfumes and spices; garish Indian silks; watches; photographic equipment; plumbing tools and religious effigies.

As you wander through the bustling streets – notably Louis Pasteur Street, Rémy Ollier Street, Corderie Street (where fabric shops and tailors' workshops proliferate), Bourbon Street and **Royal Street**, at the very heart of the Chinese quarter, you will rub shoulders with Indian ladies clad in gorgeous saris, veiled Moslem women, westernised Chinese traders, Franco-Mauritian and South African businessmen dressed in suit and tie clutching a brief case, and tourists from all over the world.

The **Jummah Mosque*** (B1) *(Royal Street. Open Saturday to Thursday, 9.30am-12noon. Closed Fridays. Appropriate dress covering shoulders and legs. No charge)*, a green and white fronted building with a finely carved **door**, was built in 1852 and is one of the island's most beautiful religious edifices. Inside, there is a lovely shaded **courtyard** that is peaceful and cool, and a realm apart from the frenetic activity of the outside world. Please note, however, that the area beyond the colonnade is the preserve of men only, and is where they carry out their ritual ablutions in silence before attending prayers.

Go back down towards the docks, strolling through Jummah Mosque Street for example and passing its attractive small houses.

The colonial heritage around Port Louis*

Approx 50km – Allow half a day by car – Map p 262.

There are a number of fine architectural monuments and sights testifying to Port Louis' colonial past scattered about the neighbouring countryside. This drive completes a circuit around the ring of hills that encircle the town starting with the Moka chain of hills that lead on to the Deux Mamelles and Pieter Both mountains, the Nicolière Lake and Ste-Croix on the other side of Longue Mountain.

Head out of town along the M2 in the direction of Rose Hill.

■ **Domaine Les Pailles** – ☎ *212 4225 Open daily, 10am-5pm. Entrance fee. Guided visits every 30min. Restaurants open for both lunch and dinner.* This tourist complex attempts – somewhat artificially – to recreate what life was like on a sugar plantation during the 18C and 19C. The first experience is a short ride in the local transport available at that time, namely an open ox-drawn carriage or a little train, to a **sugar-mill** turned by a resigned-looking ox. The next installation shows how the estate rum (on sale in the shop) is distilled in the **still**. Outside there is a miniature **spice garden**. Among the additional attractions laid on by the estate management, there are excursions on foot or horseback and cross-country drives by Land Rover.
The main draws of the Pailles Estate, however, are the casino and several renowned restaurants *(see below:* Where to eat).

Continue along the M2 towards Le Réduit, then turn left towards Moka – Mont Ory (B46). A large road-sign indicating "Eurêka la maison créole" appears on the right, just before Souillac Bridge.

■ **Eureka House**** – *Moka. Open Monday to Saturday, 9am-5pm. Closed Sundays. Entry charge includes guided tour. Shop. A Creole meal on the veranda can be ordered in advance* ☎ *433 4951.* When **Eugène Le Clézio**, a forebear of author JMG Le Clézio, discovered this 1830s colonial house in 1856, he exclaimed "Eureka!" and promptly set about acquiring it. Shortly after, his son Henri got to work decorating it. Eureka remained in the hands of the distinguished Franco-Mauritian family until 1975 when it was acquired privately and turned into a museum effectively designed to evoke the splendours of Mauritian colonial life. More than a hundred doors – the house is built from locally-found exotic hardwoods – separate the maze of interconnecting rooms in the absence of corridors and passageways. Only a proportion of the furniture is period, as many of the early pieces from the East India Company were retained by the Le Clézio family when the house was sold. Nonetheless, the glorious panels of rosewood in the drawing room, mahogany in the dining room and purple-wood, cinnamon and ebony in the music-room certainly confirm a taste for lavish interiors among the wealthy white planters at that time. A colonnaded **veranda** runs right around the house, opening out onto the carefully landscaped **grounds** and a view of Ory Mountain on one side, and a waterfall of the Moka River on the other. The small separate stone building, set apart from the house to reduce the risk of fire, accommodated the kitchen.

Head along the B46 leaving Moka behind you: at the roundabout, take the A7 right (directions for Rose Hill); at the next roundabout, take the small road to Réduit opposite (direction Rose Hill).

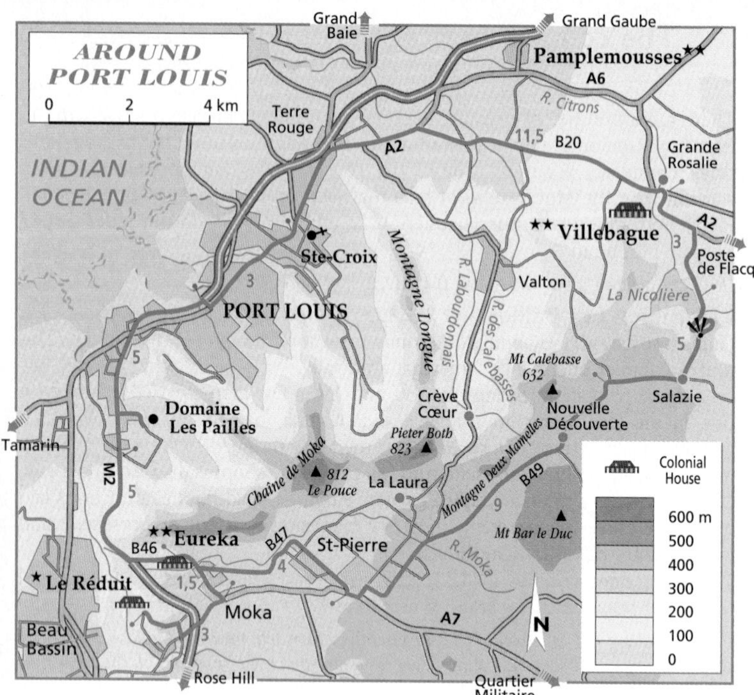

■ **Le Réduit**★ – *Open one day a year, usually the first Sunday in September. Enquire locally.* This particularly fine colonial villa (sometimes referred to as a *château*) stands proudly on a knoll at the confluence of two rivers, protected by the Moka and Corps du Garde Mountains. It was built between 1748-49, and was designated the French – then British – Governor's official residence in 1770. These days it is the formal workplace of the **President of The Republic of Mauritius**. This secluded spot was originally found by Barthélemy David, the Governor General who succeeded Mahé de La Bourdonnais, as an enchanting setting for his secret love trysts. It was also perfect for offering refuge to women and children and a safe place for squirreling away important State Papers in case of a British invasion. Throughout the 18C, the house was used to host sumptuous balls and banquets, especially when the French Navy or Army were stationed in Mauritius prior to engaging in battle with the British in India.
It was there too, under the colonnaded **veranda**, that the great French conquests in the East were planned: Madagascar, Seychelles, Indochina, the Indies.
The substantial grounds around the villa are landscaped into **formal French gardens** complete with geometric parterres with green lawns, mature trees and a well-stocked botanical garden.

The garden gently slopes down to a viewpoint called **Bout du Monde**★ – which translates as the "End of the World" – perched precariously on the edge of a steep cliff overlooking a deep gorge, and the **Manoir de la Tour Blanche** at Rose Hill opposite.

Return to the Moka roundabout back along the A7 and then take the B47 towards Nouvelle Découverte.

The road cuts through the **former residential quarter of Moka and St-Pierre**, where the loveliest houses on the island are to be found nestling in extensive grounds, at the far end of long avenues of coconut palms. A large proportion of these elegant residences date from the time of the malaria epidemic in 1865 that prompted a great number of the capital's wealthier inhabitants to flee Port Louis and build houses along the main road leading out of town and along the chain of mountains beyond, or even further out on the high plateau of the Plaine Wilhems. Just imagine how sumptuous these planter's houses must have been when captained by beautiful Creole ladies, each vying to be more elegant and coquettish than her neighbour, and a host of servants dressed in the standard livery of the East India Company.

Some few yards after the Moka roundabout, you will come across two fine **colonial houses*** on the left-hand side, one with a wood slat-roof painted in sky-blue and the other in dark grey.

On the edge of St-Pierre (100m before the roundabout), the blue roof of the **maison "Trompette"** can be seen on the right nestling among the trees at the far end of the parallel lines of coconut palms. Furthermore, a close look at the trees along the side of the road will reveal a host of bell-shaped nests built by yellow weaver birds.

At the roundabout, continue straight over in the direction of Quartier Militaire. After the St-Pierre sugar refinery (on the right of the fork), take the B49 left sign-posted "La Nicolière" and continue, turning right after Nouvelle Découverte, following directions where marked.

All the fields as far as the eye can see lying to the left-hand side of the road are dedicated to sugarcane, with the **peaks known as Le Pouce and Pieter Both** in the far distance. After Nouvelle Découverte, the scenery becomes more attractive: the vegetation thickens and the hardwood trees are more varied, as the cane fields make way for forests of Sylvester pines, *citranus*, eucalyptus, bamboo, papyrus, cryptomerias and monkey puzzle trees.

At the Salazie cross-roads, La Nicolière is signposted left (signed "Le Juge de Segrais Bridge").

As the road winds its way past flowering verges, sudden bends reveal **views*** of the landscape around Nicolière reservoir (on the left) with Île Coin de Mire and Île Ronde (opposite) and beyond to the northeastern coast (to the right). The road descends amid the sugarcane plantations interspersed with piles of accumulated black stones. Before reaching the **Nicolière Reservoir**, constructed to store and provide water to the island's northern territories, the road comes to a bridge where several small shrines and altars have been placed in honour of the main Hindu deities.

After La Nicolière, take the A2 left sign-posted for Pamplemousses (not Villebague). When the road arrives at a house with a red tin roof: turn left.

From the road, it is possible to catch a glimpse through the bamboo thicket of the pale grey wooden slats belonging to the **Château de Villebague**** *(Grande Rosalie. Private property, although one can pause briefly in the garden to take a photograph)*: home first and foremost to Mahé de La Bourdonnais himself, and later to his successor Magon de la Villebague, Governor of Mauritius at the time of the French East India Company. The private residence, the oldest on the island, became a prototype for French colonial architecture on which many subsequent houses were modelled. Strangely enough, the estate was the first sugarcane plantation on an industrial scale in Mauritius.

At the fork 10m after the château, turn left down the B20 sign posted to Port Louis. At the junction where the B20 joins the A2, you can turn right to Pamplemousses (see p 268) or left along the A2 to return to Port Louis. If heading back into town, why not continue 10m past the right turn to Baie du Tombeau, and at the Terre Rouge roundabout divert left down and along Avenue Père Laval.

■ **Ste Croix** – The main attraction of this part of town is the **Church and Shrine of Père Désiré Laval** *(regular buses from Port Louis. No charge)*. Father Jacques Désiré Laval started out as a doctor in Normandy before being ordained a priest in 1838, and setting out for Mauritius as a missionary in 1841 intent upon converting the black slaves who had recently been freed to Christianity. Before long, he earned a considerable following, largely because of his ability to heal people, and was acclaimed as a saint and miracle-worker. He died in 1864 and was beatified by Pope Jean-Paul II in 1979.

To this day, the most fervent believers gather before the shrine of "The Black People's Apostle" in order to touch the stone of his **tomb** *(6am-6pm)* with a hand or a cloth that can then transfer that contact to the face or body. Every year, on the anniversary of his death on **9 September**, a great crowd of Mauritians of all denominations gather here on pilgrimage.

The modern **church** also arouses great devotion; the crucifix hanging on the wall was carved under the direction of Père Laval, and as such entices the most ardent followers to come and touch the wall, and then rub their bodies.

The **Père Laval Centre** *(Open Monday to Saturday, 8.30am-4.45pm; Sundays and public holidays, 10am-4.15pm)* is dedicated to outlining the story of the saint's life and displaying a number of personal effects and related artefacts.

Leave the Ste Croix quarter to rejoin the main road into Port Louis.

Making the most of Port Louis

GETTING THERE

The two main access routes into the capital are the motorway to/from Curepipe and the A1, or old royal route, leading inland.

By car or taxi – Whether arriving from the north or from the south, you will enter on the expressway that runs beside the waterfront to the harbour. Leave your car or taxi in the Place du Quai (B1) or by the Cathedral square (C2). To leave town, make your way to the taxi rank near the main post office (B1) or next to Place d'Armes (B2). Port Louis is around 45min from the north and some 90min from the southern and eastern parts of the island.

By bus – A regular bus service operates at 10-15min intervals between the capital and the north or south of the island. Certain destinations may require you to change at Curepipe or Quatre Bornes.
Terminal nord, situated in Immigration Square (B1) runs buses to the north coast (Trou aux Biches, Grand Baie, Péreybère, Cap Malheureux, Grand Gaube); to Pamplemousses, Goodlands, Poudre d'Or; and the east coast (Centre de Flacq).
Terminal sud, in the former railway station in Victoria Square (A2), runs services to Rose Hill, Vacoas, Curepipe, Quatre Bornes and Mahébourg.

ADDRESS BOOK

Tourist Information – ***Tourist Office*** Caudan Waterfront, next to the central post office (B1), ☎ 208 6397, mpta@intnet.mr. 9am-4pm; closed on Saturday afternoon and Sundays.

Banks and money – Most of the banks are situated around Place d'Armes, Sir W Newton St, Queen St and Royal St.
Hong Kong Bank, Place d'Armes (B2) has a Visa ATM.
Mauritius Commercial Bank, Sir W Newton St, and Edith Cavell St (B2). Visa accepted.

Post Office – ***Poste centrale***, Place du Quai (B1) ☎ 208 2851. Poste restante. Other post offices are scattered around the town, in the bus station on Victoria Square and in the Emmanuel Anquetil office block.

Telephone – Public phone boxes can be found all around town.
For long-distance calls/faxes using phone cards: ***Mauritius Telecom***, Mauritius Telecom Tower, Edith Cavell St (B2), ☎ 208 7000. Open Monday to Friday, 8am-5.30pm; Saturdays 8am-12noon.

Health – There are a number of chemists throughout the town.
Pharmacie du port, President J F Kennedy St (B2) ☎ 208 1037.
Hôpital Dr Jeetoo, Volcy Pougnet St (B3) ☎ 212 3201/212 3202.

Airline companies – Rogers House, 5 President J F Kennedy St (B2)
Air Mauritius, Air Mauritius Centre, President J F Kennedy St (B2), ☎ 207 7070/207 7575 (reservations/confirmations), Fax 211 0366.
Air France: ☎ 208 6820.

Embassies and consulates – see Useful addresses p 236.

Immigration – see Formalities p 232.

WHERE TO STAY

Visitors generally avoid Port Louis which has few decent hotels and because the coastal resorts are far more appealing. If, however, you do need accommodation, here are a few addresses. Rates should be negotiated depending on your length of stay.

Less than US$15

Tandoori Hotel, Victoria Sq, ☎ 212 2131, Fax 212 3503 – 17rm A rather unattractive little hotel whose sole claim to fame is its unbeatable rates. The rooms are pretty basic and the place is noisy, even at night. The charm of the Indo-Mauritian owner's welcome is, however, flawless.

From US$45-60

Hôtel St-Georges, 19 St-Georges St, ☎ 211 2581, Fax 211 0885 – 60rm In the same street as the French Embassy, a fairly pleasant establishment that attempts to recapture an air of colonial times with reproduction East India Company furniture.

Over US$230

Labourdonnais Waterfront Hotel, Caudan Waterfront, PO Box 91, ☎ 202 4000, Fax 202 4040, 100100.3111@compuserve.com – 109rm Fitness centre, conference room, internet. Port Louis' most luxurious hotel, a favourite among rich business men. Hence the calm, discreet comfort that seems to be the hotel's motto. Every week the cream of the business world congregates around a jazz concert. If you've got the right gear and fancy building up your personal network of VIPs, you've come to the right place.

WHERE TO EAT

• Port Louis

Less than US$5

Street stalls and vendors. A myriad of street sellers are scattered about town with a range of mouth-watering to less than delicious snacks including dhal puri, spicy savouries, soup, and cakes. It all depends on what takes your fancy!

Patisserie idéale, 3 Old Council St (B2). Open daily, 10am-4.30pm. This tiny establishment hidden away in a minute pedestrian street bakes delicious banana pies and coconut cakes.

La Flore Mauricienne, 10 Intendance St (B2) ☎ 212 2200. Open Monday to Friday, 8.30am-4pm. Closed weekends. Snack-bar and tea-room: ideal for snatching a quick sandwich, a salad or a cake at lunch time, or for a refreshing drink sometime during the day in the shade of a parasol on the pavement – one of the few places offering such a luxury (even if rather noisy). In the basement there is a self-service restaurant, but the room is dark and gloomy. Also houses an excellent, rather smart, restaurant serving Creole and European dishes.

La Bonne Marmite, 18 Sir W Newton St (B2) ☎ 212 2403. Open Monday to Friday, 10am-4pm. Cafe-cum-sandwich-bar on the ground floor serving all kinds of delicious dishes and fresh sandwiches. Elegant, smart setting and well situated in the town centre. (For a more formal meal, see below.)

US$6-12

Le Chinois, 20 Jummah Mosque St (B1-C1) ☎ 242 8655. Lunch and dinner. Good and reasonably priced Chinese restaurant with a rather gloomy decor. Ask for a table by the window so that you can enjoy the bustle of the street outside.

Cafe du Vieux Conseil, Old Council St (B2) ☎ 211 0393. Open Monday to Saturday, 9am-5pm. Closed Sundays. A charming café to stop at and enjoy a drink under one of the large, white parasols in the peaceful garden. Also serves savoury pancakes, salads and Creole dishes.

Dragon Palace, 3 Léoville L'Homme St (B2) ☎ 208 0346. Lunch and dinner. Closed Monday evenings. Buffets Thursdays, Fridays and Sundays. Slightly more expensive than the other places listed. The polite service is somewhat aloof. Limited choice of dishes but excellent value for money. Broad clientele. It is advisable to book as the place is often teeming with private wedding parties.

US$12-25

Lai Min, 58 Royal St (B1-C1) ☎ 242 0042. Lunch and dinner. Another good Chinese restaurant, with a traditional, very pleasant decor.

La Bonne Marmite, 18 Sir W Newton St (B2) ☎ 212 2403. Open Monday to Friday for lunch. A highly popular venue especially among businessmen. Tasteful decor and civilised atmosphere. Charming establishment specialising in a delicious selection of Creole food. Cari of venison, octopus and fish. Copious portions. A few Chinese, Indian and European dishes also served. (For a snack, see above.)

Carri Poulé, Duke of Edinburgh Av, Place d'Armes (B1-B2) ☎ 212 1295. Lunch Monday to Saturday; dinner Friday and Saturday only. Closed Sunday. Buffet lunch on Wednesdays and Thursdays. One of the best Indian restaurants on the island, and probably the best in town. Frequented by knowledgeable businessmen and tourists alike. Both the cari and the tandoori dishes will quickly compensate for the rather gloomy surroundings.

• **Domaine Les Pailles**

US$12-25

Fu Xiao. ☎ 212 4225. Lunch and dinner, closed Saturday lunchtime. A delicious, varied selection of Chinese specialities, prepared by chefs from Nandjing.

Indra. ☎ 212 4225. Monday to Saturday, lunch and dinner. Closed all day Sunday and bank holidays. A wonderful venue where you will be served the most exquisite range of Indian delicacies. Live music recitals in the evening set among the fine woodwork and silk hangings.

SHOPPING

Books and newspapers – Local and international press, cards, books and guidebooks on Mauritius are on sale from the following:

Le Trèfle, Royal St (B2).

Librairie Allot, Happy World Center (2nd floor), 37 Sir W Newton St (B2).

Bloc Note, Place Foch (B2).

Tailors and dressmakers – Corderie St (B1-B2) For fabric and in particular cheap silk, go to the rows of merchants vying for trade at the heart of the Chinese Quarter. Dressmakers are also on site to make things up in the briefest of intervals: For best results, take a favourite well-fitting garment along with you to serve as a prototype.

Off-the-peg – The best choice of clothes-shops and boutiques can be found in the ***Happy World*** shopping mall on the corner of Sir W Newton St and Old Council St (B2).

Duty-free – ***Poncini***, 2 Jules Koenig St (B2) specialises in tax-free luxury items and fancy goods like watches, crockery, jewellery etc.

PAMPLEMOUSSES★★

Not to be missed
The giant water-lilies.

And remember...
Get an official guide to take you around the garden before walking about on your own.

Accessible along the A2 if coming from Port Louis, Poste de Flacq or La Nicolière; by the A5 from Goodlands if coming from the north and by the M2 if coming in from Grand Baie. Bus from Port Louis or Grand Baie.

Pamplemousses competes in the spice race

Soon after his arrival in Mauritius, Mahé de La Bourdonnais set about selecting in 1735 an extensive and fertile stretch of land on which to build his own personal residence and vegetable garden. The homestead, known as *Château de Mon Plaisir* – was eventually ceded to the French East Indies Company in 1737 and thereafter used as the official residence of the Governors of Mauritius until *Le Réduit* was built in 1742. When it came to the garden, La Bourdonnais decided to concentrate on cultivating all sorts of useful plants (like Brazilian manioc), and a broad variety of fruit and vegetables from abroad that he might be able to supply to the passing ships calling at Port Louis. A number of other early settlers were quick to follow suit, attracted to the area by its favourable climate and the opportunity of growing crops on a large scale. It was here that the first sugar plantations were established in 1745. It should be noted that new varieties of sugarcane were also being tried and tested at this time.

In 1770 **Pierre Poivre**, steward to the French king, discovered Pamplemousses and decided to acquire Mon Plaisir so that he might transform the grounds into a real botanical garden with as many new specimens as he could manage to collect. In particular, he hoped to introduce and acclimatise plants he had encountered when travelling to the Far East that were highly prized for the rare essences and spices they produced, which he hoped to harvest and export to Europe for nothing less than their weight in gold. This initiative soon proved highly successful, and merely "useful" plants were uprooted in favour of more

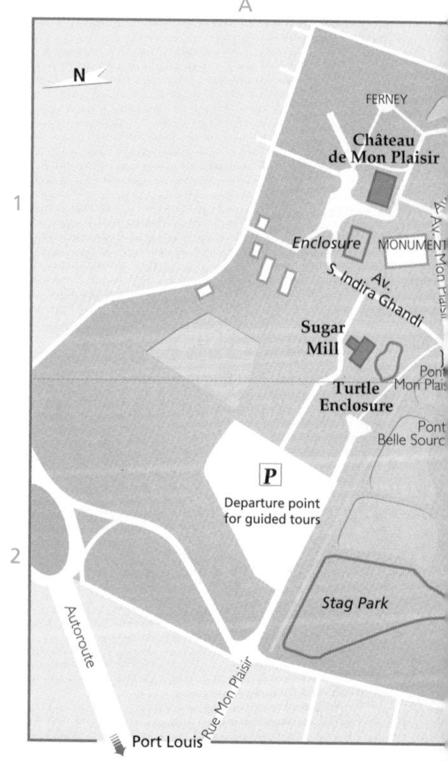

exotic species. Thus cloves, nutmeg, cinnamon and pepper were introduced. Before long, the first nutmegs to be grown on Mauritius were despatched to the King with great ceremony.

In 1775, the botanist **Jean-Nicolas Céré** was appointed keeper of "the King's garden". Over the ensuing years, he expanded the collection of rare woods and spices beyond all expectations. Fruit trees, tea, ornamental flowering species, pine trees grown from seed, Chinese pines, and special types of timber suited to building boats were introduced. By the close of the 18C, the gardens were considered to be the best and most famous in the world.

During British rule, the gardens were somewhat left to go to seed; but then, in 1849, James Duncan was made responsible for continuing the work instigated by Poivre and Céré, and so a whole new series of plants was introduced including various palms, laurels, monkey puzzle trees, ferns, orchids, bougainvillaea etc.

Sir Seewoosagur Ramgoolam Botanical Garden**

Open daily, 6am-6pm in summer; 6am-5pm in winter, ☎ *243 3531. No charge for entry but applicable to guided tours. Allow 2hr. Parking available by the side entrance.* The official name of these gardens was altered in 1988 to the *Jardin Botanique Sir Seewoosagur Ramgoolam* – the last in a list of names which since 1735 has included *Jardin de Mon Plaisir, Montplaisir, Jardin des Plantes, Jardin Royal, Jardin Botanique des*

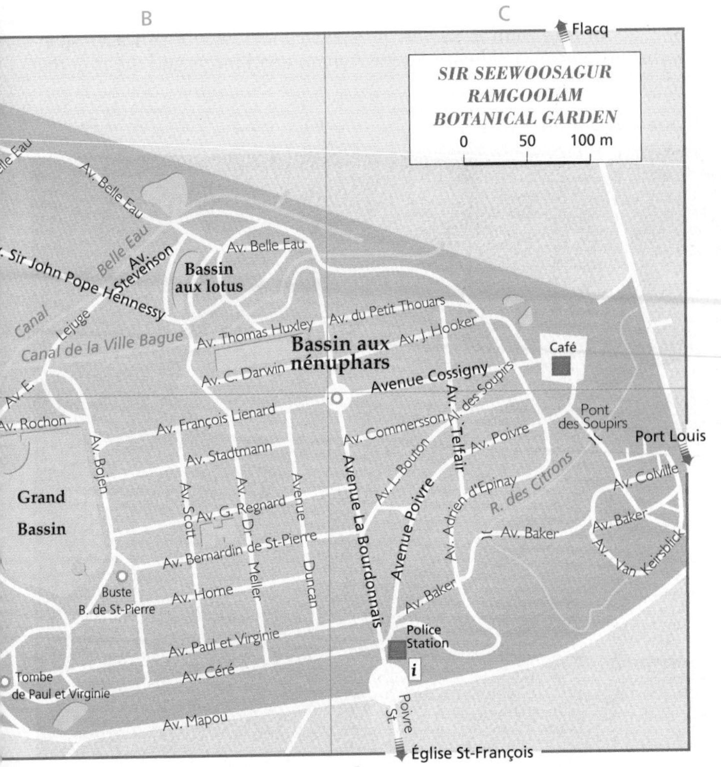

Pamplemousses, Jardin National de L'Isle de France and *Royal Botanical Garden*. To add to the confusion, the gardens are often informally referred to simply as the *Jardin des Pamplemousses*.

The official guides (A2) tend to pay particular attention to the spice trees in the course of their tour of the main groups of plants, and are liable to pluck a few leaves from a tree, rub them in their fingers and then ask you to identify the spice. Visitors are, of course, free to explore the garden on their own if they prefer.

The main gate, beautifully crafted in wrought-iron, is flanked on the right by a fine baobab tree. Straight ahead lies **Avenue La Bourdonnais** (C2) lined with mature latanier palms up which various creepers and indigenous philodendrons have been trained to grow.

The **Avenue Poivre** (C2), forking off to the right, runs between royal palms and various types of mahogany hardwoods (*Swietenia macrophylla,* Honduras mahogany; *Swietenia mahagoni,* West Indian mahogany), which provided the East Indies Company with highly-prized timber for fine furniture-making.
Across the Pont des Soupirs (a Bridge of Sighs with a difference) that spans the Citrons River lies a small area dedicated to trees imported from India and China: teak, camphor, royal guava, pagoda fig, lacquer, Indian almond and the cinnamon of Ceylon.
The section between **Avenue Telfair** (C2) and **Avenue Cossigny** (C1) meanwhile, bristles with the famous **Talipot palms** *(Corypha umbraculifera)* that take 30-40 years to grow to a height of 25m and flower just once before dying. What is remarkable about this palm is its vast pyramidal inflorescence of leaves spanning 5m that become covered with several million tiny flowers and the fruit that take a whole year to ripen.

The Victoria waterlilies

A. Picou/DIAF

At the far end of Avenue La Bourdonnais lies the **Bassin aux nénuphars***** (B1) covered with giant waterlilies. The pond accommodates three kinds of nymphea – producing white, pink or blue flowers – as well as the **Victoria amazonica,** a giant waterlily from the Amazon forest that grows great big leaves with upturned edges reaching more than 1m in diameter and strong enough to support a baby. Its flowers only last two days. When they open in the afternoon of the first day, the bloom is white; gradually this turns a strong shade of pink before wilting and dying.

Beyond the canal, at the start of Avenue Sir John Pope-Hennessy, sits the **Bassin aux Lotus** (B1), where two types of lotus grow. Their flowers – white or yellow – are regarded by Hindus as sacred.

A double row of indigenous latanier palms border the left-hand side of the **Avenue Sir John Pope-Hennessy** (B1) to its conclusion, marked by a stone bearing a fleur-de-lis which, at one time, indicated the outer boundary of the *Jardin du Roi de Mon Plaisir*.

A short way ahead sits the **Château de Mon Plaisir** (A1). This colonial homestead with its typical veranda dates from the mid-19C and was built by the British. It has nothing to do with the fabulous house constructed by Mahé de La Bourdonnais in 1735 of which nothing remains. Nowadays, the house provides a venue for formal gatherings arranged in honour of an official guest or visiting dignitary. A number of select visitors, such as Indira Gandhi and François Mitterrand, have marked the occasion of their visit by planting a special tree.

From here, follow **avenue S Indira Gandhi** (A1) on the left to the giant tortoise enclosure containing a collection of giant tortoises brought from the Seychelles island of Aldabra in 1875. Beside the pen stands one of first sugar mills to be constructed on the island.

At the heart of the garden is the **Grand Bassin** (B2), a large stretch of water surrounded with dense vegetation – clumps of bamboo, Traveller's palms, pandanus palms etc – among which nestle various small pavilions. On the western edge of the site, a folly commemorates the fanciful entombment of the famous fictional lovers **Paul et Virginie**.

Pamplemousses Village

During the French colonial era, this residential area enjoyed a certain prestige. Although the colonials have gone, the village retains a truly distinctive quality all its own.

The church, or **Église St-François**, is dedicated to the patron saint of Mahé de La Bourdonnais. Built in 1756, this church can claim to be the oldest religious building on Mauritius. It also features in the novel *Paul et Virginie* by Bernardin de Saint-Pierre as the place where the young sweethearts attended mass, a logical reference given the fact that the novelist wrote his book while living in the nearby parsonage.

The area beside the church may easily be construed to be the site of the **old Slave Market** – a haunting relic of Pamplemousses' social history.

Directly opposite the church you will notice a small grey gate leading into the **cemetery**. Although more or less abandoned, several historic figures lie interred here, namely **Abbot Buonavita** – Napoleon's personal chaplain who accompanied his master into exile on St-Helena and then spent his final years in Mauritius; the celebrated **"Creole Lady"** Emmeline de Carcenac – the muse who inspired Charles Baudelaire to write his first poem while living in Pamplemousses.

TOWNS OF THE CENTRAL PLATEAU

Pop in excess of 400 000
Alt 550m (average 300m)
Cool, humid climate (3-5°C cooler than on the coast)

Not to be missed
The view from the Trou aux Cerfs Crater.
Visiting a workshop where model boats are made.

And remember...
To take an umbrella.
Enjoy Curepipe or Rose Hill on a Saturday when it is busiest.

Inland developments

The motorway linking the capital in the southeast of the island with the north-west coast echoes the route of the old Royal Road that ran between Port Louis and Grand Port across the island's high central plateau. In 1865, when a malaria epidemic swept through Port Louis and the other coastal regions decimating the local population, those who could afford to migrated inland towards the central plateau, where temperatures were cooler and the conditions more salubrious. In so doing, they hoped to remove themselves to a safe distance from the breeding grounds of the Anopheles mosquito, which is reckoned to have been introduced in the 1860s during the great influx of immigrants from India.

And so, surprising as it may seem, the wettest region of Mauritius came to be the most densely-populated. The number of people moving into the area further increased in the 19C when the railway was built between Port Louis and Mahébourg. Gradually the remote settlements scattered along the Royal Road – often allied to a particular sugarcane plantation that has long since disappeared – grew into small villages. Since then, the onetime rural landscape has changed into an almost continuous urban agglomeration and home to a third of the Mauritian population.

The rapid transformation of the area has also boosted a considerable amount of industrial and commercial development, so even if there is little to appeal to foreign tourists, the shopping facilities – only partly rivalled by those in Port Louis – attract the island residents in droves. Here you will find tax-free shops, factory outlets selling seconds at rock bottom prices, colourful markets and ultra modern shopping malls to wander through and window-shop to your heart's content.

The "New" Towns
Beau Bassin and Curepipe

Approximately 20km – 30min drive without stopping off along the way.

Take the A1 Out of Port Louis heading southwest.

At one time, the two separate towns of Beau Bassin and Rose Hill sat midway between Port Louis and Curepipe (10km equidistant from each). In 1896, the rural councils merged to form a single municipality; a century later, the rambling suburban neighbourhood claimed to have a population in excess of 96 000, maybe because the climate here is particularly temperate and pleasant.

Turn left off the main road through Beau Bassin just before the market and the police station (Trotter Street) and continue to Balfour Street.

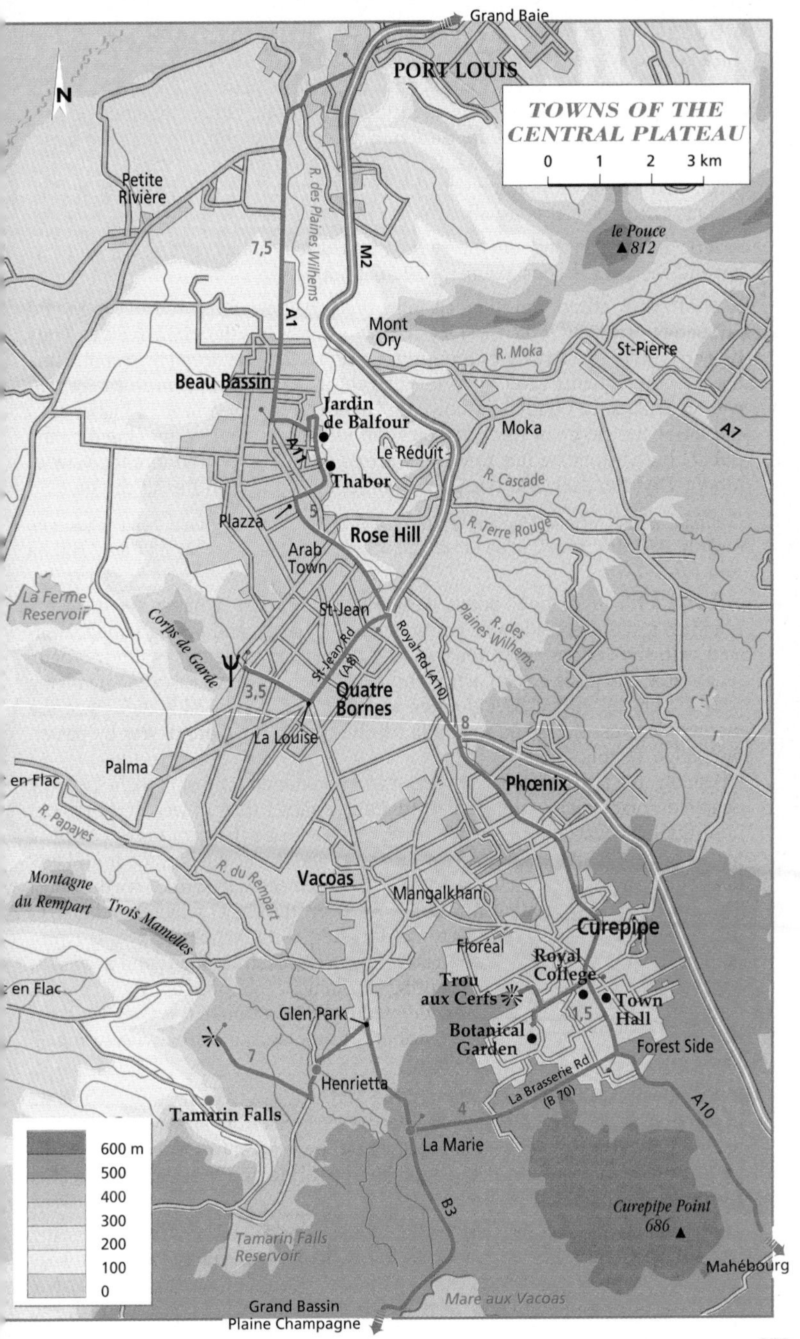
TOWNS OF THE CENTRAL PLATEAU
0
1
2
3 km
N
Grand Baie
PORT LOUIS
Petite Rivière
7,5
R. des Plaines Wilhems
M2
A1
le Pouce
▲812
Mont Ory
R. Moka
St-Pierre
Beau Bassin
Jardin de Balfour
Moka
A7
A11
Le Réduit
Thabor
R. Cascade
Plazza
5
Rose Hill
R. Terre Rouge
Arab Town
La Ferme Reservoir
St-Jean
Corps de Garde
R. des Plaines Wilhems
St-Jean Rd (A8)
Royal Rd (A10)
3,5
Quatre Bornes
8
La Louise
Palma
en Flac
Phœnix
R. Papayes
R. du Rempart
Vacoas
Montagne du Rempart
Mangalkhan
Trois Mamelles
Curepipe
Floréal
Royal College
Trou aux Cerfs
en Flac
Town Hall
1,5
Glen Park
Botanical Garden
Forest Side
7
Henrietta
La Brasserie Rd (B 70)
A10
Tamarin Falls
4
La Marie
600 m
500
400
300
200
100
0
B3
Curepipe Point
686 ▲
Tamarin Falls Reservoir
Mahébourg
Mare aux Vacoas
Grand Bassin
Plaine Champagne

■ **Beau Bassin – The Balfour Garden/Jardin de Balfour** *(Open Thursday to Tuesday, 10am-7pm between 1 November to 15 March; 10am-6pm in winter. Closed Wednesdays)* provides sweethearts with a convenient place to meet, and young children with an area for playing and running about in. Others might come here for a stroll to the far end of the garden to catch a **view** (through the wire fence) of the Sorèze Falls and the Grande Rivière Nord-Ouest as it tumbles down its green-clad gorge, with on the right Thabor Manor and Mont Ory on the left; Le Réduit, just opposite, is usually obscured by vegetation.

A little further on and on the right, (immediately after Victor Hugo Street), beyond the trees, stands a superb **colonial house**.

A short way ahead, on the left this time, Balfour Street becomes Swami Sivananda Street off which leads a narrow alleyway to the **Manoir de la Tour Blanche**, hidden in among its fine grounds high above the deep gorge containing the Plaines Wilhems River. This magnificent aristocratic residence ornamented with crenellations, otherwise known as **Thabor**, houses a college of higher education for the clergy of the Port Louis diocese. The buildings are closed to the public, but visitors are free to wander across the grounds to admire the view of Mount Ory, the deep and overgrown gorges and the sea in the far distance.

Continue along Swami Sivananda Street which after a right-hand bend leads into Ambrose Malartic Street; follow to the junction with Royal Road to find Rose Hill on your left.

■ **Rose Hill** – Without doubt, Rose Hill is the most dynamic town on the island as it has a considerable community of students and young people affiliated with the various educational establishments and religious buildings there. As a result, the place has an active and culturally diverse social scene involving people from all ethnic backgrounds and all walks of life, although since the motorway across the island was built, the area has been more or less by-passed by foreign visitors.

Originally, the resident community consisted predominantly of French-speaking people of mixed race – middle class in attitude rather than in wealth. It was not until the inter-war years (1920-30) that it came to be the very nerve centre of Mauritian culture. Not only have many artists and intellectuals come from here, Rose Hill's reputation as "culture city" has to date been safeguarded by the **Plaza Theatre** (the large open area-cum-esplanade on the right) which continues to draw a large following. This Victorian building is the venue for a varied programme of plays enacted in the main languages spoken on the island as well as concerts and operas, often featuring prominent performers from abroad. Alongside, to the left of the esplanade, stands the **Max Boullé Art Gallery** *(closed between 12noon-1pm)* which also contributes to the artistic scene by featuring all kinds of exhibitions of artistic work.

It is well worth taking a walk through the "old" parts of town around the theatre in search of the last **colonial townhouses** covered with wooden slat roofs nestling behind tall hedges or low stone walls. These are especially concentrated in the well-to-do quarter of Cascadelle, near the Town Hall, in the streets named after **Ambrose Malartic** and Dr Roux.

Those wishing to get a true feel for life in Mauritius away from the beaches and resort hotels, may like to set aside a few hours, preferably on a Saturday morning, for imbibing the atmosphere of Rose Hill when locals and island residents are out shopping. Besides the authentic vitality of the place, it is fun and rewarding to shop for any requisites. The busiest neighbourhood is **Arab Town** where a large, particularly well-stocked and lively market is held beneath a typical Creole-style **market place** covered with a green roof.

■ **Quatre Bornes** – This residential area with a population of 70 000, caught between Beau Bassin and Rose Hill, has few if any attractions to speak of save for its **fabric market** held on Wednesdays and Saturdays.

Follow St-Jean Road (A8) through town and across the La Louise crossroads turning right into Sri Velamurugan Avenue after 100m.

The name Quatre Bornes refers to the boundary marker in the centre of the modern town where the former limits of four large sugarcane plantation estates converged. To the northwest rises the peak known as the **Corps du Garde** (719m), at the base of which sits a small, raised and brightly painted **Tamil Temple** accessible up one or other flights of steps. From the windswept summit you get a view of the mountains called Pouce and Pieter Both on the left, the sea in the far distance beyond the fields of sugarcane on the right, and of the small hill known as Candos opposite.

■ **Vacoas and Phoenix** – These two industrial conglomerations united under a single municipal authority boast over 90 000 inhabitants.

Beyond the **Phœnix** brewery and bottling plant that produces the local beer, lies the Phoenix township surrounded by intensely-farmed small holdings. The majority bordering the Royal Road all the way to Curepipe are used for keeping dairy-cows and allied milk processing.

The residential quarter of **Vacoas** meanwhile, was, until Independence in 1968, the favourite haunt of British civil-servants – hence the great stretches of lawn meticulously laid out by the English, and the existence of the **Gymkhana Club** which opened as a polo ground in 1844, but was long since turned into an 18-hole golf course.

The old Royal Road (A10) cuts through Phoenix to arrive at Curepipe.

■ **Curepipe** – Curepipe is situated at 543m above sea-level. Besides being the highest town on the island, it is the coldest and the wettest. Indeed, there are some people who quip that Curepipe is renowned for the constancy of its weather, be it the season of rains or the rainy season, the short season of heavy rain and the long season of gentle rain. Either way, the place is more often than not embalmed in swirling cloud, making it rather dull and grey.

The origins of the town go back to the times when Port Louis and Mahébourg were relayed by a regular coach service that stopped at a staging-post, inn and guard-house located midway between the two. The unusual name, meanwhile, dates from when the colonial army soldiers paused there to rest their animals and slaves on the long, chaotic journey and routinely set about emptying out and cleaning their pipes (from the word 'curer' to mean to clear) to wile away the hours.

For many years the area was especially favoured by the wealthy Franco-Mauritian gentry; this came to an abrupt end with the major economic crisis at the end of the 1970s that forced a number of families to sell their principal residence on the high plateau and move into their more modest secondary home by the sea, probably located somewhere around Grand Baie. Alas many of the lovely old-fashioned wooden **colonial villas**, which cost a fortune to maintain and proved extremely vulnerable if caught in a cyclone, have either been demolished and replaced by concrete structures, or acquired for use as diplomatic residences or homes for foreign industrialists. A few of these sumptuous homesteads from the 19C survive with their magnificent green lawns in large shady grounds on the southeastern side of the town – notably off Lees Street and Rue du Jardin in the **Forest Side** neighbourhood. Most, however, are intentionally screened from prying eyes by tall thickets of bamboo.

Each weekday morning, Curepipe discharges a large part of its 76 000 resident population – mainly bureaucrats, civil servants and blue-collar workers employed in the capital and its surrounding industrial estates – along with all the other towns of the high plateau. Then, as Port Louis empties and settles down to a quiet evening, life returns to the streets of Curepipe, especially in the area where all the shops are around Rue Châteauneuf, Rue du Jardin and Rue Royale. Elsewhere, the town is deserted and of little interest.

Continue along the Royal Road (A10) through Curepipe to the southeastern edge of town (Forest Side), and turn left just before Carbonel Bridge into Rue Louis-de-Rochecouste.

The Forum is where the highly popular **weekly open-air market** is held every Wednesday and Saturday morning. Here you will find a whole range of goods including fruit and vegetables, clothes, rolls of fabric and other miscellania.

Head back into town along the Royal Road and turn down Elizabeth Avenue on the right.

The stylish stone-dressed white building with the bluish roof, a flight of steps up to the front entrance and elevated veranda is typical of 19C colonial architecture. Additional touches include the use of exotic hardwoods (teak, purple wood, ebony). Today, the building houses the Town Hall or **Hôtel de Ville**, although originally "la Malmaison" stood at Mok; it was dismantled – along with many other similar structures – and re-erected in Curepipe in 1902. Immediately next door stands the **Carnegie Library**, in which is preserved an exceptional archive of historical data relating to the Mascarene Islands. The **statue representing Paul et Virginie** in the small garden outside is by the Mauritian sculptor Prosper d'Epinay.

Proceed along the left-hand side of Royal Road.

The **Royal College** at Curepipe, founded by the British in 1913, is Mauritius' foremost educational establishment and responsible for schooling the island's elite. In front stands a **memorial** commemorating all the Mauritians who lost their lives fighting alongside French and British soldiers in the First World War.

Turn left off Royal Road into Pope-Hennessy Street, and then right into Edgar Hughes Street.

The area known as **Trou aux Cerfs**, densely overgrown with shrubs and undergrowth, nestles inside the crater of an extinct volcano 200m wide and some hundred metres deep. Its name recalls the 19C stag hunts organised in honour of visiting royal princes. A circular avenue – named after George V – leads right round the perimeter providing a variety of **views*** over the town (note an 1889 miniature model of the Eiffel Tower in the garden of "Sablonnière" house), the sugarcane plantations, and the sea in the far distance framed between the peaks of Trois Mamelles, Rempart, Corps du Garde and the Mare Longue reservoir.

Drive down from the Trou aux Cerfs along Edgar Hughes Street, turn right down Pope-Hennessy Street and then left along Kœnig Street which eventually becomes Botanical Garden Street.

This **botanical garden** *(Open daily, 9am-5.30pm. No charge. Accessible by car)* – far smaller and less remarkable than the one at Pamplemousses – makes for a pleasant outing with its fine meandering avenues of old tropical trees. It is perhaps a pity, though, that cars are allowed access.

It is also well worth seeking out the workshops where **model boats** are made. Those tempted to purchase such a thing as a keepsake will find a good selection at the most reasonable prices in Curepipe. But even if you have no intention of actually buying anything, it is fascinating to watch the craftsmen in the workshop skilfully crafting each detail with great precision *(see below Shopping)*.

■ **Floréal –** This up-market residential suburb of Curepipe, perched high on a hill to the west of the main town, enjoys a fine view out towards the island's northwest coast. Among the large houses, several are home to foreign diplomats and ambassadors, successful businessmen and wealthy Mauritians.

Around Curepipe

Approx 20km – Allow 30min to 1hr.

A short and scenic drive around the outskirts of Curepipe makes for a pleasant excursion punctuated by fine views along an attractive stretch of road through a wild forest. It also enables one to enjoy a brief but nonetheless magnificent journey en route to the south or west of the island. The most striking aspect of the present landscape is the abundance of water collected in natural lakes, reservoirs, running rivers and gushing waterfalls, a very different picture to that of the 19C when the region was covered with forest of exotic hardwoods in which bandits and runaway slaves sought refuge. The radical change came in the 19C when much of the land was stripped bare to make way for massive sugarcane plantations. Today, it is the weekend haunt of urban Mauritians intent on going for a walk or sharing a family picnic over the weekend.

Plants mentioned in bold relate to illustrations on p 16-17.

Return to Brasserie Road (B70) and continue to La Marie. Turn right onto the B3; at the Glen Park intersection (by the mosque), turn left towards Henrietta, and continue for 3km to the viewpoint.

The road picks its way past a series of glass-houses nurturing **anthuriums**, young bamboo and sugarcane plants, and a little church on the right, before reaching Henrietta bus terminal. Turn right in the midst of the sugarcane fields, and then right again after 300m. Stop by the side of the road to admire the **view**⋆ of **Tamarin Falls** which pour into a reservoir closed off by a hydraulic dam in the middle of the forest. The landscape recedes to the distant horizon on the right, all the way to the intensely blue sea.

Return to La Marie and continue straight along the B3 following directions for Vacoas-Plaine Champagne-Grand Bassin.

The road is somewhat broken and potholed but at last you come to the forest, a damp and wild place infested with wild vines scrambling up among the **traveller's palms**, maritime pines, **tree ferns**, *citranus*, Sylvester pines, wild flowers and blue convolvulus; and home to a variety of birds, monkeys and deer. Then the scenery opens out once more to reveal the **Mare aux Vacoas**, a large natural water-filled hollow formed by a crater at an altitude of 600m that has now been enlarged and transformed into a reservoir supplying the towns of the plateau. A wire-gate by the side of the road leads to a flight of steps and up to the lake above.

From here, you can either head back towards Curepipe and the north, continue down to the west coast and on to Chamarel and Plaine Champagne, or head southeast towards Mahébourg or Bois Chéri.

Making the most of the Central Plateau

COMING AND GOING

By car – The central plateau is very easy to get to by road. The old Royal Route crosses through each of the towns, and the M2 by-passes them. Both provide a direct route between the southeast (Mahébourg) and Port Louis on the north coast.

By bus – Various buses operate services across the island to Port Louis, and Mahébourg, from the west to the east coasts and vice versa, calling in on the inland towns. Additional shuttle services operate between the towns themselves.

By taxi – You will have no trouble in hailing a cab to another part of town or indeed another town.

ADDRESS BOOK

Banks / Change – Most banks are located in Curepipe, Rose Hill, and Quatre Bornes, dotted along Royal Route – the main thoroughfare.

Post Office – There is at least one post office in every town.

Telephone – Coin- and card-operated public phone-boxes are available in all the main streets.

Mauritius telecom, Manhattan shopping mall, Curepipe.

Health – *Victoria Hospital*, Candos ☎ 425 3031.

You will find a number of chemists in each town.

WHERE TO STAY

Given the choice, it is best to opt for accommodation down on the coast rather than trying one of the few hotels available in the towns of the central plateau.

WHERE TO EAT

As most of the island's population actually resides in this area, there are good restaurants specialising in a more authentic cuisine than that found in the coastal resorts.

• Curepipe

Less US$2

Ali, rue Châteauneuf (corner of rue Ferrière, opposite the "Welcome" snack-bar). This mobile Street vendor is easy to find as there is always a long queue of Mauritians around his cart, eagerly waiting to buy his delicious fresh dholl puri for their lunch.

US$7-15

Chinese Wok, 242 Royal Rd (1st floor) ☎ 676 1548. Lunch and dinner, Monday to Saturday. Closed all day Sunday. Do not be put off by the cold and rather dingy dining room as the food is excellent. Chinese set-menus for several people.

Golden Lion, rue Frère-Ignace (perpendicular to W Churchill Road, near the Shell fuel station) ☎ 674 4265. Lunch and dinner. This Chinese restaurant, like so many across the world, goes through phases of being good or mediocre depending on its chef. At the time of writing, the chef was from Peking and the food was very good despite the somewhat cold, impersonal atmosphere.

La Nouvelle Potinière, rue Frère-Ignace (perpendicular to W Churchill Road, near the Shell fuel station) ☎ 676 2648. Monday to Saturday, lunch and dinner. Closed all day Sunday. This establishment comprises two distinct parts. One area serves pancakes only, whereas the other, more formal and more expensive, offers a large selection of French and Creole dishes.

• Floréal

Over US$15

La Clef des Champs, Queen Mary Av ☎ 686 3458 or 696 1702. The Franco-Mauritian lady-owner of this restaurant proudly proclaims her "cooking to be French, but fluent in Creole" by which she implies her inspiration is French but the full-bodied flavours are Mauritian. Typical specialities include watercress soup with coconut, palm-heart millefeuille, freshwater prawns cooked with lemon balm and pearl barley, lobster medallions with vanilla, magret of duck with dried fruits served in a golden rum sauce.

• Rose Hill

Less US$2

Dewa & Sons, central marketplace in Rose Hill, Duncan Taylor St ☎ 464 5646. "The best dholl puri of the

Towns of the Central Plateau

Indian Ocean" does not fall short of the truth. If popularity is anything to go by, this place must be special as many locals order their food here when catering for large gatherings and parties. Either way, a take-away from here will more than justify a visit to the lively market.

• **Quatre Bornes**

US$7-15

Happy Valley, 79 St-Jean Rd ☎ 454 9208. Lunch and dinner; closed Sunday evenings. Take-away. If you get tired reading the long menu, you can simply point to a dish that catches your eye as it is wheeled around on a trolley. Alternatively, opt for what the Hong Kong chef proposes or choose one of the set-menus for 2-10 people that provide you with the opportunity of tasting a variety of typical Chinese dishes. Everything is excellent.

Dragon Vert, St-Jean Rd, La Louise intersection (almost next door to Happy Valley listed above) ☎ 424 4564. Lunch and dinner; closed all day Monday. Good and reasonably priced Chinese food.

King Dragon, St-Jean Road, La Louise intersection ☎ 424 7888. Lunch and dinner; closed all day Tuesday. Decorated in red velvet with booths. A little more expensive than the places listed above, but very good.

Shopping

Beware: shops tend to be closed all day Thursdays, Saturday afternoons and all day Sundays.

You will find a variety of small shops in the shopping malls at Curepipe (***Currimjee*** on the corner of Royal Rd and Churchill St; ***Salaffa*** and ***Jan Palach*** near the bus station) – Phoenix (***Phoenix Commercial Centre***) – Quatre Bornes (***Orchard Center***) – Rose Hill (***Galerie Evershine*** and ***Galerie Royale***).

Books and newspapers – Mauritian and foreign press titles, novels, reference and guide books on Mauritius.

Le Trèfle and ***Allot*** in Currimjee arcade, Curepipe.

Le Cygne, 307 Royal Rd, Rose Hill.

Clothing – There are a number of factory shops in the Mangalkhan area of Floréal. ***Floréal Knitwear***, Floréal Road: lambswool and cashmere sweaters, cotton t-shirts and casual tops. The prices are cheap, but as much of this stock is imperfect, it is advisable to check garments thoroughly before buying. Other items may include returns or unsold merchandise. Additional Floréal factory shops can be found at Port Louis, Grand Baie and Quatre Bornes.

Shibani, in the street running parallel to Floréal Road. Lambswool and cashmere knitwear: on the whole the choice is smaller but the goods are better made than those on sale from "Floréal".

Ultra-soie, Madame Feillafé, rue Dr Lallah ☎ 696 3375. Good quality classic silk ties and scarves at reasonable prices.

Duty-free shops – ***Poncini***, Royal Rd, Curepipe: tableware, jewellery and luxury giftware.

Adamas, in the street parallel to Floréal Road, Mangalkhan, Floréal. Gold and diamond jewellery. Passport and airline tickets required as proof of departure. Payment by credit card or cash.

Model ships – There are many workshops dotted around the edge of Curepipe. ***Comajora***, La Brasserie Rd, Forest Side, Curepipe. Interesting to visit and reasonable prices.

Voiliers de l'océan, W Churchill St (garden road), Curepipe. Less expensive than Comajora, although the craftsmanship is perhaps not as well-finished..

La Pirogue, Brasserie Road, Forest Side, Curepipe. Unpretentious family-run enterprise. Small models at reasonable prices.

Serinissima, 292 Royal Road, Curepipe. Much more expensive.

NORTH COAST★

BAIE TOMBEAU TO ROCHES NOIRES

Ideal conditions between April and October; unbearably hot November to March
Map p 282-283

Not to be missed
A swim off Mont Choisy Beach as the sun sets.
Mass on Sunday morning at Cap Malheureux.
An excursion to the islands offshore.
Treat yourself to an expensive café Brûlot in Royal Palm Hotel bar at Grand Baie.

And remember...
Select a hotel outside Grand Baie, preferably by Cap Malheureux or Trou aux Biches.
Beware of thieves operating along the beach and in secluded spots.

Simple beach huts and seaside resort hotels

The north coast, in the lee of the wind, is blessed with a particularly mild climate, while its lovely sand beaches dotted with a scattering of black rocks are lapped by clear sea. Together, these idyllic conditions are ideal for a range of water-sports. When malaria swept through Port Louis, many of the wealthier Mauritian gentry moved inland to large properties up on the central plateau and migrated to secondary homes by the sea during the unendurable cold winter months.

These places provided seasonal accommodation known as *campement*, crudely built out of palm fronds *(ravenala)* were easy to dismantle. The outset of winter, each family transferred almost the entire contents of their main houses by ox cart to their "camp" by the sea including furniture, cooking utensils, wardrobes full of clothes and even provisions.

These days, the seaside villas are permanent constructions and the natural building materials of yesteryear have been replaced by reinforced concrete. Over the last 10 years, the northwestern coast – where the climate is pleasantly balmy – has been invaded by major developments aimed at catering for tourists that comprise hotel complexes complete with facilities, restaurants and expensive boutiques irrespective of the needs of the local population. Only the fishing villages in the northernmost tip and northeastern parts of the island coast have managed to preserve some sort of calm and authenticity. The inland area meanwhile, is fundamentally flat and completely covered in fields of sugarcane, interrupted here and there by piles of black lava stones.

The northwestern resorts

Approx 32km from Baie du Tombeau to Pereybère – Allow 1hr without detours. Head out of Port Louis along the B29 coastal road.

■ **Baie du Tombeau** – The prime attraction of the first village north of Port Louis is its historical associations. For it was here that the Dutch Governor **Pieter Both** perished in 1615 while aboard a ship of the Dutch East Indies Company that was shipwrecked by a cyclone: hence the name of the bay alluding to a tomb. One look at the capital's harbour and the polluted state of the water will prompt you to continue on your journey north.

Keep to the B9 as this will take you onto the A4 (up a slip road on the left); after 1km, turn left onto the B40. The beach on the other side of the Tombeau River, known as the **Plage du Goulet**, is a more attractive spot for a swim despite the water being rather shallow. However, do be careful of the strong currents that have a tendency to sweep the unwary out to sea.

Go back along the A4 and turn left onto the B40.

▪ **Pointe aux Piments** – In the old days, this headland separating the **Baie de l'Arsenal** from the **Batterie des Grenadiers** was covered in pimento bushes: hence its name. The bay, meanwhile, commemorates the French arsenal that was sited there and destroyed in 1774, leaving various ruins now enclosed within the precincts of the Hotel Maritim. The old lime kiln, distillery, mill and hospital, alas, have long gone, replaced by luxury hotels. This stretch of coastline is not, however, ideal for swimming as it consists essentially of black rock interspersed with short beaches that have been claimed by the waterfront hotel behind. Far more beautiful beaches lie a little further north. *Follow the coast road B38.*

▪ **Trou aux Biches** – From this point onwards, the sea becomes progressively more inviting. The lovely long coral sand **beach*** squeezed in between the lagoon and the casuarina trees, has become very popular notably among the local well-to-do Mauritians, who in turn have helped to transform the little fishing village into one of the island's foremost seaside resorts, bristling with tight rows of hotels, bungalows and secondary seaside houses. Various facilities are now available for a whole range of water sports, and the water is delicious.

Head north through Trou aux Biches and turn right along the B36 between the hotel golf-course and the police station, circumnavigating the bus station from the right.

If heading north along the A4, turn left after the village of Triolet following signs for Trou aux Biches: look out for a discrete sign pointing left to the Shivala Temple.

▪ **Maheswarnath Hindu Temple*** – *No charge. Remove shoes before entering the temple precinct. Parking available beneath a banyan tree.* A few kilometres inland sits a collection of small shrines ornamented with colourful carvings and topped with white domes dating from 1891. After the temple at Grand Bassin, this complex imbued with a striking atmosphere of devotion is considered the most sacred on the island. Visitors should take up a discreet position in the **main temple**, and become acclimatised to the strong smells of burning incense while watching the Hindu rituals being enacted around them as the Elephant God *Ganesh*, the bull *Nandi*, and *Parvati* the wife of Shiva are honoured with dishes of banana, rice, flower petals, powdered saffron (turmeric) and other colourful sweet-smelling offerings. In the centre of the temple, the phallus-endowed figure of Shiva is sprinkled with coconut milk and his trident is wreathed with sacred yellow **allamanda** flowers *(see p 17)*. As they enter, the faithful brush against the bells suspended above the doorway to ward off jealous and hostile demons, and attract the attention the Gods. *See p 208 The Hindu Pantheon.*

Return to Trou aux Biches, and head north along the coast (B38, then B13).

▪ **Mont Choisy** – The magnificent public **beach**** extending in a great round sweep comprises 3km of fine sand. It also remains intact and unspoilt by concrete developments. During the week there are relatively few people here, but on Sundays the place is overrun by large Mauritian families out picnicking with members of all ages engaged in snoozing, participating in some ball-game or just idly listening to music. In the shade of the casuarinas, hawkers and lorry bars do their best business of the week.

▪ **Pointe aux Canonniers*** – The isthmus of land provided the French colonials with a strategic military outpost from which to survey the horizon in search of runaway slaves or signs of the English fleet. Nowadays, it has become a rather exclusive residential area boasting a few luxurious hotels overlooking the sea and a splendid **view**** of the small northern islands.

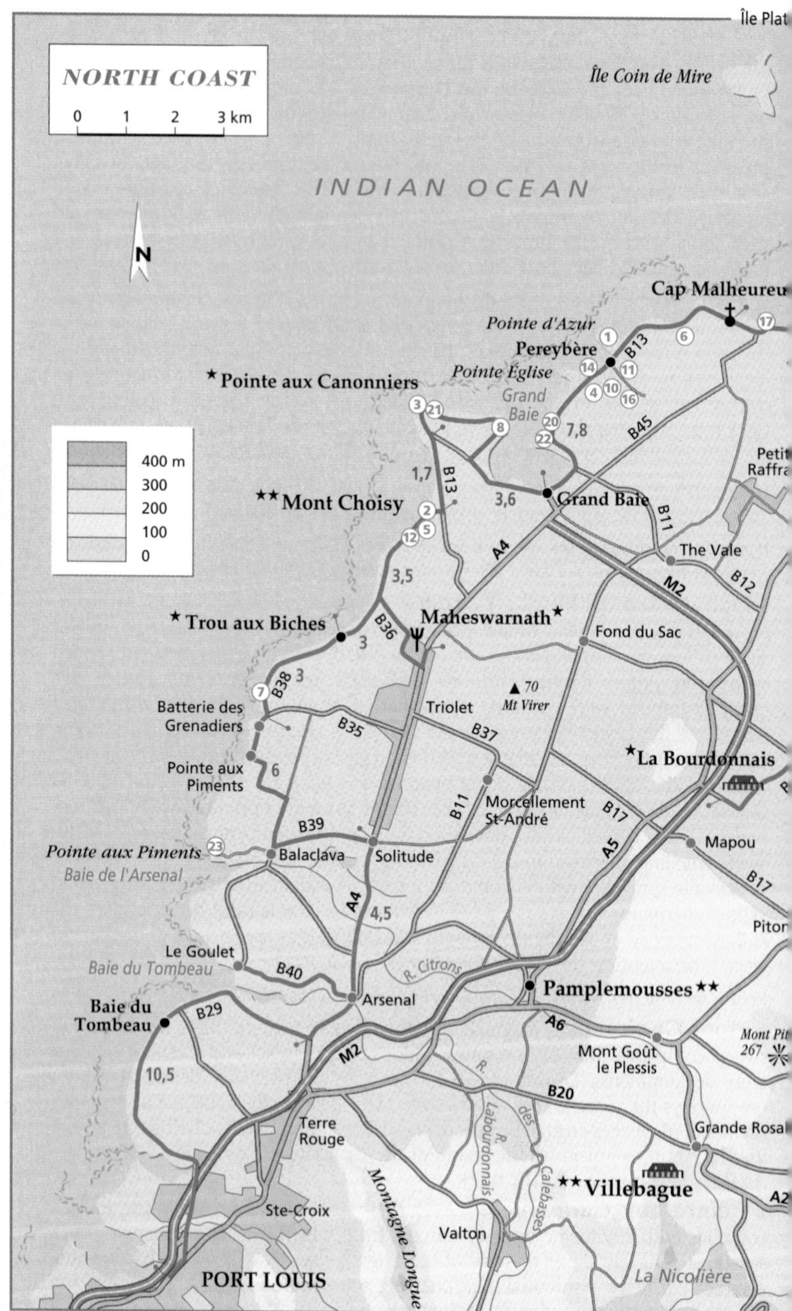
NORTH COAST
0 1 2 3 km
INDIAN OCEAN
N
400 m
300
200
100
0
Île Plat
Île Coin de Mire
Cap Malheureu
Pointe d'Azur
Pereybère
Pointe Église
Grand Baie
★ Pointe aux Canonniers
★★ Mont Choisy
Grand Baie
Petit Raffra
The Vale
★ Trou aux Biches
Maheswarnath ★
Fond du Sac
▲ 70 Mt Virer
Triolet
Batterie des Grenadiers
Pointe aux Piments
★ La Bourdonnais
Morcellement St-André
Mapou
Pointe aux Piments
Baie de l'Arsenal
Balaclava
Solitude
Piton
Le Goulet
Baie du Tombeau
R. Citrons
Baie du Tombeau
Arsenal
Pamplemousses ★★
Mont Goût le Plessis
Mont Pit 267
Terre Rouge
R. Labourdonnais
R. des Calebasses
Grande Rosa
Montagne Longue
Ste-Croix
★★ Villebague
Valton
La Nicolière
PORT LOUIS
B13
B45
B11
B12
M2
A4
B36
B38
B35
B37
B17
B39
A5
B40
B29
A6
B20
A2
1,7
3,6
7,8
3,5
3
6
4,5
10,5

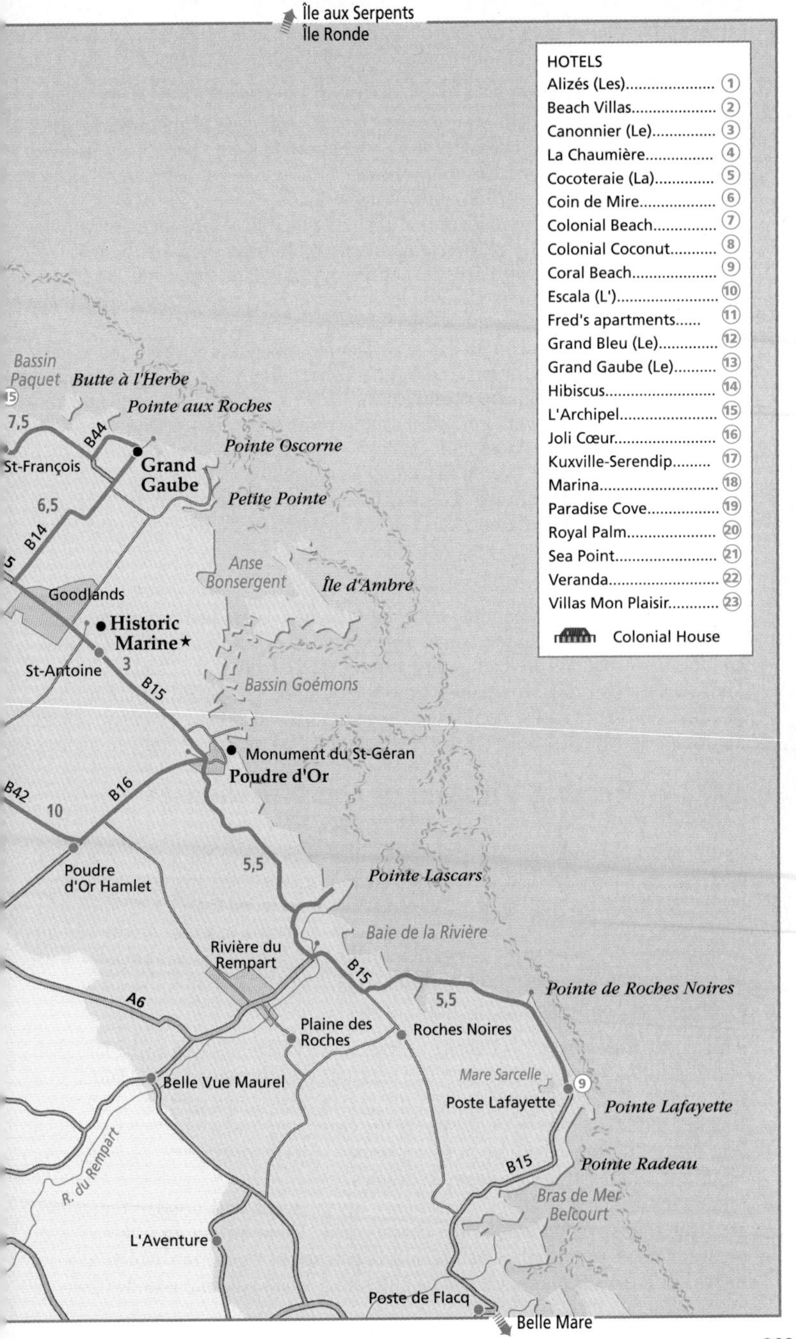

Île aux Serpents
Île Ronde
HOTELS
Alizés (Les)....................... 1
Beach Villas....................... 2
Canonnier (Le)............... 3
La Chaumière................ 4
Cocoteraie (La).............. 5
Coin de Mire.................. 6
Colonial Beach............... 7
Colonial Coconut........... 8
Coral Beach.................... 9
Escala (L')........................ 10
Fred's apartments...... 11
Grand Bleu (Le)............. 12
Grand Gaube (Le).......... 13
Hibiscus.......................... 14
L'Archipel....................... 15
Joli Cœur........................ 16
Kuxville-Serendip......... 17
Marina............................ 18
Paradise Cove................ 19
Royal Palm..................... 20
Sea Point........................ 21
Veranda.......................... 22
Villas Mon Plaisir........... 23
Colonial House
Bassin Paquet
Butte à l'Herbe
Pointe aux Roches
Pointe Oscorne
St-François
Grand Gaube
Petite Pointe
B44
B14
7,5
6,5
Anse Bonsergent
Île d'Ambre
Goodlands
Historic Marine
St-Antoine
3
B15
Bassin Goémons
Monument du St-Géran
Poudre d'Or
B42
B16
10
Poudre d'Or Hamlet
5,5
Pointe Lascars
Baie de la Rivière
Rivière du Rempart
B15
Pointe de Roches Noires
5,5
A6
Plaine des Roches
Roches Noires
Belle Vue Maurel
Mare Sarcelle
Poste Lafayette
Pointe Lafayette
R. du Rempart
B15
Pointe Radeau
Bras de Mer Belcourt
L'Aventure
Poste de Flacq
Belle Mare

Hotel Le Canonnier preserves the lofty structure of a lighthouse which, in 1855, was built on the site of an old French fort. The light was dismantled in 1932.

The B13 continues to Grand Baie: alternatively, you can also get there via the A4.

▪ **Grand Baie** – Until twenty years ago, Grand Baie – the island's most popular seaside resort – looked very different with its line of *campements* belonging to the wealthy facing onto the sea, and its rows of fishermen's shacks and peasant farmhouses looking out over the fields.
Nowadays the same thoroughfare that once bisected two very different worlds, passes between a tightly-packed assortment of untidy shops, supermarkets, rented holiday flats, cheap B&Bs, expensive hotels, night clubs and local tour-operators. There is nothing authentic left in Grand Baie, not even the Mauritians touting for business among the tourists were born here.
However, the enclosed shallow bay is perfect for water sports, protected at each end by Pointe aux Canonniers and Pointe Église. There is a large **marina** over which presides the headquarters of the Mauritian Yatch Club. Indeed the mirror-like sea is often ablaze with colourful sailing boats engaged in friendly regattas, or buzzing with water-skiers and jet-skiers. Unfortunately, the pollution such sports create does make swimming rather unappealing.
If you cannot resist swimming at Grand Baie, there is an area of clean water and sand at **Plage de la Cuvette**, squeezed in between Véranda Hotel and Royal Palm Hotel at the northern end of the bay.

Continue north along the coast road (B13).

▪ **Pereybère** – The adjoining village of Pereybère is gradually succumbing to the increased demands of tourism as a proliferation of hotels and other dubious-looking constructions are being haphazardly erected along the road.
The weekend is probably the best time to enjoy the good-natured atmosphere that prevails on the highly popular **public beach**, crowded with ice-cream sellers, Mauritian extended families and a cosmopolitan collection of holiday-makers.

North Coast

Fishing Villages of the Northeast★

Approx 48km – Allow 1hr.

As the coast beyond Cap Malheureux is more exposed to the ocean wind and currents, the landscape becomes wilder. Away from the touristy-postcard beaches of the western coast you come to a succession of secluded little coves lined with alternating stretches of golden sand and black outcrops of rock. As the climate is less arid, the vegetation grows reasonably profusely and abundantly with banyans, Indian almonds and breadfruit trees flourishing among the casuarinas.

Continue along the coast road (B13).

▪ **Cap Malheureux★** – Despite its name, the village nestling at the far north of the island is a serene little spot. The reason it was christened Cap Malheureux (the "unhappy cape") depends on your perspective. A great many ships were wrecked along this stretch of coast over the years, and it was here that the British fleet made a surprise landing on 6 November 1810 to take formal possession of Mauritius, after sailing over from Rodrigues.
Modest houses and nostalgic *campements*, small hotels and holiday bungalows are strung along either side of the coastal road. There are no great stretches of beach in these parts, only small secluded patches of sand from which to view the splendid **panorama★** over the neighbouring small volcanic islands (Coin de Mire, Serpents, Plate, Ronde).

Life here is tempered by the rhythm of fishing. On a Sunday morning, the village street is crowded with people headed for **mass**. If you are unable to spend a night at Cap Malheureux, it is well worth paying it a visit on Sunday to enjoy the gospel tunes sung by the congregation in the little **church*** with its red slat roof.

■ **Offshore islands*** – *Details of excursions to the islands are available from the local hotels and agencies around Grand Baie. Allow approx 500 Rs per person for day-trip to Île Plate including lunch.* Île Coin de Mire is difficult to get to but if you overcome that obstacle, the underwater life is fantastic, (4km from the coast), but the island itself cannot be visited.

Île Plate, a tall outcrop of land crowned with a lighthouse, is more accessible. The island is home to an old lazaretto, now a camp used by the small Mauritian military. A number of local tour operators organise picnics.

Continue along the B13, turning off onto the B44.

■ **Grand Gaube** – The road cuts through acres upon acres of sugarcane dotted with mounds of lava. In the distance rise the peaks of Pouce and Pieter Both, which will quickly become familiar landmarks. As soon as the route returns to the coastline, a sweeping **view** stretches out over the neighbouring islands. Grand Gaube is renowned for its famous **pirogues** made out of jackfruit wood. It has an endearing quality to it, distilled in part from being a genuine Creole fishing village, in part from the its relatively un-crowded seaside resort atmosphere.

Follow the B14 as it heads inland, perpendicular to the coast. Fork left onto the A5 and carry on through Goodlands before turning left into St-Antoine's industrial area.

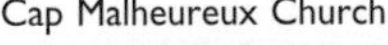

Cap Malheureux Church

M. Renaudeau/HOA QUI

■ **Goodlands –** The only claim to fame of this small inland town, with a community of 14 000, is its **Historic Marine*** workshops *(Open Monday to Friday, 8am-5pm. Closed Saturdays and Sundays. No charge)*. The workshops are considered to produce some of the island's best model ships. The workmanship is superb, and this is reflected in the prices. It costs nothing, however, to look around the very attractive boutique that sells the models, or to take a look at each phase in model construction on the first floor.

Follow signs along the B15 for Poudre d'Or. Once in the village, turn left at the junction with the stop sign, looking out for a small sign-post directing you to the monument, after a big right-hand bend.

■ **Poudre d'Or –** The peaceful little fishing village was made famous when the *St Géran* was shipwrecked off the coast there sometime during the night of the 17/18 August 1744 (and not off the Baie du Tombeau as Bernardin de Saint-Pierre claimed).

In a pretty little cove lined with black rocks and reddish sand at the end of **Avenue Paul et Virginie** stands a **stone monument** that was erected in 1944 to commemorate those who lost their lives that dreadful night.

Paul and Virginie

Bernardin de Saint-Pierre's novel was written in 1788 and tells the story of the pure, tender love between Paul and Virginie, who grew up together in Île de France. All is idyllic until the young girl is forced to leave for France to study there against her will. Not only is she heartbroken by her separation from her sweetheart, but also by the distance separating her from her beloved homeland. So after three years, she embarks on her return to the island aboard the St Géran which – and here the fiction draws upon actuality – sinks off the island of Ambre in 1744. Thus ends this tale of unhappy love, as Paul tries in vain to save his beloved from the tempest. He dies of grief soon after. Subsequently, many Mauritian artists and writers have found inspiration from this tragic story that was also to touch French readers, as much as by the tender passion and tragic ending as by descriptions of the tropical island paradise.

The attractive **chapel,** rising high above the other village buildings, sits happily among its surroundings, making for a harmonious picture as you look back from the B15 heading southward.

Rather than driving south, take the B16 out of the village, and turn right onto the B42. Follow signs on the left for "La Bourdonnais-Port Louis", and then for "La Corbeille Pépinières de La Bourdonnais".

■ **La Bourdonnais –** Besides the vestiges of an abandoned **sugar refinery,** belonging to the French East Indies Company, stands the large 19C colonial villa known as **Château La Bourdonnais***, which belongs to a wealthy Franco-Mauritian family. Like all the other privately-owned sumptuous homesteads, it is not open to the public, However, no one really minds if you walk to the beginning of the avenue of *Ficus microcorpa* that leads up to the main entrance. You can get an even better view if you walk past the anthurium greenhouses and around the old chimney on the right.

Return to Poudre d'Or and join the B15 as it follows the coast south towards Rivière du Rempart. Turn left towards Pointe Lascars.

The road cuts through a small hamlet with small, painted ramshackle houses facing onto the dirt track. At last it comes to an abrupt end before a stretch of reddish sand and a collection of black rocks. This is **Pointe Lascars** where fishing boats bob peacefully on the gently lapping water.

Go back to the B15 and follow signs left, for Roches Noires.

M Lemerle/MICHELIN

Harvesting the sugarcane

The road follows the edge of a bright green **lagoon**, which darkens as clouds pass overhead or as the outline of a far-off island, beyond **Roches Noires,** projects its shadow. The channel between the offshore coral reef and the coast gradually narrows at this point. Beyond the Pointe de Roches Noires the sea is hidden by a row of opulent *campements* nestling behind the elegant lines of fragrant oleander, *allamanda*, bougainvillaea, lilac and other flowering shrubs.

Making the most of the North Coast

Getting there

By car – A good road network makes the north coast easily accessible. A small road borders practically the whole coastline; the motorway runs from Port Louis to Grand Baie as does the former Royal Route, that passes through Pamplemousses. The North coast is a good hour and a half's drive from the airport.

By bus – Express and local bus services leave Port Louis (Immigration Sq) to all the main north coast towns (Trou aux Biches, Grand Baie, Cap Malheureux). Inquire at the bus station for timetables. If arriving from the airport, you will need to change at Port Louis.

A regular bus service operates at 10-15min intervals between the capital and the North or South of the island. Certain destinations may require you to change at Curepipe or Quatre Bornes.

Address book

Tourist Information – The tourist area along Royal Road is well-supplied in travel agents, all of whom are happy to inform tourists. ***MTTB,*** Royal Rd, Grand Baie, ☎ 263 6405.

Banks and money – Trou aux Biches, Grand Baie, Péreybère, Triolet and Goodlands all have exchange counters and branches of the main banks.

Post Office – There are post offices, generally near the police stations, in Grand Baie, Cap Malheureux, Grand Baube, Goodlands and Triolet.

Telephone – Coin operated public phone boxes are available more or less everywhere and card operated boxes can be found close to police stations or supermarkets (cards can be purchased from supermarkets and some chemists) in Grand Baie and Trou aux Biches.

Mauritius Telecom, as you drive into Grand Baie from the south.

Travel agents – All the travel agents, many of which are situated on Royal Rd between Trou aux Biches and Péreybère, offer the same range of services, activities and excursions: car hire, flat or villa rental, trips in glass-bottomed boats, under-water walking, island visits (shopping in Port Louis, Pamplemousses Garden, Chamarel landscape, Île aux Cerfs, Île d'Ambre, Île Plate, trip on a replica of the old "Isla Mauritia" yacht). Most agents are located in the hotels and along Royal Rd, towards Grand Baie.

GBTT (Grand Baie Travel and Tours), Royal Rd, ☎ 263 8771.

Car rentals – Most of the rental agencies are located in the Grand Baie area. Renting a car costs around Rs500 per day, a motorbike, around Rs200 per day and a mountain bike, Rs100. The agencies are both more numerous and cheaper in the north of Mauritius. The following have reasonable prices, a wide choice of models and will deliver your vehicle wherever you are on the island.

Dodo Gurriah, Piton, ☎ 423 7959. A small car will cost around Rs500 per day, all inclusive.

Coast Tour Ltd, Royal Rd, near the Caltex station in the town centre, Grand Baie, ☎ 263 6987/263 8050. From Rs500 for a small car. Do not hesitate to negotiate.

Health – There are chemists on the main road from Grand Baie, Péreybère, Triolet and Goodlands. The most central is ***The Grand Bay Pharmacie Ltd***, Royal Rd, ☎ 263 8403/263 7877.

SSR National Hospital, Royal Rd, Pamplemousses, ☎ 243 3661.

WHERE TO STAY

The following price ranges are calculated on the basis of a double room with breakfast in mid-season.

• Balaclava-Pointe aux Piments

US$15-30

Villas Mon Plaisir, ☎ 261 7471, Fax 261 6600 – 32rm or TV CC Basic, but very pleasant rooms. Pastel coloured premises looking onto a shady, flowery garden and a small swimming pool. Isolated and calm. The beach lacks swimming appeal due to the shallow waters and rocky bed, but a few sun-beds and parasols on the beach make sun bathing an alternative.

US$75-100

Colonial Beach Hotel, (former Hotel Calamar), coastal road, ☎ 261 5187, Fax 261 5247 – 47rm CC Half-board only. The gaily decorated rooms somewhat contrast with the sad little beach where visitors can only just manage to paddle among the rocks. Do not expect to do any serious swimming in the pool either. However the coral reef is close enough to make this shallow lagoon a paradise for snorkelling enthusiasts. Two white houses with thatched roofs, the remains of the former Hotel Calamar, are available for families or groups of friends. These prettily decorated houses have one or two double rooms, one child's room and a large sitting room. Pleasant restaurant.

• Trou aux Biches

US$45-60

La Cocoteraie, Royal Rd, ☎ 265 5694, Fax 265 62 30– 28 rm CC Split-level flats for 4 people, with an open-plan kitchen, living room and balcony. The swimming pool is just for quick dips. Cleaning and cooking extra. Amenities can prove to be a little basic.

US$60-75

Le Grand Bleu, Royal Rd, ☎ 265 5812 – 50rm TV CC Spacious flats with kitchen, living room and balcony in an attractive blue and white building. Although the road is not that noisy, it is better to ask for rooms as far as possible from the traffic. The hotel occasionally accommodates visiting Indian movie crews, which make for a lively stay. Ask for the rather unappealing but modern bungalows.

Beach Villas, Royal Rd, ☎ 263 8771, Fax 63 8274 –16rm Enjoy the independence of a rental with the facilities of a hotel (cleaning, reception, 24 hour security). Breakfast and cleaning extra. Flats with one room or more with open-plan kitchens and living rooms. Discrete, modern and clean. The balconies overlook a garden where guests can organise their own barbecues, with direct access to the sea. The nearby (a few minutes walk) Mont-Choisy beach is however much nicer to go swimming in. Guests can take advantage of the seaside sports provided by the neighbouring PLM Azur Hotel.

• Pointe aux Canonniers

US$45-75

Sea Point Beach Bungalows, ☎ 263 8604, Fax 686 7380 – 10rm Split-level flats for 4 or 5 people with kitchen, living room and a terrace shaded by an arbour of bougainvillea. Simple but comfortable and attractively decorated. The cleaning lady will prepare meals for a little extra. Barbecue available for guests in the garden. Situated on a small sandy bay with shallow waters, overlooking little islands. Residents have access to all the restaurants, activities and night-life provided by the neighbouring Club Méditerranée at a reduced price.

US$75-100

Colonial Coconut Hotel, Pointe Malartic, ☎ 263 8720, Fax 263 7116, ccoconut@intnet.mu – 34rm Half-board only. Ravenala bungalows, each with a little terrace overlooking the sea or gardens. The upper level bungalows are lighter than the ground floor ones. Each room, furnished in wood and rattan, is decorated with reproductions of scenes of Mauritian history or daily life. The pleasant lounge in the main building (bar and restaurant) is part of the remains of a former colonial *campement* and has retained a few traces of times of yore.

Over US$100

Hôtel le Canonnier, ☎ 209 7000, Fax 263 7864 – 248rm Half-board only. Rooms with individual terraces overlooking the sea, garden or the swimming pool in pastel-coloured, thatched-roofed buildings. A magnificent setting that combines brightly-coloured lush vegetation, pools and fountains and the ruins of a historic site. Three beaches border this vast hotel complex. The swimming is not ideal due to the shallowness of the waters, the rocks and all the water sports taking place, but the view over this unruly lagoon and its islands is nonetheless quite stunning.

• Grand Baie

A large number of hotels and flats for rent are located around Grand Baie, often at very competitive prices. It must however be said that it is the most touristy part of the whole island, there is not a single decent beach within walking distance and the nights are generally rowdy.

US$40-55

La Chaumière, Impasse Tajoo, ☎ 263 7351, Fax 263 6201, chaumière@intnet.mu – 7rm Located in a dead-end at right-angles to Royal Rd, between Grand Baie and Péreybère. A combination of comfort and simplicity make this little inn one of the most attractively priced of Grand Baie, if not of the whole North coast. The rooms which are clean if perhaps a little dark, are located in the main house, with the exception of two rooms in a nearby annexe. Outdoors, a small swimming pool is set in an delightful tropical garden. The owner will happily prepare excellent meals on request.

US$100-125

Veranda Bungalow Village, ☎ 263 8015, Fax 263 7369, veranda@intnet.mu – 64rm A holiday village including both independent bungalows with outdoor kitchens under over-hanging balconies and more traditional hotel accommodation. This isolated complex, located off the road, to the north of Grand Baie, is set in a pleasant garden equipped with benches and coconut trees. Wide range of services available (car rental, shops, etc). Unfortunately the shallow waters, rocks and motorboats make swimming somewhat difficult, but Cuvette beach is not too far off.

Over US$380

Royal Palm Hotel, ☎ 263 8353, Fax 263 8455, rpalm@bow.intnet.mu – 84rm Golf course, sauna, squash, fitness centre, shops, billiards, hairdressers. This hotel's sophisticated luxury make it Mauritius' most prestigious and most select hotel, favoured by stars and VIPs from the world over. Tastefully decorated, very comfortable rooms. The beach, although much cleaner than a bit further down, does not however live up to the sumptuous majesty of the gardens, lobbies and terraces. Well-known, gastronomic restaurant (open to non-residents on reservation). If you are feeling wealthy, splash out on a "*café brûlot*", a delicious concoction of coffee, fresh cream, white rum and zests of scorched orange peel.

• Péreybère

US$15-30

Joli Cœur Guesthouse, ☎ /Fax 263 8202 – 6rm This small family guesthouse is located slightly off the main road. The two rooms with a joint terrace are pleasant, but the others are relatively cramped and basic. One room does not have a private bathroom. Acceptably clean. Relaxed, welcoming atmosphere.

L'Escala, ☎ 263 7379, Fax 212 1317 – 17rm or Located on a little road, at right angles to the public beach of Péreybère. Flats with one to three rooms with kitchen, balcony or terrace, overlooking a garden. Simple and calm. Avoid the flats overlooking the sea though, because the main road is extremely busy and noisy here.

US$20-30

Fred's Apartments, Beach Lane, ☎ 263 8830, Fax 263 7531, fred.app@intnet.mu – 13rm Flats for 2 or 4 people with kitchen and terrace, set in an charming little garden. Breakfast extra. Very near to Péreybère's public beach.

US$45-60

Les Alizés, Beach Lane, ☎ 674 3695, Fax 674 3720 – 6rm Bungalows for 2 or 4 people with kitchen and terrace, on the seashore or slightly back. The garden leads down to a private pleasant little sandy beach and Péreybère's public beach is also very close by.

Hibiscus Village Vacances, ☎ 263 8554, Fax 263 8553, hibisvv@bow.intnet.mu – 15rm Bungalows with private terraces in a luscious green setting. A banyan tree rises majestically in the middle of a riot of badamier, hibiscus and coconut trees. The rooms close to the road can be a bit noisy. A mini beach and jetty have been built in front of the hotel to compensate for the absence of any real beach, but a little path takes visitors to the neighbouring beach and Péreybère's public beach is only 100m away. Pleasant restaurant with veranda by the sea.

• Cap Malheureux

US$60-95

Coin de Mire Hotel, Royal Rd, Bain Boeuf, ☎ 262 7302, Fax 262 7305, veranda@intnet.mu –74rm or Half-board only. Since a cyclone destroyed the neighbouring hotel, this former holiday village has increased its facilities. Most of the rooms are located in little white, thatched-roof cottages. Three swimming pools and a flower garden make it easier to forget the nearby road. Using the nearby Veranda Bungalow Village hotel's tennis courts at Grand Baie is free.

Bungalows Kuxville-Serendip, Royal Rd, ☎ 262 8836/262 7913, Fax 262 4707, kuxville@bow.intnet.mu – 13rm The Kuxville flats are situated on the beach, whereas the Serendip bungalows, less expensive and not half as nice, are located close to the road. The price includes a cleaning lady who can also prepare meals. A grocer stops by once a day for those who wish. Extremely convenient, on a sandy beach with a wonderful view. Ideal for those looking for a little tranquillity and solitude without the bother of household chores.

• Anse de la Raie

US$150-190

Marina Resort, ☎ 262 7651, Fax 262 7650, marinah@bow.intnet.mu – 122rm Half-board only. A peach-

North Coast

and-green coloured resort, the rooms of which are quite comparable to those of the grand hotels, some of which have a superb view overlooking the gigantic turquoise lagoon. The seafront bungalows are without doubt the most stylish.

Over US$300

Paradise Cove Hotel, ☎ 262 7983, Fax 262 7736 – 64rm Luxury hotel with the exclusive use of a little private bay, with white sands, clear waters and an enchanting view. Very stylishly decorated rooms. Stunning swimming pool. Very popular among honeymoon couples.

• Grand Gaube

US$30-60

L'Archipel Hotel, Calodyne, ☎ 283 9518, Fax 283 7910, archipel@intnet.mu – 12rm A small establishment set off from the road (follow the signs) with very reasonable rates. Calm guaranteed. Attractive swimming pool and pleasant beach, unfortunately not very accessible, due to the large rocks that make swimming difficult. If travelling with a family, the 6-person bungalows are ideal and very reasonable. Own cooking possible.

Over US$150

Le Grand Gaube Hotel, Royal Rd, ☎ 283 9350, Fax 283 9420, gg@illovo.intnet.mu – 119rm 4 hole golf practice. Somewhat impersonal holiday village. Rooms with terrace overlooking the sea, situated on a magnificent sandy beach.

• Poste Lafayette

US$45-60

Coral Beach Bungalows, route Côtière, ☎ /Fax 410 5354 – 6rm Two nights minimum. Pretty blue-and-white thatched-roof bungalows leading directly to an artificial private beach. Isolated, natural and calm. The owner is happy to prepare meals in the morning and evening on request. Residents can also do their own cooking in little kitchens. Barbecue in the garden. Bicycles, ping-pong, kayak, snorkelling gear available for guests. Excellent.

WHERE TO EAT

Most of the restaurants located along the north coast are touristy and expensive, it must however be said that their quality is gradually improving. Many do not however survive for more than a single season. The range of prices is on the basis of an average-priced meal for one person.

• Trou aux Biches-Mont Choisy

Less than US$1

The bars-on-wheels and pedestrian vendors that work their way up and down the beach of Mont-Choisy sell very welcome sandwiches, samossas, fruit and ices.

US$7-10

La Cocoteraie, Royal Rd, ☎ 265 5694. The affable Indo-Mauritian owner busies himself in the kitchen, while his daughters provide relaxed, attentive and efficient service. Mainly Mauritian and Indian cuisine (samossas, kebabs, rougail or vindaye of fish, fruit salad). Basic, good, plentiful and cheap.

US$25-60

Trou aux Biches Gourmet Club, coastal road, near the Hotel Trou aux Biches, ☎ 265 6092. Lunch and dinner; closed on Sundays and Monday lunchtime. A restaurant well-known for its fine cooking, delightful surroundings.

Le Pescatore, Royal Rd, ☎ 265 6337. Lunch and dinner. Reservations advisable. One of the best tables in Mauritius. An original cuisine in romantic, sophisticated surroundings. Diners eat on a veranda by candlelight, rocked to the sounds of soft music and the waves lapping the shorefront. If you find it difficult to choose between the specialities on the menu, ask for an "*idée du Pescatore*" (chef's selection) to taste a bit of everything.

• Grand Baie

US$7-15

Paradise, Royal Rd, Pointe aux Canonniers ☎ 263 6355. Very reasonably-priced, unpretentious Japanese restaurant. It is possible to eat on the balcony, but the street can be pretty noisy.

Quatre Epices, Royal Rd, ☎ 265 5313. Lunch and dinner; closed Sundays. A good Mauritian restaurant with wonderful fresh fruit cocktails. Although sometimes a trifle noisy during the day, it calms down in the evenings.

Don Camillo, Royal Rd, Lunch and dinner. Good Italian cooking at reasonable prices.

Palais de Chine, Royal Rd, ☎ 263 7120 Lunch and dinner. Best address in Grand Baie and one of the best Chinese restaurants in the whole island. Authentic Cantonese and Sichuan cooking.

Le Capitaine, Royal Rd, ☎ 263 6867 Lunch and dinner: closed Sundays. Reservations advisable in the evening. Good Creole, Indian and European cuisine in a pleasant setting, overlooking the sea. A restaurant popular among wealthy Mauritians.

Le Grillon, Royal Rd. Seafood, Creole and European cooking. Somewhat irregular depending on the chef's humour. Well-known for its jazz concerts.

Sakura, Royal Rd, ☎ 263 8092. If you fancy a break from Mauritian cuisine, why not try the sushi, sashimi and other Japanese specialities here?

US$25-60

Le Bateau Ivre, Royal Rd, ☎ 263 8766/263 8356. This restaurant's wonderful setting and impeccable service has not ceased to further improve its quality. Excellent seafood and desserts. A little expensive but very good.

• Péreybère

Less than US$1

Bars-on-wheels await a hungry lunchtime clientele from the public beach of Péreybère. Excellent snacks.

US$7-15

Nirvana, Royal Rd, ☎ 262 6068/262 6711 Lunch and dinner; closed Sundays. Reservations advisable on Friday and Saturday evenings. Excellent tikka, tandoori, kebabs, biryani, dhal and other Indian delicacies prepared by a Bombay chef. After a little while, diners soon relax in this immense, air-conditioned room, lit by flickering candlelight to a background of Indian music. Excellent service.

L'Auberge des Songes (chez Roland), Royal Rd, ☎ 263 8326 Lunch and dinner. Good Mauritian cooking with music for a relaxed meal. Fish, curry and vindaye can be eaten on the terrace to the sound of guitars.

US$15-30

Le Bigorneau, (Hotel Hibiscus restaurant) ☎ 263 8553. Lunch and dinner. Candlelight meals on a pleasant terrace overlooking the sea. Creole buffet every Sunday, followed by a display of *séga* dancing on the beach around a fire. Curry, stews, Moulouctany, fricassee, achards and rice.

• Cap Malheureux

US$3-7

Coin de Mire, Royal Rd, ☎ 262 8070. Lunch and dinner. Small, unpretentious establishment run by laid-back Creoles, situated just opposite, and overlooking, Cap Malheureux' red-roofed church. Terrace upstairs. Omelettes, salads, Chinese dishes. Ideal for a light lunchtime snack.

• Roches Noires

US$10-15

La Caze Carlet, coastal road, ☎ 411 5622. Lunch and dinner; closed Sundays and Monday lunchtimes. On the edge of a quiet road, this restaurant offers high-quality French and Mauritian cooking and seafood, all at very reasonable prices. Jazz groups or traditional music on Saturday evenings.

WHERE TO HAVE A DRINK

Tea rooms, cafés – ***Lotus on the Square***, Royal Rd (stop at the Café around the World sign), Grand Baie, ☎ 263 3251. Open all day, closed Sundays. Cocktails and ices served in a pleasant little garden, among a display of pottery and local crafts on sale at the store next-door.

Bars, Nightclubs – Grand Baie has most (if not all) the nightspots of the island, apart from those in hotels.

Alchemy, Les Mirabelles, la Salette Rd, ☎ 263 5314. Open midnight to the early hours of the morning depending on the evening and the season. Cocktails, grilled meat, pizzas, hamburgers or Mexican snacks available at the bar or on a pleasant, shady terrace.

Café de la Plage, Royal Rd, ☎ 263 7041. Lunchtime and evenings (until late). The "in" bar where it is best

North Coast

to stick to a drink rather than bother with the somewhat bland cooking. One of the island's few spots for night-lovers.

Banana's, Royal Rd, Grand Baie, near the Caltex station. Lively, open-air café on a beach, frequented by the island's young jet-set.

Casino – ***Trou aux Biches Casino***, Royal Rd.

SHOPPING

Books and newspapers – Papyrus, Royal Rd, Newspapers, magazines, books and tourist guides.

Off-the-peg – The vast majority of the north coast clothing stores are located in Grand Baie on Royal Rd. Large choice of well-known brand names at attractive prices (***Chipie, Hugo Boss, Ralph Lauren Habit, Bongo***), wool and cashmere sweaters (***Floréal, Bonair***). Beautiful pareos are on sale almost everywhere, but the cheapest are probably in the little stores around Péreybère beach, where a bewildering range of coloured fabrics flutters in the wind under the casuarinas.

FBI, Grand Baie Resort, Royal Rd, Grand Baie. A large choice of brand names at attractive prices. Do not hesitate to negotiate.

Gifts-souvenirs – Many boutiques, mainly in Grand Baie, offer Western style Mauritian products. They also sell Indonesian, African, etc. objects and fabric.

Art Galleries – ***Galerie Raphaël***, Royal Rd, Grand Baie, ☎ 421 2198. Open all day; closed Sundays. Work by local artists and some lovely model ships.

Galerie Hélène de Senneville, Royal Rd, Grand Baie, ☎ 263 7426/263 3738. Exhibition-Sale of work by Mauritian artists. Framing possible. Relatively upmarket.

WATER SPORTS

Lots of hotels have clubs that accept non-residents and there are also independent clubs.

Scuba diving – ***Blue Water***, Le Corsaire, Trou aux Biches, ☎ 261 7186. Hugues and Bruno will take you diving for Rs700 if you do not have your own equipment, Rs800 if it is your first dive.

Aquatic Dream, Royal Rd, Grand Baie, next to Le Capitaine restaurant, ☎ 263 9096. Two dives a day, at 9am and 2pm, at a reasonable price (Rs650, equipment included), as well as night-dives (Rs1000). Youthful, lively atmosphere.

Aquarius Diving Centre, Hotel La Véranda's diving centre, Grand Baie, ☎ 263 6260. Three dives a day at 8.30am, 11.45am and 1.45pm. Competitive prices (Rs600, equipment included). A reputable, serious club with several centres on the island offering optimum safety conditions.

Ecole de Plongée NAUI, Grand Baie. Serious reputation.

Sindbad, Bungalows Kuxville. ☎ 262 8836. Good reputation, more for experienced divers.

Deep-sea fishing – ***Organisation de pêche du nord-Corsaire Club***, Trou aux Biches, ☎ 265 5209.

Sport Fisher, Grand Baie.

Sailing – ***Yacht Club***, Grand Baie.

Croisières Emeraude and Aquacat, Cap Malheureux.

Under-water walking – ***Undersea Walk***, Royal Rd, Grand Baie (near the Caltex station) ☎ 423 8822.

Alpha II, Grand Baie, ☎ 263 9036.

Submarine – ***Blue Safari Submarine***, Royal Rd, Grand Baie, ☎ 263 3333. An hour's excursion beyond the lagoon in a little submarine. Original and reasonably priced.

EAST COAST★★

POINTE LAFAYETTE TO BLUE BAY

Pleasantly breezy in summer but cool in winter
Good scuba-diving September to May - Sailing in winter

Not to be missed
A visit to Mahébourg sometime during the week, preferably on a Monday.
Exploration of the underwater world in Blue Bay.
A glass of rum at the Hotel Le Prince Maurice.

And remember...
Set out for L'Île aux Cerfs early in the morning, taking a picnic with you.
Beware of the sun at sea.
Take something warm for the evening.

The coastal road threads its way through the lovely lush landscape of the eastern coast, for the trade winds maintain reasonable levels of humidity here and these, in turn, encourage the vegetation to thrive with vigour and profusion.
Glorious lagoons edged with long sand beaches alternate with treacherous and overgrown coves with many a story to tell.
Far removed from the hustle and bustle of Port Louis and the crowded northern seaside resorts, this area attracts holiday-makers in search of tranquillity and authenticity. The best hotels are situated overlooking the beaches in and around Flacq. Other characterful and more modest family-run hotels are to found in magical surroundings in the southeast, on the outskirts of Mahébourg.

Historical notes

The most significant event to happen on these shores had implications for the subsequent development of Mauritian history, for it was here that the Dutch first landed and laid claim to the island in 1598. By the 17C the Dutch had established their first colony there, and had begun to farm sugarcane and Java deer. In their turn the first French colonists arrived and settled in the region of Grand Port; it was only later that they made Port Louis their capital.

The shoreline around Flacq★★

Approx 18km – Allow 1hr by car.

The typical rather untamed scenery of this region, buffeted by strong trade winds and rough seas, begins at **Pointe Lafayette**. Here the ocean swells up and over the offshore coral barrier reef, gushing through any breaches to form thundering waves that crash against the basalt rocks. Even the stunted palm trees and the leaning casuarinas have been subjugated by the power of the elements.
Then the road unexpectedly comes upon the strange sight of a bay overgrown with mangroves that have invaded the water and formed various little islets.
The small market town of **Poste de Flacq**, which nestles in the crook of another bay, proudly displays its white washed **Hindu Temple★** on a spur of land surrounded by water. Here the faithful flock in their numbers, ever in awe of the stylised trident usually brandished by Shiva.

At the crossroads in Poste de Flacq, take the B62 towards Belle Mare.

Rolling fields of sugarcane extend as far as the eye can see, interrupted here and there by hillocks of lava, between which you occasionally catch a glimpse of the ocean. Elsewhere, the skyline is punctuated by the profile of the mountains.

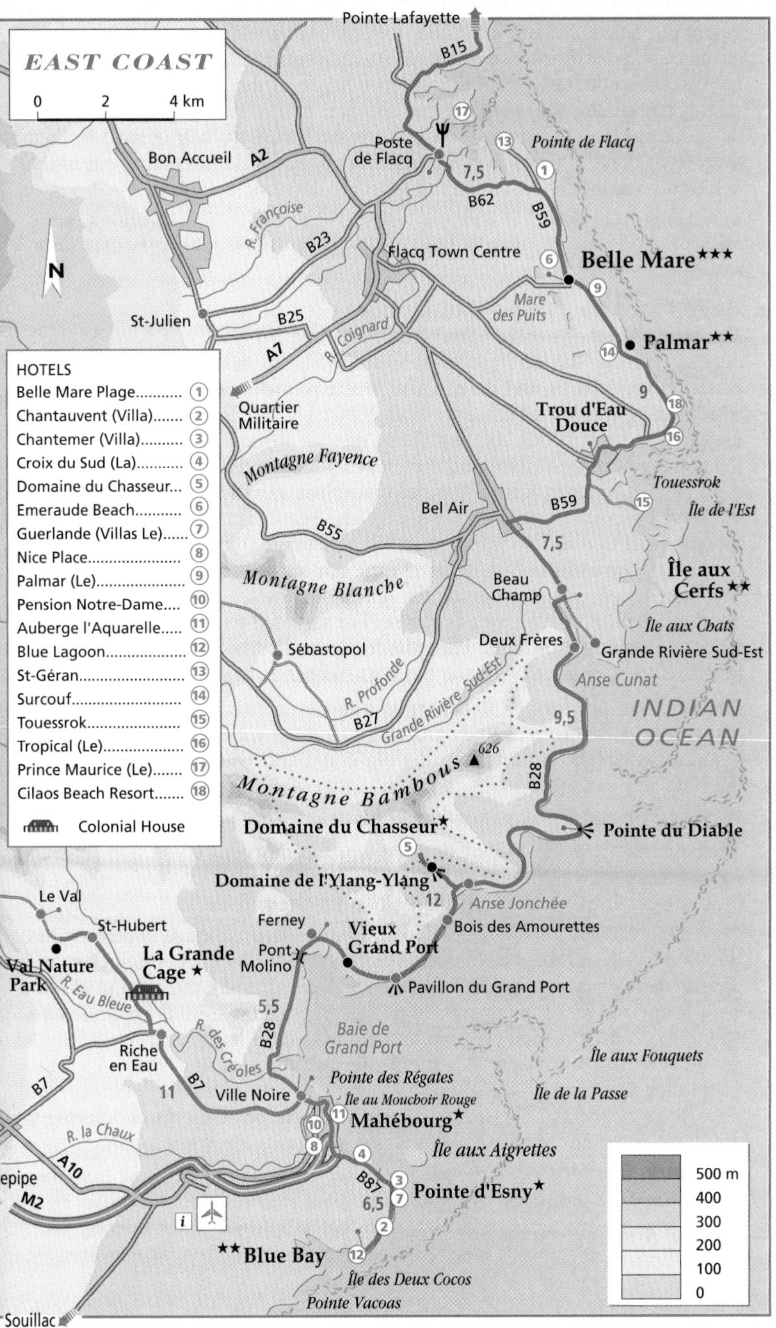
EAST COAST
0 2 4 km
N
HOTELS
Belle Mare Plage........... 1
Chantauvent (Villa)....... 2
Chantemer (Villa).......... 3
Croix du Sud (La)........... 4
Domaine du Chasseur... 5
Emeraude Beach........... 6
Guerlande (Villas Le)...... 7
Nice Place...................... 8
Palmar (Le)..................... 9
Pension Notre-Dame.... 10
Auberge l'Aquarelle..... 11
Blue Lagoon.................. 12
St-Géran........................ 13
Surcouf......................... 14
Touessrok...................... 15
Tropical (Le).................. 16
Prince Maurice (Le)....... 17
Cilaos Beach Resort....... 18
Colonial House
Pointe Lafayette
B15
Poste de Flacq
Pointe de Flacq
Bon Accueil
A2
7,5
B62
B59
R. Françoise
B23
Flacq Town Centre
Belle Mare★★★
Mare des Puits
St-Julien
B25
R. Coignard
A7
Palmar★★
Quartier Militaire
Trou d'Eau Douce
9
Montagne Fayence
Touessrok
Île de l'Est
Bel Air
B59
B55
7,5
Île aux Cerfs★★
Montagne Blanche
Beau Champ
Île aux Chats
Deux Frères
Grande Rivière Sud-Est
Sébastopol
Anse Cunat
R. Profonde
INDIAN OCEAN
B27
Grande Rivière Sud-Est
9,5
626
B28
Montagne Bambous
Domaine du Chasseur★
Pointe du Diable
Domaine de l'Ylang-Ylang
12
Anse Jonchée
Le Val
St-Hubert
Ferney
Bois des Amourettes
Vieux Grand Port
La Grande Cage ★
Pont Molino
Val Nature Park
R. Eau Bleue
Pavillon du Grand Port
5,5
B28
Baie de Grand Port
R. des Créoles
Riche en Eau
Île aux Fouquets
B7
11
B7
Pointe des Régates
Ville Noire
Île au Mouchoir Rouge
Île de la Passe
Mahébourg★
R. la Chaux
Île aux Aigrettes
A10
B87
Pointe d'Esny★
6,5
M2
i
★★Blue Bay
Île des Deux Cocos
Pointe Vacoas
Souillac
500 m
400
300
200
100
0

Before the cane is cut and harvested, sometime towards the end of June, the tall stems tasselled with flowers shimmer in the breeze. Their pinkish "plumage" contrasts harmoniously with their green foliage and the black basalt. Once the crop has been cut, the countryside is laid bare and its magic is dispelled.
As the days draw to a close, you will see the Indian women dressed in their saris, with bundles precariously balanced on their heads, streaming out of the fields and making for home, bound for more domestic duties.

After the B62 has joined the B59, you will see on the left, a line of beach-side hotels extending all the way to Pointe de Flacq. On the right, the B59 follows the coast southwards.

Belle Mare to Trou d'Eau Douce**

The lovely beaches between Pointe de Flacq and Trou d'Eau Douce continue over some 8km, shaded by casuarinas and bougainvillea. The limpid water is perfect for bathing in, and the constant breeze provides excellent conditions for wind-surfing and sailing all year round. Inevitably, the best spots are monopolised by the resort hotels. Although here, they are a good deal less concentrated than on the northwest coast; furthermore, they have been conceived with greater sensitivity in order to blend effectively into their surroundings. Unfortunately, the temptation to capitalise on this wild and beautiful corner of the island is proving hard to resist, so with demand at a premium, the open areas along the beaches are gradually becoming developed. For the present, there are almost no restaurants, bars or shops outside the hotel complexes.
The hinterland presents little of interest. The scattered remains of the odd **lime kiln** are a reminder of times when the locals made lime from coral for use in house-building and for powering the sugar refineries.

The fabulous **Belle Mare Beach***** is a favourite haunt at weekends when Mauritians gather there to enjoy great big barbecues with friends and extended families that might last late into the night and end with sleeping out under the stars.

The road continues around a Hindu temple before heading onwards along the coast.

The next beauty spot is **Palmar Beach**** which comprises a succession of pretty sandy creeks strewn with smooth basalt rocks that extend into the shallows to fleck the becalmed waters with shades of turquoise and black.

Trou d'Eau Douce is an attractive Creole fishing village, although its serenity has been somewhat disrupted by tourism, notably since the harbour began taking the pleasure boats relaying visitors to the Île aux Cerfs. Despite the handful of souvenir shops and small restaurants by the waterfront, you are still likely to come face-to-face with a roaming pig or chicken in the quiet back-streets.
To the south of the village lies the **Touessrok Peninsula**, where one of the island's loveliest hotels – the Touessrok – enjoys a prime location. Although the preserve of residents only, it is well-worth driving out there (and enjoying a drink at the bar en passant) to admire the view *(see p 308 Where to stay)*.

■ **Île aux Cerfs**** – *All the hotels and local tour operators charge the same price for an excursion to the island. Departures from Pointe Maurice (Hotel Touessrok), every 15min between 9am- 4pm in winter; 9am-5pm in summer. 5min crossing time. Alternatively, why not enjoy a longer boat trip from the jetty at Trou d'Eau or from the*

E. Valentin/HOA QUI

Île aux Cerfs

agency "Chez Vicky" at the north end of the village. Both the restaurants on the island are expensive, so you may like to take a picnic. It is advisable to take plastic shoes with you because some coves are infested with sea-urchins. Another option is to hire a boat or a catamaran in Mahébourg (or its vicinity) and explore the coast by sea under your own steam.

Whichever way they choose to get there, visitors do not tend to regret crossing the **lagoon**. For in the morning, the fishermen are often out on their boats sorting or mending their nets after landing their catch. Alternatively, the boat that heads north from the Touessrok motors past the hotel and under the little bridge linking the headland where the hotel stands, to a little islet.

Île aux Cerfs is uninhabited, and until a few years ago, must have remained a forgotten corner of paradise, surrounded by clear aquamarine waters. These days, the place is heaving with ever growing hordes of day-trippers and the sea is abuzz with increasing numbers of noisy and dangerous launches that generate wafts of smelly diesel fumes and discharge oil into the water. Nonetheless, if you manage to catch a boat early in the morning and select a private secluded spot, you will get a flavour of the island's true charm Needless to say, the majority of visitors collect on the beach beside the jetty – the most photographed stretch of sand on Mauritius – where rows of tightly-packed sun-loungers and parasols are arranged by staff from the Hotel Touessrok. On this once idyllic **beach**, sheltered from the wind, beach-hawkers selling pineapples and brightly-coloured patterned sarongs pick their way awkwardly through the all pervading smells of sun-tan lotion emanating from the outstretched bodies or of the motor boats revving-up by the **water-sports centre**.

A short walk under the casuarinas, and on past the restaurants, lies a long beach that is usually almost deserted and far more agreeable even if its sands are slightly coarser and more exposed to prevailing winds. Midway to the empty horizon lies a coral reef over which the waves break, spilling their white foam and spray with an impressive roar.

Beyond the beach, the shoreline is broken by a series of empty little **inlets**, although it is best to enquire which are subject to strong currents that might be dangerous to swim in.

The island is a popular spot for Sunday family picnics, so do not be surprised to see large groups of Mauritians setting out early in the morning with all the paraphernalia required for cooking-up a hot *cari* under the casuarinas and feeding a happy party.

Those who shun the idea of visiting the island in the company of a host of noisy day-trippers may prefer the prospect of heading out to one or more of the smaller and less frequented neighbouring islands care of a local fisherman or small boat owners. They might even be prepared to lay on a special lunch of grilled fish *(information from the hotels; also see Sports and Pastimes p 311).*

The coast of Grand Port★

Approx 35km – Allow 45min (longer if visiting the estates).

After Trou d'Eau Douce, the B59 makes its way inland. At Beau Champ follow signs on the right for Mahébourg, and cross the Grande Rivière Sud-Est (GRSE); the road becomes the B28 and once again follows the coast from Deux Frères.

The coast road weaves through a collection of colourful hamlets sandwiched between the sea and the foothills of the Bambous Mountains. This coastal region, where the island's first inhabitants once settled, is now one of the least visited. Only the odd ruins or commemorative monument dotted along the route serve to recall the many major historical events enacted here.

The broad estuary of the **Grande Rivière Sud-Est** conceals a number of spectacular gorges complete with lovely **waterfalls**. Some of the excursions to the Île aux Cerfs combine a visit to the island with a tour of the waterfalls.

At this point the coast becomes increasingly rugged as it extends southwards. The road follows the contours of shoreline as it opens out into a serene but rocky bay, or by-passes a small Indian or Creole hamlet consisting of precarious-looking shacks constructed out of breeze-blocks and corrugated-iron. None of the sumptuous *campements* found in the north and west of the island are to be seen here; for this is a wild and desolate place where the people continue to eke out an existence from one day to the next. The roadside acts like a lively meeting place, providing people with a suitable spot for selling local produce, or for exchanging news and gossip, for catching a lift from a passing truck or awaiting the delivery of some promised component. A group of men might play cards under an Indian almond tree, while a huddle of housewives in hair-curlers gather to discuss the latest rumour. On the beach below, the fishing boats lie askew on the black sand having been left high and dry at low tide, and the fishermen set about arranging their nets in the sun to dry; elsewhere, schoolchildren, still clad in uniform but fresh out of class, rush around playing ball and women quietly walk along the sand in search of crabs and shellfish for the evening soup. Each settlement looks much like the last one save perhaps for a **naval cemetery** here and a small bright white **Hindu temple** there.

JF Galmiche

The Hindu temple at Quatre Soeurs

Frangipani, *badamiers* (Indian almond) and small palm trees break the monotony of the fields upon fields of sugarcane. Then, suddenly, these give way to a broad patch where symmetrical rows of vegetables grow – onions, groundnuts and aubergines /eggplants – attended by women wearing straw hats, and holding watering-cans in each hand.

Few buses pass this way, so most people use bicycles, notably the local postman, dressed in his distinctive blue shirt, busy on completing his round of deliveries.

La Pointe du Diable (Devil's Point) proudly sports two cannons aimed at the sea, the sole remains of an old French gun battery preserved as a historic monument. The large lay-by on the left hand-side of the road enables motorists to pull-in so as to enjoy the vast **prospect*** out and over the sea to the neighbouring islands. On the opposite side of the road, meanwhile, stands the grey stone bulk of an old powder magazine complete with its observation post.

A dirt tracks leading off the main road between the villages of Anse Jonchée and Providence, continues to Domaine de l'Ylang-Ylang and on to Domaine du Chasseur (2km).

■ **Domaine de l'Ylang-Ylang** – ☎ *634 5668, 9am-5pm. No charge. Paying guided visits on foot on in 4WD. Possiblility of visiting the distillery (charge). Request a map from the restaurant or at reception. Restaurant at lunchtime.* This estate cultivates ylang-ylang, a flowering plant from which a rare essential oil is distilled for use in making perfume.

A prescribed **trail** through the natural vegetation provides a rare insight into the prevalent species of the region notably guava, traveller's palms and various precious hardwoods like ebony, macaco, black wood. Another attraction is the splendid **view**** across to the bay at Grand Port and the fabulous stretch of water dappled with ever-changing shades of watery green and blue, and the hills behind overlooked by the mountains beyond.

■ **Domaine du Chasseur*** –- *Open everyday, without a guide (Rs50) and with a guide (Rs200). Departures at 11.30am and 3.45pm. Allow 2hr. 4WD circuit (Rs200). Map available from the restaurant or at reception.(Hotel and restaurant,* *see p 308. Where to stay**).* This estate offers a green, or ecological, form of tourism that differs quite markedly from what is on offer from the usual seaside resorts elsewhere on the island. For one thing, the temperatures in the interior are decidedly cooler than by the sea. A consortium of private investors have secured an area of undulating countryside covering some 1 000 hectares, including the last surviving patch of **primary forest** where a host of endemic species of flora and fauna (specific to Mauritius) may be found thriving in their natural habitats.

The principal attraction is the opportunity of wandering about the estate among the ebony, eucalyptus and cinnamon trees and palms in search of wild orchids, shy deer and wild boar, not to mention the range of rare birds. Indeed, the last 400 **Mauritius kestrels**, one of the several species threatened with extinction, live on this estate and are fed daily at around 2pm.

A range of walks – all more or less an hour in length – take in a strategically-situated **viewpoint**** offering a wonderful prospect over the lagoon below: this is also accessible by 4WD in 25min. Shooting enthusiasts can also try their luck at hunting Java deer and other small game, and take their precious trophies home with them. Yet another way of exploring the thick and overgrown wilderness interspersed by waterfalls, is by hang-gliding, although most people are content to have lunch at the estate restaurant, in one of the thatched pavilions dotted among the greenery.

Return to the coastal road (B28).

■ **Vieux Grand Port** – As you cut through the small village called **Bois des Amourettes**, you will notice on the right of the road the remains of seven huge tanks – the largest fuel depot in the Indian Ocean – that were used to refuel the British Naval ships operating thereabouts during the Second World War.

Near **Pavillon du Grand Port**, beside the Church of Notre Dame du Grand Pouvoir on the left, sits the ruin of **Fort Hendrick**: the first fortress to be built on the island, by the Dutch. More or less in the same spot, but only clearly visible if viewed from the sea, there is a grotto (known locally as the **Salle d'Armes)** where firearms were stored and duels were fought. A few hundred metres further on, on the right, stands the village of **Vieux Grand Port**, dominated by an old **Dutch watchtower** built entirely of coral.

For it was here – as is confirmed by the **commemorative column** on the left before the Molino bridge – that the Dutch took possession of the island in 1598, and where they established their colony and where some 40 years later, they built a harbour.

Adriaen van der Stel

Adriaen van der Stel came to Mauritius as a slave in 1635, and was freed in 1638. The following year he was appointed Governor of Mauritius. Among his great achievements, he introduced the first deer to the island in 1639 that he had imported from the Indonesian island of Java aboard the ship "Capelle". Over the ensuing centuries, the deer were reared as a source of delicious meat, and for sport indulged in by the wealthy sugar planters. Today, deer farms are to be found around the foot of Morne Brabant and in the region of Rivière Noire. Indeed, venison curry is listed on many if not most restaurant menus.

The Dutchman is also credited with the introduction of sugarcane to the island; this is still the mainstay of the island's economy.

In 1722 the French arrived and reclaimed the buildings abandoned by the Dutch, and ravaged, over time, by cyclones, marauding pirates and fleeing slaves some fifty years before. The anchorage, however, proved to be exposed to the southeast trade winds and so it was not long before the French settlers gave up on the mooring – renamed Port Bourbon – in favour of Port Louis.

At **Ferney**, there is a **plaque** on the left that acknowledges the introduction of sugarcane to Mauritius by the Dutch in around 1639. A second **plaque**, this time at the entrance to the former Ferney estate sugar refinery (marked "Floréal Knitwear" on the right), commemorates Adriaen van der Stel who brought ashore the first consignment of Java deer the same year.

Several offshore islands pepper the horizon alongside the barrier reef. These are accessible by fishing-boat or by catamaran (*see p 311* Activities). Besides their historical significance, a few have been made into **nature reserves** for species threatened with extinction. Today, **Île aux Fouquets** (Shearwater Island) is home to many sea birds; but in times past (1694-96) the first French colonists were imprisoned here by the Dutch, after being accused of having stolen ambergris (a greasy substance highly prized in the perfume-making industry that collects in the intestines of sperm whales before being secreted into the sea, and is then collected from the surface).

Île de la Passe bears the ruins of a lighthouse and of French fortifications that proved highly effective during the battle of 1810.

■ Mahébourg*

Allow half a day: preferably a weekday – especially Monday – when it is at its liveliest.

The second major settlement, near Vieux Grand Port, was modelled on Port Louis under the auspices of the French Governor Decaen, and famously resisted the attack mounted by the British in August 1810. The village of Mahébourg – for it does not have the administrative status of a town – has a population of 16 000 mostly of Indian origin. Like Port Louis, the community suffered a great loss of numbers in 1865 when many of the wealthy gentry moved to the high plateaux in the wake of a malaria epidemic; later, it suffered the consequences of the railway link to the capital being closed in 1964.

Named after the first French Governor Mahé de La Bourdonnais, this endearing little place tucked away between the River Chaux and the Creole River remains somewhat old-fashioned. For here, as in many other small provincial towns and villages in the interior, life is locked in a time warp, and continues very much as it did in some past era. In among the colonial townhouses and fisherman's shacks, arranged in a grid by the French colonists, a gentle bustle pervades the streets. Hawkers meander past the street-stalls and through the central market, colourful sari shops burst with glistening fabrics, and an untidy workshop shows a tailor engaged at his sewing-machine.

The **History Museum*** *(Mahébourg Road on the right, as one heads out of town towards the airport. Open 9am-4pm and 9am-12noon at weekends, closed Tuesdays and public holidays. No charge)* is housed in the **"château*"** that was built in 1771 for Jean de Robillard, the Maritime Commander of Mahébourg and temporarily turned into a hospital for the casualties of both factions engaged in the battle of Vieux Grand Port in 1810.

It remained the property of the de Robillard family until the beginning of the 20C, when it was left as a gift to the government. After being transformed into a museum, it was opened to the public in 1950. This elegant building owes considerably more in terms of design to a Breton manor-house than to a Mauritian colonial homestead; for one thing, despite its wooden slat roof, it has an open outside terrace rather than a veranda.

The displays on the **ground floor** consist essentially of souvenirs – engravings, newspaper articles, period weapons, etc – relating to the naval battle of Vieux Grand Port fought by the French and British in 1810. Another room centres on the *St Géran* which was shipwrecked in 1744, with a scale model of the vessel, its bell, cannon-balls and other relics retrieved from the seabed.

Egg seller

C Vaisse/HOA QUI

East Coast

The **first floor** is used to show an assorted collection of colonial furniture (four-poster bed, covered litter) and porcelain made for the French East India Company. Additional material relates to the story of Paul and Virginie, and includes many old maps of Mauritius and the Indian Ocean through the ages as charted by the Portuguese, Dutch, English and French since its discovery and under colonial rule.

Come out of the museum and turn left down Mahébourg Road.

To the right rises the bell-tower of the **Church of Notre-Dame** (Rue du Bambou), with, a little further down, on the corner of rue de Suffen and rue de Délices, an attractive-looking green and white **mosque**.

Many of the principal businesses and banks are located in the **town centre**, notably in and around rue des Créoles, rue de la Chaux, rue de Maurice, rue de la Colonie, rue des Cent Gaulettes and rue du Flamant. A walk through this area and its outskirts provides ample opportunity for one to savour the local atmosphere and imbibe the laid-back attitude of a country backwater. Woven into the background noise, you may be able to pick out the mechanical sound of sewing machines going at a furious pace that emanates from the workshops above the clothes shops full of printed T-shirts and coloured sarongs. Perhaps you might like to sample the services on offer in the barbers' shops along rue du Flamant.

The tiny **market** *(corner of rue du Flamant and rue de la Colonie. Open daily, 9am-5pm or thereabouts)* is especially busy on a Monday when the stalls are piled high with rolls of cloth. Elsewhere, stalls are stacked with colourful displays of everything and anything a housewife might require – fish, fruit, vegetables, hats and baskets from Rodrigues to mention the most obvious.

Should you happen to be in Mahébourg on a Monday, you may like to take a turn around the **cloth market** held on the northern edge of town at **Pointe Canon** *(corner of rue de la Boulangerie and rue des Hollondais. Mondays all day)*. For much of the morning, things remain somewhat low-key among the stalls shaded by colourful awnings congregated around the **monument** celebrating the abolition of slavery in 1835; then, at around 12noon, business seems suddenly to take off. The cloth is unfurled and measured, clothes are removed from their hangers, plastic and metal utensils are compared for quality and price, and people jostle for bargains.

Turn down rue des Hollandais which leads down to the **Pointe des Régates**, where a **monument** stands commemorating the French and British sailors killed in the Battle of La Passe in 1810.

Opposite the tiny islet – **Île au Mouchoir Rouge** – with a little red-roofed house, stands a makeshift Hindu temple. Here, among the rocks down at the water's edge, the brightly-clad Indian women come to do their ablutions before picking their way through the heavy clouds of smoke and cloying smell of incense, to present their offerings up to the gods. The serenity of the place coupled with the constant breeze blowing in from the sea often draws groups of workmen and layabouts looking to snooze through the midday heat.

Continue down rue des Créoles, and over the Cavendish Bridge straddling the La Chaux river.

This corner of Mahébourg – known as **Ville Noire –** was where the slaves used to live. Its main attraction is the **H Rault biscuit factory** *(rue Fabien, Ville Noire ☎ 631 9559. Usually open Monday- Friday,9.30am-11.30am and 1pm-3pm, although it* *is best to ring first. Table d'hôte available if booked 2 days ahead)*: the oldest-established family-run operation on the island producing "home-made" cassava biscuits much in the same way as when production began. At first the biscuits were intended solely for home consumption; but in 1870, this unique enterprise began selling its biscuits commercially. The fundamental problem undermining the business today is the availability of manioc (grown in Brazil and imported originally to feed the slaves), a crop that takes a long time to come to maturity, and which is therefore expensive to buy on the open market. After that the roots undergo a lengthy process of washing, crushing and drying before being reduced to a fine flour that has to be sieved several times. The charming owner, a descendent of Hilarion Rault, founder of the company, is only too pleased to show people around the operation, taking care to explain all the procedures involved before the small square biscuits are baked on baking sheets heated on a cane-straw fire. The visit finishes over a biscuit tasting session and a cup of tea.

Around Mahébourg

Head out of Mahébourg through Ville Noire or Beau Vallon following signs for the B7 to St-Hubert (10km).

■ **Val Nature Park** – *Open daily, 9am-5pm. Entrance fee. Restaurant open for lunch.* The 33 hectares reservation and zoo are of no great interest. It was originally conceived as a place for people to come to for a walk in the valley among the mountains, or to see a variety of caged animals (elephants, kangaroos, ponies, leopards, zebra, deer and monkeys) and a farm of freshwater prawns *(camarons)*. The park also has watercress beds and greenhouses full of anthuriums.

Return to Mahébourg and pick up the B87 which runs southwards along the coast.

■ **Pointe d Esny** ⋆ – The southward-bound coastal road runs the length of the sandbar, right across the vast **lagoon** fringed with a lovely unspoilt **beach** and one of the island's finest beauty spots.

Cutting the stubble

The shore is lined with seaside holiday homes or *campements* that vary little in quality and type. For in its heyday, long before they were to flock to the beaches around Grand Baie and along the northern part of the island, this beach was the exclusive playground of the Franco-Mauritian aristocracy. Most of the houses are now owned by airline pilots and airport staff because of their proximity to the airport, although a few still remain in the hands of wealthy Mauritian families.

The modest villas and bungalows strung along the other side of the road are typical secondary homes, often available for holiday lets.

Off the tip of the headland sits **Île aux Aigrettes** (Egrets Island) one of Mauritius's few **nature reserves** providing a safe haven for some of the island's endemic flora and fauna.

Blue Bay** – At last the road completes its circuit around Esny Point and arrives at a pretty bay lined with a lovely – and highly popular – **public beach** shaded by casuarinas, sheltered from offshore currents and the open sea by the **Île des Deux Cocos**. The magnificent water, that ranges in colour from the deepest blue to the palest turquoise, withholds perhaps Mauritius's best preserved **marine park**** populated by an exceptional array of sea life that demands to be discovered and explored.

Notice should be drawn to the signs warning "Danger: if swimming more than 50m offshore", for bathers can suddenly find themselves out of their depth when the sea-floor suddenly falls away. The reason for the warning is that this natural occurrence tends to be rare in Mauritian waters, but this would explain why the lagoon seems to contain a dark blue inner area that markedly contrasts with the pale aquamarine water around the edge.

The road comes to a dead end at Blue Bay with no throughway around the bay. Return to Mahébourg in order to join the road at Plaisance that heads south along the coast.

Making the most of the East Coast

Coming and going

The east coast is somewhat isolated from the rest of the island.

By car– A small road runs practically all round the coastline. From Mahébourg, there is a motorway leading to Port Louis, via the central plateau towns. Depending on your exact location on the coast, it takes from 30min to an hour to get to the airport.

By taxi – Ideal for getting round the area. ***Hassen Jaunbocus***, Mahébourg, ☎ 631 9674/251 4246, is a particularly friendly driver who is also well-versed in the island's history and botany. He can come and pick travellers up at the airport if informed of their arrival time. If he's busy, contact ***Raj Chamoosing***, ☎ 631 7036/250 2502 or ***Sheere Tezooo***, ☎ 258 6616.

By bus – The east coast bus service operates less regularly than in the north or west coasts but does provide services with all of the island's main towns. Buses stop practically everywhere. A relatively frequent service operates between the airport, Blue Bay and Curepipe: departures approx. every hour for Port Louis (there is also an "express" service, less frequent services take travellers around the coast to Centre de Flacq) or southwards. Ask at Mahébourg bus station for timetables.

Address book

Tourist Information – Information counter at Plaisance airport, ☎ 637 3635, but only open on arrival of international flights; can provide information or brochures about hotels and car rentals.

Banks and money – Most banks are situated in the centre of Mahébourg. The ***State Bank of Mauritius*** (rue des Créoles), ☎ 631 9660/631 7005 and the ***Hong Kong Bank*** (Royal Rd, corner of rue des Cent Gaulettes), ☎ 631 9633, have a Visa cash dispenser. There is also a bank at Pointe de Flacq (opposite Belle Mare Hotel).

Post office – The main post office is in Mahébourg, rue des Mariannes.

Telephone – ***Mauritius Telecom***, rue de Bambou, ☎ 631 8900, open 8.30am-5pm weekdays, until 12noon Saturdays. Telephone cards on sale. Coin and card operated and public phone boxes can be found in Mahébourg bus station and on Blue Bay Beach.

Health – Mahébourg, Centre de Flacq and Trou d'Eau Douce all have chemists.
Hôpital Centre de Flacq, ☎ 413 2532.
Hôpital de Mahébourg, ☎ 631 9556.

Car rentals – Nearly all the rental agencies are located in Mahébourg on Royal Rd, but for the most part, they also have representatives in the majority of hotels.
National, ☎ 211 3191/210 1900, have a counter at the airport and although their prices are nothing special (from Rs1450), they are totally reliable.
At Pointe d'Esny, ***Tam-Tam Travels and Tours***, ☎ /Fax 631 8643, is one of the best agencies.

Where to stay

Overall, accommodation on the East Coast is more expensive than on the other coasts, with the exception of the southeastern tip of the island (Mahébourg, Pointe d'Esny), which has a number of reasonably-priced, charming little guesthouses among the best in the whole island.
The following approximate price ranges are calculated on the basis of a double room with breakfast in the mid-season.

• Poste de Flacq – Belle Mare

US$55-70

Emeraude Beach Hotel, coast road, ☎ 415 1107, Fax 415 1109– 60rm Half-board only. Slightly off the coast road (not very busy) which separates the hotel from the superb Belle Mare beach, this establishment comprises of whitewashed buildings with four rooms on two levels and little thatched cottages hidden among bougainvillea, coconut and almond trees. Pleasant, pastel-coloured rooms with private terraces overlooking the garden. Live music or shows some evenings, but calm on the whole.

Le Palmar Hotel, coast road, ☎ 415 1041, Fax 415 1043, palmar-beach@intnet.mu – 60rm Half-board only. Very conveniently located in a tidy, rather arid garden that leads down to a small, sandy beach. Set in the garden, the comfortable, clean but somewhat cold rooms are white with yellow shutters and thatched roofs and each has a terrace or balcony. Excellent value for money.

US$75-100

Surcouf Village Hotel, coast road, ☎ 419 1800, Fax 212 1361, 36rm Half-board only. Ideal for those in search of peace and quiet on an unspoilt coastline buffeted by ocean winds. This recently-renovated little hotel comprises rooms or flats of varying sizes with kitchens, all of which are spacious, clean and comfortable although not specially wonderfully decorated. Built on two levels, each has a terrace overlooking a slightly forlorn garden where the vegetation is hard put to resist the fierce trade winds. The lawn leads directly to a beach, which is unfortunately more rock than sand. Small pool around a sheltered restaurant.

US$150-300

Belle Mare Plage Golf Hotel and Resort, coast road, ☎ 415 1083, Fax 415 1082, 211rm 18-hole golf course, mini-golf, fitness centre and casino. Half-board only. Comfortable rooms spread along Belle Mare's superb beach with either a sea or garden view. Luxurious, calm, picturesque.

Over US$300

St-Géran, coast road, Pointe de Flacq, ☎ 413 9100, Fax 413 9129, – 175rm 9-hole golf course. Half-board only. One of the island's most luxurious hotels. The elegant lobby leads through arcades to a luscious, tropical garden, complete with little fountains and streams, the marble and granite interior rather lacks warmth by comparison. A superb swimming pool winds its way past through islands and coconut trees and features an island complete with bars and restaurants in the middle. The whole complex is set in a magnificent white sandy bay.

Le Prince Maurice, Choisy road, Pointe de Flacq, ☎ 415 1825, Fax 415 1983, leprince@intnet.mu – 89rm Without a doubt, the island's most beautiful and one of the world's most luxurious hotels. Comprised entirely of superbly decorated suites, the sophisticated comfort of this establishment is unmatched. The architectural style, finely-worked wood and thatch, is sumptuous and the service impeccable. The only drawback is its price, an unpleasant reminder that perfection is not necessarily within the grasp of every man. If staying there is not compatible with your budget, go and have a drink before dinner, but reservations are essential as the security service is quite intransigent.

• Trou d'Eau Douce

Under US$60

Cilaos Beach Resort, Royal Rd, ☎ 415 2985 – 10rm The owners of these little white bungalows with colourful shutters provide guests with a friendly welcome. Two possibilities: one-room flats for two or more spacious bungalows for four. All are totally independent and have a kitchen and living room. The hotel overlooks a beach, with interesting marine life. Ideal for a quiet, not too expensive holiday.

Le Tropical Hotel, La Pelouse, ☎ 419 2300/698 2222 (Reservations), Fax 419 2302, naiade@intnet.mu – 60rm All the pretty, but not enormous, rooms are located in split level white-and-yellow bungalows with terraces, overlooking the magnificent, colourful lagoon. If the seaweed, rocks and shallow waters of the hotel's beach are too uninviting, there is a free shuttle twice a day to the nearby Île aux Cerfs. Pleasant swimming pool. Timber-floored patio restaurant, whose roof is open or closed depending on the season, with a wonderful view.

Over US$300

Touessrok Hotel, ☎ 419 2451/401 1000 (Reservations), Fax 419 2025, infotsk@intnet.mu – 200rm Golf course. Half-board only. This luxurious hotel is built on a little island at the tip of Trou d'Eau Douce and joined to the main establishment by a covered bridge. Its elegant architecture comprises a maze of charming little white bungalows, bridges and arcades, reminiscent of a Greek village. The elegant rooms are situated either right on the beach or are hidden away in the gardens, all of which creates an intimate atmosphere sometimes lacking in establishments of this size. Failing staying there, go and have a cocktail or an ice around the swimming pool built on two levels, that seem to flow into each other, creating a fascinating optical illusion. The main weak point of this idyllic spot is paradoxically the beach, where the interminable shuttles to and from Cerfs Island have reduced the swimming area to a narrow band marked with buoys. The noisy motorboats can at times prove deafening.

• Anse Jonchée

US$60-70

Le Domaine du Chasseur, Anse Jonchée, ☎ 634 5097, Fax 634 5261, e-mail: dchasseur@intnet.mu– 6rm Rustic, thatched-roof bungalows hidden in the Domaine's lush vegetation. Each has a private terrace with a superb view. Ideal for nature lovers, anyone in search of a refreshing peacefulness or just for a change from the beach.

• Mahébourg

US$15-25

Nice Place Guesthouse, rue de la Bourdonnais, ☎ 631 9419 – 6rm On the corner of two quiet streets in Mahébourg, this little guesthouse, run by a welcoming Indian family, has 4 small, somewhat basic, but clean rooms, shower and WC on the landing. Overlooking the street, they are a little dark. A kitchen is available for use by guests on the ground floor. A fifth, calmer room with bathroom and small kitchen, also on the ground but somewhat stifling, is sometimes available. The best totally new room has one double bed, two bunk beds, a kitchen and a television.

Pension Notre-Dame, rue de Suffren, next to N.-D. des Anges Church, ☎ 631 9582, Fax 631 1515 – 9rm This white, square-shaped two-story building is run by nuns and indeed the sober, even Spartan surroundings, cleanliness and calm are all reminiscent of a convent. Only the close-by church bells will trouble your sleep. The nuns happily welcome guests onto the terrace where they can meditate, read or quietly talk.

Auberge L'Aquarelle, rue Shivananda, ☎ /Fax 631 9479 – 8rm One of Mahébourg's most appealing spots. Run by a Mauritian family who welcome guests simply and warmly and do all they can to make their stay pleasant. Some of the rooms are a little basic, but efforts have been taken with the decoration. If possible, ask for the independent room on the seashore; slightly more expensive, it is however more comfortable and has a wonderful view. The inn is reputed for its excellent cooking.

• Pointe d'Esny – Blue Bay

Practically the only drawback in staying near the airport is the noise of the airplanes at certain times during the day. This is however by no means unbearable and there is no air-traffic at night.

US$30-55

Villa Chantauvent Guesthouse, coast road, Pointe d'Esny, ☎ /Fax 631 9614 – 15rm This guesthouse, run by a Franco-Mauritian who make guests feel they are one of the family, is situated in a real campement with a superb ravenala wood roof. The timber patio opens directly onto the beach. The establishment has 9 simple, but clean and comfortable rooms with views of the ocean (with or without balcony). On the ground floor there is a little living-room area with a TV and a pleasant dining room where guests can have breakfast and sometimes dinner (wonderful Mauritian home cooking). There are also four larger, more luxurious, independent rooms with a kitchen but without a view, on the other side of the road.

US$50-80

Villas Le Guerlande, coast road, Pointe d'Esny, ☎ 631 9882 or ☎ /Fax 631 9225 – 14rm Modern well-equipped, comfortable independent bungalows for 2 or 4 people, with or without kitchens. Private terrace overlooking the sea. Totally calm and what appears to be an endless beach. A few cheaper rooms are available on the other side of the road.

Villa Chantemer, coast road, ☎ 631 9688, Fax 464 3964 – 4rm Tastefully decorated guest rooms in a sophisticated Indo-Mauritian style symbolise the individuality of this establishment that prefers to choose its guests and seeks to radically set itself apart from its traditional counterparts. Large or small, with or without kitchen or terrace, each room has its own individual style and charm The owner of this magical site can organise water sports for guests, together with excursions and transport to town for dinner. Meals are available (on request) for guests on certain evenings. Warm, personal welcome.

US$75-110

Blue Lagoon Beach Hotel, coast road, Blue Bay, ☎ 631 9105, Fax 631 9045, blbhotel@intnet.mu – 72rm This brand-new, luxurious, comfortable resort is one of the best located on the island, with the long unspoilt beach of Pointe d'Esny on one side and the calm little Blue Bay beach on the other. Only the noise of aircraft disturb the peace and quiet of this little corner of paradise.

US$100-120

La Croix du Sud Holiday Village, coast road, Pointe Jérôme, ☎ 631 9505, Fax 631 9603, croixsud@intnet.mu – 111rm Located between Mahébourg and Pointe d'Esny, this holiday village was built around a vast lagoon which is perfect for water sports. Luxurious rooms with terraces, located in red-and-white two-story bungalows.

WHERE TO EAT

As it is relatively undeveloped compared to the rest of the island, the east coast does not have many restaurants. But as most of the larger hotels make Half-board only, this is not such a problem.

• Belle Mare

US$2-8

Empereur, coast road (after the Pointe de Flacq crossroads), ☎ 415 1254. Lunch and dinner; closed Wednesdays. Snacks, Chinese and Creole cooking. Small, simple dining room with a few terrace tables. Take-away also available.

Symon's, next door to the above, ☎ 415 1135. Lunch and dinner. Same type of menu but the indoor room is airier and opens onto a thatched-roof terrace. Take-away meals also available.

• Bambou Virieux

US$7-15

Le Barachois, coast road, Anse Bambou, ☎ 634 5708/634 5643. Lunch and dinner (book for the evenings). Little straw huts dotted on the beach by the roadside serve the establishment's speciality, crab. The crab is chosen on the spot out of the *barachois*, that said, it is difficult to find crab more expensive on the island than that sold here and there is a wide-range of other much less exorbitant seafood.

• Trou d'Eau Douce

US$4-15

Resto 7, turn left on leaving Eau Douce southbound, ☎ 419 2766. Lunch and dinner. Small family restaurant which also organises excursions to Île aux Cerfs. Indian, Creole and Chinese cooking in pleasant surroundings.

Chez Tino, Royal Rd, ☎ 419 2769. Lunch and dinner; closed Monday evenings. Set on the roadside, this restaurant serves good, honest Mauritian cooking, and although a little gloomy during the day, it bursts into life at night. *Séga* rhythms play while you dig into a venison cari or a Creole langouste (house specialities) or delicious garlic camarons. Excellent and very reasonably priced.

• Anse Jonchée

US$12-20

Le Panoramour, Domaine du Chasseur, ☎ 634 5907 Open all day. A good restaurant that is well worth the 1km uphill walk, even if only for the superb terrace overlooking the coast and the lagoon. All the produce, venison or boar cari, salad of palmhearts and desserts, is home grown.

Le Jasmin de Nuit, Domaine de l'Ylang-Ylang, ☎ 634 5668 CC Lunch only. Hidden in a delightful tropical garden, this restaurant has a lovely view over the whole domain. The cuisine is also worth the detour: poultry livers in aspic, ostrich meat or vegetarian meals, and some delicious home-grown coffee. If you do not feel up to eating, take a seat on the charming terrace and try one of their mouth-watering fresh fruit cocktails.

• Mahébourg

Under US$3

Le Palais de la Soif, rue du Flamant (near the market). Tasty little snacks: samoussas, pastries and dhal puri.

Pâtisserie moderne, boulangerie et salon de thé Ronghen Pailly, corner of rue du Flamand and rue de Maurice (opposite the Odeon cinema). All sorts of pastries. Do not miss the banana pie.

US$3-10

Talk of the Village, Dragon de Chine restaurant, rue Flamand (opposite the market), ☎ 631 5697. Lunch and dinner. Unpretentious, little restaurant run by Chinese. Pleasant terrace opposite the market. Chinese, Mauritian and European cooking. Seafood and fish specialities.

Le Vacancier, rue Swami Sivananda (coast road, at the end of rue du Chaland), ☎ 631 9454. Lunch and dinner. Same cooking and management as the above. Delightful terrace, not as busy or noisy as the former, on the seafront with a view over the lagoon. Attentive service.

Monte Carlo, rue La Passe, Pointe des Régates, ☎ 631 7449. Breakfast, lunch and dinner. Near the bus station, a small restaurant with good home cooking at decent prices. Warm welcome and efficient service. Only shortcomings: limited choice of desserts and rather unpleasant background music.

US$10-20

Le Phare, rue Shivananda, ☎ 631 9728 CC Lunch and dinner; closed Thursday evenings. A nice little restaurant on the seashore with good Mauritian specialities and a few well-prepared European dishes. A rare luxury: the wine menu makes it possible to drink wine with the meal. Worth a visit.

Maïda Mount (chez Raymond), rue de la Bourdonnais (next to the market), ☎ 631 8563. Lunch and dinner; closed Sundays and in July. European, Mauritian and Chinese dishes, Swiss specialities, fresh grilled fish (simply divine), crunchy potato fries. Simple, tasty cooking prepared with flair by a gourmet cook, who is Swiss and married to a Mauritian. A small room with fish, coral and shells embedded in the blue walls. In this maritime setting, the friendly, but discreet owner knows how to make your mouth water without being over-pushy. Relaxed, but attentive and excellent service. Local and cosmopolitan clientele.

Le Sirius, coast road, La Chaux. ☎ 631 8906. Lunch and dinner; closed Sundays. More elegant and expensive than the previous establishment. This restaurant, located on the coast road as you leave Mahébourg, is run by a Belgian who offers a varied menu of fish, seafood, grilled meat, Mauritian and traditional "European" dishes. The delicious coq au vin, rabbit in mustard sauce and osso bucco and pleasant surroundings (oak-beam ceiling) are most appreciated among the island's Franco-Mauritian population. Good service and decent cooking.

• Blue Bay

US$7-15

Le Bougainville, coast road, ☎ 631 8299. Lunch and dinner. Reservations advisable. Another Swiss opened up this restaurant right at the end of Blue Bay. A romantic terrace under a ravenala roof, where diners can enjoy good Mauritian and European cuisine by candle-light to the tune of discreet jazz music. A few yards away from the public beach, the pizzas and salads available all day long are also very popular.

Le Jardin Créole, Pointe d'Esny, ☎ 631 5801. Lunch and dinner. An excellent restaurant with great value for money. Stylishly decorated in pastel colours which add to the refined atmosphere. Discrete, efficient service, with a varied menu of Créole dishes, pizzas and French cooking. A bit noisy, the terrace is nonetheless very pleasant.

East Coast

WHERE TO HAVE A DRINK

Le Café Créole, Jardin Créole bar, Pointe d'Esny, ☎ 631 5801. A European-style café with a cosy, intimate ambiance and good music. Delicious Ti'Punch not to be missed. Have a drink here before dinner, perhaps prior to eating upstairs. See above "Where to eat".

SPORTS AND PASTIMES

Excursions – The majority of travel agencies on the east coast organise day trips to Île aux Cerfs and other nearby islands (Île de la Passe, Île aux Fouquets, Île aux Aigrettes). Prices range from Rs400 to 500 per person, generally including drinks and food. It is also possible to charter a boat from one of the local fishermen, particularly around Mahébourg. Ask at your hotel. Most of the larger agencies have a counter at the airport as well as in the larger hotels.
Bateau Vicky, Trou d'Eau Douce, ☎ 419 2902. Shuttle service to Île aux Cerfs or day trips with barbecue. One of the most reasonably priced.
Croisières Turquoises, Riche En Eau. Day trips aboard a catamaran (buffet on board), leaving Pointe d'Esny. The boat stops at Île aux Cerfs, after having covered Mahébourg bay and Vieux Grand Port. Information from "La Croix du Sud" Hotel, ☎ 631 9835.
Croisière Océane, Trou d'Eau Douce, ☎ 416 2767 or 423 9659. Made to measure group or individual cruises along the East Coast.
Gérard Etienne Group, Mahébourg, ☎ 631 0434/499 5087. Mahébourg's best known address. This friendly Mauritian will take you to any island of your choice (Cerfs, Passe, Vacoas, Phare) and treat you to lunch on the beach. Half-day or full day trips.

Scuba diving – The best season to go scuba diving on the east coast is between September and May, in winter it's cooler and the waters are murkier. The best sites: "Roche Zozo", east of Pointe de Flacq, "Lobster Canyon" an area rich in fish and the shipwrecked Sirius in Grand Port bay (government permits must be obtained).
Cap Divers, Belle Mare Hotel, Poste de Flacq, ☎ 413 2515.
St-Géran Diving Center, St-Géran Hotel, Poste de Flacq, ☎ 415 1825.
Pierre Sport Diving, Touessrok Hotel, Trou d'Eau Douce, ☎ 419 2451. Dives from Rs800 to 1000, night dives Rs1200. Serious centre. Mario, the manager, is also quite a character.
Coral Dive, La Croix du Sud Hotel, Pointe d'Esny. ☎ 631 9505.
Coral Garden, Pointe d'Esny, ☎ 631 9614/631 5216, next to Villa Chantavent. A small, very laid-back centre with two dives a day at 9am and 2pm (from Rs700, decreasing depending on the number of dives). Also organise night dives (Rs850) and water-skiing (Rs700 for 30min).

Under-water walking – ***Alpha 2***, departures from the "Empereur" snack-bar, coast road, Belle Mare.

Golf courses – ***St-Géran***, Poste de Flacq.
Belle Mare beach, Belle Mare, ☎ 415 1083.

SHOPPING

Most of the coast's boutiques are in Mahébourg, Centre de Flacq and Trou d'Eau Douce. They stock a variety of Indian crafts, fabric, clothes, pareos, bags, t-shirts and other tourist souvenirs. Many are closed on Thursday afternoons.

THE SOUTH★★

MAHÉBOURG TO BAIE DU CAP

130km circuit -Allow a whole day.
Cool, damp climate - Map p 318-319

Not to be missed

Lunch at Le Chamarel Restaurant overlooking the lagoon.
Coastal drive to Gris-Gris and The Weeping Rock / La Roche qui Pleure.

And remember...

Leave early to complete the circuit in daylight.
The only hotel is situated at Pointe aux Roches.
Seek advice from the locals as to where it is safe to swim.
Wear plastic shoes when bathing.

The southern part of Mauritius contains some of the island's wildest scenery. Heavy downpours and constant winds blow cool air in from the southeast. More so than on the eastern side, this scarcely populated land is remote enough from the overcrowded seaside resorts in the northwest to preserve genuine identity. The hilly interior provides ample opportunity for long hikes and picturesque drives with breathtaking views over the surrounding countryside; the coast, meanwhile, is peppered with unspoilt fishing villages, rocky beaches with basalt cliffs worn by the trade winds and sculpted by the ocean swell. In between, the endless fields of sugarcane tremble in the wind, punctuated, here and there, by tall chimneys attached to pioneering – but long since obsolete – refineries.

Inland from Mahébourg to Baie du Cap★★

Approx 60km

■ **Mahébourg** – *See chapter on the East Coast: p 301.*

Head out of Mahébourg over Cavendish Bridge and through Ville Noire. Then take the B7 to Bel Air and on to Riche en Eau.

The road cuts through fields planted with endless rows of pineapples, potatoes and other vegetables, followed by great stretches of sugarcane. The cane is cut over several months (June to December), during which time the roads are busy with heavily-loaded trucks ferrying the harvest to the refineries and back. All along the roadside, birds may be seen pecking at the crushed cane stems to drink-up the sugary sap. Various chimneys across the landscape exhale large billowing clouds of black smoke blocking out the sunshine and filling the air with the delicious aroma of hot caramel.

■ **Riche en Eau** – This well-kept village belongs to the Riche en Eau sugar refinery. The neat-looking houses accommodate the factory foremen and their families, whereas the more rudimentary ones house the workers. As the road to St-Hubert heads past the last houses, you will see an avenue of latanier palms running off on the right leading up to a superb colonial villa belonging to the owner, and referred to by the local Mauritians as **La Grande Cage**★.

Go back to the mini-roundabout and turn right along the B7 bound for New Grove. At the junction with the A10, turn right towards Rose Belle; after driving through Rose Belle, turn left along the B81. At Beau Climat, follow the A9 for a short distance before turning right on to the B88. After Bois Chéri, turn left.

■ **Bois Chéri*** – At last the fields of sugarcane give way to plantations of a different kind. This time the hills are covered with parallel rows of dark green tea bushes – the only such plantation on the island.

JF Galmiche

Tea pickers at Bois Chéri

Tea Factory *(Variable opening times depending on the tea harvest: usually open, Monday to Friday, 9am-3.30pm, Saturday, 9am-12noon. Closed Sundays. Entrance fee inclusive of tea tasting. Additional attractions include the glass-houses containing anthurium and vanilla creepers, and the colonial house at St-Aubin where you can have lunch ☎ 626 1513).*

The name Bois Chéri is used to denote the market town, the factory and the tea it produces there. A visit to the factory entails learning about the cultivation and subsequent production of tea. As soon as the leaves have been picked, they are aerated and dried. The following day, the tea is crushed and fermented on a heated conveyor-belt for at least an hour; having turned a brown colour, the tea is baked in an oven at 60°C for ten minutes. After being sorted, sieved and graded, it is stored in huge silos for about 25 days until the flavours have had a chance to develop properly. It is at this point, just before being packaged, that the tea is flavoured with the addition of scented vanilla or bergamot oil.

At the end of the factory tour, visitors are invited to a tea-tasting. All varieties of tea produced by the factory are on sale in the shop.

Follow the B88 for a few kilometres.

When the tea plantations eventually peter out, the countryside dramatically changes to thick forests populated by pines, bamboo, wild vines, tree ferns and hibiscus, where deer and macaque monkeys roam.

■ **Grand Bassin** (Ganga Talao) – *No charge. The small booth beside the car-park sells religious images and cold drinks.* The site itself is of little interest, but the atmosphere that prevails there is well worth a detour.

For the Hindus in the area, the waters of this volcanic lake have become synonymous with those of the Ganges *(Ganga)* – the sacred river considered to be the mother of India. According to the legend, Shiva and his wife Parvati were flying over Mauritius and marvelling at its beauty, when a few drops of precious water fell from the vessel containing the water of the Ganges he was carrying on his head. As soon as the droplets fell down onto the earth, the extinct crater was transformed into a lake. So this place came to be regarded as sacred and the object of pilgrimages so that the faithful might come and collect the water and offer it up to the god Shiva.

J. P. Durand/DIAF

Purification ritual during the Festival of Maha Shivaratree

Almost half the island's population joins in with the annual celebrations in January or February (the thirteenth day of the month of *Magha*) associated with the **Festival of Maha Shivaratree** (Shiva's Great Night). During five consecutive days and nights, an estimated 500 000 people come to the lake bearing a *kanwar* on their shoulders, consisting of a small temple made of bamboo, decorated with flowers, coloured paper, pieces of shiny plastic and pictures of Shiva. The faithful immerse themselves in the holy water of the lake and then pour it on Shiva's *lingam* *(see p 209* Hindu Festivals).

Even if your visit does not coincide with the annual festival, the lakeside is always busy with people undertaking some kind of ritual or other on a daily basis.

In one temple, worshippers place their offerings of fruit and flowers on the altar before stepping aside to light a candle on the tray of offerings and walking backwards out of the sacred area.

Outside the entrance to the **main temple** guarded by a statue of the bull *Nandi* that Shiva once rode, some worshippers incant their prayers while walking around each of the nine planets; some chant their invocations before Shiva's *lingam* that is surmounted by a cobra and clouded in the heavy smell of burning incense. Some, meanwhile, turn their attentions to other Hindu divinities like Krishna, Parvati Buddha.

Piton Grand Bassin towers over the lake from 702m. A long stairway winds its way to the summit, where a small temple has been erected and dedicated to Hanuman (the deity with the head of a monkey and the body of a human). The place is usually overrun by monkeys who come here to steal bananas and coconuts left by devout pilgrims. In clear weather a fine **view**★ extends over the surrounding countryside.

Continue westwards along the road for 2.4km until you reach the Pétrin crossroads: turn left, and head due south. At the mini-roundabout, keep right along the tarmac road.

▪ **Parc national de la Plaine Champagne**★ – The rugged but lush plateau rises in places to a height of 750m. The area is covered with thick heather, stunted trees entwined with wild vine and a host of rare hardwoods – colophant, takamaka, tambalacoque, camphor, sideroxylon *(bois de natte)*, black wood, iron sideroxylon *(bois de fer)* etc. This precious patch of indigenous vegetation provides a rare habitat for a variety of endangered birds including the last surviving kestrels (notably those known locally as *mange poule* or "chicken eaters"), *merles cuisiniers* (blackbirds) and pink pigeons (successfully bred in the UK at the Jersey Zoo and reintroduced into the wild) as well as monkeys and deer. In winter, the roadside hedges are full of delicious Chinese guavas (red and yellow fruit).

After the first sign for "Restaurant-Bar Varangue-sur-Morne", another provides indications to the **View Point Black River Gorges**** *(Remember not to leave anything in the car).* A short path (150m) leads to a panoramic platform from which a broad view pans out across the thickly forested valley dotted with **waterfalls**.

Just after the exit from the Plaine Champagne National Park, the road engages in a sharp hairpin bend from which a fine **view**** extends to Morne Brabant and the sea glistening off the southwestern coast *(turn off the road and into the purpose-built lay-by). The road winds tortuously downhill to Chamarel which is also accessible from Baie du Cap or Grande Case Noyale.*

■ **Chamarel**** – The vegetation along the side of the road radically changes as you drop in altitude and get ever further from the Plaine Campagne. Among the main species growing here, you may recognise the traveller's palm, aloes and pandanus (used to make basketware). From Chamarel onwards, the landscape is once more given over to sugarcane plantations, relieved here and there by patches of banana trees and flourishing hedges of garish-coloured bougainvillaea.

The modest Creole mountain hamlet is dominated by the tall mass of **Piton de la Petite Rivière Noire** – the island's tallest peak that rises to 828m. For much of the year all is quiet here, although on 15 August, Catholic pilgrims stream in from far and wide to join in the celebrations of the Feast of The Assumption at the **Church of St Anne**.

Turn left past the church following signs for Terres de Couleurs and Baie du Cap. A short way further on, a dirt track forks off to the right for 3km.

The dirt track, lined with bottle and royal palms, cuts through fields of sugarcane, vetiver and coffee.

After circa 1km, as the track sweeps round in a broad bend, you will see on the left-hand side the **Cascade Chamarel***, a wonderful 100m waterfall lost among the thick and luxuriant vegetation. Eventually the track comes out at **Terres de Couleurs*** *(Open daily, 7am-5.30pm. Entrance fee. Car-park)* – an open area of undulating red-coloured dunes surrounded by green hills.

What makes this geological phenomenon so unique is how the hues seem to vary according to the light, humidity and angle of vision. Although the tones of colour range across the whole spectrum through various shades of ochre yellow, mauvy blue, coppery green, burnt amber and iron reds, you should not be deceived into expecting to see all seven distinctive colours of the rainbow. Scientifically, this feature has been brought about as a result of overlying layers of volcanic ash being compacted into hard mounds, and laid bare by erosion. The variations in colour, and the fact that the soil tends naturally to separate out as it settles, relate to the disparity in density and concentration of metal oxides contained in the volcanic fallout.

If you wish to go back to the west coast, return to Chamarel and follow the road to Case Noyale.

The road meanders down to Case Noyale, providing a series of unforgettable **views★★★** of the lagoon.

If you wish to continue the excursion around the south coast before returning to Mahébourg, turn right after driving back to the main road from Terres des Couleurs on to Baie du Cap. Do drive carefully keeping well into the left-hand side of the road during the sugarcane harvest season (June to December), so as to avoid the heavily-loaded trucks speeding along.

The road to Baie du Cap picks its way through the undulating sugarcane plantations owned by the Bel Ombre sugar refinery, rooted in a distinctively red soil. Lower down, it cuts across a magnificent jungle of mango trees, traveller's palms, flamboyants, banana trees, eucalyptus and cypress, giving way occasionally to a cleared area with **views** panning out to the sea. Before finally reaching Baie du Cap, the road passes through **Choisy** and past a colourful **Tamil Temple**.

The coast between Baie du Cap and Mahébourg★★

Approx 70km

The coastal road hugging the southern shore of the island sometimes deviates a short way inland along a water course, before winding its way eastwards through the vast stretches of sugarcane rustling in the breeze, as far as the eye can see.

The road from Chamarel comes out onto the coast level with the peaceful village of **Baie du Cap** populated by some 3 000 inhabitants including fishermen, smallholders and factory workers employed at the Bel Ombre sugar refinery. It is a pretty place ensconced between the sea and the mountains, dotted with colourful corrugated-iron houses surrounded by fertile gardens full of flowers.

Turn left along the coast road (B9), in the direction of Souillac.

Bel Ombre boasts a magnificent beach and clear turquoise water in the lee of a coral reef. The other attraction, the **sugar refinery**, is unfortunately closed to the public. A tour of the works provides a rare insight into the different stages of production, from the receipt of the freshly cut cane to the end product, all to the delicious aroma of boiled molasses.

A breach in the coral barrier reef opposite **Jacotet Bay** allows powerful – and potentially dangerous – currents to detract from the joys of a swim. Ahead sits **l'Îlot Sancho**, a small coral islet covered in bushes, which becomes accessible on foot at low tide from Ste Marie (on the right after the bridge).

Before reaching the wild and long unspoilt beach at **Pointe aux Roches**, the road passes a **seamen's cemetery**. Among the casuarinas which line the shore nestles the only hotel on the south coast *(see p 321 Where to stay)*. A concrete lookout provides an attractive **view★** of the coast lashed, at high tide, by the surf that has already crashed over the offshore reef. When the conditions are suitably calm, fishermen can be seen casting their nets right across the lagoon.

More beautiful sand **beaches** line the shore at **Pomponnette** and **Riambel**, these are best enjoyed during the week because at weekends they become crowded with people engaged in the ritual family picnic.

At Riambel, turn left (Hindu temple) and head towards Surinam. Follow the little road leading out from the centre of the village centre, by the taxi rank. The road peters into a stony dirt track as it progresses through the sugarcane. Beyond the small bridge

M Lemerle/MICHELIN

Terres de couleurs outside Chamarel

straddling the stream, level with the 2 little tombstones on the left, fork right and continue for about 500m. Park the car and walk over to the steps cut into the earth that lead down past a waterfall on the right. The alternative route from Souillac to the waterfalls, is longer, in a worse condition and badly sign-posted so you run the risk of getting lost and maybe having to walk 1km or more to find your way out of the maze.

An expedition inland to the **Rochester Falls*** which lie up the Savanne river makes for an enjoyably refreshing outing. *(Remember not to leave anything in the car. Do not forget to take insect repellent).*

Tectonic movement and erosion by the river have worn the basalt into long vertical cubic columns, over which the water tumbles in a staggered series of falls, down into a hollow pool where you can have a swim.

Drive back to the centre of Surinam, and turn left to Souillac.

▪ **Souillac*** – This seaside community comprises a number of fishermen, various small-time farmers and factory workers from the nearby St-Aubin Terracine sugar refinery. In times past, the little fishing **harbour** nestling at the mouth of the Savanne River, used to be much busier especially when boats were used to transport the refined sugar to large depots in the capital.
Continue along the coast to the **Telfair Municipal Garden** – an agreeable spot shaded by Indian almond and banyan trees, overlooking the sea – and then on to the **Robert Edward Hart Memorial Museum** or **Nef** *(Open Mondays and Wednesdays to Fridays, 9am-4pm; Saturdays and Sundays, 9am-12noon.*

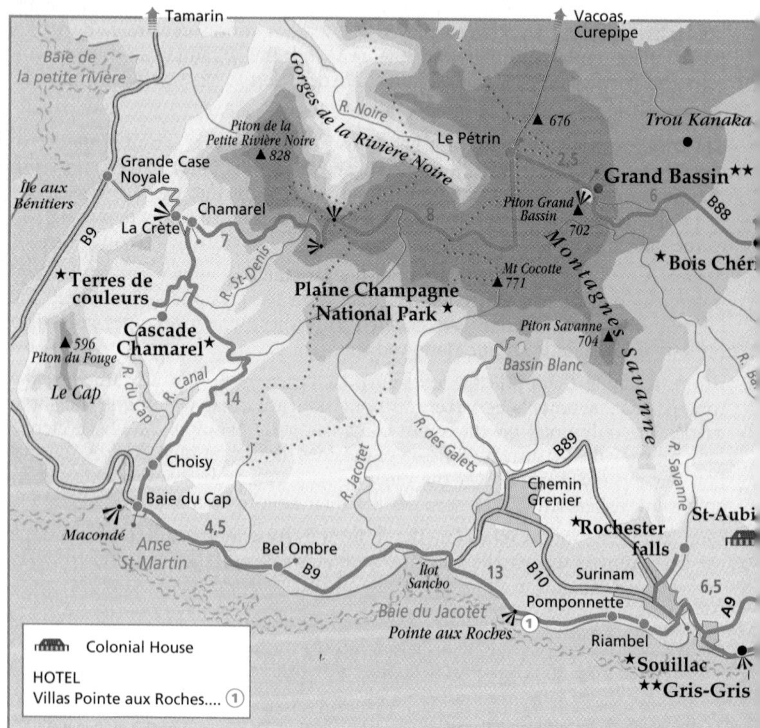

Closed Wednesdays and public holidays. No charge). The Mauritian poet Robert Edward Hart (1891-1954) retired to this modest seaside residence or *campement* in 1941 after it was given to him by close friends for his 50th birthday. After his death, the pretty little house built of concrete breeze-blocks and covered with coral, was converted into a museum that opened in 1967 housing the furniture and personal effects of the poet including treasured portraits, paintings, a violin, a hat, old postcards and a collection of shells and corals.

Turn towards the right when you come out of the museum and head for the Gris-Gris public beach (bathing dangerous) a few hundred metres further along the shoreline.

Breaches in the offshore barrier reef expose this section of the coast to the full fury of the ocean that crashes up against the **Gris-Gris cliffs**** with a great roar. A line of pavilions and benches have been placed here to allow people to come and contemplate the sea and watch the spray and the white foam play against the swirling waves of deep green and menacingly dark blue water.

The footpath leading up and along the edge of the cliff provides one with a splendid **panorama***** over the untamed scenery falling steeply down towards the sea below. The Weeping Rock or **Roche qui Pleure** jutting out of the swell up ahead is so called because of the sound made by the water that is forced into each crevice and then sucked back out again; in so doing, the rocks appear to weep.

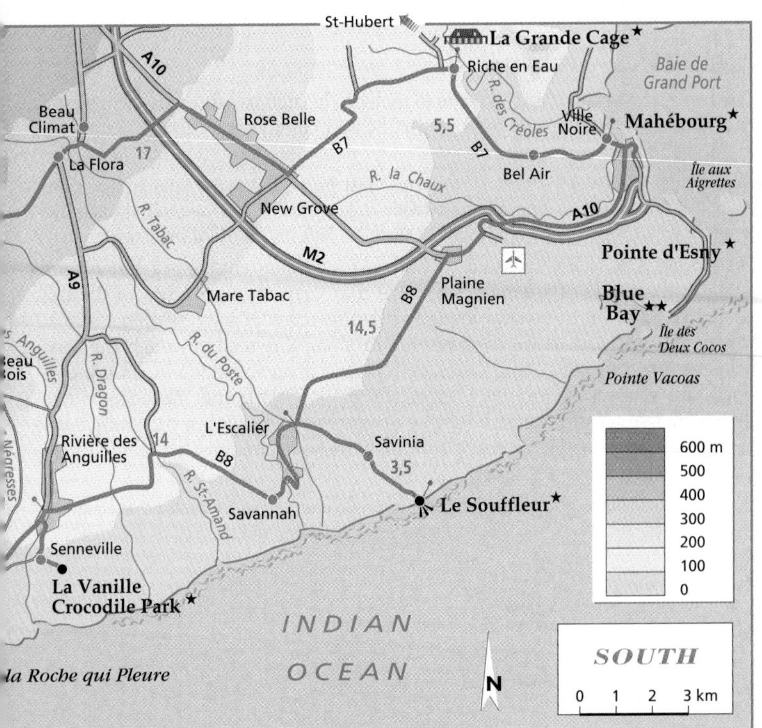

Walk back to the car and drive off along the A9 that now turns inland across the cane fields towards the back-country.

A short diversion from the main road up the track on the left provides one with a quick glimpse of the lovely **St-Aubin homestead** dating from 1819. Back on track, the road comes to the typical hamlet of **Rivière des Anguilles / Eel River** with a predominantly Hindu population. An endearing liveliness animates the main street with its brightly clad tailors' shops, jewellers and cloth merchants. This might be a good place to stop off and sample the local fare: *gâteaux piment*, samossas and *dholl puri* before continuing onwards.

Turn right towards Senneville just before the police station, and then left by the "Senneville Store". A signpost in among the cane plantations appears on the left offering directions to "La Vanille", at the next fork keep right (2km from the centre of Rivière des Anguilles)

■ **La Vanille Crocodile Park**★ – *(☎ 626 2503 Open daily, 9.30am-5pm. Entry fee. 1hr guided tour. Take insect repellent.).* Visitors are invited to wander freely among the bamboo, coconut palms and exotic orchids growing in this 6 hectare area of tropical parkland, in search of the animals collected from across the Mascarene Islands and Africa, and the enclosures containing crocodiles from Madagascar and iguanas from Central America, green lizards and giant tortoises from the Seychelles, alligators from Brazil, Japanese marbled carp, grass snakes and tame parrots from Mauritius.

If the visit has sharpened your appetite, why not order a large crocodile steak in the restaurant!

Go back to Rivière des Anguilles and turn right on to the B8.

The two main landmarks in **Savannah** include the archway through the majestic banyan trees straddling the road, and a disused chimney on the right, attached to an abandoned sugar refinery.

Once in the village of L'Escalier, turn right just before the police station signed for Savinia-le-Souffleur. Go round the Barraque sugar refinery and continue through the former Savinia sugar plant. Directions to the blow hole are provided by arrows.

On the way, it is not unusual to find farm-workers enjoying a lunch-time siesta in the shade of a banyan tree. You may even encounter one of the last ox-drawn carts on the island loaded with sugarcane at harvest time.

Having covered a distance of some 4.5km along dirt roads through the cane fields, you come to the island's most remote and unspoilt stretch of **coastline**★★. There are no limpid turquoise lagoons here, only dark and menacing waves driven by the ocean beyond breaking against the rocks with a deafening roar. Inevitably, the drama of the scene and the **blow hole**★ are most apparent at high tide, and when the sea is rough.

Go back to the village of L'Escalier, and rejoin the B8 after the police station that continues to Plaine Magnien, where you will find signs for Mahébourg and the A10 on the right.

Making the most of the South

GETTING THERE

By car– Little roads wind up and down the hilly interior and one road borders practically the whole south coastline. Finding one's way around is not always easy. It is possible to rent cars, but we recommend hiring a taxi for a day.

By bus – The interior of the country is very poorly served. Only three buses a day go to Grand Bassin and it is practically impossible to follow the recommended itinerary. Around the coast, there is a bus between Baie du Cap and Souillac and another from Souillac to Mahébourg. These are slow and few and far between. Once at Souillac you can catch another bus to Port Louis and Curepipe.

ADDRESS BOOK

Banks and money– All the main towns have at least one bank and cash dispensers are becoming more and more commonplace.

Post Office – Most villages have a post office.

Telephone – All the major towns have card or coin operated public phone boxes.

Health – If you fall ill, it is best to go to one of the large hotels on the west coast, to Rose Belle hospital or to a doctor in Mahébourg.

WHERE TO STAY

• Pointe aux roches

US$30-45

Villas Pointe aux Roches, coast road, Chemin Grenier ☎ 625 5112, Fax 625 6110, paroches@intnet.mu – 29rm CC The only hotel in the south of Mauritius. Located on a deserted beach where the waves pound the coral reef relentlessly. The wild, unspoilt beauty of this site and superb calm try their best to make up for the hotel's lack of charm. Rooms or independent bungalows, with kitchen.

WHERE TO EAT

• Plaine Champagne

US$12-25

Le Chamarel, la Crête, Chamarel. ☎ 683 6421 CC Lunch only, closed Sundays. Reservations advisable. Touristy due to its situation on the slopes of the Rivère Noire mountains. A superb, shady terrace overlooking the southwest coast offers diners one of the island's most beautiful views.

Varangue-sur-Morne, 110 Route Plaine Champagne, Chamarel. ☎ 683 6610/683 6010 CC Lunch (dinner reservations only). Popular with groups. Reservations advisable. Good French and Creole cuisine, if a little pricey. The exceptional site is however worth the chalet's prices: a large, airy terrace overlooks the stunning west coast and Morne Brabant lagoon.

• Riambel

US$1-5

Green Palm, coast road, ☎ 625 5016 CC Lunch and dinner. One of the south coast's few restaurants, in front of Riambel public beach. Fine for a quick snack or salad.

• Souillac

US$12-25

Le Batelage, Souillac Port, ☎ 625 6083 CC Lunch (dinner reservations only). Meals are served either on the terrace overlooking the picturesque port of Souillac or inside. Excellent seafood specialities (langouste, vieille rouge, camarons).

• Rivière des Anguilles

US$4-12

Le Crocodile Affamé (The Starving Crocodile), La Vanille Crocodile Park, ☎ 625 2503 CC Lunchtime only, same opening hours as the park. An opportunity to taste crocodile meat. Also serves pancakes and other simple dishes.

US$15-25

Le St-Aubin, St-Aubin, ☎ 626 1513 CC Lunch only. Sip a punch "on the house" as you relax on the veranda of this luxurious, old Creole house before you taste one of their excellent Creole specialties (set menu).

SHOPPING

Art Galleries – *L'Oasis*, coast road, ☎ 625 5330. Monday-Saturday, 9.30am-5.30pm; closed Sundays. A local artist exhibits her work, as well as that of friends. Lots of watercolours and abstract art.

WEST COAST★★

BAIE DU CAP TO FLIC EN FLAC

Approx 50km - Allow 2hr-3hr

Not to be missed

Game fishing expedition from Grande Rivière Noire (very expensive).
A swim off Morne beach or L'Île aux Bénitiers.

And remember...

Beware of sea currents in the lagoon,
even when the water looks nice and calm.
July and August are the best months for surfing in Tamarin Bay.

The west coast tends to be less crowded than the north despite its fine array of lovely (if tourist-ridden) beaches and picturesque fishing villages populated by fishermen, deer-farmers and salt-pan workers. The area is enclosed by a series of mountains, with the imposing Morne Brabant dominating the southern flank, and the chain of hills – including the peaks Vacoas and Rivière Noire – sealing-off the interior. The lagoon offers the best available conditions for water-sports as it is sheltered from strong currents and heavy swell by an offshore coral reef. Climatically, the region is subject to hot and dry weather that can be very pleasant in winter, but suffocating in summer.

Starting out from Baie du Cap, follow the B9 which runs parallel to the coast as it makes its way north. After a sharp hairpin bend, a sheer basalt outcrop rises sharply up ahead. This is the **Rocher de Macondé**, and from the small Catholic shrine (accessible by a stairway) at the top a great **view**★ extends out over the lagoon. For a brief moment, the road follows the course of the Du Cap River deviating away from the coast across the dry and arid countryside inland. Then it comes to a **ford** which after heavy rains, can be submerged by the swollen river.

Lying before you on the other side of the river is **La Prairie Beach**. After parking the car in the shade beneath the casuarinas, the beach provides an ideal spot for a picnic or a simple packed lunch although it is not really suitable for swimming. During the heat of the day, everything seems to come to a standstill save for a handful of coloured pirogues bobbing idly on the lagoon, and a horn sounded in the background heralding the whereabouts of a local market-gardener intent on selling his home-grown produce to villagers and householders along the roadside.

▪ **Morne Brabant Peninsula**★★ – The B9 continues through **Embrasure** – a small fishing community living in painted corrugated-iron shacks – as it heads eastwards to the tip of the Morne headland and then hugs the western side of the island *(illustration p 189)*.

This crooked finger-shaped protrusion of land pointing westwards towards Madagascar, is dominated by the Morne Brabant, a tall peak reaching 556m above sea-level. Its shoreline, however, is edged with several kilometres of sandy beach before giving way to what is considered to be the most beautiful blue **lagoon**★★★ of Mauritius.

A fatal mistake

The mountain was deemed a safe refuge by many runaway slaves because it was both remote and awkward to get to. According to legend, when slavery was eventually abolished in 1835, a number of the fugitives threw themselves off the top of the Morne after seeing soldiers approaching. Little did they know that instead of being charged with arresting these renegades, the soldiers were in fact bearing news of their freedom.

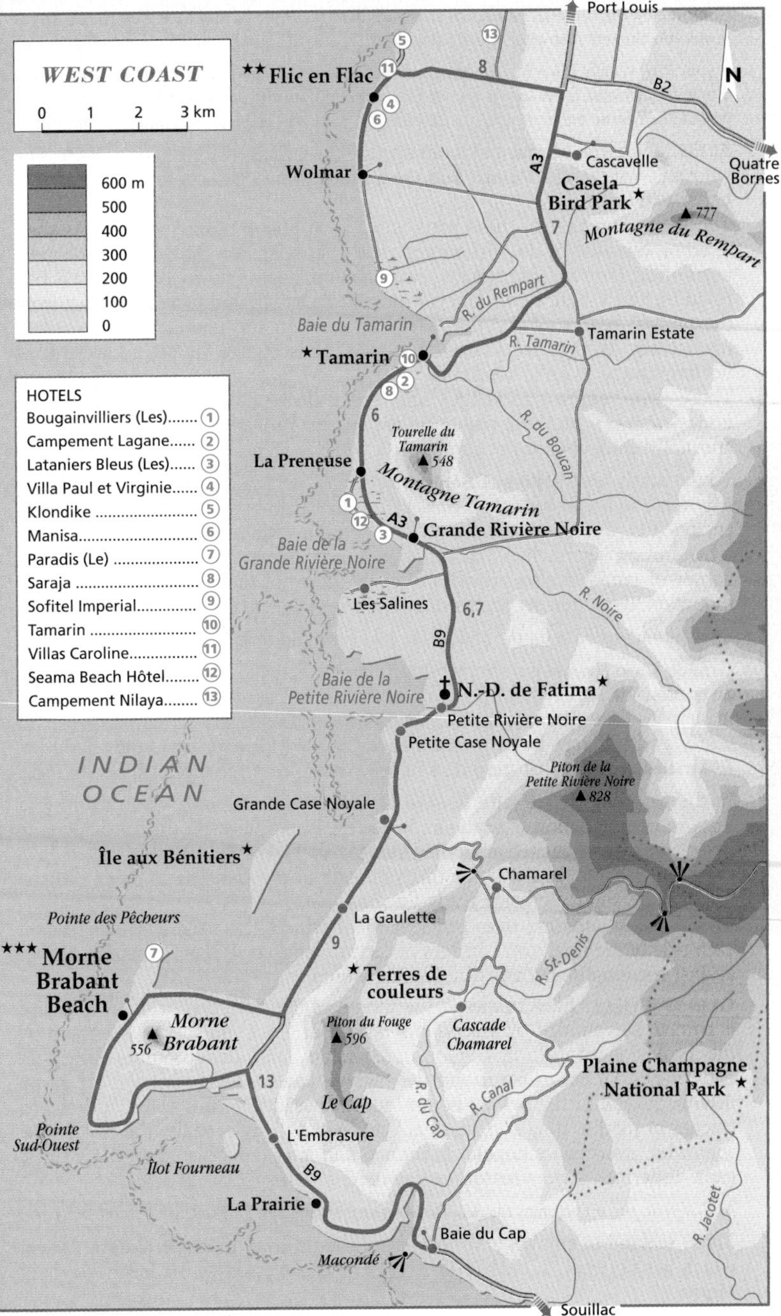
WEST COAST
0 1 2 3 km
600 m
500
400
300
200
100
0
HOTELS
Bougainvilliers (Les)....... 1
Campement Lagane...... 2
Lataniers Bleus (Les)...... 3
Villa Paul et Virginie...... 4
Klondike 5
Manisa............................ 6
Paradis (Le) 7
Saraja 8
Sofitel Imperial.............. 9
Tamarin 10
Villas Caroline................ 11
Seama Beach Hôtel........ 12
Campement Nilaya........ 13
Port Louis
N
B2
Quatre Bornes
★★ Flic en Flac
Wolmar
A3
Cascavelle
Casela Bird Park ★
▲777
Montagne du Rempart
R. du Rempart
Baie du Tamarin
★ Tamarin
Tamarin Estate
R. Tamarin
R. du Boucan
Tourelle du Tamarin ▲548
La Preneuse
Montagne Tamarin
Grande Rivière Noire
Baie de la Grande Rivière Noire
Les Salines
R. Noire
B9
Baie de la Petite Rivière Noire
N.-D. de Fatima ★
Petite Rivière Noire
Petite Case Noyale
Piton de la Petite Rivière Noire ▲828
INDIAN OCEAN
Grande Case Noyale
Île aux Bénitiers ★
Chamarel
Pointe des Pêcheurs
La Gaulette
R. St-Denis
★★★ Morne Brabant Beach
★ Terres de couleurs
Morne Brabant
556
Piton du Fouge ▲596
Cascade Chamarel
Plaine Champagne National Park ★
Le Cap
R. du Cap
R. Canal
Pointe Sud-Ouest
L'Embrasure
Îlot Fourneau
La Prairie
R. Jacotet
Baie du Cap
Macondé
Souillac

Continue on the B9 until you reach the road up to the Berjaya and Méridien Hotels (signposted on the left just after Morne Brabant).

If your hire-vehicle is a 4WD, or has good suspension, you can drive right around the Morne along a track that forks left at the foot the mountain on the outskirts of Embrasure (signposted "Le Morne public beach"). Alternatively, you can complete the circuit on horseback.

At the foot of the Morne and in among the casuarinas, there is a **deer park**. The wild and windswept **Pointe Sud-Ouest** meanwhile, attracts great numbers of hardy **wind-surfers**.
The main attraction of these parts is the long **public beach***** which is sheltered on one side by an offshore reef, and overlooked on the other by the great mass of the Morne. Unfortunately, this fabulous spot is slowly being encroached upon by newly-built resort hotels which, in time, will undoubtedly detract from the natural beauty of the finest seaside areas on the island. However, these unwelcome developments have done little to discourage the Mauritian families flocking to the place at weekends.
Those who enjoy snorkelling and scuba-diving will find plenty to see **underwater*****; for these waters are alive with a profusion of multicoloured fish and flourishing colonies of coral.

To the north lies the **Île aux Bénitiers*** *(excursions arranged through the local hotels, or privately with a fisherman from Gaulette)*; a tiny island bristling with coconut trees, encircled by a long continuous strip of beautiful white sand and populated by a handful of fishermen. What better spot for a swim and a lie in the sun! This corner of paradise also provides a lovely **view*** of the Morne and Mauritius' mountainous profile set against the sky.

After turning its back on the Morne, the B9 extends northwards.

Grande Case Noyale is a sleepy fishing village where the locals can be seen resting on a roadside bench shaded by an enormous banyan tree. Down on the sand, mangroves have spread, much to the delight of the scavenger hermit crabs and scurrying sand-crabs living there. Grande Case Noyale also marks the end of the **Chamarel road***** that meanders its way down from the mountains to the sea.

In the next hamlet – **Petite Rivière Noire** (Little Black River) – the majority of the Creole population is Catholic, hence the appearance on the left-hand side of an attractive thatched church dedicated to **Notre Dame de Fatima***. On closer inspection, you will see that one side of the building is open and the benches are aligned outside ready for mass.
An avenue of tamarind trees provides a little shade along the way, whereas on each side of the road, thick hedges of cactus plants act as a more reliable barrier against roaming **deer** than wire fencing would.

Grande Rivière Noire nestles at the mouth of the river after which the village is named, surrounded by acacias and tamarinds. Local prosperity is assured by the profusion of fish in the offshore waters, and this prompts the more entrepreneurial fisherman to tap the highly lucrative tourist market for **game fishing**. Several of the nearby hotels indeed specialise in this sport, and record catches of marlin, tuna and shark are celebrated in style. Sadly, the bay is now somewhat overrun by hopeful fishermen and anglers, and so only the keenest game fishermen have a reason to stay here.

At this point the B9 becomes the A3. Turn left at the road sign La Preneuse into the car-park.

Those seeking to enjoy a luxurious swim should head for **La Preneuse Beach**, which lies north of Grande Rivière Noire, and is blessed with a lovely **view*** of Morne.

When you come out of the car-park, turn left onto the A3 and continue to the village of Tamarin; just before the church, turn left.

■ **Tamarin**★ – The backdrop to this **village** is provided by the peaks of Rempart and Trois Mamelles, whereas before it spreads a lovely, wide and unspoilt bay, as yet mercifully preserved from tourist developments. There are a number of small family-run boarding houses (*see p 327* Where to stay).
To date, no hotels mar the outlook of this wonderful sandy **beach** at the mouth of the Tamarin River, and only Mauritians and tourists in-the-know come here with their surf-boards intent on enjoying the only big waves to break regularly on the shore (particularly in July and August). In the evening, groups of Mauritians gather on the beach and sing songs.

At the foot of the mountain Tourelle de Tamarin, the road runs beside a succession of **salt-pans**★. The scene is especially photogenic in the early morning, when the blue sky is mirrored in the rectangular stretches of shallow water and the women make the best use of the coolest time of the day to rake up the salt and empty it into large baskets. An old **lime kiln** provides a shaded spot for a well-earned rest as the sun rises high in the sky. The whole process is relatively straightforward. Sea-water is filtered and pumped into the pans and left to evaporate in the sun. The region's hot, dry weather enables these salt-works to produce enough salt to satisfy the island's entire requirement.

Follow the A3 for 7km in the direction of Flic en Flac until you come to the signs for the aviary on the right (marked with arrow).

■ **Casela Bird Park**★ – ☎ *452 0693/452 0694 Open daily, October to March, 9am-6pm; April to September, 9am-5pm. Entrance fee. Snack bar. Allow at least 1hr.*
Approximately 2 000 or so birds representing 150 different species (including various pigeons, Alexandrine parrots, hybrid lovebirds, sea eagles, sacred ibis, black-backed *radjah* and the aracacatoès from Timor) chirp away in their cages

Casela Bird Park

Collecting salt at Tamarin

M Lemerle / Michelin

among the magnificent tropical vegetation. Although every cage has a plaque with an illustration of the birds and a short text about them, it is still sometimes difficult to identify them. Despite attempts at making the cages as pleasant as possible for the birds, the arrangements of bleached wood, dry branches and black stones are not enough to make up for the accumulated mess and dirt, let alone the ugly concrete, inside some of these enormous aviaries.

Besides the birds, there are various enclosures containing a selection of **mammals** and other creatures from Africa, Australia and the Indian Ocean Islands (panthers, leopards, Bengal tigers, deer, macaco monkeys, ostriches, kangaroos, mongoose, giant tortoises, wild lemurs) as well as ducks, swans and glistening Koi carp.

Head along the A3 for 1.5km and turn left into Flic en Flac Road, which proceeds in a straight line downhill through the sugarcane plantations to the sea.

▪ **Flic en Flac** – A lovely golden **arc of sand****, lined with a long row of casuarinas, stretches around the turquoise waters of the bay into the distance where the massive bulk of Morne Brabant sits stolidly on the horizon. There are plenty of **multicoloured fish** here and so, equipped with a mask and a snorkel, it is easy to while away the hours in the water. It is important nonetheless to be aware that certain areas are subject to strong and dangerous currents.
The hamlet of Flic en Flac has managed to preserve its authenticity despite the proliferation of tourist facilities right on its doorstep. The neighbouring area of **Wolmar** for example, is entirely given over to tourism with ever increasing numbers of resort hotels, holiday homes, purpose-built apartments to let and restaurants jostling for space.

From here, the A3 continues to Port Louis.

This part of the coast has just about nothing worthy of note. The sea can be treacherous for swimming and the countryside is completely orientated towards the intensive production of sugarcane.

Making the most of the West Coast

GETTING THERE

By car – A charming little coast road links Morne Brabant and Port Louis. From the airport, take the motorway to Curepipe or Quatre Bornes, from where you can take a minor road down to the coast. Around an hour's drive.

By bus – A relatively decent bus service operates in the region, from the central towns. One bus service operates between Quatre Bornes (in the centre) and Baie du Cap (in the south) via the west coast towns. From Port Louis, you have to change at Quatre Bornes.

ADDRESS BOOK

Banks and money – Banks can be found in all the main seaside resorts, on the edge of the coast road or in hotels.

Mauritius Commercial Bank at Flic en Flac, opposite Chez Leslie restaurant.

Post Office – In all the main villages.

Telephone – In all the main seaside resorts (Grande Rivière Noire, Flic en Flac) and in the hotels.

Car rentals – Most hotels can find cars or bicycles for hire. Bicycles can also be rented at the entrance to Flic en Flac (ask at the restaurant "Chez Leslie", see p 329).
Reliable vehicles at reasonable rates can also be rented from:
Diplomat Car Hire and Tours, coast road, Flic en Flac, ☎ 250 4553/425 0980/453 9375. Two days minimum. Rates start at Rs800 for a small car and Rs900 for a larger model, mileage unlimited. Rates can be negotiated.

Itinéraire Limité, Royal Rd, Flic en Flac, ☎ 453 8475/453 9290. Vehicles from Rs1000, unlimited mileage. Negotiate rates if renting for several days.

Where to stay

• Morne Brabant

Over US$380

Le Paradis Hotel, Case Noyale, ☎ 450 5050, Fax 450 5140, parahot@intnet.mu – 293rm 18-hole golf course, casino and nightclub. Half-board compulsory. Located on the island's most beautiful beach, at the foot of Morne Brabant. The elegant architecture set amidst clumps of bougainvillea of this immense, luxury holiday village fit in perfectly with the exceptional natural site. Pleasant, tastefully-decorated rooms overlook the sea, the golf course and the Morne. It is also possible to rent luxury villas suited to a more secluded stay.

• Rivière Noire

US$45-60

Les Lataniers Bleus, Rivière Noire, ☎ 683 6541, Fax 683 6903, latableu@intnet.mu – 11rm The best value for money on the west coast. A warm welcome and a family atmosphere. Charming bungalows or a cosy Creole house provide accommodation in the heart of a quite delightful tropical garden. Guests can choose between beach or swimming- pool views, but the rooms close to the road should be avoided and, if possible ask for the "Casuarinas" bungalow that is situated right on the beach. Meals can be provided on request in the evenings. Staff can also organise outings to Bénitiers Island with a langouste lunch.

• La Preneuse

US$30-45

Auberge Les Bougainvilliers, La Preneuse, Rivière Noire, ☎ 683 6525, Fax 683 6332 – 4rm or This pleasant guesthouse offers relatively basic, but light and clean rooms on the first-floor patio of the family house. The garden leads to a little private beach, but the nearby La Preneuse beach is more suited to swimming. The establishment provides only breakfast, but there are quite a few restaurants in the vicinity. Warm welcome.

Seama Beach Hotel, La Preneuse, Rivière Noire, ☎ 683 6030/683 3031, Fax 683 6214 – 8rm Located right at the tip of the La Preneuse road, on the Rivière Noire side. The rooms are without charm and pretty basic, but the food's very decent.

• Tamarin Bay

US$10-20

Saraja Guesthouse, Anthurium Av, ☎ 683 6168 – 4rm Modest little guesthouse run by a charming Hindu family, in the heart of an unspoilt village as yet. Ideal for travellers who enjoy getting to know the inhabitants. The rooms are very plain and basic, but do have a little kitchen and a private balcony. Meals can be ordered on a day-to-day basis and can be served either on your balcony or in the family kitchen. Good, plentiful home cooking at ridiculous (low) prices. Popular among truck drivers.

Campement Lagane, main street (towards the beach), ☎ /Fax 683 6445 – 10rm Flats with kitchen and terrace for the most part. Basic but clean and functional. Relatively cramped, the success of your stay will largely depend on your room mates! At 100m from Tamarin beach, this value-for-money establishment is very popular among surfers. Young, relaxed, family atmosphere. The owner can find car rental deals at unbeatable prices.

US$30-40

Tamarin Hotel, ☎ 683 6581, Fax 683 6927, tamhot@intnet.mu – 40rm The austere atmosphere of this hotel, located on the peaceful Tamarin bay, is well-suited to the site's isolated position. The split-level rooms, arranged round a good-sized swimming pool, could do with being smartened up, but each has a pleasant terrace, from which the sea can sometimes be glimpsed through the casuarinas. The restaurant serves primarily good Chinese dishes, with a selection of European food and snacks. If you opt for the half-board formula, meals will vary between Creole, Chinese or European cuisine.

• Flic en Flac – Wolmar

US$30-40

The Nilaya, Safeland, Flic en Flac, ☎/Fax 453 9037, kitgraas@intnet.mu, – 6rm Lost in a maze of little streets, this little pink house would at first glance seem to have nothing to set it apart from its neighbours. However, once inside, a pretty little garden and small, extra clean one-room flats are quite delightful. The owners organise excursions and transport to and from the airport. Excellent value for money.

Villa Paul et Virginie, Sea Breeze Lane, ☎ 453 8537, Fax 453 – 14rm CC Small, unpretentious establishment, recently renovated. Some of the rooms, with balcony, overlook the casuarinas and the distant sea, others overlooking a little garden can be a bit stifling. Calm, set off from the main road. 1min from the beach.

US$60-75

Manisa Hotel, Coast Rd, ☎ 453 8558, Fax 453 8562, manias@intnet.mu – 50rm TV CC Separated from the beach by the road and the casuarinas, the more upmarket rooms are paradoxically less well-situated than the standard rooms, which are arranged round a flower garden with a small swimming pool.

US$75-125

Klondike Village Vacances, ☎ 453 8333, Fax 453 8337 – 33rm TV CC Half board compulsory. Extremely pleasant double rooms or family bungalows with kitchen and direct access to the beach. At the end of Flic en Flac beach, it's probably the quietest, if not the nicest, place to go swimming. Activities organised around the very decent-sized swimming-pool that almost looks as if it flows straight into the sea.

Villas Caroline Hotel, ☎ 453 8411, Fax 453 8144, caroline@intnet.mu – 70rm TV CC Half-board compulsory in summer. Ideally situated right on the long, sandy beach of Flic en Flac. A comfortable hotel, recognisable from afar by its red, iron roofs, that offers the facilities of a grand hotel at reasonable prices (slightly less expensive than the Klondike). All the rooms have a terrace on the seafront, but the view is sometimes hampered by unruly clumps of flowers. A few independent bungalows with kitchen. The dining room and orchestra are very pleasant and every week the hotel organises frenetic *séga* dancing.

Over US$155

Sofitel Imperial Hotel, coast road, Wolmar, ☎ 453 8700, Fax 453 8350, sofitel@bow.intnet.mu – 143rm TV CC 9-hole golf course. Half-board compulsory. An imposing Eastern-style architecture within which a superb swimming pool almost seems to be part of the actual building. The independent bungalows could be more romantically isolated, but one soon forgets the lack of seclusion to enjoy vivid sunsets seen over bougainvillea, coconut trees and casuarinas, with the Morne in the distance.

WHERE TO EAT

• Rivière Noire

US$7-15

Pavillon de Jade, Royal Rd, Rivière Noire, ☎ 416 2729 CC Lunch and dinner; generally closed on the first Sunday and three last Mondays of every month. Large, airy room on the first floor, over the street and a little terrace overlooking the cane fields on the other side. Typically Chinese setting, with lacquered screens, red tablecloths and assorted lanterns. Billiards. Good Hakka (Southern China) cuisine. Take-away. Pleasant welcome.

US$15-25

La Bonne Chute, La Preneuse, Rivière Noire. ☎ 683 6552 CC Lunch and dinner; closed Sundays. Candlelit dinners on the timber-floored room or in the pretty little garden outside. Unfortunately, the restaurant is a little too close to the nearby Caltex fuel station. Seafood and game specialties. Creole and European cooking.

• La Preneuse

US$4-12

Le Cabanon Créole, Royal Rd, ☎ 683 5783. Morning, noon and night. Barbecues Friday and Saturday evenings. A pretty blue-coloured restaurant serving highly commendable Mauritian cooking either in a small room or outdoors in the starlit garden. Take your own bottle, because the establishment doesn't have a licence.

• Flic en Flac

US$4-12

Chez Leslie, on the road into Flic en Flac, ☎ 453 8172 CC A few tables under a straw canopy on the roadside. A perfect place to try good, ordinary Creole cooking.

Chez Joe, Le Bois Noir, Nénuphar, ☎ 453 8820 CC Open all day; closed Thursdays. Just next door to Chez Leslie, an unpretentious establishment serving good European, Mauritian and Chinese cooking at reasonable prices. Popular among the locals.

Ah-Youn, Royal Rd, ☎ 453 9099 Open all day; closed Mondays. Situated on the roadside, this restaurant doesn't, at first glance, seem very appealing. However once seated on the terrace, overlooking the sea and after having tasted one of their delicious caris, you won't regret having stopped here. The bill will also prove a pleasant surprise.

Mer de Chine, Flic en Flac public beach, ☎ 453 8208. Lunch and dinner. Busiest at lunchtime. This is the place for a light snack at lunchtime rather than a full four-course meal. Complete with a shady terrace, it's the only restaurant on the beach. Chinese, European cuisine and seafood specialities.

Sea Breeze, coast road, ☎ 453 8143 CC Lunch and dinner; closed Tuesdays. Small, popular Peking restaurant, with a very mixed clientele. Excellent Chinese fondue.

WHERE TO HAVE A DRINK

• Tamarin

Tam Café, 7.30am-7.45pm. When you arrive in Tamarin from Flic en Flac, you will instantly recognise this little orange pastel café. Whether you stop for a bite to eat, a coffee or a cold drink, the hospitable Franco-Mauritian hosts make all their customers welcome. A favourite among Tamarin's surfing population. Relaxed atmosphere and reggae music. No alcohol.

LEISURE ACTIVITIES

Scuba diving – ***Méridien Diving Centre***, Le Morne, ☎ 450 5050.

Villas Caroline Diving Centre, Flic en Flac, ☎ 453 8450, szalay@intnet.mu Closed Sundays and bank holidays. Two dives a day, at 9.30am and 2.30pm, possibility of night dives. Around Rs800.

Klondike Diving Centre, Flic en Flac, ☎ 453 8211. Dives are Rs700 a dive, but prices decrease the more you dive. Two dives a day, at 9.30am and 1.30pm. Small groups are the best.

Sofitel Diving Centre, Wolmar, ☎ 453 8700.

Deep-sea fishing – ***Hotel Club Centre de Pêche***, Grande Rivière Noire, ☎ 683 6503/499 2353. Ask for Jacques.

Beachcomber Fishing, Le Morne.

Sofitel Imperial Hotel, Coast Rd, Wolmar, ☎ 453 8700.

Sailing – ***Yacht Club***, Grand Baie.

Croisières Emeraude and Aquacat, Cap Malheureux.

Surfing – Tamarin Bay has the best surfing waves. The hotel and guesthouses all rent out boards.

Golf – ***Le Paradis Hotel***, Case Noyale, ☎ 450 5050.

Sofitel Imperial Hotel, Wolmar, ☎ 453 8700.

Casino – ***Le Paradis Hotel***, Case Noyale, ☎ 450 5050.

Berjaya Le Morne Beach Resort, Le Morne, ☎ 683 6800.

SHOPPING

There is not an awful lot of interest in the West Coast apart from what's on sale in some hotel boutiques. There are however a few souvenir stores along the main road in Flic en Flac, selling t-shirts, pareos and shells.

Inspiration Boutique, as you enter Flic en Flac (opposite "Chez Leslie"), the shop has a nice collection of Indian print fabrics (tablecloths, bedspreads).

Métisse Boutik, Royal Rd, ☎ 453 9221. Nice clothes, if rather expensive.

Superb Ship Shop, Royal Rd, ☎ 453 9082. Closed Sundays. Excellent model ships, but also fairly expensive.

Pirate, Royal Rd, ☎ 453 9028. Closed Sundays. Next door to the other one, but better quality. A good place to buy a model ship.

ISLAND OF RODRIGUES★★

10th district of the Republic of Mauritius
Approx 36 000 inhabitants - 108sqkm
18km east-west - 8km north-south
Highest point: Mont Limon (393m)

Not to be missed

Cove-hopping down the southeast coast passing by Trou d'Argent.
The Port Sud-Est squid lancers and a view from the road down to the south coast.
Take a trip to Coco Island.

And remember...

To apply to the Administration in Port Mathurin for the permits required well before setting out for Patate cave and offshore islands.
Hire a car with driver for a trip round the island.
To pay a visit to Port Mathurin market on a Saturday morning.

The island of Rodrigues, a dependency of the Island of Mauritius, lies 563km north-east of its mainland. It is a wonderful place of rugged beauty, steeped in old-fashioned charm. It is the people, however, who make it really special, for they are warm and hospitable, and seem to be from another world and time. Lost in the middle of nowhere, the island is little but a jagged outcrop of lava protruding from the ocean, surrounded by an immense lagoon dappled with changing patterns of translucent blues and greys. It is an arid land that endures an occasionally hostile climate, but being so remote, it is a fabulously peaceful and unusual holiday destination.

To date, Rodrigues remains untouched by the ravages of invasive mass tourism. The capital remains a colonial backwater; the remote hill-villages are only accessible by tortuous, twisting roads; the deep caverns and grottoes continue to be steeped in mystery, and the numerous coves, deserted beaches and small coral islets populated by rare birds are just magical.

A strategic port of call in the Indian Ocean

Rodrigues was first charted by the **Portuguese** navigator Diego Rodriguez in 1528 - hence its name. Then, between 1601 and 1611, it was colonised by the Dutch, and from 1691, taken over by the **French.** In 1809, the territory was ceded to the British and administered as a dependency of Mauritius for the ensuing 158 years. After all of their forces in the Indian Ocean had converged on the strategic outpost, the **British** launched their victorious offensive on Mauritius (1810). The island was again occupied by the British military intelligence during the Second World War.

Since **Mauritius** was granted her independence in 1968, Rodrigues has been the new Republic's tenth administrative district. The little island is represented in the National Assembly by two delegates.

A young, Catholic, predominantly female population

More than 85% of the 36 000 inhabitants of Rodrigues are descended from Madagascan and African slaves. The majority of these **"Blacks"** are farmers living in the upland area in the centre of the island, hence the reason for them often being referred to as "Montagnards" (Mountain people). The **"Reds"**, meanwhile, are concentrated on the coasts and make their living from fishing; their forebears among the early French settlers mixed over generations with Madagascan, African and sometimes Chinese immigrants. The **"Asians"** - Chinese or Indian Moslems - represent a tiny minority of well-to-do shopkeepers who originally arrived on the island at the end of the 19C.

More than half the population is less than 20 years old. **Women**, who are in a majority, play a considerable role in society, especially when it comes to working in the fields, fishing and labour-intensive craft work. There are two centres for women set-up and managed by the Ministry of Women's Rights, as well as some fifty or so feminist associations.

Alcoholism is becoming rife among a growing number of younger people, especially among men, and constitutes a major problem. It is also the only cause for all misdemeanours appearing before the Rodrigues Court.

"Boutik" on Rodrigues

C. Pavard/HOA QUI

95 % of the population are fervent **Catholics** (the remaining 5 % are Anglicans, a few Hindus and a handful of Moslems), and so it is common to see people walking for miles attired in their Sunday-best, making their way to mass along the steep roads.

The official administrative language is English, as in Mauritius, but few people on Rodrigues actually speak it, preferring **Creole** which is more akin to French. Indeed, most understand a good deal of French.

A traditional economy in evolution

All island affairs are the responsibility of the Mauritian Prime Minister, and he is represented by a resident Administrative Secretary in situ. Until recently, the government has very much left Rodrigues to its own devices and allowed the people to eke a living from a **subsistence** economy, fishing the lagoon, enticing meagre

cultivations of maize, manioc, sweet potatoes, onions, peppers and green lemons *(limons)* to fruit in spite of droughts, devastating cyclones, and rocky terrain, and keeping a few animals such as poultry, pigs, goats and cattle for the family.
Over the past ten years, however, the authorities have been endeavouring to narrow the socio-economic gap between Rodrigues and Mauritius. Priority has been given to developing an island **infrastructure** complete with commercial harbour facilities, an airport, a network of roads, running water, electricity and international telecommunications, as well as education and health.
The islanders are conscious of the economic potential of tourism, but favour the option of promoting a different kind of tourism to that offered by Mauritius, namely a form of **"green" tourism** that is more low-key and respectful of local traditions, culture and the environment.
Despite all the investment to date, the economy continues to rely principally on agriculture, undermined by the dire consequences of soil erosion and drought, stock farming on a small scale and fishing. Indeed, the principal sources of revenue for the island are meat, salted fish and dried octopus *(ourites)* which it exports to Mauritius. Almost all the consumer goods it requires, meanwhile, have to be imported.

A flora and fauna in decline

Species mentioned in bold are illustrated on p 14-15

Little remains of the original luxuriant **flora** described by the first colonists, because it has been plundered and cleared over the centuries, although a number of unique species survive like *bois de fer (Sideroxylon ferrugineum)*, *bois chauve-souris (Neiosperma oppositifolia)*, *bois d'anémone, bois bécasse, bois-pipe, bois puant* (*Gustavia angusta* or stink wood), *bois-gandine, bois-papaye, bois-mangue, bois-cabri*, Chinese or strawberry guava *(Psidium littorale)*.
In recent years, some attempt has been made to try to reverse the relentless deforestation and to check the degradation of the soil by erosion and drought. To this end, a million trees – casuarinas, bois d'olives (*Cassine orientalis* or *Elaeodendron orientale*), indigenous plants and thorn bushes known as *piquants loulou* - have been planted over 5 years. There are practically no wild flowers left, save for clumps of orange cannas growing along the side of the road, which locally are known as "*vieilles filles*" or "old maids".

The **fauna** has fared just as badly. The *solitaire* suffered the same fate as its cousin the dodo in Mauritius. Like the dodo, the solitaire was a flightless bird and easy prey to the first colonists.
Only a few other indigenous species of bird live and breed on Rodrigues and its neighbouring islets, namely the fody *(zoizeau jaune)*, the Rodrigues warbler *(zoizeau longue bec)*, the **cardinal**, the **white-tailed tropic bird**, the **fairy tern**, the *marianne* and the *macoua*. The different kinds of land tortoises and sea turtle that once lived there have also long since been decimated to extinction, having been hunted for food during the 18C and exported as a delicacy to Reunion and Mauritius.

Festival and folklore

All the **Catholic Holy days** provide the islanders with a cause for celebration, but the most important holiday is **New Year** and this is marked with festivities lasting from 31 December to 8 January. For it is deemed good luck to celebrate the advent of a new year, and a good excuse for slaughtering a pig and visiting friends and family – beginning with the oldest. As one might expect, the rum flows freely and there is plenty of food with festivities culminating with a great party and dance – known as "lé roi boire" – attended by friends and family on the 8 January.

The other major feast day is the **Fish Festival**, which is held on 1 March when the drag-net fishing season officially opens (at the end of the fish-breeding season October to February). To mark the occasion, the fishermen take to their boats and sail out into the lagoon, singing at the top of their voices and clanking wooden poles against the sides of their pirogues. There are great shoals of mullet, so large quantities are hauled aboard the boats in the huge nets and brought ashore to satisfy everyone; for the bigger the catch, the better the prospect for the coming year.

The people of Rodrigues are by nature a happy lot, ever ready to dance, but there are not many other diversions. When there are no feast days or holidays to look forward to, a party might be organised with *séga-tambour* – a faster and primitive form of the *séga* found in Mauritius, generally sung by women, *séga-accordéon*, or other improvised dance music drawn from European archetypes like *kotis* (Scottish), *mazok* (mazurka), *polka bébé* (baby polka), Russian polka, quadrille, dance of the lancers, Boston and *laval* (waltz).

Island food

A number of the more common dishes found in Rodrigues are adapted forms of the Mauritian *cari*, *vindaye*, *daube*, *rougail* using the standard staples of fish and shellfish, usually salted and dried, accompanied by fiery bird's eye chilli condiments and **achards limon**. At one time these dishes were eaten with maize, although this has now been superseded by rice. If you want to taste the traditional maize purée with red beans served up with fish rougail or wind-dried

Sorting the drag-nets in the lagoon

Y Pitchen

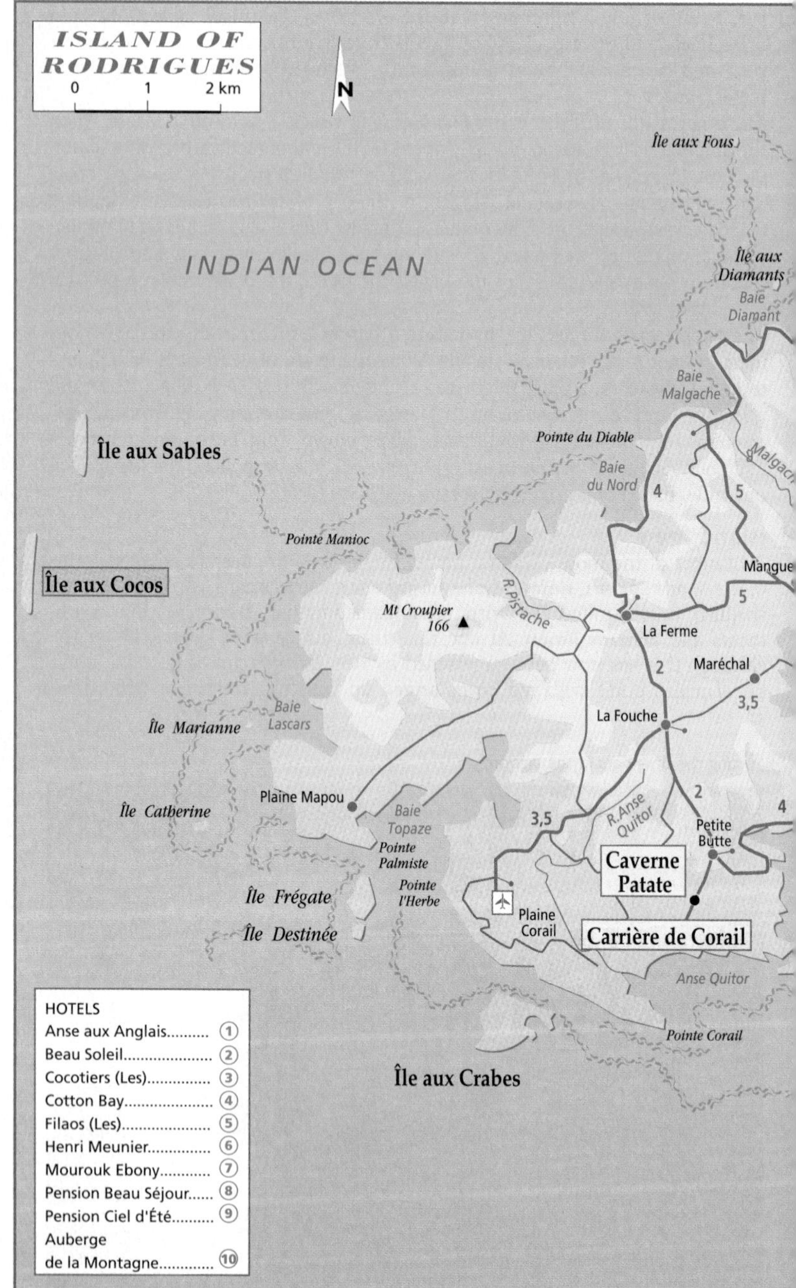
ISLAND OF RODRIGUES
0
1
2 km
N
INDIAN OCEAN
Île aux Fous
Île aux Diamants
Baie Diamant
Baie Malgache
Pointe du Diable
Baie du Nord
Malgache
Île aux Sables
Pointe Manioc
Île aux Cocos
Mangue
Mt Croupier 166
R. Pistache
La Ferme
Maréchal
Baie Lascars
La Fouche
Île Marianne
Plaine Mapou
Île Catherine
Baie Topaze
R. Anse Quitor
Petite Butte
Pointe Palmiste
Caverne Patate
Île Frégate
Pointe l'Herbe
Plaine Corail
Île Destinée
Carrière de Corail
Anse Quitor
Pointe Corail
Île aux Crabes
HOTELS
Anse aux Anglais.......... 1
Beau Soleil..................... 2
Cocotiers (Les)............... 3
Cotton Bay...................... 4
Filaos (Les)..................... 5
Henri Meunier............... 6
Mourouk Ebony............ 7
Pension Beau Séjour...... 8
Pension Ciel d'Été.......... 9
Auberge de la Montagne............ 10

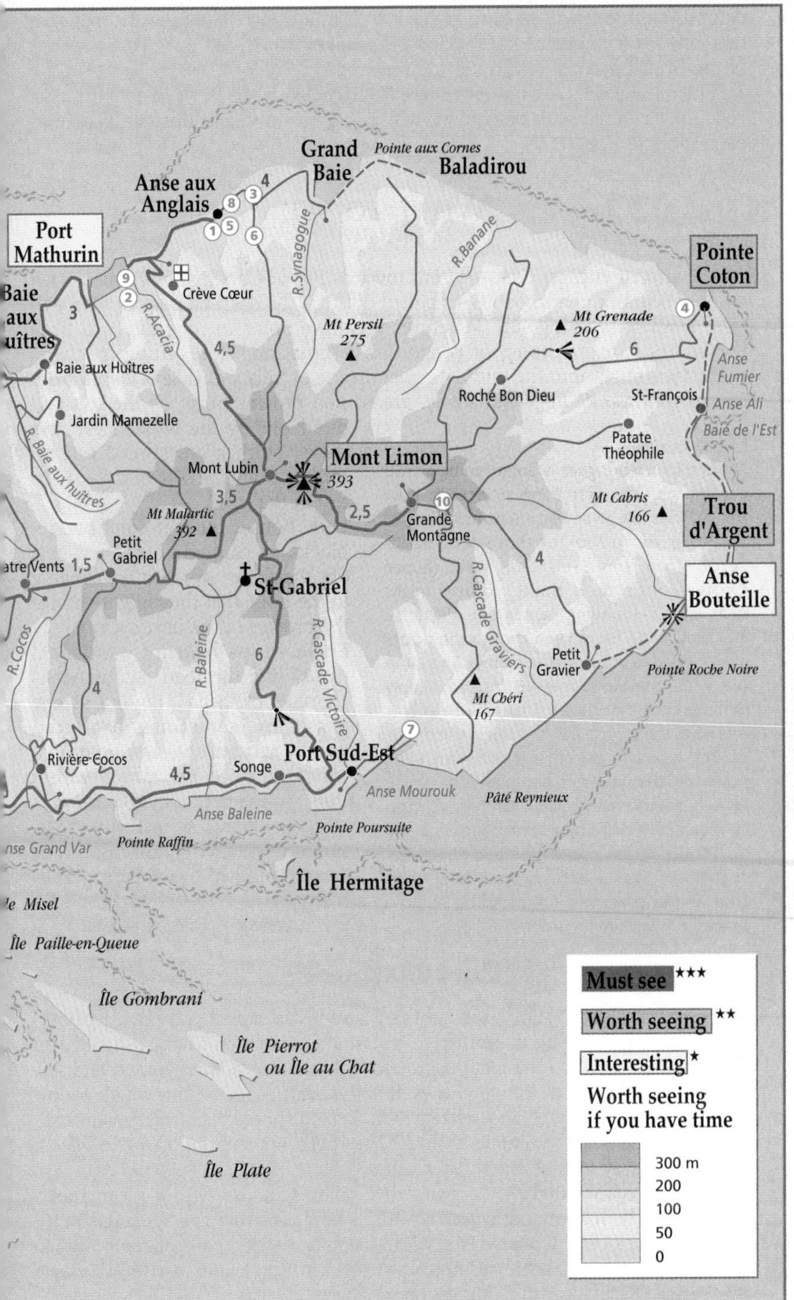
Grand Baie
Pointe aux Cornes
Baladirou
Anse aux Anglais
Port Mathurin
Crève Cœur
R.Synagogue
R.Banane
Pointe Coton
Baie aux Huîtres
R.Acacia
Mt Persil 275
Mt Grenade 206
Anse Fumier
Baie aux Huîtres
Roche Bon Dieu
St-François
Anse Ali
Jardin Mamezelle
Baie de l'Est
Patate Théophile
R. Baie aux huîtres
Mont Lubin
Mont Limon
393
Grande Montagne
Mt Cabris 166
Trou d'Argent
Mt Malartic 392
Petit Gabriel
Anse Bouteille
St-Gabriel
R.Cascade Graviers
R.Cocos
R.Baleine
R.Cascade Victoire
Petit Gravier
Pointe Roche Noire
Mt Chéri 167
Rivière Cocos
Songe
Port Sud-Est
Anse Mourouk
Pâté Reynieux
Anse Baleine
Pointe Poursuite
Pointe Raffin
Île Hermitage
Île Paille-en-Queue
Île Gombrani
Île Pierrot ou Île au Chat
Île Plate
Must see ★★★
Worth seeing ★★
Interesting ★
Worth seeing if you have time
300 m
200
100
50
0

octopus stew you will need to order it well in advance. However incongruous this may seem, another local speciality is **smoked ham** – left over from the days of the British occupation during the war.
To finish the meal, look out for **tourte Rodriguaise**, a raised pie filled with fresh coconut flavoured with cinnamon, which can be truly delicious (*see* Where to eat, *"Lagon Bleu" p 345*).

WHAT TO SEE

Allow 3 days.

As the aircraft engages in its descent towards Plaine Corail, you will be struck by how beautiful the lagoon is separated off from the deep blue ocean by a delicate band of breaking surf. Wherever you have opted to stay, the road from the landing strip crosses a good proportion of the island before getting you there, plunging straight into the undulating landscape of hills and valleys forged from strong contrasts of light and shade, greens and browns burnt by the sun and dried out by the wind. Here and there, clothes are spread out on bushes along the side of the road to dry in the sun.
Little houses built of coral breeze-blocks or painted corrugated-iron dot the flanks of the hills, clinging to the hope that they might survive the ravages of the next cyclone.
Little shops bearing whimsical names line the road. Spontaneous choruses of "hello" ring out as one passes by, sometimes proferred timidly and quietly, sometimes in a playful manner, but always with a smile. In the sleepy and picturesque villages, you may be met with stares, smiles, a tentative enquiry as to your name prompted by a mixture of curiosity and a desire to extend a warm welcome to a stranger.

Local buses

A bus trip in Rodrigues is bound to be a vivid experience. The first thing to note is how the vehicles are given fanciful names (King of the Road, Air Jumbo), or those of favourite heroes from some television serial (Super Coptère, Aigle de la Route); others might bear exotic-sounding names like Perle du Sud or Ciel de Paris. Even though the doors have a mind of their own, it is unwise to jump out while the bus is moving. Instead, simply pull the cord that runs the length of the bus, this rings the bicycle bell and alerts the driver of your intent to get off. It is recommended, however, that you give him plenty of notice as it is sometimes difficult for him to stop suddenly on a hairpin or blind bend. You will also find that the suspension and shock absorbers of these vehicles have long been shot as the roads are full of holes, but the brakes are usually considered reliable.

Port Mathurin★

The obvious place to start a tour of the island is the capital and main harbour, Port Mathurin, a small, endearingly old-fashioned colonial town suspended in time. It is here that all the main commercial businesses, administration and services are concentrated. In many ways, it is the heart of the island, where people come to do their buying and selling, their weekly shop, check their mail-boxes and watch the boats coming in to dock. The streets are laid out on a grid system and so it is easy to find one's way around.
The most elegant building - an attractive colonial house with a green roof - stands near the harbour, elbowed by various new constructions housing administrative offices (Rue Jenner). This white-painted wooden edifice, completed in 1873, has recently been restored for use as the **Island Commissioner's Residence** (Résidence du Commissaire de l'Île).

Elsewhere, various brightly coloured **Chinese-owned general stores** stock all kind of imported goods from Mauritius and small shops display hand-made hats and baskets, local honey, *achards limon* and other spicy condiments for sale. Huddles of schoolchildren smartly dressed in uniform are often to be seen wandering the streets with a basket on their arm containing their snack-lunch. Strategically situated street-vendors offer a variety of local snacks like *bonbons piments*, samossas or deep-fried fritters for a handful of rupees, while in the background, the strains of *seggae* escape from an old transistor somewhere nearby.

The most atmospheric time to savour the buzz of Port Mathurin is the early to mid-morning. For at 3pm the shops close, and everyone heads back home for the day, with the last buses departing from the capital at around 4pm.

For a proper glimpse of island life and colour, make for the covered **market** *(Fisherman Lane; Wednesdays and Sundays from 4am)* down by the harbour. Here, from well before dawn, you will find islanders coming in search of some colourful fruit or seasonal vegetable, rare foodstuffs imported from Mauritius, fresh fish and a little meat, sometimes having walked a considerable distance. Stallholders harangue the housewives in search of a bargain and haggling gets under way. It is as well to get there early, for by 7am the fresh produce has all but disappeared. This also provides visitors with a good opportunity for acquiring one of the lovely baskets or hats.

The other big event that causes a great stir is the arrival of the **Mauritius Pride**, which plies between Mauritius and Rodrigues and docks twice a month laden with supplies of food, mail, building materials, cars and anything else the little island might need. For the occasion, people stream into town from all over the island, sometimes dressed in their Sunday best, to welcome a friend or a parent, to collect any mail, to despatch goods, or simply to watch the spectacle and take part in the activities.

This is the only place capable of berthing the supply-boat, and so a few days later, cargo is reloaded aboard in preparation for its homeward journey to Mauritius. This process can also be entertaining as confused cattle are winched into the air by a crane, legs dangling, while below the local stockmen, tradesmen and craftsmen do brisk business with Mauritian merchants.

Island Tour★★ starting from Port Mathurin

Approx 20km. Allow half a day by car.

The road east out of Port Mathurin follows the coast for 2km to reach **Anse aux Anglais**, where the first English settlers landed and put up camp. It is also, according to legend, where the infamous pirate La Buse is said to have hidden his great treasure.

The next bay on the north coast is **Grand Baie**, a lovely and peaceful place where the road peters out, and where sheep and cows are to be found freely grazing under the coconut palms along the beach. If you feel like a short walk, leave the car under the trees and continue on foot to **Baladirou**, a rock-lined creek in which a secret little sandy beach nestles.

The road west out of Port Mathurin meanwhile heads along the shore to a succession of attractive coves – **Baie aux Huitres**, Baie Diamant, Baie Malgache, Baie du Nord – invaded by mangrove trees. Along the way, the road continues across

C Pavard/HOA QUI

Quarrying coral breeze-blocks for building

various streams. Drive carefully across these fords and with extreme care during the rainy season as you may encounter an assortment of debris washed down by the river.

The road climbs up to La Ferme, then on to La Fouche before coming back down towards Petite Butte, thereby crossing the island from north to south.

The houses on Rodrigues – whether built of corrugated-iron, coral breeze-blocks or concrete and covered with thatch, or now more commonly corrugated iron – are haphazardly scattered across the hillsides.

Once you reach Petite Butte, park the car and continue on foot (10min) to **Caverne Patate*** *(entrance fee. A guide is indispensable as is the requisite permit available from the Administration at Port Mathurin two days in advance: a guide can take care of this. Guided visits daily at approx 10am. Wear suitable shoes with good non-slip soles).*

A natural rift in the rock provides access to the damp and cold tunnel into the grotto, some 100m below ground. In the tangible silence of this dark and somewhat sinister cavern, strange **stalagmites** and **stalactites**, shaped into dragons, lions, Buddhas and other similar figures by the seeping water, seem petrified in the glare of the bright spot-lights.

Continue along the road as it proceeds down towards the sea.

Eventually you come across a track (on the right-hand side) that leads to a **coral quarry***, between Plaine Corail and Anse Quitor, where men cut great blocks of coral from the bedrock. These, cut into smaller units, provide an economic and weather-resistant material with which to build houses on the island.

Go back to the main road and continue to Petite Butte.

The coastal road extending to Port Sud-Est offers fabulous **views***** over the great lagoon shimmering below. You may even be lucky enough to see the fishermen of the area racing each other from time to time. Another more predictable and fascinating sight is that of the **octopus lancers**** who ritually set out from **Port Sud-Est** the night of a new or full moon on a special kind of fishing expedition. The thing to do is to get up at dawn and then follow the band of almost 600 women of all ages, known and respected, from all over the island, dressed in waders and armed with a *foëne* (a kind of pointed lance), searching among the crevices in the coral and rocks for their highly-prized prey.

The road picks its way up to St-Gabriel and Mont Lubin through a hilly landscape, fashioned into terraces and dotted with patches of lush green vegetables where women may be seen with their lovely plaited hats, bent double gathering in the onions.

As the road meanders through the countryside, a fabulous **panorama***** opens out from each bend to embrace the vast expanse of lagoon gleaming with a thousand shades of green and blue, pinpointing the whereabouts of a deeper channel, a sand bar or a rocky outcrop, the turbulence of water gushing through a breach in the coral reef, not to mention the coloured sails of the pirogues bobbing in the wind.

If time permits, why not turn left to **St-Gabriel** and make a detour to see the pretty stone **church**, one of the biggest in the Indian Ocean, before returning to the main road.

Along the way, you are likely to come across strings of people wearing crosses about their necks, dressed-up in their Sunday best, with flouncy lace dresses or tight-fitting suits, walking to mass.

At Mont Lubin, turn right. After approx 500m, a tiny, discreetly signposted track leads off to "View Point Montagne Limon" (5min). But take care, the steep path can be very slippery.

From the top of **Mont Limon**, at 393m the highest point in Rodrigues, a panoramic **view**** extends over the whole island. In the late afternoon, the sun bathes the wild hills in an extraordinary golden-coloured light, the dark green trees are thrown into deep contrast against the reddish savannah where a handful of skeletal brown cows desperately search out the meagre blades of grass.

The East Coast**

7.5km hike on foot: allow 2hr of continuous walking. Alternatively, take swimming kit and a picnic and make a day of it. It is advisable to wear good walking shoes as the rocks can be slippery.

From Mont Lubin, head down the road to Pointe Coton, where the footpath starts.

This part of the island is swept dry by the southeast trade winds. The flat black basalt rock, covered with sparse patches of burnt savannah, reveals attractive sections of bare stone textured by oblique strata. Under the banana trees along the side of the road, an improvised table is surrounded by men playing cards or dominoes.

C Pavard/HOA QUI

A little girl from Rodrigues

Beyond Roche Bon Dieu village, the **view**★★ sweeps down onto **Pointe Coton** covered with casuarinas and coconut palms, a broad stretch of white sand and an expanse of limpid water thereafter. The beautiful long **beach**★★ is fringed with shallow banks of white coral. From here onwards, a path leads from Pointe Coton to Petit Gravier, dipping and diving amid the most beautiful beaches on the island.

To the south lie a succession of sandy **coves**, sometimes nestling between coral cliffs exposed to the wind and spray: **Anse Fumier**, **Anse Ali**, St-François, **Baie de l'Est**. A track follows the coastline, set back from the edge, and threads its way through glades of casuarinas; alternatively, you can walk along the beach at low tide, although the rocks tend to be quite slippery.

Line dancing by the sea

If you go down to the green and white bungalow shaded by casuarinas down on the beach at Pointe Coton on a Sunday, you may be in for a big surprise. For this is a favourite spot for local families to come for a picnic after mass, followed by an afternoon quadrille. All that is required is a guitar, an accordion, a *ravanne* and a triangle for the music to get underway and for a rhythm to be paced. Two or three couples glide across the warm sand in an atmosphere reminiscent of some past era. Then, as the day draws to a close, the men might stay for an extra drink, or stagger around drunk while the bare-footed children play football and the women pack-up together, chattering all the way to the bus stop and heading home after a peaceful weekend.

When the tide is out, the retreating water reveals the coral reef lying a short way offshore, beaten by the crashing waves that churn the water. Then, at high tide, the ocean reverts back to its deep and intense blue highlighted by a band of pale foam as it washes over the bank of coral and into the lagoon.
As you continue southwards, the creeks become increasingly small, and the coral barrier becomes progressively shallower thereby allowing strong currents to sweep swimmers inadvertently out to sea.

Eventually, you come to the cove known as **Trou d'Argent**** *(approx 1hr walk from Pointe Coton)*: a charming little sandy beach sheltered by two magnificent great cliffs, wild and unspoilt, and regularly engulfed by waves that crash through the breaches in the offshore reef.
The sea here teems with fabulously coloured **parrot fish**. The local fishermen recount how on certain days, if the weather is right, one can make out a long metal chain leading, according to local legend, to a treasure.
The track continues along the coast to **Anse Bouteille***: a creek enclosed by cliffs that narrow to a bottle-neck. Beyond this point, the lagoon opens out: from the shady path a wide **view***** extends across the water dappled with gleaming colours and sparkling flashes. It takes an additional hour to walk to **Petit Gravier**, from where a road leads back inland *(irregular bus service)*.

Offshore islets**

There are a number of small islands dotting the 200sqkm area of lagoon surrounding Rodrigues. These are in the main concentrated in the south and west. Some provide a perfect excuse for a boat trip and are large enough to allow visitors to stroll among the coconut palms, to explore with mask and snorkel and enjoy a freshly caught fish cooked on an open fire on the deserted beach. The two most beautiful islands are Île aux Cocos and Île Hermitage.

Île aux Cocos**

Permit required through an agency or a hotel as the Administration does not issue permits to individual visitors. The largest and most interesting island in the Rodrigues lagoon shelters a **seabird nature reserve** for threatened species. Among the few survivors, there are nesting pairs of **fairy terns** *(zoizeau blanc)*, mariannes (or *mandrains*), frigate birds, boobies, *yéyés*, wedge-tailed shearwaters, **noddies** and *macoua* (or *cordonniers*). The most likely place to spot them is in the coconut grove.

A special area on the superb white sand **beach** allows the freshly-caught fish hooked on the way over to be cooked over a barbecue. To help with the digestion, enjoy a siesta in the shade lulled by the sound of chirping birds; then, there is time for a delicious adventure underwater among the fish before it is time to head home.

Île Hermitage – *Unrestricted access. 25min crossing from Port Sud-Est; 10min from Songes; 90min from Petite Butte.* According to popular legend, a fabulous treasure lies hidden on this spectacularly beautiful island.

Île aux Sables (Sand Island) – *Permit required obtainable from the Administration at Port Mathurin. 200Rs for 10 people including the cost of the boat there and back.* This little-known and little-visited island also boasts a **nature reserve**.

Île aux Crabes (Crab Island) – *Free access. 15-30min by boat from Pointe Corail.*

Offshore islets

Making the most of Rodrigues Island

WHEN TO GO

Rodrigues' climate is very similar to that of Mauritius, but the weather is drier and cyclones are more frequent.

Summertime – From November to April with average temperatures from 29 to 34°C with a peak in January. Rain is a frequent occurrence (specially in February-March) and cyclones are always a threat. The average sea temperature is 27°C.

Wintertime – From May to October with temperatures ranging from 15 to 29°C, the coldest temperatures recorded in August. The average sea temperature is 23°C.

GETTING THERE

By air – Since 1972 ***Air Mauritius*** operates 1-3 daily flights (sometimes more in the summer) between Mauritius and Rodrigues on a 46 seater ATR42. The flight lasts 1hr30 and luggage is restricted to 15kg maximum. Confirm return flights on arrival at Plaine Corail, ☎ 831 6300. Average return ticket price: US$150. The number of seats available is limited so bookings are advisable.

By boat – The ***Mauritius Pride*** cargo ship travels between Mauritius and Rodrigues roughly 3 times a month and the crossing lasts about 24hr depending on the direction and season. In addition to containers and cattle, it is also equipped to transport 264 passengers, 16 in first class cabins (US$190 return), the others are seated, similar to an airplane (US$80 return). Information and bookings: ***Mauritius Shipping Corporation***, 1 route Militaire, Port Louis, ☎ 242 5255/242 2912, Fax 242 5445 or on Rodrigues at ***Island's Services Ltd***, Port Mathurin, ☎ 831 1555, Fax 831 2089.

ADDRESS BOOK

Tourist offices – The island doesn't have a tourist office but information can be obtained from your hotel or guest-house or from one of the agents mentioned below.

Banks and money – Nearly all the banks are located in Port Mathurin, Monday-Friday, 9.15am-3.15pm; Saturdays 9.30am-11.30am.

Barclays Bank, Jenner St, Port Mathurin, ☎ 831 1533. Withdrawals possible with a Visa card.

Mauritius Commercial Bank, Douglas St, Port Mathurin, ☎ 831 1833/ 831 1832. Withdrawals possible with a Visa card.

State Commercial Bank, Port Mathurin, ☎ 831 1642.

Post Office – Jenner St, Port Mathurin. Monday-Friday, 7.30am-3.30pm; Saturdays, 8am-3.30pm. Mail takes about 2 days to reach Mauritius.

Telephone – ***Mauritius Telecom***, Johnston St, Port Mathurin. Monday-Friday, 7.30am-3.30pm, Saturdays, 8.15am-3.30pm; closed Sundays and bank holidays. To call Rodrigues from abroad, dial international + 230 + the number. To call abroad from Rodrigues, dial 00 + country code + the number. To call Rodrigues from Mauritius, dial 00 +095 + the number.

No code is necessary from Rodrigues to Mauritius.

Country codes: Australia: 61, UK: 44, USA/Canada: 1.

Police – ☎ 831 1536

Documents – Jenner St, for papers required to travel to the islands. Port Mathurin ☎ 831 2056 to 2065. Monday-Friday, 8am-3.15pm.

Airlines – ***Air Mauritius***, Douglas St, ☎ 831 1558, Fax 831 1959 (Port Mathurin). ☎ 831 6301 (Plaine Corail). Monday-Friday, 8.15am-3.30pm; Saturdays, 8am-12noon.

Health – ***Hôpital Queen Elisabeth***, Crève Coeur, ☎ 831 1583.

Travel Agencies – If intending to travel round the island or visit the lagoon's islands, the best idea is to contact an agency.

Henri Tours, Mann St, Port Mathurin, ☎ 831 1823, Fax 831 1726. All of Rodrigues knows Henri Meunier, a jovial "jack-of-all-trades", excellent diver and an irrepressible storyteller

Island of Rodrigues

A wonderful organiser, Henri can always organise the impossible at breakneck speed. Treat yourself to a boat trip with barbecue on a sublime nearby island, diving and fishing (around US$15 per person, meals, drinks and licence included). In peak season, it's best to book ahead to make sure he's free.

Rod Tours, Johnson St, Port Mathurin, ☎ 831 2449, Fax 831 2267. Airport transfers, excursions in cars or minibuses with guides. Slightly more expensive and less eccentric than the above.

Rodrigues 2000 Tours, Douglas St, Port Mathurin, ☎ 831 2099, Fax 831 1894. Same services as other agencies.

Ecotourisme, Complexe La Citronnelle, Douglas St, Port Mathurin, ☎ 831 2801, Fax 831 2800. Same services.

GETTING ABOUT

The road network has been extensively improved over the last few years and the island currently has some 100km of surfaced roads but there is still some way to go. Public transport is relatively poorly developed.

By taxi – There aren't any taxis, but visitors can rent a car with a driver (see below).

By bus – Bus services are irregular and don't cover the whole island, but the situation is improving. Destinations are indicated on the front of the bus. Shuttles for Port Mathurin or the hotels and guesthouses await passengers arriving off each flight (Rs100-300 return ticket). Most buses either leave or arrive at Port Mathurin bus station in Douglas St, and as school and office closing times coincide (between 3 and 4pm), the station is pretty hectic at this time. Buses generally run from 6am to 6pm.

By car – 4WD or Jeeps can be rented for about Rs1000, however given the state of the roads it may well be better to rent a car with a driver for the day (around US$15 extra, but petrol is included). Ask at your hotel or guesthouse. A word of warning: the island's only fuel pump is at Port Mathurin, near the station.

Henri Tours, Mann St, Port Mathurin, ☎ 831 1823, Fax 831 1726.

Ebony Car Rental, Jenner St, Port Mathurin, ☎ 831 1640, Fax 831 2030.

Rod Tours, Johnson St, Port Mathurin, ☎ 831 1249, Fax 831 1267. The cars are decent and the agency is reliable, but prices are higher than elsewhere (Rs1300).

Comfort Cars, Gordon St, Port Mathurin, ☎ 831 2092, Fax 831 1609.

Hitchhiking – Native Rodrigans often spontaneously stop when they see people walking by the side of the road. Hitchhiking is quite an effective means of transport, limited only by the fact that there are so few cars on the island.

Bicycle – Mountain bikes are well adapted to the somewhat chaotic state of Rodrigues roads and coastlines. Bikes can be rented from ***Mourouk Ebony*** or ***Cotton Bay***. Watch out for some of the hilly descents that can be very steep.

WHERE TO STAY

Rodrigues' tourist board has chosen to encourage bed and breakfast-style accommodation in order to avoid the sprawling hotel complexes that Mauritius has suffered from. To date the island has only two large hotels, guesthouses and a few houses for rent. If you've booked a room in advance, you will in theory be met at the airport.

The following price ranges are calculated on the basis of a double room for one night with breakfast in mid-season.

• Port Mathurin

US$25-40

Pension Ciel d'Eté, as you enter Port Mathurin from Anse aux Anglais, ☎ 831 1587/831 2004 – 15rm. One of the island's best value-for-money guesthouses. Rooms and the veranda where breakfast is served all overlook a pretty garden. The rooms are simple and impeccable, the welcome discreet but friendly. The nearby road has very little traffic at night.

Hotel et Restaurant Beau Soleil, Victoria St, ☎ 831 2783, Fax 831 1612 – 28rm CC Small, simple, very clean and calm even though situated right in the heart of Port Mathurin. A pleasant restaurant on the first floor serves local and international cuisine. Enquire about organised excursions.

• Anse aux Anglais

All the establishments are opposite the sea, separated by a small road. A quiet location very close to Port Mathurin.

US$15-35

Henri Meunier, ☎ 831 1823, Fax 831 1726 – 3rm Relatively basic guestrooms. Pretty little house perched up on the heights of Anse aux Anglais. Henri and his wife, who also have an excellent restaurant open at lunchtime in Port Mathurin, can provide evening meals for their guests. Warm family atmosphere.

Pension Beau Séjour, ☎ 831 1753, Fax 831 1754 – 5rm Appealing little guesthouse, calm despite being close to the road. Fairly basic, but friendly welcome. Meals can be prepared on request. Pleasant and unpretentious.

Auberge Anse aux Anglais, ☎ 831 2179, Fax 831 1973 – 22rm Each room opens onto a balcony that is pleasant, however the view is unfortunately blocked by a recent construction. Charming welcome and impeccable service. A sheltered first floor terrace serves delicious Creole and Chinese cuisine. Possibility of organising minibus or boat excursions, renting bicycles, motorbikes or a car.

Auberge Les Casuarinas ☎ 831 1644, Fax 831 2026 – 18rm A pleasant inn with clean, comfortable, recently-renovated rooms. The most expensive have a private bathroom and balcony. Pretty little garden. Local and international cooking. "Rodrigan" evenings on request. Enquire about organised excursions. The welcome is perhaps not all it could be.

Les Cocotiers, ☎ /Fax 831 1800/ 831 2866, lescocotiers@intnet.mu – 14rm CC Half-board only. Another well-run, pleasant establishment located in a recently renovated building. The top rooms have a view over the sea. The restaurant serves Rodrigues and international cuisine. A little more expensive than the above.

• Grande Montagne

US$15-30

Auberge de la Montagne, ☎ 831 4607 – 6rm Half-board recommended. For those who would like to experience the more refreshing climate of the heights of Rodrigues rather than the warmer coastal areas, this is one of the only accommodation options situated so centrally. The house is a relatively charmless house with simple rooms, the owners are however very friendly and soon make guests feel at home. Excellent value for money. The view of the surrounding hills is superb.

• Paté Reynieux Mourouk

US$100-125

Mourouk Ebony Hotel, ☎ 831 3350, Fax 831 3555, ebony@intnet.mu – 30rm CC Half-board only. Creole-style modern bungalows with private terraces overlooking the immense lagoon. The hotel's beach is very pleasant, but does have a tendency to be a bit chilly in the winter. Archery, volleyball and other beach activities are available. An attractive terrace restaurant, overlooking a small swimming pool, serves varied, delicious dishes. The hotel organises excursions and also has a few cars for hire (Rs1450).

• Pointe Coton

Over US$155

Cotton Bay Hotel, ☎ 831 6001, Fax 831 6003, cottonb@bow.intnet.mu – 48rm CC Boat excursions, horse treks, outings in glass-bottomed boats, billiards, ping-pong. Car and bicycle rentals. Boutique. This is without doubt THE hotel of Rodrigues, built on one of the island's most stunning beaches and run by Air Mauritius. Creole-style bungalows are set opposite the lagoon in the middle of bougainvillea, each has a private terrace with direct access to the beach. The restaurant and bar, which overlook a magnificent swimming pool opposite the sea, serve snacks, Creole buffets and more traditional meals. An orchestra accompanies evening diners and the hotel organises a traditional séga-drum show once a week.

Where to eat

All the hotels and guesthouses mentioned above provide half or full board at a cost of around US$4 per meal per person. Most restaurants are open from 10am-2pm to 4pm-10pm.

• **Port Mathurin**

Large numbers of little stalls selling samossas, doughnuts, spicy sweets, coconut and banana pastries abound in the centre of Port Mathurin.

Less than US$2

Restaurant du Quai, Fisherman Lane, ☎ 831 2840. This unpretentious seaside restaurant is one of the best on the island and a far cry from the artificial pomp and ceremony of other establishments. Most of the clientele is local, which explains why the cooking is so authentic and also why prices are so reasonable.

Le Lagon Bleu (chez Henri Meunier), Mann St, ☎ 831 1823 Lunch and dinner, closed Sundays. Henri goes to the market at dawn, then his wife begins cooking while he takes visitors round the island. Amusing room with marine decor. Excellent Rodrigues specialities, seafood and Chinese cuisine. Delicious fish (grilled or in a sauce), cari z'ourites, crab soup. Langouste and Rodrigues ham on request. Don't miss their delicious Rodrigues tart (also on request).

La Paille-en-Queue, Duncan St, ☎ 831 2315 Small, popular, very pleasant restaurant serving authentic Rodrigues dishes (chicken in honey, fish or ourite stews, crab soup). Simple room overlooking the street.

Le Capitaine, Johnson St, ☎ 831 1581. Lunch and dinner, closed Sundays. Small, popular restaurant. Rodrigues cuisine and seafood.

• **Mangue**

John's Resto-Pub, ☎ 831 6306 Lunch, dinner only on request. Reservations recommended. Chinese cooking and seafood specialities. Small unpretentious restaurant with terrace.

• **Mourouk**

Hotel Mourouk Ebony, ☎ 831 3350, Fax 831 3355. See the "Where to stay" section above.

Sports and Pastimes

Scuba diving – *Cotton Dive Centre*, Pointe Coton, ☎ 831 6001. One dive a day, weather conditions and bookings permitting. Ask for Jacques, who is serious and very professional.

Bouba Diving Centre, Paté Reynieux Mourouk, ☎ 831 6351. The Hotel Ebony Mourouk diving centre. One dive a day (Rs780 or less depending on how many dives), night diving possible (Rs1100). Benoît, the club's monitor, particularly likes taking visitors out to the pass where the lagoon meets the sea. Wonderful views guaranteed.

Shopping

Most stores are in Port Mathurin and are open from 7am to 7pm during the week and until 12noon on Saturdays and occasionally on Sundays.

Crafts – Local craftwork is exclusively devoted to cane and wicker work. The market and a large number of stores in Port Mathurin stock a variety of baskets and hats, together with a whole range of decorative objects made from raffia, aloes, vacoa, vétiver or bamboo.

Gastronomic specialities – Rodrigues spices, among the hottest in the world, are sold in glass bottles. However you could taste achards de limons, with spice or tamarin aromas, or dried ourite, which are easier to transport and not half as dangerous to taste buds or intestines. Rodrigues also produces a local honey well-known for its flavour and medicinal properties.

Artisanat La Colombe, Douglas St, Port Mathurin. This store provides a very good range of everything you can bring back from Rodrigues: excellent achards de limons and tamarin, Rodrigues honey, hats and baskets, etc. Sauces and honey are sold in clever little plastic tubs.

Artisanat Ebony, Jenner St, Port Mathurin, ☎ 831 2651. Rodrigues gastronomic specialities together with a large range of local crafts.

The Seychelles

Official name: The Republic of Seychelles
Area: 455sqkm
Population: 80 410
Capital: Victoria
Currency: Seychelles rupee (SRs)

Setting the scene

C. Pavard

"Botanical Gardens" (detail), Michael Adams

AN ARCHETYPAL ARCHIPELAGO

Geographical location

The Seychelles Islands are to be found scattered over a large area between 4°-11° latitude south and 46° to 57° longitude east. Their closest neighbours include Madagascar (930km south-west) and the Mascarene Islands – Réunion, Mauritius and Rodrigues (south-east). The African mainland lies some 1 590km to the west and the Indian subcontinent 2 800km to the east. There are 115 islands in all which, together, have a total land area of 455sqkm, spread across 400 000sqkm of ocean. The location of this fragmented micro-state has become increasingly strategic as international trade in crude oil from the Middle East has boomed. Today, petrol tankers ply their way north up the Red Sea and the Suez Canal as well as south along the East African coast through the Mozambique canal and westwards beyond the Cape of Good Hope.

Early beginnings

The archipelago comprises a collection of granite and coral outcrops that range in size from the very tiniest uninhabited crag (Les Mamelles, Chauve-Souris Island) to the largest island (Mahé). The granitic islands were probably formed several hundred million years ago and rank among the oldest land-masses on earth. There are two distinct hypotheses as to their origin. Some suggest that the islands could be the remains of the lost continent of **Gondwana,** which became submerged when the tectonic plates of Africa and India moved apart and the intervening area was flooded; whereas others argue that the group resulted from a massive cataclysm that inundated the region, leaving only the highest peaks poking through the sea, like isolated outcrops apparently adrift in the middle of the Indian Ocean.

The islands fall into two distinct geological categories, each with its peculiar, yet readily identifiable types of relief, vegetation, population density and economic importance.

Forty granite islands (including the main islands Mahé, Praslin, La Digue, Ste-Anne, Silhouette, Cousin, Cousine, Curieuse, Frégate) comprise over half of the entire land mass of the Seychelles. Over time, these last vestiges of Gondwana have come to evolve and support their very own ecosystems and interdependent flora and fauna. The tallest rocky outcrops rise fairly steeply on Mahé (905m), to form a high region covered in luxuriant tropical vegetation, including impenetrable forests of exotic trees and flowering plants only a short distance from the sea. The islands are edged with alternating stretches of rugged coastline and long white beaches of the finest sand, scattered here and there with massive and smoothly contoured rocks, fashioned and time-worn by nature, or sharply puckered boulders known locally as *glacis.* The powerful momentum of the huge ocean waves is in part absorbed by the coral reefs out at sea, so that less violent rollers break onto the exposed beaches and gentle ripples wash into the shallowest bays. Tranquil lagoons give way to deserted beaches shaded by coconut palms and *takamakas.* Elsewhere, in unprotected spots, the coast is exposed to the full force of the ocean's fury. A large proportion of the local population subsists on these more fertile islands, which for the most part are grouped reasonably close to each other.

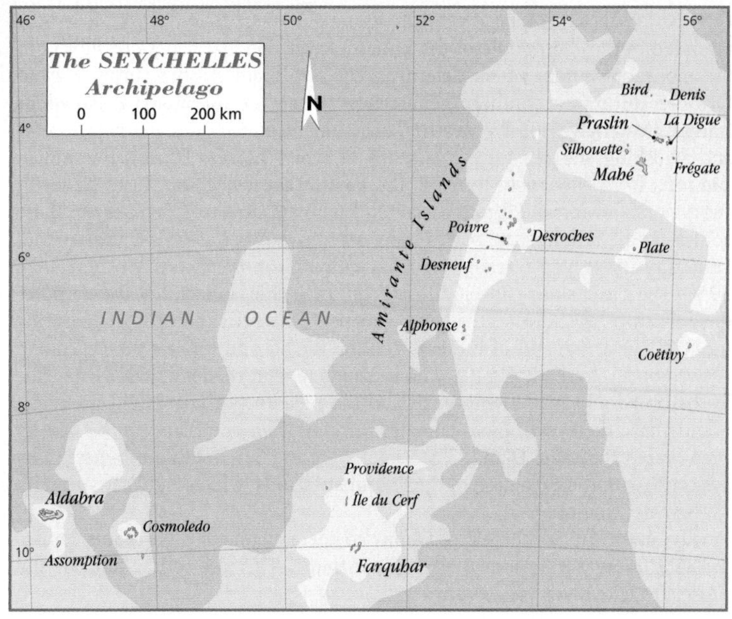

Each island endeavours to preserve its autonomy and to be as self-sufficient as possible by having its own fruit tree plantations, fishing fleets and ambitious entrepreneurs.

Far removed from any major land mass, the granite islands are blessed with abundant rainfall, after which the precious fresh water collects into pools, springs, streams and waterfalls before flowing freely through the landscape. However, these rains can also cause considerable damage, notably great landslides, fissures in the asphalt roads and unhealthy swamp areas.

Seventy-five coral islands make up the outlying islands (Denis, Bird, the Amirantes, Aldabra, Farquhar and a host of others) which are more widely dispersed. These account for just under half of the national territory, but only 500 people live there, out of a total population of 84 410 for the whole of the Sychelles.

Geologically, the **coral islands** were formed much more recently than the granite outcrops, and consist simply of exposed sections of flat coral banks emerging from the warm shallows of the lagoons. In certain cases, they form huge atolls of ring-shaped reefs, each enclosing a lagoon connected to the sea. They project but a few metres above sea level, and the water gently laps at broad white fine sand beaches. Their very remoteness has encouraged great colonies of sea birds to nest and breed there in complete safety, thereby increasing the size of flocks and allowing for a considerable accumulation of **guano** (mixture of bird droppings and fish scraps). This very rich natural fertiliser, once blended with a scattering of loose earth, has enabled the diverse vegetation to proliferate unchecked – most especially that king among palms, the coconut, whose seed is carried from afar by the sea.

An equatorial ocean climate

Stranded out in the middle of the Indian Ocean, the Seychelles are subject to the monsoon winds, which determine the two main seasons. From May to October, during the southern-hemisphere winter, the **south-east trade winds** bring refreshingly cool dry weather, occasionally stirring the winds into gales and whisking the sea into cavalcades of white horses. During the Indian summer, from November to April, the **north-west monsoon** causes frequent, short bursts of torrential rain to fall and temperatures to soar. Despite these contrasts, the temperature varies little, staying between 24-31°C year round. Humidity levels also remain constant, with an annual average of more than 80 %. The clear skies can cloud over unexpectedle and give way to unpredictable tropical showers; the most violent downpours tend to occur during the night or at the end of the day, cooling the air and leaving the vegetation revived and refreshed. On the whole, winds remain moderate. However, due to the broad expanse of empty sea and the breadth of the archipelago, many islands have their own micro-climates, varying from one island to the next or even across the same island. The majority of the Seychelles are bypassed by cyclones, with the exception of the Farquhar Islands, which regularly succumb to their devastation.

Finally, given the Seychelles' proximity to the equator, daylight hours remain constant (around 12hr a day) all the year round. This also causes sunrises and sunsets to take place very swiftly.

A UNIQUE FLORA

To date, the Seychelles have been spared from any major natural catastrophes, and so most of the indigenous plant and animal species have survived intact – despite man's predations – over the last three centuries. The variety and rarity of the Seychelles flora is exceptional, with some 2 000 different species growing there, of which at least 250 are indigenous and 80 endemic *(see inset Definitions p 27)*. The government is conscious of this precious natural heritage and has maintained an efficient policy in controlling the spread of tourist facilities, as well as halting the merciless deforestation that has denuded so many other islands of the Indian Ocean. By now, stringent regulations have been imposed upon 46 % of the territory, transforming both dry land and marine habitats into areas designated as National Parks, Nature Reserves or Protected Zones. These efforts have been given additional financial support by the Seychelles Bank, world charities (the Royal Society for Nature Conservation: Aldabra Atoll and the Vallée de Mai on Praslin are World Heritage Sites) and ecology-sensitive philanthropists.

Change through evolution

The luxuriant vegetation seen today only partly resembles what the first colonists discovered when they landed in the archipelago. Early accounts record how the first settlers found an impenetrable jungle on most of the islands, and set about clearing the original woodland to make way for plantations, and extracting the hardwoods for building boats and houses. In this way certain **indigenous species** became extinct and others have become rare. Efforts to regenerate forest areas by propagation and transplantation have boosted stocks and re-introduced certain species to particular islands.

A number of species have become established in the Seychelles over the course of centuries, which are now considered **endemic** to the archipelago. Although many seeds were brought from distant countries by migrant birds and ocean currents, the presence of some is still a mystery. Among these are six types of palm tree, the most unusual being the *coco de mer*, which only grows in its wild state on Praslin and Curieuse.

Among the other species to grow in restricted areas, let us mention the sandalwood tree – so prized for the scent it releases when burnt and for its exotic-smelling fragrant oil – which thrives on Silhouette, and Wright's gardenia *(Rothmannia annae or bois citron)*, *peponium* and pisonia *(bois mapou)* which are found only on Aride and Cousin.

M. Renaudeau/HOA QUI

Coco de mer

The third and last category of vegetation, the **exotic flora**, includes all the foreign species introduced by man for their commercial value, medicinal or gastronomic qualities, or simply as ornamental garden plants.

The species mentioned in bold type appear in the plates on p 16-17.

A tree for all occasions

From the root is extracted a powder with diuretic and anti-scurvy properties. The trunk is used in building and burnt as fuel. The bark is shredded and blended with earth to make special compost used in orchid cultivation. The palm fronds are used to cover roofs and to make brooms, baskets and hats. The hairy husk provides filling for mattresses and the shell is burnt as fuel and made into useful and decorative objects. The actual flesh of the nut, rated for its flavour and nourishing milk, is also used to tenderise meat in cooking (especially octopus!). The toddy or palm sap, collected from the Indian wine palm (*Caryota urens*) in bamboo tubes below shallow incisions, is fermented into an alcoholic drink and enjoyed with abandon by the Seychellois. Finally, copra oil relieves aches and rheumatism; and being rich in vitamin A, it is a nourishing cosmetic for the skin and hair. A more specialised application in medicinal circles includes the use of the naturally sterile coconut for growing cultures and developing plasma substitutes.

A king among palms

Most visitors will be struck, as they approach the islands, by the profusion of tropical vegetation that blankets each land mass – especially when seen from the air. The full impact of its lushness and diversity, however, can only be appreciated at close hand, perhaps when out walking.

Pride of place is given to the coconut palm which reigns over 40 % of the land area, and which the Seychellois have come to exploit in every way imaginable.

Coastal regions

Mangroves encroach upon the shorelines of Mahé and Silhouette in several places (Anse Boileau, Port Glaud; Grande Barbe), but the largest and densest stretches are on Aldabra. Along the shore, you will find groves of *takamakas* (Alexandrian laurel or *Calophyllum inophyllum*), *bois de rose (Thespesia populnea)* with large yellow flowers, *filaos* (Casuarina pines), – planted in reforested areas and to counter soil erosion, and *veloutiers (Scaevola sericea)*, which stabilise shifting sand dunes; as well as *badamiers* (Indian almonds) so beloved by the fruit-bats, *bonnets carré* (barringtonia or fish poison tree) which produce fat four-sided fruit, and the silvery-leafed *bois de table* (looking glass tree or *Heritiera littoralis*).

Few are indigenous, however, having probably sprouted from seeds or fruit landed by ocean currents. Several are endemic species, including four types of pandanus **(vacoa)**, and the three-leafed *bois cafoul (Allophyllus pervillei)*, *bois rouge (Dillenia ferrugenia)*, and *bois dur (Canthium bibracteatum)*. Latanier palms, raphia, Betel palms, and the distinctive banyans with their aerial roots also line the coastal roads.

The uplands

An increased number of endemic species thrive on the hillsides. They include six types of palm, among them the *latanier feuille* or thatch palm *(Phoenicophorium borsigianum)* – so called because it is frequently used to thatch building – , the stilt-rooted *latanier millepattes (Nephrosperma vanhoutteanum)* with finely fringed leaves, which produces a kidney-shaped nut, and the tall *palmiste* palm *(Deckenia nobilis)*, which once only grew along the coast itself, and which is felled for its highly prized smooth, pale green crown or "palm heart", formerly used in Millionaire's salad, but now a protected species.

The birds and the wind together have helped to spread indigenous trees among the rocky glacis at the base of the hills. A variety of common shrubs cover the granite hillsides, namely a number of comparatively spindly specimens of northea (named after Marianne North of Kew Gardens fame): *bois de natte*, *bois de ronde*, *bois de chandelle*, *bois calou*, and *bois de lait* or *bois jasmin rouge*; the Seychelles pandanus, Horne's pandanus *(Vacoa parasol)* and the lethally armed *Multispicatus (Vacoa rivière)* or Balfour's screwpine; as well as mahogany and tabebuia (or *Tabebuia pallida*) a perfectly acclimatised exotic known locally as *calice du pape* and prized for its silvery timber). Among the flowers and ferns, keep an eye out for wild orchids like the Seychelles' national flower – the waxy white-and-green *paille-en-queue* or tropic-bird orchid – and the large sweet-scented white flowers of the wild vanilla, which tend to be less showy than those found in Indonesia.

Virgin forest

Untouched stretches of forest survive in the mountains of Mahé and Silhouette, and in the Vallée de Mai on Praslin. There are many kinds of rare scented woods like *bois rouge*, *bois de fer*, the primitive and very rare **Jellyfish tree** *(bois méduse* or *Medusagyne oppofitifolia)*, Wright's gardenia (*bois citron*, found on Aride and Sans Souci Forestry Station), Pisonia *(bois mapou)*, the lovely Albizia whose outline can be made out on the top of the hills, and the dark-leafed *capucin*, which grows in clumps high up among the most inaccessible mountain slopes. Here, you will also find a host of ferns and creepers, as well as the Pitcher plant, a mysterious-looking climber which, like its cousin the venus flytrap, sets dreadful traps for unsuspecting insects. Perhaps the most extraordinary, however, is the Dragon's Blood Tree *(sandragon)*, which can grow to great heights (30m tall and 1.5m in diameter) on the tallest slopes of certain islands. The reason for its distinctive local name is that the trunk oozes blood-red sap when cut.

Beware of the poisonous juice of the white and innocent-looking Star of Bethlehem, and the scent of the trumpet-shaped flowers of the thorn apple growing freely along the side of the road. Both are dangerously toxic.

Flowering species

This category encompasses a mass of orchids, multicoloured **bougainvillea**, pink and yellow **hibiscus**, sweet-smelling white gardenias and **frangipani**, vivid red **flame trees** *(flamboyants)*, and heady-scented yellow and purple allamanda, together with a profusion of other brilliantly coloured creepers (Rangoon, coral and railway creepers, sky flower, ipomoea). There are also many exotics, such as flowering ginger, poinsettias, canna lilies, lobster claw, portulacas coleus plants – and foreign imports that have happily established themselves in the wild.

Fruit

A broad range of exotic fruits grows easily in the Seychelles: mangoes and bananas (fifteen or so different varieties of each), pawpaw or papayas, pineapples, lychees, guavas, passion fruit, custard apples, *cœurs de bœuf (Annona reticulata)*, the wild orange-yellow santol fruit, crunchy pink – and – white Jamalac or Barbados cherries (delicious as jam), oranges and lemons, breadfruit (General Gordon's Tree of Life) and jackfruit (whose enormous fruit goes into many speciality dishes), not to mention the luscious avocado. Almost all can be bought in the market, or from someone's garden, others – like the rather tasteless coco plum *(prune de France)* – may be picked from the wild.

Spices

The standard spices used in Creole cooking are turmeric or Indian saffron, cinnamon, cloves, pepper and nutmeg. Cinnamon *(Cinnamomum cassia)*, which, like the others, was introduced into Mahé's Jardin du Roi in 1772 by Pierre Poivre, has played the most important role in the economy of the Seychelles. Today, the pink-leafed young shoots of evergreen bastard cinnamon are still harvested for their sweet fragrant bark, which curls when dried in the sun, although historically, centred around the pungent oil obtained by distillation, after macerating the leaves in sea water. On the other hand, demand for the prized vanilla pod, once a significant commercial export, declined considerably after a synthetic substitute was discovered in 1902.

Cardamom and lemon grass grow abundantly along the side of the road, while small plantations of ylang-ylang are being set up to rival those of the Comores, and satisfy the market for the essential oil extracted from the flowers and used in perfumery.

Capucin House and its tropical gardens

A PROTECTED FAUNA

Land animals

Few mammals

After sundown, visitors may be startled by the shrill cries of the large Seychelles fruit-bats (also known colloquially as flying foxes) and the shadow of their great black wings as they swoop into the trees – usually mangoes. Their high-pitched call is amplified by the male's special ability to use his cheeks as a resonance chamber. The giant fruit-feeding bats, together with the very rare insect-eating sheath-tailed bats, are the only mammals endemic to the archipelago. For the more daring, the tender and rather sweet-tasting meat of the fruit-bat appears as a a local delicacy on many restaurant menus.

The other common mammal is the nocturnal hedgehog-like **tenrec**, which was introduced from Madagascar (via Réunion) as a source of food.

Many reptiles

The giant land tortoise is only found in the Seychelles and the Galapagos Islands. The giant tortoise, which traditionally has been hunted for its meat and its shell, has been saved from extinction in the nick of time and is now thriving once more in a wild state on Aldabra, where one of the largest land tortoise sanctuaries in the world boasts a staggering 100 000 specimens. Those seen on the other islands like Mahé and Curieuse also come from Aldabra, although these are often penned to protect them from poachers. It is claimed that these tortoises can live 300 years, weigh up to 500kg and measure 1.5m in length by 1m in height!

There is a profusion of harmless lizards that busy themselves catching small insects; look out for the almost fluorescent green geckos, the bronze geckos, cayman lizards, skinks and chameleons. It may be reassuring to know that there are no poisonous snakes in the Seychelles, only the occasional small and harmless grass snake.

M. Lemerle/MICHELIN

Aldabra Giant Land Tortoise

Insects and spiders

Many of the 3 500 species of insect recorded in the Seychelles are unique to the archipelago. The majority present absolutely no danger whatsoever; only the 8cm nocturnal scorpions found on Frégate, an angry yellow wasp, the occasional tarantula and the 25cm millipede, with its painful bite, are to be feared. Airborne rhinoceros beetles, however, can be unnerving. Thousands of large innocuous yellow-legged palm spiders (the females can reach 10cm) spin their webs overhead among the trees and electricity wires, and a variety of decorative multicoloured butterflies and hawk moths flutter in the gardens. You should also look out for stick insects, praying mantises and the *Seychelles leaf insect*, which camouflages itself against the foliage.

Birds

The Seychelles provide a unique habitat for a broad range of birds. Not only do the isolated islands provide the various species with a safe environment in which to feed and breed, but the late colonisation of the area by man has allowed a number of conservation measures to be implemented before its fragile ecosystems were damaged beyond repair. Of the 29 endangered species of bird found on Indian Ocean islands, eight are unique to the Seychelles. It is estimated that the bird population of the Seychelles, comprising more than 200 species, exceeds seven million. The majority frequents the same nesting areas all year round; although others migrate from cold climes in the Northern Hemisphere, in search of warmer temperatures and the plentiful food on offer in the tropics. Furthermore, in the absence of predators, most birds are relatively sociable, making these islands a veritable paradise for ornithologists and keen bird-watchers.

The species mentioned in bold can be found on the colour plates p. 14-15.

Sea birds

Most of the spectacular bird colonies are comprised of seabirds with webbed feet who live on a diet of fish, caught either on the water or up to 20m below the surface, which they regurgitate to feed their fledglings.

Residents – There are several different native species, among which a number nest only on specific islands. The dark shiny shearwaters – the large wedge-tailed shearwater *(fouquette)* and Audubon's or dusky shearwater *(riga)* – nest underground in burrows, on the rat-free islands of Cousin and Aride; they can also be seen hovering over the surface of the sea around the Amirantes, Aldabra and various small granitic outcrops. The boobies, members of the gannet family, have a white plumage edged with large, black bills and webbed feet. The common masked or blue-faced booby *(fou général)* and the brown booby *(fou capucin)* breed on Aldabra and the Amirantes, whereas the vagrant red-footed booby *(fou bête)* is a rare visitor.

The frigate birds *(frégates)* – the common, larger, great frigate and the lesser frigate – are veritable pirate birds gliding majestically over the rocky coastlines of Aride, Frégate and especially Aldabra, sometimes aggressively harassing other birds on the wing and forcing them to regurgitate the catch reserved for their young, or stealing unattended eggs. Their most distinctive features include a forked tail and big black wings with a span of up to 2m.

Terns are a dainty subspecies of the gull. They have fairly elongated bodies, short webbed feet and long slender wings that enable them to fly quickly and gracefully above the water. Colour and plumage vary considerably according to type. The white tern or **fairy tern** *(goéland blanc)* is without doubt the most beautiful of all. It has a blue-black beak and small dark round eyes, in striking contrast to its immaculate white plumage. In addition to its endearing goods looks on the ground, the white tern is also the most graceful in flight. Look out for it on Aride and Cousin, Bird Island, the Amirantes and Aldabra. The crested tern *(goéland sardine)*, meanwhile, is a vagrant. Impressive colonies of roseate terns *(diamants)* live on Bird, Aride and Desnœufs.

Unlike the other terns, **noddies** – the lesser (black) and the common (brown) noddies (*cordonnier* and *maqua*) – are a smooth dark charcoal grey colour with a white head patch; they have long and thin pointed beaks and striking black eyes ringed with white. Large colonies live and breed on Aride and Cousin in among the Pisonia trees.

The lovely long-tailed **tropic bird** *(paille-en-queue)* includes two different sub-species. The more common one is yellow-billed with a long white tail. They can be seen sitting on their eggs in the shelter of a rock or in the stump of a tree on Aride, Cousin and Aldabra, or flying high above the forests of Mahé. The red-beaked bird with red tail streamers *(quelec)* is a great rarity except on Aride.

Migrants – Various seafaring visitors come to the Seychelles in successive waves for the egg-laying season, usually April-May and October-November. These are simply and collectively known locally as *z'alouettes*. Little islands such as Bird or Cousin are suddenly invaded by millions of birds, performing great acrobatic displays in the sky before squawking and flapping their wings in a skirmish over a rocky ledge on which to build a nest. Among the more exotic species to be spotted frequenting the islands are the European roller, the turnstone *(baise roche)*, the green-backed heron *(mannique)* and such waders as the **grey plover**, the crab plover, the Siberian ring plover and the great sand plover; a small member of the curlew family called the whimbrel *(petit corbigeau)*; various stints; and small sandpipers, as well as the larger common sandpipers *(chevalier)*.

Land birds

There are birds everywhere in the Seychelles, in the forests, parks and gardens, and as they are not hunted or persecuted, they may appear remarkably tame. Despite this, several species are threatened with extinction and are rigorously protected. The magpie robin *(pie-chanteuse)*, a black-and-white thrush, lives only on Frégate; and the Seychelles (grey) white-eye *(oiseau banane)*, one of the most threatened birds of the archipelago, breeds exclusively in the high forests of Mahé, where dwindling numbers of a rare little mountain bird, the Seychelles bare-legged scops owl *(scieur)* also live. The endangered **Seychelles black paradise flycatcher** *(veuve)* is brown or blue-black, depending on sex and season, with streamer tail-feathers; it lives among the Indian almond trees on La Digue. The **Seychelles fody** *(toc toc)* – a dull-looking weaver when compared to its cousins on the African mainland – is found on Cousin and Frégate, the Seychelles brush warbler *(petit merle de ville)*, long-tailed and long-billed and has so far avoided extinction only on Cousin. The endangered African barn owl *(hibou)* is also protected, even though it hunts the endemic fauna and sea birds (especially fairy terns). Finally, the Vallée de Mai, on Praslin, harbours the last specimens of the black parrot *(catau noir)*, now the last of the parrot species on the archipelago to survive.

Bird Island, one of the coral islands, is a highly accessible bird sanctuary, although the rarest species may be sighted only on the very remote atoll of Aldabra: the Aldabra sacred ibis, the Seychelles kestrel *(katiti)*, the Madagascar coucal *(toulou)*, the rather drab-looking sunbirds – the Souimanga sunbird and its larger counterpart, the Seychelles sunbird *(colibri)* – the Aldabra drongo *(moulin ban)*, the Aldabra fody (not to be confused with the common red-headed forest fody), the Madagascar bulbul *(merle)* and the pied crow *(corbeau)*, illustrations of which appear only in specialist bird books. The **flightless white-throated rail** *(chiumicho)* is perhaps Aldabra's most precious bird, being the last surviving flightless bird of the Indian Ocean, although a far younger species than the dodo.

Among the more common birds are a number of imports: the common or Indian **mynah** *(martin)*, with its brown underside and a yellow patch on the side of its head; the fearless **scarlet fody** (or Madagascan cardinal), with its scarlet or brownish-grey plumage; the orange-billed Seychelles bulbul with its sombre plumage; the turtle-dove *(tourterelle des îles)*; and the barred ground dove *(tourterelle coco)*, which wanders about residential areas in search of seeds and crumbs. Clustered around the fish section of the market in Victoria strut a number of rather elegant white **cattle egrets** *(Madame Paton)*. Rumour has it that early in the morning, grey-headed love birds *(petit cateau vert)* can be seen in the trees around town and later on, near Port Launay, Anse La Mouche and Anse Boileau, but sightings are now exceedingly rare. The pretty red-billed and finch-like common waxbill *(bengali)* enjoys a more marshy habitat, as found on la Digue and in western parts of Mahé. Other endemics include the black Seychelles moorehen *(poule d'eau)* with its red patch on the forehead; the Seychelles blue pigeon *(pigeon hollandaise)*, and the little Seychelles cave swiflet *(hirondelle)*.

Colourful marine life

The warm waters shelter a rich and fertile habitat – a different world that can be explored effortlessly by means of excursions in a glass-bottomed boat, snorkelling around shallow rocks, or scuba-diving expeditions by day or night.

The species mentioned in bold can be found on the colour plates p. 12-13.

Sheltered lagoons

Coral reefs surround most of the islands, protecting them from strong currents and large predators. Here, the shallow lagoon waters are warmer, allowing plant life to proliferate and sustain fabulous colonies of exotic fish, corals, crustaceans, sponges and shellfish. It is in these shallows that one might inadvertently come upon a large lobster or a turtle. Four national marine parks preserve the fauna around Mahé and Praslin (Port Launay, Baie Ternay, Ste-Anne and Curieuse). Almost every species of tropical reef fish found in the Seychelles and thirty or so kinds of coral have been recorded there. The easiest way of attracting attention is to produce a piece of bread, and soon fish of every colour, shape, size and temperament will be coaxed into view. To help with identifying them, take a heat-sealed illustrated chart showing such creatures as surgeon fish, zebra fish, damsel fish, **butterfly fish**, Picasso fish, razor fish (long, slender fish that swim vertically with their head facing downwards), soldier fish, **parrot fish** (which feed on coral), stone fish (deadly poisonous if trodden

Living coral

Corals sustain very fragile ecosystems. In simple terms, they consist of colonies of microscopic organisms that secrete a calcareous substance – corallum – which hardens to form a brittle skeleton. They will only flourish in warm, reasonably salty, clear, shallow water, with the help of plenty of sunlight and a constant temperature (18°-30°C). The tiny polyps feed on plankton, which they catch with their sticky tentacles. Four fundamental types of coral – stone, soft, fan and leather – form different structures on the banks or reefs. Breeding is another of nature's miracles; for one night after the full spring moon, each polyp secretes what is required to fertilise the available eggs. After hatching, the new polyps attach themselves to the colony, helping it to grow about a centimetre a year. Specialist dendochronologists can date corals by counting the layers of hard skeleton.

on), anemone fish (never far from the swaying sea anemones), harlequin fish (tame playmates), **emperor angelfish**, porcupine fish (which puff themselves into a ball when threatened) or the Sergeant-Major fish (with its fabulous aerodynamic profile).

Most of the coral that was present until only recently in the lagoons and which provided for a fascinating variety of underwater landscapes, has unfortunately disappeared. In 1996, El Ninõ resulted in a sudden increase in the temperatures of the planet's oceans, thereby destroying many of the more fragile organisms, sensitive to changes in their environment.

Despite efforts by the Seychelles Government to protect them, four species of endemic **turtle** are threatened with extinction. For generations, their flesh has been regarded by locals as a delicacy and their shells as a valuable trade commodity, especially in Victorian times. There is perhaps no greater thrill than to glimpse one of these large creatures, usually so shy and ungainly on land, swim with effortless grace off the shores of Aldabra, Curieuse, Cousin, Mahé, Praslin or La Digue. On Desroches, it is sometimes possible to witness the amazing spectacle of eggs being laid, when the turtles wait for evening before returning to the very same beach where they were born, in order to crawl up the beach, dig holes and bury their eggs (up to 500 each) under 50cm of sand. All the eggs hatch together several weeks later, producing offspring of the same sex (dependent, apparently, on the period of incubation and the ambient sand temperature). Sadly, most young turtles will fall prey to numerous predators, allowing but a fraction to reach maturity.

Despite temptation, it is strictly forbidden to collect shells. You will have to content yourself with leaving them on the sand for others to enjoy, or for nature to grind them in to sand. Beware of handling living shells: several will sting and impart a poison that can be dangerous. Certain kinds are for sale in the market in Victoria or from the tourist craft shops. Look out for the giant clams that can reach a metre wide; **cowries**, black, white, yellow, speckled or striped with an enamel surface; **cones** (be careful of the poisonous kinds); **helmets**, **tritons**, *Vasum* (shaped like tops), long tapering *Terebreras* or **murex**, *Spondyles*, Spiny Oysters, and *Preroceres* with mother-of-pearl protrusions.

Deep-sea predators

Beyond the coral barrier reefs extends the vast ocean; and in a world where onmy the fittest survive, the shark reigns supreme. These fearsome creatures come in various forms including white sharks, tiger sharks, maiden sharks, basking sharks, black sharks, hammerhead sharks, blue sharks and the enormous whale shark, all of which contend for supremacy. Because of the abundance of food available, it is possible, and quite safe, when diving with registered diving leaders to observe groups of the more passive sharks basking in a cove.

The Seychelles' reputation for deep-sea fishing is unparalleled. The archipelago holds the world records for size for barracuda, marlin, swordfish, *wahoo*, tuna (yellowfin, *bonito*), amberjack, giant ray, bream, kingfish, sailfish, and snapper *(bourgeois)*. Grilled on a fire or simmered in a coconut curry, these will delight the most refined gourmet. When at sea, keep your eyes peeled for joyful bottlenose dolphins.

COVETED ISLANDS

851	First mention of the Seychelles in Arab documents.
1502	The Portuguese commander **Vasco de Gama** discovers the Amirantes Islands on his way back from India.
1609	First English landing.
1742	First French expedition led by **Lazare Picault**.
1756	**Nicolas Morphey** takes official possession of the "Séchelles" in the name of the King of France.
1814	The Seychelles are ceded to the English, who make them a dependency of their colony Mauritius.
1835	Abolition of slavery.
1903	The Seychelles become a British Crown Colony, independent of the Mauritian administration.
1964	Founding of the first political parties: the **SPUP** and the **SDP**.
1975	The Seychelles secure their autonomy.
1976	Independence: birth of the Republic of Seychelles with **JR Mancham** as President.
1977	JR Mancham toppled by a coup which brings **FA René** to power.
1993	Democratic elections and a new Constitution.
1998	The SPPF party wins the general elections again. France Albert René is re-elected President with 66.7 % of the votes.

Uncertain discoveries

Ancient Egyptian, Indian and Chinese texts allude to an established trade route between India and Africa from 2000 BC; Polynesians and Phoenicians also certainly crossed the Indian Ocean. It is possible, therefore, that long-haul sailors discovered the Seychelles very early on.

The earliest actual mention of the islands appears in manuscripts from 851 AD, when Arab merchants from the Persian Gulf were criss-crossing the Indian Ocean between the Gulf of Oman, Madagascar, the Comores, Mauritius and Réunion. Various indications confirm the presence of Arabs, including inscriptions found on rocks on North Island and graves discovered on Silhouette. Some historians claim that the coconut palm was introduced by these Arab navigators.

First accounts

In 1501, a Portuguese navigator probably discovered Farquhar Island while searching for direct access to the Indies. The following year, **Vasco de Gama** charted the existence of islands he called the Amirantes ("the Admiral's islands") situated somewhere between the Maldives and Madagascar. Soon, maps charted the existence of another archipelago that is identifiable as the Seychelles. In 1517, during further explorations, the Portuguese discovered an additional group of islands, the "Seven Sisters", where they were afraid to land lest they should fall foul of the formidable coral reefs.

Sometime later, in 1609, a **British East India Company** expedition came upon the "Seven Sisters" and anchored safely off the largest of the islands. Their accounts tell of abundant coconut palms, birds, giant tortoises and many terrifying caymans (crocodiles) in the rivers.

Pirate safe haven

At the end of the 17C, roaming pirates were hunted out of the Caribbean. They sailed for the Indian Ocean, intent on plundering the boats plying to and from the Indies bearing spices, tea, exotic woods, silks, gold and precious stones. The Seychelles provided a safe haven and ideal hiding places for concealing their loot. The most infamous pirate to cause terror on the high seas was probably **Olivier Levasseur** – nicknamed La Buse (meaning buzzard) – who occasionally teamed up with the Englishman **George Taylor**. The Frenchman's antics earned him a considerable fortune before he was ambushed, arrested and condemned to death. Calm was soon restored to the islands (*see* La Buse's treasure, *p 420*).

Under French rule

The story of the Seychelles really begins on 19 November 1742, when **Lazare Picault** and **Grossin** were sent to explore the region by Mahé de La Bourdonnais, governor of Île de France (modern-day Mauritius). First they landed on the island of Ste Anne before venturing across to the larger mountainous island densely covered in vegetation, which they named "Ile d'Abondance" – island of abundance. The following year, the name of the island was changed to "Mahé", and the archipelago was called "La Bourdonnais" in honour of the governor. As his research continued, Lazare Picault found Frégate and Praslin, which he called "Palm Island" on account of the astounding number of palm trees growing there. The charting of the area was interrupted for twelve years due to the death of Picault and the humiliation of La Bourdonnais; research was resumed at last under the auspices of the new governor of L'Ile de France named Magon. On 1 November 1756 **Captain Nicolas Morphey** claimed ownership of the archipelago in the name of the King of France. A stone bearing a dedication to the French forces was laid on a rock above his anchorage (now in the History Museum in Victoria), the royal colours were flown over the future port of Victoria and a nine-gun salute was sounded to mark the inclusion of Mahé into the Kingdom of France. The archipelago assumed the name Séchelles after Louis XV's finance minister, **Moreau de Séchelles**.

Some years later (1768) **First Lord of the Admiralty, Gabriel de Choiseul**, Duke of Praslin, commissioned one of his officers, **Captain Marion Dufresne,** and his fleet to explore the islands and make a detailed inventory of the various resources available. The other objective was to study more closely the famous *coco de mer*, whose fruit, when marketed to the Far East as possessing aphrodisiac and medicinal properties, promised to become a highly lucrative commodity. Dufresne took official possession of "Palm Island" and named it Praslin after his minister.

Forty-one years of French colonisation

The first thirty colonists and slaves from Île de France (Mauritius) settled on Ste-Anne in 1770. Early attempts to grow basic crops soon proved promising. Encouraged by the taste of success, the French established a second colony on Mahé and set about clearing the land to make way for large-scale plantations. In 1772 a Royal garden (*see p 423*) was created on a trial basis at Anse Royale, under the supervision of **Pierre Poivre**, to see if spices and vegetables could be introduced and cultivated commercially. The enterprise ran into difficulties through mismanagement, largely as a result of the white men's abuse of power over the black workers, and this inevitably had serious repercussions on the fragile economy of the young colony.

In 1778 **Romainville** was appointed as the new commander of the Seychelles by the governor of Île de France and he was promptly sent there with instructions to restore peace, unite the colonists, and restructure the young colony so as to make it prosper. Ten years later, he imposed strict measures for the protection of the indigenous flora and fauna which, until then, had been abused, exploited and threatened with eradication. First priorities were to ban the hunting of the giant tortoises and sea turtles.

Repercussions of the French Revolution were only felt in the Seychelles in 1792, when two emissaries arrived charged with reorganising the political and administrative systems of the colony. They introduced universal suffrage and instituted a national guard; they then set about forming a Colonial Assembly before which the local population could air their grievances. Soon it became clear that the general consensus was for the disparate archipelago to be granted independence from the administration of Île de France.

Anglo-French rivalry

The arrival in 1794 of a new governor of the Seychelles, **Chevalier Jean-Baptiste Quéau de Quinssy**, coincided with the first wave of intimidation from the English, who saw the turbulent years following the French Revolution as a perfect opportunity for undermining the French colonies in the Indian Ocean. After all, the Seychelles were strategically situated when it came to gaining supreme control over the sea route to India. Several events marked the period 1794-1810, including the forced exile of a number of **Jacobins**, deported to Mahé under susoicion of having plotted Napoleon's assassination in Paris in 1801. The British increased their offensives, but each time their ships approached land, they were duped by de Quinssy, who temporarily replaced the French tricolour with a British flag until the enemy had departed. For fifteen years Mahé managed to switch allegiance between the French and the English according to the colours of the flag flown by the ships at anchor there Meanwhile locally-owned trading ships continued to ply their trade across the Indian Ocean under the protection of their blue-and-white standard. At last, after some ten or more attempts, the English established their sovereignty over the archipelago.

160 years of British rule

The Seychelles were officially secured by the British in 1810; de Quinssy was retained as governor and anglicised his name to **de Quincy**. The new masters inherited a prosperous territory with an expanding economy, and a promising agriculture that already had attracted new colonists and many slave workers from the African mainland. According to separate censuses, the population consisted of some 680 inhabitants and 6 600 black slaves.

In 1814, the Seychelles, Mauritius and Rodrigues were ceded to the English by the **Treaty of Paris**: only Réunion remained French. The Seychelles, meanwhile, became a dependency of Mauritius, and attracted a number of new, predominantly British, colonial prospectors to their shores. Ever increasing numbers of vessels called at the islands for supplies of fresh food and drinking water, or for shelter while whaling in the stormy seas.

During the 1830s several major reforms were initiated. In 1833 a decree was passed forbidding the trade in slaves, which in turn led to the eventual **abolition of slavery** in 1835. The implementation of this radical policy caused a serious economic crisis, since the main commodity being traded at that time was cotton, a labour-intensive crop which depended on cheap manpower. As growing numbers of emancipated slaves refused to work for their former masters, plantation owners were obliged to switch to cultivating other crops, the most popular being coconuts for copra oil. Those who elected to struggle on with producing cotton were singled out for further problems, as rapidly falling prices on the world markets accompanied a flood of raw cotton from America. Financial hardship at home prompted some of the Seychellois workforce to sail to the parent island of Mauritius, where lucrative fields of sugarcane were being grown for export. Dwindling numbers rapidly meant that Seychelles' plantation owners began to recruit Indian immigrant workers. Ignoring the governor of Mauritius' refusal, the first **Indians**, most of whom were tradesmen, arrived in the archipelago from the mid-19C onwards.

In desperation and despite the government's reticence, the Catholic Church began to broaden its influence throughout the colony in 1851. Soon the British were forced to concede their failure to impose Protestantism on the Francophile population or to anglicise the local language and culture. Parallel to their missionary work, the Church took responsibility for public education and began funding schools around the island. At the end of the 19C a serious economic crisis was to plunge the whole country into poverty and malnutrition and disease wreaked their dire consequences. Things went from bad to worse, when, first, in 1862, a terrible storm hit Mahé and Praslin, leaving ruin behind it. Then, in 1883, a tidal-wave flooded the archipelago as a result of a volcanic eruption in the Indonesian island of Java, causing considerable casualties and extensive damage.

Steps towards independence

1903 marked the first step towards self-government. The Seychelles were granted independence from the jurisdiction and administration of Mauritius, and became a **British Crown Colony** ruled by its own governor. Fragile hopes and prosperity returned briefly, only to be suspended by the First World War and the embargo imposed on maritime movement and trade in the Indian Ocean. The few volunteers sent to fight in Africa returned in ever depleted numbers. Regeneration began at the end of the Second World War, in part with the help of British Government funding; then, as investments were made in teaching, health, public works and agriculture, the well-being of the Seychelles took on a new momentum.

Entrance into politics

In 1948 a basic electoral system was put into place. The first political parties were formed in 1964, with the principal players being the **SPUP** and the **SDP**. The Seychelles People's United Party, founded by the socialist-inclined lawyer France Albert René, declared itself to be dedicated to a national liberation movement towards independence. The more conservative Seychelles Democratic Party run by another lawyer, James Mancham, was committed to a closer relationship with Britain. The first step towards true independence came in 1970, when internal autonomy was granted. A democratically elected Council of Ministers and a 15-member Legislative Assembly were formed to work alongside the Governor. The SDP leader was made Prime Minister when his party won the 1974 legislative elections. Soon, thousands of Seychellois were strongly voicing their claims for independence; at last the British Protectorate abandoned its rights over the colony, according it the status of "autonomous colony" in 1975.

On 28 June 1976, British colonisation was officially terminated. The independent **Republic of Seychelles** was born on 29 June, governed by a coalition led by Mancham as President and René as Prime Minister.

Towards a totalitarian socialist republic

Within a year of the Republic's proclamation, a bloodless **coup** brought the reigning President, France Albert René, to power on 5 June 1977.

In consequence a new party, the **SPPF** (Seychelles People's Progressive Front), formed in 1978 on state socialist principles, quickly replaced the SPUP and in 1979, the Seychelles were proclaimed, in a new constitution, to be the **United Sovereign Socialist Republic**.

Since then, the SPPF Congress has designated the presidential candidate and those of the Popular Assembly. The President is elected by universal suffrage for a 5-year term; he shares executive and legislative powers with the 25-member Popular Assembly, drawn from the SPPF. He also nominates a Council of Ministers to carry out the policies defined by the SPPF Congress. The judiciary is completely independent.

Re-elected in 1979, 1984 and 1989, France Albert René announced the creation of a **"multi-party political democracy"** in 1991. However, the newly created parties did not score enough votes to remain on the political scene. As long as the opposition remained divided, it was ineffective in contesting policy decisions.

Democratic Communism

During the two decades that followed the coup, a growing patriotism unified the people as René managed to guide the country out of crisis. Modelling his methods on procedures carried out in the USSR, Cuba and China, he found ways to satisfy the majority of the population by finding food and employment for them. Many landowners were expropriated and fled the country. Great swathes of land were handed over for use as state-owned farms. A state-controlled economy was imposed to combat social inequality, to create employment for all, and to establish a social security system. Other prime objectives of the President included essential priorities such as education, health and housing. Unlike what happened elsewhere among "sister" states, this socialist revolution was brought about peacefully, despite a series of failed attempts to overthrow René. In 1993 the President finally bowed to local, international and Catholic pressure to adopt a new Constitution, which clearly opened the way to a **pluralist democracy**. Presidential and legislative elections followed and, once again, **France Albert René** and the **SPPF** scored an overwhelming majority. Thereupon, René relaxed his policies and moved towards greater democracy, authorising the creation of new political parties and inviting exiles to return home. In the 1998 elections, it must however be noted that there was no alternative to the current regime.

Despite a centralised state-run economy and a one-party government, this democratic communism has managed to attract the goodwill and financial aid of many foreign powers.

The Seychelles today

The Seychelles are divided into **twenty-four administrative districts**: twenty for Mahé, two for Praslin, one for La Digue and one for the remaining islands. Six State Secretariats and the Presidential Office come under the direct control of the President of the Republic. The President also nominates seven ministers responsible for internal affairs, political organisations, transport, education and information, health, employment and social security and national development.

CHANGING FORTUNES

The economy of the Seychelles is an extremely fragile affair, depending on a small population, with no natural mineral resources and low agricultural productivity. To the world at large these islands are famous only for their intrinsic beauty and their endearingly nonchalant people – both of which, in turn, have reinforced the image of the place as a magical paradise holiday destination.

The economic policies implemented during the 1960s and 1980s have assisted the islands in levering themselves out of poverty. Evidence of the ongoing financial recovery that was largely triggered by tourism continues to be reflected in reasonably stable unemployment figures, an ever-improving quality of life and a fairer distribution of wealth. Furthermore, the Seychelles can be proud of their stable currency, the strongest in the Indian Ocean.

The local economy, which for so long precariously depended on unpredictable yields from farming and fishing, has benefited from a more sustainable income since 1971, when the international airport was built to handle a steady flow of foreign visitors.

Until that time, the main source of revenue was the export of copra, vanilla and cinnamon, and the islands were able to be self-sufficient in producing their own foodstuffs, notably fish and vegetables. Since then, although the growth of tourism has boosted the strength of the local currency, it has compelled the country to import large quantities of building materials, goods (domestic appliances) and food – mainly from the Far East and South Africa – thus causing the cost of living to soar. Today, the State has become the major employer, and the economy relies consistently on the success of financial service industries such as offshore banking, shipping registration and insurance.

In other sectors, where foreign investment has been crucial to the nation's early infrastructure, government-sponsored agencies, aided by relevant legislation, are beginning to compete effectively on their own. Nowadays, the main weakness of the Seychelles' economy lies in the poor exchange rate for currency held in reserve within the county.

Exclusive tourism

Tourism is the main driving force of the Seychelles' economy. It makes up nearly a quarter of the GNP (or around US$100 000 in 1998) by exploiting the country's natural attributes – sun-drenched beaches and rare flora and fauna – while providing employment both directly in the hotel and transport industries, and indirectly in improved education and health facilities. At present, the majority of tourists are drawn from the most affluent parts of Europe (Britain, France, Germany, Italy) and South Africa.

The government is highly conscious of the high stakes in this sector and the potential dangers of mass tourism. It has therefore adopted a long-term policy that will encourage entrepreneurs to improve services required to attract a sustainable number of holidaymakers, while safeguarding the country's most precious and vulnerable natural assets. The number of visitors to the islands is therefore limited to 150 000 a year, or 4 500 at any one time. This quota intentionally confines the Seychelles to being an exclusive, expensive destination, saving the islands from insensitive commercialisation, which would be so detrimental to local ecology. Even the building industry is strictly regulated limiting the height of structures erected outside Victoria to that of the average coconut palm, implementing designs that relate to and integrate with their vernacular surroundings, especially along the coast, and discouraging the use of concrete wherever possible. In the hotel and catering industries, the authorities are vigilant about maintaining the highest standards in order to satisfy the most discerning tourists. Meanwhile, special encouragement has been given to small family-run establishments, as they help to promote an **ecological form of tourism** whereby the natural environment is preserved and the local population is employed in providing the warm and informal hospitality associated with the Seychelles.

Vital improvements in agriculture

An ambitious farming programme has been implemented by the government in the hope of making the islands more self-sufficient in food production. Although for the most part the soil looks fertile, the islands are composed of granite or coral, and the shallow topsoil is therefore easily washed away by the heavy and abundant rainfall. When slavery was abolished, many of the expensive labour-intensive practices aimed at improving soil quality had to be abandoned. Impoverished growers sold their large estates to the government. Experimental farms and agricultural research centres were set up so as to educate a new generation of farmers and growers in new, improved intensive farming methods. Stronger strains of crops have been bred or imported to boost productivity and revenues from market gardening as a whole. Over time, it is hoped that such measures will help to reduce the need to import perishable fruit and vegetables from Europe and Africa.

For many years the dried kernel of the coconut, commonly known as **copra**, has been the Seychelles' main trading commodity. Indeed, it has an international reputation for being among the best in the world, although the financial returns are being badly affected by falling commodity prices on the world markets and rises in production costs. Landowners are therefore increasingly choosing to abandon the cultivation of coconuts in favour of a more lucrative income from the tourist trade. A similar fate is affecting the extraction and export of **cinnamon** (dried bark of the cinnamon tree) and **vanilla** as a result of increased competition within small markets. Vanilla was introduced in 1886 and was soon underpinning the country's fortune. Then, in 1904, synthetic vanillin was invented, and since then the demand for the expensive pods has dwindled, as drought and blight have largely crippled the commercial cultivation of the vine everywhere but on Praslin and La Digue. A less exotic yet important commodity is **tea**, which is grown most particularly on the higher slopes of Mahé.

Fruit and vegetables, herbs and spices grow easily but tend to be grown on a small scale. The only form of intense farming is **rearing animals** – poultry, goats, sheep and cattle – for food.

The management and administration of all agricultural issues, from production to distribution, has long been the responsibility of the Seychelles Marketing Board **(SMB)**. It is their duty to coordinate the sale of crops from independent growers, cooperatives and state-run farms. Since 1990 it has gradually become easier to sell home-grown produce and this, in turn, has encouraged growers to increase production.

Extracting the copra

Commercial fishing

The government is very keen to exploit the Seychelles' rich territorial waters. As growing numbers of small boats continue to satisfy an ever larger demand for fresh fish from the islands themselves, efforts are now being channelled into more economically efficient commercial fishing fleets, so as to capitalise on the potential for exporting both fresh and tinned fish. Resources have been directed into modernising boats, improving docking facilities and training specialist crews. Such investments are already bearing fruit, and Victoria's new harbour, the most important tunaport of the Indian Ocean, is now regarded as ranking among the best in the world. A large canning factory just outside the capital processes the tuna quickly, while a new freeze-works nearby handles the other fish for despatch by air or sea. The profits from these investments, however, continue to be eroded by threats from hard-line competition and variable market forces. In 1978 the authorities stated their claim to **exclusive fishing rights** in a large area covering a band of some 320km around perimeter of the entire archipelago. This equates to a territory of 1 300 000sqkm, reserved for ocean fishing. While increased canning facilities are being developed, concessions made to countries like Japan, Russia and Korea provide a regular revenue. In 1998, exports of tuna increased spectacularly, primarily due to investments by the Heinz company.

Emerging industries

In the absence of natural energy resources and mineral wealth, the Seychelles have concentrated on small cottage industries like boat-building, woodworking, fibreglass moulding, brewing under licence, and production of paint, leather, detergents, plastics, packaging, soap, cigarettes, salt, clothes, mineral water, fruit juices, etc. Anything, in fact, that will reduce imports. Looking to the future, local demand will continue to remain limited, and in the absence of any legislation that would encourage entrepreneurs to manufacture goods for export, it is unlikely that industry will develop in the Seychelles to any great extent.

Meeting the People

J. Malburet/VISA

Children celebrating their first communion

A MELTING POT

A young population

The population of the Seychelles is unevenly spread across its territory, with some 80 % of the total figure (80 410) resident on Mahé. The ratio of people to land area across the entire archipelago should be 243 people per square kilometre; in reality it is 400/sqkm on Mahé, 100/sqkm on Praslin and 150/sqkm on La Digue.

The average age is 27, although this figure is bound to change given the steadily improving life expectancy of the inhabitants. Until recently, a quarter of all mothers were under 18. Since the 1970s, the mortality rate has been sizably reduced by free and improved health care and education; infant mortality is dropping and life expectancy has now risen to 72.

The national growth rate (now estimated to be 0.8 % per year) is also in general decline, partly because of policies implemented by the government on family planning, and partly because a considerable number of people continue to emigrate (1-1.5 % of the population per year) to Australia, Britain, Canada, and South and East Africa.

Racial harmony

The extremely varied racial mix of the Seychellois population is a direct consequence of its history. The harmonious integration of different ethnic groups reflects the interrelationships of fortune-hunters, colonial occupiers, rescued slaves, foreign entrepreneurs and passing traders in a remote land.

A close-knit community evolved, largely in the 19C, when French and English colonists lived with African and Madagascan freed slaves and prosperity attracted immigrant workers from the Indian and Chinese sub-continents. The result is that each person has a unique family background and they all live happily among their neighbours, with whom they share the Creole language, Catholic creed and Seychellois nationality.

Note the skin colour of the people who wander about the streets of Victoria. You will see every shade imaginable from the very black to the very white. The principal ethnic types groups have evocative names. The majority of the population is made up of **Mozambiques**, who are descended from the original black slaves brought from Africa and Madagascar over the last three centuries. The **grands Blancs** are the "great white" families whose ancestors were among the French or English planters who colonised the islands in the 19C. These individuals are not always white-skinned, and the term usually refers to the wealthy hereditary landowners.

Among the Blancs are also the **Blancs coco** (coconut whites) – the poor, illiterate people who were exploited by the plantation owners for collecting coconuts; the **Rougeons** or **Blancs rouillés** (literally the rusty whites), of mixed blood; and the **Blancs pourris** (rotten whites), a nickname they earned due to their questionable hygiene. The ethnic kaleidoscope took on new dimensions with the arrival during the 1850s of the Indian shopkeepers and of the Chinese from 1866 onwards. The many varietiesof interbreeding gave rise to the **Mulatto Creoles**, who have European blood, the **Chinese Creoles**, born of Chinese stock, and the **Malabar Creoles**, of Indian descent. It is important to note, however, that many Seychellois of Indian origin tend to be Moslems. They live in closely guarded communities in which arranged marriages continue to be the norm, which precludes any further ethnic cross-breeding.

Faith and religion

The Seychellois population is predominantly Christian with two important minorities of Hindus and Moslems. The largest faction by far is formed by the **Roman Catholics** (90 %) with a small number of Anglicans, Seventh-day Adventists, Jehovah's Witnesses and Pentecostal making up the balance. Most people are devout and may be seen crossing themselves before every church or calvary. On Sunday mornings church choirs celebrating Mass replace the more usual radio broadcasts of *séga* and reggae music. Out in the far-flung villages, families congregate in church dressed in their Sunday best.

Undoubtedly, the religion handed down from the first European settlers has been tempered over the years by the integration of beliefs revered by the slaves from Madagascar and Africa. A deep-rooted reverence for the **Occult** is still widespread throughout the islands. Despite a law passed in 1958 banning **witchcraft,** it continues to persist in daily life. Many Seychellois are highly superstitious and earnestly believe in the forces of magic and the supernatural, against which lucky amulets or *gris-gris* are invoked.

The people's inherent fear of evil spirits (*dondozias* or *zombies*), bad luck, vengeful spells and nasty fetishes is exploited by the sorcerers, known as *bonhommes di bois* (men of wood), who purport to be able to cure all ills and to possess magic powers. They use medicinal plants to concoct potions for love, luck and vengeance. Despite the government's great attempts to publicise free medical care, it seems unable to curb the deeply ingrained local practices.

Devotion and gaiety

The Seychellois are happy for the excuse to hold a party and therefore celebrate all the Catholic festivals with great zeal. Some feast days are marked by processions and banners, others by contests or musical events. Every Catholic family religiously honours its dead on **All Saints Day** *(Toussaint)*, brightening up the cemeteries with more flowers than usual. **Christmas** in the sun is a particularly merry affair. For it to be a success, everyone has to eat, drink and dance to his heart's content. As marriages are relatively rare, occuring but once in a lifetime, baptisms and first communions provide for more feasting and heartiness. The local brew *(calou)* flows liberally and the dancing takes off.

15 August (Feast of the Assumption)

C. Pavard/HOA QUI

A melting pot

DAILY LIFE

Creole architecture

The houses in the Seychelles, be they little shacks or elegant colonial villas, are usually harmonious combinations of forms, colours and materials. As the State sets about providing sufficient housing to suit demand, it must also weigh up the consequences on the environment. To date, even concrete has been used with discretion so as to blend in with the surroundings, although the temptation to construct tower blocks may undermine this. The buildings of the 18C reflected the taste and technical know-how of the first European settlers, as well as the preferences of middle-class people from Île de France (Mauritius) and Île de Bourbon (Reunion), and of slaves from Africa and Madagascar. These eclectic elements, together with the practical needs of providing shelter from the local climate, have combined to form a wholly unique style of architecture.

See illustrations, p 18-19

Traditional homes

Most of the houses tend to be built in rural settings, scattered along the coasts or perched up on the granite slopes surrounded by the dense, but refreshing, vegetation.

The climate demands that houses should be well ventilated with many openings. Where possible, a covered **veranda** with elegant columns or a balustrade stretches across the front of the house, or around the whole building, overlooking the garden. Adjustable *latanier* screens or wooden-slatted Persian blinds are fitted to keep the glaring sun or the pouring rain out, or simply to provide a little privacy during the siesta hours. The veranda is a vital feature of the house because it is here that the ambient temperature will be the most comfortable and thus where the family and friends will gather, to snatch a snooze, eat a snack, work or play. Many houses are raised on a stone platform in case of flood and to prevent damp. The main room very often serves a dual purpose, as a dining-room and sleeping area. The kitchen, meanwhile is traditionally located in a separate outbuilding to minimise the risk of fire. If the house is built of more modern materials, like corrugated iron or cement breeze-blocks, however, then the cooking area is integrated into the main building. The occasional roof is to be found thatched with coconut fronds, latanier leaves or branches of screw pine, although these have largely been replaced by more durable sheets of corrugated iron, painted in bright colours (often the red and green of the national flag) or pastel shades, that tend to rust in the high humidity.

Each morning, the house-proud Seychelloises are out sweeping the beaten earth yard around the house, bent double with the left arm folded behind the back and the right hand clutching the short palm-leaf broom seen everywhere. This daily ritual is enacted with precision, for the outward appearance of the house and garden are matters of great pride to all the family, as each tacitly vies with his or her neighbour for the best array of plants and flowering shrubs.

Plantations

The large homesteads that survive from a forgotten era tend to nestle in lush gardens and so are hidden from view. A few on the outskirts of Victoria can be seen, but this involves trekking up the back roads. Each family compound comprised the main house and a series of outbuildings (kitchens and storehouses), an extensive vegetable patch and a working farm area complete with

mills, copra-fired ovens, distillery, and more. The slaves were put up in little one-room houses raised on stone piles and roofed with layers of leaves, on the edge of the estate, whereas the paid hands (labourers and workers) lived in rather more sophisticated houses with verandas.
The owners whiled away their days in their big house which they called a **gran lakaz**, an imposing mansion set in a large, well-cared for garden, preceded by a tree-lined drive. These elegant houses are a testimony to the bygone lifestyle of the colonial age. What is especially striking is the skill with which the various woods are used as flooring or in finely-made furniture.
Sadly, these houses do not weather the ravages of time and fire, and many are falling to rack and ruin due to lack of love and expensive maintenance. However, the State has implemented measures to safeguard this heritage. In 1980, a law was approved for funds to be allocated to restoring and preserving the finest surviving examples. It was under this initiative that the Craft Village complex, the houses at Plaine St-André and the Creole Institute in Mahé *(see p 421-422)*, the Yellow House that now forms part of La Digue Island Lodge and the secondary presidential residence at L'Union on La Digue *(see p 465 and 459 respectively)*, were saved from dereliction.

Education

The prime objective of President René's egalitarian programme is to provide better education facilities (free) to all children. As a result 97 % of children go to school. For children aged four to six, there are voluntary crèches. Thereafter, school becomes compulsory for all children until they reach 16. To ensure conformity, parents of children who skip class for more than three weeks without a valid excuse are liable to a heavy fine or up to three months in prison. Formerly, at 16, most adolescents spent a year in the **National Youth Service,** a highly disciplined training scheme introduced in 1981 which was used to initiate young people in to the doctrines of communism. By the age of 18, the young adults were ready to go into public-spirited service. At that point, those who managed to qualify with diplomas quickly sought to emigrate.
In 1990, the NYS, renamed S5, became optional, and the emphasis was on imparting practical skills rather than political

Ironing clothes

C. Pavard/HOA QUI

Education

indoctrination. Abolished in 1998, there is now an extra year of Secondary School Education for all. Now, at 17, a young Seychellois must choose either a career path along specialist lines (like the hotel and catering industry), advanced academic training at a **polytechnic**, or an active life working the land.
This remote and scattered archipelago, devoid of any natural resources save its appeal to tourism, hardly needs to impose military service on its young. This having been said, the country employs a considerable **army** of 1 200 or so men and, since the 1977 coup, a specialist **paramilitary unit**.

Women

Women play an important role in society, and are considered the head of their families whether or not they are actually married. Furthermore, they must be adept at making all the decisions, raising the children, and finding time to go out to work so as to feed the family. It is no surprise therefore to find women with a strong sense of independence.
Despite the admonishments of the Church, many couples prefer not to marry but to live together, break up and move on. This has been common practice since time immemorial, when the men were likely to spend long periods at sea, and as the Church is reluctant to grant divorces, the overwhelming majority of new babies, maybe three-quarters of births, are born out of wedlock. Indeed, it is not uncommon for families to consist of eight to ten children born to different fathers, mothers often bearing children when still adolescents. The situation is further exacerbated by the fact that the law requires fathers who admit paternity to pay between 20 % and 50 % of their salary towards the upbringing of their children.

Leisure

The Seychellois attitude to work is limited to earning enough for their daily needs, rather than putting away savings or making a profit. Instead, they prefer to make the most of the time available and enjoy life to the full. Visitors are often struck by just how sociable these people are, for everyone seems to know everyone – and their business – on these small islands. The climate, together with the fact that the people have only themselves to rely on to get things done, lends a certain nonchalance to the prevailing attitudes and practices. There is always time for a chat on the street corner, or a game of cards, draughts or dominoes and a cool beer under the *takamaka* trees by the beach. Night falls very quickly in the tropics, and since the relaxation of the political regime, the people of Mahé flock to crowded casinos and noisy gaming halls for an evening's entertainment. Even here, in this remote island paradise, slot machines have taken hold and thousands dream of winning the lottery.

Openness and modern living

Until 1971, the Seychelles were extremely isolated from the rest of the world; since the international airport was built, however, tourism has boomed, influences from abroad have flooded in, and with them has come a craze for consumerism. Hi-fi equipment, televisions and electrical appliances have made a sudden appearance in shops and homes everywhere. The number of cars has shot up over the last few years, causing severe congestion in the capital, which until recently, would have been quite inconceivable! Imported ready-to-wear clothes have overtaken locally made articles.

A Game of Dominoes

ART AND FOLKLORE

Music and dance

Music and dance are an integral part of daily life in the Seychelles. The people have an innate sense of rhythm, and will take up the opportunity of expressing themselves in dance or song at the slightest excuse. Snatches of *séga*, *moutia* and reggae are to be heard emanating from the most unexpected corners and remotest backwaters. European, Madagascan and especially African influences have given the music of the Seychelles a distinctive quality.

Although these traditional tunes have been somewhat re-interpreted and remastered, the very sound of the catchier numbers is enough to make the Seychellois heart race. Unfortunately, it's impossible to see any shows, except in the large hotels.

Moutia

The *moutia* was probably brought to these shores by the black slaves, who were able to forget their trials and tribulations when gathered in the moonlight around a fire on the beach. The repetitive strains are reminiscent of the *maloya* of Reunion and the *séga* of Mauritius and Rodrigues. First the drums are warmed by the fire so that the goatskin membrane is stretched tight; for this dance, three round, flat **moutia-drums** are required. The actual songs are intoned by a man and a woman like a spontaneous and improvised dialogue. The words speak of exile, the hardships of slavery and exploitation in the plantations, and aspirations for a better life. Social satire, laments and love stories are woven together with humour. With a little encouragement from alcohol, the slaves were thus able to exorcise their frustrations and alleviate their anger by lamenting their plight.

After the abolition of slavery, the Church was quick to censor the dance, which imititated sexual intercourse – the dancers use suggestive hand gestures and the male reaches down over the woman, though without ever touching her. After being condemned as debauched and an outrage to public morality, the *moutia* was strictly regulated: the fire could be lit and drums played only in places prescribed by law, so as to preserve the peace of mind of the Whites.

Séga

The *séga* of the Seychelles is similar to the *moutia*. The dancers face each other and – without touching – enact the game of seduction and mutual sexual attraction. Many movements parody the rituals of ordinary life. Several percussionists beat the rhythm on the long and thin **séga-drums**, made out of hollow coconut palm trunks held between their legs. In response, the **ravanne** (big box), triangle and **maravanne** (maracas) are sounded.

The **séga tremblé** (trembling séga) is slightly different from the normal *séga* in that it derives from Madagascar, and has more staccato rhythms. Furthermore, the beat of the drums seems to hypnotise the dancers, who move as if in a trance.

Camtolé

The *camtolé* dances are European in origin and include the waltz, the mazurka (or masok), the berlin, the écossaise, the polka – which gave rise to many variants , or scottish and the contredanse or quadrille (popular in France, at the Court of Louis XIV). The dances are accompanied by two violins, a mandolin, a banjo, an accordion, a large drum, a base drum, cymbals and the inevitable triangle. The gay mood of these tunes is truly infectious, and so *camtolé* is frequently played at weddings, dances, popular festivals and other special celebrations.

Song

The traditional airs, sung with the backing of stringed instruments, are an important part of the Seychelles' cultural heritage.
In the old days the **makalapo** (from Africa) and the **bobre** (an arched African instrument with one string) were used to beat time to the onomatopoeic African chants. Songs of everyday life were accompanied by the **zez**, a Madagascan instrument resembling a single-string sitar, with a music box provided by a calabash gourd. In this way, the lonely sailors sought consolation when out wandering the remote and deserted islands on turtle-hunting expeditions.
If singers chanted popular stories, they might use the **mouloumba**, another Madagascan sitar, as they intoned all sorts of staccato sound effects, groans, onomatopoeia, gnashing of teeth and hiccups.

Sokwé and Boya

Sokwé and *boya* originated in Africa and Madagascar. Both are traditional forms of entertainment that border on theatre, song and dance. **Sokwé** was performed by six men dressed up in grass, their faces covered by black masks, with eyes ringed in red and lichen beards. Thus attired, they set about enacting a burlesque story of a king and his court. The **boya** – which has all but died out – dealt with healing and resurrection.

There is little chance of visitors being treated to any of these traditional art forms, although occasionally shows are put on by hotels for tourists. Although such events may lack authenticity, the performances are usually contrived to convey some of the atmosphere, mood and sound of the real thing.

Flamboyant paintings

The art of painting in the Seychelles, which is best summarised as naive, celebrates the simple pleasures of island life, the profusion of colour and the fabulous richness of the local flora and fauna. Each canvas encapsulates a moment in the daily life of the Seychelles in a riot of bright colours: fishing, children playing, the flight of birds, Creole houses, the sea, people and above all the luxuriant vegetation.
Many painters have fallen in love with the scenery, the strong colours and the clear light of the Seychelles and made the islands their home. Among the first was Michael Adams *(illustration p 348-349)* with Donald Adélaide, Gérard Devoud, Christine Harter and others following suit; all open their studios to the public (addresses and opening times available from the Victoria Tourist Office) and exhibit their work in galleries, notably in Victoria, Beau Vallon and La Digue. Since 1988 a **biennial exhibition of fine and applied art** is held to show works by the best artists from across the Indian Ocean.

Craftsmanship

The Seychellois show neither the enterprise nor the ambition to seek financial profit from selling handmade artefacts using the scarce resources available to them locally. One reason is that people are used to making things for their own personal use in the home. This tradition is being revived, however, as people are encouraged to sell handcrafted goods through such State-sponsored initiatives as the Craft Village *(see p 422)*, at the market in Victoria and in souvenir shops.

The most popular and widely available example of handiwork are the **basket-work** hats, baskets, mats and such-like, made from plaited and occasionally dyed palm leaves. Shell and coral have now replaced tortoiseshell in **jewellery** since the latter was banned in 1995. Polished **coconut shells**, particularly those of the coco de mer, are used to make unusual containers. The applied use of **wood**, although still in its infancy, is becoming progressively more original as artisans experiment with carving, marquetry, decorative sculpture, Creole furniture and, above all, the production of superbly crafted model boats *(see p 422)*.

Batik clothes and sarongs, as well as **textiles**, hand-blocked or painted with vibrant tropical motifs, are becoming increasingly popular. There are also plenty of opportunities to browse through the stalls in the streets of Victoria for masks, statuettes and jewellery imported from Africa.

Popular literature

Until recently, just about all myths and stories were transmitted orally by the illiterate population. Today, things are very different, with various literary forms being fashioned by a blend of influences as diverse as the multi-ethnic population. The most popular genre is poetry, closely followed by storytelling, proverbs, riddles and word games. Among the favourite themes are the joys of nature, evocations of daily life, ancient legends and old wives' tales, gris-gris and other superstitions.

This oral tradition, handed down from generation to generation is one the wane due to the rise in literacy and increasing access to the media. Nonetheless, this declining oral tradition and the upgraded status of Creole language have boosted the fashion for the written word. Now at last, novels, articles and plays, mostly English or French, are beginning to be translated into Creole.

Creole identity

In many colonial or ex-colonial countries, an awareness of Creole identity developed with the first stirrings of independence. In the Seychelles, national identity is intertwined with thinking, speaking and being Creole. Since independence, therefore, the language has been revived and adopted as the appropriate language of the press, radio, political life and school. It is now the official language of the Seychelles, and has played a considerable role in reawakening an interest in traditional folklore – dance, music and literature – which in turn is being assimilated into popular culture. Let it be said that the State has also played its part in encouraging this to happen.

If you happen to be in the archipelago at the end of October, you will have a chance to attend the **Creole Festival**, which was inaugurated in 1985 across most of the Creole-speaking countries. In the Seychelles this day soon became a week of celebration with a succession of events involving all the arts, including arts and crafts, architecture, music and dance, literature and poetry, theatre, food and fashion, in ajoyful celebration of the wealth of Creole culture.

SOCIAL ETIQUETTE

A visit to the Seychelles is not only about discovering and enjoying the splendid natural features of the island, but also about meeting the local people.
Perhaps the surge of national pride that followed independence provoked a certain resentment of whites similar to that felt for the former colonists, but natural Creole hospitality and the need for tourism have overcome past rancour. Nevertheless, it is rare for the Seychellois to approach one spontaneously, and first impressions can be a little off-putting, with the people seeming cold, indifferent or indeed disdainful. But it is really a case of nonchalance mixed with shyness. To start up a conversation and get beyond first impressions one needs to take time and show one's interest and curiosity.

How to mix with the locals

• Contact is established fairly easily as most Seychellois have mastered English or French. Otherwise, with a little patience and good sense one can say a few words in clear English and try to interpret the reply phonetically.
• One gets to know the people better in family-run guest-houses, many of which give a more authentic view of daily life in the Seychelles than the large, standard hotels.
• To engage in conversation, you will not be short of gambits, since the Seychellois are proud of their country. They are bound to be thrilled with a compliment or flattering observation relating to their beautiful islands. Alternatively, you could ask a question about the flora and fauna, what is growing in their garden or what fish they have just caught. Why not ask what they do on Sunday or what local specialities they cook, the music they like etc?

In front of the "boutik" at Quatre Bornes

Roudinalexandre/DIAF

• Explore the small, steep roads leading to the remote villages; greet the young people at work, the old people taking the air in their gardens, the shopkeepers on the doorstep, especially in the more out-of-the-way places. But do remember to be discreet so as not to intrude too much in their private lives.
• Religious gatherings and celebrations provide the perfect opportunity to meet locals and share in the joyful spirit of the occasion.

Forewarned is forearmed

• The people of the Seychelles have an innate sense of fun and enjoy hearing jokes. They will therefore be delighted to share a story with you and laugh with good humour.
• If you are lucky enough to be invited to a celebration (baptism or marriage, for instance), it will be an honour for the hosts to have you there; be at ease and enjoy the food and drink offered.
• Do dress appropriately when visiting churches, especially if you wish to attend Sunday Mass, because the locals will be smartly turned out.
• The heavenly, deserted beaches can tempt women to go topless, but do not be surprised if this provokes unwanted attention.
• Foreigners should avoid causing offence by pointing a camera lens at someone and taking their photograph without their consent; older people in particular may prefer not to feature in someone's holiday snaps. Children, however, will not need much encouragement, but catching a spontaneous pose may be difficult. In Victoria Market, the women often tend to hide behind their stalls, but the fishermen, on the other hand, are usually proud to show off their catch when they unload their boats.
• Do not refer to groups by names such as Chinese, Blacks or Whites. The Seychellois feel themselves to be one people regardless of skin colour or ethnic origin.
• Avoid talking about politics in the Archipelago, as most people prefer to avoid the subject by sighing in resignation, or giving an awkward or stilted reply.
• In public the Seychellois never argue or lose their cool. The local people look askance at tourists who raise their voices or lose control.

EATING & DRINKING

Creole cuisine

The creole cooking of the Seychelles is without doubt the best in the Indian Ocean. African, English, French, Chinese and Indian heritage, coupled with plentiful fresh ingredients, have created an original and varied cuisine, albeit somewhat adulterated by catering to tourist tastes.

The most popular staples are chicken and **fish** (shark, barracuda, swordfish, *job*, red snapper, marlin, tuna, grouper, jack fish, etc), and these are prepared in a number of different ways: with fruit or vegetables, herbs and spices, simmered in coconut milk *(kari coco)*, cooked with tomatoes and onions *(daube, rougay)*, or simply marinated in lightly spiced lime juice and grilled on an open fire. Alternatives might include crayfish, crabs, octopus *(zourit)* and, more occasionally, beef or pork.

Potatoes are scarce so rice is usually served as an accompaniment alongside **breadfruit** (puréed or in fritters), simmered Indian spiced lentils *(dhal)* or some local vegetables (aubergines or eggplant, known as *brenzel*, *chouchou*, boiled greens known as *bred*, or pumpkin, called *zironmon*, etc). There will also be some kind of relish like *satini*, which comprises an excellent assortment of grated fruit - papaya, coconut or green mango - steeped in lime juice or coconut milk.

You may also be given the opportunity of taste specialities such as the sweet and tender flesh of the vegetarian **fruit-bat** served roasted, curried or in a coarse paté. It will be as well to save a space for a mouth-watering dessert or a refreshing bowl of exotic fruit salad (various kinds of mango and banana, Java plums, custard apples, *corasols*, passion fruit, guava, pineapple, etc). If you fail to catch these fruits at breakfast in the large hotels, you will find seasonal varieties on sale in the market in Victoria; elsewhere, any spare produce tends to be shared out among the community.

For a quick midday snack, why not buy a few **gato piman** and a bag of the little savoury deep-fried Indian pastries known as **samossas** *(see p 224)* available from the bakeries in Victoria or roadside grocery stores.

Local drinks

A variety of bottled drinks are made under licence in the Seychelles, including three kinds of thirst-quenching light beer *(Seybrew, Célébration and EKU)*. After a large meal, you may wish to sip a lemon balm infusion to help digestion, or opt for a pot of cinnamon- or vanilla-flavoured tea from the slopes of Morne Seychellois (Mahé), or a coffee grown in one of the outlying islands.

At parties, family celebrations or *séga* and *moutia* sessions, the Seychellois often open a bottle of locally brewed and highly intoxicating beverages like **bacca** (fermented sugarcane juice) or **kalou** (fermented coconut palm sap). The other favourite is **coco d'amour**, a heady liqueur sold in a suggestively shaped bottle and reputed to be an aphrodisiac from the *coco de mer*.

LANGUAGE

90 % of **Kreol Seselwa** is old French and as such, it resembles the Creole spoken in Mauritius, but differs markedly from that spoken in Réunion.

The language was developed in the 18C as a means of communication between the early colonists and their African or Madagascan slaves, and to allow the slaves of different nationalities, who spoke a host of separate dialects, to understand each other. In formulating Creole, the slaves not only had to simplify the form and structure of French, they also had to devise descriptive or phonetic expressions for hitherto unfamiliar concepts like "slavery" and "mixed race". Over time, additional words have been assimilated from the African, Indian, Madagascan and English tongues, making a hybrid and oral language. It is only relatively recently that the grammatical structure and spelling have been standardised, largely as a result of the need for a national voice with which to express a new-found identity.

Those with a good grounding in French will understand a number of onomatopoeic and evocative words, and smile at their derivations. Others should be content to listen to the mellifluous sounds and musical intonations.

Throughout colonial times, Creole was banned from schools, churches and other public institutions in favour of French or English, but it continued to be spoken in the family home. Then, when the British imposed the use of English in schools in 1944, the Creole language became even more firmly entrenched. With Universal Suffrage in 1967, politicians and the media were obliged to address the electorate in Creole. After the 1977 coup, a Creole national anthem was composed, and in 1981 the new government made Creole the official national language.

Most people in the Seychelles speak fluent **English** or **French**, some both. At school, children are taught to read and write their Creole mother tongue, before embarking on learning English in the second year of primary school and French four years later. So the three languages are heard side by side every day. The administration, courts and business use English, the Church uses French, and the media alternate between all three.

Short Creole lexicon

Pronunciation

See p. 60.

Everyday expressions

Bonzour	Good morning/Good afternoon
Koman sava?	How are you?
Ki kote?	Where?
Kiler?	When?
Ki li ki la?	Who's there?
Ki mannyer ou apele?	What's your name?
Ki sa?	What's that?
Ki sa sa?	What do you want?
Kombyen sa?	How much is it?

Kote ou reste?	Where do you live?
Mon appel...	My name is...
Mon byen mersi	Thank you very much
Mon kapa ganny en labyer silvouplé?	Please may I have a beer?
Mon kontan	I really like...
Mon pa kompran	I don't understand
Mon swaf	I'm thirsty
Oli..?	Where is...
Oplezir	See you again
Sa I byen zoli	It's very beautiful
Taler	Later

Useful words

Baka	Cane liquor.
Bazar	Market.
Bwa (bois)	Describes many woody plants.
Bonbon	Sweet or savoury snack.
Boukan	Formerly a small fisherman's shack: now a tin-roofed barbecue.
Bred	Local greens eaten braised or in soup.
Brenzel	Aubergine/egg plant.
Gato piman	Spicy savoury fritter made of pulses.
Glasi	A sloping, rocky, eroded ledge or granite boulders washed by the sea.
Gwano	Sea bird droppings.
Kalou	Alcohol made from fermented coconut sap.
Kap	Large rock or headland.
Kari	Curry, an important Creole dish from India.
Kaz/Lakaz	Tin or cement breeze-block house. Even the largest keep this name. Only a really grandiose house is a château.
Kopra	The shelled coconut flesh, pressed for oil.
Kour	Garden.
Lavarang	Creole veranda, open or screened on one/several sides.
Limon	Lime.
Morn	Small, rounded-hill in the middle of an eroded valley.
Rougay	Either a simmered dish (rougail marmite), or a spicy condiment (rougail pilon).
Sanmousa	Small deep-fried pastry filled with meat, fish or spicy vegetables.
Zil	Island.
Zironmon	Red pumpkin/squash
Zourit	Squid or octopus.

Practical Information

L. Pozzoli/HOA QUI

Underwater landscape

BEFORE GOING

• Local time

The Seychelles are 4hr ahead of London in the winter and 3hr ahead in the summer and 9hr ahead of Eastern Standard Time (EST). So when it is 9am in Britain, it's either 12noon or 1pm in the Seychelles, depending on the season, and when it is 9am in New York, it is 5-6pm in the Seychelles, again depending on the season.

• How to call the Seychelles

Dial international + 248 + the number you wish to call (without the zero).

• When to go

The Seychelles have an equatorial tropical climate with monsoons. Lying outside the cyclone zone (with the exception of the Farquhar Atoll), the archipelago enjoys a relatively constant climate due to the Ocean. The best period to visit is **from March-May**, but temperatures are extremely pleasant throughout the year, ranging from 24°-30°C and the humidity is around 80 %. The ocean is responsible for a large number of microclimates on many of the islands.

Daytime lasts from 6am-6pm throughout the year.

Southern summertime

From October-March, northwest monsoon breezes bring a heavy, humid heat with occasionally violent storms. This is the best time to go fishing. Short tropical storms can hit the islands all year long, but the heaviest, shortest and the most sudden occur in January, primarily on Mahé and Silhouette. The vegetation is at its lushest at this time of year.

Southern wintertime

From April-September, the weather is at its coolest and driest due to the southwest trade winds. This is the best time for sailing, diving and surfing. July and August are the driest months. Although the term mass-tourism does not really apply, the islands' peak tourist periods are in **December-January** and **July-August**, when prices are consequently higher. April, when the migratory birds return, is the beginning of the best season for keen bird watchers.

• Packing list

Dress codes in the Seychelles are relaxed. Given the climate, all you will need are lightweight garments and a swimsuit. Plastic sandals will be useful protection against sea urchins, stonefish and coral. Warm trousers and a light sweater may be a good idea for the evening breezes in winter and in particular to protect against mosquitoes. Sunglasses are essential. A wide variety of sun-hats are available locally, made out of straw, coconut fibres or fabric. Most of the local inhabitants wear them.

• A trip for everyone

Travelling with children

The quality of the islands' facilities and the absence of illnesses make it easy to travel with children. The only precautions required will be protection against the sun and the sea.

Women travelling alone

Women travelling alone may experience more unwanted attention in the Seychelles than in Réunion or Mauritius, but travelling alone is neither dangerous nor difficult.

As the Seychelles are traditionally a destination for couples, the locals may simply be surprised to see someone travelling alone.

Elderly people

As with children, the facilities and hygiene are such that elderly people can travel without difficulty in the Seychelles, providing of course that they are prudent regarding the sun and the heat.

Disabled people

Some of the hotels located on very steep hill sites have many staircases. It is advisable to check with potential hotels beforehand to make sure that it will be easy to get about on the premises. Otherwise, only travelling by boat may prove somewhat difficult.

Pets

All pets are subjected to a quarantine period of six months before being admitted to the Seychelles.

• Address book

Tourist Information Offices

United Kingdom – 111 Baker St, second floor, London W1M 1FE, ☎ 171 224 1670 Fax 171 486 1352

USA (& Canada) – 235 East Fortieth St, Suite 24A, New York, NY 10016, ☎ 212 687 9766, Fax 212 922 9177

Web Sites

Seychelles official tourist board site: www.seychelles.net

Travelocity: www3.travelocity.com

Embassies and Consulates

Australia – 18 Dansu Court, Hallam, 3803 ☎ 39 796 4010, Fax 39 796 3577

Canada – 67 rue Ste Catherine Ouest, fith floor, Montreal, Quebec, ☎ 514 284 3322, Fax 514 845 0631

United Kingdom – 111 Baker St, second floor, London W1M 1FE, ☎ 171 224 1660 Fax 171 487 5756

USA – 820 Second ave, Suite 203, New York, NY 10017, ☎ 212 687 9766, Fax 212 922 9177

• Formalities

Identity Papers

A valid passport and a return or onward ticket are all that is needed to travel to the Seychelles. A visa valid for one month will be supplied free of charge on arrival on condition that visitors can prove they have enough money to remain for the duration of their visit. Anyone wishing to extend their visa (up to one year) should contact the **Immigration Office**, Independence House, on the corner of Independence ave and 5th June ave, Victoria ☎ 224 030, Monday-Friday, 8am-4pm (two passport photos, sufficient funds and a return ticket are required).

Customs

There are no restrictions on importing foreign currencies into the Seychelles. Tourists can bring in one litre of spirits, one litre of wine, 200 cigarettes (or 250g of tobacco), 125ml of perfume and 250ml of eau de toilette. Drugs, firearms and munitions are prohibited, as are food or agricultural products.

The export of shells, coral, fish, tortoises, etc from the Seychelles is prohibited and an official export certificate is required to leave with *coco de mer*.

Sanitary regulations
A sanitary certificate from the Ministry of Agriculture is necessary to import any plants.

Vaccinations
No particular vaccinations are required. However, nationals of African states or anyone having spent time on this continent will be required to produce up-to-date vaccination certificates for cholera and yellow fever.

Driving licence
A current national driving licence is required to rent a car.

• Currency

Cash
The national currency in the Seychelles is the Seychelles Rupee (SRs), a healthy currency which is equivalent to approximately US$1 = SRs5.

Currency exchange
Money can be changed in foreign exchange offices at the airport on arrival or departure of international flights, at all tourist sites, in Victoria, in the larger villages of the three main islands, and in most hotels. Most foreign currencies are accepted. The exchange rate, fixed daily by the Central Bank of Seychelles, is identical in all banks. Visitors should however note that, at the time of going to press, the Seychelles government had announced that visitors would be required to pay hotel bills in foreign currency (credit card, travellers' cheques or cash).

Travellers' cheques
Travellers' cheques can be changed practically everywhere. The rate is better than for foreign currency, but a commission is taken on each exchange.

Credit cards
The main hotels, restaurants, souvenir shops and banks accept American Express, Diner's Club, Master Card and Visa, except on the island of Silhouette, where only Visa and Master Card are accepted. The only cash dispensers on Mahé are in Victoria and at the airport; at Baie Ste-Anne and Grand'Anse on Praslin, they can be found.

• Spending money
Life is more expensive in the Seychelles than in Réunion and much more expensive than in Mauritius. Prices can double depending on the season, and practically all prices increase by 20-30 % between 15 December and 15 January. For two people travelling together, a hotel will cost a minimum of US$30 per person per day and it is possible to eat out for around US$15 per meal. More upmarket accommodation and restaurants, without being luxurious, will cost around US$75 per day per person including meals.

Travelling by bus is by far the cheapest form of transport, but it involves the inconvenience of not stopping exactly when or where you want. Renting a car costs around US$50-55 a day on Mahé and more like US$60 on Praslin. Taxis are expensive. Regular boatfares and airfares are relatively reasonably priced. For more details, see the transport, accommodation and restaurant sections in this chapter.

• Booking in advance
Because of the limited number of beds in the archipelago, and because the climate is so pleasant throughout the year, it is more than advisable to book accommodation in advance, whatever the season you intend to travel. During

the Christmas season and summer months (July-August), it is also a good idea to book a car in advance, if that is how you've decided to get about, together with any air tickets between islands. Hotel rates are generally cheaper if the accommodation is arranged through a travel agency.

• Repatriation insurance

Remember to take out repatriation insurance. You may be able to do this through your bank: some bank cards include special insurance policies. If you booked through a tour operator, emergency/repatriation insurance is often included in the price of your trip. The following may however prove useful.

Travel Insurance Agency, Suite 2, Percy Mews, 755B High Rd, North Finchley, London NI2 8JY, UK, ☎ 181 446 5414, Fax 181 446 5417, info@travelin-surers.com

Travel Insurance Services, 2930 Camino Diablo, Suite 200, PO Box 299, Walnut Creek, CA 94596, USA, ☎ 800 937 1387, Fax 925 932 0442, webinfo@travelinsure.com

• Gifts to offer

The Seychelles Islands were cut off from the western world by communist rule for a long period, which explains the inhabitants' current fascination with all things modern. They are perhaps inevitably attracted to things which they see on television or in the possession of foreign tourists, but which are generally out of their reach. If you want to take a gift to friends or to new acquaintances, you could take souvenirs of your city and country, photos of your family and home, little gadgets, makeup, cosmetics, music cassettes, T-shirts or anything else that is trendy. A bottle of wine or spirits may also be a good idea.

GETTING THERE

• By air

Scheduled flights

The direct London-Mahé flight lasts 9hr; it is also possible to fly direct from Johannesburg. Travellers from Australia, Canada or the United States will have to stop in Europe or South Africa and catch a connecting flight.

British Airways operate two flights a week between London and Mahé. Information: callers within the UK ☎ 0345 222 111, callers outside the UK ☎ 44 141 222 2222, www.britishairways.com

Air Seychelles operate four weekly flights from Paris and two from London. Information: Head Office, Victoria House, PO Box 386, Mahé, ☎ 248 381 000, Fax 248 225 933, www.airseychelles.net

Condor Airlines fly to the Seychelles via Frankfurt.

Charter flights

While there are no charter flights to the Seychelles, some travel agencies do offer promotional rates on regular flights.

Flights between the Seychelles, Mauritius and Réunion

Air Austral offer one to two flights a week between the Seychelles and Réunion and between the Seychelles and Mauritius.

Seychelles – Victoria House, Victoria, Mahé ☎ 225 300, Fax 211 1411

Mauritius – Roger's House, 5 Pres John F Kennedy St, Port Louis, ☎ 212 2666,
Réunion – 4 rue de Nice, St-Denis, ☎ 909 090, Fax 909 091.

Air France operate three weekly flights between the Seychelles and Réunion and Mauritius.
Seychelles – Independence ave, Victoria, Mahé.
Mauritius - Roger's House, 5 Pres John F Kennedy St, Port Louis, ☎ 208 6820
Réunion – 7 ave de la Victoire, 97477 St-Denis, ☎ 403 838

Air Mauritius operate three flights a week from the Seychelles to Mauritius.
Seychelles – Kingsgate House, PO Box, Victoria, Mahé, ☎ 322 414
Mauritius – Roger's House, 5 Pres John F Kennedy St, Port Louis, ☎ 208 7700
Réunion – 13 rue Charles Gounod, 97400 St-Denis, ☎ 948 383.

Air Seychelles operate two weekly flights between Mauritius and the Seychelles (Tuesdays and Saturdays).
Seychelles – Victoria House, PO Box 386, Mahé ☎ 381 000, Fax 225 933
Mauritius – Roger's House, 5 Pres John F Kennedy St, Port Louis, ☎ 208 6801, Fax 208 3646
Réunion – Air France, 7 ave de la Victoire, St-Denis, ☎ 403 838

British Airways have two weekly flights between London and the Seychelles.
Seychelles – Kingsgate House, PO Box 292, Victoria, Mahé, ☎ 224 910
Mauritius – Ground floor, IBL House, Caudan, Port Louis, ☎ 202 8000
Réunion – Air Liberté, 13 rue Charles Gounoud, St-Denis, ☎ 947 210

International airport

All international and domestic flights arrive at Mahé airport, which is built on the sea at Anse Talbot, 10km from the capital, Victoria. Taxis and representatives of the major car rental companies, as well as a currency exchange, souvenir shop, duty-free shop and a cafeteria can all be found open at the airport on the arrival of international flights, and there is a cash dispenser in the airport.
Most hotels provide a shuttle service to their premises. If you arrive on a domestic flight, however the airport can, depending on the time, be totally deserted. A telephone is available that you just have to pick up to order a taxi. There are no car rental companies on hand at weekends or in slack periods, but public transport buses stop by the airport approximately every 20min.

Confirmation

It is highly recommended that you reconfirm your return flight on arrival and arrive 2hr before the scheduled departure time, because overbooking is pretty systematic.

Airport tax

Keep US$40 to pay the departure tax on leaving the Seychelles.

• Package deals

A wide range of agencies offer a wide range of vacations. It is becoming more and more advantageous to purchase deals which include the air ticket, full board and accommodation and even a rental car, than to organise a trip individually.

See the list of specialised tour operators, p 72-73.

THE BASICS

• Address book

An independent English language magazine, *Treasure Every Moment*, is published monthly free of charge.

Tourist Information Centre

Tourist Office – *Independence ave, PO Box 92, Victoria,* ☎ 225 313, Monday-Friday, 8am-5pm; Saturdays, 9am-12noon.

Embassies and consulates

United Kingdom – PO Box 161, Victoria Hose, Victoria, ☎ 225 225
USA – PO Box 251, Victoria House, Victoria, ☎ 225 256

• Opening and closing times

Banks

Victoria has a large number of banks (open Monday-Friday, 8.30am-2/3pm; Saturdays, 8.30am-11.30am.

At the airport they open on the arrival of each international flight. Banks are also available in Beau Vallon, on the road from Victoria (open during the week, 9am-12.30pm; Saturdays, 8.30am-10.45am), at Grand Anse and at Anse Boileau. You can change money at all hotels but at a less advantageous exchange rate. The only cash dispensers on Mahé are located in Victoria and at the airport.

Post offices

Post offices are open Monday-Friday, 8am-4pm; Saturdays, 8am-12noon.

Shops

Shops are open from 8am-5pm; Saturdays 8am-12noon.

Restaurants

Opening days and times vary from one establishment to another.

Offices

Office opening hours are Monday-Friday, 8am-12noon, 1pm-4pm.

• Museums and gardens

Hours

Most museums are stated run and generally open from 9am-5pm, often closing for an hour for lunch. Private places of visit are subject to varying opening hours.

Admission fees

Prices vary from US$1.50 to US$3, and a reduction is often available for children.

• Postal service

The Seychelles postal service works well. Although you will find post offices in most of the main villages, it is advisable to wait and post your mail from Victoria's central post office. Stamps can only be purchased from post offices, but some hotels do provide them for their guests. It is possible to airmail packages.

• Phone and fax

The Seychelles are equipped with a modern telephone network. This network covers the islands of Mahé, Praslin, La Digue, Silhouette, Bird, Fregate and Desroches.

International calls

You can call anywhere in the world from the **Cable and Wireless** office in Victoria, Mahé, which also offers telex, telegraph and fax services.

Local calls

The streets of Victoria and all the main villages of Mahé, Praslin, La Digue, Silhouette and Cerf have coin – or card – operated public phone booths. 30, 60, 120 or 240 unit telephone cards can be bought at the airport, from the **Cable and Wireless** office in Victoria and from most shops and post offices.

Codes and rates

To call abroad from the Seychelles, dial 00 + country code + phone number. **Codes for other countries –** United Kingdom: 44, USA/Canada: 1, Australia: 61.

Directory enquiries

Local directory enquiries: dial 181.
International directory enquiries: dial 151.

• Public holidays

National holidays

1-2 January	New Year
1 May	Labour Day
5 June	Liberation Day
18 June	National Reconciliation Day
29 June	Independence Day

Religious holidays

March/April	Good Friday and Easter Sunday
June (var)	Corpus Christi
15 August	Assumption
1 November	All Saints' Day
8 December	Immaculate Conception
25 December	Christmas Day

GETTING AROUND

• By car

The best way to visit Mahé, and possibly even Praslin, is to rent a car for a few days.

Car rentals

To rent a car, you must have a current international driving licence and be 18 years of age or over. On Mahé, the main rental companies have representatives at the airport and in the hotels. on Mahé, as on Praslin, the smaller rental companies offer competitive rates, but it is worthwhile checking the condition of the vehicle and the insurance clauses carefully before renting. Keep the breakdown service number close at hand.

The national vehicle, the legendary *mini-moke*, is the most adapted to the islands' narrow, winding lanes. You can also rent 4WD vehicles and closed cars, more appropriate in case of storms. Mileage is unlimited. All the companies will deliver the vehicle to where you are staying, but the fuel tank is generally empty. Renting a car costs between Rs300–350 a day on Mahé and Rs350-400 on Praslin.

A few useful addresses in Mahé:
Nelson's Car Hire, St-Louis, ☎ 266 923, Fax 266 032. Friendly welcome, but check the car before renting.
Meins, St-Louis, ☎ 266 005/266 366, Fax 375 732.
Hertz, Revolution ave, ☎ 322 447/322 669, Fax 324 111. Reliable vehicles but more expensive than the local agents.

Road network

The island of Mahé boasts a network of some 150km of good surfaced roads and over 100km of unsurfaced roads. Most of the roads on Praslin are surfaced, but watch out for potholes. Driving on the other islands is most often a case of off-road driving and a 4WD is definitely the best choice in this case. Signposting is fairly sparse, but given the size of the islands, it is almost impossible to get lost.

Driving

You must drive on the left side of the road and give way to vehicles coming from the right. The locals drive very fast and a large number of accidents happen at night on the unlit roads. Drivers will need to watch out for children on the roadsides, particularly in the afternoon, when the schools finish.
Signs remind drivers that seat belts are compulsory and that the speed limit is 40kph in villages and 65kph on open roads.

Fuel

On Mahé, there are fuel stations in Victoria, Beau Vallon, Baie Lazare, Anse Royale and at the airport. On Praslin, there is a fuel station at Grand Anse and one at Baie Ste-Anne. Fuel prices are more or less equivalent to those in Europe.

H. Choimet

• By taxi

Taxis can be found on Mahé and Praslin. Prices are high. If planning on a taxi on a Sunday or in the evening, it is best to book ahead, either by phone or via your hotel, and agree on the rate beforehand.

• By bus

Although the Mahé bus service is good, Praslin is not so well equipped. Bus stops are indicated by marks on the edge of the road. When you want to get off, just shout *"Devant!"* and the driver will try to stop as soon as possible. Tickets can be bought in the bus (US$0.75). A regular service runs between 5.30am-7pm but is less frequent on Sundays.

• By ox cart

An amusing form of transport, found only on La Digue, enabling tourists to relax as they discover the island. It is, however, relatively expensive.

• Renting a bike

Motorbikes and scooters are forbidden in the Seychelles for safety reasons. You can, however, rent bikes on Praslin and La Digue.

• Organised tours and excursions

Travel agencies organise transfers and excursions leaving the hotels to most of the main islands. They have offices on Mahé *(see p 414)*, Praslin and La Digue, and are also represented at the airport and in some hotels. Check with your hotel.

• From island to island

Domestic flights

Air Seychelles organise regular services between Mahé and the archipelago's main islands. The number of flights varies depending on demand.
Mahé-Praslin (15min): frequent flights daily.
Mahé-Fregate (15min), flights nearly every day.
Mahé-Denis (25min) and Mahé-Desroches (1hr): two weekly flights.
Mahé-Bird Island (30min): one flight per day.
Passengers must arrive 30min ahead of departure time and are allowed a maximum of 10kg of luggage.
For information and reservations, contact **Air Seychelles** in Victoria, Victoria House, opposite the clock tower (☎ 225 159/381 300), at Mahé airport (☎ 373 311) or on Praslin (☎ 233 214).

Helicopters

Helicopter Seychelles operate services between all the islands, except Bird. Regular flights are progressively replacing boat crossings for visitors to Silhouette and to Digue Island Lodge Hotel. Special transfers are organised between Mahé and Praslin, La Digue, Silhouette, Denis and Fregate. Departures are from the airport, Mahé Heliport, Victoria Helistop, Plantation Helistop, or from hotels.
Helicopter Seychelles, PO Box 595, Victoria, Mahé, ☎ 373 900, Fax 373 055, victor@seychelles.net

Maritime transfers

A regular schooner service operates between Mahé (Victoria's new port), Praslin (Baie Ste-Anne) and La Digue (La Passe). There is no regular service with the other islands. Boats can be chartered directly or by contacting an agency. The sea can be pretty choppy, especially from May to October: take seasickness pills and some waterproof clothing.

Organised tours and excursions

Several agencies organise minibus tours of Mahé and Praslin, and excursions to the main islands of the archipelago.

BED AND BOARD

• Where to stay

Over 75 % of the available accommodation is on Mahé. Praslin also has a large number of hotels. Guesthouse and family accommodation is becoming more and more frequent on La Digue. On the whole, however, there is limited accommodation available, so it is advisable to book in advance and to reconfirm a short time before you plan to arrive.

• Various categories

The government carefully controls the number and quality of hotels, via the *Seychelles Tourist Board* (STB). All accommodation must observe a certain number of comfort standards in order to be able to receive tourists.

Camping

Camping is not allowed in the Seychelles.

Guesthouses

This is aa far-reaching term that can cover small basic hotels, private luxury bungalows or typical bed & breakfast accommodation. Whatever the degree of luxury, this type of accommodation is very common in the Seychelles and enables tourists to get a much more authentic feel for the country than they would in a traditional hotel. The government encourages this type of accommodation in preference to the larger, grander hotels. Many guesthouses have a restaurant or can provide meals.

Hotels

Hotels are generally more luxurious than guesthouses, often equipped with a restaurant, bar, gift shop and leisure facilities.

Private accommodation

It is possible to rent a furnished, fully equipped bungalow or villa. This is by far the cheapest solution, especially if you are travelling with a family.

• Eating out

In hotels and guesthouses

All hotels have a restaurant, and nearly all the guesthouses can provide half board, generally with a set menu.

In restaurants

With the exception of a few little restaurants in Victoria and a few snack bars or pizza houses near the most popular beaches, eating out is expensive. A meal in a guesthouse – where the cooking is often excellent – will cost around US$14 and you will pay at least US$15 in restaurants. If you get bored with the excellent Creole-style Seychelles cooking, you can always choose from a variety of Chinese, Indian or even Italian restaurants.

In the street

You will find sandwiches and *samossas* in some of the little grocery shops in Victoria and in the villages, but this type of "eating out" phenomenon has yet to really catch on.

Drinks

Tap water is drinkable and bottled mineral water is very expensive. Soft drinks, fruit juices and beer are widely available. Restaurants do serve relatively expensive wine, imported from South Africa, Australia or France.

SPORTS AND PASTIMES

• The sea

All the beaches in the Seychelles are public, with the rare exception of the few private islands. Most of the more touristy beaches on Mahé (Beau Vallon) and Praslin (Anse Volbert) have diving clubs, either independent or attached to the hotels.

The temperature and colour of the water naturally invite visitors to **swim** (don't forget to bring plastic sandals to protect against coral and sea urchins) and to explore the islands' fantastic marine wildlife (wear a T-shirt to avoid sunburn). If you don't have your own equipment, masks, snorkels and flippers can be rented from all the diving clubs or can be borrowed from some hotels.

It is also possible to go water-skiing (on Mahé, in the Beau Vallon bay, from May-October, and on the East coast from November-April), **windsurfing** or even **parasailing** (at the beach of Beau Vallon on Mahé).

H. Choimet

Scuba diving

Extremely severe environmental regulations have enabled the Seychelles to protect its fauna, and the seabeds are among the best-preserved in the world, particularly in the national parks. Underwater hunting is not allowed, whether for coral, shells or fish. The tourist office in Victoria has a full list of all the scuba-diving clubs; see also the regional practical information sections for a list of the main clubs on each island. The clubs cater to enthusiasts of all levels: introduction, PADI, night diving, etc.

April-November is the best scuba-diving period. The rest of the year, the sea is rough and murky.

Underwater walking

Accessible to all (from seven years up), underwater walking is a good alternative to scuba-diving if you want to explore the seabed. No prior knowledge of diving or even swimming is necessary. Wearing a panoramic helmet fed with oxygen and a weighted lead belt, and attached to a platform from which they climb down, walkers are free to walk about on the sea bottom at a depth of about 3-4m *(see illustration p 243)*. Ask at your hotel.

Glass-bottom boats

If you would rather explore the seabed without getting wet, try an outing in a glass-bottom boat, available in particular in the marine parks of Ste-Anne and Baie Ternay (departures from Victoria or Beau Vallon beach). For best visibility, choose a sunny, windless day and check the condition of the "glass bottom" for scratches before embarking.

Deep sea fishing

Record catches are regularly recorded in the exceptionally fishy waters of the Seychelles. The waters around Bird, Denis and Desroches literally team with marlin, tuna and barracudas.

Sailing enthusiasts should head for Silhouette, an ideal site if the number of catches recorded between April and August and in December is to be believed.

Marine Charter Association, Victoria Port, ☎ 322 126. Night trips are also possible.

Chartering sailing boats

Rentals of yachts and catamarans are developing fast. However it must be remembered that sailing in the Indian Ocean is not to be undertaken lightly, even by experienced sailors. Wind, currents and the coral reef represent very real dangers. Passages and coastal canals have recently been marked out, but on the whole, it would be better to set sail with an experienced Seychelles skipper. More information from the **Marine Charter Association**, Victoria Port, ☎ 322 126, Fax 224 679.

• Other activities

Walking

Eager to develop ecotourism in the Seychelles, the government marks and maintains hiking paths. A dozen or so brochures, published by the Ministry of Tourism and sold in the Tourist Information Centre in Victoria (SRs5 each), describe itineraries, as well as the fauna and flora you're likely to discover out walking. Of varying lengths and difficulty, most of these walks are nonetheless accessible to all, but if you don't feel too adventurous, private guides are available to accompany walkers. Contact **Basil Beaudoin**, Coral Strand Hotel, Mahé, ☎ 241 790.

The Seychelles have practically no dangerous plants, insects or snakes, but walkers should always take protection against the sun, drinking water and waterproof clothing in case of rain.

Riding

Riding treks are organised by:

Domaine du Château d'Eau, Barbarons, Mahé, ☎ 378 577.

Union Estate, La Digue *(see p 458)*.

Tennis

Most hotels are equipped with a tennis court.

Golf

There is a nine-hole course at the **Reef Hotel** (Anse aux Pins, Mahé), open to visitors. On Praslin, a second golf course has been built next to the Hotel Lémuria.

• Helicopter rides

Hélicoptère Seychelles, ☎ 373 900, organises panoramic flights over Mahé or the neighbouring islands. An hour's flight will cost around SRs4 000. Departures are from Mahé airport, Victoria Helistop, Plantation Helistop or your hotel.

• Night-life

Night-life is virtually nonexistent in the Seychelles and most activity seems to come to a total halt as soon as the sun sets. Mahé does, however, boast the only cinema together with a few bars and nightclubs.

Some hotels organise barbecues or dancing evenings, or put on shows featuring Seychellois music and dancing, sometimes attended by local young people. If you like gambling, a casino has recently opened in Victoria, and some of the larger hotels also have casinos.

SHOPPING

• What's on offer

Arts and crafts

The islands' complete range of natural resources is employed in the arts and crafts trade. Straw hats and baskets, decorative objects made out of pottery, wood or coconut, shell jewellery. Some statues and jewellery are among the more popular items also imported from Africa.

Paintings and batiks

A large number of artists live in the Seychelles and are happy to sell their work. Some art galleries do have work by painters, but you can also visit most of them directly in their studios.

Model ships

The country's sole factory, **La Marine** at La Plaine St-André *(see p. 422)*, will delight all lovers of model ships and sailing. Although far more expensive than in Mauritius, these entirely handmade models of vintage ships are quite stunning.

Perfume

The three **Kréofleurage** perfumes are sold at the manufacturer's, in most of the boutiques in Victoria and at the main tourist sites *(see* Shopping section, *p 437).*

"Coco de mer"

The *"coco de mer"* coconut or *"coco-fesse"*, is without a doubt the rarest souvenir you can bring back. Depending on the number of nuts available at any given moment, however, they can sometimes prove difficult to find. This is because the government, wishing to avoid speculation and protect the species, has regulated the sale of this precious fruit. The number and price of the nuts on sale is fixed by the government. Make sure you obtain a certificate of sale, because you will be asked for it when you exit through customs.

"Coco d'amour"

This creamy alcohol, with its delicate coconut flavour, is sold in a bottle shaped like a *coco-fesse*. Add an ice-cube and savour the memory of relaxed Seychelles evenings when back home. Available in large or miniature bottles.

Spices

The markets are full of vanilla, patchouli, cinnamon and chillis, as well as tea and vanilla essences, all of which will make your mouth water. Good gift ideas to take home to the family and friends or for any budding Creole cook.

• Where to shop

Spices and essences can be found in Victoria market, one of the only markets of the archipelago. Victoria has several well-established souvenir and craft boutiques. Most of the arts and crafts on offer can be found in the Craft Village at Anse aux Pins on Mahé. You will come across a number of art galleries as you explore. Elsewhere you won't find much on offer. The best place to buy *cocos de mer* is Praslin, on the road through the Vallée de Mai.

• Bartering

See p 403.

• Duty and regulations on certain items

Only buy *cocos de mer* with a certificate of sale; otherwise they will be confiscated by customs when you leave the country.

HEALTH AND SAFETY

• Precautions

There are no tropical illnesses in the Seychelles. The only dangers are from the sun or the sea. Although the mosquitoes may prove ferocious, there are no cases of malaria.

• Medical kit

Take an insect-bite lotion and protective sun cream. If you are prone to upset stomachs, also take along anti-diarrhoea pills.

• Health services

First aid

Go to the infirmary of a large hotel. If necessary, ask your hotel to contact a doctor.

Hospitals

The main hospital, located on Mahé, at Mont Fleuri, near Victoria's Botanical Gardens (24-hour emergency service: ☎ 388 000) – has a good consulting service for the major specialities and also has a dental surgery.

Doctor Jules Gedeon is regularly called on to treat tourists.

Praslin and La Digue each have a clinic.

Pharmacies

The main chemists are in Victoria. Praslin doesn't have a pharmacy but medicine is available from Baie Ste-Anne hospital (☎ 232 333).

• Emergencies

Call ☎ 999 and ask for the required service (fire brigade, police, ambulance).

FROM A TO Z

• Bartering

The price of car rentals and some hotel accommodation in the low season can be negotiated, but prices indicated in shops are fixed.

• Conversion table

The Seychelles use both the imperial and the metric measurement systems. *See Units of Measurement on p 248.*

• Credit cards

Some establishments take a 5 % commission on bills paid by credit card.

• Drinking water

The tap water is drinkable.

• Electricity

Electricity is 240 volts. All rooms are equipped with British three-point plugs and standard two-point adapters. If this isn't the case, adapters can be bought from hardware shops in Victoria.

• Laundry service
Most hotels and guesthouses provide a laundry service.

• Newspapers
Most of the local newspapers are in a mixture of Creole, English and French. Finding the foreign press is difficult in the Seychelles, except in some hotels in Victoria and a few rare bookshops.

• Photography
Films can be bought everywhere and can be developed in Victoria and in some tourist locations at reasonable prices.

• Radio and television
Programmes are broadcast in Creole, English or French depending on where they are from. English news is broadcast on the radio daily at 7pm and on TV at 6pm. There is only one television channel in the Seychelles, SBC, and one radio station, Paradise FM.

• Smoking
Cigarettes are expensive in the Seychelles and the choice is limited, which probably explains why so few people smoke on the islands. It is best to buy any cigarettes or tobacco products at the duty-free shop at the airport, or perhaps try the local brand, *Mahé'king*.

• Thefts
To be on the safe side, don't leave valuables in your car. Most hotels have a safe where you can leave valuables (request a receipt).

• Tipping/gratuities
Tipping is not compulsory. A 10 % service charge is already included in all restaurant and hotel bills.

• Weather forecasts
Call ☎ 373 377.

LOOK AND LEARN

• General
CARPIN Sarah, ***Illustrated Guide to Seychelles***, Odyssey, 1998. Photos and maps.
GEORGES Eliane, **Indian Ocean**, B Taschen Verlag, Germany, 1998. Coffee table book.
GILHAM Mary E, ***Islands of the Trade Winds; An Indian Ocean Odyssey***, Minerva Publications, 1999.
SKERRETT Adrian, ***Beauty of Seychelles***, Camerapix, 1991. Photos.
SKERRETT Adrian, ***Journey through Seychelles***, Camerapix, 1994. Photos.
TINGAY Paul, ***Beautiful Seychelles: An illustrated traveller's companion***, C. Struik, S. Africa, 1996.

• Children's books
PENNY Malcolm, ***The Indian Ocean***, Raintree Publications, 1997. Children's nature guide.

• Flora and fauna

CASTLE GILLIAN E, ***Flora of Aride Island, Seychelles***, Eco Tech, 1994.

HENKEL FW, ***Amphibians and Reptiles of Madagascar, the Mascarenes, the Seychelles and the Comoros Islands***, RE Krieger Publishing Co, US, 1998.

NOLTING Mark, ***Africa's Top Wildlife Countries: With Mauritius and Seychelles***, Global Travel Publishers, 1997.

PAOLILO Vincenzo, **Seychelles**, Swan Hill Publishing, 1997. Guide to the fish of the Seychelles.

ROBERTSON SA, ***Flowering Plants of Seychelles***, Royal Botanic Gardens, Kew, 1989.

SKERRETT Adrian & Judith, ***Beautiful Plants of Seychelles***, Camerapix, 1991.

SKERRETT Adrian, ***Birdwatcher's Guide to Seychelles***, Prion, Huntingdon, 1992.

WISE Rosemary, ***Fragile Eden: Portraits of Endemic Plants of the Granitic Seychelles***, Princeton UP, 1998.

• History

SCARR Deryck, ***Seychelles Since 1770: History of a Slave and Post Slavery Society***, C Hurst, 1999.

DUCROTOY Athalie, ***Beautiful Isles, Beautiful People: Family in Olde Seychelles***, Rawlings Publications, 1995.

• Literature

MANCHAM James, ***Reflections and Echoes from Seychelles***, available from Victoria library. Poetry collection by the first president of the Seychelles.

• Maps

Maps can be bought before leaving or on arrival from the Map Division, Independence House, 5th June ave, Victoria.

Seychelles, Globetrotter tourist map, 1:33 000, 1995.

Seychelles, Mahé, Ordnance Survey Map, 1:50 000, 1989.

Seychelles, Praslin, Ordnance Survey Map, 1:30 000, 1986. Also covers La Digue and other neighbouring islands.

Seychelles: Traveller's Map, Macmillan Educ, 1990.

• People and Culture

FRANDA Marcus F, ***Seychelles: Unquiet Islands***, Gower Pub. Co, 1983.

SAUER Jonathan D, ***Plants and Man on the Seychelles Coast***, University Wisconsin P, 1967.

• Sports

HEIKELL Rod, ***Indian Ocean Cruising Guide***, Imray, 1999.

JACKSON Jack, ***Diving in the Indian Ocean***, Rizzoli Publications, 1999.

WOOD Lawson, ***Diving and Snorkeling Guide to Seychelles***, Pisces Books, US, 1997.

Exploring the Seychelles

G. Simeone/DIAF

Anse Takamaka, Mahé

VICTORIA★

Capital of the Seychelles and Mahé's harbour
Pop 24 700
Map p 410-411

Not to be missed
A walk round the market.
A drink or an ice-cream at Kaz Zanana.

And remember...
The town is at its busiest during the morning up to noon.
Avoid Sundays: the town is dead and all the restaurants are closed.
Park the car and explore the town on foot.

Since Victoria can be visited on its own, it is treated independently of the itineraries around the Island of Mahé.

A miniature capital

The capital of the Seychelles, one of the tiniest in the world, is like no other, nestling as it does in a large sheltered bay encircled by a majestic ring of granite mountains covered with lush vegetation. Victoria is the only real town of the archipelago, and a rather provincial kind of town it is at that, although a third of the entire population of the Seychelles is resident there. It is also the islands' principal administrative and economic centre. Over the last few years, an ever increasing number of traffic jams has come to clog the handful of streets, especially during early morning and noon rush hour periods; traffic lights have recently been introduced and seem to be effective in streamlining the growing congestion of people and vehicles. Despite this, the overall atmosphere is laid-back, the drivers remain courteous, the pedestrian movement is orderly, if at times almost feverish, and the streets are almost irreproachably clean.

A morning stroll through this tiny city is sufficient to provide a clear insight into the ongoing development of the Seychelles as a whole; the walk will also impart a real feel for Victoria which is quite different not only from the rest of the island, but from anywhere else in the archipelago. The town cannot be called beautiful as such, given the many recent constructions (including some soulless supermarkets crammed with ever increasing numbers of foreign imports) it is the last vestiges of colonialism that preserve a peculiar charm, the slightly dilapidated wooden houses with ornate ironwork balconies, or the old-fashioned shops packed with a thousand Indian or Chinese treasures like Ali Baba's cave.

The town throngs with people at lunch-time and when the offices close for the day at around 4pm, and casually-dressed workers do that last bit of shopping before going home.

Port Royal to Victoria

Lazare Picault landed in the bay at Victoria in 1744 and named it Port Royal. Two years later Captain Corneille Nicolas Morphey took official possession of Mahé and dedicated a stone above the port to the French army. In 1778 it was rechristened Etablissement du Roi. Eventually, the town took the name Victoria in 1838, in homage to Queen Victoria of England who was crowned that day. Victoria became the capital of the Seychelles in 1903.

The small, drowsy administrative and commercial centre long stood in a time warp, forgotten and unchanged as if time stood still. By all accounts the town was rank and lacked proper drainage and pavements until the Second World War. Independence and the construction of Mahé's airport combined to energise the island and make it into what is now a strikingly clean, airy, bustling and well-cared for provincial town.

Tour of the town

Allow half a day.

The **Clock Tower** (B1) – known locally as *l'horloge* – has marked the centre of town since 1903, when it was erected in celebration of the Seychelles becoming a British Crown Colony, and Victoria as its new capital. The "Little Ben" clock tower is in fact an amusing replica of the one outside Victoria Railway Station in London, and was once the tallest structure in town. Regularly repainted in silver, it looks singularly like something from toytown presiding over the traffic from its isolated position at the very heart of Victoria, a few metres from the Central Post Office.

Find Albert St and turn left into Market St.

Sir Selwyn Clarke Market* (B1) – which is known simply as the market *(open Monday-Friday, 6am-5pm; Saturdays, 5.30am-3pm)* – is set up early each morning in the shade of a giant mango tree. Small crowds gather around the lottery ticket sellers, the lottery being very popular here. Alternating between a sleepy quiet and noisy bustle, the market is at its liveliest at lunchtime and in the early evening. At these times it bursts into a harmony of colours, scents and sounds.

The Clock Tower in Victoria

M. Renaudeau/HOA QUI

Pretty housewives in bright dresses jostle side by side Jamaican rastamen in dreadlocks and Seychelles yuppies in suits, a bunch of bananas and a string of sardines in one hand, their briefcase in the other. Here, also, in between the colourful fruit and vegetables, fresh fish, spices, tea, bottles of vanilla essence and stalls with shells for tourists, is where you will see the most cattle egrets, the elegant white, yellow-beaked birds that are such a familiar sight in the capital. It is well worth wandering around **Market Street** *(theoretically reserved for pedestrians)* and around the market, for this is probably the liveliest and most popular district of Victoria. Note the elegant, if dilapidated, vestiges of the colonial era here, especially the wooden houses with coloured corrugated tin roofs and wrought-iron balconies. At street level, the small but prosperous shops are run by the present generation families of Chinese and Indians.

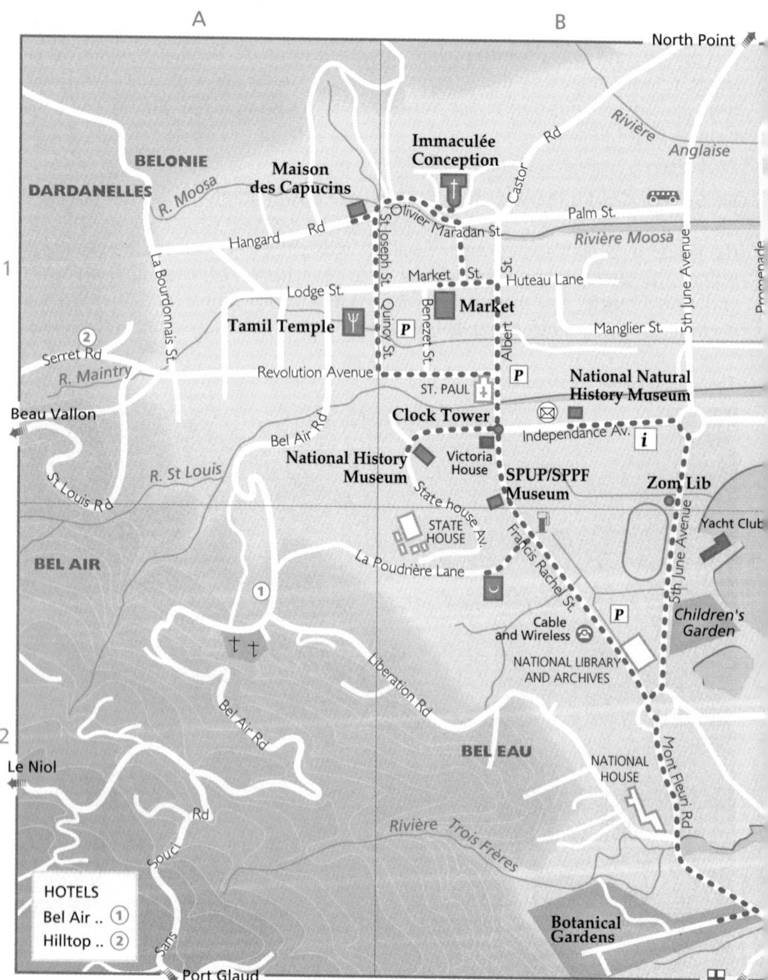

North of here, on Olivier Maradan St, stands the **Roman Catholic Cathedral** (l'Immaculée Conception – B1) with its painted beige façade shaded by lovely flowering trees. The separate **bell-tower** set back from the main body of the church has four bells which mark the passing of every hour by tolling twice, once before the hour as a 'wake-up' call and once on the hour to indicate the time. The congregations are always dressed in their best clothes and in fine voice for Sunday morning mass. These are informal as well as reverential occasions, however, with children capering about the gardens eating snacks while their parents come and go, stopping for a chat before going inside to sing a hymn or listen to the sermon. Several of the women, neatly dressed in colourful floral prints, hats and matching shoes, will loiter after the service outside in the shade before the statue of the Virgin to have a nip of whisky and a cheery gossip.

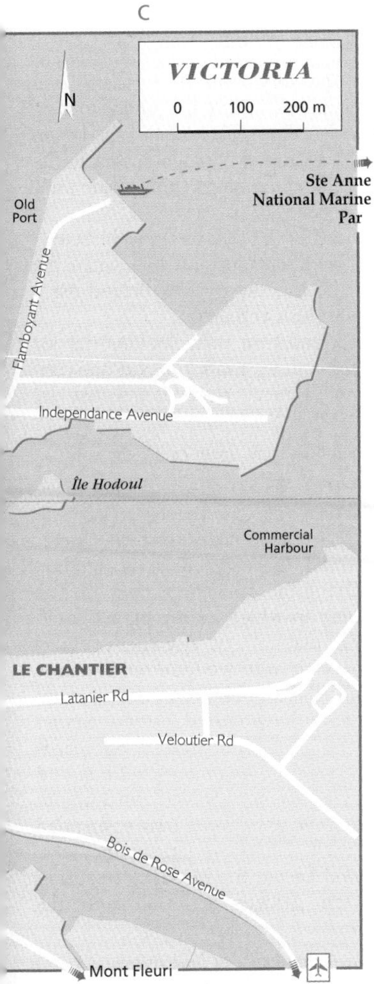

Next to the Cathedral stands **Capucin House*** (Maison des Capucins – A1), which houses a small community of elderly Swiss monks. The Portuguese-style house was built in 1933 and has elegant verandas and a graceful colonnade *(see illustration p 356)*.

Turn back down St-Joseph St, which soon becomes Quincy Street.

In passing, why not pop into the **Tamil Sri Navasakthi Vinayagar Temple** (A1) *(closed Sundays; no charge; remove shoes and leave by the entrance)* and discreetly observe the ritual centred around the effigy of Ganesh, an elephant-headed god surrounded by Hindu divinities painted in pale colours.

Continue along Quincy St and turn left onto Revolution ave. At the Clock Tower take State House ave.

The fine early 20C building that once served as the governors' offices presently houses the **National History Museum** (B1) *(open Thursday-Tuesday; closed Wednesdays and holidays; 8.30am-4.30pm (12noon on Saturdays); admission fee)*. Among the eclectic collection of exhibits displayed is the **Possession Stone** erected by Captain Morphey in 1756 to celebrate French ownership of the islands. Documents and relics relating to the discovery and conquest of the archipelago are shown along with early maps and fortune-hunters' charts, as well as portraits of important historical Seychellois figures. A second room displays mundane objects from daily life.

One glass case encloses a range of products made from coconut: hats made of *tami coco* (a vegetable fibre also used to filter liquids), brooms, toothpicks, mats, rope, brushes, fibre mattresses and stoppers. The rather splendid spiral staircase leads upstairs to an exhibition of photographs recording the changing hairstyles of the Seychellois since 1949.

At the end of State House ave, some 10m to the left of the museum.

The **State House** (Palais Présidentiel – B2) *(authorised visits only)*, which sits in spacious grounds, was designed as the headquarters for English government representatives. Although little can be seen from the street, it was built in the old colonial style around 1910.

Return to the Clock Tower and turn right down Francis Rachel St.

Another colonial-style wooden house, used as the headquarters of the SPUP (Seychelles People's United Party) between 1964-77 now houses the **SPUP/SPPF Museum** (B1, B2) *(Monday-Friday, 8am-4pm; Saturdays, 9am-12noon; closed Sunday; free entry; guided visit by an eager party member)*. The glory of the SPUP is celebrated in the Creole language from its earliest beginnings in 1964. Posters, rousing slogans and the original offices used by President René, his acolytes, the Union and the Party newspaper are all here. Upstairs, a series of photographs retells the history of the Party, the fight for independence, and the preparations made prior to President René's coup on 5 June 1977 (*see p 366-367*).
A short way beyond the museum, at the end of *Poudrière Lane* on the right, stands the small green and white **Sheikh Mohamed bin Khalifa Mosque** (B2), where the faithful quietly undertake their ablutions before entering to pray. Behind rise a number of steep granite outcrops covered with lush vegetation.
Retrace your steps back to Francis Rachel St and turn right, looking out for further old-fashioned wooden **colonial houses** with tin roofs, the odd one converted into small Chinese- or Indian-run general store frequented by schoolchildren on their way home.

At the roundabout, turn right onto Mont Fleuri Rd, then right again before the hospital.

The **Botanical Gardens*** (Jardin Botanique – B2) *(☎ 224 644, open daily, 9am-6pm; no charge. Snack bar. Souvenir shop. Parking. Take insect repellent and wear shoes fit for scrambling up muddy tracks. Best time to visit: June-August and October (flowering time); avoid December and January (rain). Leaflet on sale at the entrance)* are a must for anyone interested in identifying the indigenous species. The gardens were conceived in 1901 as a nursery in which **exotic plants** could be nurtured and acclimatised before being planted out elsewhere. Today Rivaltz Dupont's landscaping is fully mature, with over two hundred **endemic** and **indigenous** species including the Round Island bottle palm, the elephant apple, the octopus tree and the drumstick tree. Signposted paths meander through the shaded glades of different palm species, fruit trees, exotic hardwoods, multicoloured flowering trees and climbers, bamboo, orchids and spice trees (nutmeg, kapok, flowering ginger). This is a good opportunity to see giant tortoises from Aldabra, wild fruit-bats, and russet bats suspended upside-down in their enclosure until nightfall. The more patient may also glimpse various birds such as the rare Kestrel falcon, the Madagascan turtle-dove and the blue pigeon. Although the gardens are well-kept, the identification and labelling of plants is poor.

Return to Victoria. At the roundabout continue straight along 5th June Avenue.

Note the **Zom Lib Monument** (B1) on your left, representing a man freed from the chains of slavery, his arms raised in a sign of victory. It was erected to celebrate the independence of the Seychelles after the coup of 5 June 1977.

At the next roundabout, turn left onto Independence ave.

The **Natural History Museum** (B1) *(open Monday-Friday, 8.30am-4.30pm, Saturday 8.30am-12noon; closed Sundays and holidays; no charge)* has a number of stuffed giant tortoises from Aldabra to welcome visitors. Inside are displayed various fine specimens of *coco de mer*, a collection of shells, insects, butterflies, fauna and coral. A recording of different Seychellois birdsong *(zoiseaux seselwa)* may help to reassure the squeamish that most sounds to be heard in the forests are quite natural! The museum is, however, scheduled for refurbishment so exhibits are likely to change. On the second floor, admire the paintings by the English painter Marianne North (1830-1890), painted during her stay in the Seychelles in 1883.

Ste Anne Marine National Park*

For information on access, contact any TSS, Creole Holidays or Mason's Travel agent (see below).

The islands opposite Victoria harbour have been designated a protected marine park since 1973. Together with their surrounding lagoon, they extend over an area of some 15sqkm. There are various ways of enjoying the full impact of this fabulous underwater world, the most accessible being a day's excursion in a glass-bottom boat or a swim with mask and snorkel.

Remember: it is forbidden to go fishing or collect shells and coral.

Ste Anne was the first island of the Seychelles to be settled, and preserves a disused whaling station that was abandoned in 1915. The island now accommodates the headquarters of the Marine Parks Authority and is therefore closed to visitors. The neighbouring **Long Island** is similarly off-limits, as it is houses a prison and a quarantine station .

The four smaller granitic islands, Moyenne, Round Island, Cerf and **Île Cachée**, provide perfect conditions for diving and snorkelling. The larger three have restaurant facilities and may be visited with ease. **Moyenne Island** (Île Moyenne) is probably the most interesting, and belongs to a retired English journalist. A walk across the island *(45min)* may even include an encounter with a giant land tortoise roaming free. The isaland also has two excellent restaurants and fabulous snorkelling, with butterfly fish and red soldier fish to be found off the northern coast. **Cerf Island** (Île au Cerf), named after Corneille Nicholas Morphey's ship, which landed here in 1756, has a population of around forty inhabitants who make a living from growing market produce. Cerf is 15min by boat from Victoria; allow 2-3hr to walk around the island trail. Fabulous grilled fare for day-trippers. **Round Island** (Île Ronde), once a leper colony complete with chapel and prison, now accommodates a small restaurant; being tiny, it may be circumnavigated in 10min.

East of Ste Anne lies **Beacon Island** (Île S che), where colonies of noddies breed.

Making the most of Victoria

GETTING THERE

By car – The northeastern and southeastern parts of Mahé are linked with Victoria by a coastal road; other roads cut across the island from Sans Souci (to Port Glaud) and from St-Louis and Bel Air (to Beau Vallon).

By bus – The central bus station is located on Palm Street, ☎ 323 315 (B1). Bus timetables and itineraries are available from there.

ADDRESS BOOK

Tourist office – Independence ave (B1), ☎ 225 313. Monday-Friday, 8am-5pm; Saturdays, 9am-12noon.

Travel agents – Day trips to Ste Anne National Marine Park, fishing, island boat tours.

Mason's Tours and Travel, Revolution ave (A1), ☎ 322 642, Fax 324 173/ 325 273.

Travel Services Seychelles (TSS), Victoria House, Francis Rachel St (B1), ☎ 322 414, Fax 321 366.

Créole Holidays, Kingsgate House, Independence ave (B1), ☎ 224 900, Fax 225 111.

Marine Charter Association, next to the Yacht Club (B2), ☎ 322 126, Fax 226 79.

Telephone – ***Cable and Wireless***, Francis Rachel St (B2), 7am-9pm.

Post office – ***General Post Office (GPO)***, Liberty House, Independence ave (B1). Open Monday-Friday 8am-4pm; Saturdays 8am-12noon. *Poste restante*.

Banks and money – Most of the banks are located in Victoria around the Clock Tower, in Albert St and on Independence ave.

Airlines – ***Air Seychelles***, Francis Rachel St (B1), ☎ 225 159.

Air France, Victoria House, ☎ 322 414/225 048/373 176 (airport), Fax 321 366 (B1).

British Airways, Independence ave, ☎ 224 910, Fax 225 596 (B1).

Medical services – ***Mont-Fleuri Hospital,*** ☎ 388 000, has a good reputation. Chemists on Market St and in Palm Passage.

WHERE TO STAY

None of the hotels are to be found in Victoria itself, but in the surroundings areas. It is also advisable to check prices of accommodation as part of an all-inclusive package deal before departing for the Seychelles. Prices given here are based on the cost of a double room with breakfast for two.

Less than US$60

Hilltop Guesthouse (A1), St-Louis, ☎ 266 555, ☎ /Fax 266 505 – 11rm The three rooms in the main house are charming, with polished wooden floors and walls. There is a communal lounge area and the windows look out over Victoria and the islands beyond. The rooms in the annexe, however, are in need of renovation. Delicious, plentiful breakfasts are served on the terrace overlooking the garden, complete with giant tortoises. See also "Marie-Antoinette" p 415.

US$75-95

La Louise Lodge, La Louise (see map of Mahé p 404-405) ☎ /Fax 344 349 – 9rm Situated on the higher ranges of Mont Fleuri, this comfortable boarding-house enjoys splendid views over the Ste Anne National Marine Park and the commercial harbour. Only the lower rooms have private balconies with views. Pleasant restaurant with terrace.

Pension Bel Air (A2), Bel Air Road ☎ 224 416, Fax 224 923 – 7rm Family atmosphere. Rooms small and basically furnished, but impeccably clean. Those overlooking Victoria and the sea also face onto the Sans Souci road, which can be noisy at busy times of the day; for greater peace and quiet, request a room at the back with views of the garden and the green hills beyond. A little on the expensive side. Discounts available for those flying with Air France and for those spending more than four nights.

US$95-110

Louis XVII, La Louise, route de la Misère (see map of Mahé pages 404-405) ☎ 344411, Fax 344428 – 10rm Charming hotel overlooking the Ste Anne National Marine Park. Local history claims Louis XVII may have stayed here during the

Victoria

years of the Revolution. Several independent bungalows with terrace. *See also Where to eat.*

Over US$230

Mountain Rise Hotel, Sans Souci (see map of Mahé p 404-405), ☎ 225 145, Fax 225 503 – 5rm CC Enchanting family hotel overlooking Victoria. Old building with thick walls which keep the place surprisingly cool. Rather stark but spacious rooms with atmosphere. Large veranda and warm sitting-room.

WHERE TO EAT

Less than US$2

Lai Lam, Market St (B1) stays open all day for take-away snacks, doubling as a baker and cake shop in the busy thoroughfare by the market. Especially popular at lunchtime. Various types of bread, sanmousas, sandwiches and cakes. The coconut nougat is to be recommended.

US$2-6

King Wah, Benezet St (B1), ☎ 323 658. Lunch and dinner; closed Sundays. Small dark room near the market, always crowded with local clientele at lunch-time. Lunch menu includes pork with noodles, chicken and rice, vegetable stews *(kari)* and other Chinese-style dishes; ample portions and good value. Take-away food not as good.

US$7-15

Marie-Antoinette (restaurant attached to the Hilltop Guest House) (A1), ☎ 266 222. Lunch and dinner; closed Sundays. CC Set menu includes a variety of Creole dishes, mostly fish-based (tuna steak, parrot fish), aubergine / eggplant fritters and other home-grown vegetables with tomatoes and onions. Meals served in Mrs Fonseka's lovely old-fashioned house; walls covered with photos, pictures and postcards.

US$15-30

Vanilla 2000, Independence ave, (B1), ☎ 324 628. Lunch and dinner. CC A sophisticated setting for this restaurant which serves fish, prawns in garlic, cream and spices or grilled steak. Good cooking and pleasant music, but the service is a bit slow.

Louis XVII, La Louise, route de la Misère (see map of Mahé p 404-405), ☎ 344 333, Lunch and dinner. CC Tasty fish and shellfish dishes. Terrace facing Ste Anne.

HAVING A DRINK

US$3-10

Kaz Zanana Café and Art Gallery, Revolution ave (A1), ☎ 324 150. Monday-Saturday, 9am-5.30pm; closed Sundays. Attractive wooden building. A good place to enjoy a freshly squeezed fruit juice or nibble at a snack – depending on the time of day – or have an ice-cream, pastry, salad or sandwich out on the veranda or in the garden. Pictures and printed fabrics for sale.

SHOPPING GUIDE

Souvenirs and crafts – Souvenir kiosks lining Francis Rachel St offer various knick-knacks for sale: postcards, carved ebony from Kenya, jewellery, trinkets, T-shirts and polished shells.

Sunstroke, Market St, (B1). Monday-Friday, 9am-5pm; Saturdays, 9am-1pm. T-shirts, pareos, local art work, jewellery and other souvenirs.

Artizan-de-Zil, Albert St (B1) is a retail outlet for the Codevar (Company for the development of arts and crafts). Scale models of ships, mother-of-pearl, needlework dolls, basketwork, ceramics, lithographs, shells.

Museum shop – Le Jardin du Roi 1771, Independence ave (behind the Pirate Arms bar) (B1). Good selection of gift ideas: tea, perfume, scented soap and candles, bags etc. Quite expensive.

Duty-Free shop, Camion Hall, Albert St (B1) Monday-Saturday 9am-5pm (1pm Saturdays). Proof of travel required (passport and departure ticket). The advantage of shopping here is that plenty of time may be spent browsing and all goods purchased can be collected at the airport when you leave. Choice is limited, however.

Bookshops and newsagents – ***Antigone,*** Palm Passage, Francis Rachel St (B1) offers a good selection of cards and various books – general, photographic and reference on the Seychelles. English language newspapers.

SPACE, Huteau Lane (extension of Market St) (B1) Some local newspapers and guidebooks.

Imprimerie St-Fidèle, Huteau Lane (B1). A selection of international newspapers and magazines. Not always up to date.

MAHÉ★★★

Granitic island rising to 905m (Morne Seychellois)
154sqkm (27km north-south by 3-8km east-west)
Pop 67 248 – Map p 418-419

Not to be missed

A walk from Danzilles to Anse Major.
A drive through La Gogue, Dame Le Roi and Val d'Endor.
The road and the beach at Port Launay – Anse Intendance – Anse la Liberté.
Saturday evening entertainment at the Hotel Casuarina.

And remember...

Hire a mini-moke to tour the island.
Do not leave any valuables in the car or lying around while on the beach.
Take plenty to drink and a water proof jacket when out hiking.

The first French settlers arrived on the largest island of the Seychelles in 1742, and by 1770 had established a colony there. Since then, Mahé has become the most densely populated island, accounting for some 80 % of the archipelago's total population, with many migrants from the other islands. This is where the country's government is based, together with all its socio-economic organisations (health, education and welfare) and private businesses. It is also from here that all the principal communications and transport services are operated. Not only does it have the Seychelles' only international airport large enough to receive international passenger jets, but its harbour is the only one equipped with the requisite facilities for processing incoming and outgoing commercial sea freight. Mahé is therefore the main point of entry and departure for almost all visitors and goods alike.

The landscape is dominated by an imposing and uneven granite relief that is blanketed by a variety of dense vegetation. The coastline is scalloped by a succession of broad beaches and small deserted inlets, washed by an ever-changing clear turquoise sea. Unlike the coral atolls, the beaches of this granite island are nearly all shaded by palm trees and *takamakas* and scattered with tumbles of grey-brown boulders, smoothed over time by ocean waves, which take on a pink blush when caught by the rosy rays of the setting sun.

A narrow road threads its way between the sea and the hills along the entire length of the island coastline, save for a short section on the northwest coast. This is a land of supreme natural beauty, an island paradise basking in the sun, skirted with soft sands and an azure sea. A land of walks in unspoilt landscapes, of traditional fishing villages, little multi-coloured iron kaz' perched on the edge of steep mountainsides and surrounded by lush vegetation and ruins of past colonial splendour. Mahé's diversity is such that it requires visitors willing to take the time to discover its treasures.

The North peninsula★★

Victoria to Beau Vallon

20km – approx 2hr drive.

Leave Victoria by the road leading north (5th June ave).

The best time to drive up and around the north cape is at sunset, when the scenery is bathed in a soft gentle light and the rounded boulders, or *glacis,* along the white sandy shore take on the loveliest pink hues. Although the sea can be

tempting, it is important to choose a swimming place with care. Although the water might appear innocuous and shallow from the surface, the underlying seafloor may conceal razor-sharp outcrops of bedrock; it may even fall away suddenly and cause the unwary to be swept off by the strong and dangerous tidal currents breaking over the coral reef offshore. Why not simply head for one of the splendid sandy bays like **Anse Carana**** *(access by Carana Beach Chalets)*. And do feel free to park in the hotel parking lots, which appear to monopolise the access to what in theory is a public beach.
The village of **Glacis** suddenly teems with life at the end of the school day as swarms of identically dressed chattering schoolchildren make for home. Most carry their schoolbooks on their backs and are impeccably turned-out in uniforms coloured according to the class and grade. However, at this time of day, all their attention is likely to be concentrated on devouring an ice-cream or devising plans for playing on the beach. A little later, as the youngsters return indoors and prepare for bed, the roads briefly thunder with the sound of jogging office workers who have traded jackets and trousers for sports gear.

Chemin la Gogue**

Opposite the Manresa Hotel by Anse Étoile on the east coast, a road heads inland and eventually comes out before the Glacis police station or opposite the Northolme Hotel on the west coast. Distance: 4km (20min by car or 2hr on foot). Narrow, potholed road with some difficult stretches; test the state of your brakes before you set out.

Anyone with any sense of adventure will enjoy exploring this little road that runs across the north cape, through a quiet and somewhat forgotten corner of the island, and winds its way through the most fabulous, lushly green and

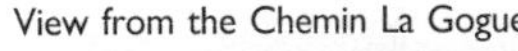

View from the Chemin La Gogue

M. Lemerle/MICHELIN

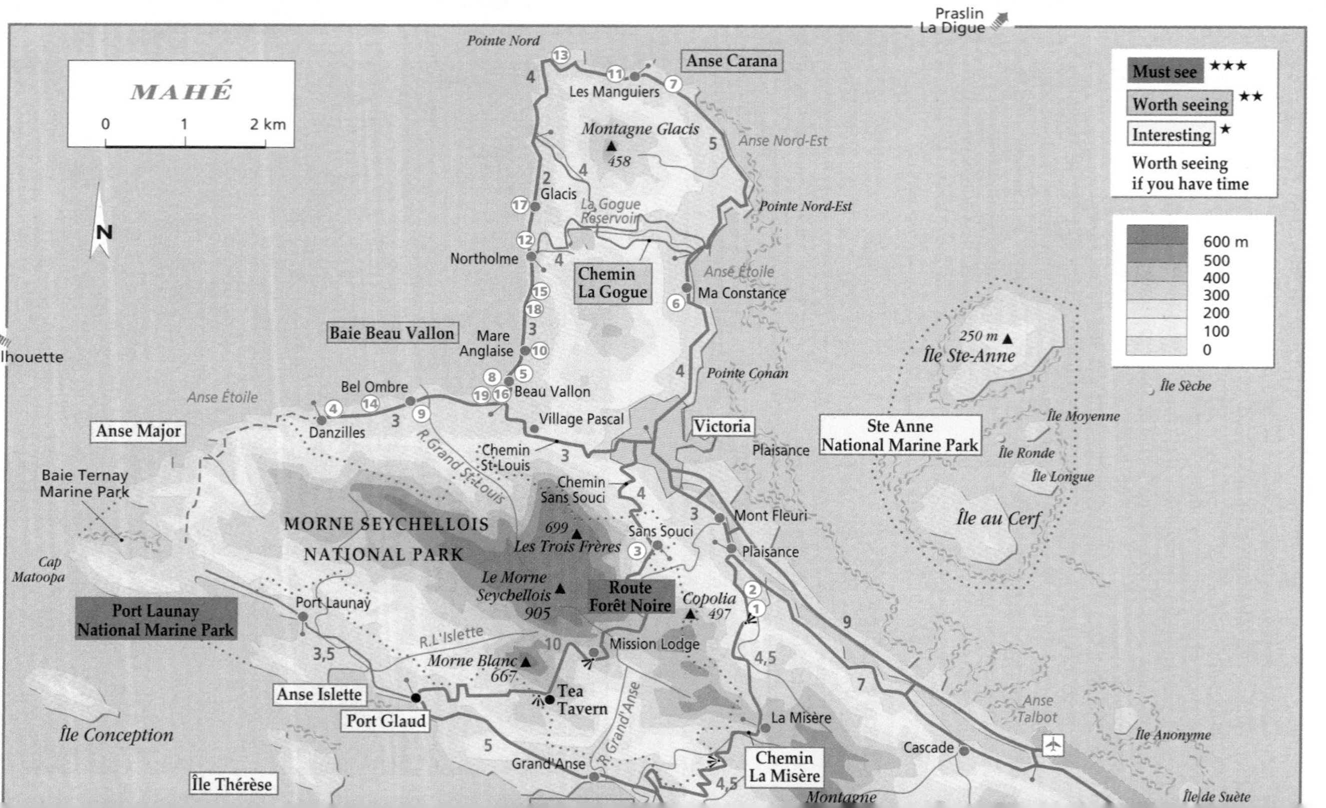
MAHÉ
0
1
2 km
N
Pointe Nord
Praslin
La Digue
Anse Carana
Les Manguiers
Montagne Glacis
458
Anse Nord-Est
Glacis
La Gogue Reservoir
Pointe Nord-Est
Northolme
Chemin La Gogue
Anse Étoile
Ma Constance
Baie Beau Vallon
Mare Anglaise
Silhouette
Beau Vallon
Pointe Conan
Bel Ombre
Anse Étoile
Danzilles
Village Pascal
Anse Major
Victoria
Plaisance
Chemin St-Louis
R. Grand St-Louis
Chemin Sans Souci
Baie Ternay Marine Park
MORNE SEYCHELLOIS NATIONAL PARK
699
Les Trois Frères
Sans Souci
Mont Fleuri
Plaisance
Cap Matoopa
Le Morne Seychellois
905
Route Forêt Noire
Copolia
497
Port Launay
Port Launay National Marine Park
R.L'Islette
Mission Lodge
Morne Blanc
667
Tea Tavern
Anse Islette
Port Glaud
Île Conception
R. Grand'Anse
La Misère
Grand'Anse
Chemin La Misère
Île Thérèse
Montagne
Cascade
Anse Talbot
Must see ★★★
Worth seeing ★★
Interesting ★
Worth seeing if you have time
600 m
500
400
300
200
100
0
250 m
Île Ste-Anne
Île Sèche
Ste Anne National Marine Park
Île Moyenne
Île Ronde
Île Longue
Île au Cerf
Île Anonyme
Île de Suète

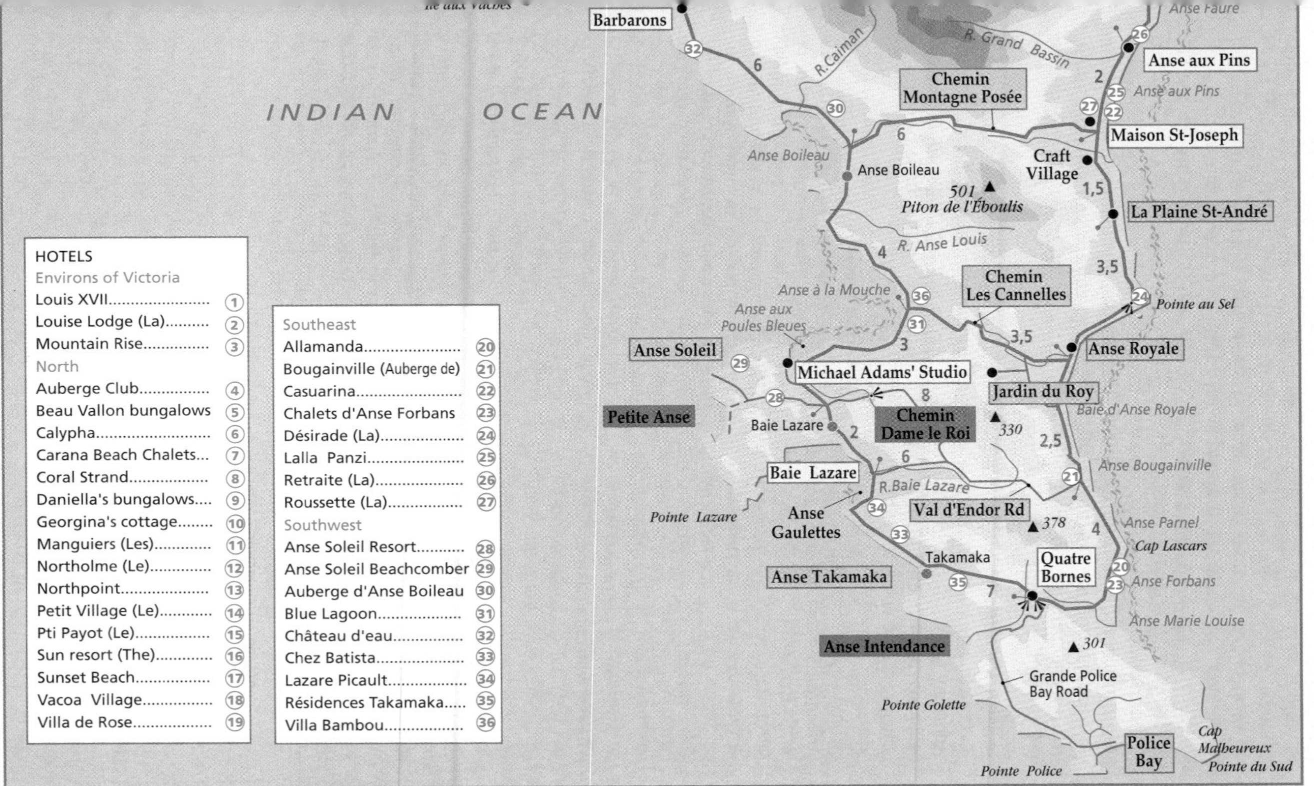

INDIAN OCEAN
HOTELS
Environs of Victoria
Louis XVII 1
Louise Lodge (La) 2
Mountain Rise 3
North
Auberge Club 4
Beau Vallon bungalows 5
Calypha 6
Carana Beach Chalets 7
Coral Strand 8
Daniella's bungalows 9
Georgina's cottage 10
Manguiers (Les) 11
Northolme (Le) 12
Northpoint 13
Petit Village (Le) 14
Pti Payot (Le) 15
Sun resort (The) 16
Sunset Beach 17
Vacoa Village 18
Villa de Rose 19
Southeast
Allamanda 20
Bougainville (Auberge de) 21
Casuarina 22
Chalets d'Anse Forbans 23
Désirade (La) 24
Lalla Panzi 25
Retraite (La) 26
Roussette (La) 27
Southwest
Anse Soleil Resort 28
Anse Soleil Beachcomber 29
Auberge d'Anse Boileau 30
Blue Lagoon 31
Château d'eau 32
Chez Batista 33
Lazare Picault 34
Résidences Takamaka 35
Villa Bambou 36
Barbarons
R.Caiman
R. Grand Bassin
Anse Faure
Anse aux Pins
Anse aux Pins
Chemin Montagne Posée
Maison St-Joseph
Craft Village
Anse Boileau
Anse Boileau
501 Piton de l'Éboulis
La Plaine St-André
R. Anse Louis
Chemin Les Cannelles
Anse à la Mouche
Anse aux Poules Bleues
Pointe au Sel
Anse Soleil
Anse Royale
Michael Adams' Studio
Jardin du Roy
Petite Anse
Baie Lazare
Chemin Dame le Roi
330
Baie d'Anse Royale
Baie Lazare
R.Baie Lazare
Anse Bougainville
Pointe Lazare
Anse Gaulettes
Val d'Endor Rd
378
Anse Parnel
Cap Lascars
Takamaka
Anse Takamaka
Quatre Bornes
Anse Forbans
Anse Marie Louise
Anse Intendance
301
Grande Police Bay Road
Pointe Golette
Cap Malbeureux
Police Bay
Pointe Police
Pointe du Sud

vigorous vegetation bristling with *flamboyants*, *takamakas*, breadfruit, mango and palm trees. Here and there, the scarred grey rock is left exposed, bared by temporary but nonetheless torrential waterfalls laden with broken debris following heavy rain. As the road sweeps from side to side with each successive bend, great sweeping **views*** open out across the islands dotting the horizon, surrounded by a restless sea glinting in the sunshine. It is amazing to stop and wonder at how the locals have managed to build their houses so high up on the mountainside in the thick forest. Eventually the road makes its descent, coming out before the flower-filled cemetery of **Glacis,** or alternatively, depending on the route taken, by the beach below the **Northolme Hotel,** further south.

▪ **Beau Vallon**** – This wonderful crescent of white sand (1.5km long) is considered by many to be the finest beach on the island, especially in the early morning when no one else is about and the spectacular landscape can be claimed exclusively for oneself. A more practical consideration is the shade provided by the groves of coconut palms and *takamakas* that line the beach, into which sunbathers can retreat when the midday sun becomes increasingly intolerable. On Sundays, however, the area is taken over by groups of men who collect there in order to indulge in a noisy session of dominoes and a string of drinks before sundown. Then, at dusk, the picture-postcard landscape takes on a different appearance; the sky is flushed with the colours of the sunset and the white sand turns pink; the birds have gone quiet and the evening promises to be balmy. The beach is abandoned by people and the hermit crabs come out to scavenge for food, pausing a moment as they emerge from their holes before darting across the cooling, dew-dampened sand and disappearing again. Only then does one become aware of the sounds of the night beginning to reverberate from the dense canopy of vegetation covering the hills behind.

La Buse's treasure

Olivier Levasseur, nicknamed La Buse (the buzzard), is probably the most infamous pirate ever to have terrorised the Indian Ocean; furthermore, he is known to have ardently defended his territory around the stormy waters and precipitous coasts of the Seychelles. Having mastered the dangers, he was to regard the archipelago as his safe-hold from which to scour the seas in search of all gold-bearing ships. The prize could be worth major fortunes, as in the case of the "Virgin of the Cape", which sailed from the Indies in 1721 loaded with strings of diamonds, precious stones, gold ingots and prized vases, and fell foul of La Buse and his terrible accomplice Taylor. According to legend, before being executed on the gallows in 1730 on Réunion, La Buse threw a mysterious map into the crowd, exclaiming: "Whoever manages to decipher it inherits my treasure!". The race is still on to find the treasure; each island, convinced that it might conceal a valuable chest or two, seeks to check out every clue in the hope of a miraculous discovery.

Besides its beauty, the beach at Beau Vallon is one of the safest places for children and nervous swimmers to enjoy the water. Not only is it shallow and warm, but the large bay is unaffected by dangerous currents when stormy weather is blowing in from the north and west. The complete range of **water sports** is on offer including paddle boats, windsurfing, water-skiing, parasailing, glass-bottom boats, scuba-diving and deep-sea fishing.

Where the road forks in front of the police station, turn right and head back towards the coast.

Bel Ombre is a small sleepy fishing village that often appears abandoned save for its gaily painted boats, drawn high up on the sand at low tide or left to bob about nonchalantly at high water. It is also most particularly associated with the fruitless search for La Buse's treasure.

The road terminates at Danzilles, so either turn around and drive back or stop the car and continue on foot.

Danzilles to Anse Major**

The easiest way to find the right path is by asking around for directions. A good footpath traces its way along the rocky shoreline to the lovely beach nestling in **Anse Major*** *(1.5km; 90min there and back; remember to take plenty of drinking water)*. Pass before the houses set back from the track before venturing onto the *glacis* – rounded dark granite boulders that tumble down to the sea – to enjoy the **view***** of Beau Vallon with Silhouette and North Island beyond. The path continues through glades of different exotic trees like patchouli and cinnamon, and on past great big boulders worn smooth by the gently lapping turquoise water.

The more adventurous may continue inland and on to **Baie Ternay***** *(see p 427). It is well worth checking whether it is possible to follow this track to its end as it tends to get so overgrown that it becomes impassable.*

The East Coast*

Victoria to Anse Forbans

Approx 28km – 45min drive.

Leave Victoria by the road leading south (5th June ave, then Mont Fleuri Road).

Mont Fleuri is the most fashionable residential "suburb" of Victoria. Note in passing the sun-filled **cemetery***, often filled with flowers, rising up the hillside. The road continues through a rather desolate (and smelly) salt-marsh that was created when the speedway to the airport was reclaimed from the sea. The best time to come upon the village of **Cascade** from the north is at the end of the day, when the front of the church and the great granite cliffs beyond are briefly caught by the last colourful rays of the setting sun.

■ **Anse aux Pins*** – With a bit luck, you might see the fishermen landing their catch on the beach, bringing ashore whole nets of multicoloured fish, including tuna and the odd young shark. Such an event always attracts a group of inquisitive onlookers and prospective buyers. The excitement incites cries of glee and laughter, news and gossip are exchanged, jokes are shared, then the crowd breaks up as various locals depart with strings of fish hanging from each hand.

■ **Maison St-Joseph*** – The striking, sky blue-and-white villa on the right is the **Creole Institute** (Linstiti Kréol): *open Monday-Friday, 8am-4pm; closed Saturdays and Sundays; no charge*), which, since 1986, has served as a research station for documenting translations and changes in the Creole language. The traditional former planter's house, complete with its fine verandas on both levels, is open to the public.

Carry on a little further of, till just after Montagne Posée Rd on the right.

M. Lemerle/MICHELIN

The cemetery at Glacis

▪ **Craft Village** – ☎ 376 100, open daily 9.30am-5pm; no charge. Vye Marmit restaurant, see *Where to eat, p 435*. The *Village artisanal* consists of a cluster of small pastel-coloured traditional houses or *cases créoles*, converted into workshops for craftsmen practising their various skills. There are no actual indigenous handicrafts as such, and the authorities are only too aware of the dangers inherent in encouraging the use of such rare commodities as tortoiseshell from the endangered hawksbill turtle, mother-of-pearl from the over-exploited green snail, coral, and the slow-growing hardwoods. Among the foreign artists who have settled in the Seychelles, most can afford to buy precious timber from authorised sources for carving or use in making model ships, and charge suitably high prices accordingly. It is of vital importance, however, that visitors respect the ecological implications of buying coral and shell jewellery, bleached shark's jaws and suchlike. Best to seek out the infinitely more practical – and transportable – baskets, embroideries and hand-painted T-shirts.

At the centre of this village, conceived specifically for tourists, stands a rather fine old-fashioned **Plantation House*** painted in pale blue and white. Inside, the floors are original but the furniture in the sitting room, dining room and bedroom are modern reproductions. The other rooms are used as offices.

Continue along the coast and turn right where signposted.

▪ **Plaine St-André Ecomuseum**** – ☎ *371 878, open Tuesday-Friday, 10am-5pm; Saturday-Sunday, 1pm-5pm; closed Mondays. Admission fee includes guided tour.* This elegant planter's house, built of wood on coral piles, has recently been restored to accommodate the recreated interiors of a typical 18C family home. The entrance is through an attractive **veranda** shaded from the sun by lovely white shutters. Inside, most of the furniture consists of reproductions as the original pieces perished in a fire. Many of the utensils in the pantry are identical to those still in use today by the Seychellois. The kitchen is built at the back of the house to minimise the risk of fire. The rooms upstairs were reserved for the daughters and the maid; the sons of this family of sixteen children would have slept in an annexe in the garden. Guests would have been accommodated in another little villa.

■ **La Marine*** – *Plaine St-André. ☎ 371 441, open Monday-Friday, 7.30am-5pm; Saturday, 8am-3.30pm; closed Sundays. No charge.* A disused copra warehouse next door to the ecomuseum was converted in 1979 into a workshop, where exquisite scale models of sailing boats are now made. In the beginning, the operation was launched with a special team of craftsmen brought in from Mauritius, since their skill in this field is considered to be the best; since then, a number of Seychellois craftsmen have served their apprenticeship and assumed control of production for themselves. Each person is specialised in his own domain: cutting the wood, planing it, assembling it, gluing it or varnishing it; while the women take on the task of sewing the sails and threading up the rigging.

The road continues to wind its way along the coast, past small rocky inlets and a deserted beach here and there, sometimes flanked by a lonely fisherman's shack.

In places the shore is dotted with young men fishing with spears. Coloured pirogues bob on the water, while in the distance the sea rumbles over the reefs.

■ **Anse Royale**** – As the road begins to make its way back down towards sea level, it sweeps into a broad bend; a spectacular **view**** stretches beyond the coconut palms, taking in the long white beach and the glorious turquoise lagoon below.

It is possible to swim across to the islet sprouting a few coconut palms, known as **Île Souris****. This is a particularly good spot for snorkelling.

Turn right into Cannelles Rd, opposite the first church (signposted), then fork left by the signpost and climb steeply up (stay in low gear!) to L'Enfoncement.

If the car gives out on you, park it conscientiously by the side of the road and continue on foot. For this is a private and peaceful place, lost among the abundant vegetation, where the occasional strain of *séga* is carried up from the houses. This is the back country where laughing children play, and women, their heads covered in rollers, put the finishing touches to their hair while the men have a sip of beer before returning to work.

■ **Jardin du Roy**** – ☎ *371 313, open daily, 10am-5pm. Admission charge. Allow 1-2hr for visiting.* Armed with a map of the garden and a plant list, most people can

An unfortunate mistake

Sometime in May 1780, a French frigate was sailing off the coast of Mahé when its captain realised that they might have ventured into British waters. In order to allay any fears among the enemy faction, the captain decided to hoist the British ensign. Meanwhile, the garrison duty officer Romainville, charged with keeping the spice garden a secret and under strict orders from the governor to burn all evidence of the plantations at the approach of any enemy ship, espied the vessel flying the British flag and set to scrupulously executing his orders. The entire spice garden went up in smoke. Fortunately, by then, birds had managed to convey the seeds of the cinnamon tree to other parts of the island and the species established itself, and multiplied so as to become a vital export product.

while away the time with ease in these wonderful gardens, wandering through the nutmeg, cinnamon, clove, pepper, orange, banana and Indian coral trees, looking out for orchids and flowering ginger or watching the birds, tortoises and other reptiles. This is a reconstruction of the original secret spice nursery designed by **Pierre Poivre** in the 18C to acclimatise all kinds of spice plants imported from Indonesia and India to the conditions prevalent on the islands of the Indian Ocean, and laid out by Anse Royale where the soil was deeper and there were more abundant supplies of water.

A glorious **view**★★ extends from the top of the estate out over the sea and the surrounding landscape. The small **colonial house**★ was built by the great-grandfather of the present proprietor in about 1860. It currently displays a secondary collection of shells, old engravings, stamps, letters, decorative objects and furniture.

This is a good place to pause for a refreshing drink of home-made punch or fresh fruit juice, and maybe even a pancake or some other speciality prepared with ingredients grown on the estate.

Go back down to Anse Royale.

The road threads its way tortuously down through the rocks, narrowing where necessary *(be careful of cars parked on bends)*, circling a shallow bay in which the water seems to change colour with each passing cloud. The vegetation becomes gradually more extravagant and the number of houses dwindles to none as you go further south. One inlet follows another, the coral reef gets closer and the sea becomes increasingly wilder.

The road then climbs its way across the island from east to west

C. Pavard/HOA QUI

Pierre Poivre (Album de Roussin)

Mahé

The West Coast★★★

Quatre Bornes to Port Launay

Approx 30km – 50min drive.

▪ **Quatre Bornes**★ – The road passes right through Quatre Bornes, the southernmost village of the island that sits more or less midway between the east and west coasts. It is a peaceful, sleepy place, populated with coloured houses shaded by hibiscus and banana palms, which enjoy extensive **views**★★ over the ocean.

Fork left downhill by Grand Police Bay Rd, and continue straight on at the fork until you come to a dead end.

■ **Police Bay**★★ – Visitors should restrain themselves from swimming off this temptingly deserted beach lapped by turquoise water, as its benign appearance masks dangerously overwhelming currents and powerful waves.

Go back the way you came and turn left at the junction (Intendance Rd).

■ **Anse Intendance**★★★ – The long, white sandy beach shaded by rows of swaying coconut palms, lapped by the clearest water, is just as wonderful as the brochures make it out to be. It does, however, attract bathers and surfers – depending on the height of the waves. Do take care, especially with young children, as currents can be deceptively strong here.

Return to Quatre Bornes and continue (left) on down to the west coast.

As the road descends to the sea, it passes a number of simple wooden houses covered in latanier palm leaves; before each one, trays of cinnamon bark are laid out to dry in the sun.

■ **Anse Takamaka**★★ – This fabulous bay is especially spectacular at sunset. It does attract enthusiastic surfers, however, almost as soon as the waves show signs of becoming rollers. As before, be aware of the risk of strong currents.

The narrow road continues to pick its way past great granite boulders on one side and, between the trees on the other, an ever-changing perspective of the rocky coastline and the empty horizon beyond.

Anse Gaulettes and **Baie Lazare**★ are sheltered from the ocean by coral reefs. Although the narrow band of sand with its dappled shade looks tempting, the water here is too shallow for a good swim.

The road then pulls up and away from the coast to climb to a village with a pretty **church**, sheltering in Baie Lazare.

In the village, turn right between the telephone kiosk and the police station.

Chemin Dame le Roi★★★

The best way to "do" this excursion is on foot when it is not too hot (remember to take some drinking water), but be warned, the road does rather go up and down! The alternative is to drive, but do check the reliability of your mini-moke's brakes and tyres before setting off – just in case you meet an oncoming vehicle.

From the outset, the **view**★★★ over the wide open sea is quite splendid. Then, the track quickly ducks down into the lush scenery so typical of the Seychelles, dotted with an assortment of multicoloured shacks put together with corrugated iron, wood or concrete, each nestling amid plantations of pineapples, *brenzels* (aubergine or eggplant), sugar cane, papayas and banana trees. Life continues at its leisurely pace here in suspended animation, removed from the constraints of time and place.

At last, the Chemin Dame le Roi comes out onto **Val d'Endor Road**★★: to the left lies the east coast and Anse Bougainville. To the right the West Coast and Anse Gaulettes.

Go back to Baie Lazare village and turn left off the main road along Anse Soleil Road (signposted "Beachcomber Guest House"). Fork right (driveable but difficult).

■ **Anse Soleil**★★ – A narrow track leads to what is probably the nicest beach on the island. It is isolated enough to remain uncrowded, and is only overlooked by green vegetation and granite rocks.

Where Anse Soleil Rd forks, stop and park the car (only 4x4s should attempt to go any further) and walk down to the left; ask for directions if you feel unsure of the way.

Homeward bound with the catch

■ **Anse la Liberté (or Petite Anse)***** – A short walk leads to another beautiful and remote beach, even less frequented than the preceding one. The sand is incredible, its texture as fine as flour. Be prudent when swimming, however, as the currents can be deceptive and help is far away.

Make your way back to the village at Baie Lazare and follow the main road down left. Turn left just before Anse aux Poules Bleues.

■ **Michael Adams Studio*** – *Normally open Monday-Friday, 10am-4pm; Saturday, 10am-1pm; closed Sundays.* ☎ *361 006.* An enchanting white house, surrounded by an informal garden, shelters the studio of the Seychelles' most celebrated (and modest) painter. Michael Adams' style conveys the vibrancy and colour of his beloved country, where the light sparkles through the rustling palm fronds *(see illustration on p 348-349)*. Full descriptions and explanations of the watercolours and prints may be requested from the artist himself or his wife.

The coast road leads on through **Anse à la Mouche** and **Anse Boileau**, an attractive village collected around the fine **Church of Notre-Dame**. Beyond the coconut palm plantation lie the sandy beaches of **Barbarons*** – monopolised by a large hotel – and **Grand' Anse****, which shelters another great expanse of pale sand. Grand'Anse is not protected by an offshore coral reef and therefore is liable to strong tidal currents. Do not be alarmed if the almost tangible tranquillity of the place is suspended by the sound of children playing. This will be but a temporary interruption before school classes resume.

From here onwards, the mountains inland begin to rise, and the lush tropical vegetation sweeps down to the coast.

■ **Port Glaud*** – This little fishing community has come to specialise in tuna fishing. On occasion you may hear the school choir singing in the church, girls on one side of the aisle, boys on the other, intoning the hymns and psalms as if they were poetry.

Anse Islette* is a broad and rocky bay, deceptively shallow and apparently enclosed by **Islette**, a rocky outcrop (with a good restaurant) that is more or less accessible on foot at low tide, and its neighbour **Île Thérèse***. The latter forms part of the estate of the Berjaya Mahé Beach Hotel, which organises day trips to the island with lunch on the beach and the opportunity of swimming, snorkelling etc.

Suddenly, the scenery changes quite dramatically. A tangle of mangroves emerges from a marsh irrigated by little inland rivers providing the ideal conditions, one might say, for a menacing crocodile to break the surface and chase a pirogue...

Park the vehicle opposite the entrance to the former National Youth Service camp (NYS).

■ **Port Launay***** – The shining white sand extends in a gentle arc shaded here and there by an uneven row of large *takamakas*, *badamiers* and *bois de rose* trees. In the translucent water, myriad fish can be clearly seen darting about in search of food. In the heat of the day, the beach is very often deserted and so provides a perfect spot for a swim or a picnic. Should someone else be there before you, there is a completely private little inlet at the north end of the beach.

To the south, a series of inaccessible coves with turquoise water succeed one another where perhaps some solitary Robinson Crusoe still roams.

To make the most of the scenery, drive slowly back and enjoy the differing perspectives of the landscape at each bend in the road.

The views from the stretch of road between **Port Launay and Baie Ternay***** must surely rank among the most spectacular on Mahé's. As it progresses, the road narrows, its path encroached upon by the exuberant vegetation emanating from the side of the hill, and squeezes its way along a ledge that falls precipitously down to the sea below. As there is not enough room for another car to pass, you might as well adopt the local custom of stopping in the middle of the road to admire the view! Note the houses precariously poised among the bushes on the right-hand side, from where gregarious snatches of *séga* emerge from time to time. Do not be alarmed if the occasional Seychellois comes out from the darkness brandishing a machete: he will no doubt be in quest of coconuts or some other wild fruit for dinner. Below, the shining sea glints restlessly, ever altering the ranges of turquoise, blue and azure as the water churns and breaks against the rocks.

A little further on, a dappled limpid **lagoon**, rocky and shallow, may be discerned through the foliage.

The spellbinding sense of adventure is cut short when the road comes abruptly up against a somewhat awesome pair of wire gates which formerly belonged to a military youth camp. Plans are afoot to turn the site into a 4-star hotel complex.

The island interior**

At one time Mahé was a lonely volcanic outcrop surrounded on all sides by miles of ocean. Over time, the landscape has been changed by accumulated layers of fertile soil which, in turn, provide a variety of habitats for plants, birds and animals. The hinterland is bisected by several roads running east to west that cut right through great swathes of unspoilt and protected countryside, abounding with rare species and providing an easy means of access to a network of footpaths. Several invigorating expeditions in the cool of the forest can even be scheduled between swims! Footpaths are usually well maintained and carefully arranged so as to ease the climb up the green hills or *monts* through the fantastically diverse landscape to specially-built viewing platforms. These, in turn, are designed to offer the opportunity of contemplating a different, but no less remarkable, prospect of the Seychelles.

To save being blinded by the sun, it is advisable to follow the roads across the island from east to west in the morning, and from west to east after noon. This simple piece of advice will allow you to better enjoy the view and avert the danger, and discomfort, of having the glaring light shining straight into your eyes.

Route de la Forêt Noire***

The road that runs between Port Glaud and Victoria *(approx 14km – 30min)* edges its way around the tallest peak on the island, skirting a protected area of 30sqkm known as the **Morne Seychellois National Park**. As the road winds its way uphill, superb **panoramic views**** open out onto the lagoon and the islands off the west coast.

The **Tea Tavern** (☎ *378 221 open Monday-Friday, 8.30am-12noon; closed Sundays. Admission charge; tea/souvenir shop and snack bar open until 4pm)* serves as a visitor's centre for the tea plantation and provides a full description of how the tea is grown, picked and processed through the drying, sieving and flavouring stages, before being packaged for sale. The factory itself is set among the tiers of parallel rows of tea bushes undulating in harmony with the relief of the hillside. Tea-tastings are laid on for visitors to try the different flavours: cinnamon, vanilla, orange, lemon or mint.

The **view***** takes in the whole southwestern coast: the forest's intense green in the foreground, stretches of pale sand further on and a gradual range of blues extending into the distance, as the sea assumes an ever more intense colour before merging completely with the clear sky above the horizon.

As the road climbs upwards, ever steeper and steeper, almost all the endemic trees and plants of the Seychelles *(bois de fer, bois méduse, etc)* may be identified, including such exotics as cinnamon, *albizia* and vanilla. Immediately after a hairpin bend, a path leads off to the left between rows of *sandragon* trees to **Mission Lodge**. Only the ruins now survive of what was once a school, founded by missionaries for the young slaves freed by the English slave ship overseers after the abolition of slavery. Park the car to one side and walk up to the viewpoint to admire the **view***** of jagged coves lacing the west coast and the densely-covered hills, or *morns*, of the park.

Walking in the Morne Seychellois National Park

All trails are marked; either acquire one of the special leaflets available or hire a guide *(see* Activities, *p. 401).*

Mahé

Rocky inlet, Mahé

Morne Seychellois (alt: 905m) – *Allow 6-8hr there and back; difficult in places; guide strongly recommended.* The circuit can include a climb up to the highest point of the Seychelles.

Morne Blanc (alt: 667m) – *Approx 1.2km, 250m climb, 2hr there and back; medium difficulty.* The path branches from opposite the Tea Tavern, off the Chemin Sans Souci, some 250m above the road. This walk picks its way through the tea plantations before entering the dense, humid forest.

Copolia (alt: 497m) – *Allow 2hr there and back; fairly difficult.* Follow the track off the Chemin Sans Souci, beyond the Bureau des Forêts (forestry office) which leads eastwards from Val Riche, some 6km from Victoria. Although this walk covers a short distance, it does climb fairly steeply to the top from where fine views stretch inland towards the heart of Mahé.

Trois Frères (alt: 699m) – *Approx 4km, allow 3hr there and back. Be careful: the path can be very slippery after heavy rain.* The path starts from the Sans Souci Forestry Department bureau on the Route de la Forêt Noire, some 5km from Victoria. Turn right at the sign marked "Forestry Department" and leave the car in the car park about 250m further on. The going is steep up to the pass (signed Le Niol). To reach the summit, turn right (approx 1.8km from the car park): the panoramic view is well worth the climb, unless it is lost in cloud. Look out for the *creeper pitcher plant* with its carnivorous flower about halfway to the summit. Either come down the same way or, alternatively, opt for the path which comes out at the village of Niol, between Beau Vallon and Victoria (5km from the summit).

Chemin La Misère*

Approx 9km – 20min. The Chemin La Misère begins at Plaisance on the east coast (at the roundabout south of Mont Fleuri) and goes all the way to Grand'Anse on the west coast. Stop on the left-hand side of the road outside Victoria to admire the **panoramic view**** across to Cerf Island and Ste Anne (especially when it is caught by the light of the evening sunset). Another fabulous view extends from the far side of the Col de la Misère over to the west coast and the lush forest.

Chemin Montagne Posée**

Approx 6km – 15min. Several **viewpoints**** punctuate the road between Anse Boileau on the west side and Anse aux Pins on the eastern coast. Whether on foot or in a car, it is well worth making the effort to check out the three **viewing stations**** overlooking the west coast. The track leaves from the *Cable and Wireless* station and quickly crosses into the dense forest.

Chemin Les Cannelles**

Approx 3.5km – 15min. This attractive little road, named after the cinnamon trees that once lined the way, links Anse la Mouche on the west coast with Anse Royale on the eastern shore.

Making the most of Mahé

GETTING THERE

See p 393, "Getting there"

GETTING AROUND

By car – All the larger car rental companies operate on the island in addition to a number of smaller local operators. To rent a vehicle, enquire at your hotel. However, it may be more convenient and less expensive to book a car as part of your travel arrangements prior to departure. Do not expect to rent a car at the weekend, as most agencies are closed. Petrol/gas stations are located outside the airport at Victoria and at Anse Royale, Beau Vallon and Port Glaud.

By taxi – Available 24hours a day, although it is advisable to book one in advance for an evening out or for an airport transfer. Ranks are located in Victoria, outside the airport's international arrivals terminal, and by the main hotels.

By bus – The island's main bus station is on Palm Street in Victoria. Timetables and itineraries are available there. Request stops are marked along the main roads; once aboard, indicate to the driver where you want to get off (other passengers will also be delighted to help!). Buses run between 5.30am and 6.30pm or thereabouts; a more restricted service is in operation on Sundays.

ADDRESS BOOK

Tourist office – See p 414

Travel agents – See p 414

Telephone – See p 414

Post office – For any mail in need of weighing, you need to go to the central post office in Victoria (see p 414). Stamps may be bought in shops selling cards or from hotel lobbies; letters and cards can be posted in the red letter boxes dotted around the island and in hotel lobbies.

Banks and money – The major banks have their headquarters in Victoria (see page 414). Subsidiary branches are located at Beau Vallon, on the road to Victoria (open Monday-Friday, 9am-2.30pm; Saturdays, 9am-11.30am), at Grand'Anse and Anse Boileau. All the hotels change money at a less advantageous rate. Automatic cash dispensers are only available in Victoria and at the airport.

Medical services – see p 414

WHERE TO STAY

Prices given here are based on the cost of a double room with breakfast for two.

• Northern peninsula

Less than US$45

Calypha, Ma Constance, ☎ /Fax 241 157 – 7rm The house is perched up on the hillside, overlooking Ste Anne and its surrounding marine park. Enchanting little rooms. Lounge and dining room decorated with characteristic Seychellois knick-knacks; dining room open to non-residents. Warm family feel.

US$45-60

Georgina's Cottage, Mare Anglaise, ☎ 277 016, Fax 247 945– 7rm. This rather ornate house accommodates an eclectic set of rooms ranging from the simplest single to the vast family suite. Depending on the room allocated, additional facilities may include a TV, radio, small kitchenette, or balcony where a copious breakfast will be laid out for you in the morning. The affable owner prefers to dispatch guests to the neighbouring eateries – whose job it is to cook – rather than prepare anything herself.

US$60-75

Les Manguiers Guesthouse, Machabée ☎ 241 455 – 3rm. Three small units available to rent, simply furnished, done up to local tastes, comprise bedroom, seating area, small old-fashioned kitchen and small veranda. One, perched up on the side of a hill, forms a distinctive part of the local community; the second, situated on the side of the road, is less desirable and the one overlooking the sea is the most pleasant.

Northpoint Guesthouse, Fond des Lianes, Machabée ☎ 241 339, Fax 241 850 – 8rm. Small bedrooms with adjoining kitchen area, private balcony and view over the sea. Occasionally encroached upon by over-exuberant vegetation. A small path leads downhill to a private creek.

US$75-95

Le Pti Payot, Mare Anglaise ☎ 261 447, Fax 261 094 – 3rm. Individual bungalows tucked into the hillside available to rent, each with double room sitting area with beds for two children, kitchen and balcony overlooking the sea. Perfect place for a family or a group of friends wishing to stay together.

Villa de Rose Guesthouse, Beauvallon, ☎ 247 455, Fax 241 208 – 3rm. Bed and breakfast or comfortable self-contained flats with two rooms and equipped kitchen. Peaceful garden 200m from the beach.

Daniella's Bungalows, Bel Ombre ☎ 247 212/247 914, Fax 247 784 – 10rm Two-room cottages; rather unattractive from the outside, with private balcony giving onto a rather mean garden. Pretty and spotless interiors. Situated among the upper reaches of Bel Ombre.

US$110-125

Vacoa Village, Mare Anglaise, ☎ 261 130, Fax 261 146, vacoasv@seychelles.net – 11rm Comfortable twin-bedroom studios or flats with kitchen facilities, seating area and balcony stacked among granite boulders and lush tropical vegetation. Quality fixtures. Nice pool; Beau Vallon Beach 5min away.

Beau Vallon Bungalows, Beau Vallon ☎ 247 382, Fax 247 955, bvbung@seychelles.net – 8rm Small rooms or bungalows with kitchenette and veranda overlooking the garden. Avoid the bungalows on the road. Warm welcome and convivial atmosphere. A little on the expensive side.

US$125-140

The Sun Resort, Beau Vallon ☎ 247 647, Fax 247 224, sun@seychelles.net – 12rm Luxurious bedrooms with kitchenette, sitting area and private balcony or veranda, arranged over two floors around the attractive pool. Within 200m of Beauvallon Beach.

Le Petit Village, Bel Ombre ☎ 247 474, Fax 247 771 – 10rm Comfortable two-bedroom studios or flats with kitchen and private veranda. Built of wood in the style of a Swiss chalet right on the beach: peaceful location, perfect for snorkelling; better beach 50m further on.

US$140-155

Carana Beach Chalets, North East Point ☎ 241 041, Fax 241 649, carana@seychelles.net – 16rm Attractive wooden bungalows with modern kitchen and large veranda giving onto a fine panoramic garden. Fabulous private beach lapped by limpid turquoise water.

Auberge Club, Danzilles ☎ 247550, Fax 247703, e-mail: acds@seychelles.net – 40rm Very attractive spot. Tastefully decorated circular bungalows and bedrooms surrounded on all sides by exuberant plants growing from among the rocks. Lovely long veranda, pleasant pool excavated from the base rock overlooking the sea; private path cut from the granite down to the seafront.

Coral Strand, Beau Vallon, ☎ 247 036, Fax 245 717, coralres@seychelles.net – 147 rms. Prestigious hotel with a relaxed atmosphere, situated right on Beau Vallon beach. Small rooms laid out in four storeys around an impressive swimming pool. Balconies with sea views. Small, pleasant beach bar. Reputable diving centre.

Over US$230

Northolme Hotel, Glacis ☎ 261 222, Fax 261 223 – 20rm Small but very comfortable hotel with private arc of sand. Rooms with private balconies that have wonderful views over the sea and Beau Vallon Beach. Open-air restaurant on glorious panoramic veranda. Opportunities to enjoy full range of water sports at Beauvallon.

Sunset Beach Hotel, Glacis ☎ 261 111, Fax 261 221, sunset@seychelles.net – 25rm Comfortable rooms with balcony and view over the bay. Pool overlooking the sea; small private beach.

• East Coast

US$40-45

La Retraite Guesthouse, Anse aux Pins ☎ 375 816, Fax 375 243 – 4rm Small family-run guesthouse: basic facilities only. Run by an outgoing warm-hearted and genuine Creole lady who will be happy to prepare meals by prior arrangement. The house is right by the sea and there is a small beach alongside.

Lalla Panzi Guesthouse, Anse aux Pins ☎ 376 411, Fax 375 633 – 4rm or Family-run guesthouse comprising an elegant wooden house built on piles at the water's edge. Essential to book in advance as knowing visitors return. Meals on request.

US$60-70

Auberge de Bougainville, Anse Bougainville ☎ 371 788, Fax 371 808, audebou@seychelles.net – 11rm or Colonial planter's house owned by descendants of the same family for which it was built. Entirely surrounded by magnificent bougainvillaea hedges, the house perches above a steep road overlooking the sea. The charming old-fashioned bedrooms on the first floor are tastefully decorated and each has an enclosed balcony. All the fixtures are made of wood, including the floor; the furniture includes locally made Creole armchairs and the odd family heirloom. Those who prefer a modern style of comfort should ask for one of the newer rooms with terrace giving onto the garden.

US$75-95

La Roussette Hotel, Anse aux Pins ☎ 376 245, Fax 376 011, chantal@seychelles.net – 10rm. Bungalows painted in pastel shades, complete with veranda overlooking the garden. Opportunity to play golf and various water sports at the Reef Hotel nearby (200m or so).

La Désirade, Pointe au Sel ☎ 225 714, Fax 225 736 or 371 611, doffy@seychelles.net – 3rm Modern bungalows with kitchenette and veranda overlooking the sea. Close to a number of remote – and therefore deserted – small inlets.

Chalets d'Anse Forbans, Anse Forbans ☎ 366 111, Fax 366 161, forbans@seychelles.net – 12rm Modern and comfortable individual cottages with kitchen facilities and private veranda. Location may be slightly remote but meals can be eaten at the Hotel Allamanda next door. Alternatively, why not shop down the road at Quatre Bornes (1km) for a simple picnic in the garden or on the long unspoilt beach that extends along the front of the rooms. Snorkelling equipment and bicycles provided.

US$110-125

Casuarina Beach Hotel, Anse aux Pins ☎ 376 211/376 026, Fax 376 016, casarina@seychelles.net – 20rm Attractive bedrooms with private terrace dotted around the garden that leads straight onto the beach. Bonus open-air Jacuzzi set in among the rocks above the sea. Occasionally on Saturday nights, the hotel organises special evenings with a sumptuous Creole buffet followed by a show of traditional dancing around the fire; dance evenings also provide visitors with the opportunity of learning the basic steps of the *séga* dance from the young and energetic Seychellois.

Hôtel Allamanda, Anse Forbans ☎ 366 266, Fax 366 175, amanda@seychelle.net – 10rm Large well-appointed, newly furbished rooms on the first floor with or without balcony, and with view over the sea or the garden. Spacious communal areas that are comfortable even if rather stark. Creole buffet one evening a week. Private sandy beach, secluded and perfect for snorkelling.

• West Coast

US$60-75

Résidences Takamaka, Anse Takamaka ☎ 366 049, Fax 366 303 – 10rm Pleasant bungalows with veranda arranged informally in a large peaceful garden where goats roam freely! Casual family atmosphere. Largely Italian clientele. 5min walk from Takamaka Beach.

Auberge d'Anse Boileau, Anse Boileau ☎ 375 660, Fax 376 406 – 9rm Attractive rooms in a thatched building. Pleasant veranda runs right around the house, opening out onto the garden; locally ade wooden deck-chairs and cane garden furniture. Restaurant **Chez Plume** (see Where to eat p 436).

Blue Lagoon, Anse à la Mouche ☎ 371 97, Fax 371 65 – 4rm Two-bedroom cottages, large sitting area decorated with colourful Sri Lankan batik hangings, equipped kitchen and terrace. Well-kept garden from which it is possible to glimpse the sea. Cleaning and airport transfer included in price. Cook available for hire on request. For those prepared to share communal facilities, the cost of renting half a cottage is half that of the two-bedroom unit.

Anse Soleil Resort, Anse Soleil, Baie Lazare, ☎ 361 090, Fax 361 435 – 4rm Excellent for quiet family holidays. Fully equipped bungalows built against the mountain, 20min walk from Anse Soleil and Petite Anse, two of Mahé's most beautiful beaches. The owner prepares a selection of excellent Seychelles cuisine himself. Book early.

US$75-95

Lazare Picault Hotel, Anse Gaulette ☎ 361 111, Fax 361 177 – 14rm or Attractive building nestling among profuse vegetation. Rooms with balcony set into the hillside. More expensive rooms are larger and more modern, have kitchen facilities provided and a spacious balcony overlooking the whole of Anse Gaulette and Baie Lazare: one of the finest views in Mahé.

Anse Soleil Beachcomber, Anse Soleil ☎ 361 461, Fax 361 460 – 8rm This lost corner of paradise is quite wonderful, although a car is essential. Rooms with their own balcony overlook a small beach with dazzlingly white sand. Reservations are vital as the rooms are often booked well in advance.

Chez Batista, Anse Takamaka ☎ 366 300, Fax 366 509, batistas@seychelles.net – 9rm Two-bedroom cottages with large terrace, lost in among the vegetation at the foot of the mountain. Sea or garden view. Most attractive and pleasant. Restaurant on Takamaka Beach (see Where to eat).

US$95-110

Villa Bambou, Anse à la Mouche ☎ 371 177, Fax 371 108 – 3rm Picturesque Creole house with awnings, completely surrounded by a cool, open veranda furnished with attractive African chairs. Small, simply furbished rooms, immaculately clean, brightened by colourful lithographs by Michael Adams. Comfortable seating area with cane furniture. The adorable owner is happy to provide meals by prior arrangement. The only drawback is that the villa works practically exclusively with a tour operator, ***Trauminsel Reisen***, 08152/93190

Over US$155

Chateau d'Eau, Domaine de Barbarons, Dans Galet ☎ 378 339/378 177, Fax 378 388 – 5rm Luxurious guest rooms in an old-fashioned planter's house. Quiet and spacious. Wonderful garden with scented flowering shrubs. Lovely pool situated midway between the house and the sea. The two slightly isolated bungalows down by the water-line tend to be reserved for couples on honeymoon. Refined accommodation with a strong personal touch, making this a more exclusive place to stay than any of the main hotels. Access to private beach. Fabulous sunsets!

WHERE TO EAT

• Northern peninsula

US$5-10

Baobab, Beau Vallon ☎ 247 167. Lunch and dinner Popular pizzeria on the island's favourite beach and a favourite among an eclectic crowd. Tables are often hard to come by at weekends when occupied by large Sechellois families and friends.

Maxim's Jade House, coastal road, Ma Constance ☎ 241 489. Lunch and dinner; closed Sundays. Chinese dishes served in large or moderate portions depending on how hungry you are.

US$10-12

Boat House, Beau Vallon ☎ 247 898. Dinner (book tables during the day); closed Sundays. Delicious, generous and varied Creole buffet. Different kinds of curry, grilled fish, green mango salad, coconut combinations. Great range of fish depending on the morning's catch. Friendly staff. Affable place and tasty food.

Lafontaine, Beau Vallon, ☎ 247 841. Lunch and dinner. Situated between Boat House and the Baobab, a little off the road, this very pleasant restaurant has a covered terrace. To the beat of reggae or séga music, you can eat good Creole cooking (fish curry, tuna fish steak Creole style, grilled prawns) at very reasonable prices.

US$15-30

La Perle Noire, Beau Vallon ☎ 247 046. Dinner CC Varied menu verging on the predictable. Pleasant tables outside. A little on the expensive side.

La Scala, Danzilles ☎ 247 535. Dinner; closed Sundays. Suitably smart but casual dress CC Italian dishes cooked Seychelles-style by an Italian chef. Fresh pasta with fish and shellfish. Lovely terrace with view of the sea.

• East Coast

US$7-15

Carefree, Anse Faure, ☎ 375 237. Lunch and dinner. One of the establishments closest to the airport. Serves varied and delicious Creole cuisine with fish and seafood specialities (grilled prawns in garlic and butter, shark steak, ourite cari). The relaxed family atmosphere makes it a very pleasant place to stop.

Ty-Foo, La Plaine, opposite Pointe au Sel, ☎ 371 485. Lunch and dinner. This unpretentious little restaurant with rather insipid decor is one of the most popular restaurants among the locals. Excellent choice of chop suey, pork curry; you can even drink your coffee while playing billiards.

Vye Marmit, Village Artisanal, Anse aux Pins, ☎ 376 155. Open all day. CC Located on the largepainted wood veranda of a colonial house. Guests are invited to taste the best of Seychelles cooking (including bat stew or skate kari with green saffron). Discrete service, relaxed at lunch-time, more sophisticated in the evening.

Kaz Kreol, Anse Royale ☎ 371 680. Tuesday-Thursday, lunch only; Friday-Sunday, lunch and dinner; closed Mondays CC Small informal restaurant on the beach. Variety of pizzas and pasta dishes.

• West Coast

US$10-25

Jolie Rose, Anse Intendance ☎ 366 060 Food served all day. Set back 100m or so from the fabulous often deserted beach in Anse Intendance. Relaxed venue decorated with fishing nets, straw hats and a miscellany of goodies made of coconut. Salads, curries, fish and crayfish.

Sundown Restaurant, Port Glaud ☎ 378 352. Food served all day; reservations required for dinner; closed Sundays (or Mondays depending on the season) CC Small restaurant facing onto the lagoon opposite l'Islette. Fish soups, mixed crayfish specialities, grilled fish, bat curry; restricted selection of sandwiches.

Chez Batista, Anse Takamaka ☎ 366 300. CC Food served all day. Likeable little shack on the beach. Enjoy a completely mellow meal with your feet in the sand. Delicious fresh fish. Creole buffets on Sundays.

La Sirène, Anse aux Poules Bleues ☎ 361 339. Food served all day. Quiet desert island restaurant on the water's edge. Good selection of fresh fish and crayfish, roast bat, wonderful home-made ice-creams.

Anse Soleil Café, Anse Soleil, Baie Lazare, ☎ 361 085. Open all day. One of the island's most pleasant secluded and quiet spots. Located right on Anse Soleil beach, this little restaurant provides both a magical setting and excellent cuisine (crab curry and tuna steak).

Chez Plume, Auberge d'Anse Boileau (Where to stay p 434) ☎ 376 660. Closed Sundays to all save hotel guests CC Excellent Creole buffet for residents on Sundays, occasionally open to non-residents on application. Authentic cooking with good blends of flavour, friendly service, pleasant decor. Menu lists bat terrine and various fish, each served with its own particular sauce: passion-fruit for capitaine, turmeric or *safran* for bourgeois, ginger for vieille, green pepper for swordfish, tarragon for shark, and a composite (sauce matelot) for barracuda! Keep enough room for the coconut flan with chocolate sauce.

Oscar – au Capitaine Rouge, Anse à la Mouche, ☎ 371 224. Lunch and dinner; closed Wednesdays. It's always a pleasure to lunch on the terrace, which directly overlooks Anse à la Mouche. Simple, very tasty fish specialities. Worth a trip.

SPORTS AND PASTIMES

Glass-bottom boats – off Beauvallon Beach, by the Coral Strand (***Teddy*** ☎ 521 125) and Berjaya Hotels. Monday-Friday: half-day excursions to the marine park at Baie Ternay (or Ste Anne from December to February when the winds are too strong); Saturday-Sunday: a full day out including barbecue lunch on one of the small offshore islands. Snorkelling equipment provided. 150RS for half day; 300RS for full day, including lunch.

Walking underwater – See p 400.

Jules Verne Dive Center, Hotel Berjaya, Port Glaud ☎ 378 451/361 450. A shuttle transfers trippers from their hotel to the floating platform where they can don a complete pressurised dry suit before taking the plunge and exploring the depths (240RS for 30-45min). Day trips to Île Thérèse (50RS), to Playboy Beach (accessible only by boat: 100RS) or Petite Anse (125RS).

Boat trips – The ***Blue Bird*** is usually anchored at Port Glaud in the early morning and off the beach at Port Launay during the day. Daylong excursions in the marine park or around the neighbouring islands (approx 500RS per day for four people).

Offshore fishing – ***Fishing***, coastal road in Beau Vallon ☎ 24 78 98. Day trips to Silhouette or North Island, including fishing, barbecue lunch, a walk and a swim (100-500RS per person).

Scuba-diving – Everything from induction courses to advanced standards, BSAC and PADI. Excursions to wrecks and coral reefs; night diving. Bottles, buoyancy jackets and basic wet suits provided.

Big Blue Divers, Mare Anglaise, northern part of Beau Vallon, ☎ 261 106, bigblue@seychelles.net Deep-sea diving (Rs220, reduced rates depending on the number of dives), beach barbecues, excursions. Friendly, serious and professional staff.

Le Diable des Mers, Beau Vallon Beach (opposite Beau Vallon Bungalows) ☎ 247 104.

Underwater Center Seychelles ☎ 247 357. This organisation, possibly the most reputable in the Seychelles, operates a number of centres on Mahé: Coral Strand, Beau Vallon ☎ 247 357; Reef Hotel, Anse aux Pins ☎ 376 251. Dives from Rs250-330.

Hiking – ***Basil Baudoin*** ☎ 241 790. Usually to be found at the Coral Strand Hotel on Monday evenings at 6pm. A very knowledgeable local guide arranges various walks across the island.

Mason's Travel (see p 414) regularly organises different walks.

Tourist Office (see p 414) provides a good range of leaflets describing the options available, with comprehensive directions and information on flora and fauna to be seen.

Casino – ***Berjaya Universal Casino***, Berjaya Hotel, Beau Vallon ☎ 247 400. Open until 3am. Slot-machines and betting tables.

Planter's Casino, Plantation Club Hotel, Baie Lazare ☎ 361 361.

Other entertainment – Casuarina Beach Hotel (see p 433).

WHERE TO SHOP

Souvenirs and handicrafts – A number of little shops are to be found in and around Beau Vallon.

Craft Village, Anse aux Pins (see p 422).

Maison Coco, Craft Village, Anse aux Pins. Open daily. All kinds of things made from coconuts and their by-products.

La Marine, la Plaine St-André, ☎ 371 441. Scale ship models (prices start from Rs3 000). See p 422.

Kreolfleurage, coastal road, Pointe Nord-Est. This perfume business blends various essential oils of flowers, herbs and spices to make three different scents (Bwanwar, Bamboo, Ambre vert). Packaged in attractive little wooden bottles available from the manufacturers and from various tourist shops elsewhere.

Artists' studios and art galleries – ***Michael Adam's Studio***. See p 426.

Donald Adelaide Studio, Baie Lazare ☎ 361 067. Open Monday-Saturday, 9am-6pm; closed Sundays. Seychellois painting.

Gérard Devoud Studio, Baie Lazare ☎ 361 313. Coloured paintings and lithographs.

Tom Bowers, Les Cannelles, Anse à la Mouche ☎ 371 518. Monday-Saturday, 9am-6pm. Bronze sculpture.

Zimaz Kréol, Colourful quality paintings on silk, paper, batiks, bath/beach towels, T-shirts, bags, etc available from a small boutique on the road to Victoria at Beau Vallon, and from Market Street in Victoria.

PRASLIN★★★

Granitic island rising to 367m (Praslin Island)
40km northeast of Mahé
Approx 38sqkm (11km east-west and 4km north-south)
Pop 6 091 – Map p 440-441

Not to be missed

White beaches in Anse Lazio, Petite Anse Kerlan and Anse Georgette.
Birdwatching on the islands of Aride or Cousin.
Tour of the Vallée de Mai.
Stroll along Baie Ste Anne or Grand'Anse late afternoon.

And remember...

Hire a car for a day to go round the island.
Make the most of the islet St-Pierre before 2pm (when groups arrive).
The north coast is best from April-September, the south coast from October-March.

Island of Palms

Lazare Picault named Praslin the "île des Palmes" when he landed there in 1744, impressed by the profusion of palm trees covering the island. In 1768, **Captain Marion Dufresne** claimed possession of the island for the French, calling it Praslin in honour of the naval minister **Gabriel de Choiseul**, Duke of Praslin. Whether approached from the sea or from the air, the most striking aspect of Praslin is its vivid green mantle of dense vegetation, interrupted here and there by a patch of rusty red bare earth or a group of mighty grey granite boulders. For obvious reasons the island provided pirates and Arab merchants with a safe hideaway.

Praslin has a seductive, unhurried pace of life and swathes of unspoilt countryside. Holidaying here might include venturing into the hills, sunbathing on deserted beaches, or discovering countless species of fish in the clear waters. For a long period of time, the island's economy depended on eking a revenue from the cultivation of coconuts, vanilla and patchouli, and exploitation of the granite quarries; today, the most lucrative industry is tourism. Still, the way of life for the local population is entirely rural, with people concentrated in one of the only two villages: Grand'Anse on the west coast and Baie Ste Anne on the eastern side. Between the two shores rise the hills that comprise the **Vallée de Mai National Park** with its unique forest of *cocos de mer*.

North Coast★★

Baie Ste Anne to Anse Lazio

Approx 10km – 30min by road.

■ **Baie Ste-Anne★ –** Schooners from Mahé and La Digue put in at Baie Ste Anne, a large sheltered bay in which nestles Praslin's most important village. The main buildings are scattered around the white church: these include the school, the only hospital on the island, the post office, banks and various businesses. Vividly coloured fishing boats wait patiently moored along the jetty. The odd roof thatched with coconut fronds peeped through the undergrowth, although the number of these is dwindling, as they are largely superseded by corrugated tin painted garish yellows, reds, greens and blues which are picked out from the green backdrop by the sun.

Turn right out of Baie Ste Anne after walked up from the landing stage.

■ **Anse Volbert**★★ – The fabulously long beach (3km) separates the sea from the largest concentration of hotels on Praslin, and provides facilities for a broad range of water sports. The shallow water laps almost imperceptibly on the sand, its clear aquamarine colours gradually growing to a pale turquoise as far as the eye can see.

Beyond the coconut trees, clumps of vivid hibiscus and bougainvillaea, and lines of multicoloured tropical plants (birds of paradise and canna lilies) sits the **Café des Arts**, where quality handmade goods and works of art are sold (*see* Shopping, *p 453*).

Excursions to **ilslet St-Pierre**★★ are regularly organised by the local diving school and fishing boats. For this rather unassuming outcrop presides over a veritable natural **underwater aquarium**★★★ (*see* Travel Agents *and* Water sports, *p 448 and 453. Avoid day trips taking in several islands at a time: the tiny islet soon becomes overwhelmed by groups and it is impossible to see anything*).

Return to the main tarmac road.

The road soon climbs its way steeply up the hillsides, offering an ever changing perspective of the landscape from fine **viewpoints**★ at every bend: below stretch views over the dappled waters of the lagoon and the greyish or pinkish glacis, depending on the time of day, gently lapped by the gentlest of wavelets.

At the end of the coast road, turn left after the shop selling souvenirs and snacks.

The buses terminate at **Anse Boudin**, from where it is easy to continue on foot; if you are travelling by car, follow the road until it becomes impassable (*4-wheel drive vehicle recommended; check the state of the brakes, as it becomes very steep*). The climb to the top of **Morne Grand Fond** at a modest 340m above sea level provides an extensive **view**★★ of the rugged coastline and the deep blue sea.

Back in Anse Boudin, take the dirt road which climbs up into the forest.

The track of red earth penetrates a tunnel of undergrowth. At last, it leads to the edge of the forest and a great **view**★★ over the thick vegetation thrown into relief by the red earth, the island of Curieuse and the deep blues of sky and sea in the distance. Having taken in the space, the light and the stillness, walk down to the coast (energy levels permitting!).

■ **Anse Lazio**★★★ (Chevalier Bay) – This huge beach is among the most beautiful of the granite beaches of the Seychelles. Transparent turquoise water and spotless sand surrounded by rounded rocks give it a little touch of paradise. It is a favourite sheltered mooring for sailing boats.

South Coast★★

Baie Ste Anne to Anse Georgette

Approx 20km – 40min by road.

Take the road south up from Baie Ste-Anne (turn left if coming from the landing stage).

The South Coast has a wilder beauty, protected by far-off reefs. Access is via a steep, narrow, winding road that sometimes follows the contours of the hill and sometimes hugs the coastline, passing the succession of peaceful little coves bordered by fishermen's shacks. The *glacis* glow a pale grey, sometimes tinted with rosy hues, whether in bright sunlight or under a dark monsoon sky.

The faded golden sands of the lagoon are interspersed with black rocks: the scene becomes an amalgam of marbled colours with blues, greens and shades of black contrasted with the lightest froth of the sea foam.

■ **Grande Anse**★ – The second village on Praslin stretches out from around a "village square" in which sits the **Monument to Independence** – which consists of a female *coco de mer* encircled by two male fruits. One side is in part taken up by the small **marketplace**, which comes to life when the fishermen return with their catches. If the atmosphere appears somewhat charged as you pass through, it is well worth venturing down to the beach. It may be that the fish-laden boats have been tied up, the bulging nets have been landed and crowds of housewives are jostling with farm-workers in their attempts to collect a bunch of identical fish hanging from a string, or a single, more meaty specimen suspended by the tail.

The main road is lined with small **Indian stores** ornamented with wonderfully kitsch Hindu portraits, stuffed full of everything imaginable ready to be weighed on the large brass trays of scales suspended above the counter.

Although the majority of shops are closed on Sundays, the area bubbles to life after mass, at around 10am, when all self-respecting Seychellois Christians, dressed in their Sunday clothes, file out of church and stop for a quick exchange of gossip in the shade of a tree or to pick up those last groceries required for the family picnic on the beach.

Sundays are also the day for First Communion so look out for small groups of pretty little girls in immaculate dresses and polished shoes with ribbons in their hair, gadding about giggling.

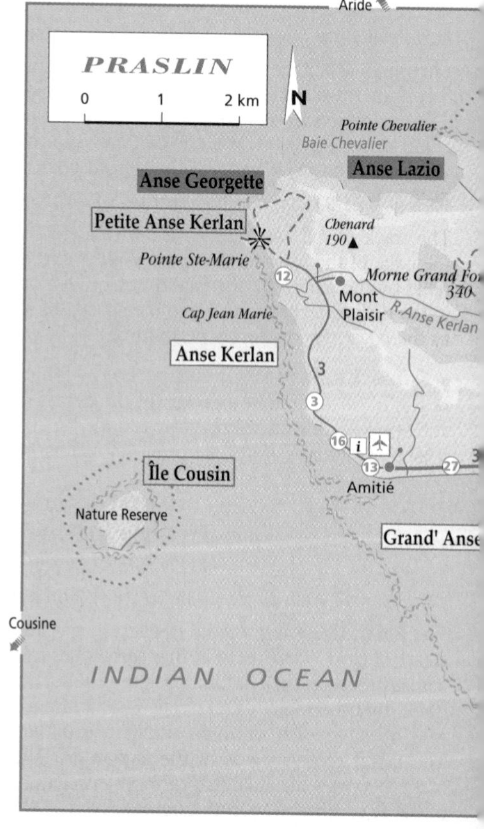

HOTELS

- Archipel (L')........ 1
- Beach Villa........ 2
- Beach Villa annexe........ 3
- Britannia (Le)........ 4
- Beaudamier (Le)........ 5
- Cabane des Pêcheurs (La) 6
- Chalets Côté Mer........ 7
- Coco de Mer........ 8
- Colibri (Le)........ 9
- Cuvette (La)........ 10
- Grand Bleu (Le)........ 11
- Islander (The)........ 12
- Maison des Palmes........ 13
- Paradise Sun........ 14
- Réserve (La)........ 15
- Tropique Villa (Le)........ 16
- Vanille (La)........ 17
- Villa Flamboyant........ 18
- Village du Pêcheur........ 19

Across the island*

Find the track opposite the church at **Grand'Anse** that leads inland (in the direction of the Hotel Britannia). Follow it for some 45min to the highest point, where it forks. The footpath off to the left is known as the **Pasquière track** and it leads to **Anse Possession** on the north coast (3km from Grand'Anse) in less than an hour. The one forking to the right is the **Salazie track** and it comes out at **Anse Volbert** (5km from Grand'Anse).

■ **Anse Kerlan*** – The road skirts the bays of Grand'Anse and Anse Kerlan, past an assortment of hotels, restaurants and shops, small colonial houses with verandas and shabby – or occasionally spanking new – tin shacks.
To one side, the sea can be glimpsed through the trees, gently lapping the sequence of long sandy beaches broken now and then by little coves and a tumble of black boulders. Out at sea sit the neighbouring islands of **Cousin** and **Cousine**, their profiles the only interruption on the horizon. On the landward side, clumps of magnificent granite boulders protrude from the fallen leaves of the trees: mangoes, breadfruit, banks of brightly coloured bougainvillaea, casuarinas and

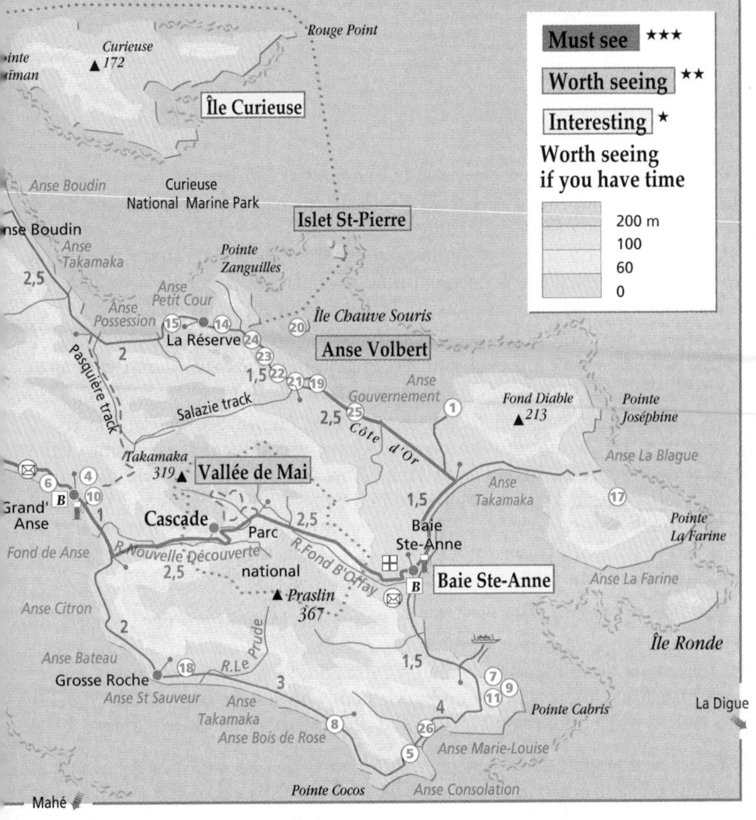

South Coast

H. Choimet

A little house on Praslin

palms; additional texture is provided by the intermittent bare patches of reddish earth. The cheerful sound of Creole conversations or local music may be heard in snatches coming from the numerous *kaz* and their colourful front gardens. Should you hear the sound of shuffling fronds from above, you may catch a man up a coconut tree skilfully collecting the sap from an incision in the trunk. When fermented, it becomes the local alcoholic brew known as *calou*.

The coastal road comes to an abrupt end at a fork marked with a no entry sign; park the car and follow the earth track straight ahead, leaving the road, which climbs up to the right. Walk for 5min.

The shaded track leads off to the left towards **Pointe Ste Marie**, the rocky promontory projecting into the ocean to form the most westerly point of the island, dividing Anse Kerlan from Petite Anse Kerlan. The little **shrine** with a white cross dedicated to the Virgin commemorates the tragic drowning of a child in the rough waters hereabouts. On a fine day, a great **panoramic view★★** is unfurled to include Cousin and Cousine on the left, with Mahé beyond blocked out on the horizon, while to the right sits the island of Aride.

■ **Petite Anse Kerlan★★** – From Pointe Ste Marie the water is especially tempting, glimpsed as it is through the needles of the casuarinas! This bright emerald sea is almost always absolutely calm and, for some reason, warmer than anywhere else. On the beach, a multitude of tiny opalescent crabs scamper across the sand – almost indiscernibly – before precipitating themselves down a hole.

■ **Anse Georgette★★★** – *Access only on foot; wear shoes with a good grip as there are a few tricky stretches; avoid setting off alone. Approx 15min there and back.*

Climb over the rocks at the edge of Petite Anse Kerlan (right when facing the sea). The magical **view★★★** back through the palm fronds takes in the beach and calm sea beyond. There is no real path, but it is quite easy to continue over the granite boulders emerging from the vegetation, and follow the line of the coast. The objective is to reach one of the most idyllic beaches on Praslin. Shining white sand, mesmerisingly pure turquoise water and not a soul with whom to share the spellbinding solitude. *However, take care when bathing lest the currents carry you offshore; keep close to the beach because no help is at hand should you run into difficulties.*

There is a second rather longer but easier route back *(approx 30min)*. Follow the path inland and around the hillock between the two coves. The way narrows where overgrown; however, rest assured, the only signs of life will be the odd isolated shack nestling in the vegetation or the occasional man working with a machete cutting firewood.

■ Vallée de Mai National Park★★

Halfway along the road between Baie Ste-Anne and Grand'Anse. Open daily 8am-5.30pm. Admission charge. Guided tours (advisable - 1hr-90min) on request. Well-maintained and clearly signed paths; map available for the more independent visitor. Allow 1hr (longer for exploring all the different tracks). Wear shoes with a good grip and insect repellent. Shopping and refreshments.

A natural heritage of uncertain origin

Praslin's main attraction, the Vallée de Mai, was classed a World Heritage Site in 1983. It extends over some 20 hectares of undulating landscape at the heart of the island's southern section. It also forms part of the **Praslin National Park**. Most importantly, this exuberant forest includes 4 000 or so giant **coco de mer palms**, among which are some estimated to be more than 300 years old. Even before the tree was discovered, giant coconuts weighing up to 20kg were washed up on the shores of the Indian Ocean. Since no one knew where they came from, they became known as "cocos de mer" and, having perhaps come from mysterious trees growing underwater, they were attributed mythical origins and magical powers.

Coconuts worth millions

The nut of the "coco de mer" was introduced to Europe by merchants and navigators trading in the Indian Ocean; before long, it had become highly prized as an object of rare quality, to the point where kings vied to pay considerable fortunes for a specimen. It is said that Rudolph II of Habsburg, Emperor of the Holy Roman Empire, offered 4 000 florins to the heirs of the Dutch Admiral W Hermanssen for a coco de mer but in vain. Long considered to be a luxury item, the nut was often mounted in gold or silver and transformed thereby into an objet d'art worthy of a museum.

Although once endemic on all five granitic islands of the Seychelles, the *coco de mer* only grows wild now on Praslin and Curieuse. Male and female trees grow side by side in equal numbers. The rounded female nut is suggestive of a woman's buttocks (from which comes the name "coco fesse") or pelvis – depending on your imagination. The long catkin flecked with little yellow flowers of the **male** plant, meanwhile, is decidedly phallic in appearance.

These curiosities have inevitably inspired all maner of folkloric interpretations, most often erotic, but sometimes religious and scientific as well. Local legend relates how the palms of both

The Garden of Eden

In 1881 a certain Charles Gordon identified the Valleé de Mai as a vestige of the Garden of Eden, an earthly Paradise where Man would still be living had he not succumbed to temptation. Furthermore, the "coco de mer" was the tree of Knowledge described in the Bible, the fruit of which God forbade Adam and Eve to taste lest they should gain knowledge of Good and Evil.

sexes couple with each other on stormy nights, and that misfortune befalls anyone unlucky enough to witness such forest trysts. It may come as no surprise, therefore, to learn that the white flesh of the fruit is said to be a powerful aphrodisiac.

A unique microcosm

The warm and humid conditions allow these trees to grow to great heights – up through the gloom to sunshine – forming a thick canopy 30m above the ground. When beams of sunlight manage to break through the foliage and pierce the hazy dimness of the forest, the feathery fronds are picked out against deep shadows. The slightest draft is picked up by the sail-like pleated leaves of the tangled palms, making them rustle mysteriously, while in the rain, the fan shaped fronds amplify the sound of falling drops, drowning out the gentle chirping of the birds.

In no time at all, the footpaths meander among over 50 **indigenous plants**, including the six species of palm that are endemic to the Seychelles. Some of this flora and fauna is unique to this valley. Other **exotic plants** found in these parts range from a variety of fruit trees, *albizia, sandragons, flamboyants* and acacias to the vanilla vine and flowering orchids. However, current policy is to remove species introduced by man, so as to return the forest to its original state.

This unique natural reserve shelters an **endemic fauna** that is just as exceptional.

In the thick of the Vallée de Mai

G. Simon/SCOPE

Praslin

The rare and elusive black parrot and the scarce examples of the blue pigeon, as well as the more common *bulbul*, have made their home here, as have many multicoloured insects and versatile reptiles such as the bronze gecko, green lizard, Tiger chameleon and Seychelles boa.

After completing a tour of the actual park, it is well worth taking a stroll along the road towards Grand'Anse to see the **waterfall***, which pours down through a profusion of palm trees and is all the more spectacular after rain.

Praslin's sister islands

Day trips are organised by the main tour operators (Creole Holidays, TSS, see p 449), as well as by some hotels and other smaller family-run structures, which are less well-known and often friendlier. The favourite combination takes in the islands, Cousin, Curieuse and St-Pierre, with barbecue lunch on Curieuse and the opportunity to snorkel around St-Pierre (see p 454).

Note: the species of birds mentioned in bold are shown on the illustrated plates p 14-15.

Cousin**

Open to visitors Tuesday-Friday. The best time to visit is April-May. Compulsory guide. Access charge. Swimming, picnics and collection of shells and plants are forbidden. A zoom or telephoto lens as well as light-sensitive photographic film, suited to taking pictures of the wildlife shaded by thick vegetation, are advised, as are binoculars.

The smallest granitic island of the Seychelles (a mere 600m x 800m) lies 3km west of Praslin. Since 1975 Cousin has become an important **natural reserve for sea birds** administered by the International Council for Bird Preservation (ICPB), having originally been acquired with the help of the World Wildlife Fund in 1968 to save the Seychelles warbler from imminent extinction. As conservation is the principal consideration in this initiative, visits to the island are strictly controlled. Only ten or so people are allowed to live there, namely a warden, an ornithologist and their respective families, while the permanent bird population numbers some 500 000 land and sea birds, with 200 000-300 000 visitors flying in to nest and breed in greatest numbers in April and May.

The guide is both knowledgeable and passionate about "his" domain. He will happily identify the various creatures wandering in the undergrowth between palms, pisonias *(bois mapou)*, fruit-bat trees *(bois sousouri)*, Balfour's pandanus and tortoise trees *(bois tortue)*. Plant enthusiasts may be intrigued to recognise cotton, which was once grown here commercially, castor oil plants, pawpaws, coffee, bamboo, chillis, lemon, jamalac and mango from plantation days. The guide will help you discover the **white-tailed tropic bird** *(paille-en-queue)*, with its elegant black and white plumage and the long, slender tailfeathers that make it so distinctive when in flight, sitting on its egg nestled in the stump of a tree; the **noddy** (brown or lesser), with its velvety grey plumage, which nests in pisonias and coconut trees or among the rocks; the lovely **fairy tern** – with its translucent wings, spotless plumage and dark blue beak; the wedge-tailed shearwater *(fouke)* and the Audubon shearwater *(riga)*, which skims the water or floats on the waves to catch fish that it will later regurgitate as feed for its young; or the Seychelles brush warbler, which is no longer rare. Moorehens, the frigatebird (which breeds exclusively on Aldabra), the Seychelles fody *(toc-toc)*, sunbirds, the **scarlet fody** *(cardinal)*, Seychelles turtle-doves, ruddy turnstones, and **bridled terns** – to mention but a few complete the picture.

Other residents who will come out to watch the stream of visitors will no doubt include *Georges*, a giant 150-year-old tortoise, and a profusion of coloured lizards and curious skinks. The endangered hawksbill turtle, however, is rather shy.
Two kilometres from Cousin sits the privately owned and uninhabited **Cousine Island**, access to which is even more restricted.

Curieuse*

Open to visitors Tuesday-Friday. It is strictly forbidden to collect shells or coral. This island half a mile (1km) northeast of Praslin is the fifth largest granite island of the Seychelles (2.5km x 3.5km) and was once known as Île Rouge. Although it has been badly exploited by man, a reforestation programme is restoring the landscape to its original state. Additional measures have been imposed to conserve the marine life thereabouts, including the creation of **Curieuse Marine National Park**, which extends from Praslin's Pointe Chevalier to Pointe Zanguilles. There is a proliferation of fish, corals, molluscs, octopus, and crabs here, partly because of the depth of the channel and partly because of the mangroves. Sanctuary is also provided to breeding hawksbill turtles and giant land tortoises.

The former leper colony provides some of the most idyllic anchor-holds for sailing boats and cruisers. Local guides are on hand for those looking to identify the flora and fauna, although well-marked trails across the island can be explored by visitors alone.
Rounded boulders eroded by the sea and coral fossils indicate that part of Curieuse was once submerged by the ocean. Furthermore, early accounts record the island marshes as being infested with crocodiles. Today, little footbridges link the dry mangroves, which provide labyrinthine underground homes for great extended families of land crabs tunnelled in the red earth.
Among the indigenous trees found on Cousin, look out for the *tabebuia* (*Tabebuia pallida* or *calice du pape*), *bois rouge* and *capucins*. A fragment of hardwood forest, a rare survivor from the beginning of the century when the area was stripped to make way for a coconut plantation, is now protected and being expanded by the National Parks authority. Two of the six palm species endemic to the Seychelles are well established here, namely the *coco de mer* and the mountain screwpine, while cinnamon trees, the endemic wild vanilla orchid, *takamakas*, *badamiers* and *latanier-feuilles* are positively common.
To round off the tour, stop at the giant tortoise breeding centre where tortoises of all ages, like all those seen elsewhere on these islands, are from Aldabra.

Aride***

Visitors may land on the island only between October and April; excursions Wednesday-Friday and Sundays. Tours accompanied by warden. Landing charge. Moorings, picnics and collection of shells and plants are all strictly forbidden. Remember to take insect repellent and comfortable walking shoes.

The most northerly granitic island of the Seychelles lies 16km north of Praslin (50km northeast of Mahé) and measures 1.5km by just over 0.5km wide. There are seven inhabitants. It was only discovered in 1756 and earned its name from its rugged and arid appearance; today it is one of the lushest islands and is considered to be the sea-bird sanctuary of the Indian Ocean; an interdependent relationship, since it is the layers of guano (sea birds' manure and fish waste), deposited over time and diluted with natural plant compost, that have enriched the red soil.

In 1973 the island was purchased by Christopher Cadbury on behalf of the Royal Society for Nature Conservation, in accordance with conditions dictated by the Chenard estate (the island's owners for a century). In June 1975 it became classified a Special Reserve and its status was secured. Indeed Aride is recognised as the most exceptional **Natural Reserve** in the archipelago after the more remote Aldabra, on account of its unique combinations of both fauna (the most lizards and geckos in the world; one of the most productive natural underwater ecosystems in the world) and flora (it is the only place in the world where **Wright's Gardenia** or *bois citron* grows naturally, following its sweet-scented, magenta-spotted, trumpet-shaped white flowers with shiny green fruit).
Aride boasts ten breeding species of which six are terns: **fairy (white) terns**, sooty terns, roseate terns, bridled terns, and lesser (black) and common (brown) **noddies**. Also in residence are an impressive number of white-tailed **tropic birds** and their rarer counterpart with red beak and red tail streamers.

Fairy Tern (goéland blanc)

Making the most of Praslin

GETTING THERE

By air – ***Air Seychelles*** fly ten to fifteen small propeller-driven 20-seater aircraft daily from Mahé to Praslin (Rs343 return). The 15min flight passes at a low altitude over Ste Anne, Cousin and Cousine before landing smoothly on the runway.

By boat – Three schooners shuttle between the principal islands (3hr crossing). Departures from Victoria harbour Monday-Friday, 11am-1pm depending on the tide; be there one hour before the scheduled departure time. Arrival at the landing-stage in Baie Ste Anne where taxis will be waiting to take passengers on their onward journey. Tickets are sold from the harbour office prior to departure or on board ship (Rs50 one-way). There is also a more expensive high-speed boat that does the crossing in less than a hour.

All-inclusive package – Check with the travel agencies: Mason's, TSS or Creole Holidays – see p 414.

GETTING AROUND

By car – The larger car rental companies do not have agents on Praslin, but smaller independent operators will be happy to supply the car of your choice (enquire at your hotel reception). The mini-mokes on Praslin have a bad reputation. Check the vehicles over carefully before signing any agreement and remember to try out the brakes, for there are a number of steep roads on the island. Four-wheel drive cars are required only in exceptional conditions. Hardtop cars are preferable in case of heavy rain storms. Prices are a little above the rates on Mahé due to the lack of rival competitors: budget Rs300 to Rs350 per day (do not hesitate to strike a bargain). There are only two service stations, located at Baie Ste Anne and Grand'Anse, open Monday-Saturday, 7.30am-6.30pm; Sundays 7.30am-12noon.

Standard Car Hire, St-Joseph, ☎ 233 555.

Explorer Cars, Grand'Anse, ☎ 233 311/513 706. Rents out fun little 4WD beach buggies.

These rental agents will deliver vehicles all over the island. Ask for a reduction if renting for several days.

The only two fuel stations are at Baie Ste-Anne and Grand Anse. Open every day from 7.30am to 6.30pm, Sundays until 12noon.

By taxi – At the landing-stage in Baie Ste Anne (☎ 232 209) cars wait the arrival of each schooner from Mahé or from la Digue. Others are available at the airport after the arrival of each plane (☎ 233 228). For additional trips, ask the hotel reception to call one for you. Journeys incur set prices which tend to be expensive.

By bus – Small Indian ***Tata*** minibuses circumnavigate the island and provide visitors with the opportunity of travelling with local people. Timetables are available from travel agents and from some hotels – although beware, the times given will be a mere approximation of services available. Similarly, if a bus charges past without stopping, it may be full.

The ***RT61*** route runs from Mont Plaisir to Anse Boudin via the airport, Grand'Anse, Vallée de Mai, the jetty at Baie St-Anne, Anse la Blague and La Réserve in an hour. Departures every 30min on the hour, from 6am-6.30pm.

The ***RT62*** route runs from Mont Plaisir to Zimbabwe via the airport, Grand'Anse, Anse Consolation, the landing-stage at Baie Ste-Anne, La Réserve and Anse Boudin in around an hour. There are only six or seven departures every day in each direction, between 6-7am and 4.30-5.30pm. Less frequent on Sundays.

By bicycle – This is perhaps the most pleasant way of exploring the island, when it is not too hot. The roads are relatively flat on the whole with the occasional steep climb or descent; check the state of your brakes before setting out. Bicycles are available to hire from an agent in Anse Volbert, one in

Grand'Anse and from certain family-run guesthouses (Rs50 per day). To rent good quality mountain bikes, contact ***James Collie***, Amitié (near the airport), ☎ 511 233. James can also deliver bikes if required. Around Rs50 a day, but you can always ask for a reduction.

On foot – The island trails are not especially well maintained, but several circuits can provide for a good couple of hours' easy walking. Remember to take a reliable map and some drinking water.

Hitchhiking – Locals will often stop by the side of the road and offer a lift, especially on Sundays when buses are scarce.

ADDRESS BOOK

Tourist office – A small office at the airport distributes a limited range of material (☎ 233 346).

Travel agents – All three main agents have representatives on Praslin, and organise excursions to the neighbouring islands of Cousin, Curieuse, Aride and La Digue, as well as special guided tours of the Vallée de Mai.

Mason's, on the right-hand side of the coastal road between the Vallée de Mai and Grand'Anse ☎ 233 211.

TSS, on the right-hand side of the coastal road, between Grand'Anse and the airport ☎ 233 438.

Creole Holidays, on the coastal road just opposite the airport ☎ 233 223.

Telephone / Fax – Pay phones/call-boxes are to be found along the main road in built-up areas. Phonecards are sold in some small shops and at the post office. Only hotels and a limited number of guesthouses have faxes.

Post office – There are two post offices on the island: one at Baie Ste Anne, the other by the police station at Grand'Anse. Certain village grocery stores also sell stamps.

Banks and money – There is one bank at Baie Ste Anne, one in Côte d'Or and there are three at Grand'Anse. Open 8.30-3pm weekdays and 9am-11am Saturdays.

Airlines – ***Air Seychelles*** have an agency in the airport ☎ 233 214.

Bookshops and newspapers – There are no bookshops or newsagents as such on Praslin. A small selection of newspapers and magazines are on sale in certain large hotels. Local newspapers can be purchased from Grand'Anse police station.

Medical services – ***Grand'Anse Clinic*** ☎ 233 414.
Baie Ste-Anne Hospital ☎ 232 333.

WHERE TO STAY

Price are calculated on the basis of one night in a double room with breakfast.

• North Coast

US$60-75

Rosemary's Guesthouse, Anse Volbert, ☎ 232 176 – 3 rm Without a doubt one of Praslin's least expensive establishments. A quiet family atmosphere with very basic, clean rooms. Easy access to Anse Volbert beach is one of this charming little guesthouse's main attractions. Rosemary also cooks in the evening, if she's not too tired.

Les Lauriers, Anse Volbert, ☎ 232 241, Fax 232 362 – 5 rm CC Unpretentious little guesthouse. The bungalows have much more appeal than the characterless rooms. Set in a tropical park, the rooms are clean and comfortable. Despite the very friendly welcome, the complex has a slight tendency to be disorganised. It nonetheless remains one of the least expensive establishments opposite Anse Volbert beach.

US$95-110

Le Colibri, Baie Ste Anne ☎ /Fax 232 302 – 9rm CC This attractively thatched house nestles among the trees and rocks overlooking the sea, and can be spotted from the schooner as she sails into Baie Ste Anne. Each of the rooms bar one has its own distinctive character: one is smallish, has a balcony and is furnished with a four-poster bed facing the sea; the one over the dining-room is grander but is tucked under the sloping roof, with a balcony faces the sea. Others, each enjoying a splendid view from its own little terrace, are carefully and tastefully furnished. Be warned: the Swiss owner and his Seychellois wife sometimes take their

Making the most of Praslin

success for granted and may fail to pay attention to all guests equally. Excellent spreads at dinner help to ensure a convivial evening.

Le Grand Bleu, Pointe Cabri ☎ /Fax 232 437 – 4rm Good if the Colibri is booked up or if you prefer to be a little more isolated. Kitchen, sitting-room and large terrace are shared by the two guesthouses. Dinner available from the Colibri. The only thing that might obstruct the view is the flourishing bougainvillaea.

Chalets Côté Mer, Baie Ste Anne ☎ /Fax 232 367 – 12rm Bedrooms or two-storey family cottages with kitchen and sitting-room. Clean and modern. All rooms have private balconies with a fabulous view over the bay. The French chef and his Seychellois wife will lay on excellent meals in the small dining area that looks out onto the sea. A solarium below the terrace is the most perfect place for sunbathing: from here it is possible to scramble over the rocks down to the sea.

US$100-125

Le Duc de Praslin, Côte d'Or, ☎ 232 252, Fax 232 355 – 14 rm Situated 100m from Anse Volbert beach, this guesthouse has a selection of pretty, calm bungalows, each with a private terrace overlooking a sumptuous tropical garden. The only drawback is the proximity of the rooms.

Hôtel du Café des Arts, Côte d'Or, ☎ 232 170, Fax 232 155, paultur@seychelles.net – 4 rm The Café des Arts was recently turned into a hotel and now has very comfortable, attractively decorated rooms with individual terraces. Calm and friendly atmosphere guaranteed. The owner lays on meals nearly every Thursday, with excellent fish specialities (book as early as Monday). As it's a popular place with only a few rooms, bookings are most advisable.

US$125-230

La Vanille, Anse la Blague ☎ 232 178, Fax 23 22 84 – 6rm Unusual building set back into the hillside overlooking the sea. The granite bedrock is integrated into the actual interior spaces to provide a headboard for one room, a wall dividing off the bathroom in another. The bar and restaurant also makes good use of the rock to which they are adjoined. You may require a rental-car if staying at this hotel as it is quite isolated.

Village du Pêcheur Hotel, Anse Volbert ☎ 232 224, Fax 232 273, village@seychelles.net – 13rm Unpretentious detached whitewashed thatched cabins and bungalows surrounded by garden or by the beach in Anse Volbert. Attractive bar area complete with comfortable secluded corners for an intimate tête-à-tête over an aperitif before dinner. The restaurant is set on the actual beach and ranks amongst the best on the island (see Where to eat, p 453)

Acajou Hotel, Côte d'Or, ☎ 232 400, Fax 232 401, acajou@seychelles.net – 28 rm These mahogany wood bungalows, perched high up and surrounded by takamakas and casuarinas, overlook the whole region. The rooms are tastefully decorated. Total calm guaranteed, providing you get a room close to the beach.

US$230-300

Château des Feuilles, Baie Ste-Anne, ☎ 233 316, Fax 233 916, reserv@chateau.com.sc – 9 rm This magnificent establishment is the only *Relais-Château* hotel in the Indian Ocean. It is of course both luxurious and quite charming. In addition, it has a superb view over the sea, which can be reached by a small path. The hotel's rooms are more stylish than its bungalows. The hotel restaurant serves only fish and seafood.

Over US$300

La Réserve, Anse Petit Cour ☎ 232 211, Fax 232 166, lrmk@seychelles.net – 32rm or Minimum 5-day stay. Secluded bungalows with terrace shaded by palm-covered roof, or luxurious suites in a villa on the edge of the sea. Old colonial-style furnishings including four-poster beds. The compound is carefully arranged in a lovely peaceful garden planted with palms, mango trees, orchids, hibiscus and bougainvillaea

Praslin

between the hillside and the beach. The hotel bar area is situated on the large veranda overlooking the bay. See Where to eat p 453.

Paradise Sun Hotel, Anse Volbert ☎ 232 255, Fax 232 019 – 80rm Half-board accommodation only. Handsome rooms built of wood and stone arranged in bungalows or two-storey cottages facing out onto the sea or onto the garden. These bungalows have a distinctive quality about them, be it the lovely wood flooring extending out onto the veranda, the slatted shutters, the bamboo blinds that can be unfurled to screen out the blazing sun or the inclement rain, or the attractive batik pictures on the walls. Lunches on the beach under a parasol with toes dug into the sand; dinner with music beneath the great thatch.

L'Archipel, route des Cocotiers, Anse Gouvernement ☎ 232 242, Fax 232 072, archipel@seychelles.net - 16rm An irregular stack of separate large cottages, each with its balcony backing onto the hillside. Tracks weave down from the lovely gardens to the secluded beach of this remote little bay. Well-known restaurant.

• South Coast

US$55-70

La Cabane des Pêcheurs, Grand'Anse ☎ /Fax 233 320 – 5rm Small and simple hotel nicely redone by the new Franco-Italian owner. Pleasant rooms, moderate rates. Discreet and efficient service.

Beach Villa Guesthouse, Grand'Anse ☎ 233 445, Fax 233 098 – 9rm Simply furnished large rooms with private balcony surrounded by a wonderful garden stretching down to the sea. Owned by an elderly and warm-hearted Creole who will cook up an inexpensive meal on request.

Beach Villa Bungalows, Amitié ☎ 233 216, Fax 233 098 – 3rm The two main rooms tend to be slightly stuffy, located as they are around an internal veranda area. The little thatched bungalow with a terrace facing the sea, and another looking out onto the garden are by far the best. The lovely owner, who is married to the man managing the main guesthouse, is happy to take guests back "home" for a meal on request.

La Cuvette Hotel, Grand'Anse ☎ 233 219/233 005, Fax 233 969 – 8rm Comfortable modern rooms arranged around a small swimming pool. The owner enjoys sharing his love of food with his guests by preparing fabulous and generous assortments of Creole dishes.

US$100-115

Le Beaudamier, Anse Marie-Louise ☎ 233 066, Fax 233 159 – 9rm Isolated bungalows (car recommended) stacked up against the hillside above a rocky creek on the seashore. Each room has a balcony and most enjoy a view over the sea. Panoramic dining-room closed.

Villa Flamboyant, Anse St-Saveur ☎ /Fax 233 036 – 8rm Family-run guesthouse operating from a lovely house surrounded by a garden shaded by flame trees. An attractive wooden veranda surrounds the building on two levels. If possible, put in a request for either of the two rooms with terrace overlooking the sea on the ground floor. Informal and convivial atmosphere at dinner when all guests dine at the same long wooden table. Meals are prepared with fruit and vegetables from the garden. Breakfast is laid out in the garden overlooking the sea. The owner – an Englishman married to a Seychelloise – paints in the studio upstairs.

The Britannia Guesthouse, Grand'Anse ☎ 233 215, Fax 233 944 – 12rm Well-furnished rooms with private balconies overlooking the garden. For some the place may lack warmth and homeliness.

The Islander's Guesthouse, Anse Kerlan ☎ 233 224, Fax 233 154 – 10rm Two-suite bungalows with kitchen and terrace. Lovely beach at the bottom of the garden.

US$110-140

Le Tropique Villa, Amitié ☎ /Fax 233 027 – 6rm Two recently built two-storey wooden blocks with large rooms and kitchen facilities. All the private balconies face onto the sea. The two rooms overlooking the garden may be less expensive but are closer to the road. The landlady will very occasionally cook a meal.

Hotel Maison des Palmes, Amitié ☎ 233 411, Fax 233 880 – 24rm CC Bungalows thatched with fronds of latanier shelter among the trees. Some of the prettily-appointed, welcoming rooms have views over the sea; the drawback to the others, set slightly back, is their proximity to the road. The restaurant has a good reputation (see Where to eat p 454)

Indian Ocean Lodge, Grand'Anse, ☎ 233 324, Fax 233 911, iol@seychelles.net – 24rm TV CC A very pleasant hotel comprised of attractively decorated bungalows. All the rooms have a sea view. The suites are extremely comfortable, with wonderful bathrooms. Good value for money.

Over US$230

Hotel Coco de Mer, Anse Bois de Rose ☎ 233 900, Fax 233 919, cocodeme@eychelles.net – 40rm TV CC Most of the rooms of this luxurious hotel are well-situated: some have a view of the sea, others are aligned in a row between the hotel drive and the coastal road. The spacious suites include a sitting area in the corner where two children could sleep and a private balcony overlooking the sea. Siesta times may be savoured in a hammock slung between coconut trees, where you will be lulled by the gentle sound of the sea on the beach.

• Chauve Souris Island

Over US$230

Chauve-Souris Club, ☎ 232 200, Fax 232 130 – 6 rm CC Full board compulsory. Elegant, sophisticated and luxurious rooms: original parquet floors, colonial furniture, bathrooms with inlaid rock, Jacuzzi. You can also play tennis at the Côte d'Or Lodge Hotel, which belongs to Chauve-Souris Club.

WHERE TO EAT

• Côte d'Or

US$25-45

Tante Mimi, ☎ 232 500. Dinner and Sunday lunch, closed Sunday evenings. Located above the casino in a magnificent Creole house, this restaurant's luxury and setting are quite remarkable: original parquet floors, superbly laid tables, European-style deco. The food is also impeccable: pastries stuffed with shrimps and black olives, thermidor or tandoori chicken in onion sauce, and to finish, white chocolate mousse with dark cherry sauce. Excellent service.

• Anse Volbert

US$4-15

La Goulue (on the tarmac road parallel to the beach) ☎ 23 22 23. Open all day, closed Sundays. Small, unpretentious restaurant well-suited to visitors wanting a salad or light lunch between swims; excellent cooking. Tables available outside (by the side of a road) or inside the dining area.

US$15-30

Les Lauriers ☎ 232 241. Lunch and dinner. Small open-air restaurant serving sandwiches, salads or simple curries at lunch-time and a broad range of extravagant Creole dishes in the evening (set menu).

Village du Pêcheur Hotel ☎ 232 224. Lunch and dinner. Creole buffet Thursdays from 7.30pm (advance booking advisable for non-residents). Tasty cooking to be enjoyed while sitting out on the superb sandy beach of Anse Volbert. Good selection of smoked, marinated raw fish and crayfish.

• Baie Ste-Anne

US$3-7

Le Coco Rouge, ☎ 232 228. Closed Sundays. Don't be misguided by the "take-away" look of this little restaurant, which serves very good, plentiful food.

• Anse Petit Cour

US$18-40

La Réserve ☎ 232 211. Lunch and dinner (advance booking advisable for non-residents). Generous selection of dishes that changes daily according to the supplies available and the mood of the chef that day! Dining-room with romantic decor, candles and background music with tables laid out on a semi-covered pontoon.

• Anse Lazio

US$15-30

Bonbon Plume ☎ 232 136. Lunch (book the morning ahead for a table on the beach). A good place to have lunch, on perhaps the most magical beach of the Seychelles. Informal atmosphere; service can be a little offhand if you order the minimal. Varied menu that changes daily with great selection of fish and crayfish. The only pity is that the restaurant does not serve sandwiches, healthy salads or light meals at reasonable prices. Fabulous freshly squeezed fruit drinks/shakes and excellent "banana caramel" for those with a sweet tooth.

• Grosse Roche

US$25-45

Les Rochers, La Pointe, ☎ 233 910. Lunch and dinner. Recently taken over by a pleasant German couple, this restaurant used to be reputed as one of the island's best. Today, although it is without doubt full of charm and the cooking is very good, the high prices are far from justified. Seafood specialities served in a beach restaurant, opposite the sea.

• Grand'Anse

Under US$7

Steve's Café, ☎ 233 215. Open Monday-Saturday all day; closed Sundays. Sandwiches, salads, baked and stewed dishes. Go early as this establishment is highly popular among locals. It's located by a busy junction, so it is a good idea to order a take-away (cheaper option) and eat it on the beach nearby.

Briz Take-away,. ☎ 233 454. Open all day. Salads, sandwiches, simple dishes (tasty curry made of goat or some other meat, grilled fish, eggplant, aubergine, etc) may be eaten outside, slightly back from the road.

US$15-30

Le Capri, ☎ 233 337. Lunch and dinner. Italian and Creo-Italian cuisine. Pizzas at lunch-time. In the evenings the restaurant serves fresh home-made pasta, chicken cari Seychelles-style, beef with shallots, grilled fish with garlic and ginger or octopus cari. Pleasant setting and excellent service.

• Anse Kerlan

Under US$3

Jessie's Icecream (well signposted: between the Beach Villas annexe and the Islander) ☎ 233 184. Recommended for real ice-cream junkies! This place, operated from a German-Seychellois couple's private veranda, specialises in home-made ice-creams. Massive dilemma as to what to taste in which order: cinnamon, kiwi, banana, passion-fruit, papaya, melon, Chinese gooseberry *(carambole)*, coconut, mango, guava, pineapple, lime, sour sop *(corrosol)* orange, avocado, blackcurrant, cherry... to name but a few. Freshly prepared fruit juices and salads. They also have a fantastic selection (as good as their ices) of delicious jams and preserves.

US$15-30

Hotel Maison des Palmes, Amitié ☎ 233 411. Lunch (light snacks) and dinner (fixed menu or à la carte if ordered before 6.30pm). Buffet with live music certain evenings. Á la carte: crab and lobster clear soup, fresh home-made pasta with seafood flambéed with rum, fillet of snapper stuffed with greens and crab liquor, octopus stewed in coconut milk, king prawns in sherry sauce, giraffe crab with ginger, seafood gratin.

SPORTS AND PASTIMES

Water sports – A collection of activity centres operates on the beach at Anse Volbert organising, and hiring out equipment for, all kinds of sporting pursuits: introductions to diving with bottles, PADI and BSAC courses, night dives, excursions by boat to the neighbouring islands or for offshore fishing.

Diving in Paradise, Anse Volbert (next to the Berjaya Pizzeria) ☎ 232 222, ☎ /Fax 232 148. Diving (about Rs200 per outing), windsurfing, water-skiing, hobby-cat, catamaran, fishing, etc. Excursions to La Digue (Rs100); Cousin, Curieuse, St-Pierre including barbecue lunch (Rs400); Aride (Rs400), Sœur (Rs325), St-Pierre (Rs45), Curieuse (Rs75). Offshore fishing (Rs500 per person).

Octopus, Anse Volbert ☎/Fax 232 350 (shack opposite La Goulue Restaurant). Good diving facilities (from Rs225 per outing). Daily expeditions from 9am-2pm. Véronique and Baba also organise boat trips to Anse Lazio (Rs100), St-Pierre (Rs50), Cousin (Rs250), Curieuse (Rs125) and La Digue; and offshore fishing (Rs400-600). They will also charter out their boat for the day (Rs1 200).

Underwater Center Seychelles, Anse Volbert, Paradise Sun Hotel Centre ☎ 232 255. Good reputation.

Savuka, Anse Bois de Rose ☎ 233 900. Coco de Mer Hotel Diving Centre. Diving and offshore fishing.

Sagittarius, Anse Volbert, near the Café des Arts, ☎ 512 137. Excursions, deep sea fishing. Friendly staff.

Casino – ***Casino des Îles,*** next to the Côte d'Or Lodge Hotel, ☎ 232 500, is located on the main road from Anse Volbert, on the sea-side of the road.

Golf – An 18-hole course has recently been developed at Hotel Lemuria, at Anse Kerlan.

WHERE TO SHOP

Souvenirs and handicrafts – There are no traditional crafts as such that are special to Praslin. Small shops centred around Anse Volbert, Grand'Anse, Anse Kerlan, and Baie Ste Anne sell the usual assortment of sarongs, T-shirts, books and shells.

Chez M Albert Durand, Baie Ste Anne, ☎ 560 053. Workshop and gallery selling carved fish and wooden ship models.

Cocos de mer – The sale of cocos de mer is strictly regulated by the government: this straightforward little memento may set you back a small fortune, with prices starting at 2 000RS. See Shopping p 402.

Art galleries – Praslin seems to attract more artists than the other islands of the archipelago.

Café des Arts, Anse Volbert ☎ 232 170. Open Tuesday-Sunday, 9am-5pm; closed Mondays. Famous gallery run by Christine Harter displaying a good selection of local artwork. The small shop opposite sells a range of things: candles, perfume, objects made of wood or pottery by Seychellois craftsmen.

Villa Flamboyant studio and art gallery, Anse Sauveur ☎ /Fax 233 036. Open 8am-6pm. Verney Cresswell has his studio on the first floor of his fine family-run guesthouse. A warm welcome is extended to residents and non-residents alike. The house alone is worth a visit, not to mention the watercolours and lithographs that are on sale at surprisingly affordable prices.

G. Simeone/DIAF

Praslin

The Praslin Coastline

LA DIGUE★★★

Granitic island rising to 333m (La Digue Island)
6km east of Praslin and 43km from Mahé
10sqkm (5km north-south and 3km east-west)
Pop 2 450

Not to be missed
The rocks of Anse Source d'Argent at sunrise and sunset.
A walk from Grand'Anse to Anse Cocos.
Dinner at Château St-Cloud (if you don't stay there).

And remember...
Spend at least one night on the island.
Avoid the rainy season: April-September is best.
Avoid Anse Source d'Argent between 11am-2pm when it is invaded by day-trippers.
Explore the island by bike.

Beyond the reaches of time

Lazare Picault named the island of La Digue "île Rouge" after discovering it at sunset in 1744; its present name was borrowed from the boat captained by Duchemin, who led the French expedition of 1768 under the orders of Marion Dufresne.

La Digue, which is accessible from Mahé and Praslin by schooner, is probably the most charming and singular of the granitic islands. Although a handful of cars has recently appeared along the dirt roads, the main means of transport is by ox cart, bicycle, horseback or on foot.

A tall hill rises from the central part of the island leaving an extensive area of flat land on its western flank. It is here, among traditional wooden houses raised on piles, brightly painted Creole tin shacks and more recent concrete houses, that the population and their cultivated plots are concentrated.

The Diguois have preserved their traditional rural way of life, scratching a meagre livelihood from the cultivation of copra, vanilla, patchouli, Indian saffron (turmeric) and fishing. Elsewhere, the landscape from coast to mountaintop is covered with *takamakas*, *badamiers*, latanier palms, banana trees and above all coconut palms. Encircled by a ring of protective reefs, La Digue is fringed with sandy beaches scattered with spectacular arrangements of sculpted rock formations hewn by the forces of nature. Unfortunately, the benign-looking shallow waters are not ideally suited to bathing because of latent strong undercurrents. The only sign of civilisation to encroach upon these wild and deserted beaches is a scattering of fishing boats, gently bobbing on the water to the cadence of the waves. This truly "forgotten" island seems so unspoilt as to be beyond the reaches of time. A small faction of locals insists on pursuing the idea of independence from the rest of the Seychelles, and it is true that the Diguois are regarded as being quite distinctive from the other islanders.

Northern Coast★★

Approx 5km – 90min on foot one way.

■ **La Passe★** – The atmosphere of this sleepy village is tempered daily by the arrival of the schooners from Praslin and Mahé disgorging their loads of trippers onto the coral jetty. This is one's first view of La Digue on arrival. Those with a reservation at a local hotel or guesthouse will probably be met;

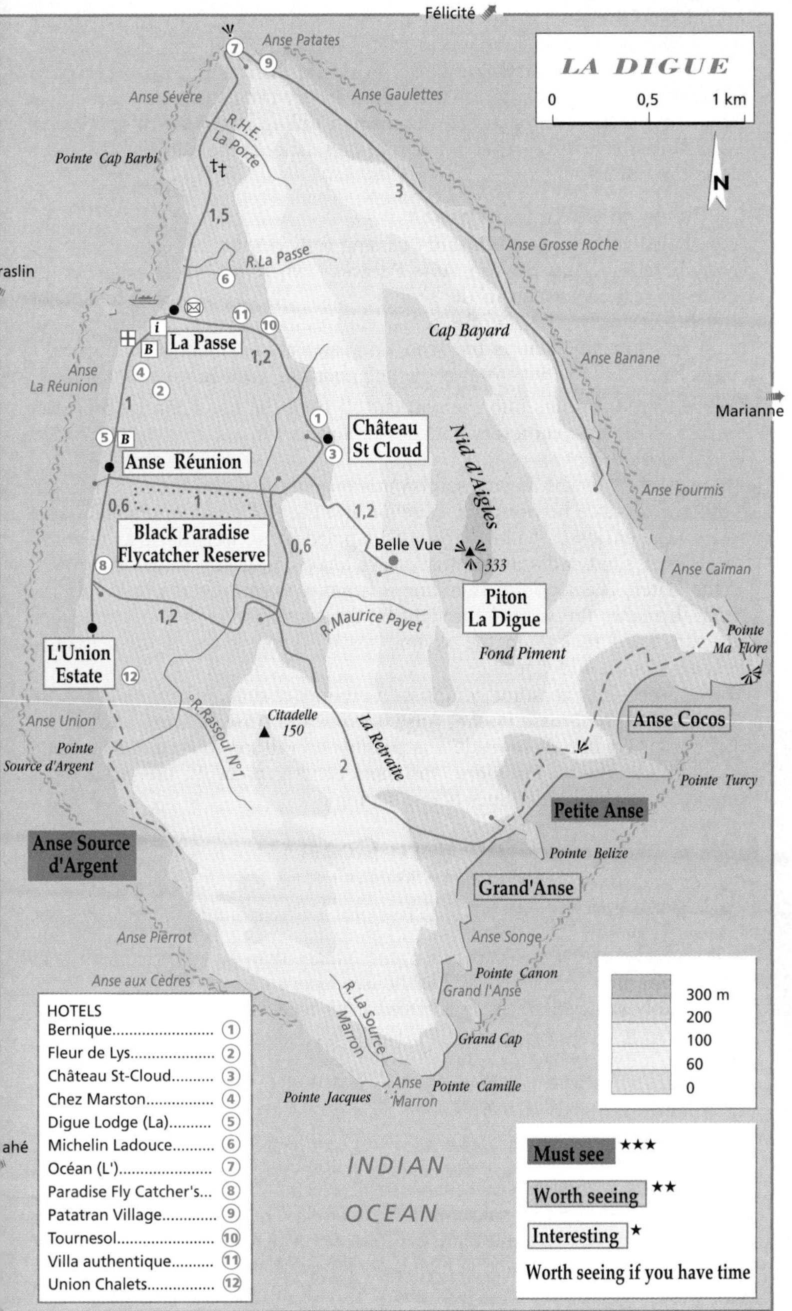
Félicité
LA DIGUE
0 0,5 1 km
N
Anse Patates
Anse Sévère
Anse Gaulettes
Pointe Cap Barbi
R.H.E.
La Porte
1,5
3
Anse Grosse Roche
R.La Passe
Praslin
La Passe
1,2
Cap Bayard
Anse Banane
Anse La Réunion
1
Marianne
Château St Cloud
Nid d'Aigles
Anse Réunion
Anse Fourmis
0,6
1
1,2
Black Paradise Flycatcher Reserve
0,6
Belle Vue
333
Anse Caïman
Piton La Digue
1,2
R.Maurice Payet
Pointe Ma Flore
L'Union Estate
Fond Piment
Anse Cocos
R.Rassoul N°1
Citadelle 150
La Retraite
Anse Union
Pointe Source d'Argent
2
Pointe Turcy
Petite Anse
Anse Source d'Argent
Pointe Belize
Grand'Anse
Anse Pierrot
Anse Songe
Pointe Canon
Grand l'Anse
Anse aux Cèdres
R. La Source Marron
300 m
200
100
60
0
Grand Cap
HOTELS
Bernique ①
Fleur de Lys ②
Château St-Cloud ③
Chez Marston ④
Digue Lodge (La) ⑤
Michelin Ladouce ⑥
Océan (L') ⑦
Paradise Fly Catcher's ⑧
Patatran Village ⑨
Tournesol ⑩
Villa authentique ⑪
Union Chalets ⑫
Pointe Jacques
Anse Marron
Pointe Camille
Mahé
INDIAN OCEAN
Must see ★★★
Worth seeing ★★
Interesting ★
Worth seeing if you have time

others should make for one of the ox carts that serve as local taxis! Among the crowd there might be the odd nun dressed in white, shielded from the sun by a straw hat, carrying a brace of fish on a string instead of a rosary. Meanwhile, life goes on as usual on the harbour-front; perhaps a fisherman might be casting a line between the moored sailing boats, and it is business as usual for the housewives at home or in attendance at the gaily painted shops along the waterfront.

La Passe to Anse Fourmis**

A potholed road leads northwards passing a succession of rocky inlets and sandy beaches – **Anse Sévère, Anse Patates** – where bathing is hampered by the loose seaweed tossed in the shallow water. The monotony is broken by stretches of lovely *glacis* and the occasional wind-worn coconut palm punctuating the horizon; then as the road undulates along small promontories, a serene **view** extends out towards the neighbouring islands.

Pointe Cap Barbi juts into the sea, cut off from the mountain by the road; there, a serene little **cemetery** dotted with flowers and white tombstones basks in the sunshine.

The road then makes its way southwards once more down the eastern coast; while the distance between the shoreline and the reef becomes gradually narrower. The enclosed shallow lagoon is dappled by an irregular patchwork of rock, coral, sand and seaweed that sways forever restlessly below the surface of the water. The sound of rumbling is heard as ocean rollers break onto the reefs; thereafter the water is brought by the gentle waves in to shore to lick the sun-tinted rocks. On the skyline sits the green mass of three islands: Félicité, Cousin and Cousine.

The last section of coastline comprises a number of shallow bays named **Anse Gaulettes**, **Anse Grosse Roche**, **Anse Banane** and **Anse Fourmis** after which the road peters out. At low tide it is possible to walk on to **Anse Caïman** and eventually to **Pointe Ma Flore**, the most easterly point on the island; it is important to check tide times before setting out.

Southern Coast***

Approx 5km – 90min on foot one way.

Follow the road right from the jetty at La Passe that leads southwards parallel to the coast.

■ **Anse Réunion*** – This is a livelier village than La Passe, consisting as it does of a number of hotels, guesthouses, shops and art galleries stretched out untidily along the recently surfaced main road.

Continue down the asphalt road south following the western shoreline.

■ **L'Union Estate*** – *Every day, 8am-6pm. Wellworth visiting before the arrival of the hordes of trippers at 10am. Entrance charge. Horse-riding.*

A small abandoned **colonial cemetery*** beyond the entrance to L'Union Estate is where the early settlers of La Digue are buried. Little remains of the former colonial spice plantation other than a small selection of the plants once grown: vanilla, turmeric (Indian saffron) and patchouli. The main area, however, is given over to a vast **coconut palm plantation**** which at one time would have supplied its share of copra, that mainstay of the archipelago, for export. Accept a taste of coconut milk or indeed the tender flesh of a freshly-opened nut if they are offered to you. This will serve as a good introduction to the other stages in the process seen in the **copra factory**: although the display is put on for tourists, the methods used are entirely traditional.

By the mill, but in front of the magnificent collection of rounded mouse-grey granite boulders, stands a **pen of giant tortoises*** shaded by swaying palms.

From palm to copra oil

Women workers at L'Union sit among piles of coconuts breaking shells with a single well-aimed swing of the machete. The split nuts are arranged in an insulated room to dry, thus allowing the shrunken flesh to be detached more easily. This is then cut into pieces known as copra before being ground in the last surviving mill on the island. Grinding stones have been in use here for almost a hundred years and continue to be worked in the age-old fashion by an ox which, when it slackens its pace, is goaded on by its eagle-eyed Seychelloise keeper. Approximately 35kg of coconuts, ground for at least two hours, are required to produce a single bucket of oil. Small pots of the precious unguent are for sale at the entrance to the estate.

Beyond the factory stands **Union Plantation House*** *(closed to visitors)*: an elegant wooden colonial house complete with veranda and thick latanier palm thatch. This is reserved for use by **President France Albert René** (or special friends like the Pope and the Blair family) when he stays on La Digue; the house also featured in the making of the film *Emmanuelle*.

A path skirts the building before continuing on down to **L'Union Beach*** at the end of the garden. There, under the trees, craftsmen can be seen hewing fishing boats from the trunks of teak or *takamaka* trees in the old-fashioned way, a dwindling skill that continues to be practised on the island.

Cycle along the sandy track parallel to the beach or walk along the sand at the water's edge.

■ **Anse Source D'Argent***** – This blissful beach is one of Mother Nature's wonders: a timeless place where rocks seem at one with the sand, serene below the swaying palm trees that rustle their fronds in the breeze. Depending on the time of day, the rounded granite boulders take on pink or greyish hues. Asymmetrically arranged and counterbalancing one another, these great sculpted masses seem almost artificial, like plaster props arranged as a backdrop for the filming of a big-screen movie. Photographers and filmmakers are in their element here.

Be it day or night, in bright sunlight or torrential rain, by a waxing or waning moon, this perfect landscape remains quite mesmerising and tirelessly beautiful. When the tide is out, hollows in the sand retain shallow pools of water warmed by the sun – just ideal for idling away the time. If swimming when the tide is in, you may catch a glimpse of the flat outline of a stingray, the graceful shadow of a giant turtle or the stray flicker of an as yet inoffensive baby shark.

M. Lemerle/MICHELIN

L'Union Estate to Anse Cocos★★★

The steep road from L'Union Estate to the beach at Grand'Anse, whether climbed on foot or by bicycle, cuts through the most wonderfully thick vegetation. Although the coconut tree reigns supreme, *takamakas*, *badamiers*, latanier palms and banana trees break through the exuberant undergrowth reaching for the sky. These lordly trees form a great vault over the road, sealing in either the dry fresh air or the warm and sticky tropical humidity generated by the plants, depending on the season.

By travelling across the island from west to east, you will penetrate the truly authentic scenery at the very heart of La Digue. Here, a dilapidated wooden house sits back from a bend in the road; there, a faded red corrugated tin roof indicates a house nestling in the shrubbery. When the slope becomes a challenge, the haunting rhythm of a snatch of *séga* music might drift across and drive you on before you reach the top and go freewheeling downwards, exhilarated by the heady rush of warm air and the muffled sound of a reggae tune emanating apparently from nowhere. The effort is soon rewarded by the spectacular descent into **Grand'Anse**★★, the most fabulous beach on the island, where the road peters out. Emerging suddenly from the gloom of the shaded road, the glare of the white sand and sparkling turquoise water seem to assault the senses.

Means of reproduction

It is difficult to determine the sex of a tortoise, except when the female is in heat. Mating takes place during the warm season and can last up to five hours. The females lay a dozen or so eggs by digging a nest up to 30cm deep, covering it in warm sand, excrement and urine, then leaving the eggs to "fend" for themselves. The incubation period lasts around 6 months when only a very few eggs hatch. The sex of the baby tortoises depends on the incubation temperature. If over 30°, they are female, if under, they are male.

The beach is regularly swept by the southwest trade winds and is unprotected by any coral reef. It is therefore open to the assault of every angry force of nature. The waves crash onto the shore. The foam is transported by the wind. The salty spray stings the eyes. Do not let the temptation to swim make you forget the invisible undercurrents, which are both unpredictable and treacherously strong. It is better to remain at the water-line and allow the water to wash gently over you, like the swarms of busy little crabs who right themselves after being swept along for a tumble or turn.

Seek out the path that leads from the top of the beach, following the shoreline northwards (fairly easy 5min walk).

The track down from **Pointe Belize** to the beach nestling in **Petite Anse**★★★ is quite wonderful. This long lick of white sand, framed between monolithic granite boulders and washed by regular breakers, is often deserted save for flocks of lovely fairy terns, those elegant white terns that love to circle above one. The same safety precautions should be applied as at Grand'Anse if you are tempted to swim.

Continue along the track running above the beach and between the rocks (fairly easy 15min walk).

The track that links the two bays cuts across the rocky promontory **Pointe Turcy**. Here and there, gaps in the palm fronds and shrubbery provide a great plunging **view**★★★ of the rugged coastline trimmed with white foam.

G. Simeone/DIAF

Anse Source d'Argent

Eventually, you come out onto the beautiful **Anse Cocos**** with its scattering of granite boulders reaching right down into the sea. Concealed in the folds of the scenery at the northern end of the beach are a series of natural swimming pools formed by the receding tide caught in bowls formed by the rocks.

At last the sun begins to sink towards the horizon and the coconut palms sway gracefully in the wind, allowing the shadows of their great fronds to dance effortlessly on the sands Although the calm sea here may look more benign, the hidden dangers are as prevalent here as elsewhere.

At the most northerly end of the beach the path continues to pick its way parallel to the shoreline and on among the rocks.

A scramble up and over the rocks will take you to the heights of **Pointe Ma Flore**, from where a broad panoramic view extends to take in Anse Cocos, the northeastern coast and the rocks beaten by the swirling sea *(swimming very dangerous)*. In theory, it is possible to continue on to **Anse Caïman** on the northeastern coast, but the path is not always very clearly indicated and there is some risk of going astray.

The island interior*

Three tracks lead inland towards the heart of the island from La Passe, Anse Réunion and L'Union respectively, and converge outside the grey and white façade of **Château St-Cloud***, which has been handed down through six generations of the Saint-Ange family (*see* Where to stay, *p 465*). If you are unable actually to stay there, it is still well worth going for the warm welcome and to soak up the atmosphere over a drink or dinner. There are plans to transform the large room on the ground floor into a small family museum.

Take the Belle Vue road up to the highest point on the island.

If the weather is right and the sky is clear, you can climb up (even if the summit is 333m above sea level!) to **Piton La Digue***, at the top of **Nid d'Aigles**.

An unreasonable amount of effort may be required to make the ascent by bicycle, it is therefore advisable to go up on foot *(approx 90min there and back)*. The best time is towards the end of the afternoon, when the heat of the day has subsided and when you can catch the sunset.

Chance encounters along the way may provide an insight into the daily routines of the most remote islanders. As the track meanders its way, a different **view**** opens out ever further over the sea. Praslin, Curieuse, Aride, Mahé and Felicité encroach upon the skyline.

Closer to hand, the island appears cloaked in thick forest dotted with the odd coloured *kaz*, scattered on the sides of the hill. The distinctive umbrella-shaped trees outlined against the sky are *albizias*.

Just before you reach the top, a lovely family is happy to welcome you onto their **terrace** to admire the view, catch your breath, enjoy a cool drink and watch the decline of the setting sun.

15 August

The Feast of the Assumption is cause for a most popular annual celebration on La Digue. The order of the day is merrymaking and music is sounded to accompany the parade as it makes its way around the island followed by banners and flaming torches. Every islander partakes in the event and a number of Seychellois from Praslin and Mahé come to join in the festivities.

The dirt track leading inland from Anse Réunion also leads past the following nature reserve.

Black Paradise Flycatcher Reserve* – *(Free entry. Best visited early in the morning. Binoculars advised).* An area predominantly populated by *takamakas* and giant *badamiers* provides a habitat for the last remaining specimens of the **Seychelles black paradise flycatcher** *(see illustration p 14)*. The last of this species, which is threatened with extinction, are thought to number about seventy-five.
Marked trails and the sound of its song will dictate which route to take, and you will slowly, silently, seek out the rare bird. The male is distinguished by its long tapering tail and shimmering blue-black plumage which earned it its Creole name, *veuve (pronounced vev)* meaning widow. The female, meanwhile, has a black head, chestnut upper parts and a shorter tail; in contrast, its breast and under-parts are a creamy white. To see this bird requires a pair of sharp eyes and a great deal of patience. Be warned, many visitors come away disappointed at not having seen this elusive bird.

Neighbouring islands

Enquire at a travel agency or hotel reception as to how to arrange an excursion.

All the islands and rocky islets off La Digue – namely **Coco**, **Petite Sœur**, **Grande Sœur**, and **Marianne** – are renowned for their fishy waters and wonderful coral formations, which delight divers and fishermen alike. In the main these outcrops are uninhabited and so preserve some vestiges of indigenous virgin forest, home to such rare birds as the Souimanga sunbird on Marianne. Extraordinary *glacis* tumble down onto the beach, lost among the untouched rambling vegetation.

Felicité* – *For additional details about this privately owned island, enquire at La Digue Lodge Hotel located in Anse Réunion. Three days minimum stay.* Félicité lies 3km north-east of La Digue and has a land area of 27 hectares. Its highest point reaches 227m and is largely covered with *takamakas*, coconut palms and other fruit trees right up to the edge of the cliffs that plunge directly down into the sea. There are two luxury **plantation houses** located on a secluded beach (*see* Where to stay, *p 466*).

Making the most of La Digue

GETTING THERE

By boat – A schooner service operates between Mahé and La Digue, crossing 3hr. Departures from Victoria port, Monday-Friday around 11am. When you arrive at La Passe jetty at La Digue, ox carts await visitors. The vessel leaves La Digue for the return journey around 6am. Tickets can be bought on board or at Victoria port, around 45min prior to departure (Rs50 one way). Those in more of a hurry can take the express boat that links the islands in only an hour (Rs140 one way). Information: ***Inter Island Ferry Service***, ☎ 232 329/ 234 254.

Two other boats shuttle between Praslin (Baie Ste Anne) and La Digue up to five times a day, Monday-Sunday. This crossing takes 30min. Tickets may be acquired on the quayside or on board (Rs35 one way). It may be worth making prior reservations, as many tourists opt for a day trip and catch the first boat out (☎ 233 229 / 233 874).

Departures from Praslin daily at 7am, 9.30am, 10.30am (except Sundays), 2.30pm and 5pm. Departures from La Digue at 7.30am, 10am, 11.30am (except Sundays), 3.30pm and 5.30pm.

Day trips – Various agencies arrange day trips to La Digue from Praslin, but it is a shame not to stay at least one night on the island.

By helicopter – ***Helicopter Seychelles*** runs a series of flights a week (☎ 373 900, Mahé and ☎ 234 222, La Digue).

GETTING AROUND

By ox cart – An ideal means of conveying luggage from the landing-stage to where you will be staying. It is also a slow but pleasant way of wandering across the island and surveying the landscape. Bartering is quite permissible as prices are relatively high.

By taxi – The motorised vehicles on the island can be counted on the fingers of a single hand. They are especially convenient for transferring luggage from the landing-stage to one's hotel.

By bus – A small open truck-cum-public bus will drop passengers off at their hotels and then return to collect groups of tourists wishing to speed their way around the sight.

By bicycle – The best way of exploring the island must be by bike: the tracks are relatively flat, it will cost up to 25RS a day to hire, and it provides complete freedom to go wherever and do whatever you choose. The largest selection available is from ***Michelin Ladouce*** at La Passe, opposite the landing-stage.

On foot – The size of the island allows one to visit the main attractions on foot.

ADDRESS BOOK

Tourist office – La Passe, near the jetty. ☎ /Fax 234 393. Open Monday-Friday, 8am-12noon/1pm-4pm; Saturday 9am-12noon.

Banks and money – ***Barclay's Bank***, Anse Réunion (opposite La Digue Island Lodge). Open Mondays, Wednesdays and Fridays, 10.30am-2pm.

Seychelles Savings Bank, Anse Réunion (opposite the hospital) ☎ 234 135. Open Monday-Friday, 8.30am-2.30pm; Saturdays 9am-11am. No credit cards.

Post Office – La Passe, opposite the landing-stage. Open Monday-Friday, 8am-12noon/1pm-4pm.

Telephone – There are several public phone boxes at La Passe and Anse Réunion. Only the hotels and certain guesthouses have fax machines.

Medical services – ***Logan Hospital***, La Passe ☎ 234 255.

Travel agents – The main travel operators have representatives at La Passe.

Mason's, Anse Réunion, ☎ 234 227.

TSS, La Passe, ☎ 234 411.

WHERE TO STAY

Be warned: most of the small hotels and family-run guesthouses do not accept payment by credit card. The prices given here are based on the cost of a double room with half-board.

US$60-75

Chez Marston, La Passe ☎/Fax 234 023 – 5rm (half-board only). The cheapest rooms on the island. Simply furnished, clean and comfortable bedrooms with basic kitchen facilities, arranged along the edge of a garden. Nice, informal family atmosphere.

US$75-110

Château St-Cloud, La Passe ☎ 234 346, Fax 234 545 –10rm (half-board only). Myriam represents the sixth generation of the well-known white Seychellois family, Saint-Anges. Having grown up in the wonderful house, which was converted into a hotel almost 20 years ago, she is rather sentimental about the place and is more than willing to share her memories with her guests. The old rooms on the first floor bear the names of those who helped build the place some two centuries past. The polished floors and original furniture reinforce the comfortable homeliness of the hotel. For those who prefer more modern facilities, there are a series of newly built rooms. The owner, a warm and generous person with a lovely sense of humour, will need little prompting before embarking on descriptions of her family, her island or even her homeland. As lady of the house, she greets every guest personally. It will be almost impossible for you to set off in the morning without having tasted her delicious home-made jams, and in the evening you will return to the most sumptuous spread of varied and mouth-watering Creole dishes. Furthermore, you are not allowed to leave any left-overs!

Villa Authentique, La Passe ☎/Fax 234 413 – 3rm This Seychellois family has only recently opened its house to paying guests. It is easy to be assimilated into the household after sipping a refreshing fruit punch in the cluttered lounge or the shaded garden.

Tournesol Guesthouse, La Passe, ☎ 234 155, Fax 234 364 – 6rm Bungalows split into two rooms with private terrace. Attractive garden from which you can pick ripe mangoes in season. Light and spacious dining room.

Bernique Guesthouse, La Passe ☎ 234 229, Fax 234 288 – 17rm Cottages containing two or three bedrooms arranged in a line around a communal terrace area. Some look out over the garden and the restaurant. Others are more secluded, set in amongst the large and attractive garden. Avoid, if possible, the cramped rooms without balconies in the main building.

US$110-140

Pension Résidence Michelin Ladouce, La Passe ☎ /Fax 234 304 – 6rm Make enquiries at the bicycle hire shop belonging to Michelin Ladouce (who humorously compares himself to the Michelin man Bibendum) opposite the landing-stage. He owns a series of two twin-roomed wooden bungalows a short way from his shop. Each house has a sitting area, kitchen and large terrace amply suitable for four people, although none offers much privacy as all the houses face each other.

Fleur de Lys, Anse Réunion, ☎/Fax 234 459 – 4rm Located just 150m from the beach, these pleasant bungalows, with a veranda overlooking the garden, are all very comfortable. Each has a kitchenette, enabling guests to be independent, but the charming owner will prepare meals on request in the evenings.

Paradise Fly Catcher's Lodge, Anse Réunion ☎ 234 423, Fax 234 422– 8rm Large spacious cottages with open-plan dining-cum-sitting room and American-style kitchen. Each opens out onto a broad wooden veranda and the garden beyond. Each has two self-contained rooms which can be rented independently. The whole is extremely well looked after. Meals on the premises by request.

Patatran Village, Anse Patate ☎ 234 333, Fax 234 344 – 18rm These units backing into the mountainside are strung along the northern section of the coastal road and surrounded by natural vegetation. Each has its own balcony facing out over the sea. The highest ones, more spacious and modern, all have a large terrace overlooking a charming little inlet.

Over US$155

Hotel L'Océan, Anse Patate ☎ 234 180, Fax 234 308,hocean@seychelles.net – 8rm A single stairway provides access to the tiers of rooms set into the hillside above the coastal road. Each has a terrace which opens out towards the sea and the islands – Grande Sœur, Petite Sœur, Coco and Félicité – after which the rooms are named. Comfortable and peaceful.

La Digue Island Lodge, Anse Réunion ☎ 234 232, Fax 234 100, lilodge@seychelles.net – 60rm The row of separate cottages with private terraces facing onto the beach is perfect for young families, with room for the children upstairs under the thick thatch of latanier leaves that extends right down to the ground, keeping the heat out. On the other side of the road there is a garden in which are arranged a number of round bungalows with a terrace, an attractive colonial-style house painted in yellow and accommodating various rooms, and an annexe housing yet more rooms without air-conditioning. Despite being rather heterogeneous, the compound and its buildings are well-designed and make an effective whole.

Over US$300

L'Union Chalets, Union Estate at Anse Réunion, ☎ 234 232/234 233, Fax 234 100/234 132 – 4 rm These luxurious bungalows for four are situated near Anse Source d'Argent, La Digue's most well-known beach. Built in the heart of the estate, their current claim to fame is the fact that the British prime minister, Tony Blair, occasionally stays there. Discreet and very pleasant establishment. Ideal if it's within your budget. Possibility of ordering meals.

WHERE TO EAT

Less than US$2

Various bakeries in La Passe, Anse Réunion and elsewhere along the side of the road sell a selection of locally made samossas, patties, pasties, doughnuts and cakes for next to nothing. These are perfect as a mid-morning snack or as part of a picnic on the beach. You will find one such shop offering a good range of vegetable and meat sanmousas tucked in behind Michelin Ladouce's bicycle hire business, opposite the landing-stage at La Passe.

US$2-5

Café Tarosa, La Passe, ☎ 234 250. Open daily, 10am-6pm. Small and informal place at the rear of a grocery store next to the jetty. Convenient for a salad, omelette, sandwich or fried chicken and chips; shaded from the sun by the sea. It is worth getting there early if you want to avoid having a long wait during the busy lunch-hours.

Chez Mme Payet, Anse Grosse Roche, ☎ 234 200. This tiny snack bar hidden away in the north of the island is ideal to savour a cold drink, a mango from Mme Payet's garden or other munchies.

US$5-12

Zerof Take Away, Anse Réunion, ☎ 234 439. Very good little snack bar that serves excellent chutneys and sausage rougail, as well as a large selection of other dishes at moderate prices. It is also possible to eat on the shady terrace or in the garden, for a little extra.

Tournesol Guesthouse, La Passe ☎ 234 155. Although the menu is restricted, this place offers great value. Spacious and airy dining-room set in a garden. Creole cuisine.

Bernique Guesthouse, La Passe ☎ 234 229. Lunch (à la carte) and dinner (fixed menu). Shaded terrace overlooking a small garden. Live musical entertainment some evenings. Creole buffet on Saturdays.

Loutier Coco, Grand'Anse. Closed in the evenings. Beach house right on the sands of Grand'Anse. After the exertion of cycling, taking a long walk in the sun or a strenuous swim in the sea you will feel the need for a cool drink and something tasty to eat. Iced soft drinks or coconut punch usually do the trick, followed by a sandwich, a grilled fish, a salad or some fresh fruit. It is a pity that the service can be grouchy and the lack of competition allows prices to be inflated without reason.

US$15-30

Patatran, Hotel Océan, Anse Patate. Lunch and dinner CC Perfect for a reviving refreshment, a light meal or something more substantial. Lovely terrace with broad outlook over the sea and the offshore islands. Creole specialities including fish and crayfish.

Le Pêcheur, La Digue Lodge, Anse Réunion. Lunch and dinner CC The restaurant attached to the largest hotel on the island is situated right on the beach, shaded by latanier palm fronds. Idyllic place to eat with sand beneath your feet, watching the sun go down over the ocean and the darkening profile of Praslin looming on the horizon. Barbecue and *séga* dancing once a week.

SPORTS AND PASTIMES

Aquatic sports – *La Digue Dive Center*, La Digue Lodge, Anse Réunion. Windsurfers, hobie-cats, masks and snorkels for hire. Diving excursions.

Gérard Payet, La Passe, ☎ 234 073. Deep sea fishing and excursions to Coco and Grande Sœur, as well as to all the other islands near La Digue. Gérard and his team will make your day out a success as they take you from one island to the next. Prices can be reduced depending on the number of participants and the destination.

Horse-riding – Fabulous way of exploring the island. Stables at L'Union Estate ☎ 234 240.

WHERE TO SHOP

Souvenirs – Shops selling the usual selection of cards, souvenirs, locally made handicrafts, coloured sarongs, jewellery and shells may be found at La Passe and Anse Réunion.

Art galleries – *Green Gecko*, Anse Réunion, ☎ 234 402. Monday-Saturday, 9am-5pm. Watercolours and silk screen paintings.

Barbara Jenson Studio, Anse Réunion, ☎ 234 406, e-mail: jenson@seychelles.net Open Monday-Saturday, 9am-5pm.

THE OUTER ISLANDS

The species of birds mentioned in bold appear in the illustrations on p 14-15.

Silhouette★★

Take comfortable walking shoes.

The third largest island of the archipelago, after Mahé and Praslin measures some 20sqkm and lies 17km off Beau Vallon *(45min by boat)*. It has a population of 400 or so, which is dependant on fishing and the commercial production of tobacco, coffee, cinnamon, patchouli and avocados.

This rather rugged granitic island culminates with Mont Dauban (750m) and is for the most part covered with very dense virgin forest often lost in swirling cloud. The heavy rainfall makes this the only **primary equatorial forest** of the Seychelles group. Gardeners and plantsmen out walking will be thrilled to recognise the carnivorous pitcher plant creeper, various understated orchids, rare woods *(bois rouge, bois noir, bois de natte*, sandalwood, *bois de table, bois méduse), calices du pape, veloutiers* with white flowers, cedars and jackfruit trees. Eighty species among these are endemic.

It is said that a cutthroat named **Pirate Hodoul** took refuge here in times past and that he hid treasure here somewhere in the jungle, among the great granite boulders worn smooth by innumerable rivers and waterfalls.

There are no cars on Silhouette, so its secrets are revealed only to those prepared to explore the place on foot. A coastal track runs around the north of the island and several others cross it from side to side between La Passe and Grande Barbe, cutting through the stiflingly humid forest.

A coral reef runs parallel to the northeast coast, safeguarding it from deep swells, while another protects a large section of the west coast (Anse Grand Barbe), to provide a lagoon ideally suited for swimming and snorkelling. The bungalows of the only hotel are located by a magnificent beach.

A short distance further on lies the **Pointe Ramasse Tout Cemetery** in which stands a rather incongruous-looking **funeral monument commemorating the Dauban Family** (long-time owners of the island) of a Greek temple.

A little way south, a group of **graves** has been uncovered at **Anse Lascars**; the scant remains appear to indicate that these graves belong to the Arab seafarers who landed on the island in the 9C. The only other attraction worthy of note is the former **planter's house** which stands in the vicinity of **La Passe**.

Frégate★★

Two days minimum stay.

The tiny granitic island of Frégat (2sqkm) lies 56km east of Mahé and has about 30 permanent residents, who make their livelihood from fishing and farming a huge variety of fruit and vegetables, coffee, tobacco, vanilla, cinnamon and sugar cane.

The island essentially consists of a flattened rock which rises to 125m, wooded with breadfruit trees, casuarina pines, *takamakas*, latanier palms, *sandragons, badamiers*, coconut palms and banyan trees. The forest also abounds with wondrous varieties of flowering shrubs and an extremely rich fauna. While the giant tortoises tramp the islands undisturbed, two species of turtle visit the island's beaches to deposit their eggs.

The outer islands

Overhead, the skies are ever full of birds on the wing; approximately 50 different species nest here including some that are unique to the shores of Frégate. A walk on the island may provide the opportunity to catch a glimpse of the endangered magpie robin *(pie-chanteuse)*, a black thrush with a bluish sheen and white markings on the wings, or the blue-throated thrush – one of the rarest birds in the world. More common sights include the **cardinal** (scarlet fody), the **fairy tern**, the frigate-bird – after which the island is probably named – the shearwater, the Seychelles fody or *toc toc*, and the brightly coloured Dutch pigeon. On the ground, look out for various kinds of lizards and insects: spiders, millipedes, scorpions, May-bugs, and giant beetles.

Most of the island is edged with beautiful unspoilt beaches, the majority protected by coral reefs and the clarity of the water allows one to make out the fabulous colours and textures of corals, shells and innumerable fish. Deep-sea fishing here is always a successful and rewarding experience.

Bird Island★★★

The world-famous Bird Island, which consists of 1sqkm of coral and which is the most northerly island of the Seychelles group, lies 96km north of Mahé. From the air it looks like a green speck in the ocean: completely flat, ringed with dazzlingly white sand, and surrounded on all sides by limpid, shallow turquoise water and a sea-floor visibly variegated with corals.

The island once was known by the name "Ile aux Vaches", and appears as such on certain outdated maps or charts. This name was attributed to it by the French in 1756 when a profusion of "sea cows" or *dugongs* used to live here (they have long since gone). The largest creatures to roam the shaded glades of coconut palms, casuarinas, mangoes and papayas are the giant tortoises. Among them resides the 150-year-old *Esmeralda*, who weighs 300kg. She is the largest tortoise in the Seychelles, perhaps in the world, and is also reputed to be the oldest as well.

Above all else, Bird Island provides a paradise home for residential colonies of black-napped terns, **cardinals**, ground doves, Mascarene **martins**, white-tailed **tropic birds**, crested terns, elegant sea swallows etc.

Numbers are boosted by the arrival of land migrants and waders seeking refuge from the European winter. The best time to come bird-watching, however, is between April-October when nigh on three million **sooty terns** gather here to breed. At this time, a veritable cacophony (and potent smell) accompanies the feverish activity on land, sea and sky.

Denis Island★★

Three days minimum stay.

Denis lies 80km northeast of Mahé; it has a land area of 1.5sqkm and is populated by some 50 inhabitants. Shaped like a flattened croissant, this coral island is densely covered with coconut groves that give way to dazzling beaches and sparkling shallows filled with fish. Scuba-diving and deep-sea fishing are reputed to be quite exceptional here especially during May and between October-December. Several paths crisscross the woodland made up of casuarinas, *takamakas*, banyans and papayas; but be warned, these tracks are to be shared with the resident tribes of giant tortoises. In the village survive the ruins of a **copra factory** and an old lighthouse.

Far-flung atolls★★★

An additional 60-odd coral islands, largely uninhabited, are scattered over a 1 000km stretch of the Indian Ocean. Their size and remoteness make them havens for a highly specific flora and fauna, including a number of truly unique species. These far-flung, often featureless islands are blessed with a fresher and dryer climate than the granite islands, with a constant temperature of 26-30°C all year round. In the main, they form three distinct groups: the Amirantes, Aldabra and Farquhar.

The Amirantes★★

The group of 24 islands that make up the Amirantes lies some 200-300km southwest of Mahé. Stretched over a distance of 100km like a string of beads, these flat coral areas (Poivre, Boudeuse, Desneuf, Rémires, Daros, Desroches etc) appear to float precariously on the sea. Only four are inhabited, and of these only **Desroches** has the infrastructure for accommodating tourists. It has been cleared and planted with coconut trees that provide the communities with a sustainable income. Interestingly, it has been found that the copra extracted here is of a quality superior to the norm. Other commodities to have been exploited on these shores include turtles, sharks, *bois blanc*, shells (for their mother-of-pearl) and guano (the excellent fertiliser made from sea-bird manure).

Pockets of casuarina pines shade grazing areas and handsome *takamakas* edge the beaches. The warm shallow waters, especially around the rocks at low tide shelter a rich assortment of marine life. Visitors fly to **Desroches** (4sqkm, population approx 50) to enjoy the tangible tranquillity of the place as well as the opportunity of swimming with turtles, tickling lobsters, diving among sharks or fishing offshore for *wahoo,* bonito or swordfish. Excursions to **Poivre** (1sqkm) – one of the most beautiful atolls of the Amirantes, with a central lagoon ringed with reefs – may also be arranged from Desroches.

Aldabra★★★

Stranded in mid-ocean, 1 000km from Mahé, lies Aldabra. Like a beaded necklace, the coral atoll encloses the largest lagoon in the world, making it into a contained sea dotted with little outcrops. Some have compared the place to a coronet of coral that barely rises 8m above the sea, surrounding and preserving a unique habitat in which a range of specific plants and animals has evolved. For example, it has the largest colony of giant tortoises in the world, with 70 000-180 000 living in a wild state in the shade of the *takamakas*. The same territory is shared by colonies of large land-crabs which can open a coconut by simply snapping their claws together. Meanwhile there is space enough for a multitude of birds: **terns**, ibis, red-footed boobies, frigate-birds, Madagascan kestrels, herons and pink flamingos. Turtles clamber up the sands to lay their eggs between December-March in greater numbers than on any other island. As the tide draws out from the lagoon, large mushroom-shaped pieces of coral are exposed to the sun-attracting ever-keen sea birds in search of the finest delicacy. Despite its apparent arid desolation, the land mass hosts a variety of ferns, flowering bushes, whistling pines, assorted palms, mangroves and acacias that thrive on the guano-enriched soil. Formidable sharks inhabit the rich waters around the atoll and sometimes slip into the lagoon at high tide through breaches in the reefs. Aldabra's low-key tourism is strictly controlled by the Seychellois authorities and visits remain largely scientific. It is a nature reserve designated a "World Heritage Site" by Unesco.

C. Pavard/HOA QUI

Flying over Aldabra

Far-flung atolls

Farquhar★

This archipelago, 700km from Mahé, covers some 8sqkm. Its remoteness is reinforced by its location in the path of violent cyclones that regularly devastate the area between December-February. Approximately 100 people live on two of the islands, eking their meagre subsistence from fishing and extracting copra. Farquhar is government-owned and no accommodation is available on the island for visitors.

Making the most of the outer islands

GETTING THERE

There are no regular services in operation to the outer islands. The cost of flights is usually included in the price of the accommodation.

• Silhouette
Connections by boat from Mahé (1hr from Victoria; 30min from Beau Vallon) or by helicopter (12min, Thursday-Tuesday). Private charter (4-seater) daily, 8am-6pm.

• Frégate
Three flights per week (15min) from Mahé to fulfil hotel reservations.

• Bird Island
Air Seychelles fly from Mahé (30min), Monday-Saturday. Flight plus hotel deal.

• Denis
Four flights per week from Mahé (25min) to fulfil hotel reservations.

• Desroches
Four flights per week from Mahé (45min).

• Aldabra
No scheduled flights, fly to Assomption from Mahé (2hr), then take a boat to the other islands (3hr).

• Farquhar
No regular service. Four or five day crossing by boat from Mahé (rare) or by air (3.5hr).

ADDRESS BOOK

Mason's Travel, P O Box 459, Victoria, Mahé ☎ 322 642, Fax 325 273. Day trips or longer stays on Silhouette (by boat), Bird island and Frégate (by air).
Travel Services Seychelles (TSS), Victoria House, PO Box 356, Victoria, Mahé ☎ 322 414, Fax 321 366. Overnight stays.
Fondation des îles Seychelles, Ministry of Tourism, PO Box 92, Victoria, Mahé ☎ 225 313, Fax 224 035. Provides special authorisation to visit places outside the norm (essential for access to Aldabra).
Marine Charter, Victoria Harbour, PO Box 469, Victoria, Mahé ☎ 322 126, Fax 224 679. Arranges transfers by boat to certain islands.
Air Seychelles ☎ 381 000. Details of scheduled flights and private hire of a helicopter (expensive!); see also ***Helicopter Seychelles*** ☎ 375 400.

WHERE TO STAY

Each of these islands has one hotel. In each case accommodation consists of luxurious private bungalows with full amenities. Prices given are based on the cost of a double room with full board (as there are no independent restaurants available). Rates vary according to the number of nights booked, each hotel has a representative in Victoria to answer any queries in detail.

US$150-300
Bird Island Lodge, ☎ 323 222/ 224 925, Fax 323 335/225 074 – 25rm CC

US$230-450
Silhouette Island Lodge ☎ 224 003/ 344 154, Fax 344 178 – 12rm CC
Plantation House, Frégate ☎ 323 123, Fax 324 152 – 10rm CC
Denis Island Lodge ☎ 321 143/ 321 010, Fax 334 405 – 25rm CC golf.
Desroches Island Lodge ☎ 229 003/ 322 414, Fax 321 366 – 20rm CC

The outer islands

Notes

Notes

Notes

NOTES

Notes

Notes

Notes

If you have just come back from holiday or vacation, we would like you to share your travel experiences with us.

Please write to:

Michelin Travel Publications
The Edward Hyde Building
38 Clarendon Road
Watford, UK

or

Michelin Travel Publications
P.O. Box 19008
Greenville, SC 29602-9008
USA

There may be a restaurant or hotel you particularly liked and which is not in the guide. Perhaps you came across some delightful village or discovered a pleasant walk in the country. If so, please let us know for our future editions. Please feel free to comment on the presentation and content of the guide if you think it can be improved. We would be grateful if you could point out anything which seems out of date. Don't forget to mention the page number and publication date.

INDEX

Anse Lazio: description of curiosity, geographical name
La Bourdonnais (Mahé de): person
Scuba diving: practical information Spices: explanation of a term

A

B

C

D

E

F

G

H-I

J-K

L

M

N-O

P

Q-R

S

T

U-V

W-Z

MAPS AND PLANS

Manufacture Française des Pneumatiques Michelin
Société en commandite par actions au capital de 2 000 000 000 de francs
Place des Carmes-Déchaux – 63000 Clermont-Ferrand (France)
R.C.S. Clermont-Fd B 855 200 507

Dépôt légal avril 2000 – ISBN 2-06-855301-5 – ISSN 0763-1383

Printed in the EU 03-00/1
Compograveur : Nord Compo – Villeneuve d'Ascq
Imprimeur : IME – Baume-les-Dames

Cover illustrations :
Traditional fishing boat. M. Huet/HOA QUI
Little girl from Rodrigues. P. Hausherr/HOA QUI
Tamil temple in Réunion (detail). G. Guittot/DIAF